Lecture Notes in Computer Science　　　9740

Commenced Publication in 1973
Founding and Former Series Editors:
Gerhard Goos, Juris Hartmanis, and Jan van Leeuwen

Stephanie Lackey · Randall Shumaker (Eds.)

Virtual, Augmented and Mixed Reality

8th International Conference, VAMR 2016
Held as Part of HCI International 2016
Toronto, Canada, July 17–22, 2016
Proceedings

 Springer

Editors
Stephanie Lackey
Federal Solutions Division
Design Interactive, Inc.
Orlando, FL
USA

Randall Shumaker
Institute for Simulation and Training
University of Central Florida
Orlando, FL
USA

ISSN 0302-9743 ISSN 1611-3349 (electronic)
Lecture Notes in Computer Science
ISBN 978-3-319-39906-5 ISBN 978-3-319-39907-2 (eBook)
DOI 10.1007/978-3-319-39907-2

Library of Congress Control Number: 2016940337

LNCS Sublibrary: SL3 – Information Systems and Applications, incl. Internet/Web, and HCI

Printed on acid-free paper

This Springer imprint is published by Springer Nature
The registered company is Springer International Publishing AG Switzerland

Foreword

The 18th International Conference on Human-Computer Interaction, HCI International 2016, was held in Toronto, Canada, during July 17–22, 2016. The event incorporated the 15 conferences/thematic areas listed on the following page.

A total of 4,354 individuals from academia, research institutes, industry, and governmental agencies from 74 countries submitted contributions, and 1,287 papers and 186 posters have been included in the proceedings. These papers address the latest research and development efforts and highlight the human aspects of the design and use of computing systems. The papers thoroughly cover the entire field of human-computer interaction, addressing major advances in knowledge and effective use of computers in a variety of application areas. The volumes constituting the full 27-volume set of the conference proceedings are listed on pages IX and X.

I would like to thank the program board chairs and the members of the program boards of all thematic areas and affiliated conferences for their contribution to the highest scientific quality and the overall success of the HCI International 2016 conference.

This conference would not have been possible without the continuous and unwavering support and advice of the founder, Conference General Chair Emeritus and Conference Scientific Advisor Prof. Gavriel Salvendy. For his outstanding efforts, I would like to express my appreciation to the communications chair and editor of *HCI International News*, Dr. Abbas Moallem.

April 2016   Constantine Stephanidis

HCI International 2016 Thematic Areas and Affiliated Conferences

Thematic areas:

- Human-Computer Interaction (HCI 2016)
- Human Interface and the Management of Information (HIMI 2016)

Affiliated conferences:

- 13th International Conference on Engineering Psychology and Cognitive Ergonomics (EPCE 2016)
- 10th International Conference on Universal Access in Human-Computer Interaction (UAHCI 2016)
- 8th International Conference on Virtual, Augmented and Mixed Reality (VAMR 2016)
- 8th International Conference on Cross-Cultural Design (CCD 2016)
- 8th International Conference on Social Computing and Social Media (SCSM 2016)
- 10th International Conference on Augmented Cognition (AC 2016)
- 7th International Conference on Digital Human Modeling and Applications in Health, Safety, Ergonomics and Risk Management (DHM 2016)
- 5th International Conference on Design, User Experience and Usability (DUXU 2016)
- 4th International Conference on Distributed, Ambient and Pervasive Interactions (DAPI 2016)
- 4th International Conference on Human Aspects of Information Security, Privacy and Trust (HAS 2016)
- Third International Conference on HCI in Business, Government, and Organizations (HCIBGO 2016)
- Third International Conference on Learning and Collaboration Technologies (LCT 2016)
- Second International Conference on Human Aspects of IT for the Aged Population (ITAP 2016)

Conference Proceedings Volumes Full List

Virtual, Augmented and Mixed Reality

Program Board Chairs: **Stephanie Lackey, USA, and Randall Shumaker, USA**

- Sheryl Brahnam, USA
- Jessie Y.C. Chen, USA
- Jesse D. Flint, USA
- Gino Fragomeni, USA
- Panagiotis D. Kaklis, UK
- Fotis Liarokapis, Czech Republic
- Gordon Mair, UK

- Crystal Maraj, USA
- Marius Preda, France
- Olinda Rodas, USA
- Julie Salcedo, USA
- Jose San Martin, Spain
- Peter A. Smith, USA
- Marjorie Zielke, USA

The full list with the program board chairs and the members of the program boards of all thematic areas and affiliated conferences is available online at:

http://www.hci.international/2016/

HCI International 2017

The 19th International Conference on Human-Computer Interaction, HCI International 2017, will be held jointly with the affiliated conferences in Vancouver, Canada, at the Vancouver Convention Centre, July 9–14, 2017. It will cover a broad spectrum of themes related to human-computer interaction, including theoretical issues, methods, tools, processes, and case studies in HCI design, as well as novel interaction techniques, interfaces, and applications. The proceedings will be published by Springer. More information will be available on the conference website: http://2017.hci.international/.

General Chair
Prof. Constantine Stephanidis
University of Crete and ICS-FORTH
Heraklion, Crete, Greece
E-mail: general_chair@hcii2017.org

http://2017.hci.international/

Contents

Perception, Cognition, Psychology and Behaviour in VAMR

Multimodal Interaction in VAMR

Novel Devices and Technologies in VAMR

VAMR Applications in Aviation, Space and the Military

Medicine, Health and Well-Being Applications of VAMR

VAMR in Industry, Design and Engineering

Novel Virtual Environments

Usability, User Experience and Design in VAMR

Comparing Objective and Subjective Metrics Between Physical and Virtual Tasks

S.N. Gieser[1]([✉]), Caleb Gentry[1], James LePage[2,3],
and Fillia Makedon[1]

[1] Heracleia Human Centered Computing Laboratory, Department of Computer
Science and Engineering, University of Texas at Arlington, Arlington, TX, USA
{shawn.gieser,makedon}@uta.edu,
caleb.gentry@mavs.uta.edu
[2] Veteran Affairs North Texas Health Care System, Dallas, TX, USA
james.lepage@va.gov
[3] University of Texas Southwestern Medical Center, Dallas, TX, USA

Abstract. Virtual Reality (VR) is becoming a tool that is more often used in various types of activities, including rehabilitation. However, studies using VR rehabilitation mainly focus on comparing the performances of participants, but not their opinions. In this paper, we present a virtual version of the Box and Blocks Test. We also present the results of a pilot study where participants completed a physical version of the Box and Blocks Test and the virtual version, comparing their scores and opinions. We also compare how the participants viewed the passage of time while performing both versions as a way to see how engaged they were during the task.

Keywords: Box and blocks test · Leap motion · Upper extremity rehabilitation · Gamification · Virtual reality · Time perception

1 Introduction

The onset of low-cost, off-the-shelf sensing equipment, such as the Leap Motion [1], have made Virtual Reality (VR) more easily accessible to everyone. It has also expanded the use of VR and virtual environments into many different fields, such as driving simulations, cooking, vocational training, and rehabilitation [2–5]. When VR is used in rehabilitation, exercise programs can provide more interesting and engaging tasks, causing patients to perform better and recover quicker than traditional rehabilitation [6]. Research has shown that therapists would use certain types of VR technology in a home environment without their presence, creating a form of tele-rehabilitation [5].

However, with this advent of VR rehabilitation, would people want to perform a VR version of exercises and tasks, or would they rather do the traditional physical version? Also, other questions can be asked too, such as which version do people find more fun, more frustrating, or which would they rather do again? This paper aims to answer these questions by presenting a virtual version of an Occupational Therapy assessment task called the Box and Blocks Test using the Leap Motion. This virtual version was then

© Springer International Publishing Switzerland 2016
S. Lackey and R. Shumaker (Eds.): VAMR 2016, LNCS 9740, pp. 3–13, 2016.
DOI: 10.1007/978-3-319-39907-2_1

compared to the tangible and traditional physical version by having participants perform both tasks and recording their performance. We will also compare how participants perceive the passage of time to see which version they were more engaged by. Lastly, we will compare their subjective opinions of the participants to see which version they prefer and why, as well as their overall opinions of the technology being developed.

2 Background

The Box and Blocks Test is an assessment used in Occupational Therapy used to evaluate gross manual dexterity [7]. This is done by having a participant sit in front of a box with a partition in the middle, and having them move blocks from one side to the other. The goal is to move as many blocks as the participant can in a one minute time period. Blocks can only be moved one at a time. The test is at first uses only the participant's dominant or non-affected (for people with disabilities) hand, moving blocks from the same side as the dominant hand to the other. The participant get a point for each block they move over. Carrying multiple blocks over at once only counts as one point. If the hand does not completely cross the partition (i.e. the block is thrown over), that block is not counted towards the score. If a block bounces out of the box and lands on the table or the floor, that block is still counted and the participant does not have to pick it up. After one minute has passed, the blocks are counted and the test is reset to be repeated with the person's non-dominant or affected hand.

The assessment of activity engagement can be done by simply asking participants to what degree they enjoyed the activity; however this can create expectation demand which bias the participants' self-reports. To avoid these demand characteristics, more indirect means of assessing engagement is required. A relatively simple way of indirectly assessing engagement is through the assessment of perceived time while performing a task.

Characterized by the idiom "time flies when you are having fun," research has shown that being exposed to engaging positive activities or stimuli results in individuals underestimate the amount of time that has passed, while individuals tend to overestimate time passing when under negative conditions [8–10]. In practical terms, being exposed to positive stimuli such as pictures of desserts or pleasurable tactile stimulation [11] result in an underestimation of exposure time. Factors such as pain [12] and fear [13] have been associated with an overestimations of the time passed.

3 Related Work

Using VR has been shown to have many strengths when applying it to rehabilitation, as it provides stimulus control, consistency, and real-time performance feedback. VR also allows the adaptation to a patient's abilities, and the ability to distract and motivate a patient [14]. In fact, VR can be used for patients of all ages, helping adults regain the ability to perform activities of daily living [15] to children with Cerebral Palsy to improve motor performance [16]. The Leap Motion has been evaluated for game based therapy. Clinicians and therapists have shown positive feedback when viewing the

Leap Motion's use for therapy [17], and that it has the potential to be used in a home environment with younger users [5].

The Box and Blocks Test has been used in many stages of studies that involves VR rehabilitation, such as evaluation of VR tasks or even being the task performed. The performance of people performing VR tasks and games created is correlated to the scores of that same person performing the Box and Blocks Test [15]. The scores from the Box and Blocks Test are also used as inclusion and exclusion from studies that involve VR games as well [18]. There have been versions of the Box and Blocks Test created in a virtual environment using both a Wii and a Kinect [19, 20]. However, these two studies only showed the performance between the different versions, and did not consider the opinions of the participants performing the task.

Not surprising, video and computer games have also demonstrated distortions in perceived time passing while engaged. For example, when time performing the activities were the same, the perceived time playing a video game was shorter than reading on a computer [21]. Additionally, in a comparison of expert and novice gamers, expert gamers perceived time as passing more quickly than novices after 30 and 60 min of play. While initially novice gamers perceived time as going slower while they were learning the game after 90 min they had similar time experiences as experts as their experience increased [22].

4 Experimental Setup and Procedure

For this experiment, we had participants perform two different versions of the Box and Blocks Test. The first version was a traditional version that could be touched. The second version was a virtual version done on a computer, lacking any tactile feedback. All participants participating in this pilot study were from a healthy general student population. The rest of this section will describe the two different versions followed by the experimental procedure.

4.1 Physical Version

The physical version used in the study was 3D printed. The goal with the physical version of the test was simply to recreate the size and shape of the original test. The box has a partition dividing it in half with all of the blocks on one side, where the subject was asked to move all blocks from one side of the partition to the other in one minute [7]. The goal was to see their ability to reach and grab the blocks, and quickly move them over the partition to drop them into the other side. The physical setup used for this experiment is shown below in Fig. 1 Left. The box and blocks were designed using SolidWorks CAD software, and printed using Makerbot Replicator 2 and Polyprinter 229 3D printers. The reason for this design was centered around some physical goals for the equipment.

Firstly, it was desired that the physical version be mobile, and easy transport to the different subjects in the test. Thus, it was decided that rather than making the box and blocks out of wood, which would be heavy, plastic puzzle pieces would be light,

Fig. 1. (Left) Physical version that was 3D printed. (Right) Virtual version that was created in Unity using the Leap Motion.

and easy to place into a box for easy transportation. Additionally, if any piece of the box broke, a repair would be easy, requiring only that the broken part be reprinted and then the experiment could easily continue. Thus, this design was more mobile and robust, allowing the experiment to be performed accurately on a continuous basis. In order to accomplish this, the parts needed to be designed using dovetails for a "puzzle-piece" fitting process. This allowed the parts to be easily printed, easy to assemble, and easy to transport.

4.2   Virtual Version

A virtual version of the Box and Blocks test was developed using the Unity Game Engine [23], which can be seen in Fig. 1 Right. All components were developed to be a scale model of the physical version in comparison to the size of a virtual hand. This allowed the virtual version to be an accurate recreation of the physical version and would require participants to perform the exact same actions to complete the Box and Blocks Test. This virtual environment was displayed on a computer monitor.

A Leap Motion was used to capture the motion of the hand. Grabbing the blocks in the virtual world is done in a similar fashion to that of the physical version. When a participant's fingers were near a block and then brought their fingers close together in a pinching fashion, a block was bound to the participant's thumb on their virtual hand. When they moved their fingers apart, the block would be released from the thumb and fall from the hand. This prevented multiple blocks to be picked up at once. The physics model for the hand was turned off to make it easier for the participant to move their virtual hand and pick up blocks without causing other blocks to fly around the environment. The score was automatically tracked and increased each time a block was placed in or fell into the other side of the box.

For gameplay, timers were implemented for the fifteen second practice and the sixty second full sessions that turn off sensor input upon completion. During the full session, the data from the Leap Motion is recorded so that it can be analyzed later and turned into a report for therapists. These data points include, but not limited to, the wrist position, palm position, fingertip positions, and joint angles.

4.3 Experimental Procedure

Twelve participants took part in this pilot study. After obtaining consent, the participants were given a survey asking the following questions:

- Demographic questions, such as age, gender, and ethnicity
- Have you had any experience playing video games? Significant/Some/No Experience
- Have you had any experience with virtual reality? Significant/Some/No Experience

Then, the concept of the Box and Blocks Test was described to the participants. Afterwards, the participants performed both the physical and virtual versions in one minute and five minute formats. The order of the tasks were complete were balanced in order to not show any bias towards a certain version. The order of tasks can been seen in Table 1.

Table 1. Order of tasks completed by participants

Participant number	Task 1	Task 2	Task 3	Task 4
1, 5, 9	Physical One-Minute	Virtual One-Minute	Physical Five-Minute	Virtual Five-Minute
2, 6, 10	Virtual One-Minute	Physical One-Minute	Physical Five-Minute	Virtual Five-Minute
3, 7, 11	Physical One-Minute	Virtual One-Minute	Virtual Five-Minute	Physical Five-Minute
4, 8, 12	Virtual One-Minute	Physical One-Minute	Virtual Five-Minute	Physical Five-Minute

Both the one minute physical and virtual versions were similar to the original procedure [24], with the physical being exact, and the virtual having minor modifications. The one minute tasks consisted of an optional practice period followed by the actual test. The practice period for the physical version followed the standard rules of fifteen seconds. The virtual version's practice period did not have a time limit, but lasted until the participants had a firm understanding of how to pick up blocks in the virtual world. After the practice period, the participants than performed the Box and Blocks Test with both hands with both versions. The participants' score was recorded after each one-minute tasks.

After the one-minute tasks, the participants were given another survey to see what their opinions were of the two different versions. The questions can be seen in Table 5 in Sect. 5, along with the results of the survey.

Once the survey was completed, the participants were then asked to do a five minute version of both the virtual and the physical tasks. If they ran out of blocks on one side of the box, the participants started moving blocks back to the other side without changing hands. The participants were not told when five minutes were over, but were told to stop whenever they felt five minutes have passed. All other rules of the one minute version still applied to the five minute version. The five minute tasks were performed with both hands. The scores and the elapsed time since the start of the task till the participants stopped were recorded.

A short video explaining the procedure and technology used can be seen here: https://youtu.be/ej5ZQBTGDWU .

5   Analysis and Discussion

Below, in Table 2 is the demographic information of the student population that participated in this study. The rest of this section will detail the rest of the results obtained.

Table 2. Demographic information of student participants

Population characteristics	Number of participants	Percentage
Male	9	75 %
Age		
18– 24	6	50 %
25– 34	4	33 %
35– 44	2	17 %
Ethnic or racial minority	3	25 %
Bacherlors Degree or Higher	6	50 %
Right Handed	10	83 %

5.1   Experience with Video Games and VR

Experience with video games and virtual reality was assessed on a three point self-report measure: No Experience, Some Experience, and Significant Experience. Though this was a very crude evaluation tool, it does allow students to easily classify their experience.

As shown in Table 3, there was a fair amount of variability in the response of the students with only one student reporting "Significant Experience" with virtual reality.

To improve the interpretability of the results, scores were coded: No Experience = 0, Some Experience = 1, and Significant Experience = 2. The two scales were summed. Students were then split into two groups, Low Experience (scores of 0 or 1, N = 5) and High Experience (scores greater than 1, N = 7).

Table 3. Participants experience with video games and virtual reality

Level of experience	Number of participants	Percentage
Video Game Experience		
No Experience	3	25 %
Some Experience	3	25 %
Significant Experience	6	50 %
Virtual Reality Experience		
No Experience	5	42 %
Some Experience	6	50 %
Significant Experience	1	8 %

5.2   Comparison of Scores on Physical and VR Tasks

As expected, students scored higher,, in the physical task compared to the virtual task, as seen in Table 4. At the one minute mark using the dominant hand, students physically moved 53.6 (sd = 7.1) blocks compare to 19.3 (sd = 5.0) moved through the computer interface. The results on the non-dominant had were very similar with 55.7 (sd = 6.7) moved in the physical task and 19.5 (s.d = 5.1) moved in the computer task. Paired comparisons between modalities were significantly different (p < .001).

Table 4. Number of blocks moved by each participant

Participant number	Physical		Virtual	
	Right	Left	Right	Left
1	44	48	26	21
2	55	57	24	25
3	58	50	27	28
4	49	46	21	17
5	62	61	16	24
6	56	69	20	21
7	58	52	12	12
8	60	55	13	14
9	63	60	20	13
10	45	46	20	18
11	45	51	21	15
12	59	62	15	24

Overall the it appeared that experience with video games and VR was associated superior ability to perform the computer task as the level of video game/VR experience was positively correlated with total blocks moved in the computer task, r = .834, but not in the physical task, r = .101. Contrary to expectations, the association between the total moved with both hands was insignificant p > .5.

5.3   Time Perception

Students, when asked to stop when they perceived five minutes had passed, spent approximately the same amount of time on the each modality. Total time spent of both dominant and non-dominant hands were 545 s (sd = 204) for the physical task and 536 (sd = 227) for the computer task, p > .5.

When the analysis was done between Low and High Experience students, there was a significant difference in the time spent performing the computer task. Those with High Experience performed the task for 427 s (sd = 169) compared to the Low Experience students who performed the task for 689 s (sd = 223), 2 min more.

5.4   Student's Subjective Experience

The subjective experiences of the students were evaluated. Table 5 presents the questions asked and the preferences of the students. As can be seen, the physical task was viewed as easier and less frustrating by the majority of students. Of note, the majority of students felt that technologies like the one used here should be developed to improve rehabilitation and would recommend this type of system to a family member.

Table 5. Subjective comparison of physical and virtual based tasks

	Physical		Computer		No preference	
	n	%	n	%	n	%
Which version was more fun?	6	50 %	4	33 %	2	17 %
Which version was more frustrating?	0	0 %	10	83 %	2	16 %
Which version was more stressful?	3	25 %	6	50 %	3	25 %
Which version make you more tired or worn out?	5	42 %	5	42 %	2	17 %
Which version required more work?	2	17 %	9	75 %	1	8 %
Which version would you rather do again?	7	58 %	3	25 %	2	17 %
Ratings on 1–10 with 10 being the highest					Average	SD
How useful do you think the tehcnology would be in assisting in rehabilitation?					7.1	2.1
If you were asked to use this type of technology for rehabilitation at home, how likely would you use it?					7.2	2.1
How strongly do you feel these types of technologies should be developed?					9.4	0.9
Would you recommend a friend or family member to use this technolgoy in their rehabilitation?					N	%
Yes					9	75 %
No					0	0 %
No Opinion					3	25 %

One interesting finding was that the subjective ratings appear, in part, related to the amount of experience the student had in video games/VR. In the item "Which version was more fun?" zero (0 %) of students in with Low Experience felt the virtual task was more 'fun'; this is significantly lower than the High Experience students where four (57 %) reported the virtual task was more fun, $X2(2, N = 7) = 8.6$; $p = .004$).

There were two common comments that were received by the participants about why the virtual version was harder and more frustrating. The first was that it was very difficult to grab the blocks at times in the virtual version. The second was that it was sometimes hard to perceive where the fingers were and what block you would be picking up.

6 Conclusions

In this paper, we have presented a virtual version of the Box and Blocks Test. We compared the scores and opinions of student volunteers who performed both the physical and virtual versions of the test. We showed that the amount of experience with video games and VR was positively correlated with their performance of the virtual task. We also compared their time perception during the two different tasks, showing that students with less video game and VR experience perceive time going slower than students with more experience. Lastly we showed that students, even though they found the virtual version more frustrating, would rather do that version again instead of the physical version. Also students with more VR experience found the virtual activity more fun than students with less experience.

7 Future Work

Future plans for this work include conducting a clinical versions of this study to get the opinions of patients who are actually undergoing therapy and whether they would want to use VR technologies or not. The target populations for future studies could include patients who are post-stroke, have significant hand pain due to arthritis, or children with cerebral palsy. Besides just gathering their opinions of the technology and comparing the performances between the two versions, we would also be comparing their pain levels between the two versions to see if patients feel less pain performing the virtual version.

We also plan to develop analysis tools to process the data obtained by Leap Motion during the one and five minute sessions. The data and results will be presented in a user interface designed for therapists. We will meet with therapists and discuss the data that is collected and how to visualize the data in a way that is useful to them.

Lastly, we will improve the ability for the person to interact with the virtual environment, mainly the ability to grasp blocks. There are two possible solutions being considered. The first is to improve how the game interprets the pinching motion of the hand while picking up the blocks. The second is to either change sensors or include other sensors to get a more accurate reading of the hand, fingers, and joints.

Acknowledgements. The authors wish to acknowledge the work of Benjamin Chebaa for assisting in the creation of the surveys, Raith Hamzah for developing the background elements to the virtual environment, and to Rebekah Roskens for editing the video. Also, we would like to thank the Dallas VA Research Corporation for providing partial support for this study. This work was also partially supported by the following NSF grants: 1041637, 1035913, 1338118 and 1439645. Any opinions, findings, and conclusions or recommendations expressed in this publication are those of the author(s) and do not necessarily reflect the views of the National Science Foundation.

References

1. Leap Motion Controller SDK. https://developer.leapmotion.com/
2. Tudor, S., Carey, S., Dubey, R.: Development and evaluation of a dynamic virtual reality driving simulator. In: Proceedings of the 8th ACM International Conference on PErvasive Technologies Related to Assistive Environments, pp. 55:1–55:5. ACM, New York (2015)
3. Nakamoto, T., Otaguro, S., Kinoshita, M., Nagahama, M., Ohinishi, K., Ishida, T.: Cooking up an interactive olfactory game display. J. IEEE Comput. Graph. Appl. **28**(1), 75–78 (2008)
4. Bozgeyikli, L., Bozgeyikli, E., Clevenger, M., Raij, A., Alqasemi, R., Sundarrao, S., Dubey, R.: VR4VR: vocational rehabilitation of individuals with disabilities in immersive virtual reality environments. In: Proceedings of the 8th ACM International Conference on PErvasive Technologies Related to Assistive Environments, pp. 54:1–54:4. ACM, New York (2015)
5. Charles, D., Pedlow, K., McDonough, S., Shek, K., Charles, T.: Close range depth sensing cameras for virtual reality based hand rehabilitation. J. Assistive Technol. **8**(3), 138–149 (2014)
6. Sveistrup, H.: Motor rehabilitation using virtual reality. J. NeuroEngineering Rehabil. **1**(1), 1–8 (2004)
7. Mathiowetz, V., Volland, G., Kashman, N., Weber, K.: Adult norms for the box and blocks test of manual dexterity. Am. J. Occup. Ther. **39**(6), 386–391 (1985)
8. Angrilli, A., Cherubini, P., Pavese, A., Manfredini, S.: The influence of affective factors on time perception. Percept. Psychophys. **59**(6), 972–982 (1997)
9. Droit-Volet, S., Brunot, S., Niedenthal, P.M.: Perception of the duration of emotional events. Cogn. Emot. **18**(6), 849–858 (2004)
10. Gable, P.A., Poole, B.D.: Time flies when you're having approach-motivated fun: effects of motivational intensity on time perception. Psychol. Sci. **23**(8), 879–886 (2012)
11. Odgen, R.S., Moore, D., Redfern, L., McGlone, F.: Stroke me for longer this touch feels too short: the effect of pleasant touch on temporal perception. Conscious. Cogn. **36**, 306–313 (2015)
12. Odgen, R.S., Moore, D., Redfern, L., McGlone, F.: The effect of pain and the anticipation of pain on temporal perception: A role for attention and arousal. Cogn. Emot. **29**(5), 910–922 (2015)
13. Fayolle, S., Gil, S., Droit-Volet, S.: Fear and time: fear speeds up the internal clock. Behav. Process. **120**, 135–140 (2015)
14. Keshner, E.: Virtual reality and physical rehabilitation: a new toy or a new research and rehabilitation tool? J. NeuroEngineering Rehabil. **1**(1), 1–2 (2004)
15. Khademi, M., Hondori, H.M., McKenzie, A., Dodakian, L., Lopes, C.V., Cramer, S.C.: Free-hand interaction with leap motion controller for stroke rehabilitation. In: CHI 2014 Extended Abstracts on Human Factors in Computing Systems, pp. 1663–1668. ACM, New York (2014)
16. Bryanton, C., Bosse, J., Brien, M., Mclean, J., McCormick, A., Sveistrup, H.: Feasibility, motivation and selective motor control: virtual reality compared to conventional home exercise in children with cerebral palsy. Cyberpsychology Behavior. **19**(2), 123–128 (2006)
17. Gieser, S.N., Boisselle, A., Makedon, F.: Real-time static gesture recognition for upper extremity rehabilitation using the leap motion. In: Scholz, S.-B., Duffy, G.V. (eds.) DHM 2015. LNCS, vol. 9185, pp. 144–154. Springer, Heidelberg (2015)

18. Broeren, J., Claesson, L., Goude, D., Rydmark, M., Sunnerhagen, K.S.: Virtual rehabilitation in an activity centre for community-dwelling persons with stroke. J. Cerebrovascular Diseases. **26**(3), 289–296 (2008)
19. Saposnik, G., Teasell, R., Mamdani, M., Hall, J., McIlroy, W., Cheung, D., Thorpe, K.E., Cohen, L.G., Bayley, M.: Effectiveness of virtual reality using wii gaming technology in stroke rehabilitation: a pilot randomized clinical trial and proof of principle. J. Stroke. **41**(7), 1477–1484 (2010)
20. Cho, S., Kim, W.S., Paik, N.J., Bang, H.: Upper-limb function assessment using VBBTs for stroke patients. IEEE Comput. Graph. Appl. **36**(1), 70–78 (2016)
21. Tobin, S., Grondin, S.: Video games and the perception of very long durations by adolescents. Comput. Hum. Behav. **25**(2), 554–559 (2009)
22. Rau, P.P., Peng, S.Y., Yang, C.C.: Time distortion for expert and novice online game players. Cyberpsychology Behavior. **9**(4), 396–403 (2006)
23. Unity Game Engine. http://unity3d.com/5
24. Box and Blocks Test Instructions. http://www.rehabmeasures.org/PDF%20Library/Box%20and%20Blocks%20Test%20Instructions.pdf

Avatar Types Matter: Review of Avatar Literature for Performance Purposes

Irwin Hudson[1]([✉]) and Jonathan Hurter[2]

[1] U.S. Army Research Laboratory, Orlando, USA
irwin.hudson@us.army.mil
[2] Institute for Simulation and Training, University of Central Florida, Orlando, USA
jhurter@ist.ucf.edu

Abstract. The use of avatars as learning agents is becoming increasingly popular in the sports, education and military domains due to the rapid advancement in distributive technologies (e.g., internet, virtual worlds, etc.). When it comes to military and sports, Simulation-Based Training has proven to be cost-effective, due largely to restrictions on time, costs and safety [1]. As virtual reality and virtual worlds have become cheaper and more powerful in computer terms, the subject of how an avatar relates to an avateer (the avatar's controller) is becoming increasingly popular. More precisely, interest rests on how an avatar's appearance may promote or disrupt training objectives, by affecting the behavior or the psychology of a user, and thus subsequently raising or degrading learning. Virtual simulations for training have often shared the aspect of avatars found in Virtual Reality, video games, and Virtual Worlds. This paper examines how avatar representation can provide insight into manipulating avatar appearance for training demands. Existing literature suggests avatars act as drivers for affective changes in attitude and motivation, and can be integrated into an instructional strategy.

Keywords: Agent · Avatar · Doppelganger · Virtual environments · Virtual reality · Instructional systems design · Motivation · Attitude · Simulation

1 Introduction

Simulation-Based Training (SBT) is often carried out through a Virtual Environment (VE), where a user (or learner) is situated in a synthetic environment for carrying out authentic tasks. Aspects of military training, due largely to restrictions on time, cost, and safety, have the potential to be cost-effectively enhanced by SBT [1].

As in other uses of digital and interactive media, such as video games, an avatar in SBT represents the learner as a virtual substitute. An avatar is a stand-in for the person, which may be represented by a human character, another animal, a vehicle, or any other image. Specific human examples include a generic virtual human, a subject matter expert (SME), and a doppelganger or look-alike - an avatar that realistically matches its owner's features (Fig. 1). A user typically inhabits an avatar in a Virtual Reality (VR) system, enacting as an entity within the environment. In contrast, a user's icon in a text-based Internet message forum also acts an avatar. Ultimately, a range of media can afford avatar

© Springer International Publishing Switzerland 2016
S. Lackey and R. Shumaker (Eds.): VAMR 2016, LNCS 9740, pp. 14–21, 2016.
DOI: 10.1007/978-3-319-39907-2_2

usage. Avatars, for our research purposes, do not include digital actors, such as Digital Emily [2], or agents endowed with artificial intelligence, such as intelligent tutors and virtual assistants. As VEs have become cheaper and more powerful in computing terms, interest in how an avatar relates to an avateer (i.e., the avatar's controller) has spawned research questions in the natural sciences, social sciences, and arts. While other aspects of avatar behavior lag in development (e.g., nuanced and spontaneous facial movements correlating with a user), basic avatar appearance has been spotlighted as it can be flexibly customized. Namely, this paper's interest is in how an avatar's appearance may be manipulated to promote training objectives. Through changing the behavior and psychology of a user, avatars could aid in raising positive transfer to a real-world task. Virtual reality experiments consisting of virtually embodied avatars have elicited user behaviors, after experimental exposure, which corroborate the idea that avatar appearance can affect one's beliefs, attitudes, and perspective. Avatars manifested in other forms of VEs, too, can shape user performance. What follows is a brief review of how avatars' appearances affect behavior, and the consequent implications for SBT.

  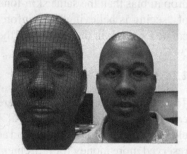

Fig. 1. Avatar types (from left to right): a generic avatar, a military SME avatar, and a doppelganger avatar (shown with corresponding avateer) (Doppelganger photograph replicated with permission from Hudson and Badillo-Urquiola [24]).

2   Avatar Appearance Effects in Virtual Reality

A VR system allows a user to be submerged within a synthetic space, or alternate reality. Key features of VR include interactivity within said space, displays (i.e., sensory dimensions of seeing, hearing, touching, and so on) providing feedback for interactions within that space, and a contrived world that allows for immersion, or the feeling of "losing oneself," in an experience [3]. Pure VR technology is concerned with constructing a replacement of real elements; a holistic illusion of some real or fantastical idea and/or environment. This type of virtuality is in contrast to forms of mixed reality: augmented reality, where virtual objects are injected into real-world environments; and augmented virtuality, where real-world elements are placed in a predominately virtual environment [4]. Researchers using virtual simulations have applied the strengths of VR to influence user behaviors.

Manipulating avatar appearance, in conjunction with VR capabilities, is a specific type of research that offers insight into facilitating performance. Avatar-appearance has been a factor for altering racial bias, exacerbating musical body-movements, and improving susceptibility for choosing long-term retirement savings. All these experiments involved immersive VR, where humans had some level of control over their embodied avatars. Additionally, improved exercise motivation has been attributed through vicariously watching a doppelganger run.

2.1   Racial Bias

Employing VR, negative bias towards African-Americans was lowered for users that embodied a dark-skinned avatar, in comparison to wearing the "skin" of either a Caucasian person or a purple alien [5]. Importantly, one experimental group had black-skinned avatars that matched each user's coincident real-life body movements, as shown in a virtual mirror. However, another experimental group had black-skinned avatars that lacked the mimicking features of the virtual mirror. This type of interaction had a significant difference, where those with reciprocating body movements having a higher drop in bias than the same skin-tone avatars without the mirror effect. Here, the maxim of "seeing is believing" is reinforced, where the non-reciprocating avatars may have created a break in the illusion of the VR system.

2.2   Retirement Savings

The effects of embodying a different version of a human were also replicated in an experiment by Hershfield et al. [6]. Users who spent time embodied in a photo-realistic, elderly version of themselves, and accessed aforementioned aspects of mirror-matching, reserved more money for retirement. A hypothetical task given before and after the VR intervention served to detect changes in monetary savings behavior. The condition where users did not view an elderly version while in the VR had little effect on this task.

2.3   Musical Body Movements

Finally, again adopting a mirror-matching paradigm, users who embodied a dark-skinned and casually dressed avatar were more likely than other avateers to have a wide range of body movements while playing a djembe drum [7]. The other avatars consisted either of a light-skinned person wearing a formal suit, or a pair of opaque, white, floating hands. This experiment suggests social cues are inferred and internalized during body ownership.

2.4   Exercise Motivation

Attitudes toward exercising have been a source of interest in terms of avatar manipulation. In two experiments, highly realistic doppelgangers and generic avatars were viewed in three conditions: a doppelganger running, a generic running, and a doppelganger loitering [8, 9]. In the first experiment, users who watched their avatar double run were the most likely to perform more exercise within 24 h after the experiment. A second, companion experiment inspected these conditions (with an added fourth condition of a generic loitering), with objective, physiological measures of arousal serving as variables. The highest rates of arousal were found in doppelgangers exercising and generics loitering. The doppelganger effect may point to imagining oneself running from previous experience, or perhaps higher engagement by vicariously watching oneself exercise. The generic loitering may have raised nervousness and lowered comfortability.

2.5 Implications for Training from Virtual Reality

The central question to our research was, "Does avatar appearance effect learning?" To answer this, we review the evidence built from the foothold of VR avatar literature. The associations, bonding, and/or empathy elicited in some of the VR experiments can cascade into behavioral changes. Specifically, perspective and attitudes have been altered due to the control, feedback, and illusion of an avatar, in what Slater and Sanchez-Vives term "body semantics" [10]. Further, a learner watching their doppelganger avatar running impacts the user to increase exercise. The act of "becoming" a different race, an elderly version of one's physical self, or an athletic self (indirectly), resulted in changes within a value system. If a learning objective is to teach one to exhibit a certain behavior that is attitudinal in nature, avatar usage appears appropriate. Ultimately, supporting motivation can be integral for any objective. The terms attitude and motivation are used in the sense of being part of the user's affective domain. According to Hays [11], affective behaviors can play a role in orienting the learner's system to receive content: affective behaviors "primarily influence interactions among the learner's decider subsystem, input transducer, associator, and memory to open the input screen to the material to be learned" (p. 208). In common terms, learning occurs because one is open to learning, or is in an accepting mood for learning. If a student does not want to learn, the process for learning becomes arduous.

The requirements of time, personnel, space, and equipment can drain project resources for a VR experiment or training setup. Clark [12] proposes a replaceability challenge to compare differing types of media, and decide if a cheaper or more convenient avenue is available. The experiment where users interacted with their digitally-aged doubles had an impact on saving behavior, yet came with hefty technology. The authors thus decided to simplify their results using only a 2-D aged-self or present-self on an online application [6]. The aged avatar would smile if money was reserved for retirement, or frown (in gradations) for placing less amounts of money in retirement. The opposite facial features roles existed in the present-self condition. The aged-self participants, as in the original VR experiment, placed more money in a retirement fund. Here, an avatar still exists (if in the abstracted form of a floating head), while retaining avatar-appearance effects for effectively considering future finances. Practical use of a VR may be limited, thereby inviting innovation with other forms of media and VEs for behavior modification.

3   Avatar Appearance Effects in Other Virtual Environments

Virtual Reality is one type of VE. To give adequate depth to avatar research, other VEs involving avatars deserve mention. These include video games in a broad sense (entertainment-oriented or learning-oriented), and Virtual Worlds (VWs). A recent game-based turn in training has caused serious games to be criticized for their potential benefits [13, 14]. Since serious games blend aspects of entertainment with formal instruction, one part of these games' efficacy may rest on avatar appearances.

3.1   Video Games

Given an endless runner game, users who played as an avatar that resembled themselves had more intrinsic motivation than users who played as a random avatar for their character [15]. The former group identified highly with their avatar, a sign of character attachment that aligns with Banks and Bowman's [16] view of users creating an "avatar-as-Me" projection.

Applying a serious game for math and programming skills, an experiment by Kao [17] allowed users to be represented either by a geometric shape, or by a human cartoon character. The cartoon character was extracted from the Nintendo Wii's mii catalog to resemble a user's likeness. The abstract shape group outperformed the other group, which might signal that the mii group was over-attached to their likeness avatars (attributing failure to themselves), that the avatars were distracting, or that the avatars reinforced stereotypes (given that the game used was a programming and math game, females may have subscribed to the stereotype of being bad at math).

3.2   Virtual Worlds

Virtual sandboxes, or VWs, are another type of VE where avatar appearances are connected to human behavior. These systems are sandboxes in the sense of being coordinated by user and community guidelines, rather than the necessarily enforced rules of games. In Second Life (SL), avatars socialize, play, learn, and shop via avatars. Within SL, many users feel less inhibited, choose preferred body sizes, and don virtual drag that portrays their ideal identity [18].

3.3   Implications for Training from Other Virtual Environments

There are signs of avatar appearance effects on learning within types of VEs, but the avatar functions can be contradictory. For example, doppelgangers helped performance in the endless runner game, yet were connected to hindering performance in the programming game. Even proposals for avatar utilization clash: Fox, Bailenson, and Ricciardi [9] believe using a doppelganger to show ideal behaviors may improve self-efficacy (i.e., the learner's belief they can complete a task), but Yim and Graham [19] contend that an ideal doppelganger would lower self-efficacy. The difference is that the ideal behavior in the former is for social anxiety (the avatar would perform social behaviors), whereas the latter is for exercising (where a thinner version of the self would induce negative feelings of inadequacy, and lead to demotivation). Ultimately, the task and how an audience would react to an avatar should be analyzed. To illustrate, an ideal-weight self may be appropriate in SL for socializing or shopping, but questionable in a work-out simulation. Additionally, a work-out simulation may circumvent building a negative sense of self by removing both a 3rd-person and mirror-image view of the avatar completely, or by adapting a non-human character.

4   Limitations and Future Directions

Instead of a global review, this paper investigated a few crucial points, in an economical look at existing avatar phenomena. The Proteus Effect, for example, is a topic warranting substantial consideration as a driver of performance in future research. The Proteus Effect explains that a person will change their behavior in accordance with the expectations a community places on that person's avatar appearance [20].

As a limit, the experiments discussed involved short periods of avatar use in experimental settings. This artificial setup ignores that avatar-relations can develop over long periods of time, and strengthen with investment in a character. There are also many combinations of avatars, and therefore many variations are ignored for the sake of an experiment. For instance, clothing has had effects in the real-world on improving cognition [21], begetting investigation for changes in avatar clothing. Another future tangent is determining if, and when, avatar appearance does not significantly matter.

Tweaking avatar appearance suggests a suitable vehicle for improving motivation. Baylor [22] has noted the important link between motivation and avatar appearance. In the realm of instructional design, instilling motivation in a trainee serves as a critical step in the learning process. The Attention, Relevance, Confidence, and Satisfaction (ARCS) Model of Motivational Design was developed by Keller [23] to address motivational needs. This model serves as a starting point for mapping types of avatars to types of motivation. Hypothetically, a goal in a serious game may be more relevant to a person if the avatar is a doppelganger, and student attention may be gained by a soldier SME avatar in a VE for warfighter tasks. Such applications would require testing for their effectiveness. A next step towards understanding avatar-appearance training factors is to find the ways avatar types map to a motivational framework.

5   Conclusion

This paper addressed whether avatar appearances can function as a tool for improving performance. Various studies on VR and other VE applications have shown that avatar appearance can change behaviors, such as attitudes and motivation. These types of applications suggest avatars as part of a larger instructional strategy. That is, changing an avatar may support performance, rather than completely predicting performance. The early stage of research on avatar types leads to pertinent illustrations and strong evidence, rather than a complete concrete framework, for adapting avatar appearances towards a learning objective.

Acknowledgements. This research was sponsored by the U.S. Army Research Laboratory – Human Research Engineering Directorate Advanced Training and Simulation Division (ARL HRED ATSD), in collaboration with the Institute for Simulation and Training at the University of Central Florida. The views and conclusions contained in this document are those of the authors and should not be interpreted as representing the official policies, either expressed or implied, of ARL HRED ATSD or the U.S. Government. The U.S. Government is authorized to reproduce and distribute reprints for Government purposes notwithstanding any copyright notation hereon.

References

1. Wilson, C.: Avatars, virtual reality technology, and the U.S. military: emerging policy issues. Congressional Research Service (CRS) Reports and Issue Briefs (2008)
2. Alexander, O., Rogers, M., Lambeth, W., Jen-Yuan, C., Wan-Chun, M., Chuan-Chang, W., Debevec, P.: The digital emily project: achieving a photorealistic digital actor. IEEE Comput. Graph. Appl. **30**(4), 20–31 (2010)
3. Craig, A.B., Sherman, W.R.: Understanding Virtual Reality: Interface, Application, and Design. Morgan Kaufmann, London (2003)
4. Milgram, P., Takemura, H., Utsumi, A., Kishino, F.: Augmented reality: a class of displays on the reality-virtuality continuum, SPIE, vol. 2351, pp. 282–292. International Society for Optical Engineering (1995)
5. Peck, T.C., Seinfeld, S., Aglioti, S.M., Slater, M.: Putting yourself in the skin of a black avatar reduces implicit racial bias. Conscious. Cogn. **22**(3), 779–787 (2013)
6. Hershfield, H.E., Goldstein, D.G., Sharpe, W.F., Yeykelis, L., Carstensen, L.L., Bailenson, J.N.: Increasing saving behavior through age-progressed renderings of the future self. J. Mark. Res. **48**, 23–37 (2011)
7. Kilteni, K., Bergstrom, I., Slater, M.: Drumming in immersive virtual reality: The body shapes the way we play. IEEE Trans. Vis. Comput. Graph. **19**(4), 597–605 (2013)
8. Fox, J., Bailenson, J.N.: Virtual self-modeling: The effects of vicarious reinforcement and identification on exercise behaviors. Media Psychol. **12**(1), 1–25 (2009)
9. Fox, J., Bailenson, J.N., Ricciardi, T.: Physiological responses to virtual selves and virtual others. J. Cybertherapy **5**(1), 69–72 (2012)
10. Slater, M., Sanchez-Vives, M.V.: Transcending the self in immersive virtual reality. Computer **47**(7), 24–30 (2014)
11. Hays, R.: The Science of Learning: A Systems Theory Perspective. BrownWalker Press, Boca Raton (2006)
12. Clark, R.E.: Media will never influence learning. Educ. Technol. Res. Dev. **42**(2), 21–29 (1994)
13. Connolly, T.M., Boyle, E.A., MacArthur, E., Hainey, T., Boyle, J.M.: A systematic literature review of empirical evidence on computer games and serious games. Comput. Educ. **59**(2), 661–686 (2012)
14. Gunter, G.A., Kenny, R.F., Vick, E.H.: Taking educational games seriously: using the RETAIN model to design endogenous fantasy into standalone educational games. Educ. Technol. Res. Dev. **56**(5/6), 511–537 (2008)
15. Birk, M., Atkins, C., Bowey, J.T., Mandryk, R.L.: Fostering intrinsic motivation through avatar identification in digital games. In: Proceedings of the SIGCHI Conference on Human Factors in Computing Systems (CHI 2016). San Jose (2016, in press)

16. Banks, J., Bowman, N.D.: Close intimate playthings? understanding player-avatar relationships as a function of attachment, agency, and intimacy. Sel. Pap. Internet Res. **3**, 1–4 (2013)
17. Kao, D., Harrell, D.F.: Toward avatar models to enhance performance and engagement in educational games. In: Proceedings of the 2015 IEEE Conference on Computational Intelligence & Games (CIG), pp. 246–253 (2015)
18. Messinger, P.R., Stroulia, E., Lyons, K., Bone, M., Niu, R.H., Smirnov, K.: Virtual worlds-past, present, and future: new directions in social computing. Decis. Support Syst. **47**(3), 204–228 (2009)
19. Yim, J., Graham, T.N.: Using games to increase exercise motivation. In: Proceedings of the 2007 Conference, Future Play, pp. 166–173 (2007)
20. Yee, N., Bailenson, J.: The proteus effect: the effect of transformed self-representation on behavior. Hum. Commun. Res. **33**(3), 271–290 (2007)
21. Adam, H., Galinsky, A.D.: Enclothed cognition. J. Exp. Soc. Psychol. **48**(4), 918–925 (2012)
22. Baylor, A.L.: Promoting motivation with virtual agents and avatars: role of visual presence and appearance. Philos. Trans. R. Soc. Lond. Ser. B Biol. Sci. **364**(1535), 3559–3565 (2009)
23. Keller, J.M.: Motivational Design for Learning and Performance: The ARCS Model Approach, 2010th edn. Springer, New York (2010)
24. Hudson, I., Badillo-Urquiola, K.: Virtual approach to psychomotor skills training: manipulating the appearance of avatars to influence learning. In: Shumaker, R., Lackey, S. (eds.) VAMR 2015. LNCS, vol. 9179, pp. 292–299. Springer, Heidelberg (2015)

A Tool for Assessing User Experience
of Fit of a Virtual Workplace

Ursula Hyrkkänen[1(✉)], Suvi Nenonen[2], and Carolyn Axtell[3]

[1] Turku University, Turku, Finland
ursula.hyrkkanen@tuas.fi
[2] Aalto University, Helsinki, Finland
[3] Sheffield University, Sheffield, UK

Abstract. The aim of this article is to formulate theoretical premises for a virtual workplace fit/misfit assessment tool as well as pilot the tool with a preliminary study. The theoretical basis lies in the environment-person fit theory applied in the field of worker-workspace relationship. The categories of Frequency, Atmosphere, Familiarity, Functionality, Narrative and Meaning of the place were developed and used for assessing the fit of a virtual workplace. The pilot research showed that the categories systematically sorted out the features of the virtual workplace in a way that might be useful for illustrating the differences of various virtual workplaces and thus assessing the fit of various virtual workplaces.

Keywords: Virtual workplace · Fit and misfit of virtual workplace · Person–environment fit theory · Worker – workspace relationship

1 Introduction

Working anytime and anywhere is a reality which will become more and more prevalent [1–3]. Mobile employees work many hours per week outside of the primary workplace and constantly use information and communication technologies for collaboration and have a requirement to be connected to shared resources for achieving joint goals [e.g. 4–6]. Because mobile work happens in ever-changing situations and bears the need to collaborate with other workers and customers, it expands the working environment as well as the need to master and control both many physical and virtual spaces used for work [5]. According to Bailey, Leonardi and Barley [7], virtuality occurs when digital representations stand for, or in some cases completely substitute, the physical objects, processes or people they represent. The virtual workplace provides connectivity through different sizes of devices and is accessed by different interfaces when supporting the performance of both individual and collaborative work activities [8].

However, the research considering virtual space as a working place is still rare. There is research connected to the performance of a virtual team [9, 10], the management of the virtual team [11, 12], and developing the virtual team processes [13]. But when talking about the virtual workplace, virtual workplace development or the management of it, the research is almost lacking or takes only the tools or interfaces into consideration. For example Popma [3] states that place-independent screen work

S. Lackey and R. Shumaker (Eds.): VAMR 2016, LNCS 9740, pp. 22–34, 2016.
DOI: 10.1007/978-3-319-39907-2_3

which is a characteristic feature of New Ways of Working (NewWoW) is more than the workstation. The environment around the station should also be taken into account when ensuring the healthiness and safety of work: behind the screen, there is a new world with its features and behavioral demands.

Whilst the contemporary literature shows that the most research concerning the fit between the person and the work environment has been approached from the psychosocial point of view [14] a growing number of studies on virtuality approach it from the technology- or system-oriented views [15]. In the technology-oriented approach, virtuality is usually measured as the amount, frequency and quality of ICT-mediated communication. In addition to technology, the system-oriented research takes into account the intra-group processes and work processes generating the need to collaborate virtually [16].

The interest of this article is to initiate the definition for virtual workplace fit and formulate a structure for virtual workplace fit assessment. The aim is to formulate theoretical premises for a virtual workplace assessment tool as well as pilot the idea with a preliminary study. The theoretical basis lies in the environment-person fit theory applied in the field of worker-workspace relationship [17–20]. In prior studies Hyrkkänen, Nenonen and Kojo [21], Hyrkkänen and Nenonen [22] have used Visher's [18, 19] model of fit or misfit in worker-workplace relationship and expanded it to also cover virtual work. The other premise of this article is in the field of assessing user experiences of workplace and especially in the studies where Diller's et al. [23] classification for workplace assessment has been modified and modelled to six dimensions of workplace experience assessment [24, 25].

The article will proceed as follows. The background section will present the prior research where Vischer's model of a three-level assessment of fit and misfit of workplace has been modified for virtual workplace assessment as well as Diller's et al. classification modified for assessing experiences of the workplace. Section three deals with the methodology. Section four deals with the piloting and the results. The final section includes the conclusions, the limitations of this research and suggestions for future steps for enhancing the assessment of virtual workplace fit or misfit.

2 Background

The Person–Environment (PE) fit theory states that fit or compatibility between an individual and work environment occurs when their characteristics are well matched. The match i.e. fit has alternatively been conceptualized as equilibrium between needs and satisfaction or between demands and abilities [26]. The fit may be complementary or supplementary. The PE theory asserts that the fit between individual characteristics such as needs, abilities and values and environmental characteristics such as job supplies, job demands and organizational values affect employees' attitudes and behaviors such as satisfaction, commitment and turnover [14].

Based on the ideas of PE fit, Vischer [17–20] has formulated a model of worker–workspace relationship according to which the elements in the physical workspace can affect fit or misfit between a person and the environment at work. In her studies, fit or misfit is the cause of the relationship between the physical environment and users' needs, or in the demands which environment places on users. When the environment sets inappropriate or excessive demands to users, in spite of their adaptation and adjustment behaviours, it manifests the concept of misfit. In a good fit there is a balance between a person's abilities, skills, degree of control and decision latitude and the work environment's demands, complexity, expectations and challenges. The nature of person–environment transactions arouses the sensation of either comfort or stress. Comfort may be considered as the fit of the user to the environment in the context of work [17, 18, 27]. The fit or misfit which originates from the transaction between an employee and her/his work environment can be observed from three different levels, i.e. physical, functional and psychological [17–20]. Physical comfort of physical space includes basic human needs such as safety, hygiene and accessibility. Functional comfort is defined in terms of support for users' performance in work-related tasks and activities. Psychological comfort contains feelings of belonging, ownership and control over workspace.

Hyrkkänen, Nenonen and Kojo [21, 22], expanded Visher's model of fit or misfit to cover also virtual work and explored the elements of the virtual workplace that either hinder or enable productive mobile virtual work [22]. Physical fit consisted of physical features of ICT tools and applications for the virtual work as well as the physical places where the virtual work was executed, including ergonomics. Physical fit was also determined from the appropriateness of the virtual place to the human sensory system. The functional fit consisted of connectivity issues such as the availability, speed and functionality of the internet connection. Hyrkkänen et al. [21, 22] concluded that the substantial threshold of virtual work lies at the functional fit level. The work of an employee stops completely if the worker has connectivity problems, i.e. problems at the functional level. The discourse concerning the psychosocial fit of virtual places dealt with the concepts of territoriality, privacy and control. Territoriality was related to the need of belonging and the proper selection of interactive communication tools and channels. The need of privacy was challenged with dual and multi-presence demands arising from simultaneous use of many virtual places as well as also physically being in some social space. Need of control emerged from the demand of being continuously virtually available. The fit at the psychosocial level was found to be a mixture of physical and virtual worlds [21].

Nenonen and Kojo [24, 25] modified and tested a framework for assessing the user experience of workplace through abductive reasoning of Diller's et al. (2005) classification of experience. The developed model was aimed as a physical workplace assessment tool and it has six dimensions: the frequency, atmosphere, familiarity, functionality, narrative and meaning of the place.

According to the researchers, the frequency experience of a place refers to activities happening at a certain rhythm and tempo in the place [24]. The dimension of the frequency of the place is connected with the use of time, sense of time and rhythm of time in the place. The atmosphere is related to how the solutions fit and affect humansenses, e.g. seeing and different cognitive symbols (such as signs) relate to this dimension [24]. The dimension of familiarity [24] of the place refers to the ease of use of the place and how to learn to use the place. The dimension of the functionality [24] of the place indicates how the place supports the activities and the performance. The dimension of narrative [24] of the place means the constancy and coherency of the story of the place, e.g. identity, brand and purpose of the place. The dimension of meaning [24] expresses the significance of the place for its users. It relates to tangible and intangible values as part of the place experience, e.g. ownership. Nenonen and Kojo [24] conclude that the six dimensions of experience of place can be clustered according to Vischer's [18–20] model of physical, functional and psychological levels of fit or misfit of the working place, as in Table 1. Frequency and atmosphere can be used for assessing the physical features of the place; familiarity and functionality for studying the functional features of the place, and the dimensions of narrative and meaning for assessing the psychosocial features of the place.

Table 1. Clustered dimensions of the experience of place (mod. Nenonen & Kojo 2013)

Experiences related to physical features of the place	Experiences related to functional features of the place	Experiences related to psychosocial features of the place
Frequency	Familiarity	Narrative
Atmosphere	Functionality	Meaning

In this study the clustered themes combining the theories of fit and physical workplace experience assessment were modified as categories for assessing the virtual workplace fit or misfit. Further the formulated themes were tested against the interview data concerning virtual meeting in virtual settings.

3 Method

Because the aim was to develop a framework and structure of themes for virtual workplace fit assessment a constructive study was used as a methodological frame for this preliminary case study [28]. The case study was commenced as an iterative process between empirical interview data and the selected theory bases of PE-fit as well as Diller's classification of user experiences.

The experience category related themes for virtual work place assessment were developed based on the above-mentioned theories and results of prior studies [21, 22, 24] in focus group sessions. The participants of the three focus group sessions represented researchers from ICT science, constructed environment science, facility management science, work and organisational psychology and ergonomics.

For testing the developed frame semi-structured interview data was gathered. Because user experience is a holistic and all-encompassing concept including the user, the product and the contexts of use [30], the interviews (N=10) were carried in the physical workplace of each interviewee while she/he was working in the virtual workplace, i.e. when she/he used the programme and the virtual meeting place for collaboration. The interviewees were selected purposively. They all worked either in international R&D projects or arranged international eLearning sessions and used the same software meant for a Web conferencing platform for Web meetings, eLearning, and webinars. The platform allows creating, customising and branding digital meetings according to you or your organisation's needs. With the software it is possible to securely store files, documents, layouts and notes in a consistent manner. eLearning sessions may be conducted in virtual classes across devices. In webinars it is possible to communicate a message with, for example, dynamic multimedia content, social media integration and real-time engagement monitoring. The interviewees used the programme and virtual space for conducting meetings or collaborative eLearning sessions and had prepared the virtual place as a meeting or learning room (Table 2).

Table 2. Themes used for coding

	Experience category	Themes	Example
Physical	Frequency	Use of time, sense of time and time in the place.	*When there is a discursive lecture where the participants can chat, write and ask questions all the time, there are so many things you must constantly be aware of that you become exhausted after 60 min.*
	Atmosphere	Sense-experience of the place, sight, hearing and also cognitive symbols.	*If there are many participants, your voice easily starts to echo. That quickly makes you feel nervous and annoyed. On the other hand, people are somehow a bit reserved here because they know that there are buzzing microphones...*
Functional	Familiarity	Ease of entering and using the place.	*I gave instructions on the functions of the meeting application, about how to behave, what is allowed and what you should not do. Then I gave them time to try out things on their own. Still they were nervous about coming here...*
	Functionality	Ease of operating in the place for achieving the purposes of the session.	*You can also share presentations and documents. This means that when somebody has prepared a paper, you can view it through here. We can discuss a paper, but we cannot actually work on it here together.*

(Continued)

Table 2. (*Continued*)

	Experience category	Themes	Example
Psychosocial	Narrative	Story of the identity, brand and purpose of the place.	*I do not long for organisation symbols. It is in line with constructivism that when people are globally present in a workspace in different countries, the more familiar the workspace appears, the better people will adapt to it.*
	Meaning	Significance and meaning through belonging, ownership, control and privacy	*When using the system, you somehow feel that everybody is working together in the same space. The time when you come together is devoted to shared work. I think it is important in that sense.*

The interviews were recorded, transcribed and encoded according to six dimensions with the help of the AtlasTi programme. Accordingly the categories and category-related themes were further shaped and the examples for guiding the interpretation were derived (see examples taken from the transcribed texts). Then the focused coding was then used to extract passages related to these six main themes. The coding was an iterative process between the two researchers in order to increase validity.

4   Outcomes

4.1   Frequency of the Usage of the Place Was Short, Intended and Scheduled

The interviewees arranged either a meeting or learning sessions in the virtual meeting room. The frequency they used the place for varied from weekly to once a month. All the interviewees had used the tools and the virtual meeting programme for at least two years.

The use was characterised as intended, planned and scheduled carefully beforehand. The virtual meeting or learning place was not used unsystematically, such as asking for help for an acute or sudden problem. The preparation phase before the session was done thoroughly and for that reason it was time-consuming (several hours, even days).

The actual session was then straightforward, intense and brief. The interviewees described the rhythm of the virtual workplace as hasty and filled with no nonsense issues. Compared with face to face meetings there were no normal minor breaks caused, for example, by normal body motions. The rhythm of the meetings and learning sessions was altered also due to a minor amount of non-verbal communication. The lack of non-verbal communication and dominance of verbal official communication gave the impression of formality. Due to the intense character of the session, the leaders explained that time felt long and they felt nervous when there was too long a silence or they had to wait for somebody writing a comment. They also had to remind other participants to take it easy when there were activities other than talking going on.

All the interviewees thought that they had to concentrate on the virtual meetings in a way that exhausted them in an hour. So for that reason also the meetings or learning sessions lasted typically no longer than an hour. They also explained that the nature of the virtual session was fact-oriented and as they had prepared it carefully, the hour was enough to meet fact-oriented goals. There were no normal breaks caused by informal communication—or they were very minor, normally at the beginning or at the end of the session. After the meeting, the leaders also spent some time in the virtual place arranging, saving and sending documents and other meeting or learning material to participants. Others had then already left the place.

4.2 The Atmosphere of the Place Based on Official Grey Rectangles and Texts

The layout of the place is divided into rectangles, where there is a space for video which participants send (mainly a video of the participant's face), a place for shared documents (e.g. slides), a board for notes and shared ideas and plans and a space for chat. The layout can be modified according to the needs of the session or according to the preferences of the leader or the participants. During the meeting participants could talk, make notes, chat, raise a hand to take the floor and different polling activities could also be organised.

The pertinence was a dominant feature whereby the interviewees described the physical characteristics of the virtual meeting or learning place. A grey background colour, rectangles for different activities and functions and only minor marks illustrating the organisation moulded the feeling in the space as business-like. Some of the interviewees were satisfied with the simplified, even dull, official look of the place. They respected the simple look so as not to get one's interest in unnecessary secondary matters. A plane look was preferred because it does not cause visual interruptions.

The interviewees could see the texts and fonts properly. The problem with the view was in perceiving simultaneous and different functions taking place in the multiple rectangles on the screen (e.g. simultaneous chat and sharing notes going on and you have also to act as a moderator). The audio-talking connections sometimes acted up and that was a substantial problem, which even hindered participation in the session.

Sharing the facial video picture was considered important—a shared face manifested active involvement in the meeting or learning session. If somebody was not sending video, other participants felt that she/he was not actively in attendance and sometimes she/he was thought to be even disrespecting the meeting. However, sending facial video overloaded the connection and caused disturbances. The facial video helped participants read a little non-verbal communication. Mainly, however, they used it to determine who was willing to talk next.

The leaders advised the participants to use the hand raising function when asking to address the meeting, especially when there tended to be an echo due to multiple talking connections. They then instruct participants to mute the line and after raising a hand turn the line on for talking. However, muting the line if not talking changed the atmosphere of the place. Interviewees thought that it was more difficult to reach the feeling of shared space because of not hearing others, such as "hmmm" – sighs for approval or encouragement for the speaker.

The interviewees described situations where one cannot get rid of one's physical existence. Some of them felt that they could not sit still for a long time and they preferred to move when they were talking. A wireless headset allows movement during a meeting, but then you have to send only a still picture of your face. Problems with following, for example, shared documents also arose. These problems affected the atmosphere.

4.3   Familiarity of the Place as the Responsibility of the Other Participants

Those interviewed quite frequently used the virtual meeting or learning space. The leaders of meetings or learning sessions felt that the virtual working place was easy to access, but they had to struggle to teach other attendees to use the place as well as to behave in the place. The interviewees worked a lot beforehand and after the meetings or learning sessions. Before the session, they ensured that the participants had proper devices (e.g. headsets) and that the participants knew how to enter the meeting room and how to use the programme properly during the meeting. They informed the participants on how to test entering and participating actions and provided help for them, if they had difficulties or questions. After the virtual session, they took care of the notes and delivered them to participants. Often the interviewees felt stress before and during the sessions, because they had to be able to quickly react to whatever kind of problem came up.

The interviewees criticised the unfamiliar symbols used in the drag down menus of the space. For adding familiarity, the need for standardised symbols was expressed. The interviewees also found fault with the programme for not giving enough instructions on how to use it.

4.4   The Functionality of the Place was Threatened by a Lack of IT Support

The meeting or learning room was a place for sharing information as well as for checking and agreeing that the work is in progress. It was not used for collaborative developmental work or sketching out ideas.

It is possible to modify the layout of the place according to, for example, the preferences of the leader, the needs or aims of the session or the wishes of the participants. The interviewees, however, had made only minor modifications, mainly with the places of rectangles for different activities.

The interviewees were able to build up the meeting or learning session – they knew how to bring documents to a meeting, they were able to start sharing the voice and video, they were able to make minor repairs with the connections during the meeting and they could save the meeting or learning documents as well as the whole session to the programme for later views. However, they felt bad ICT support to be the main threat to functionality. Due to distributed and global work or eLearning, the session times did not follow office hours and it was not possible to get any help. The interviewees felt tense from the expectation to manage the tools, the programme and the virtual space by themselves. Multiple demands to be able to prepare the virtual session, check the functioning of the tools, the programme, find the best layout, etc., and solve the problems occurring during the meeting stressed the users a lot. All of the interviewees expressed the need for virtual place management.

4.5 The Narrative of the Place Represented the Software not the Organisation

The interviewees arranged the virtual room layout and, for example, the documents and pictures needed for the windows of the place beforehand. The shared documents reflected the meaning of the place for the participants: it was for meeting or learning. The official preparation duties took so much time from the leaders that they seldom thought about the narrative nature of the place. Only a tiny and unnoticeable logo was communicating about the organisation. Because of the international character of the sessions, the interviewees felt the neutral look was good.

However, advantage was taken of infiltrating features from the physical place to the virtual place. Because of the simple and official look of the virtual place, the interviewees used the signs from the physical place for moulding the atmosphere of the session and the narrative of the meeting or learning room. They might have a cup of coffee in the meeting for signalling the informality and intimacy of the session. They took notice of how they were dressed and what was seen in the background of the shared video, they used tried to highlight the culture of the town or country or identify the features of season. They also struggled with placing the camera in such a way that it would mediate the feeling of talking face to face and meet other participants' eyes.

4.6 Meaning of the Place Mediated Equal Belonging Over the Meeting Span

The value and meaning of the place related strongly to the distributed working or learning mode. Because there were only rare opportunities for face to face meetings, the virtual meeting place was really needed for achieving the goals set for the joint project or learning. The meeting room was a place for checking and agreeing that the work was in progress. After checking and commenting on the work, the reconstructions and reforms were done in the "physical world". The concept of meaning is further analysed through the concepts of belonging, control and privacy.

The virtual place was not used for adding the feeling of belonging. However, the way the attendees were joined to the meeting showed the belonging to the project or learning group: the invited got the address beforehand and they had to sign in with their names—and the leader accepted them as participants in the session. The place was not meant for outsiders. Belonging lasted for the session time, but also the stored materials —which may be used beforehand—highlighted the feeling of belonging to the group.

In spite of the feeling of equality, the host had control over the place and this was pointed out by minor signs in the place. The host might, after some consideration, give rights to other attendees to control the place. Assignment of the place to other participants was made interim.

In this software, there were no private virtual rooms for participants—the place and its areas were shared. If they wanted to, for example, make private notes, they had to simultaneously use other software. However, in a broader sense, the interviewees executed the need for privacy during the meeting by muting the microphone and camera and escaping from the screen to, for example, get some coffee from the kitchen. Privacy was found in the physical environment.

Table 3. Summary of experiences of a virtual workplace and factors of fit in each category

The comfort and fit of the workplace	Experience category	Experience of the virtual workplace	Fit of the examined virtual workplace
Physical	Frequency	Verbalism shapes the time brief.	Brief sessions
	Atmosphere	Shared texts shape the atmosphere official.	Official sessions
Functionality	Familiarity	Familiarity is host-related.	Competent host
	Functionality	Functionality is help- and support-related.	Support available
Psychosocial	Narrative	Stick to issues in international sessions. Narratives of physical places in background	Pertinence in international collaboration, point in affairs.
	Meaning	A shared place for checking and agreeing for defined group	Distant belonging to project or learning group

5 Conclusions

By categorizing the experiences according to the six-dimensional model, it is possible to show the differences and idiosyncrasies of virtual workplaces provided by different software. In Table 3, there is a summary of the experiences related to the virtual meeting and learning place created by the assessment selected software. The table shows the experience categories, the tense experience of the virtual place and the main ensemble illustrating the experience of fit. Physical environment-related experiences were frequency and atmosphere [24]. The examined software provided the virtual place, which emphasized the short time frequency of the use of the place and the official atmosphere in the place. Familiarity was very much dependent on the abilities of the host for the session. Her/his duty was to familiarize the other participants with the place and direct the behavior of others in the place. The possibility to get ICT support affected greatly the experiences of functionality of the place. Psychosocial features that characterized the virtual place were multifaceted. The main and, from interview to interview, repetitive factor of the narrative of the place was the minor indications of the host organization communicating to the international participants "keep to the issues, stick to the point". The factor of the meaning of the place highlighted the equality of the international participants in the virtual place. During the meeting or learning session, the place was equally owned although the host had the main responsibility for ensuring that everything was proceeding smoothly during the meeting. So the place was mainly permitted and controlled by the host. The place was used for checking and agreeing that the work was progressing with those belonging to the group.

So it can be concluded that this software provided the virtual workplace with a fit for brief and official sessions, if the host is competent and if there is ICT support available. The virtual room encouraged participants to stick to the point and showed them that they belong to a group, which had to meet the objectives of learning and developing.

Limitations and suggestions for future research. The categories systematically sorted out the features of the virtual workplace in a way that might be useful for illustrating the differences of various virtual workplaces. However, in this study the categories and their descriptions were tested only using one software programme provided for the virtual workplace. There is a need to gain more test-based information and knowledge with different virtual places for ensuring the validity of the categorization [see 30]. Only after analyzing many different virtual workplaces by using the categories will it be possible to judge the validity and power of the categories.

Because this study was the first pilot, there is work to do in ensuring and validating the categories of the used model. From this research perspective the names and the spheres of each category of the used model [24, 25] should be further developed and studied for ensuring the concept validity of each category [e.g. 31]. As the ergonomic demands of the physical workplace are well known, there is a need to gain understanding and development of the ergonomics of the virtual workplace. Structured outcomes of user experiences in virtual workplaces are needed and may be used as first steps in developing the ergonomics of virtual places as well as the competencies of self-management.

References

1. Eurofound: New forms of employment. Publications Office of the European Union, Luxembourg (2015)
2. Holtgrewe, U.: New new technologies: The future and the present of work information and communication technology. New Technol. Work Employ. **29**(1), 9–24 (2014)
3. Popma, J.: The Janus face of the 'New Ways of Work': Rise, risks and regulation of nomadic work. Working Paper 2013.07. Brussels: ETUI (2013)

4. Gareis, K., Lilischkis, S., Mentrup, A.: Mapping the mobile eWorkforce in Europe. In: Andriessen, J.H.E., Vartiainen, M. (eds.), pp. 45–69. Springer, Heidelberg (2006)
5. Vartiainen, M., Hyrkkänen, U.: Changing requirements and mental workload factors in mobile multi-locational work. New Technol. Work Employ. **25**(2), 117–135 (2010)
6. European Commission: The increasing use of portable computing and communication devices and its impact on the health of EU workers. Publications Office of the European Union, Luxembourg (2010)
7. Bailey, D.E., Leonardi, P.M., Barley, S.R.: The lure of the virtual. Organ. Sci. **23**(5), 1485–1504 (2012)
8. Nenonen, S., Airo, K., Bosch, P., Fruchter, R., Koivisto, S., Gersberg, N., Rothe, P., Ruohomäki, V., Vartiainen, M.: Managing Workplace Resources for Knowledge Work, the final report of ProWork-project (2009). http://www.proworkproject.com/prowork/final-report
9. Lin, C., Standing, C., Liu, Y.: A model to develop effective virtual teams. Decis. Support Syst. **45**, 1031–1045 (2008)
10. Ferreira, P.G.S., de Limaa, P., de Costaa, S.E.G.: Perception of virtual team's performance: A multinational exercise. Int. J. Prod. Econ. **140**(1), 416–430 (2012)
11. Curseu, P.L., Schalk, R., Wessel, I.: How do virtual teams process information? A literature review and implications for management. J. Manag. Psychol. **23**(6), 628–652 (2008)
12. Hertel, G., Geister, S., Konradt, U.: Managing virtual teams: a review of current empirical research. Hum. Resour. Manag. Rev. **15**, 69–95 (2005)
13. de Guinea, A.O., Webster, J., Staples, D.S.: A meta-analysis of the consequences of virtualness on team functioning. Inf. Manag. **49**, 301–308 (2012)
14. Kristof-Brown, A.L., Zimmerman, R.D., Johnson, E.C.: Consequences of individuals' fit at work: A meta-analysis of person-job, person-organization, person-group, and person-supervisor fit. Pers. Psychol. **58**, 281–342 (2005)
15. Raghuram, S., Tuertscher, P., Garud, R.: Mapping the field of virtual work: A Co-citation analysis. Inf. Syst. Res. **21**, 983–999 (2010)
16. Gibson, C.B., Gibbs, J.L.: Unpacking the concept of virtuality: the effects of geographical dispersion, electronic dependence, dynamic structure, and national diversity on team innovation. Adm. Sci. Q. **51**, 451–495 (2006)
17. Vischer, J.C.: Space Meets Status: Designing Workplace Performance. Routledge, New York (2005)
18. Vischer, J.C.: The effects of physical environment on job performance: towards a theoretical model of workspace stress. Stress Health **23**, 175–184 (2007)
19. Vischer, J.C.: The concept of workplace performance and its value to managers. Calif. Manage. Rev. **49**(2), 62–79 (2007)
20. Vischer, J.C.: Towards an environmental psychology of workspace: how people are affected by environments for work. Architectural Sci. Rev. **51**(2), 97–108 (2008)
21. Hyrkkänen, U., Nenonen, S., Kojo, I.: The virtual reality of work - how to create a workplace that enhances well-being for a mobile employee. In: Lanyi, C.S. (ed.) Virtual Reality and Environments, in Tech, pp. 192–204 (2012)
22. Hyrkkänen, U., Nenonen, S.: The virtual workplace of a mobile employee – how does vischer's model function in identifying physical, functional and psychosocial fit? In: Jacko, Julie A. (ed.) Human-Computer Interaction, Part III, HCII 2011. LNCS, vol. 6763, pp. 69–75. Springer, Heidelberg (2011). http://www.springer.com/computer/hci/book/978-3-642-21615-2
23. Diller, S., Shedroff, N., Rhea, D.: Making Meaning: How Successful Businesses Deliver Meaningful Customer Experiences. New Riders Press, Berkeley (2005)

24. Nenonen, S., Kojo, I.: Experience of Places – Six dimensional model for capturing the user experience. 12th EuroFM Research Symposium, 22 – 24 May 2013, Prague Congress Center, Czech Republic (2013)
25. Kojo, I., Nenonen, S.: Workplaces for social ecosystems; User experiences in coworking places. In: Proceedings of EFMC 2012, 23rd – 25th of May, 2012, Copenhagen Denmark (2012)
26. Kristof, A.L.: Person-organization fit: An integrative review of its conceptualizations, measurement and implications. Pers. Psychol. **49**(1), 1–49 (1996)
27. Dainoff, M., Mark, L., Ye, L., Petrovic, M.: Forget about aesthetics in chair design: ergonomics should provide the basis for comfort. In: Dainoff, M.J. (ed.) Ergonomics and Health Aspects of Work with Computers. LNCS, vol. 4566, pp. 19–25. Springer, Heidelberg (2007)
28. Lehtiranta, L., Junnonen, J.-M., Kärnä, S., Pekuri, L.: The constructive research approach: problem solving for complex projects. In: Basian, B. (ed.) Designs, Methods and Practices for Research of Project Management. Gower (2016). http://www.gpmfirst.com/books/designs-methods-and-practices-research-project-management/constructive-research-approach
29. Battarbee, K.: Co-experience: Understanding User Experiences in Social Interaction, Ph.D. thesis, University of Art and Design Helsinki, Helsinki (2008)
30. Patton, M.: Qualitative Research and Evaluation Method, 3rd edn. Sage, Thousand Oaks, CA (2001)
31. Kerlinger, F.N., Lee, H.B.: Foundations of Behavioral Research, 4th edn. Harcourt College Publishers, Fort Worth (2000)

Preliminary Review of a Virtual World Usability Questionnaire

Crystal S. Maraj[1(✉)], Sushunova G. Martinez[1],
Karla A. Badillo-Urquiola[1], Jonathan A. Stevens[2],
and Douglas B. Maxwell[3]

[1] Institute for Simulation and Training, Orlando, FL, USA
{cmaraj,smartine,kbadillo}@ist.ucf.edu
[2] University of Central Florida, Orlando, FL, USA
jonathan.stevens@knights.ucf.edu
[3] US Army Research Laboratory, Orlando, FL, USA
douglas.maxwell3.civ@mail.mil

Abstract. Improving performance through training in virtual environments has led to identifying the best methods associated with enhancing human-computer interaction. This paper provides a description of a usability questionnaire for Virtual World training, by focusing on experiential U.S. Army Warrior Leader Course tasks performed using an input desktop device (i.e., a mouse and keyboard). The usability questionnaire was developed by integrating established usability subscales. A Likert scale for both user experience (for game genre and controller type) and usability levels were implemented, along with free response questions, to gain insight into the controller interface(s). Descriptive statistics and determination of internal consistency (using Cronbach's alpha) are reviewed for establishing the reliability and validity of the novel questionnaire. Proposed changes to the questionnaire include removal of superfluous items and consolidation of subscales. Tradeoffs for types of controllers are discussed, in light of the results.

Keywords: Usability · Video game controller · Survey · Human-Computer interaction · Interface design · Virtual worlds · Experiential learning · Technology acceptance · Instructional technology · New media · Military simulation

1 Introduction

Military personnel require training throughout their career. Programs, such as the Warrior Leader Course (WLC), provides Non-Commissioned Officers (NCO) with training for enhancing squad leadership skills. The WLC is a four-week experiential learning course covering topics such as tactical operations, combat orders, casualty evacuations and land navigation through the use of classroom training, field exercises, and subsequent assessments [1]. Advancements in technology have provided a method for supplementing traditional classroom training through virtual platforms. A common part of utilizing virtual platforms is the user's controller interface for a system: an input

© Springer International Publishing Switzerland 2016
S. Lackey and R. Shumaker (Eds.): VAMR 2016, LNCS 9740, pp. 35–46, 2016.
DOI: 10.1007/978-3-319-39907-2_4

device supporting maneuvers within generated scenarios, through some form of manipulation. Virtual platforms such as Virtual Battlespace 3 (VBS3) support scenario-based training that can replicate field exercises using the virtual environment. It is vital that the most appropriate input devices are used to maximize effort on completing the training task, and minimize throughput time. This paper identifies several input devices as possible alternatives to the traditional keyboard and mouse, focusing on human performance within a Virtual World (VW).

The user interface is the first interaction between a product and the Soldier, making the interface a critical training attribute to be examined. If this step of engagement is difficult, problematic, or confusing to its users, the product risks not achieving its intended purpose or goal [2]. Several methods of input (such as a traditional keyboard and mouse or gaming console controllers), or interfaces, can be used for virtual platforms. Research has expanded to testing the usability of wearable controls, such as a head mounted display [3]. Ultimately, a highly intuitive device is sought to reduce the time impediment of learning or performing device operation, therefore allowing more time for conducting training tasks.

Pairing a device suitable to a task allows easier interaction, and video game users have been found to prefer an input device that fits the type of gameplay [4]; although a naturally interactive device might not necessarily bode well for performance [5]. User preference can also depend on familiarity and comfort [4, 6]. Unfortunately, the simulation interface is oftentimes an afterthought during the design and development phase of a system; it is only after initial user testing that the interface is substantially analyzed, because collected user feedback is not typically positive.

A summative survey can be conducted to ensure the usability of such input devices. Researchers often use questionnaires to find the usability of commercial off-the-shelf input devices [3, 7]. These questionnaires have adapted a Likert scale and can provide beneficial assessment if tailored to the training situation correctly [6]. The scale can follow either an odd- or even-numbered system, though it has been found that an odd-numbered scale prevents the halo effect, limits impairing validity, and provides appropriate balance for sensitivity and efficiency [8–10]. Additional research recommends a 7-point Likert scale due to optimal reliability [11–13]. For this research initiative, one set of questions contained a 5-point scale (ranging from novice (1) to expert (5)) and was modified to assess user experience with regards to game genre and controller type. Similarly, the usability rating for the controller consisted of a 7-point Likert-scale (ranging from strongly disagree (1) to strongly agree (7)). Additionally, free response questions were integrated to gain meaningful insight through additional coverage of controller usage.

In effort to assess the reliability of the questionnaire, Cronbach's alpha was used to determine the effectiveness of the questions. To assemble the usability questionnaire, an in-depth literature of usability questions (including topics such as usefulness, satisfaction, and ease of use of the video game controllers) were compiled to determine which were most applicable. With permission from the source authors [3, 7, 14, 15], the questions were modified to assess the usability of the VW navigation devices. The subscales that were incorporated included aspects of Usefulness, Ease of Use, Ease of Learning, Satisfaction, Device Comfort, and Overall Device Satisfaction. The definitions used are according to the original sources: Usefulness refers to a device's capability to accomplish a task efficiently; Ease of Use focuses on the simplicity of a device, and denotes the level of effort and difficulty when utilizing a device; Ease of Learning applies to comprehending how the device works and to adopting the skills required to use the device; Satisfaction determines whether the device is suitable for the virtual simulation; Device Comfort refers to operating the device by assessing levels of fatigue and comfort; and Overall Device Satisfaction identifies whether the device appeared to be difficult or easy to use for completing the task.

The purpose of this usability research initiative is twofold. First, the usability questionnaire was developed to assess the reliability of the questions. Second, the data collected from the NCOs was evaluated to assess the effectiveness of the VW navigation devices used for training.

2   Method

2.1   Participants

Fifty U.S. Army Soldiers, in the rank of Corporal or Sergeant, served as participants in the data collection events. Each Soldier was a student enrolled in the U.S. Army's Warrior Leader Course at Camp Blanding Joint Training Center, Florida. The aggregated sample was composed of 37 males and 13 females. All individuals were U.S. citizens, between the ages of 18 and 40 ($M = 27.02$, $SD = 4.77$), with normal or corrected-to-normal vision, and full color vision. No compensation, in any manner, was provided for participation.

2.2   Survey Design

Within the VW training, Soldiers were asked to complete four collective tasks (i.e., reacting to contact while dismounted, to a near ambush, to a far ambush, and to an improvised explosive device (IED)) through the Army's VBS3 software, while being supervised by the Small Group Leaders (SGLs). The usability questionnaire assessed the reliability of its subscales as well as documented the Soldier's reaction to the virtual simulation, in reference to using a standard desktop with a keyboard and mouse.

2.3   Measure

The usability questionnaire was a 44-question individual-level survey that asked participants to subjectively rate their gaming experience, their experience with the simulation, their interaction with the simulation's game controller, their interaction with other interface devices, and their overall response to the VW training scenario. The questionnaire was recreated from previously published works that examined the type of video game controller, controller use, satisfaction, gaming experience, and user interface experience [3, 7, 14, 15]. The majority of questions followed a 7-point Likert scale, with three questions reserved for free-text response. Additionally, the questionnaire consisted of several items that were reverse-scale scored.

2.4   Procedure

The data was conducted at the Florida Army National Guard's 211th Regional Training Institute (Camp Blanding, Florida). At the Army training facility, each Soldier was pre-assigned to a squad (46, 47, and 48 respectively) and then asked to read and sign the consent form. Following the consent forms, all three squads were transported to the computer lab (on-site) where under the direction and guidance of the SGL's to complete the four previously mentioned tasks using VBS3. After completing the virtual simulation training, the experimenter administered the usability questionnaire and then provided each participant with a debriefing form.

3   Results

In order to obtain meaningful results, a minimum of 30 participants was needed in accordance with the behavioral science sample size standard [16]. Data collection efforts revealed a sample of fifty participants who completed the usability questionnaire. The questionnaire was evaluated to determine the reliability of the subscales including Usefulness, Ease of Use, Ease of Learning, and Satisfaction. Additionally, the usability data was analyzed using statistical means to explain participant's Game Experience with several different interfaces, as well as experience with genre types, including First Person Shooter, Massively Multiplayer Online, and Virtual World. Finally, an examination of each participant's free responses regarding the overall interaction with the system was logged to add insight through anecdotal evidence.

3.1   Reliability of the Questionnaire Subscales

Usefulness.   To assess the internal consistency reliability of the Likert-type subscales created for the usability questionnaire, the Cronbach Alpha was calculated and reported. The first subscale focused on questions examining Usefulness. The Statistical Package for the Social Sciences (S.P.S.S.) output for the three items revealed a Cronbach's alpha = .77 A closer look at the *Corrected Item-Total Correlation*

Table 1.   Corrected Item-Total Correlation for Usefulness

	Scale Mean with Deletion	Scale Variance with Deletion	Corrected Item-Total Correlation	Squared Multiple Correlation	Cronbach's Alpha if Item Deleted
It is useful	8.681	6.570	.692	.552	.586
Makes things I want to accomplish	9.277	6.248	.670	.543	.604
Does what I expect	8.894	7.619	.455	.208	.842

(Table 1) revealed all three items had a correlation greater than .5, which established a reliable correlation between each item and the total. Additionally, in instances where there are few items listed on a scale, the inter-item correlation is also reported. In this case, the *mean inter-item correlation* was .53, with values ranging from .41 to .73. This suggests a strong relationship among the items, furthering the support for validation of the scale.

Ease of Use. The next subscale examined for internal consistency was Ease of Use. The Cronbach's alpha reported for all 11 items = .93. The *Corrected Item-Total Correlation* revealed all items had a strong correlation (> .5) between each item and the total score from the questionnaire. The *mean inter-item correlation* value reported was .55, with a range from .21 to .91 (Table 2). The results suggest a strong relationship among the items.

Table 2. Corrected Item-Total Correlation for Ease of Use

	Scale mean with deletion	Scale variance with deletion	Corrected item-total correlation	Squared multiple correlation	Cronbach's alpha if Item deleted
Simple to use	44.750	154.362	.704	.688	.923
Using is effortless	45.271	155.138	.653	.751	.925
I can recover from mistakes	44.604	154.372	.720	.665	.922
I can use it successfully	45.042	151.488	.733	.769	.922
Difficult to learn Movement	44.646	151.553	.651	.850	.926
Difficult to learn View	44.646	147.893	.750	.896	.921
Difficult to perform Movement	44.438	147.315	.808	.878	.918
Difficult to perform View	44.500	147.021	.833	.888	.917
Requires fewest steps possible	44.708	154.594	.784	.742	.920
Occasional users would like it	44.875	154.878	.665	.677	.925

(Continued)

Table 2. (*Continued*)

	Scale mean with deletion	Scale variance with deletion	Corrected item-total correlation	Squared multiple correlation	Cronbach's alpha if Item deleted
Regular users would like it	44.396	158.031	.534	.560	.931

Ease of Learning. Following the analysis of the Ease of Use subscale, Ease of Learning was examined for internal reliability. The results suggested a Cronbach's alpha value = .81 for all three items. The *Corrected Item-Total Correlation* revealed that the correlation between each item and total score had a strong correlation (> .5) (Table 3). Furthermore, the *mean inter-item correlation* value reported was .59, and ranged from .52 to .67. Overall, the results suggest a strong relationship amongst the items that contributed to the Ease of Learning subscale.

Table 3. Corrected Item-Total Correlation for Ease of Learning

	Scale mean with deletion	Scale variance with deletion	Corrected Item-Total Correlation	Squared multiple correlation	Cronbach's alpha if Item deleted
It is easy to learn	9.420	7.147	.676	.471	.727
Easily remember how to use it	9.280	8.655	.610	.377	.799
Quickly became skillful	9.540	6.090	.725	.528	.678

Satisfaction. The final subscale assessed for measuring reliability was Satisfaction. The Satisfaction subscale revealed a Cronbach's alpha value = .71. The *Corrected Item-Total Correlation* showed a relatively strong correlation between each item and the total score (reported values > .5) (Table 4). Despite the small number of items, the *mean inter-item correlation* was also reported as .56, which suggests a strong relationship between the items (despite that the *Cronbach's alpha if item deleted* reported no item value).

Table 4. Corrected Item-Total Correlation for Usefulness

	Scale mean with deletion	Scale variance with deletion	Corrected item-total correlation	Squared multiple correlation	Cronbach's alpha if Item deleted
12 Works the way I want	4.490	2.547	.556	.309	.
13 User control	4.408	2.205	.556	.309	.

Game Experience. Part I of the Game Experience section of the usability questionnaire asked participants to indicate their experience with seven different interfaces, or controller inputs. The focus of the Game Experience section was essential to understanding the level of familiarity a participant had with a specific interface. Each participant rated their user experience with each device, ranging from novice to expert. Included in the usability questionnaire was the use of a standard desktop keyboard and mouse; devices with consoles, and a pad. Preliminary analysis from the questionnaire indicated that participants were most experienced with a keyboard and mouse, and least experienced with a joystick. Equal experience was found between the steering wheel and pad. Table 5 illustrates the controller type and the averages for the participants' usage.

Table 5. Averages for Controller Types

Controller type	Mean (M)
Keyboard/Mouse	3.51
Game Pad	3.09
Joystick	2.33
Steering Wheel	2.51
Motion Controller	2.60
Gun	3.26
Pad	2.51
Average Interface Experience	2.88

Part II of the Game Experience section of the usability questionnaire asked participants to indicate their experience with eight game genres. The eight genre types included First Person Shooter, Massively Multiplayer Online, Virtual World, Strategy, Role Playing Games, Simulation, Puzzles, and Racing. The answers revealed which genre a participant had the most experience with, in order to get deeper insight into a participant's likely gaming preference or interaction style. Each participant rated each genre from novice to expert. Preliminary analysis of the means indicated that the participants had the most experience with racing games, and equal experience among the First Person Shooter and Puzzle genres. The least amount of experience appeared to be in the Virtual World Genre. Table 6 shows each genre and the averages for genre experience. Interestingly, a preliminary analysis of the highest mean controller type and the highest mean genre experience indicated an unexpected pairing of the keyboard and mouse with the racing genre.

Table 6. Averages for Genre Experience

Genre	Mean (M)
First Person Shooter	3.19
Massively Multiplayer Online	2.82
Virtual World	2.24
Strategy	2.90
Role Playing Game	3.11
Simulation	2.51
Puzzles	3.19
Racing	3.42
Average Game Genre Experience	2.88

Free Response. The Free Response section of the usability questionnaire allowed participants to describe their overall interaction with the system. All 50 individual were given an opportunity to pinpoint specific issues faced while conducting the training task in the VW. Approximately 10 % of the participants indicated a positive interaction with the VW using the keyboard and mouse system. Alternatively, 14 % described the keyboard and mouse as disruptive and the overall desktop computer was limited making it difficult to use. With regards to meeting expectations, 16 % indicated the keyboard and mouse controls was favorable and functional. On the other hand, 18 % viewed the controls with increase difficultly and not easy to use. Interestingly, four participants explicitly stated that an Xbox control would be a preferred choice. The last free response question gauged the overall impression of the system. Approximately 34 % of the participants view the overall system as useful and a good learning tool while 12 % felt that the system was ineffective and needed more time to familiarize themselves with the keyboard and mouse. Finally, eight participants recommended incorporating a video game controller or game pad to enhance the overall training experience.

4   Discussion

The research initiative examined a usability survey in the aim of determining the appropriate controller for virtual world training, and determining the reliability of the usability questionnaire. Several subscales resulted in a high Cronbach's alpha, including Usefulness, Ease of Use, Ease of Learning, and Satisfaction. The Ease of Use subscale signaled a valuable relation: the subscale had the highest Cronbach's alpha (.93) and the most questions (a total of 11). This indicates that the variation in questions may be enough to satisfy the subscale [17]. Even though the subsequent subscales had between two and three questions, the Cronbach's alpha combined for each subscale was above .70. The questions may have been phrased appropriately to gather useful information [18].

The results showed that the Device Comfort and Overall Device Satisfaction subscales were not statistically significant. Specifically, the Overall Device Satisfaction subscale included a single statement for completing (i.e., "Overall input device was…") which could have been a source of low reliability for the subscale. Gliem and Gliem [17] noted that unreliable measurements may occur with individual scores. Consolidating the Overall Device Satisfaction subscale with the Satisfaction subscale is posited as a potential method to increase reliability. Further, the subscale of Device Comfort failed to provide significant results, which could be due the limited amount of time provided within the system. The Device Comfort section asked participants about fatigue of the wrist, arm, and fingers. However, the time spent in the simulation was not sufficient for the onset of such symptoms. Fagarasanu and Kumar [19] report that repetitiveness is a factor that contributes to carpal tunnel syndrome. The time participants spent was limited to a total of four hours, including a ten-minute break. Thus, this subscale may be better suited for a longitudinal study or training involving a longer time in the simulation.

Lastly, the 7-point Likert scale forms were presented to users with an additional Not Applicable (N/A) option. Throughout the course of refining the survey, the need for this option was defeated by generalizing the questions, affording multiple input types for inclusion. For instance, the original survey pertained to providing two sections of similar questions that participants answered based on the controller used (e.g., keyboard/mouse vs. game controller). However, having generalized the questions, the N/A seemed to be used by participants to avoid questions. The University of Washington Office of Educational Assessment [20] recommends using N/A if appropriate, but sparingly for opinion items. Further, the time allotted for as much training as possible, so time taken for filling out the survey information was limited. This may have promoted the use of the N/A option. Future studies will change the N/A option to only include the 7-point Likert scale within the questionnaire, in order to retain a higher sense of control.

Additionally, the usability data was analyzed using statistical means to explain participant's game experience with several different interfaces, as well as experience with genre types. Specifically, the highest means from Tables 5 and 6 indicate that the racing genre and the keyboard/mouse interface have the highest controller and genre experience levels, respectively, among the participants. This is an unexpected discovery. Previous studies [21, 22] show that the realism of a steering wheel and pedal interface used in a racing game enhances the overall gaming experience. However, these previous studies did not account for the economy of using an interface that comes "standard" with a console or computer. Although these more realistic interfaces may indeed enhance a user's gaming experience, the devices are limited in their applications. For example, a steering wheel must be used primarily for a racing genre and cannot be effectively or conveniently mapped to another game genre, such as a first person shooter or a puzzle game. The utility of a keyboard and mouse or console controller allows the user to apply the interface to multiple genres, without requiring the gamer to use additional financial resources for perceived realism. The user can also customize the control settings to suit his or her process of gameplay. It may be implied that the utility of certain devices, such as the keyboard and mouse or console controller, allows the user to fluidly map device control settings across multiple genres without having to arduously re-learn a different interface for each game genre.

Further, game controller implementation shows advantageous traits, in comparison to traditional desktop setups, in several ways. Game controllers such as the Xbox have a smaller design that affords the user the ability to maintain both hands in close proximity on one device, unlike a keyboard and mouse which requires two hands that may be a substantial distance apart. The increased distance may add to the difficulty experienced by the user, especially when moving. This would likely be observed when a task or action requires the combined use of the mouse with a button on the far left side of the keyboard. With a game controller, the use of joysticks close to each other reduce the difficulty associated with movements. The keyboard has an additional disadvantage: there are many keys that are not utilized, yet are still able to be pressed, therefore potentially disrupting the user's flow of actions within the game. A game controller has a limited amount of buttons with each serving a specific purpose. This purposeful advantage coupled with a smaller design gives the user an ability to quickly sequence multiple buttons to manipulate, move, and interact within the game when needed. Overall, a more user-friendly game controller, such as the Xbox controller, will likely reduce the amount of time the user needs to become oriented to the controls. The less time that is needed for practice, the more time the user is able to focus on achieving the desired training effects.

5   Conclusion

The preliminary results serve as a foundation for future research on the usability of VW navigation devices. Modifications to the usability questionnaire will include removing the N/A option that coincided with the Likert scale, adjusting the future length of training time to legitimize the Device Comfort subscale, and combining the Overall Device subscale with the Satisfaction subscale. Finally, future research initiatives will seek to incorporate additional types of controllers to usability testing, as this paper did not exhaust all interfaces (e.g., motion-sensors for body-based interactions, touch-screens, and trackballs). The objective of incorporating these adjustments will be to confirm the reliability of the questionnaire, discover questionnaire aspects that need to be augmented, and reveal interfaces beneficial for VW tasks. Although this questionnaire is currently focused on gaming controllers for VWs, future testing could expand to other applications.

Acknowledgements. This research was sponsored by the U.S. Army Research Laboratory – Human Research Engineering Directorate Advanced Training and Simulation Division (ARL HRED STTC), in collaboration with the Institute for Simulation and Training at the University of Central Florida (IST-UCF). This work is supported by ARL HRED STTC contract W911NF-14-2-0012. The views and conclusions contained in this document are those of the authors and should not be interpreted as representing the official policies, either expressed or implied, of ARL HRED STTC or the U.S. Government. The U.S. Government is authorized to reproduce and distribute reprints for Government purposes notwithstanding any copyright notation hereon.

Finally, ARL HRED STTC and the IST-UCF research team would like to express profound gratitude to the dedicated men and women of the RTI/211th without whom this work could not have been performed. Thank you for your service to our country.

References

1. United States Army. (n.d.). Soldier life. www.goarmy.org: http://www.goarmy.com/soldier-life/being-a-soldier/ongoing-training/leadership-training/warrior-leader-course.html
2. Barnum, C.M.: Usability Testing Essentials. Morgan Kaufman, Burlington (2011)
3. Taylor, G.S., Barnett, J.S.: Training Capabilities of Wearable and Desktop Simulator Interfaces. Army Research Institute for the Behavioral and Social Sciences, Arlington (2011)
4. Thorpe, A., Ma, M., Oikonomou, A.: History and alternative game input methods. In: Mehdi, Q., Elmaghraby, A., Moreton, R., Yampolskiy, R., Chariker, J. (eds.) The 16th International Conference on Computer Games, pp. 76–93 (2011). doi:10.1109/CGAMES. 2011.6000321
5. McMahan, R.P., Alon, A.J., Lazem, S., Beaton, R.J., Machaj, D., Schaefer, M., Bowman, D. A.: Evaluating natural interaction techniques in video games. In: Hatchet, M., Kiyokawa, K., LaViola, Jr., J.J. (eds.). IEEE Symposium on 3D User Interfaces 2010, pp. 11–14. IEEE, Waltham (2010)
6. Gerling, K., Klauser, M., Niesenhaus, J.: Measuring the impact of game controllers on player experience in FPS games. In: Proceedings of the 15th International Academic MindTreck Conference: Envisioning Future Media Environments, pp. 83–86 (2011). doi:10. 1145/2181037.2181052
7. Natapov, D., Castellucci, S.J., MacKenzie, S.I.: Evaluation of video game controllers. In: Gooch, A., Tory, M. (eds.) Graphics Interface Conference, pp. 223–230. Association for Computing Machinery, British Columbia (2009)
8. Finstad, K.: Response interpolation and scale sensitivity: Evidence against 5-point scale. J. Usability Stud. 5(3), 104–110 (2010)
9. Tsang, K.K.: The use of midpoint on likert scale: the implications for educational research. Hong Kong Teachers' Cent. J. 11, 121–130 (2012)
10. Worcester, R.M., Burns, T.R.: A statistical examination of the relative precision of verbal scales. J. Mark. Res. Soc. 17(3), 181–197 (1975)
11. Symonds, P.M.: On the loss of reliability in ratings due to coarseness of the scale. J. Exp. Psychol. 7(6), 456–461 (1924)
12. Miller, G.: The magical number seven, plus or minus two: Some limits on our capacity for processing information. Psychol. Rev. 63(2), 81–97 (1956)
13. Nunnaly, J.: Psychometric Theory. McGraw-Hill, New York (1978)
14. Lund, A.M.: Measuring usabiltiy with the USE questionnaire. Usability Interface 8(2), 3–6 (2001)
15. Castelucci, S.J., Teather, R.J., Pavlovych, A.: Novel metrics for 3D remote pointing. In: Proceedings of the 1st Symposium on Spatial User Interaction, pp. 17–20. ACM (2013). doi:10.1145/2491367.2491373
16. Cohen, J.: Statistical Power Analysis for the Behavioural Sciences, 2nd edn. Academic Press, New York (1988)
17. Gliem, J.A., Gliem, R.R.: Calculating, interpreting, and reporting Cronbach's alpha reliability coefficent for Likert-type scales. In: 2003 Midwest Research to Practice Conference in Adult, Continuing, and Community Education, pp. 82–88 (2003). https://scholarworks.iupui.edu/handle/1805/344
18. Boynton, P.M., Greenhalgh, T.: Hands-on guide to questionnaire research: Selecting, designing, and developing your questionnaire. BMJ. Br. Med. J. 328(7451), 1312–1315 (2004)
19. Fagarasanu, M., Kumar, S.: Carpal tunnel syndrome due to keyboarding and mouse tasks: A review. Int. J. Ind. Ergon. 31, 119–136 (2003)

20. University of Washington Office of Educational Assessment. Tips for writing questionnaire items (2006). https://www.washington.edu/oea/resources/surveys.html
21. Schmierbach, M., Limperos, A.M., Woolley, J.K.: Feeling the need for (personalized) speed: How natural controls and customization contribute to enjoyment of a racing game through enhanced immersion. Cyberpsychol. Behav. Soc. Netw. **15**(7), 364–369 (2012)
22. Williams, K.D.: The effects of dissociation, game controllers, and 3D versus 2D on presence and enjoyment. Comput. Hum. Behav. **38**, 142–150 (2014)

Smart Prototyping - Improving the Evaluation of Design Concepts Using Virtual Reality

Mathias Müller[1(✉)], Tobias Günther[1], Dietrich Kammer[1], Jan Wojdziak[1],
Sebastian Lorenz[2], and Rainer Groh[1]

[1] Chair of Media Design, Technische Universität Dresden, Dresden, Germany
{mathias.mueller,tobias.guenther2,dietrich.kammer,
jan.wojdziak,rainer.groh}@tu-dresden.de
[2] Center for Industrial Design, Technische Universität Dresden, Dresden, Germany
sebastian.lorenz3@tu-dresden.de

Abstract. The evaluation of innovative user interface concepts using virtual reality technology faces many challenges. In this paper, we discuss current limitations regarding the integration of virtual reality in a participatory design process. Furthermore, we propose guidelines including visualization and interaction techniques that address aspects such as presence and awareness in virtual worlds. We introduce agricultural machinery and automotive industry as application scenarios for virtual reality prototyping. In order to ascertain the feasibility of the proposed techniques, we present prototypical implementations. Our experience report concludes with implementation issues of current frameworks and open research questions.

Keywords: Virtual reality · Virtual prototyping · Interface design · Product design · Participatory design

1 Introduction

Traditional product development involves many stages, which address crucial design decisions. The most important method to acquire user feedback, communicate core design concepts, and compare different designs is prototyping [1]. In the context of industrial product design, e.g. automotive industry (cf. Fig. 1), mobile machinery (cf. Fig. 2) or architecture [2], usually physical prototypes are created to visualize a specific aspect of the current concept. Due to the increasing availability of process information, products for professional applications such as agricultural machinery, e.g. harvesters or tractors, contain an increasing number of displays, touch screens and controls. Traditional physical prototypes are not capable of reproducing the functionality of these virtual elements and thus it is difficult to evaluate the interaction between product and user interface. Integrating virtual elements in prototypes such as clay models is costly and time-consuming. Moreover, the limited flexibility of the prototype itself renders this tool unusable for quickly testing a design idea or evaluating a rough concept at an early design stage. Virtual Reality (VR) technologies can aid in assessing the interplay of

© Springer International Publishing Switzerland 2016
S. Lackey and R. Shumaker (Eds.): VAMR 2016, LNCS 9740, pp. 47–58, 2016.
DOI: 10.1007/978-3-319-39907-2_5

devices, controls, and displays in the product under development. In general, two different approaches are possible:

- augmentation of physical prototypes with (interactive) virtual content
- virtual simulations of physical prototypes

Fig. 1. Visualization for a HUD-concept and gesture-based control in an automotive context.

Due to the current technological advancement, virtual prototypes are affordable, quickly realized and easy to modify. Hence, these prototypes provide an option to overcome the deficits of physical prototypes, which are typically created when the design is already quite mature.

In the next section, we present related work and afterwards discuss virtual prototyping in more detail. We then address research questions and propose a set of guidelines including interaction and visualization techniques to overcome current limitations. Moreover, we address practical issues we experienced during the development of prototypes in the context of agricultural machinery and automotive industry. We discuss the integration into the design workflow and conclude with future work.

2 Smart Prototyping

Digital modelling, simulation and communication has long been an integral part of product development. VR technologies and especially Virtual Prototyping can be used to define design specifications [3] or as methods for participatory design [4]. VR has also been investigated as a design tool for quick evaluations [2, 5]. Hence, users can evaluate the usability of product interfaces using VR, which acts as a means to communicate design decisions and alternatives. Moreover, virtual training scenarios allow users to experience a tool, machine, or process without the need to stop operations of devices and factories or risking health threats [6, 7]. Heydarian et al. worked on a study comparing immersive virtual environments with their physical equivalent focusing on the user performance in test activities. The results show that the participants' performance was only slightly influenced by the type of the environment and they also felt a strong sense of presence within an interactive Virtual Environment [8].

Although no complete and evaluated approaches to virtual prototyping have been proposed, previous research projects provide valuable starting points that show how to proceed in this area. For instance, Frund et al. use augmented reality as a design tool in order to blend virtual objects such as 3D models or user interfaces with partial physical prototypes [9]. Zwolinski et al. focus on early design stages, using VR technologies to define basic product structures based on functional requirements [10]. Architectural visualization has already been investigated as a field of application for virtual prototyping, involving users in the planning process of a participatory design process [11, 12].

Using VR to present early design concepts offers several opportunities to aid the participatory design process. The communication between users and designers is significantly enhanced with interactive prototypes [13]. Ideas and concepts are easier to understand if the user can experience the intended effects of the design interactively. Another idea behind virtual prototypes is to constantly gather feedback from users during the whole design process by using VR prototypes containing only elemental parts to visualize a design concept. When the design and the entire product become more mature, existing VR models can be extended to facilitate an in-depth evaluation. During our interdisciplinary research, we identified another advantage: VR helps to communicate the different requirements and priorities of participating disciplines and boosts the collaboration within the development team by providing an easily comprehensible and dynamic form of visual communication.

For a long time, the immersive presentation of VR content has been very costly, involving large power walls or CAVE settings. With the introduction of lightweight and powerful consumer electronics such as current Head-Mounted-Displays (e.g. Oculus Rift [14]) or smartphone-based VR headsets (e.g. Samsung Gear VR [15]), VR Prototyping and the immersive presentation becomes a reality for a wide range of developers and end-users. This addresses another requirement for virtual prototyping: portability. Using smartphones in combination with Google Cardboards [16] as low level VR Experience proved to be very effective for communicating ideas to project partners, visualize concepts or simply exchange ideas. This represents a huge advantage for the participatory design process: Instead of evaluating design concepts in the laboratory, a variety of users can be equipped with portable VR-prototypes for evaluation in a familiar environment and generate feedback directly from the potential customer.

3   Research Challenges

Apart from the visualization a main challenge of VR prototyping is the interaction with virtual models and interfaces. In the next sections we discuss the importance of multimodal approaches and several interaction prototypes, which we developed to study their suitability for different application scenarios and their effects on the user's perception.

3.1   Multimodality

The visualization of 3D models for use with VR is still not a straightforward task but solutions for most issues are available (cf. Sect. 5). Including other modalities remains problematic. Sound represents a minor issue, although we experienced that the design workflow seems to be very visual, and therefore it is quite difficult to obtain authentic sounds for a VR simulation. This situation may be specific to the scenario of agricultural machinery where sound design is not a core aspect of the design process. With haptics, the situation is different: Current solutions to simulate haptic sensation are expensive, complex, and not very portable.

As VR prototypes focus on simulating only certain aspects of the design concept, especially for evaluating the visualization or interaction design with touch interfaces, missing haptics and other modalities may be acceptable. For evaluation of physical controls, physical prototypes seem to remain the most feasible option, however VR can be used to combine these physical controls with virtual elements, e.g. for information visualization aspects. Another approach goes one step further by replacing concrete physical objects with dummy objects, which incorporate a similar, but not necessarily identical shape and materiality in order to simulate these aspects with VR visualizations. The question remains, whether the optical illusion of authentic shape, texture and material is sufficient to trick the human perception.

3.2   Interaction with VR Prototypes

Besides the difficulties to simulate certain modalities, interaction with VR content represents another major issue. For our idea of interactive prototypes, we concentrate on basic tasks, such as (guided) navigation, selection and basic manipulation tasks. As we target an early design phase, exact simulation of complex interactions is not necessary, especially when evaluating visualization parameters or the spatial layout of interactive elements in the cockpit as well as identifying opacity or occlusion issues typically found in Augmented Reality (AR) scenarios.

Fig. 2. Head-based interaction in context of mobile machinery.

Especially for portable systems, options for interaction are spare. Zhu et al. investigate head movement and eye tracking as natural forms of interaction [17]. The authors show that head movements can be more easily tracked and do not cause the Midas touch problem, which is present when using eye movement as a means for interaction. Eye movement is primarily needed to investigate the surroundings, which can be in conflict with interaction. However, head movement as a tool to interact imposes greater physical strain on the user. In any cases of eye and head tracking, applying a dwell time before triggering actions in the virtual world is necessary in order to avoid unintentional actions [18, 19].

One of our prototypes demonstrates the feasibility of this approach for simple navigation tasks (entering a vehicle, moving around based on leaning forward/ backwards/to the side) and interacting with control elements inside the cockpit of the machine (cf. Fig. 2). Even basic steering actions of the vehicle could be performed, although reaction was very high and accuracy quite low. This illustrates the core problem of dwell-time based interactions: it is simply not suitable for time-critical interaction steps.

Gesture-based interaction seems another option for more or less portable VR systems. However, in VR the absence of the user's body represents a serious issue for this type of interaction. The integration of an egocentric avatar in the virtual environment represents a possible solution and offers several additional advantages. Due to representation of the user's body and knowledge about real world scales, the predictability of size relations and virtual distances can be improved [20, 21] which is highly relevant for virtual prototyping. In addition, it can be assumed that the depth of presence increases in Virtual Reality applications, if the body of the user operates according to his real world movements [22]. A strong sense of presence is a desirable feature for virtual prototyping, as you want the user to perceive the model and world as natural as possible.

4 Virtual Reality Prototyping Guidelines

Especially interaction techniques for prototypical VR experiences are an open research field. We present several approaches, realized in the depicted examples. Furthermore, the feasibility of current 3D frameworks to quickly create a reasonable VR experience and their integration in the design workflow/toolchain are discussed.

4.1 Interaction Techniques

One goal of virtual reality prototyping is the substitution of physical prototypes by using virtual models [3] in order to reduce efforts in building complex functional physical prototypes. Using VR or AR techniques, they therefore can be realised much cheaper and in early phases of the development process. This enables a better integrated evaluation and participation when designing new products. The layout of interfaces elements such as steering wheels, pedals, monitors, buttons etc. can be evaluated by using the VR simulation. We propose a wide range of interaction techniques which enable the utilization of different interaction techniques depending on the specific needs of the simulation. Available options in our prototypes are:

- gaze-based interaction, simulated by head movements
- leaning-based interaction, using torso movements
- use of gestures, especially hand and finger movements
- interaction techniques using existing devices such as steering wheels

To address specific needs of virtual prototyping applications we present an overview of the mentioned interaction techniques and the corresponding suitability to different tasks and requirements according to our experience (cf. Table 1).

Table 1. Interaction techniques and the suitability to different tasks and requirements: ++: excellent, +: good, ○: neutral, −: poor.

	Gaze	Leaning	Gestures	Devices
Manipulation tasks	+	−	+	++
Selection tasks	++	−	+	○
Simple movement tasks	○	++	○	−
Complex navigation tasks	−	+	−	−
Mobility	++	○	+	−
Authenticity	○	+	+	++
Ease of use	+	++	○	+
Haptic feedback	−	○	○	++
Ergonomics	○	+	−	++
Universality	+	○	+	−

Gaze and head-based interaction can be used for simple, not time-critical tasks. Their main advantage is that they represent functionality built into the most devices, are applicable to most scenarios and do not require additional wiring or tracking. Gestures, and leaning as special gesture, do need additional, lightweight tracking. Leaning is suitable for navigation tasks as it is easy to learn and understand. Depending on the complexity and suitability for the associated task, gestures are more demanding both for the user and the tracking hardware. Devices are the least universal solution. However, as they are designed for one specific purpose they are unmatched in terms of ergonomics, ease of use and efficiency.

Another approach utilized in our prototypes is to reduce complexity of the interaction by mapping complex real-world interactions to simple inputs to trigger these actions in VR. Although this approach does not completely reflect how the user would interact with the according system in reality, the efficiency of visualizations, or the user interface design in general can be quickly evaluated. On the other hand, these interactive prototypes can serve as playground for designer to try concepts for novel interaction techniques and iteratively refine existing concepts.

4.2 Visualization Techniques

Still a problem at present is the artificial character of virtual avatars. We found tendencies for the intensification of mental immersion once users perceive their own individual body in virtual environment. Thus, we developed a prototypical application, which superimposes a captured video stream of the user's current view on the virtual scene in real-time. By means of a chroma-keying segmentation method only skin tones will be displayed, such that the user is able to see his authentic hands form, colour, pigmentation and hairiness (cf. Fig. 3). [23] According to our research, the user experience can be enhanced with this system. Evaluation results show significant improvements regarding stimulation and originality scales [24]. It can be assumed that Virtual Prototyping can benefit of the increased hedonic quality and experience-oriented focus of the application. In combination with markerless tracking systems, freehand gestures will allow the user to interact with virtual objects or navigate through virtual scenes. Current technological developments even allow a portable tracking when using a small depth camera mounted at the VR headset for hand tracking purposes (cf. [25]). Therefore, we recommend the integration of an animated user avatar or the adaption of the proposed video overlay technique for virtual prototyping. In our opinion the benefits in terms of size and distance estimation, the deeper sense of presence and the increasing user experience are important key points for a successful prototyping and design process.

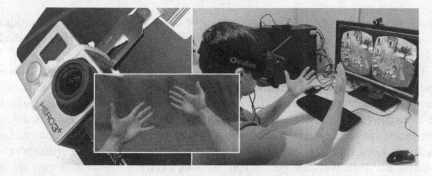

Fig. 3. Visualizing the user's body in virtual environments (Günther, Franke & Groh 2015).

We created several prototypes visualizing several different types of agricultural machinery and the interaction with these machines, especially different cockpit layouts and control paradigms. For a better understanding of the functionality of these complex machines, we developed interactive visualizations that show different types of harvesters. The resulting VR prototypes used different visualization techniques to reveal the technical components inside the harvester and the parameters to control the harvesting process to reveal the inner components of the machine (cf. Fig. 4, left):

- transparency
- wireframes
- dynamic masking of the machine hull (hiding unnecessary parts of a complex system based on the user interaction, position or view direction)

This example shows one advantage of interactive VR prototypes for presentation purposes and training scenarios. Existing CAD-Models can be used and enhanced by interactive components and visualization techniques to visualize functionality of a complex system and interaction between components. Furthermore, interactive proto-types can be used for customers to show the technical evolution and advantages of upcoming systems. Especially for these scenarios, we encourage the use of special

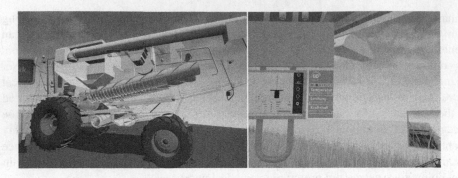

Fig. 4. Examples of prototypes visualizing components of harvesters (left) and UI-concepts for controlling the machine (right).

capabilities found in VR, such as annotations or overlays, transparency or masking of elements, as well as stylized rendering techniques such as outlines or special shading techniques.

Prototyping innovative user interface concepts for controlling complex machinery, especially visualizing parametrisations of system components and their side effects, represents another use case. Nowadays, agricultural machinery (or at least parts of it) are often controlled using touch sensitive screens. The transition from traditional hardware-based interaction techniques towards the interaction with virtual content leaves much space for improvement of the visualization and interaction. Furthermore, AR concepts find their way into the cockpit. Although current AR technologies are quite limited, basic questions on future AR visualization techniques and solutions for typical problems such as text legibility, the amount of information which can be presented, contrast or occlusion represent typical design parameters which need to be considered.

One approach is to use VR to simulate typical behaviours of AR visualizations (cf. Fig. 5). One benefit of this method is, that concepts can be evaluated which circumvent current technical limitations offering the opportunity to focus on the benefits which AR offers for visualizing virtual information integrated into the physical environment. By doing so it is possible to develop interaction and visualization concepts for future AR

Fig. 5. Simulation of AR concepts using VR.

implementations. Additionally, the combination of different visualization and interaction techniques are in focus: questions like interoperability between touch control and AR visualizations can be evaluated.

4.3 Technology and Frameworks

Computer Graphics Frameworks have been evolved over the last couple of years. Modern graphics engines, which are available (and affordable), allow to create interactive 3D scenes without large programming overhead. This represents an advantage for design prototyping, because development times are shorter, the implementation is less error prone, easier to debug and, due to the use of visual scripting tools, interactive content can be created even without programming skills. This allows designers and programmers to work closer together and facilitates the interdisciplinary collaboration. Additionally, it helps to work with small iterations on the intended prototype or design solution.

In our recent prototypes, we relied mainly on the Unreal Engine 4 [26] and Unity 5 [27]. These frameworks consist of powerful editors for material editing, mesh import and customization as well as scripting functionality to easy make a static 3D scene interactive. Furthermore, they provide a convenient integration of VR components, especially in regards to the integration of VR headsets. They also grant access to an exhaustive collection of materials, models and plugins through their inbuilt stores. These assets, some of them are freely available, can be used to augment the virtual environment with additional elements to make the VR experience more authentic (e.g. foliage, landscape presets) without additional development overhead. Further advantages are a very active community which helps to solve technical issues, an extensive technical documentation which help to explore the more sophisticated features of the frameworks and continuous technical development.

Integration of common tracking devices is achieved by using existing plugins. Custom plugins for the framework can be implemented in order to support devices. Especially with regards to the Unreal Engine, the opportunity to integrate C++ code offers the opportunity to reuse existing frameworks by writing wrappers that grant access to the core functionality to be used by the engine. Existing state-of-the-art libraries like OpenCV [28] or ARToolkit [29] can be integrated in this way.

5 Integration into the Design Workflow

To face the complex HMI design development and the urge to exploit the advantages of evaluation and decision-making in early stages of design and development processes, frameworks for rapid prototyping are needed, which allow frequent changes of content, easy adaption of UI-designs or altering the interaction design. Additionally, VR prototyping frameworks should provide a seamless integration into the design workflow, one area which is currently still problematic, due to different technological approaches of CAD-Software and Real-Time Systems, and incompatible file formats or incomplete interchange formats. One core issue represents scaling down the existing CAD models for use with real-time systems. As CAD is often based in curves and the goal is to create as exact curvature as possible, a straightforward tessellation creates a very high polygon count. This makes it impossible to render the content with high frame rates that are needed for VR. Simple reduction is possible, but sometimes creates artefacts, as specific parts of a model may require a higher level of detail whereas other parts can be reduced even further. Reducing the level of detail for use in VR is therefore work-intensive and requires a clear communication by the VR experts about constraints regarding the rendering capabilities.

Another issue relates to the rendering of the materials. CAD software uses different mathematical models for rendering materials (mostly due to the missing real-time requirement) and therefore a different parameterization for creating a specific look. Especially when using the Unreal Engine 4, its in-built Physically-Based Material approach makes it necessary to recreate the materials after importing the model. Although the editor offers a WYSIWYG experience, material networks for authentic materials can become quite complex. A related issue is the number of possible materials, which is typically constrained in a real-time 3D scene to keep performance acceptable. Depending on the interchange format and software used, duplicate materials or large amounts of material with slightly different parameters require an additional overhaul of imported models or an additional revision of the source materials before exporting.

Rapid prototyping works for creating a more or less authentic VR experience, however, rendering performance, especially for high resolution rendering used with the oculus rift requires powerful hardware or a reduction of detail when used with less powerful hardware (e.g. mobile rendering for use with Google Cardboard). However, the code created by rapid prototyping tool provided by the editor is not optimized for performance. Additionally, the current frameworks need to mature to become more stable and deliver more predictable rendering results. Especially the Unreal Engine 4, which is under active development with rapidly changing and improving software versions, is still not very stable and suffers from performance problems especially when exporting to mobile devices.

6   Future Work

In the early design phase, a core requirement is a context-based, individual and flexible simulation. In contrast, the demands on realistic simulation and completeness of the environment are lower than for other scenarios, such as training or in-depth evaluation. Current graphics engines make this less work-intensive, however, making a VR scene interactive is still a demanding task. Especially when using proprietary tracking software or hardware, the translation between tracking result to intended interaction is tedious and error prone. There is a need for abstract interfaces between tracking hardware and VR software and for a general human interaction model. Another related issue is represented by the integration of traditional UI-Interaction (e.g. touch panels in a harvester) in a VR scene. Design concepts and UI-prototypes often use standard UI technologies such as HTML5. Integrating these prototypes in a VR experience is currently simply not possible or requires a complete reimplementation using UI-frameworks suitable for

VR. This issue – integrating 2D UI in 3D scene – remains unsolved for a long time. Additional work is needed to find methods to integrate or convert user interfaces created classic UI-technologies into 3D graphics engines without breaking the complete implementation.

Interaction with VR content remains another critical issue. In some use cases, current technologies are at least usable – e.g. if the goal is to determine the most convenient spatial layout of controls or UI-elements. However, for usability evaluations or similar demanding tasks incorporating a concrete interaction of the user with the system, current systems and interaction are simply not accurate enough, are too inflexible or do not provide adequate feedback.

To explore the described technologies and guidelines as well as their potentials and usability in development based prototyping, several projects are planned. An interdisciplinary project discusses innovative approaches for future cabins for excavators. In cooperation with an industry partner, the goal is to collaboratively design a new cabin or vital components using digital and physical prototypes for testing evaluation and communication. Another project deals with the location of different types of digital enhanced prototypes within the different phases of the design process. Therefore, a wide range of technologies and forms of enhancement will be contrasted with the demands, settings and capabilities of crucial milestones within the process.

References

1. Yang, M.C.: An examination of prototyping and design outcome. In: ASME 2004 Computers and Information in Engineering Conference (DECT 2004). ACM, New York (2004)
2. Shiratuddin, M.F., Thabet, W.: Utilizing a 3D game engine to develop a virtual design review system. J. Inf. Technol. Constr. **16**, 39–68 (2011). CIB, Rotterdam
3. Bordegoni, M.; Ferrise, F.; Lizaranzu, J.: Use of interactive virtual prototypes to define product design specifications: a pilot study on consumer products. In: Proceedings of the ISVRI 2011, pp. 11–18. IEEE, New York (2011)
4. Bruno, F., Muzzupappa, M.: Product interface design: a participatory approach based on virtual reality. Int. J. Hum Comput Stud. **68**(5), 254–269 (2010). Academic Press, London
5. Bao, J.S., Jin, Y., Gu, M.Q., Yan, J.Q., Ma, D.Z.: Immersive virtual product development. J. Mater. Process. Technol. **129**, 592–596 (2002). Elsevier, Amsterdam, New York
6. Guo, H., Li, H., Chan, G., Skitmore, M.: Using game technologies to improve the safety of construction plant pperations. Accid. Anal. Prev. **48**, 204–213 (2012). Elsevier, Amsterdam
7. Hoberman, P., Krum, D.M., Suma, E.A., Bolas, M.: Immersive training games for smartphone-based head mounted displays. In: Virtual Reality Short Papers and Posters (VRW 2012), pp. 151–152. IEEE, Piscataway (2012)
8. Heydarian, A., Carneiro, J.P., Gerber, D., Becerik-Gerber, B., Hayes, T., Wood, W.: Immersive virtual environments versus physical built environments: a benchmarking study for building design and user-built environment explorations. Autom. Constr. **54**, 116–126 (2015). Elsevier, Amsterdam
9. Frund, J., Gausemeier, J., Matysczok, C., Radkowski, R.: Cooperative design support within automobile advance development using augmented reality technology. In: Proceedings of the CSCW 2004, vol. 2, pp. 492–497. ACM, New York (2004)

10. Zwolinski, P., Tichkiewitch, S., Sghaier, A.: The use of virtual reality techniques during the design process: from the functional definition of the product to the design of its structure. CIRP Annals – Manuf. Technol. **56**(1), 135–138 (2007). Elsevier, New York

11. Bullinger, H.-J., Bauer, W., Wenzel, G., Blach, R.: Towards user centred design (UCD) in architecture based on immersive virtual environments. Comput. Ind. **61**(4), 372–379 (2010). Elsevier, New York

12. Poplin, A.: Playful public participation in urban planning: a case study for online serious games. Comput. Environ. Urban Syst. **36**(3), 195–206 (2012). Elsevier, New York

13. Tversky, B., Morrison, J.B., Betrancourt, M.: Animation: can it facilitate? Int. J. Hum.-Comput. Studie **57**(4), 247–262 (2002). Elsevier, New York

14. Oculus Rift. www.oculus.com

15. Samsung Gear VR. www.samsung.com/global/galaxy/wearables/gear-vr

16. Google Cardboard. www.google.com/get/cardboard

17. Zhu, D., Gedeon, T., Taylor, K.: Head or gaze? controlling remote camera for hands-busy tasks in teleoperation - a comparison. In: Proceedings of the OZCHI 2010, pp. 300–303. ACM, New York (2010)

18. Jacob, R.J.K.: What you look at is what you get: eye movement-based interaction techniques. In: Proceedings of the CHI 1990, pp. 11–18. ACM, New York (1990)

19. Jacob, R.J.K.: Eye movement-based human-computer interaction techniques: toward non-command interfaces. In: Advances in Human-Computer Interaction, vol. 4, pp. 151–190. Ablex Pub. Corp., Norwood (1993)

20. Mohler, B.J., Creem-Regehr, S.H., Thompson, W.B., Bülthoff, H.H.: The effect of viewing a self-avatar on distance judgments in an HMD-Based virtual environment. Presence: Teleoperators Virtual Environ. **19**(3), 230–242 (2010). MIT Press, Cambridge

21. Ries, B., Interrante, V., Kaeding, M., Anderson, L.: The effect of self-embodiment on distance perception in immersive virtual environments. In: Proceedings of the ACM Symposium on Virtual Reality Software and Technology, pp. 167–170. ACM, New York (2008)

22. Slater, M., McCarthy, J., Maringelli, F.: The influence of body movement on subjective presence in virtual environments. Hum. Factors: J. Hum. Factors Ergon. Soc. **40**(3), 469–477 (1998). Pergamon Press, New York

23. Günther, T., Franke, I.S., Groh, R.: Aughanded virtuality: the hands in the virtual environment. In: 3D User Interfaces (3DUI 2015), pp. 157–158. IEEE, New York (2015)

24. Günther, T.: Aughanded Virtuality. Diploma Thesis. TU Dresden, Dresden (2014)

25. Leap Motion for Virtual Reality. https://www.leapmotion.com/product/vr

26. Unreal Engine 4. www.unrealengine.com

27. Unity 5. www.unity3d.com

28. Open CV. http://opencv.org

29. ARToolkit. http://artoolkit.org

Interaction Fidelity: The Uncanny Valley of Virtual Reality Interactions

Ryan P. McMahan[✉], Chengyuan Lai, and Swaroop K. Pal

University of Texas at Dallas, Richardson, TX, USA
{rymcmaha,Chengyuan.Lai,sxp142730}@utdallas.edu

Abstract. Interaction designers often strive to create more-realistic and natural interactions for virtual reality (VR) applications. However, due to hardware and system limitations, they often settle for semi-natural interaction techniques. Using the concept of interaction fidelity and the Framework for Interaction Fidelity Analysis (FIFA), we present several case studies that provide empirical evidence that semi-natural interactions are worse for user performance than low-fidelity interactions that do not resemble real-world actions and high-fidelity interactions that do. We discuss these case studies and how interaction fidelity generally acts as the uncanny valley of VR interactions in terms of user performance. We also consider different reasons for this phenomenon and conclude with a guideline to avoid designing semi-natural interaction techniques that lack similarities to established techniques or real-world actions.

Keywords: Virtual reality · Interaction fidelity · Uncanny valley

1 Introduction

Interaction designers often strive to design realistic and natural interactions when developing VR applications because naturalness has been associated with increased usability and improved user performance [1]. However, when working with VR systems with limited capabilities, designers often resort to creating or using semi-natural interaction techniques. While many designers may intuitively believe that these techniques should afford better user performances than non-natural techniques, we present evidence in this paper that suggests otherwise.

First, we must clearly distinguish the differences among natural, semi-natural, and non-natural interaction techniques. To do so, we use the concept of *interaction fidelity* —the objective degree of exactness with which real world actions are reproduced in an interactive system [2]. Additionally, we present an updated version of the Framework for Interaction Fidelity Analysis (FIFA) [3], which can be used to assess the degree of interaction fidelity provided by a technique compared to a real-world action. FIFA consists of three broad categories of fidelity aspects. First, biomechanical symmetry is used to analyze the anthropometrics, kinematics, and kinetics of an interaction technique. Second, the input veracity of a technique concerns the accuracy, precision, and latency of the input devices used to implement it. Finally, control symmetry represents

© Springer International Publishing Switzerland 2016
S. Lackey and R. Shumaker (Eds.): VAMR 2016, LNCS 9740, pp. 59–70, 2016.
DOI: 10.1007/978-3-319-39907-2_6

the transfer functions that translate input data into meaningful system functions and simulation outcomes.

In this paper, we present a series of case studies in which we used FIFA to analyze the degrees of interaction fidelity provided by different techniques in prior research studies. Across the varying case studies, we found two common results. First, high-fidelity interaction techniques usually outperform mid-fidelity techniques. This was not surprising given the intuitive notion that usability improves with more naturalness. However, the second common result was that low-fidelity interaction techniques also usually outperform mid-fidelity techniques. This result directly contradicts the intuition that more naturalness is good. Additionally, it indicates that increasing interaction fidelity may produce a U-shaped curve in terms of user performance.

Considering these results, we propose that interaction fidelity is similar to the uncanny valley phenomenon regarding aesthetics in robots [4]. In general, we hypothesize that increasing interaction fidelity from traditional, non-natural techniques will initially result in worse user performances. As interaction fidelity continues to increase, and the overall degree of fidelity becomes relatively high, user performances will rebound and be comparable, if not better, than those afforded by the low-fidelity techniques. We discuss potential reasons for this phenomenon and conclude that familiarity is the most likely cause. We also present a new guideline concerning the design of mid-fidelity and semi-natural interaction techniques.

2 Framework for Interaction Fidelity Analysis (FIFA)

FIFA was originally introduced by McMahan [3]. Since then, it has been used by researchers to analyze the interaction fidelity of various techniques (e.g., [5]). Recently, we have updated the framework to account for nuances that the original version did not account for and to make it easier to use. We present that updated version here.

FIFA consists of three major categories of components—biomechanical symmetry, input veracity, and control symmetry. Each corresponds to one of the aspects of the User-System Loop, as seen in Fig. 1. In addition to these three categories, the new version also emphasizes the importance of three phases of interaction. Below, we define the three categories, their components, and the three phases of interaction.

2.1 Biomechanical Symmetry

Biomechanical symmetry is the objective degree of exactness with which real-world body movements for a task are reproduced during interaction. It consists of three subcomponents. First, *anthropometric symmetry* is the objective degree of exactness with which body segments involved in a real-world task are required by an interaction technique. Second, *kinematic symmetry* is the objective degree of exactness with which a body motion for a real-world task is reproduced during an interaction technique. Third, *kinetic symmetry* is the objective degree of exactness with which the forces involved in a real-world action are reproduced during an interaction technique.

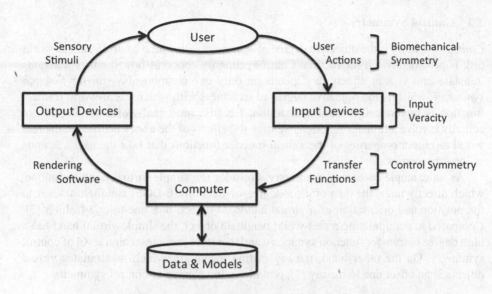

Fig. 1. The User-System Loop and the three categories of FIFA

For an example, consider the March-and-Reach technique [6], in which the user uses both hands and both feet to climb a virtual ladder. March-and-Reach has a high degree of anthropometric symmetry to real-world ladder climbing since both involve using the hands, forearms, upper arms, thighs, legs, and feet. Additionally, the interaction technique has a high level of kinematic symmetry because it reproduces most of the arm and leg motions involved with climbing a real ladder. However, it has a low level of kinetic symmetry, as it lacks the tactile and force feedback stimuli involved with grabbing and stepping on actual ladder rungs. Considering all three subcomponents, March-and-Reach has a moderately high degree of biomechanical symmetry.

2.2 Input Veracity

Input veracity is the objective degree of exactness with which the input devices capture and measure the user's actions. It also consists of three subcomponents. First, *accuracy* refers to how close an input device's readings are to the "true" values that it attempts to measure. Second, *precision* concerns a device's ability to reproduce the same results when repeated measures are taken in the same conditions. Finally, *latency* is defined as the temporal delay between user input and the sensory feedback generated by the system in response to it.

Input veracity depends solely on the quality of the input devices and is independent of the user's actions. Consider a Vicon motion capture system for an example. Most Vicon systems offer sub-millimeter accuracy, sub-millimeter precision, and latencies of a few milliseconds. Hence, these systems provide a high degree of input veracity. On the other hand, some tracking devices do not offer the same quality of input data, such as the Microsoft Kinect. Therefore, such devices provide less input veracity.

2.3 Control Symmetry

Control symmetry is the objective degree of exactness with which control in a real-world task is provided by an interaction. Control primarily concerns how the user's actions translate into system effects. It depends on only one component—*transfer function symmetry*, which is the objective degree of exactness with which a real-world transfer function is reproduced through interaction. Because most real-world actions do not actually involve a transfer function, we treat the effects of the user's actions on the real world as output properties of theoretical transfer functions that take the user's actions as input properties.

As an example of control symmetry, consider the simple virtual hand technique, which directly maps the data of a six-degree-of-freedom (6-DOF) handheld tracker to the position and orientation of a virtual handheld object, in a one-to-one fashion [7]. Compared to manipulating a real-world handheld object, the simple virtual hand has a high degree of transfer function symmetry and therefore provides a high level of control symmetry. On the other hand, the ray-casting technique, which manipulates virtual objects at an offset due to the ray [7], provides a low degree of control symmetry.

2.4 Interaction Phases

In the updated version of FIFA, we have adopted the practice of analyzing techniques across three phases of interactions: (1) the initiation phase, (2) the continuation phase, and (3) the termination phase. The initiation phase includes all of the biomechanical, input, and control aspects required to begin using a technique. The continuation phase encompasses all of the aspects involved with continuing the interaction. Finally, the termination phase indicates what is required to stop the interaction.

Consider the Walking In Place (WIP) technique [8]. During the initiation phase, the user starts the travel technique by lifting and stepping in place with one leg. The continuation phase involves continuously alternating steps in place to continue virtual travel. Finally, the termination phase only requires the user to stop stepping in place.

3 Case Studies of Interaction Fidelity

Using FIFA, we have conducted several case studies to investigate the effects of interaction fidelity on user performance in prior research studies. We have found two common results. First, we have found the intuitive result that those techniques with high degrees of interaction fidelity in biomechanical symmetry, input veracity, and control symmetry, generally afford better user performances than mid-fidelity interaction techniques that are lower in one of the three categories. However, our second result is not as intuitive. We have also found that low-fidelity techniques, with little interaction fidelity in any of the three categories, also generally afford better user performances then the mid-fidelity techniques. Together, these two results indicate that moderate levels of interaction fidelity often yield the worst user performances and that increasing interaction fidelity produces a U-shaped curve. We present three subsets of case studies below that exemplify this phenomenon.

3.1 Moderate Levels Worse Than High Levels

The following case studies provide results that indicate mid-fidelity interaction techniques are worse than high-fidelity techniques in terms of user performance. Hence, these case studies demonstrate that user performance increases as interaction fidelity increases from moderate to high levels.

For Manipulation Tasks. Mine et al. [9] conducted a study comparing three 6-DOF virtual hand techniques for a 3D manipulation task. One of the three techniques was a simple virtual hand technique with a direct, one-to-one mapping. However, the other two techniques used transfer functions that created offsets between the physical handheld tracker and the user's virtual hand position.

The two offset techniques afforded only moderate levels of interaction fidelity. Both provided high degrees of biomechanical symmetry with high anthropometric, kinematic, and kinetic symmetries to the real-world action of manipulating a handheld object. However, both only had moderate control symmetry due to their transfer functions intentionally producing offsets between the physical tracker and virtual hand. On the other hand, the simple virtual hand was a high-fidelity interaction technique with high degrees of both biomechanical symmetry and control symmetry, with its one-to-one transfer function directly mapping the virtual hand to the physical tracker.

During the study, Mine et al. [9] found that the high-fidelity technique afforded significantly faster completion times for the task of manipulating a virtual cube and docking it (i.e., positioning and aligning it with) another target cube. In a similar study, Ware and Rose [10] also found that the high-fidelity simple virtual hand outperformed a mid-fidelity offset technique. Therefore, both of these studies indicate that high-fidelity interaction techniques afford better user performances than those with moderate levels of interaction fidelity.

For Search Tasks. Pausch et al. [11] conducted a study comparing two view control techniques for the task of visually searching a room for a target. One of the techniques simply relied on mapping the 6-DOF head tracker of a head-mounted display (HMD) to the user's viewpoint. However, the second technique involved placing a 6-DOF tracker within a handheld object and using the same one-to-one transfer function to translate the tracker's position and orientation into the user's viewpoint. Additionally, for the handheld technique, Pausch et al. mounted the HMD to the ceiling to prevent users from attempting to physically look around.

The handheld view control was a mid-fidelity interaction technique. It essentially afforded no biomechanical symmetry, as users would move their hands to control their viewpoints instead of moving their heads. However, its control symmetry was relatively high as it used a direct, one-to-one mapping from the tracker's input to the viewpoint's position. On the other hand, the head-tracked technique afforded high levels of interaction fidelity as it afforded both biomechanical symmetry and control symmetry to the real-world action of looking around to visually spot a target.

During the study, Pausch et al. [11] asked users to sit and visually search a surrounding virtual environment for a target letter and verbally inform the experimenter when they found the target or determined that it did not exist. The researchers found that the high-fidelity head-tracked technique afforded faster completion times for non-present targets than the mid-fidelity handheld technique. Hence, the results of this study also indicate that high-fidelity interaction techniques provide better user performances than mid-fidelity techniques with moderate levels of interaction fidelity.

3.2 Moderate Levels Worse Than Low Levels

The following case studies provide results that indicate mid-fidelity interaction techniques are worse than low-fidelity techniques in terms of user performance. Hence, these case studies demonstrate that user performance can decrease as interaction fidelity increases from low levels to moderate levels.

For Steering Tasks. McMahan et al. [12] conducted a study comparing four steering techniques for driving a virtual vehicle in the Mario Kart Wii game for the Nintendo Wii. Two of the techniques employed traditional joystick controls for racing games and only differed in terms of the form factor of the game controller. One used the Wii Classic controller while the other used the GameCube controller. The remaining two steering techniques used the orientation reported by a Wii Remote to determine the steering direction. Their only difference was also form factor, with one technique using only the Wii Remote and the other using the Wii Wheel prop.

The two joystick techniques yielded low levels of interaction fidelity. Because the user's thumb performed the steering actions, all three components of biomechanical symmetry were low for both techniques compared to using a real-world steering wheel to drive a vehicle. Additionally, their levels of control symmetry were low due to using a force-to-direction transfer function instead of the real-world position-to-direction function that steering wheels employ.

The Wii Remote and Wii Wheel techniques only provided moderate degrees of interaction fidelity to using a real-world steering wheel. Because the user could change the steering direction by manipulating the orientation of the relevant handheld device, both techniques yielded high degrees of anthropometric and kinematic symmetry. However, the kinetic symmetries of these techniques were low due to users having to exert additional forces to hold and re-center the devices in the absence of a powered steering column. The control symmetries of the techniques were low due to also using a force-to-direction transfer function to translate the Wii Remote's accelerometer data into a steering direction. Additionally, McMahan et al. [12] questioned the latency of the accelerometer-driven orientation tracking, which indicates that the techniques may have had only moderate input veracity compared to a real-world steering wheel.

In the within-subject study, McMahan et al. [12] found that the low-fidelity joystick techniques afforded significantly faster driving times and significantly fewer driving mistakes (i.e., running off course) than the two mid-fidelity interaction techniques. Hence, these results support our findings that low-fidelity techniques provide better user performances than mid-fidelity interactions.

For Navigation Tasks. McMahan [3] conducted a study comparing two travel techniques for navigating a path from one location to another throughout a large virtual environment. The first travel technique was similar to traditional keyboard-and-mouse controls for first-person desktop games. The second travel technique was the Human Joystick [2], which uses the center of the tracking area and the user's tracked head position to define a 2D horizontal vector. This 2D vector defines the direction of travel and its magnitude controls the speed. To avoid constant virtual locomotion, the Human Joystick employs a small no-travel zone at the center of the tracking area.

The keyboard-and-mouse technique obviously provides only a low level of interaction fidelity. It lacks biomechanical symmetry due to not incorporating the user's thighs, legs, and feet. Additionally, its control symmetry is low due to using a velocity-based transfer function, instead of the position-based function of real walking. On the other hand, the Human Joystick offers a moderate degree of interaction fidelity. It has high anthropometric symmetry to real-world walking. During the initiation phase, when stepping outside of the no-travel zone, it also affords high kinematic and kinetic symmetries. Though these are low during the continuation and termination phases. The Human Joystick also provides moderate control symmetry due to employing two transfer functions. In the no-travel zone, a one-to-one, position-to-position function offers a high degree of transfer function symmetry. However, outside of the zone, another position-to-velocity function provides little control symmetry.

McMahan [3] varied the two travel techniques within-subject during his study. The results of his study showed that the low-fidelity keyboard-and-mouse technique afforded significantly faster travel times than the mid-fidelity Human Joystick technique, which supports our hypothesis that mid-fidelity techniques are generally worse than low-fidelity techniques, in terms of user performance.

3.3 Moderate Levels Are the Worst

The following case studies provide results that indicate mid-fidelity techniques are worse than both low-fidelity and high-fidelity interaction techniques. These case studies support our theory that mid-fidelity techniques are the worst and that interaction fidelity is a U-shaped curve with user performance first decreasing and then increasing as interaction fidelity increases from low to high levels.

For Manipulation Tasks. Zhai and Milgram [13] conducted a study comparing four interaction techniques for a 3D manipulation and docking task. The first technique was an isometric rate approach, in which force applied to a 6-DOF Spaceball directly controlled the direction and speed of the object's velocity. The second technique was an isometric position technique that allowed the user to directly manipulate the object's position by moving the Spaceball and using a button for clutching. The third interaction was an isotonic rate technique, in which the user manipulated the velocity of the object by freely moving a 6-DOF glove. Finally, the fourth technique was an isotonic position approach that allowed the user to directly manipulate the position of the object by freely moving the glove device.

The isometric rate technique yielded the lowest level of interaction fidelity among the four techniques. Its anthropometric symmetry to manipulating a handheld object in the real world was low due to not incorporating the forearm or upper arm. As such, its kinematic and kinetic symmetries were also low. Additionally, its control symmetry was low due to its force-to-velocity transfer function.

The isometric position and the isotonic rate techniques were both moderate in terms of interaction fidelity. Like the isometric rate technique, the isometric position interaction was low in biomechanical symmetry, but its position-to-position transfer function provided it with greater control symmetry. On the other hand, the isotonic rate technique had a high degree of biomechanical symmetry due to the ability to freely move the glove device, but its control symmetry was low due to a velocity-based transfer function similar to the isometric rate technique's function. The isotonic position technique was the only high-fidelity interaction with both high biomechanical symmetry and high control symmetry to the real-world task.

For the task of manipulating and docking a virtual pyramid with another target pyramid, Zhai and Milgram [13] found that the low-fidelity isometric rate technique and the high-fidelity isotonic position technique were nearly identical in terms of task completion times. However, they found that both mid-fidelity interaction techniques were significantly worse than the low and high-fidelity techniques. They also determined that the mid-fidelity isometric position technique yielded the worst task completion times. Hence, the results of this study reinforce our theory that mid-fidelity interaction techniques are generally worse than both low and high-fidelity techniques.

For Navigation Tasks. In a more recent study, Nabiyouni et al. [5] compared three travel techniques for a path navigation task. The first travel technique was based on the traditional gamepad interface for first-person console games, in which one joystick controls translations while the other joystick controls view orientation. The second travel technique was the Virtusphere technique, which allows the user to physically walk in any direction within a large "hamster ball" sphere mounted on casters. For the third technique, Nabiyouni et al. [5] used the real walking technique, in which a 6-DOF head tracker updates the user's view as if walking through the real world.

The joystick-based technique used in the study was a low-fidelity interaction technique. It afforded no biomechanical symmetry to real-world walking and little control symmetry, as its transfer function mapped the forces applied to the joysticks to the direction and speed of the user's velocity. The Virtusphere technique provided more interaction fidelity due to higher degrees of anthropometric and kinematic symmetries. The kinetic symmetry of the Virtusphere was low though due to extra forces being required to start and stop the rolling of the large sphere. Additionally, its transfer function symmetry was low due to translating the sphere's velocity into virtual movements. The real walking technique afforded the highest degree of interaction fidelity with high levels of biomechanical symmetry and control symmetry.

For the navigation task of walking along a path, Nabiyouni et al. [5] found that the mid-fidelity Virtusphere technique resulted in the worst user performances for path deviations and task completion times. Both the low-fidelity joystick technique and the high-fidelity real walking technique outperformed the Virtusphere technique. Hence, this case study further supports the theory that mid-fidelity interaction techniques are generally the worst and that interaction fidelity yields a U-shaped curve of user performance as it increases from low levels to high levels.

For Search Tasks. In another recent study, Pal et al. [14] compared three travel techniques for visual and navigation-based search tasks with an HMD. The first travel technique was gaze-directed steering, in which users used a handheld device to activate movements relative to the current gaze direction of the HMD. The second technique was similar to real walking for translational movements, but required users to use the handheld device to activate virtual turning within the environment. The third technique was real walking, which did not require any use of the handheld device.

The gaze-directed steering was a low-fidelity interaction technique. It lacked biomechanical symmetry as users primarily used their fingers instead of their thighs, legs, and feet to move. Additionally, its control symmetry was low due to its transfer function translating button presses into velocity through the virtual environment.

The virtual turning technique afforded only a moderate level of interaction fidelity. Its biomechanical symmetry to real-world walking was high due to using the thighs, legs, and feet to move around, though the inability to physically turn did lower the overall kinematic symmetry. With regard to control symmetry, the technique had a high degree of transfer function symmetry with its one-to-one, position-to-position mapping. However, the control symmetry was not entirely high, as the handheld device buttons controlled the forward direction of virtual movements. The real walking technique afforded the highest degree of interaction fidelity, as it did in the prior case study of Nabiyouni et al. [5].

For both visual search tasks and navigation-based search tasks, Pal et al. [14] found that the mid-fidelity virtual turning technique yielded the worst user performances in terms of search times and errors. Both the low-fidelity gaze-based steering and the high-fidelity real walking outperformed the mid-fidelity technique. These results further reinforce our theory that moderate levels of interaction fidelity provide the worst user performances and that interaction fidelity is a U-shaped curve.

4 Discussion

4.1 Interaction Fidelity Is an Uncanny Valley

In robotics, the term "uncanny valley" represents the phenomenon that, after a certain point, as a robot's human likeness increases, familiarity with and empathy toward the robot decreases, unless human likeness is at a very high level [4]. At high levels, reports of familiarity and empathy rebound and increase to levels higher than any previous degree of human likeness. We see a similar U-shaped curve with regard to the effects of interaction fidelity on user performance, as seen in our case studies. Hence, interaction fidelity appears to be the uncanny valley of VR interactions.

However, it is important not to overgeneralize our theory that moderate levels of interaction fidelity yield the worst user performances. There are obviously exceptions to this phenomenon. For example, mid-fidelity interaction techniques are not always worse than their low-fidelity counterparts. Consider the study conducted by Peck et al. [15], in which they compared a low-fidelity joystick technique, a mid-fidelity Walking In Place technique, and a high-fidelity redirected walking technique. For their navigation and wayfinding tasks, Peck et al. [15] found that the high-fidelity travel technique significantly outperformed both the low and mid-fidelity techniques. However, they did not find any significant differences between the low-fidelity joystick technique and the mid-fidelity WIP technique. Hence, the interaction fidelity uncanny valley is likely applicable to many subsets of interaction techniques, but not necessarily every subset or technique.

4.2 Potential Causes of the Interaction Fidelity Uncanny Valley

In addition to recognizing the phenomenon, it is important to understand what might be the cause of the interaction fidelity uncanny valley. In discussing the implications of their study, Nabiyouni et al. [5] suggested that the phenomenon is due to users attempting to employ mid-fidelity interaction techniques in the same manner as high-fidelity ones and the brain needing to adapt to the non-natural parts of the mid-fidelity techniques. However, if this were the case, we could expect to see a consistent and linear decrease in user performance for every component of interaction fidelity that a mid-fidelity technique differed from its high-fidelity counterpart. Also, this does not explain why many low-fidelity techniques outperform their mid-fidelity counterparts.

Instead, we believe the cause of the interaction fidelity uncanny valley is primarily due to a lack of familiarity. High-fidelity interaction techniques benefit from being similar to real-world actions and therefore are familiar to users. This is why they are often referred to as natural interactions. On the opposite end of the spectrum, many low-fidelity interaction techniques are similar to preexisting computer interfaces, such as keyboard-and-mouse techniques, joystick-based techniques, and game-controller techniques. These types of interfaces are familiar to many users nowadays, especially those that play videogames. Hence, like high-fidelity interaction techniques, low-fidelity interfaces also benefit from being familiar to users.

However, most mid-fidelity interaction techniques do not benefit from familiarity amongst users. Most interfaces that offer moderate levels of fidelity are not similar to preexisting computer interfaces or real-world actions. Hence, users cannot leverage prior experiences and familiarity with these techniques to achieve better user performances. When they can leverage such experiences, we have seen that users perform better with mid-fidelity techniques than predicted by the uncanny valley. For example, in the study conducted by Peck et al. [15], we believe that the lack of significant difference between the joystick and WIP techniques was due to most of the users being familiar with marching in place, which is the basis of the mid-fidelity WIP technique. As further evidence of the importance of familiarity, Lai et al. [6] found that users with many real-world experiences climbing ladders performed better on a virtual ladder climbing task using the moderately high (but not high) fidelity March-and-Reach technique than users without such real-world ladder climbing experiences.

Furthermore, it is important to note that familiarity with distinct components of a mid-fidelity interaction technique may not be enough to ensure better user performances. Consider the study conducted by Pal et al. [14]. The mid-fidelity virtual turning technique was essentially the combination of a low-fidelity joystick technique and a high-fidelity real walking technique. However, the researchers found that the mid-fidelity technique yielded the worst user performances. Therefore, we hypothesize that a user's familiarity with a whole interaction technique, and not just its components, is necessary for better user performances.

4.3   Guideline for Interaction Designers

Given the uncanny valley phenomenon related to interaction fidelity, and our hypothesis that the cause of the U-shaped curve is due to a lack of familiarity, we suggest that interaction designers should avoid developing mid-fidelity, semi-natural interaction techniques that lack overall similarities to well-established user interfaces or common real-world actions. At the surface, this may seem limiting. We are not suggesting that interaction designers should stick to low-fidelity techniques that are similar to other computer interfaces or high-fidelity techniques that mimic real-world actions. We are, however, suggesting that designers should start at one of these two ends of the uncanny valley and think of ways to maintain familiarity with users while designing new techniques with moderate levels of interaction fidelity.

5   Conclusions and Future Work

We have discussed the concept of interaction fidelity and why it is important to interaction designers when creating natural and semi-natural interaction techniques. We also presented the latest version of FIFA, a framework for analyzing the level of interaction fidelity that a technique provides when compared to a real-world action. Using FIFA, we have presented several case studies that demonstrate the effects of interaction fidelity on user performance. We have repeatedly provided evidence that moderate levels of interaction fidelity can result in the worst user performances. We refer to this U-shaped phenomenon as the uncanny valley of VR, which appears to be caused by a lack of familiarity with whole interaction techniques. Given this, we have offered a new design guideline concerning mid-fidelity interaction techniques.

For future work, we plan to conduct a series of studies that will provide more empirical evidence of interaction fidelity's uncanny valley and hopefully insights into the effects of familiarity and how designers can overcome system limitations to deliver semi-natural techniques that are more effective than their low-fidelity counterparts.

References

1. Bowman, D.A., McMahan, R.P., Ragan, E.: Questioning naturalism in 3D user interfaces. Commun. ACM **55**, 78–88 (2012)
2. McMahan, R.P., Bowman, D.A., Zielinski, D.J., Brady, R.B.: Evaluating display fidelity and interaction fidelity in a virtual reality game. IEEE Trans. Vis. Comput. Graph. (TVCG) **18**, 626–633 (2012)
3. McMahan, R.P.: Exploring the Effects of Higher-Fidelity Display and Interaction for Virtual Reality Games. Computer Science, vol. Ph.D. Dissertation. Virginia Tech (2011)
4. Mori, M.: The uncanny valley. Energy **7**, 33–35 (1970)

5. Nabiyouni, M., Saktheeswaran, A., Bowman, D.A., Karanth, A.: Comparing the performance of natural, semi-natural, and non-natural locomotion techniques in virtual reality. In: IEEE Symposium on 3D User Interfaces, pp. 3–10 (2015)
6. Lai, C., McMahan, R.P., Hall, J.: March-and-reach: a realistic ladder climbing technique. In: IEEE Symposium on 3D User Interfaces (3DUI), pp. 15–18 (2015)
7. Bowman, D.A., Kruijff, E., LaViola Jr., J.J., Poupyrev, I.: 3D User Interfaces: Theory and Practice. Addison-Wesley, Redwood City (2005)
8. Usoh, M., Arthur, K., Whitton, M.C., Bastos, R., Steed, A., Slater, M., Brooks Jr., F.P.: Walking > walking-in-place > flying, in virtual environments. In: Annual Conference on Computer Graphics and Interactive Techniques (SIGGRAPH), pp. 359–364. ACM Press (1999)
9. Mine, M.R., Brooks Jr., F.P., Sequin, C.H.: Moving objects in space: Exploiting proprioception in virtual-environment interaction. In: Annual Conference on Computer Graphics and Interactive Techniques (SIGGRAPH), pp. 19–26. ACM Press (1997)
10. Ware, C., Rose, J.: Rotating virtual objects with real handles. ACM Trans. Comput. Hum. Interact. (TOCHI) **6**, 162–180 (1999)
11. Pausch, R., Proffitt, D., Williams, G.: Quantifying immersion in virtual reality. In: 24th Annual Conference on Computer Graphics and Interactive Techniques (SIGGRAPH), pp. 13–18. ACM Press (1997)
12. McMahan, R.P., Alon, A.J.D., Lazem, S., Beaton, R.J., Machaj, D., Schaefer, M., Silva, M.G., Leal, A., Hagan, R., Bowman, D.A.: Evaluating natural interaction techniques in video games. In: IEEE Symposium on 3D User Interfaces (3DUI), pp. 11–14. (2010)
13. Zhai, S., Milgram, P.: Human performance evaluation of manipulation schemes in virtual environments. In: IEEE Virtual Reality Annual International Symposium (VRAIS), pp. 155–161 (1993)
14. Pal, S.K., Khan, M., McMahan, R.P.: The benefits of rotational head tracking. In: IEEE Symposium on 3D User Interfaces (3DUI), Greenville, SC (2016)
15. Peck, T.C., Fuchs, H., Whitton, M.C.: An evaluation of navigational ability comparing Redirected Free Exploration with Distractors to Walking-in-Place and joystick locomotio interfaces. In: IEEE Virtual Reality Conference (VR), pp. 55–62 (2011)

Guidelines for Graphical User Interface Design in Mobile Augmented Reality Applications

Carlos Santos[1(✉)], Brunelli Miranda[1], Tiago Araujo[1], Nikolas Carneiro[1],
Anderson Marques[2], Marcelle Mota[1], Jefferson Morais[1], and Bianchi Meiguins[1]

[1] Federal University of Pará, Belém, Brazil
gustavo.cbcc@gmail.com, brunelli.miranda@gmail.com,
tiagodavi70@gmail.com, nikolas.carneiro@gmail.com,
cellemota@gmail.com, jeffersonmorais@gmail.com,
bianchi.serique@gmail.com
[2] Federal Rural University of Amazon, Capanema, Brazil
andmarques2006@gmail.com

Abstract. The technological advancement of mobile devices allowed the entry of innovative technologies in users' daily lives, due to miniaturization and advancement of sensors, cameras and computer resources. These technologies make it possible to increase the user's interaction and perception about places and objects around him, allowing, for example, the use of augmented reality. However, this opportunity presents new challenges, such as application design and development, aspects to this new context of ubiquitous devices, heterogeneity of mobile devices, and how the user interacts with these applications. Thus, this paper aims to present the results of Mobile Augmented Reality application usability evaluation, identifying a list of problems in the application Graphical User Interface and propose some guidelines for building Graphical User Interfaces to avoid these problems. The chosen usability evaluation is the Think Aloud protocol, which was performed with 20 participants in the Mobile Augmented Reality application named ARguide.

Keywords: Mobile augmented reality · Usability evaluation · GUI design guidelines

1 Introduction

The technological development of mobile devices has brought many advantages to the development of Mobile Augmented Reality (MAR) applications, which search and explore Points of Interest (POI). Smartphones and tablets allow users to carry a range of applications with Internet access, location and movement sensors, and sufficient computational resource for playing multimedia content.

Augmented Reality (AR) can enhance user's daily lives activities using a hardware that people already own and at various locations, such as at work, at home, or during a trip. The AR uses technological resources aiming to expand the user's senses in relation to a given task, generally using visual content. An example of task that can be enhanced by AR is to discover and visit nearby sights. When a device extends the user's sense of

© Springer International Publishing Switzerland 2016
S. Lackey and R. Shumaker (Eds.): VAMR 2016, LNCS 9740, pp. 71–80, 2016.
DOI: 10.1007/978-3-319-39907-2_7

direction highlighting POIs with virtual markers over the real sight, augmented reality helped the user to accomplish his task.

The MAR applications context presents challenges, such as: the lack of applications' developing standards, some applications have limited flexibility withstanding the use in other areas, the demand for improvement in accuracy of location and pattern recognition technologies, shortage of available screen space to display virtual information, and the necessity of testing the acceptance of these new features [1].

This paper aims to present the results of MAR application usability evaluation, identify a list of problems in the application's Graphical User Interface (GUI), and propose guidelines for building GUIs for MAR applications to avoid the problems found in this work.

The evaluation performed is the Think Aloud Protocol, which was conducted with 20 participants, mainly aged from 18 to 30 years, and with experience on smartphone usage. To analyze the results, the significant verbalization of participants was extracted from evaluation videos. Finally, to propose guidelines all participants' verbalizations are transformed on usability problems and guidelines are proposed to avoid these problems.

The paper is organized according the following: Sect. 2 cover the background of MAR applications and introduces ARguide, which are the system used on tests, the Sect. 3 explains the usability evaluation used and its results, Sect. 4 presents the proposed guidelines, and Sect. 5 concludes the paper and points future works.

2   Mobile Augmented Reality and ARguide

The MAR is the employment of AR concept in mobile devices, which means increasing user perception about the real world with virtual elements over and synchronized to that real world, visualized through mobile devices [2]. Providing a good user experience is essential in this technology, which implies studies about GUI design are as important as innovative studies in this area [1, 3–5].

Among the main challenges identified in the development of MAR applications, the following can be highlighted [1, 3]:

- Appropriate use of devices' sensors;
- Low accuracy of tracking technologies;
- A range of hardware and software features and limitations;
- User interface design variability;
- Lack of standards adopted by application developers RAM;
- Energy consumption;

With these challenges in mind, it is important to evaluate MAR applications, so the identification of usability problems allows proposals for improvements and evolutions for more robust and adoptable applications that directly impact the user experience when using MAR applications.

ARguide [6] is the application used in the evaluation test. ARguide is a MAR application that uses technologies such as sensors, camera, GPS, and Internet to provide an intuitive discovery of Points of Interest (POI) through three modes of operation: AR Browser, Map and QR Code Scanner. The main ARguide's GUI is presented in Fig. 1.

Fig. 1. Screenshot of ARguide Application showing a POI through AR browser. The numbered areas highlight some GUI's widgets and visual items.

Figure 1 (1) shows two tabs used for change the exploration mode between map and AR browser. In (2) shows a virtual marker overlapped on the real POI, indicating the direction of the POI in the real environment. In (3) shows POIs radar and a slider widget to control the distance of interest. The area (4) has two buttons: clean and help. The area (5) has a button that starts the QR Code Scanner.

The user can read QR Codes with codes that is related with applications database. These codes makes possible to select a POI that is very close from others. After reading a QR Code, the application performs a POI selection automatically if the code is related to a POI, or shows a media directly to the user.

The Fig. 2 shows a screenshot of ARguide's GUI with the map tab selected. In this tab the user can navigate through the map and identify POIs touching their graphic representation (red balloon) according to Fig. 2 (1). Another important function in this application is the route that user can draw building circuits or a path to a particular POI.

The map functionality can be very helpful when the user decide to visit a POI's sight and want to know how he could reach the POI location. The AR Browser is complementary with map providing directions of POIs.

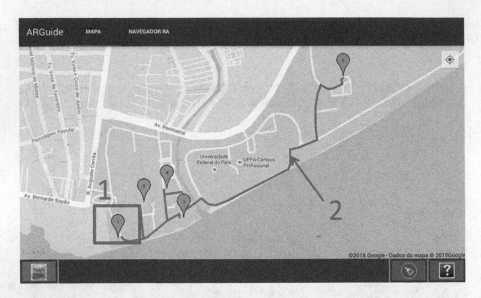

Fig. 2. Screenshot of ARguide Application showing POIs through Map tab. The numbered area (1) highlights the visual representation of a POI in the map while the area (2) highlights a circuit between POIs.

3   Usability Evaluation

This section shows the uability evaluation setup used on ARguide to extract usability problems from the GUI and shows the results of this evalution.

3.1   Evaluation Setup

The usability evaluation chosen is the Think Aloud Protocol [7], due to its good performance in usability factors evaluation [8]. The evaluation was conducted with 20 participants, mainly aged from 18 to 30 years; almost all participants have used the Android operating system before, according to charts in Fig. 3. All participants declared having already used smartphones and their daily frequency of smartphone usage is high.

The tasks were performed in a room in the university campus and the POIs refer to locations and buildings of this campus. The tasks were recorded on video and audio focusing on tablet screen used and participants' hands. Specially, the participants' speeches were recorded for later analysis of theirs unaware opinions triggered by the application usage.

The evaluation was conducted with six tasks and users had free time to perform them. The six tasks are listed below.

- **Task 1**: Select the local of central library to know about it.
- **Task 2**: Visualize a media (image or video) of conventions center.
- **Task 3**: Trace a route from your position to the University Hospital.

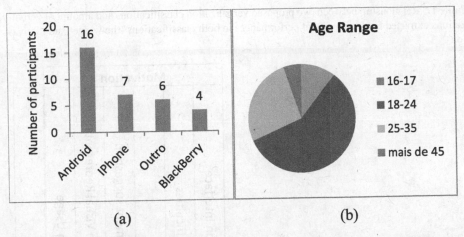

(a)   (b)

Fig. 3. Profile of participants in usability evaluation. Chart (a) shows the number of participants who have used the each of operating systems in smartphones and the chart (b) shows the proportion of participants in each the age range.

- **Task 4**: Find the university president's building through RA Browser.
- **Task 5**: Decrease the interest radius to visualize only nears POIs.
- **Task 6**: Scan a QR Code, visualize the provided content and say what it is about.

Before starting tasks, the evaluation conductor explained the application's functionality and characteristics to participants, and then each participant had 2 min to test the application by himself. After this, the conductor explained the tasks to participants and asked them to verbalize any difficulty, question or suggestion during the test performance.

To perform the tests we used a tablet model Samsung Galaxy Tab III with Dual-Core Processor of 1.5 GHz, 1.5 GB of RAM and 8 inches of screen size. The application was previously installed on this tablet and all participants used the same tablet.

3.2 Evaluation Results and Discussions

In the think aloud protocol evaluation is fundamental an analysis of the recorded video and audios of participants performing the suggested tasks. Hence, the first step into analysis of results is extract significant verbalization of participants. After obtaining all the significant verbalizations, each of these is classified according to the two following criteria: the widget or graphical component that the verbalization is related to and what is the motivation for this.

Table 1 shows the amount of verbalizations correlating the two criteria defined above. The amount of verbalizations in map and in its route functionality shows that usability problem in this function is very noticeable. Table 2 has some of the participants' verbalizations, whereas the first column has the raw participants' speeches associated and the second column has the speeches itself.

Table 1. Relationship between two proposed verbalization classifications and amount of verbalizations extracted from experiment performances in both classifications (the widget and motivation).

		Motivation						
		Doubts on Interface	Usage difficulties	bug	Improvement suggestion	Doubt on Visual Representation	Doubt on Usage	Total
Related Widget	Markers on Map	0	4	0	4	12	2	22
	Route on Map	0	0	0	2	1	13	16
	Markers on AR Browser	0	0	4	1	3	2	10
	Media Visualization	0	1	3	2	0	0	6
	Radius of Interest	0	0	0	1	0	5	6
	Map-details Balloon	1	1	0	1	0	1	4
	QR Code Scan	0	0	0	3	0	1	4
	AR Browse Radar	0	0	0	1	0	0	1
	Web Media Button	0	0	0	0	0	1	1
	Total	1	6	7	15	16	25	70

Table 2. Some participants' speeches obtained from evaluation and the related GUI component

GUI Component	Participants' raw speeches
AR Browser	"How am I going to find the Rectorate here?!"
Radar	"I had not paid attention that could see the distance here…"
Interest distance slider widget	"I do not understand."
Map	"I think I am lost…"
Virtual markers	"The Rectorate is behind the Convention Center? How does it work?"
QR Code Scanner	"OK … it did not give me any information, which was supposed to give me…"
POI's details panel.	"How do I close this?!"

The verbalizations concerning the map details balloon are related to the fact that the balloon covers the map, and overlap some markers. Since there was no close button, users got confused. To close that balloon, the user had to click anywhere else on the map, however this interaction was not intuitive to almost all participants.

Markers on map cause 22 verbalizations from participants. Analyzing the recorded videos, it is clear that these verbalizations are often related to the absence of text labels on the markers. The markers are labeled with a number that indicates a suggested visitation sequence. However, the participants did not notice this sequence and did not want this information.

The trace route application's functionality is the most problematic in tab map according to recorded videos. The verbalizations are usually referring to questions of where and how to trace route. To make a route in the application the only action needed is to select a POI marker and the system traces a route between your position and the clicked marker. Therefore, participants did not realize that the route was already drawn, and verbalized phrases, such: "The route is already done?!".

Problems encountered in AR Browser are mainly related to the adjustment of radius of interest, and with the arrangement of markers on the screen. Participants did not understand how to operate the moving slider (Figs. 1, 2, 3) and its effect on the application. One possible reason is that the slider only gives feedback on the radar, which is a very small component, turning the up and down movement a non-intuitive process.

The arrangement of the markers hinders is confused when there is more than one marker in the same direction and the algorithm tries to spread them, aiming that the user can view all markers. However, this spreading does not always occur in a satisfactory way and ends up placing markers far above or far below from the horizon.

The verbalizations related to the QR Code Scanner occurred mainly for not providing appropriate feedback to users when they were performing the reading of a QR Code. The system updates the bottom bar with buttons that gives access to media content of the selected POI; however, participants did not notice these updates and therefore, did not notice what have occurred.

The chart in Fig. 4 visually shows the amount of participants' verbalizations as the height of each bar, the rows from left to right represent each widget or graphical representation related to a verbalization and each color represents the verbalization motivation.

Two outliers are clear in the chart: the user's doubt on tracing a map route and the doubt about the visual representation of the markers on the map. These outliers mean that many participants commented about these problems, therefore representing the two major interface design problems on ARguide's GUI interface.

Another clear factor in chart is that there was usage doubt for almost all widgets, highlighting the slider of radius of interest. Two components that get minor attention are the AR Browser's radar (Figs. 1, 2, 3) and the Web Media button. This was expected for Web Media Button, because it is not mentioned explicitly on the tasks and its functionality is insignificant to accomplish the tasks, but the same cannot be said about the AR Browser's radar. Finally, the graph shows that the participants gave suggestions for improvement during the course of the test for almost all graphical components.

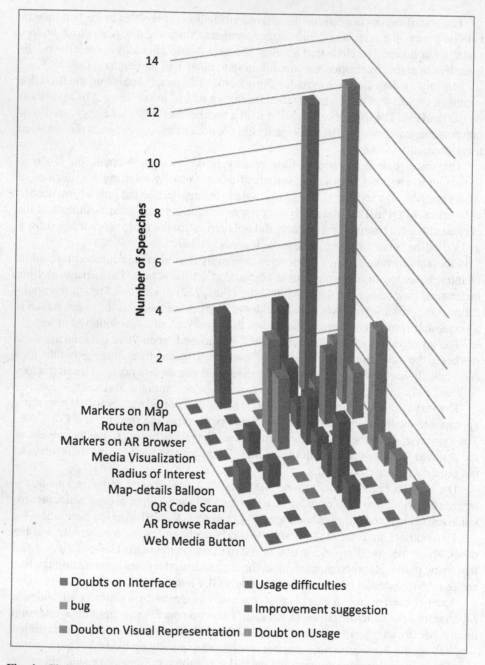

Fig. 4. Chart of the amount of verbalization encountered in Thinking Aloud Protocol usability evaluation

4   Proposed Guidelines

To propose guidelines based on encountered problems in usability evaluation, first all 70 verbalizations were listed from the recorded participants' performance and were translated to usability problems on ARguide interface. Next, a merge operation has been made with similar problems or with problems that may have the same solution. And after this, the resulting problems were discussed out on a brainstorm with ARguide's development team and specialists in GUI design and usability.

After the brainstorm reunion, for each suggested solution, it was evaluated what could better satisfy the conditions reported by participants, according the analysis of the captured videos and verbalizations. At least, a summary of the encountered problems and their recommended solutions was proposed, aiming to meet the participants' evaluation and subsequent users in general.

Table 3 shows in the first column the identified GUI problem and in the second column, the proposed guideline to mitigate the related problem. The GUI issues are in form of a heuristic, such that it can be modified and adapted to a variety of contexts.

Table 3. Found GUI issues and related proposed guidelines

GUI issue	Proposed Guideline
Not understand the application on first use.	Provide a tour guide on first use, stating the purpose of the application and how to use widgets.
Slide to control interest distance is not understandable.	Use known interactions on mobile touchscreen devices, for example the pinch gesture.
Map and AR browser without any POIs or direction indicators.	The application cannot run out of POIs, even if there is not any in the area. The direction of POIs can be suggested with arrows in the corner.
Textual distance information may go unnoticed by users.	The application should provide visual feedback for distance information. For example, draw the POI as if they were on the horizon.
Update text labels to inform the selection of POIs.	The application should draw the user's attention. One suggestion is to shrink the exploration space to present the details of the POI.
Use popups to show details of POIs.	Popups can be difficult to close and overlaps navigation. The details of POIs should be presented in a space apart.
Scanner or Discover POIs automatically without proper notify the user or suggest what he could do next.	When a scanner or automatic selection occurs, the system must notify the user and suggest what to do next.

The proposed guidelines follow the same style as the GUI issue and are suggestions based on what was observed both in video recorded as in extracted verbalizations of evaluation participants. Notwithstanding, the proposed guidelines are not absolute and can be considered as a suitable approach for designing MAR applications' GUI.

5 Conclusion and Future Works

This paper presented a MAR application that use georeferenced points to show POIs by AR Browser, map, and Scanning QR Code. Thinking Aloud Protocol usability evaluating was performed to identify possible problems with the application's GUI, and based on participants' verbalizations and actions in recorded tests, some guidelines were proposed to mitigate these problems.

The guidelines may be useful for designing MAR applications' GUI and analog for applications that have innovative interfaces such as multimodal interfaces that are used for operating and navigating through POIs. The guidelines were developed in general terms and are flexible in the context of adjustments and changes that solve the problems. At least, the proposed guidelines can be used as either heuristics or checklist for a pre evaluation of RAM applications.

For further research, we plan to use other usability evaluations aiming to find other types of GUI design problems, apply this evaluation in MAR applications with multimodal interfaces, such as, voice commands and hand gesture recognition. An update in ARguide application using these guidelines will be conducted to verify the benefits of the proposed guideline, as well as the drawbacks.

References

1. Martínez, H., Skournetou, D., Hyppölä, J., Laukkanen, S., Heikkilä, A.: Drivers and bottlenecks in the adoption of augmented reality applications. J. Multimedia Theor. Appl. 1, 20–26 (2014)
2. Bimber, O., Raskar, R.: Spatial augmented reality: merging real and virtual worlds. In: Peters, A.K. (ed) CRC Press by Taylor & Francis Group, Danvers, MA (2005)
3. Wasserman, A.I.: Software engineering issues for mobile application development. In: Proceedings of the FSE/SDP Workshop on Future of Software Engineering Research, pp. 397–400. ACM, Nova York (2010)
4. Dünser, A., Grasset, R., Seichter, H., Billinghurst, M.: Applying HCI principles in ar systems design. In: Proceedings of the IEEE Virtual Reality Conference: Mixed Reality User Interfaces: Specification, Authoring, Adaptation Workshop (MRUI 2007), pp. 37–42. IEEE, Charlotte, NC (2007)
5. De Sá, M., Churchill, E.F.: Mobile augmented reality: a design perspective. In: Huang, W., Alem, L., Livingston, M.A. (eds.) Human Factors in Augmented Reality Environments, pp. 139–164. Springer, New York (2013)
6. Araujo, T., Carneiro, N., Miranda, B., Santos, C.G., Meiguins, B.S.: Android augmented reality applications in extensible, flexible, and adaptable architecture. In: Proceedings of the XI Brazilian Symposium on Information Systems (SBSI 2015), pp. 63–70 (2015)
7. Lewis, C.: Using the "thinking Aloud" Method in Cognitive Interface Design. IBM T.J. Watson Research Center. (Research report) (1982)
8. Mahrin, M.N., Strooper, P., Carrington, D.: Selecting usability evaluation methods for software process descriptions. In: Proceedings of the 16th Asia-Pacific Software Engineering Conference. Penang: [s.n.], pp. 523–529 (2009)

The User Experience of Disney Infinity

Do Smart Toys Matter?

Shelly Welch[(✉)] and Peter Smith

School of Visual Art and Design,
University of Central Florida, Orlando, FL 32816, USA
shelly.welch@knights.ucf.edu, peter.smith@ucf.edu

Abstract. This study investigated what factors come into play when looking at the user experience involved with the commercial video game Disney Infinity (2.0 Edition), and sought to determine if the unique combination between sandbox and smart toy based gameplay present in gameplay offers an additional level of immersion. This study analyzed the effect of Disney Infinity (2.0 Edition) on immersion utilizing a Game Immersion Questionnaire modified to analyze play preference as well as video game experience. The study methodology analyzed 48 users while playing in "Toy Box" mode both with and without the associated smart toys, or Disney characters. Results show that while there was no significant difference in immersion for either group, nor were there any significant correlations between variables, there was a preference for playing the game with the associated smart toys in both groups. Recommendations were made for continued research building on modifications to this study as well as future research exploring the potential for smart toys in other areas.

Keywords: Pervasive games · Smart toys · Immersion · Disney infinity · Virtual worlds · Sandbox games · User experience · Usability · Human-computer interaction

1 Introduction

A user experience designer's role is to understand how to make a game appealing to users. This research addresses what factors come into play when looking at the user experience (UX) involved with the video game Disney Infinity (2.0 Edition), also referred to as Disney Infinity: Marvel Super Heroes (2.0 Edition). Disney Infinity (2.0 Edition) is more than just a virtual world playable on a video game console– it is a unique combination of vast virtual worlds, sandbox modes, and smart toys all playable across multiple platforms and linked through the Internet.

While the potential for further research utilizing smart toy based games is vast, this research focused on two specific aspects of UX in order to determine if the unique combination between sandbox and smart toy based gameplay present in Disney Infinity (2.0 Edition) offered an additional level of immersion. Additionally, this research goes on to discuss whether users prefer gameplay with the tangible objects incorporated into the Disney Infinity (2.0 Edition) experience, and offers explanations why this may be the case.

© Springer International Publishing Switzerland 2016
S. Lackey and R. Shumaker (Eds.): VAMR 2016, LNCS 9740, pp. 81–91, 2016.
DOI: 10.1007/978-3-319-39907-2_8

2 Literature Review

Smart toys in video games have much to add to UX. Research on informal learning suggests smart toys can add educational benefits, which aid users in learning, assist in developing positive social skills, and promoting motivation and engagement in the classroom [6, 8]. This research suggests the value users' associate with smart toys in games like Disney Infinity (2.0 Edition) extends beyond monetary value or justification. While some users may suggest that smart toy based games are more valuable simply because there is a physical object to help justify a less tangible digital purchase, others may see the more personal value these smart toys bring to gameplay. As supported in the qualitative feedback in this research, many users already have some sort of familiarity and preference to play with the Disney characters present in Disney Infinity (2.0 Edition) gameplay, suggesting that perhaps there may be additional intangible value to these characters.

2.1 Defining User Experience

As the name suggests, UX is all about the users' experience with a device or emerging media, focusing on both qualitative and quantitative data from users. Many UX designers and researchers define UX as focusing on both a users' emotional response as well as their perceptions on more practical aspects, such as usability. While UX can be defined in many ways, sometimes very empathetically, for the sake of this research UX is defined based off an industry standard definition for the term: every aspect of the users interaction with the video game that make up the user's perceptions of the whole, in order to allow for the best possible interaction by users [11].

As shown in research on serious educational games, video games can have a major impact on a user's experience. The level of fun and excitement in video games can motivate or even distort perception, and the opportunities for social interaction in video games can inspire feelings of relatedness and belonging [2]. Furthermore, the pervasive nature of many video games, like Disney Infinity (2.0 Edition), can blur the line between the physical reality and the virtual world invoking an even different experience for its users.

In contrast to research on flow and engagement, Brown et al. conducted research in order to define immersion using grounded theory, and concluded that immersion has three stages: engagement, engrossment, and total immersion [1, 4, 12]. Similarly, Ermi et al. broke down immersion into three components: sensory, challenge-based and imaginative immersion [5]. These two definitions of immersion are very similar, with overlapping concepts in several areas as seen with the component of imaginative immersion as well as the engrossment and total immersion stages. This research focused on these overlapping aspects of immersion. Specifically imaginative immersion, in which "players empathize with the characters and/or enjoy the fantasy and virtual reality of the game" as well as the engrossment and total immersion stages, in which players' "perceptions of their physical surroundings and physical needs become lower and their emotions are directly attached to the game" as well as the players' sense of attachment towards in-game characters and empathy towards those characters' situations [2].

This research focused on play preference as it relates to use of smart toys during gameplay. Play preference was measured utilizing responses collected during a post-survey. This research focused specifically on play preferences during gameplay and allowed users to interpret the questions based on their own definition of smart toy based video game play.

3 Experiment

3.1 Objective and Goals

The objective of the research this was to determine if the unique form of gameplay involved in Disney Infinity (2.0 Edition), specifically the addition of smart toys, had an effect on UX. This research analyzed the effect of Disney Infinity (2.0 Edition) on immersion while playing in "Toy Box" mode, as well as play preference during Disney Infinity (2.0 Edition) gameplay. This research had the following research goals in mind: determine if the smart toys included with Disney Infinity (2.0 Edition) have any effect on immersion, and determine if users prefer playing Disney Infinity (2.0 Edition) with the smart toys.

3.2 Hypotheses

This research purposes the following hypotheses: (H1) immersion will be higher in the Disney character group compared to Control group, (H2) there will be no significant difference between either group for preference playing with smart toys, (H3) there will be a small or larger correlation between number of game element used and immersion– the higher the number of game elements used, the higher the immersion ($r = 0.2$ or greater), (H4) there will be a small or larger correlation between average amount of gameplay experience and immersion– the higher the gameplay experience, the higher the immersion ($r = 0.2$ or greater), and (H5) there will be a small or larger correlation between number of smart toys used and immersion– the higher the number of smart toys used, the higher the immersion ($r = 0.2$ or greater).

3.3 Methodology

The research design targeted young adults aged 18–25. A total of 53 users were recruited for this research, 5 of which were excluded from data analysis due to technical complications during testing.

The research design evaluated gameplay in Disney Infinity (2.0 Edition) "Toy Box" mode both with and without the associated smart toys. Users were divided into two groups: Disney character group, and Control group. Alternating conditions for each user randomized distribution into groups. The Disney character group was assigned gameplay using Disney Infinity (2.0 Edition) including the smart toys. The Control group was assigned gameplay using Disney Infinity (2.0 Edition), but lacking the physical presence of smart toys and was provided with a selection sheet, which depicted visual representations of the physical smart toys. Users in the Control group could select a character for gameplay by pointing to the character on the selection sheet, or by saying so verbally. The research proctor would then place the appropriate Disney character on the Disney base.

Both groups were provided access to the same selection of smart toys, including eight Disney characters and eight Power Discs. Disney characters were selected based on four types: (1) villains, (2) heroes, (3) minorities, and (4) non-human characters of both male and female genders (where applicable). An additional Disney character, Sorcerer's Apprentice Mickey, was used during the tutorial portion of the research session and was not available for selection during the gameplay portion of the research session.

Users were allowed 30 min of uninterrupted play with the game in "Toy Box" mode, allowing users the freedom to interact with the game as they preferred utilizing sandbox style or adventure style game features.

A 5-point Likert scale and free response questions were used to measure survey responses ranging from 1 (Strongly Disagree) to 5 (Strongly Agree). A positive (i.e., yes) response was indicated by a Likert scale score of four or five. A negative (i.e., no) response was indicated by a Likert scale score of one or two. A neutral response was indicated by a Likert scale score of three. Survey responses were collected using Google Forms and analyzed using SPSS.

A single PS3 gaming console was used including a wireless controller, Samsung 32" High Definition (HD) TV, the commercial video game Disney Infinity (2.0 Edition) as well as the associated smart toys Additionally, a Hauppauge 1212 HD PVR was used to record gameplay during each session. A laptop computer was used to run video capture software included with the HD PVR.

3.4   Independent Variables

The independent variables utilized in this research study include: (1) immersion and (2) play preference.

In order to measure immersion, a post survey was offered based off similar research on serious educational games, shown in Table 1 [2]. The Game Immersion Questionnaire (GIQ) was modified for this research. The immersion section contained 24 items consisting of three dimensions: engagement (A), engrossment (B) and total immersion (C). The subcategories were included and compiled as a single immersion score. An additive score was utilized for data analysis with a minimum score of 24 and a maximum score of 120, based on a similar questionnaire [13].

Additional subcategories were included for play preference (P) and average amount of gameplay experience (E). These sections included Likert scale and free response questions. Responses for smart toy use (S) were analyzed manually and coded based on frequency of response categories. User responses that fell into multiple categories were counted once for all applicable categories.

Table 1. Modified Game Immersion Questionnaire item and descriptions

A1	I would like to spend time playing the game.
A2	I like the appearance and style of the game.
A3	I like to play the game because it is novel and interesting.
A4	Generally, I can handle the game as the degree of its difficulty is appropriate.
A5	It is easy for me to control the game.
A6	The user interface of the game makes me feel comfortable.
A7	I like the type of the game.
A8	I would like to spend time collecting the information of the game and discussing it with friends.
A9	The time I spend playing the game is more than I expected.
B1	My ability to perceive the environment surrounding me is decreased while playing the game.
B2	I would be impatient when someone interrupted me to play the game.
B3	I feel nervous or excited because of the game.
B4	I forget the passage of time while playing the game.
B5	I feel I could easily forget my schedule and/or to-do things in the real world while playing the game.
B6	While playing the game, I would feel unhappy if someone interrupted me.
C1	When I am playing the game, I feel as if I have experienced the context of the game in person, just like I am who the Disney Character is in the game.
C2	My consciousness completely transfers from the real world to the game world while playing the game.
C3	I lose perceptions of time and the real world surrounding me, as if everything just stops.
C4	I feel happy or sad according to what the Disney Character experiences, and sometimes I even feel as if I am who the Disney Character in the game is occasionally.
C5	I feel so integrated into the Disney Character in the game that I could feel his/her feelings.
C6	All of my senses, including vision, learning, and my mind, are concentrated on and engaged in the game.
C7	I lose the ability of perceiving the surroundings around me; however, it seems natural for me to be totally immersed in the atmosphere of the game.
C8	I used to feel that the Disney Character in the game is controlled by my will, and not by the controller, so that the avatar does just what I want to do.
C9	It seems like the thoughts and consciousness of the Disney Character and me are connected.
P1	I prefer playing the Disney Infinity video game with the Disney Characters (i.e. Smart Toys) physically present.
P2	I would interact the Disney Characters even when I'm not playing the Disney Infinity video game.
P3	I care about or am interested in the Disney Characters I played with during this research session.
P4	I am very knowledgeable about the Disney Infinity characters I played with prior to this research session.
S1(a-b)	(a) Which Disney Character/s did you play with? If you played with more than one, please list them all. (b) Why?
S2(a-b)	(a) Which power disc/s did you play/interact with? If you played with more than one, please list them all. (b) Why?
S3(a-b)	(a) Of the Disney Characters available, which character did you like the most? (b) Why?

E1	Place rate your experience with video games.
E2	Have you played the video game Disney Infinity prior to this research session?
E3	Please rate your experience with the video game Disney Infinity.
E4	Please rate your experience with the video game Disney Infinity and/or video games similar to it.
D1	What is your gender?
D2	How old are you?
D3	Is English your first language?
D4	What is your ethnicity?

3.5   Dependent Variables

The dependent variables utilized in this research study include: (1) game element used, (2) average amount of gameplay experience, and (3) number of smart toys used.

Game element used was defined as the number of digital game elements used while accessing the "Toy Box". A game element was defined as any object the user placed into active gameplay through use of the "Toy Box", or any object that was customized by the user during active gameplay through use of the "Magic Wand".

The "Video Game Experience" subcategory asked about the users' average amount of gameplay experience including general video game experience as well as experience with Disney Infinity and games similar to it.

The number of smart toys used included all Disney characters and Power Discs outlined previously. The "Smart Toys" subcategory asked users' to list the number of smart toys used while playing Disney Infinity (2.0 Edition). Number of smart toys used was measured manually and was utilized for quantitative data analysis. Use of a smart toy was defined as any Disney character or Power Disc and was counted when a user placed the smart toy on the Disney base for gameplay and the smart toy appeared virtually during the gameplay session.

3.6   Results

An independent samples t-test was used to analyze the results for both hypothesis one (H1) and hypothesis two (H2). A Pearson's r correlation was used to analyze the results for hypothesis three (H3), hypothesis four (H4) and hypothesis five (H5). A total of 53 users participated in the research study. Five users (n = 5) were excluded from data analysis due to technical issues during testing. Reasons for exclusion were outlined in Sect. 3. A total of 48 users (n = 48) were recruited for data analysis, including 24 males (n = 24) and 24 females (n = 24). Users were divided randomly into two conditions: the Disney character group (n = 24) and the Control group (n = 24). A total of 12 males (n = 12) and 12 females (n = 12) participated in the Disney character group. A total of 12 males (n = 12) and 12 females (n = 12) participated in the Control group. The Disney character group participated in 30 min of gameplay with smart toys, and the Control group participated in 30 min of gameplay without the associated smart toys.

Table 2 provides descriptive statistics for both independent and dependent variables, where applicable.

Table 2. Descriptive statistics for independent and dependent variables

Variable	Min.	Max.	Positive Response	Negative Response	Neutral Response	Mean	Std. Deviation
Immersion	39	110	-	-	-	76.83	14.406
Play preference	1	5	28	10	10	3.50	1.20
Average game experience	-	-	35	5	8	-	0.857
Number of smart toys used	1	15	-	-	-	5.6	4.088
Game element used	0	54	-	-	-	9.00	12.237

For hypothesis one (H1), an independent samples t-test revealed there was no significant difference between immersion scores for either group ($M1 = 75.88$, $SD1 = 13.671$; $M0 = 77.79$, $SD0 = 15.340$; $t = -0.457$, $p = 0.650$, $df = 46$). Hypothesis one (H1) is not upheld, shown in Tables 3 and 4.

Table 3. Descriptive statistics for hypothesis one

Variable	Condition	N	Mean	Std. Deviation
Immersion	Disney Character	24	75.88	13.671
	Control	24	77.79	15.34

Table 4. Independent samples t-test for hypothesis one

Variable	df	t	p
Immersion	46	-0.457	0.65

For hypothesis two (H2), the average score for users in both groups revealed there was a neutral to positive preference for playing with smart toys ($M1 = 3.58$, $SD1 = 1.18$; $M0 = 3.42$, $SD0 = 1.25$), shown in Table 5. An independent samples t-test revealed there was no significant differences between play preferences for either group ($t = 0.476$, $p = 0.636$, $df = 46$), shown in Table 6. Hypothesis two (H2) is upheld.

Table 5. Average score for hypothesis two

Variable	Condition	N	Mean	Min.	Max.	Std. Deviation
Play preference	Disney Character	24	3.58	1	5	1.18
	Control	24	3.42	1	5	1.25

Table 6. Independent samples t-test for hypothesis two

Variable	t	df	p
Play preference	0.476	46	0.636

For hypothesis three (H3), a Pearson's r was computed to assess the relationship between game element used and immersion. There was no significant correlation between the two variables ($n = 48$, $M = 9.00$, $SD = 12.237$, $r = -0.077$, $p = 0.601$). Hypothesis three (H3) is not upheld. See Tables 7 and 8.

Table 7. Descriptive statistics for hypothesis three

Variable	N	Mean	Std. Deviation
Game element used	48	9.00	12.237

Table 8. Pearson's r for hypothesis three

Variable	r	p
Game element used	-0.077	0.601

For hypothesis four (H4), a Pearson's r correlation revealed the correlation is not significant ($n = 48$, $M = 1.23$, $SD = 0.857$, $r = 0.143$, $p = 0.333$). While a small or larger correlation was found ($r = 0.143$), the results indicate the correlation was not significant ($p = 0.333$). Hypothesis four (H4) is not upheld, shown in Tables 9 and 10.

Table 9. Descriptive statistics for hypothesis four

Variable	N	Mean	Std. Deviation
Average game experience	48	1.23	0.857

Table 10. Pearson's r for hypothesis four

Variable	N	r	p
Average game experience	48	0.143	0.333

For hypothesis five (H5), the largest number of smart toys used was 15 ($n = 15$) and the smallest number of smart toys used was one ($n = 1$). In the Control group ($M = 2.83$), the largest number of smart toys used was seven ($n = 7$) and the smallest number of smart toys used was one ($n = 1$). In the Disney character group ($M = 8.38$), the largest number of smart toys used was 15 (n = 15) and the smallest number of smart toys used was two (n = 2). Pearson's r correlation analyzing data in both conditions revealed the correlation is not significant (n = 48, M = 5.60, SD = 4.088, r = 0.065, p = 0.659). While a small or larger correlation was found when analyzing data from both conditions (n = 48, r = 0.065), the results indicate the correlation was not significant (p = 0.659). Pearson's r correlation analyzing data in the Control group revealed the correlation is not significant (n = 24, M = 2.83, SD = 1.685, r = 0.180, p = 0.399). Pearson's r correlation analyzing data in the Disney character group revealed the correlation is not significant (n = 24, M = 8.38, SD = 3.910, r = 0.164, p = 0.445). Hypothesis five (H5) is not upheld, shown in Tables 11 and 12.

Table 11. Descriptive statistics for hypothesis five

Variable	Condition	N	Mean	Min.	Max.
Number of smart toys used	Disney character	24	8.38	2	15
	Control	24	2.83	1	7

Table 12. Pearson's r for hypothesis five

Variable	Condition	N	r	p	M	Std. Deviation
Number of smart toys used	Both	48	0.065	0.659	5.60	4.088
	Disney character	24	0.164	0.445	8.38	3.910
	Control	24	0.180	0.399	2.83	1.685

3.7 Discussion

Overall, results from data analysis show hypothesis one (H1), hypothesis three (H3), hypothesis four (H4), and hypothesis five (H5) was not upheld. While both hypothesis four (H4) and hypothesis five (H5) show a small or larger correlation (r = 0.2 or larger), the data analysis indicated the correlation was not significant. Therefore, data is not adequate to conclude that the small or larger correlation was not due to chance. While these hypotheses were not upheld, both qualitative and quantitative data supports hypothesis two (H2), showing preference for playing with smart toys was present in both groups.

In addition to analyzing data quantitatively, various observations were noted during research sessions. This qualitative analysis aids in fully understanding UX, shedding light on various areas of the users' experience such as emotional responses, perceptions, and usability issues.

Qualitative analysis does show users prefer playing the game with the smart toys, and analysis of free response questions could shed light on some reasons why this preference exists. During the gameplay session, some users played with specific smart toys due to personal preferences and associations with the character or associated movie. For example, one user made note, "Tangled is my favorite movie" when using the Rapunzel's Birthday Sky Power Disc. Another user stated, "My best friend is obsessed with Frozen, so I feel very connected with Elsa." Several others made note of liking Disney characters because they remembered them from movies or TV shows growing up. These comments support the quantitative data and help explain, to a certain degree, why these play preferences exist for specific users. For these users, connectedness, relatability, and reminiscence played a role.

3.8   Limitations

Given the complexity of Disney Infinity (2.0 Edition) gameplay and mixed methods research, several limitations arise. UX can be very challenging, often requiring multiple methods of analysis as well as several iterations before yielding a positive user experience. Thus, these limitations should be seen as a stepping-stone to further research, aiding the field of UX and helping to improve gameplay with smart toys.

This research was designed utilizing a predesigned area of Disney Infinity (2.0 Edition) gameplay called "Introduction to the Toy Box". This area of gameplay was designed to be a tutorial space, teaching users how to use the game in "Toy Box" mode. This area also includes intermittent voice prompts, directing the user verbally to speak to certain "Toy Box" hosts or complete specific tasks within the tutorial area. These voice prompts could have influenced or guided user actions. While this selection was made specifically in order to promote autonomy and volition during the gameplay session quantitative analysis was not conducted in this research.

This specific research design also utilized a selection sheet. This sheet provided users with a visual representation of the smart toys available to them during gameplay. Users in the Control group may have been inhibited because they are required to ask the researcher proctor in order to access the smart toys. Additional analysis is needed to determine if these factors and any confounding effects.

3.9   Conclusion

As described, this research sought to determine if the unique gameplay environment formulated with Disney Infinity (2.0 Edition) increased immersion by studying the affect of associated smart toys. However, the research design could be expanded upon for future research possibilities. Research could be conducted to study gameplay and learning or social disorders, such as children with autism, or gameplay could be controlled or modified to teach scientific concepts. Additionally, given the vast array of platforms available for gameplay, there are a number of research possibilities comparing game-play UX between platform types and/or input styles.

Games like Disney Infinity, already offer the medium and the tether needed to write new immersive stories. While physical location may be the primary tether connecting the virtual world to physical experience, smart toy based games like Disney Infinity (2.0 Edition) may take that argument a step further. While some may argue that these new expansive virtual worlds will destroy distance by destroying closeness, this research argues that these new video games can help to further develop this connection between a seemingly impersonal and geographically independent virtual worlds and the physical experience by utilizing smart toys.

References

1. Brown, E., Cairns, P.: A grounded investigation of game immersion. In: Paper presented at the Computer-Human Interaction Extended Abstracts on Human Factors in Computing Systems (2004)
2. Cheng, M., She, H., Annetta, L.: Game immersion experience: Its hierarchical structure and impact on game-based science learning. J. Comput. Assist. Learn. 31, 232–253 (2014). doi:10.1111/jcal.12066. Advance online publication
3. Coulton, P.: Skylanders: Near field in your living room now. Ubiquity J. Pervasive Media 1(1), 136–138 (2012)
4. Csikszentmihalyi, M.: Flow: The psychology of optimal experience, 41. HarperPerennial, New York (1991)
5. Ermi, L., Mäyrä, F.: Fundamental components of the gameplay experience: Anaysing immersion. Worlds Play Worlds Play Int. Perspect. Digit. Games Res. 37, 37–53 (2005)
6. Garrido, P.C., Miraz, G.M., Ruiz, I.L., Gómez-Nieto, M.Á.: Use of NFC-based pervasive games for encouraging learning and student motivation. Paper Presented at the 3rd International Workshop on Near Field Communication (NFC) (2011)
7. Jennett, C., Cox, A., Cairns, P., Dhoparee, S., Epps, A., Tijs, T., Walton, A.: Measuring and defining the experience of immersion in games. Int. J. Hum Comput Stud. 66(9), 641–661 (2008)
8. Lampe, M., Hinske, S., Brockmann, S.: Mobile device based interaction patterns in augmented toy environments. Paper presented at the Pervasive 2006 Workshop Proceedings Third International Workshop on Pervasive Gaming Applications, PerGames 2006, Dublin, Ireland (2006)
9. Magerkurth, C., Cheok, A.D., Mandryk, R.L., Nilsen, T.: Pervasive games: Bringing computer entertainment back to the real world. Comput. Entertainment (CIE) 3(3), 4 (2005)
10. McGonigal, J.: A real little game: The performance of belief in pervasive play. In: Proceedings of DiGRA (2003)
11. User Experience Professionals' Association. Usability Body of Knowledge Glossary (2012). http://www.usabilitybok.org/glossary
12. Wiebe, E.N., Lamb, A., Hardy, M., Sharek, D.: Measuring engagement in video game-based environments: Investigation of the User Engagement Scale. Comput. Hum. Behav. 32, 123–132 (2014). doi:10.1016/j.chb.2013.12.001
13. Witmer, B.G., Singer, M.J.: Measuring presence in virtual environments: a presence questionnaire. Presence Teleoperators Virtual Environ. 7(3), 225–240 (1998)

Using Qualitative Data Analysis to Measure User Experience in a Serious Game for Premed Students

Marjorie A. Zielke[✉], Djakhangir Zakhidov, Daniel Jacob, and Sean Lenox

The University of Texas at Dallas, Richardson, USA
margez@utdallas.edu

Abstract. The University of Texas Transformation in Medical Education Portal (UT TIME Portal) is a game-based learning platform for select premed students, with a particular emphasis on communication and professionalism. In addition to quantitative data on system usage and user performance, the UT TIME Portal generates rich sets of qualitative data collected through discussion board posts and pre- and post- surveys. Using NVivo 10's built-in tools, our team used this qualitative data to measure game experience outcomes in many ways by building and testing out hypotheses about our user experience design. The ability to tag, code and organize themes to then be analyzed in the context of quantitative data generated by the UT TIME Portal adds an important dimension to understanding the user experience and generates insights not possible to glean from quantitative data alone.

Keywords: Qualitative analysis · Discussion boards · Nvivo · Serious game · Medical education · Online learning portal · Education and training · Asynchronous access · Asynchronous practice · Adaptive learning · Emergent learning systems · Intelligent agents

1 Introduction to the TIME Program

With 17.6 million Americans insured under the Patient Protection and Affordable Care Act as of September 2015 [1], it has been noted that there will be a shortage of primary-care doctors available in the foreseeable future [2]. To address these concerns, education curricula are focusing efforts to accelerate clinician programs [3]. In conjunction with the acceleration, curricula are providing a larger focus on patient-centered care by emphasizing patient safety and evidence-based practices [4, 5].

In collaboration with the University of Texas Southwestern Medical School (UT Southwestern), the University of Texas at Dallas (UT Dallas) joined the Transformation in Medical Education (TIME) initiative. The goal of this initiative is to increase the amount of clinical caregivers through the dual admission into the undergraduate BA in biology and MD training program. Through this initiative, students accepted into the program will have exposure not only to the traditional premed classes typically offered, but they will also engage in material that is designed to enhance their medical professionalism so that the students are better prepared in administering clinical care [6].

© Springer International Publishing Switzerland 2016
S. Lackey and R. Shumaker (Eds.): VAMR 2016, LNCS 9740, pp. 92–103, 2016.
DOI: 10.1007/978-3-319-39907-2_9

2 What Is the UT TIME Portal?

The University of Texas Transformation in Medical Education Portal (UT TIME Portal) was developed to complement the clinician programs at UT Southwestern. The UT TIME Portal is asynchronously accessible via a web dashboard and consists of: a pre-survey to gather demographics and obtain general knowledge/attitude levels, an intro-ductory episode on platform usage, two instructional gameplay episodes, a discussion board, and a post-survey to gain feedback and measure knowledge/attitude change. The UT TIME Portal gives premed students the opportunity to interact with a virtual patient in the scenario of a medical interview, as well as engage in a scenario regarding a medical professional's interaction with social media. As a complement to the learning modules of the UT TIME curriculum, the UT TIME Portal was tasked with offering the premed students the opportunity to practice interpersonal skills with asynchronous access.

The first gameplay episode that is experienced is the "Medical Interview Episode." In the Medical Interview Episode, students assume the role of a practicing clinician who is responsible for interviewing a patient named Walter and his wife Susan. Walter self-reports the symptom of a painful headache while his wife, Susan, interjects subjective statements. The premed student's responsibility is to conduct the medical interview using rapport, empathy, and active listening. Using these techniques will enable the premed student to: extract the relevant information from Walter, professionally respond to Susan's interjections, and, ultimately, diagnose Walter's ailment.

The second gameplay episode, the "Social Site Episode," covers behavior in commu-nications on a simulated social media site and illustrates potential harmful consequences to patient privacy. In the scenario, the premed student is presented with the opportunity to post vaguely about an interaction with a patient on an interactive social media site. The premed student then experiences a simulation of peers' comments and conversations regarding their social media post. The conversation leads to the premed student divulging sensitive medical information for a patient, only to see the situation unfold into a serious HIPAA violation. The episode is designed to be unwinnable in order to demonstrate the dangers of posting to social media sites about patient care and how closely one's professional life is tied to unprofessional social media conduct.

The UT TIME Portal offers a large variety of engagement measures, both quantita-tive: player and team score, badges, stars, and usage metrics; and qualitative: open-ended survey questions and a moderated discussion board to motivate and support learning objectives.

The impact of education-oriented serious games depend not only on the content they are designed to teach, but also the proficiency of the teacher and the context in which they are presented in the curriculum [7, 8]. In order for serious games to appropriately deliver their intended subject matter, the students need to be actively engaged in the software [9] in order to facilitate learning. By presenting students with the chance to actively engage in the material, effects such as self-reference enable stronger encoding processes [10]. By leveraging students' motivation to learn the material and their role of active participation with the learning platform, one can facilitate deeper learning [11]. The learning portal is intended to engage active participation from the premed students, where users cannot simply click through dialogue trees; users must attend to the contextual scenario and respond appropriately in the given episode.

The UT TIME Portal is integrated within a summer curriculum where the students engage in a variety of learning modules, including the opportunity to conduct a standardized patient interview. With the placement of the UT TIME Portal in this curriculum, student engagement with the material and depth of learning practical clinical skills could be enhanced.

3   The Changing Nature of Media and Data Analysis

The development of new technology brings new forms of data [12]. As an example of new technology, since 2006, the platform of smartphones has been adopted by consumers, manufacturers, and developers, becoming a normal part of everyday use and an integral part in data collection [13]. Further, social networks– such as Facebook, Twitter, and LinkedIn – track user interactions, interests, and the creation of content to the degree where an individual's online identity mirrors their real world identity to a striking degree [14].

Large searchable databases have enabled researchers to easily query to stored results and pull from datasets [15] that have unprecedented size and growth; Twitter stores upwards of 340 million tweets per day [15]. While the size of these datasets is immense, the syntactic nature of the stored data is difficult to analyze using traditional methodologies, as they were designed for much smaller sample sizes and number of variables. Novel analyses are still under development and review that are better capable of handling the size and complexity of these emerging datasets [15]. Our research here contributes to exploring new relationships between data gathered through the traditional i.e., survey, and emerging data collection methods, i.e., gameplay and qualitative metrics, collected through the UT TIME Portal.

4   Benefits of Quantitative Data

In spite of the changing nature of data and data analysis, quantitative data still serves as an important foundation for data collection in the UT TIME Portal. Quantitative research has been the standard for the collection of empirical data and "it is also known as the scientific research paradigm," [16]. User metrics enable researchers to analyze the sample that has been collected through descriptive and inferential measures [17]. The design of the UT TIME Portal enabled the opportunity to collect large amounts of quantitative data. The implementation of the portal enabled quantitative data to be captured using objective instructions and stored in a structured database, which is paired to a corresponding user. Through purposeful design, researchers can capture every meaningful interaction that a given user has within the portal. These measures can give the researcher insight into user behavior which can address questions with precision and accuracy.

In the case of the UT TIME Portal, numerous usage metrics were quantified and captured. Details such as number of repeated sessions played, length and scores of the session, and badges received from each user session were informative as to how the UT TIME Portal affected self-reported knowledge gains on the post-TIME survey. Users' discussion board posts were also categorically labeled with stars by the instructor of the course; the stars were awarded to students' posts that were considered insightful in relation to the question posed by the instructor.

5   Unique Applications of Qualitative Data

The UT TIME Portal was also designed to capture users' qualitative data. Qualitative research is carried out with the same goals as quantitative design – to yield data that is systematic, reproducible, and cumulative [18]. Many methods exist for qualitative data analysis, such as: constant comparison analysis, classical content analysis, keyword-in-context, word count, domain analysis, taxonomic analysis, and componential analysis [19]. Qualitative research seeks a better understanding of the context of a given dataset that a quantitative exploration may not capture. Qualitative data analysis software tools also ensure accuracy of the performed analyses by minimizing analyst errors [20].

While quantitative metrics are largely informative of a group of participants' performance with the UT TIME Portal, quantitative data has difficulty capturing the experiences the user has through their interaction. Anecdotally, researchers at the Rotterdam Eye Hospital carried out a qualitative study on software designed to educate and support children suffering from an eye disorder; the researchers found that the qualitative study better captured the users' interactions with the portal compared to what their quantitative data would have been able to yield [21]. Interviews revealed that children with the disorder were largely unaffected by it and felt little need to use the software, whereas quantitative data alone would only indicate low usage, which could have been attributed to a knowledge or technological barrier as opposed to a fundamental disinterest in the software.

In a similar manner, the impact of the UT TIME Portal on a user would have less depth if the portal was designed to exclusively capture quantitative usage metrics. In order to address this limitation, the researchers at UT Dallas also collected the participants' qualitative data provided by their discussion board posts and responses to open-ended survey questions. These data offer opportunities in a variety of different areas that are of benefit to researchers. Each user's qualitative data would help measure their engagement with the content, as the response the students' provide will offer their level of awareness of the scenarios presented to them. Posts can also be used as a measure of how the students learned – i.e. were the students thinking critically about the material presented. As shown in Fig. 1, immediate emotional responses could also be recorded, as the students were asked for their reactions after experiencing the episodes. Finally, the posts were reviewed by a professor who was given the opportunity to award stars to posts that were deemed insightful; using this information, it was possible to evaluate the quality of posts the students were making.

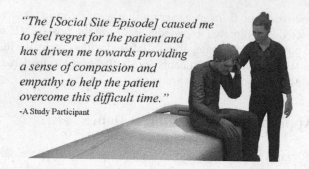

"*The [Social Site Episode] caused me to feel regret for the patient and has driven me towards providing a sense of compassion and empathy to help the patient overcome this difficult time.*"
-A Study Participant

Fig. 1. The UT TIME Portal captured student emotional response to help analyze their engagement and experience. Students demonstrated empathy towards the virtual characters and evoked strong emotions, indicating that they were actively engaged with the UT TIME Portal.

6   Mixed Methods

Through the utilization of both quantitative and qualitative techniques, one can address the limitations of each methodology. In the UT TIME Portal, there were a total of 2572 lines of text from 423 discussion board posts, and two self-reported surveys completed by 74 premed students. Due to the text-based and syntactic nature of qualitative data, the sheer amount of possible records would be difficult to analyze. With qualitative data analysis software, it was possible to quickly organize and categorize this data in an efficient and thorough manner.

While a single user's self-report of their experience is quantifiable, when a learning platform is intended to be experienced by larger samples or populations, more deliberate methodologies can be implemented in order to account for user behavior. To this end, the qualitative data received from the UT Time Portal was analyzed using the software suite NVivo 10. A review of 763 empirical articles has found that the number of studies reporting use of qualitative data analysis software is increasing each year, is published primarily in health sciences journals, and is most commonly used for data management and analysis [22].

The ability to meaningfully quantify emotional qualitative data is in its early stages, as researchers provide methods to capture and semantically assess qualitative entries [23]. Using prototypes for emotional categorization – a hierarchy of basic-level and subordinate-level emotions outlined by Shaver [24] – researchers have been able to develop automatic emotional identification algorithms in media analysis by implementing a combination of large training datasets and machine learning algorithms [15].

In spite of these developments, qualitative methodologies have largely been ignored by researchers as a method for analyzing serious games. A literature review of 129 papers reporting empirical evidence of serious games showed that only 8 of those papers reported qualitative data [25]. This could be attributed to a multitude of factors, such as the daunting datasets, lack of proven software and analytical methodologies, or a disregard of qualitative data as a whole.

7   Methodology

The data gathered from the 74 premed students using the UT TIME Portal was captured over the course of two annual sessions: in 2014, 54 students were enrolled, and 20 students were enrolled in 2015 [26].

NVivo 10 is a qualitative data analysis software package released in 2012. NVivo's tools are designed to help users organize and evaluate large amounts of quantitative and qualitative data. NVivo's "node" functionality allows users to collect and categorize important pieces of data into nodes that may easily be compared to datasets or each other. Through the use of nodes in conjunction with review and visualization tools, users may use NVivo to test hypotheses or correlations in large datasets, regardless of their type of data [19]. With this functionality, it is possible to evaluate this dataset in its entirety with its context intact, leading to a greater understanding of the process and experience of the participants, as a whole.

The UT TIME Portal – with its discussion board and post-surveys – generated numerous reports of qualitative data. NVivo's "node" functionality was used to collect data pertaining to certain emotions and reactions. Nodes – such as, "Strong emotional response," "Frustrated," "Attitude change," and "Attachment to Virtual Characters" – were created to test hypotheses and assess the effect the learning portal had on the premed students. These nodes made it possible to keep track of important pieces of data and generated new insights through comparisons to quantitative data.

When creating these nodes, NVivo's word search functionality was used to quickly sift through discussion board posts to find particular themes and emotions. The broadness of a word search may be adjusted to include synonyms and/or related words, speeding up the process and highlighting instances of a word that may otherwise have been missed. These word searches helped to determine if the episodes were having the desired effect, as well as test hypotheses in regards to participants of different demographics reporting certain feelings or thoughts.

After importing and organizing the data and using word searches to fill in nodes, analyses could then be drawn by comparing qualitative nodes to quantitative data. By assigning gender and age attributes to the data, potential correlations between nodes and these attributes could also be tested. NVivo's tools were used to quickly organize and sort data, validate hypotheses, observe data correlations, and gain new insights in an efficient and thorough manner.

8   Results

NVivo was used to search for commonly occurring themes in the data and create 11 nodes, grouping responses in ways that evoked engagement, displayed affection or attachment to virtual characters, and provided other insights into user experience. For example, a node titled "Attachment to Virtual Characters" was created to analyze if and how participants reacted to virtual characters. Searching for keywords such as "feel" when used in conjunction with the names of the virtual characters revealed that many users explicitly expressed attachment by empathizing with the characters, feeling bad for them, and often referring to them as if they were real.

The students shed much light on useful design considerations and improvements for keeping both the patient and the caregiver engaged during the Medical Interview Episode. As stated earlier, in this episode the student conducts a medical interview with Walter, and his wife, Susan. The student must keep the interview focused on Walter and his symptoms in spite of Susan's interjections. Some students suggested non-verbal techniques like using body language and eye contact as means to switch attention back to the patient from the overly helpful caregiver.

Even though the caregiver Susan was modeled as a distractor in the medical interview, students still emphasized her importance and helpfulness in their discussion board posts, as well as concern for her feelings and making her feel included in the interview. For example, one student remarked that, "It is important to acknowledge the caregiver and use their input to ask appropriate questions so that the patient history is more complete." Students also stressed being "respectful" to the caregiver and avoiding being "rude."

These discussion board posts were also informed by the quantitative pre- and post-survey data. Both surveys asked the students to rate their agreement with the following statement: "I consider a caregiver a significant source of information during a medical interview." In 2015, five out of 20 students reported negative movement in this area, meaning their ratings went down from pre- to post-survey (they rated "Strongly Agree" on the pre-survey, and went down to simply "Agree" on the post-survey). Even these students – whose opinions of a caregiver's importance seemed to be affected by the Medical Interview Episode – qualitatively agreed that the caregiver was still an important source of information and that both her helpfulness and her feelings should be taken into account. One of these students wrote, "I would definitely take Susan's observations of the chief complaint into account, as she brings an entirely different perspective of the chief complaint and can give information about the chief complaint that Walter either is not comfortable sharing or is not aware of."

The Social Site Episode, as previously mentioned, simulates a social media site and demonstrates how sharing medical information online can lead to breaches of patient privacy. In this episode, Walter's daughter, Wendy, learns that her father had a stroke when people start posting about it on social media. When analyzing the data for the Social Site Episode, NVivo's built-in chart functionality was used to compare the "Attachment to Virtual Characters" node to quantitative demographic user attributes, such as gender and technological inclination, to discover that a user's technical inclination or gender did not influence the level of engagement. Most responders, regardless of their technical inclination, preferences, or gender were concerned for Susan's feelings, frustrated at the Social Site Episode, and wary of posting important things online for others to see. Notably, the least technological savvy respondent showed clear empathy while describing feelings for "poor Wendy" and her situation with Walter.

The majority of students had strong negative emotional reactions to the Social Site Episode dealing with professional online behavior, using words like "frustrated," "hopeless," and "despair" in their discussion board posts. These strong emotional responses also led many students to discuss professional behavior in general and the importance of keeping information private in any situation [26]. Some students took this as an opportunity to research and better understand laws regarding de-identification of patient information. Many students felt appalled by how quickly sensitive information can be compromised and disseminated, and agreed that it is best to not share any information if possible.

All students sympathized with the patient and some felt a need to show empathy: "this result caused me to feel regret for the patient and has driven me towards providing a sense of compassion and empathy to help the patient overcome this difficult time." Another node, titled "Strong Emotional Responses," consisted of references such as: "helpless," "overwhelmed," "very sad," "out of control," "frustrated," "distressed," "extremely irritated," "angry," "upset," "shocked," "uncomfortable," "annoyed," "frightened," and displayed that most students (74 % from 2014; 90 % from 2015) had strong negative emotional responses to the Social Site Episode.

A substantial number of all discussion board posts were awarded stars by the instructor: 43 % of posts from 2014 received stars (133 out of 306), as did 51 % of posts from 2015 (59 out of 115). This categorical data provided by the instructor shows that a large portion of discussion board posts evoked engagement through their quality and insight.

Quantitatively, students were asked the question "Do you believe that a medical student should be held accountable for unprofessional behavior discovered through postings on his/her personal social networking page(s)?" and prompted to answer "yes," "no," or "not sure" on pre- and post-surveys. This question was posed in both the 2014 and 2015 UT TIME Portal sessions and yielded contrasting results. In 2014, there was a positive movement between the pre- and post-surveys: 74.55 % of students answered

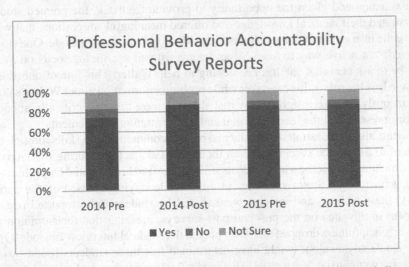

Fig. 2. In 2014, Students reported positive movement on the question, "Do you believe that a medical student should be held accountable for unprofessional behavior discovered through postings on his/her personal social networking page(s)?" In 2015, however, students reported no movement between pre- and post-surveys. However, analyzing qualitative data gives us additional insight into student learning gains.

"yes" on the pre-survey, and 86.96 % of students answered "yes" on the post-survey, indicating a trend toward "yes." However, in 2015, students reported no movement at all on this question, with 85 % of students reporting "yes" on both surveys, as shown in Fig. 2 [26]. As stated earlier, students received other learning modules outside of the UT TIME Portal within this timeframe as part of their educational experience.

9   Discussion

The qualitative data collected provided insight into the effect the episodes had on the 74 premed students in our study. Through analysis of quantitative and qualitative data generated by the UT TIME Portal, a deeper understanding of the students' experience could be gleaned.

Emotional responses were consistently presented across the premed users, demonstrating an opportunity to capture and understand the interactions and impact of the learning platform in a way that quantitative methods would not allow. If the UT TIME Portal was not designed with a feature-set capable of providing both a suitable learning environment and a meaningful interaction with its users, the emotional responses from the users would not have been captured.

Technological predisposition had no effect on an individual's ability to be engaged with the virtual characters and the scenarios presented to them. In the case of these premed students, having the opportunity to access meaningful content provided them additional hands-on experience.

The Medical Interview Episode was one learning module available to help students gain insight on how to provide meaningful clinical care for patients. When presented such a situation and given the opportunity to provide feedback, the premed students demonstrated their medical knowledge and offered meaningful suggestions that would improve the interaction with the patients in the Medical Interview Episode. One student suggested: "an active way to keep Susan happy without sacrificing focus on Walter would be to ask her what she has been doing to help Walter. This line of questioning acknowledges her role as his caretaker while probing information about Walter's health simultaneously." These insights show that students were thinking critically about the situations presented in the learning portal and demonstrating engagement.

Students also demonstrated empathy and patient communication skills through their responses to Susan, the caregiver. Even though Susan's actions during the interview were distracting and overbearing, students still emphasized her potential helpfulness and offered ways to keep Susan's feelings in mind while staying focused on the patient. Notably, these feelings and insights were shared by students who reported negative movement in this area on the pre- and post-surveys, meaning that their opinion of a caregiver's helpfulness dropped after they played the Medical Interview Episode. Quantitative data analysis alone might have determined that these students found Susan's overbearing nature to be detrimental to the medical interview, but qualitative data shows that their discussion board posts still emphasize Susan's helpfulness and the importance of treating her respectfully, in spite of their negative movement between the pre- and post-surveys. This combination of qualitative and quantitative data generated new and important insight about the students' experience and opinions.

The Medical Interview episode presented students with a difficult, nuanced situation. In such an interview, the clinician must extract relevant information from the patient and the caregiver while keeping the interview focused and efficient. The clinician must stay focused on the patient while keeping the caregiver's feelings in mind and making them feel included. They must also think critically about the information they receive and quickly determine its relevance and implications. While the quantitative results show that students performed well and understood the concepts, the qualitative data is especially informative in that it gives insight into the students' depth of understanding. Discussion board posts detailing strategies for the interview or additional questions to ask demonstrate deep learning and a thorough understanding of the nuances present in the interview. In this sense, the qualitative data informs the quantitative data and offers potential explanations of why students performed well or gave certain answers. Students may have performed well because they thoroughly understood the situation and the strategies necessary to work through it.

The Social Site Episode elicited a strong emotional response from the students, emphasizing the importance of electronic professionalism on social networking sites. The Social Site Episode presented students with a plausible scenario that was relevant to their future careers and the hyper-connected world they currently live in. To these students, this scenario unfolding for these virtual characters was emotionally impactful. This emotional response may have been noticeable through pre- and post-survey questions regarding social media and accountability, but through qualitative data collection and analysis the magnitude of these emotions could begin to be understood. Discussion board posts showed that students felt great empathy for the virtual characters and frustration towards the events in the Social Site Episode. Some students even made strong declarations about the potential dangers of social media and the importance of keeping the details of one's medical career off of public forums – no matter how small. Qualitative data collection and analysis showed the true impact of the episode and allowed for assessment of its personal and emotional effects.

Quantitative pre- and post-survey data was informed by qualitative data. As mentioned earlier, when asked the question "Do you believe that a medical student should be held accountable for unprofessional behavior discovered through postings on his/her personal social networking page(s)?" students reported positive movement in 2014 but no movement at all in 2015. When looking at quantitative data alone, this seems to indicate that the Social Site Episode had little impact on the 2015 students. However, qualitative data shows that these students still reported empathy and strong emotional reactions to the episode, and understood the importance of information privacy. In this instance, the qualitative data reveals information about the students' experiences that the quantitative data does not seem to indicate. In contrast to survey responses, the Social Site Episode still had a strong effect on the students, even if they did not report positive movement.

The stars add an interesting layer to the dataset, in the sense that this variable can be evaluated in both a quantitative and qualitative sense. As a quantitative metric, the stars provide a measure as to which students were thinking critically. When evaluated as a qualitative variable, one can quickly see which posts were considered as perceptive.

10 Summary

Through both qualitative and quantitative data analysis, a deeper understanding of student knowledge gains enhanced through learning interventions can potentially be obtained. In our study, qualitative data analysis indicated that students understood nuances of the gameplay episodes and possibly experienced deep learning – observations that could not be drawn through quantitative data analysis alone. New and developing media – such as serious games – provide a mix of qualitative and quantitative data and will likely continue to provide new types of methodologies to more fully understand participant experiences.

Acknowledgement. The research team would like to thank colleagues from the UT Southwestern Medical School and the students from the UT TIME program and UT Dallas for their support of this research.

References

1. Howell, T., Jr.: HHS: Number insured under Obamacare swells to 17.6 million. (2015, September 22). Retrieved January 4, 2016. http://www.washingtontimes.com/news/2015/sep/22/hhs-number-insured-under-obamacare-swells-176-mill/
2. Susan, B.: New Physician Workforce Projections Show the Doctor Shortage Remains Significant. (2015, March 3). Retrieved January 6, 2016. https://www.aamc.org/newsroom/newsreleases/426166/20150303.html
3. Utdallas.edu. UT-PACT BA/MD Program - Health Professions Advising Center (HPAC) - The University of Texas at Dallas (2015). http://www.utdallas.edu/pre-health/ut-pact. Accessed July 28, 2015
4. Cooke, M., Irby, D., Sullivan, W., Ludmerer, K.: American Medical Education 100 Years after the Flexner Report. The New England Journal of Medicine. Boston: Sep 28, 2006. vol. 355, Iss. 13, pp. 1339–44 (6 pp.)
5. Leape, L., Berwick, D., Clancy, C., Conway, J., Gluck, P., Guest, J., et al.: Transforming healthcare: a safety imperative. Qual. Saf. Health Care **18**(6), 424–428 (2009). doi:10.1136/qshc.2009.036954
6. Transformation In Medical Education (TIME): A multi-institutional initiative within the University of Texas system. (n.d.). Retrieved January 6, 2016. http://www.utsystem.edu/initiatives/time/
7. Ke, F.: A qualitative meta-analysis of computer games as learning tools. Handb. Res. Effective Electron. Gaming Educ. **1**, 1–32 (2009)
8. Breuer, J.S., Bente, G.: Why so serious? On the relation of serious games and learning. Eludamos J. Comput. Game Cult. **4**(1), 7–24 (2010)
9. Sitzmann, T.: A meta-analytic examination of the effectiveness of computer-based simulation games. Pers. Psychol. **64**, 489–528 (2011). doi:10.1111/j.1744-6570.2011.01190.x

10. Rogers, T.B., Kuiper, N.A., Kirker, W.S.: Self-reference and the encoding of personal information. J. Personal. Soc. Psychol. **35**(9), 677–688 (1977). doi: 10.1037/0022-3514.35.9.677
11. Vos, N., Van Der Meijden, H., Denessen, E.: Effects of constructing versus playing an educational game on student motivation and deep learning strategy use. Comput. Educ. **56**(1), 127–137 (2011)
12. Dalbello, M.: A genealogy of digital humanities. J. Documentation **67**(3), 480–506 (2011)
13. Smith, A.: U.S. Smartphone Use in 2015 (2015, April 01). Retrieved February 26, 2016. http://www.pewinternet.org/2015/04/01/us-smartphone-use-in-2015/
14. Aggarwal, C.C.: Social network data analytics. Springer, New York (2011)
15. Gandomi, A., Haider, M.: Beyond the hype: Big data concepts, methods, and analytics. Int. J. Inf. Manag. **35**(2), 137–144 (2015)
16. Ochieng, A.P.: An analysis of the strengths and limitation of qualitative and quantitative research paradigms. In: Problems of Education in the 21stcentury, 13, 13–18 (2009). Retrieved January 20, 2016. http://oaji.net/articles/2014/457-1393665925.pdf
17. Taylor, C.: Descriptive and Inferential Statistics: How Do They Differ? (2014, December 16). Retrieved February 26, 2016. http://statistics.about.com/od/Descriptive-Statistics/a/Differences-In-Descriptive-And-Inferential-Statistics.html
18. Kazdin, A.: Research design in clinical psychology. Allyn and Bacon, Boston (2003)
19. Leech, N.L., Onwuegbuzie, A.J.: Beyond constant comparison qualitative data analysis: Using NVivo. School Psychol. Q. **26**(1), 70 (2011)
20. DeLyser, D., Sui, D.: Crossing the qualitative-quantitative divide II Inventive approaches to big data, mobile methods, and rhythmanalysis. Prog. Hum. Geogr. **37**(2), 293–305 (2013)
21. Van't Riet, A., Berg, M., Hiddema, F., Sol, K.: Meeting patients' needs with patient information systems: potential benefits of qualitative research methods. Int. J. Med. Inf. **64**(1), 1–14 (2001)
22. Woods, M., Paulus, T., Atkins, D.P., Macklin, R.: Advancing qualitative research using qualitative data analysis software (QDAS)? Reviewing potential versus practice in published studies using ATLAS. ti and NVivo, 1994–2013. Social Science Computer Review, 0894439315596311 (2015)
23. Wang, W., Chen, L., Thirunarayan, K., Sheth, A.P.: Harnessing twitter "big data" for automatic emotion identification. In: Privacy, Security, Risk and Trust (PASSAT), 2012 International Conference on and 2012 International Conference on Social Computing (SocialCom) (pp. 587–592). IEEE (2012, September)
24. Shaver, P., Schwartz, J., Kirson, D., O'connor, C.: Emotion knowledge: further exploration of a prototype approach. J. Pers. Soc. Psychol. **52**(6), 1061 (1987)
25. Connolly, T.M., Boyle, E.A., MacArthur, E., Hainey, T., Boyle, J.M.: A systematic literature review of empirical evidence on computer games and serious games. Comput. Educ. **59**(2), 661–686 (2012)
26. Zielke, M.A., Zakhidov, D., Jacob, D., Hardee, G.: Beyond fun and games: toward an adaptive and emergent learning platform for pre-med students with the UT TIME portal. In: IEEE SeGAH 2016 Conference Proceedings Paper presented at IEEE 2016 International Conference on Serious Games and Applications for Health, Orlando, Florida. In press (2016, M)

Perception, Cognition, Psychology and Behaviour in VAMR

A Holistic Evaluation of Task View Format for Training a Simulated Robot-Assisted EOD Task

James P. Bliss[1(✉)], Eric T. Chancey[1], Alexandra B. Proaps[1], and Peter Crane[2]

[1] Old Dominion University, Norfolk, VA, USA
{jbliss,echan004,aproaps}@odu.edu
[2] A2-T2, Inc., Orlando, FL, USA
pcrane@a2-t2.com

Abstract. Recent decreases in psychophysiological recording method cost have enabled researchers to more easily supplement questionnaire and performance based indices of cognitive constructs like workload and situation awareness. The current paper describes the results of an experiment to compare single- and dual-view task interfaces for simulated unmanned vehicle navigation and object manipulation. Testing ten ROTC students in a within-condition experiment, researchers found that task completion time and eye gaze data revealed general learning trends and preferences for the dual-view condition. The results align with prior documentations of dual-view advantages and provide useful estimates of simulator learning speed.

Keywords: Robot · Simulation · View · Training · Control · FRAM

1 Introduction

Researchers have demonstrated that experts cognitively process information differently than novices. Early research by Chase and Simon [1] demonstrated that expert chess players could recall the position of pieces on a board more accurately than novices due to their advanced domain knowledge. With regard to unmanned vehicle control and monitoring, operators have been shown to verbalize aspects of the control task in different ways depending on their level of expertise [2].

The structure and delivery of task training often influences the rapidity and comprehensiveness of mastery. In some cases, unmanned vehicle operators may have complete classroom training with minimal operational practice. Others, however, may receive comparatively little classroom training but considerable practical experience. The variability of practice may be compounded by interfaces used for vehicle control. In particular, the visual displays used to depict task elements may facilitate knowledge building or may inhibit it.

With current interface evaluation methods, experts use the interface and fill in questionnaires many times to identify negative system traits. Unfortunately, novice users often display confusion and frustration, and commit errors when encountering embedded negative system traits. This outcome is especially true in reduced manning level environments where each individual has more and different types of tasks.

© Springer International Publishing Switzerland 2016
S. Lackey and R. Shumaker (Eds.): VAMR 2016, LNCS 9740, pp. 107–115, 2016.
DOI: 10.1007/978-3-319-39907-2_10

The purpose of this research was to use the Fused Realities Assessment Modules (FRAM) system to measure novice operator opinions and performances during a simulated unmanned vehicle operation scenario. By assessing physiological data in a low-cost fashion, FRAM represents a neuroergonomic approach for construct measurement [3]. FRAM scenarios reflect critical knowledge, skill and ability components and may allow comprehensive performance tracking. Specific neuroergonomic data sources are meant to enable real-time assessment and tracking of critical cognitive constructs such as mental workload and situation awareness.

For workload, pupil gaze has been used as a diagnostic indicator of workload in two ways. First, dwell time may be an indication that the individual is extracting information from certain areas. Dwell times differ by level of expertise, where novices dwell longer than experts as a function of workload. Second, in multitask environments fixation points indicate the task that is the greatest source of resource allocation and thus workload [4]. The reliance on eye tracking within FRAM should allow estimation of workload, especially in combination with assessment of task performance and data from a questionnaire such as the NASA-TLX [5].

With regard to situation awareness, there are several methods available to assess a user's environmental element perception (Level 1 SA), comprehension (Level 2 SA) and projection across time (Level 3 SA) [6]. Wickens & Hollands [4] have suggested that the construct of SA is domain specific; this frequently impacts the way in which it is measured. FRAM allows for estimation of workload by considering data from subjective questionnaires such as the Situation Awareness Rating Technique [7] as well as by examining eye tracking behavior and conventional task performance data such as reaction time and task success.

To determine the potential for FRAM to reflect the growth of task expertise in novices, we measured task speed and accuracy, operator workload, and situation awareness as operators interacted with a single-screen and a dual-screen display.

The use of methods and tools to assess and identify cognitive factors that impact human-technology performance must be carefully evaluated. For the current research, the FRAM tool leveraged a variety of neuroergonomic measures to supplement the use of task measures and traditional paper-and-pencil measures to comprehensively reflect human-technology performance. After consulting available published research, our team selected a focused range of the most pertinent cognitive components related to UGV operator performance: mental workload and situation awareness.

One purpose for this research was to demonstrate the utility of the FRAM tool suite for measuring cognitive constructs in real time during complex task performance. Standalone measures of mental workload and situation awareness have faced criticism because of questionable validity and challenges related to data collection [8, 9]. Recently, researchers have devoted effort successfully to triangulate measures for complex constructs such as workload [10]. The data reported here represent an initial attempt to demonstrate the ability of FRAM to accomplish such triangulation.

The second purpose for this investigation was to investigate the ability of FRAM to assess and track the growth of expertise within the context of simulated small UGV performance. This goal was approached with the specific intent of comparing task view format as an independent variable of interest. Prior researchers have demonstrated performance gains and subjective preference for multiple screen views [11]. However, such research has not documented changes in such data across the task learning continuum. For this reason, we made no specific hypotheses regarding superiority of view format.

2 Method

2.1 Experimental Design

To ensure adequate statistical power with a relatively small sample of task experts, the experimenters employed a one-way, repeated-measures design. Screen view format (single-screen or dual-screen view) was manipulated within participants. Dependent measures included several performance based and neuroergonomic data streams within the FRAM suite. First, the experimenters measured task performance speed in seconds. Task accuracy was reflected by the number of charges successfully placed within a designated area. Neuroergonomic measures included eye tracking gaze time for particular screen regions (in seconds), electroencephalograph energy bands, and questionnaire data for cognitive workload (NASA-TLX) and situation awareness (SART). The experimental task required simulated UGV navigation and manipulation of a simulated detonator using an arm. Participants relied on a single-screen view to accomplish this in one session and a dual-screen view in a second session (see Figs. 1, 2 and 3).

Fig. 1. Experimental layout with task and monitoring stations

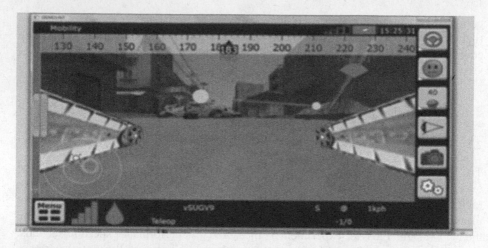

Fig. 2. Task interface – single screen view

Fig. 3. Task interface – dual screen view

2.2 Participants

Ten ROTC students from Old Dominion University participated for class credit (9 male, 1 female). Average age was 20.9 years (20-24). Eight of ten reported no prior experience using robots.

2.3 Materials

Questionnaires included the Informed Consent Form, Demographics Questionnaire, the SART situation awareness questionnaire [7], the NASA-TLX workload questionnaire [5], and a post-scenario questionnaire. The SART and the NASA-TLX have been widely used by researchers for decades and have demonstrated acceptable psychometric properties. Eye tracking was reflected as gaze duration in seconds within pre-defined areas of interest (task screen and birds-eye map). Task performance data included time (in seconds) to pick up a simulated detonator and total time to complete a navigation course with it.

The experimental task scenario was designed to resemble a common occurrence: using an unmanned ground vehicle to approach explosive charges, pick up the charges, and transport them to a safe location. The scenario was designed systematically through task analytic interviews with U.S. Marines and Army experts. That process included determining the behaviors, skills, and abilities necessary for completing the task. The research team also completed a comprehensive error analysis pertinent to the particular visual task interface used. Pilot testing of the scenario was accomplished by testing military expert personnel at Fort Benning, Georgia.

2.4 Procedure

After arriving at the laboratory, participants first completed the Informed Consent form and Demographics Questionnaire. The demographics questionnaire included items to determine participant sex, age, and experience with robotic devices. After completing the questionnaire, participants were randomly assigned to a task session sequence (single screen or dual screen first) and were trained to navigate the UGV within a practice virtual environment. After they indicated that they could effectively move the UGV in all directions, they were trained to use the simulated robotic arm to grasp and hold the simulated charges.

Following task training, participants were asked if they had any questions or needed clarification about the required task. Once participants' questions had been answered, they then completed two task sessions, separated by a five-minute break. Participants were free to take as much time as necessary to complete the task. During the break between sessions, participants completed the SART and the NASA-TLX questionnaires. Following the second session, participants completed an opinion questionnaire to describe the strategies they employed, their estimation of their own performance, and their preferences for each display condition. After completing the opinion questionnaire, participants were debriefed and dismissed.

3   Results

Because of the novel nature of this research, $p < .10$ was used as a significance criterion. For the analyses below, data from the one female participant were excluded because of difficulty acquiring EEG signals.

Few performance and subjective differences were evident between Single and Dual Screen conditions.

Participants did prefer the Dual Screen layout based on written and verbal comments. They perceived the dual screen layout to be less confusing than the single screen layout ($p = .035$). The effort factor of the NASA-TLX approached significance, indicating that participants expended more effort to process task imagery on two screens ($p = .107$). There were no significant differences found between single and dual screen conditions for situation awareness, time on task, time taken to pick up the C4 charge, and eye gaze duration ($p > .05$).

With regard to training, differences in time on task were significant ($p = .06$) and time taken to pick up the C4 charge ($p = .085$) between the first and second sessions, regardless of screen layout (less time required for the second task; see Figs. 4 and 5). It is also important to emphasize that the relative amount of time participants devoted to viewing the primary task view and the birds-eye map varied between the single- and dual-screen formats. Specifically, participants focused longer on the birds-eye map when completing the task in dual-screen format (see Fig. 6).

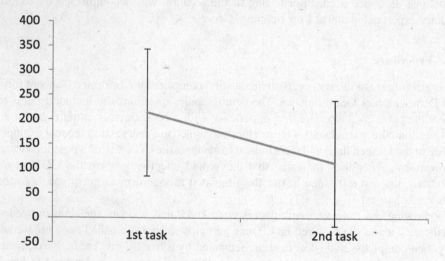

Fig. 4. Total time (in seconds) taken to pick up the C4 charge between first and second task (N= 9). Note: Error bars indicate standard errors.

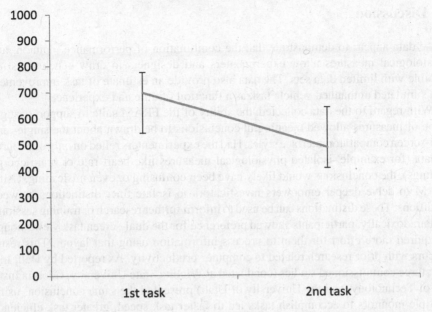

Fig. 5. Total time (in seconds) taken to complete task between first and second tasks (N= 9)

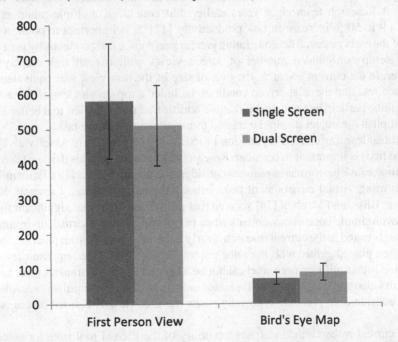

Fig. 6. Means and standard errors for gaze duration on First Person Shooter view and Bird's Eye Map view for Single and Dual screen layouts (N= 9).

4   Discussion

These data appear to demonstrate that the combination of performance, opinion, and physiological measures allow experimenters and designers to draw conclusions not possible with limited data sets. The data also provide an estimate of task improvement on a simulated unmanned vehicle task as a function of time and experience.

With regard to the data collected, the ability of the FRAM suite to support triangulation of measures allowed meaningful conclusions to be drawn about the single- and dual-screen comparator interface styles. Had the experimenters relied on only one source of data (for example, isolated physiological measures like heart rate or brain energy readings), the conclusions would likely have been confusing or even misleading. Using FRAM to delve deeper empowers investigators to isolate finer distinctions between conditions. These distinctions can be used to inform further research or training sessions.

Paradoxically, participants showed preference for the dual-screen task view, though it required more effort for them to process information using that layout. This result concurs with prior research related to computer productivity. As reported by Dell, Inc. [11], three commissioned studies (conducted at Wichita State University, Georgia Institute of Technology, and the University of Utah) presented the same conclusion: using multiple monitors to accomplish tasks led to faster task speed, greater task efficiency and higher user satisfaction. This finding echoes similar research conducted by the Microsoft Research team eight years earlier that concluded multiple monitors may enable a 9 to 50 % increase in task productivity [12]. It is important to point out that much of the early research demonstrating greater preference and productivity for a dual-display setup confounded number of screen views with overall task display size. However, in the current research, the overall size of the task view was equivalent; the difference was that the dual-screen condition included a top-down view of the task. By all accounts, participants concluded that the addition of this view led to a better ability to accomplish the object manipulation and transport aspects of the task.

The clear learning effect from Session 1 to Session 2 (regardless of which view layout occurred first) is important to consider. Researchers have for decades demonstrated that psychomotor task performance requires considerable time to master [13]. Early military research using virtual environment tasks echoed the early findings. Lampton, Knerr, Goldberg, Bliss, and Moshell [14] showed that participants required significant time to master even simple control movements when performing tasks in virtual environments. Participants tested in the current research clearly benefitted greatly from practice, though many often played games with the same control device used. One important lesson to be learned is that military personnel cannot be assumed to simply transfer prior knowledge with video games to unmanned vehicle control and object manipulation. Such skills require considerable practice, especially when the task view is divided among visual displays.

The current research demonstrates the utility of the FRAM tool suite for assessing and understanding complex tasks. Future researchers may benefit from examining further the FRAM method of neuroergonomic measurement to isolate the bounds of its utility.

References

1. Chase, W.G., Simon, H.A.: The mind's eye in chess. In: Chase, W.G. (ed.) Visual Information Processing, pp. 215–281. Academic Press, New York (1973)
2. Andre, T., Hunt, J., Crews, A., Gluck, K.: Effect of fatigue and type of training strategy on UAV simulator performance. In: Proceedings of the Human Factors of UAVs Workshop. Mesa, AZ: Cognitive Engineering Research Institute (2007)
3. Parasuraman, R., Rizzo, M.: Neuroergonomics: The brain at work. Oxford University Press, London, UK (2008)
4. Wickens, C.D., Hollands, J.G.: Engineering Psychology and Human Performance, 3rd edn. Prentice Hall, Upper Saddle River, New Jersy (2000)
5. Hart, S.G., Staveland, L.E.: Development of NASA-TLX (Task Load Index): Results of empirical and theoretical research. In: Hancock, P.A., Meshkati, N. (eds.) Human Mental Workload. North Holland Press, Amsterdam (1988)
6. Endsley, M.: Toward a theory of situation awareness in dynamic systems. Hum. Factors **37**(1), 32–64 (1995)
7. Taylor, R.M.: Situational awareness rating technique (SART): The development of a tool for aircrew systems design. In: Proceedings of the AGARD AMP Symposium on Situational Awareness in Aerospace Operations, CP478. Seuilly-sur Seine: NATO AGARD (1989)
8. Miller, S.: Literature review: Workload measures. (Final Report No. N01-006). Iowa City, IA: National Advanced Driving Simulator (2001)
9. Salmon, P., Stanton, N., Walker, G., Green, D.: Situation awareness measurement: A review of applicability for C4i environments. J. Appl. Ergon. **37**(2), 225–238 (2006)
10. Rusnock, C., Borghetti, B., McQuaid, I.: Objective-analytical measures of workload – the third pillar of workload triangulation? In: Schmorrow, D.D., Fidopiastis, C.M. (eds.) AC 2015. LNCS, vol. 9183, pp. 124–135. Springer, Heidelberg (2015)
11. Dell, Inc. Dual monitors boost productivity, user satisfaction [online] (2011). www.dell.com/downloads/global/products/monitors/en/dual_monitors_boost_productivity_whitepaper.pdf, January 30, 2016
12. Ross, S.: Two screens are better than one [online] (2003). http://research.microsoft.com/en-us/news/features/vibe.aspx, January 30, 2016
13. Reynolds, B.: The effect of learning on the predictability of psychomotor performance. J. Exp. Psychol. **44**(3), 189–198 (1952)
14. Lampton, D.R., Knerr, B.W., Goldberg, S.L., Bliss, J.P., Moshell, M.J.: The Virtual Environment Performance Assessment Battery (VEPAB): Development and evaluation. (Technical Report No. 1029). Alexandria, VA: U.S. Army Research Institute for the Behavioral and Social Sciences (1993)

The Effects of Automation Error Types on Operators' Trust and Reliance

Svyatoslav Guznov[1(✉)], Joseph Lyons[1], Alexander Nelson[1], and Montana Woolley[2]

[1] Air Force Research Laboratory, WPAFB, Ohio, USA
{svyatoslav.guznov.1,joseph.lyons.6,
alexander.nelson.2}@us.af.mil
[2] CSRA, Virginia, VA, USA
montana_woolley@sra.com

Abstract. This study examined the joint effects of automation error type and error severity on operators' trust and reliance during a simulated unmanned aerial vehicle (UAV) mission. Participants were asked to search for improvised explosive devices (IEDs) with the help of an automated aid (AA). Four combinations of error types (miss and false alarm) and severity (mild and severe) were used, but with the same rate of error across all conditions. The results did not confirm the original hypothesis that severe false alarms would result in the lowest levels of trust and reliance, while the mild miss condition would result in the highest levels. No significant differences in self-reported trust were found among the conditions and the mild false alarm condition resulted in the lowest levels of reliance on the AA. In addition, reported perception of reliability of the AA was significantly lower in the severe miss condition compared to all other conditions. Finally, the mild false alarm condition produced the worst IED search task performance. Overall, results indicate a complex interaction between error types and error severity.

Keywords: Unmanned systems · Automation errors · False alarms · Misses · Trust · Reliance · Multi-tasking

1 Introduction

Operators' interaction with unmanned systems is becoming increasingly complex. In order to maintain optimal performance of human-machine teams, automation is heavily implemented. Multiple studies demonstrate the benefits of automation reflected in improved decision making, performance, and reduced workload [1]. At present, these systems are not perfectly accurate and may commit errors thus requiring the operators to maintain supervisory control over them. The operators must be "in the loop" to make the final decision on when to trust or distrust the automation, consequently leading to their decision to use or not use the automation (i.e., rely on automation). The major factor that forms the decision to rely on the system is trust [2] which is defined as an individual's (1) belief that the system will accomplish a certain objective and (2) willingness to accept vulnerability and uncertainty [3]. Trust is particularly important in a situation when the

© Springer International Publishing Switzerland 2016
S. Lackey and R. Shumaker (Eds.): VAMR 2016, LNCS 9740, pp. 116–124, 2016.
DOI: 10.1007/978-3-319-39907-2_11

operators need to use imperfect automation (e.g., low reliability automation) to accomplish the task [3].

A key characteristic of system reliability is the number of errors it commits. Previous studies show that more reliable systems (i.e., the fewer errors made) result in higher trust and reliance [4]. These studies primarily concentrated on the effects of error rates on human interaction with automation [5]; however, few studies have explored such effects of different types of errors. One study [6] examined the effects of error difficulty on trust and reliance. They found that obvious errors made by automation produced larger reduction in trust and reliance. Additionally, [7] found that more severe automation errors – the errors with the largest negative outcome – resulted in a larger decrease in trust. In addition to error severity, research by [5, 8, 9] suggested that false alarms (FAs) and misses differentially affect reliance behavior: FAs had a more negative effect on trust than did misses, which is possibly due to FAs being more noticeable. Finally, [10] examined the effects of error type on automation reliance. In cases when automation produced FAs, participants (1) did not rely on automation during states when alerts (i.e., automation suggestions) were provided and (2) over relied on automation when alerts were not provided. The impact of an automation that produced misses had the opposite effect.

Previous studies examined the effects of error types and severity on trust and reliance. However, none of them explored their joint effect in a realistic task environment. For example, in a military mission an automated system that monitors and classifies improvised explosive devices (IEDs) and non-IEDs can commit errors in multiple ways: by committing false alarms or misses and by making errors with different levels of severity. Thus, the goal for this study was to examine the effects of these types of errors on operators' trust and reliance in the automated system within a generic IED search mission. During the study, the participants performed an IED search task in the Mixed Initiative eXperimental (MIX) testbed [11, 15], which simulated controlling an Unmanned Aerial Vehicle (UAV). The participants were given an Automated Aid (AA) that provided information about the location of the IED and non-IED units on a separate map. Depending on the condition, the AA committed distinct error types including IED miss (severe miss), non-IED miss (mild miss), IED false alarm (severe false alarm), and non-IED false alarm (mild false alarm). It was expected that severe false alarm errors would result in the lowest levels of trust and reliance, while the mild miss errors would result in the highest levels of trust and reliance.

2   Methodology

2.1   Participants

Sixty-eight participants were recruited for this experiment (23 men and 45 women). Participants ranged in age from 18 to 52 years ($M = 23.79$, $SD = 8.61$). All participants reported normal or corrected-to-normal vision and hearing, normal color vision, and no history of neurological disorders.

2.2 Design

The experiment employed a 2 (Error Type) × 2 (Error Severity) between-subjects design. The Error Type factor included Miss (M) and False Alarm (FA) levels. The Error Severity factor included Mild Error (ME) and Severe Error (SE) levels. Thus, 17 participants were assigned at random to one of the four experimental conditions (MME, MSE, FAME, and FASE). The dependent variables for the study were IED search performance, reliance on the AA, state trust, perceived reliability of the AA, and perceived workload. Additionally, trait trust was measured.

2.3 Apparatus and Materials

The experiment was conducted using a computer that ran the MIX testbed which simulated a UAV control task. The MIX interface was comprised of the UAV videofeed window that showed a UAV camera view, the AA window which classified the objects by placing icons on the map, and the Ground Troop Report (GTR) window which provided feedback on the decision made by the participants (Fig. 1).

Fig. 1. MIX testbed screenshot

During the task, the UAV moved autonomously along a pre-determined path. The operator monitored a limited area through a UAV videofeed and searched for IEDs using the AA suggestions. The path contained IEDs and non-IEDs (similar looking but harmless objects) further referred to as *Boxes*. The UAV periodically stopped and the participants were prompted to make a decision by pressing one of the three buttons to classify IEDs, Boxes, or no IED/Box situations in the GTR window. The simulator logged the UAV coordinates, events on the AA map, and user mouse clicks within the MIX interface. Throughout the course of the search task, the AA provided the participants with suggestions about the locations of the IEDs and Boxes by placing corresponding icons in the AA map. The AA was not entirely reliable, producing errors in 15 % of suggestions for all conditions. However, the conditions varied based on error type and severity. Miss and FA error types contained two separate severity levels of errors, thus exposing participants to four error conditions. The AA committed Miss error types by either reporting no IED icon when there was an IED in the environment (severe error) or reporting no Box icon when there was a Box in the environment (mild error). Similarly, the AA committed FA error types by either reporting an IED icon when there was no IED (severe error) or reporting a Box icon when there was no Box (mild error). The AA made a total number of 20 classifications in each condition. Specifically, the AA in the MSE condition contained seven IED icons, ten Box icons, and three miss errors. The AA in the MME condition contained ten IED icons, seven Box icons, and three miss errors. The AA in the FASE condition contained ten IED icons (three of which were FA errors) and ten Box icons. Finally, the AA in the FAME condition contained ten IED icons and ten Box icons (three of which were FA errors). The environment contained either 17 or 20 total objects depending on the condition. Specifically, the MSE and MME conditions contained 10 IEDs and 10 Boxes, the FASE condition contained 7 IEDs and 10 Boxes, and the FAME condition contained 10 IEDs and 7 Boxes. The participants received feedback in the GTR window immediately after making a decision. The length of the route was set to 20 min. In this study, the following metrics were used: the Perceived Reliability metric measured participants' accuracy at evaluating the reliability of the AA [12], the Reliance Intentions Scale (RIS) measured participants' state trust [13], the Propensity to Trust Machines (PTM) metric measured trait trust [12], and the NASA-Task Load Index (NASA-TLX) measured perceived workload [14].

2.4 Procedure

Upon arrival, each participant was asked to read and sign the informed consent forms followed by completion of a color blindness test. Next, the participants filled out the demographics questionnaire and PTM metric. The participants were trained on how to perform the experimental task in the MIX testbed. In particular, they were trained on how to search for the IEDs and how to use the AA that assisted in the IED search. Participants were informed that in the actual experimental task the AA might make errors; however, no other information regarding number or type of errors was provided. Near the end of the training phase, the participants performed a short scenario to practice the skills. This short training scenario's AA made no errors. Next, the participants performed the experimental task in the MIX testbed. At the end of the experimental phase, the participants filled out the RIS, Perceived Reliability Scale, and NASA-TLX questionnaires. Upon completion of the experiment, the participants were debriefed and dismissed.

3 Results

3.1 Perceived Reliability

Between-subjects ANCOVA with the PTM variable as a covariate showed a significant interaction between the Error Type and Error Severity factors, $F(1, 63) = 7.41, p < .05$, $\eta^2 = .11$. Post-hoc comparisons using the Tukey HSD criterion for significance showed significantly lower perceived reliability for MSE ($M = 51.47$, $SD = 26.73$) when compared to MME ($M = 72.53$, $SD = 13.22$) and FASE ($M = 70.70$, $SD = 17.40$) conditions with $p < .05$ for both comparisons (Fig. 2).

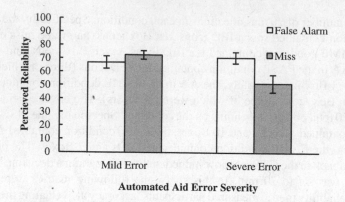

Fig. 2. Perceived reliability of the AA across the error types. Error bars are standard errors

3.2 State Trust

Between-subjects ANCOVA with the PTM variable as a covariate showed no significant main effects or interaction for the Error Type and Error Severity factors for the state trust. The average trust level across all conditions was 36.12 ($SD = 10.46$), with the maximum possible score of 70. The Cronbach's alpha for the metric was .83.

3.3 Reliance

Reliance percentages (i.e., percentage of agreements with the AA) were calculated for each condition. Between-subjects ANCOVA with the PTM variable as a covariate revealed a significant interaction between Error Type and Error Severity factors, $F(1, 63) = 19.30$, $p < .001$, $\eta^2 = .24$. In addition, there was a significant main effect for Error Type, $F(1, 63) = 22.93$, $p < .001$, $\eta^2 = .27$ and Error Severity, $F(1, 63) = 12.91$, $p < .001$, $\eta^2 = .17$. Post-hoc comparisons with the Tukey HSD criterion for significance showed FAME condition ($M = 76.99$, $SD = 4.51$) produced significantly lower reliance

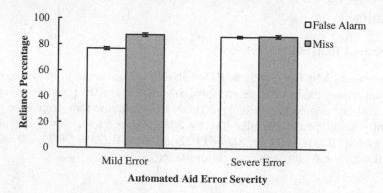

Fig. 3. Reliance on the AA across error types. Error bars are standard errors

when compared to MSE ($M = 86.69$, $SD = 5.15$), MME ($M = 87.62$, $SD = 5.42$), and FASE ($M = 86.17$, $SD = 3.61$) conditions $p < .001$ (Fig. 3).

3.4 IED Search Performance

Percentages of hits (i.e., percentage of correctly identified IEDs) were calculated for each condition. Between-subjects ANCOVA with the PTM variable as a covariate revealed a significant interaction between Error Type and Error Severity factors, F (1, 63) = 17.70, $p < .001$, $\eta^2 = .22$. In addition, there was a significant main effect for Error Type, F (1, 63) = 8.74, $p < .05$, $\eta^2 = .12$ and Error Severity, F (1, 63) = 4.87, $p < .05$, $\eta^2 = .07$. Post-hoc comparisons with the Tukey HSD criterion for significance showed FAME condition ($M = 52.94$, $SD = 15.72$) produced significantly lower hit percentage when compared to MSE ($M = 72.35$, $SD = 19.85$), MME ($M = 81.18$, $SD = 15.36$), and FASE ($M = 78.15$, $SD = 16.06$) conditions $p < .05$ (Fig. 4).

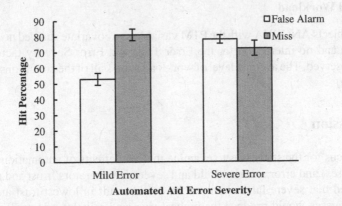

Fig. 4. IED hits across the error types. Error bars are standard errors

Percentages of false alarms (i.e., percentage of objects incorrectly identified as IEDs) were calculated for each condition. Between-subjects ANCOVA with the PTM variable as a covariate revealed a significant interaction between Error Type and Error Severity factors, F (1, 63) = 9.66, $p < .05$, $\eta^2 = .13$. In addition, there was a significant main effect for Error Type, F (1, 63) = 7.30, $p < .05$, $\eta^2 = .10$ and Error Severity, F (1, 63) = 17.28, $p < .01$, $\eta^2 = .22$. Post-hoc comparisons with the Tukey HSD criterion for significance showed FAME condition ($M = 4.76$, $SD = 1.60$) produced significantly higher false alarm percentage when compared to MSE ($M = 1.00$, $SD = 1.86$), MME ($M = 1.63$, $SD = 3.15$), and FASE ($M = 0.88$, $SD = 1.51$) conditions $p < .01$ (Fig. 5).

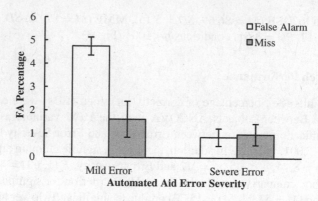

Fig. 5. IED false alarms across error types. Error bars are standard errors

3.5   Global Workload

Between-subjects ANCOVA with the PTM variable as a covariate showed no significant main effects and no interaction for the Error Type and Error Severity factors for the workload observed. The average level of workload across all of the conditions was 44.12 ($SD = 12.70$).

4   Discussion

The main focus for the study was to examine the joint effects of automation error type (FA and misses) and error severity (mild and severe) on operators' trust and reliance. It was predicted that severe false alarm errors would result in lowest trust and reliance while mild misses would produce the highest trust and reliance as found in previous studies by [5, 8, 9]. The results did not confirm the original hypothesis. The participants did not report any significant differences in trust for all conditions, with trust being moderate on average. The participants relied on the AA the least in the FAME condition when compared to the other three conditions. In this condition, participants relied on the AA in approximately 75 % of the cases (however, not necessarily correctly) while the other three conditions had reliance levels of slightly above 85 %. The lowest level of perceived reliability was observed in MSE condition, not in the FASE condition as suggested by previous research, with perceived reliability rated slightly above 50 %. The participants' evaluations of reliability were closer to the actual AA reliability (85 %) for the other three conditions. The MSE reliability value was significantly lower when compared to the MME and FASE conditions. Finally, in terms of performance, the FAME condition produced the lowest number of hits and highest number of FAs indicating unexpected consequence of a mild error on performance.

Overall, results from our study indicated complex interactions between error types and error severity. Trust literature suggests that there is a one-directional relationship between perceptions of automation trustworthiness (in this study, measured by perceived reliability metric), trust in automation, and reliance on the automation (agreement with the suggestions of the AA) [3]. For example, the perception of an automated system being low in reliability is expected to be accompanied by low trust and, consequently decreased use of the system. The results indicate that there may not necessarily be a positive correlation between trustworthiness, subjective trust, and trust outcome reliance behavior. In this study FAME was rated the lowest in perceived reliability; however, we did not observe matching outcomes in trust and reliance. Moreover, it appears that mild error FAME produced lowest system reliance as well as the poorest performance; however, it was not rated in the lowest reliability and trust. This finding indicates that errors irrelevant to the primary task (IED search) might have a detrimental effect on the task performance. The participants tended to under-rely appropriately (meaning agree with the AA when it was correct). Minor failures can cause a negative impact on reliance calibration and performance. Ultimately, this study provides insight into the patterns of trust and reliance on the systems that commit different types of errors which may negatively affect performance in human-machine teams. These results suggest that human-machine systems should be tailored to account for automation errors.

There are limitations associated with the experiment. The effects of error and severity types can be task-dependent. For example, [5] used a collision avoidance task in a simulated agricultural environment. In that study, the consequences for both types of errors (Misses and FAs) were equated to remove selection bias. We attempted to equate the consequences for both error types by using verbal instructions during the training. However, if the instructions were insufficient, the participants might have had their bias set to weight misses as more important when compared to FAs, thus affecting the results. The duration of the task could have been longer to allow for the capturing of changes in trust as participants become more familiar with the aid. Also, it would be beneficial to introduce pauses during the task to measure changes in trust and reliance as the task progresses. In addition, psychophysiological measurements such as eye-tracking and electroencephalogram could provide additional information on the neurophysiological processes occurring in relevance to the task.

Acknowledgments. The authors would like to thank Dr. Nathan Bowling, Wright State University (Dayton, Ohio) for support of this research and for comments on this manuscript.

References

1. Parasuraman, R., Sheridan, T.B., Wickens, C.D.: A model for types and levels of human interaction with automation. IEEE Trans. Syst. Man, Cybern. **30**, 286–297 (2000)
2. Lee, J.D., Seppelt, B.D.: Human factors in automation design. In: Nof, S. (ed.) Springer handbook of automation, pp. 417–436. Springer, New York, NY (2009)
3. Lee, J.D., See, K.A.: Trust in automation: Designing for appropriate reliance. Hum. Factors **46**(1), 50–80 (2004)
4. Bailey, N.A., Scerbo, M.W.: Automation- induced complacency for monitoring highly reliable systems: The role of task complexity, system experience and operator trust. Theor. Issues Ergon. Sci. **8**, 321–348 (2007)
5. Sanchez, J.: Factors that affect trust and reliance on an automated aid (Unpublished doctoral dissertation). Georgia Institute of Technology, Atlanta, GA (2006)

6. Madhavan, P., Wiegmann, D., Lacson, F.: Automation failures on tasks easily performed by operators undermine trust in automated aids. Hum. Factors **48**(2), 241–256 (2007)
7. Khasawneh, M.T.: Effect of error severity on human trust in hybrid systems. In: Human Factors and Ergonomics Society 48th Annual Meeting Proceedings. New Orleans, LA, pp. 439–433 (2004)
8. Dixon, S., Wickens, C.D.: Automation reliability in unmanned aerial vehicle flight control: A reliance-compliance model of automation dependence in high workload. Hum. Factors **48**, 474–486 (2006)
9. Geels-Blair, K., Rice, S., Schwark, J.: Using system-wide trust theory to reveal the contagion effects of automation false alarms and misses on compliance and reliance in a simulated aviation task. Int. J. Aviat. Psychol. **3**, 245–266 (2013)
10. Sanchez, J., Rogers, W.A., Fisk, A.D., Rovira, E.: Understanding reliance on automation: Effects of error type, error distribution, age, and experience. Theor. Issues Ergon. Sci. **15**(2), 134–160 (2014)
11. Barber, D., Davis, L., Nicholson, D., Chen, J.Y.C., Finkelstein, N.: The mixed initiative experimental (MIX) testbed for human robot interactions with varied levels of automation. In: Proceedings of the 26th Annual Army Science Conference, December 1–4, ADA505701 (2008)
12. Merritt, S.M., LaChapell, J., Lee, D.: The perfect automation schema: Measure development and validation. Technical report submitted to the Air Force Research Laboratory, Human Effectiveness Directorate (2012)
13. Lyons, J.B., Koltai, K.S., Ho, N.T., Johnson, W.B., Smith, D.E., Shively, J.R.: Engineering trust in complex automated systems. Ergonomics in Design (in press)
14. Hart, S.G., Staveland, L.E.: Development of NASA-TLX (Task Load Index): Results of empirical and theoretical research. In: Hancock, P.A., Meshkati, N. (eds.) Human Mental Workload. North Holland Press, Amsterdam (1988)
15. Guznov, S., Nelson, A., Lyons, J., Dycus, D.: The effects of automation reliability and multitasking on trustworthiness, trust, and reliance in a simulated unmanned system control task. In: Proceedings of 17th Human-Computer Interaction Conference, pp. 616–621 (2015)

Modeling Human Comprehension
of Data Visualizations

Michael J. Haass[✉], Andrew T. Wilson, Laura E. Matzen,
and Kristin M. Divis

Sandia National Laboratories, Albuquerque, NM, USA
mjhaass@sandia.gov

Abstract. A critical challenge in data science is conveying the meaning
of data to human decision makers. While working with visualizations,
decision makers are engaged in a visual search for information to support their reasoning process. As sensors proliferate and high performance
computing becomes increasingly accessible, the volume of data decision makers must contend with is growing continuously and driving the
need for more efficient and effective data visualizations. Consequently,
researchers across the fields of data science, visualization, and human-
computer interaction are calling for foundational tools and principles to
assess the effectiveness of data visualizations. In this paper, we compare
the performance of three different saliency models across a common set of
data visualizations. This comparison establishes a performance baseline
for assessment of new data visualization saliency models.

Keywords: Visual saliency · Visualization · Modeling · Visual search

1 Introduction

A critical challenge in data science is conveying the meaning of data to human
decision makers. While working with visualizations, analysts or decision makers
are engaged in a visual search for information to support their reasoning process.
As sensors proliferate and high performance computing becomes increasingly
accessible, the volume of data that analysts must contend with is growing continuously. The resulting bloom of data and derived data products is driving the
need for more efficient and effective means of presenting data to human analysts
and decision makers. Consequently, researchers across the fields of data science,
visualization, and human-computer interaction are calling for foundational tools
and principles to assess the effectiveness of data visualizations [9]. In this paper,
we describe the need for a computational model of bottom-up, stimulus-driven

Sandia National Laboratories is a multi-program laboratory managed and operated
by Sandia Corporation, a wholly owned subsidiary of Lockheed Martin Corporation,
for the U.S. Department of Energy's National Nuclear Security Administration under
contract DE-AC04-94AL85000. SAND2016-1685 C.

ⓒ Springer International Publishing Switzerland 2016
S. Lackey and R. Shumaker (Eds.): VAMR 2016, LNCS 9740, pp. 125–134, 2016.
DOI: 10.1007/978-3-319-39907-2_12

visual saliency that is appropriate for abstract data visualization. We compare the performance of three different saliency models across a common set of data visualizations to establish a performance baseline for assessment of new data visualization saliency models.

Human visual processing is guided by two parallel processes: bottom-up and top-down visual attention [16]. When viewing an image, a person's eye movements are guided by both the visual properties of the image that capture bottom-up attention (e.g. color, contrast, motion) and top-down processes such as task goals, prior experience, and use of search strategies [8]. Many bottom-up models are based on the neurophysiology of human and primate visual systems [1]. These models construct a number of features from the image data and then highlight differences in the features across multiple scales of image resolution. The chosen features are based on the response of neurons in the visual processing system to certain image characteristics such as luminance, hue, contrast and orientation. Various models have explored the use of different visual features at different scales to predict where humans will look in natural scene imagery.

Maps of bottom-up visual saliency have been valuable tools for studying how people process information in natural scenes, and could also be useful for evaluating the effectiveness of data visualizations. Ideally, the most important information in a data visualization would also have high visual saliency. This evaluation approach has been demonstrated with scene-like data visualizations [12], but it is unclear whether or not it is applicable to abstract data visualizations. In addressing this question, it is important to consider how visual search may differ between natural scene visualizations and abstract data visualizations. For the latter, viewers are engaged in drawing conclusions about causality, efficacy or consequences rather than identifying objects or properties of objects. The visual appearance of their target (information) may not be well defined or known ahead of time. The vast majority, if not all, existing computational models were developed and optimized to predict visual saliency for image-like, or natural, scenes and may not perform as well when applied to abstract data visualizations. In fact one published taxonomy of visual stimuli used in studies of gaze direction lists only three types of stimuli: psychophysics laboratory stimuli, static natural scenes, and dynamic natural scenes [15]. To date, we have been unable to find any published examples of bottom-up saliency models designed explicitly for data visualizations. In the following sections, we compare the performance of three high performing natural scene saliency models across a common set of data visualizations.

2   Method

The MIT Saliency Benchmark [7] is an online source of saliency model performance and datasets. The site scores and reports performance on author-contributed saliency models on datasets where the human fixation positions are not public. This approach prevents model performance inflation due to over-fitting of the test dataset. We selected three saliency models, described below, listed on the MIT Saliency Benchmark site that span a range of performance on natural scenes when measured on standard stimuli with a common set of human gaze data. For baseline performance on natural scenes for each model, we used results for the cat2000 data set [4] because it is the most recent (introduced Jan 2015). MATLAB or Python code for each model was downloaded from saliency.mit.edu and saliency maps were constructed with each model on a set of data visualizations. We measured the performance of each model for the data visualizations using the same eight metrics used for the saliency benchmark project. We selected 184 example data visualizations from the Massachusetts (Massive) Visualization Dataset [6] with corresponding eye-movement data [5] from 33 viewers (average 16 viewers per visualization, minimum of 11, maximum of 22). Figure 1 shows an example data visualization and corresponding human fixation map. The MASSVIS samples were selected from infographic blogs, government reports, news media websites and scientific journals.

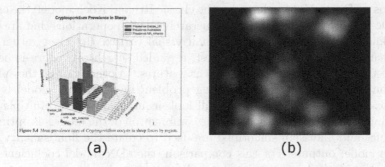

(a)   (b)

Fig. 1. Example data visualization (a) and human fixation map (b).

2.1   Saliency Models

Itti, Koch and Nieber. Numerous saliency prediction models have been developed in recent years, taking a variety of approaches to predict which parts of an image are likely to draw a viewer's attention. Several of these approaches involve the creation of feature maps that are weighted, combined, and filtered to produce a visual saliency map. The most prominent of these models, the Itti, Koch and Niebur model [11], is based on the properties of the human visual system. The model detects changes in low-level features such as color, intensity, and orientation at varying spatial scales. It then weights those features and uses an iterative spatial competition process to create feature maps that are then summed to produce the saliency map. More recently, other researchers have developed new approaches to create saliency maps. When compared using the MIT Saliency Benchmark, two visual saliency models that consistently perform well with images of natural scenes are the Boolean Map based Saliency model [20,21] and the Ensembles of Deep Networks model [19].

Boolean Map Based Saliency. The Boolean Map based Saliency model (BMS) [20] creates a set of Boolean maps to characterize images. It relies on the Gestalt principle of figure-ground segregation and the idea that visual attention will be drawn to the figures in an image rather than the background. The model randomly thresholds an image's feature maps, such as the color map, to generate a set of Boolean maps. For each Boolean map, the model uses the feature of surroundedness [21] (a connected region with a closed outer contour) to identify figures within the image and to create an attention map. The attention maps are then normalized and combined to form the full-resolution attention map. This approach differs from many other saliency models because it utilizes scale-invariant information about the topological structure of the images. It does not use multi-scale processing, center-surround filtering, or statistical analysis of features. Thus, it is a relatively simple model that focuses on identifying figures within images.

Ensebles of Deep Networks. Like the classic Itti and Koch model, the ensembles of Deep Networks (eDN) model is hierarchical with operations that are based on the known mechanisms of the human visual cortex. However, rather than hand-selecting visual features of interest, a guided search procedure is used to optimize the model for identifying salient features. In other words, the saliency prediction task is a supervised learning problem in which the model is optimized for predicting where humans will look in natural scenes. Multiple high-performing models are identified and the combination of the models is optimized. Center bias and Gaussian smoothing are used to create the final saliency maps from the model outputs. For this comparison, the eDN model coefficients provided by Vig et al., learned using natural scene stimuli rather than data visualizations, were used to illustrate the difference in feature sensitivity across the two stimuli types. Future comparisons of learned model coefficients across the stimuli types could inform the development of saliency models for data visualizations. Figure 2 shows examples of each saliency model applied to the data visualization shown in Fig. 1.

(a)   (b)   (c)

Fig. 2. Example saliency maps, (a) Itti, (b) BMS, (c) eDN, for data visualization shown in Fig. 1.

2.2   Comparison Metrics

Many different metrics have been proposed for comparing saliency and fixation maps. Riche et al. provide a thorough review and taxonomy of published comparison metrics [17]. The authors use a two-dimensional taxonomy to organize the various metrics. Along one dimension, they categorize the metrics as "value-based," "location-based" or "distribution-based." Along the other dimension, they categorize the metrics as "common," "hybrid" or "specific." Metrics categorized as common are generalized and were not originally designed for saliency comparisons. Metrics categorized as hybrid are adapted from other fields to work with saliency and fixation data. Metrics categorized as specific were developed directly for application to saliency comparisons. In order to compare model performance on natural scenes and data visualizations, we elected to use the eight comparison metrics used by the MIT Saliency Benchmark project. Of the eight metrics, one was value-based, three were location-based, and four are distribution-based, as described in more detail below.

Value-Based Metric. The normalized scanpath saliency metric (NSS)[2] first standardizes saliency values to have zero mean and unit standard deviation, then computes the average saliency value at human fixation locations. When NSS is greater than one, the saliency map exhibits significantly higher values at fixation locations compared to other locations.

Location-Based Metrics. Three of the comparison metrics are based on the receiver-operator characteristic (ROC). For these metrics, the human gaze positions are considered positive examples and all other points are considered negative examples. The saliency map is treated as binary classifier to separate the positive and negative example sets at various thresholds and the area under the resulting ROC curve (AUC) is computed. As the saliency map and fixation map become more similar, AUC values approach one. Random chance agreement results in an AUC value of 0.5. For all three implementations, the true positive rate is the proportion of saliency values above the threshold at all fixation locations. For the AUC-Judd implementation the false positive rate is the proportion saliency values above the threshold at non-fixated locations and the thresholds are sampled from the saliency map values [17]. For the AUC-Borji implementation, the false positive rate is based on saliency values sampled uniformly from all image pixels and the thresholds are sampled with a fixed stepsize [3]. For the shuffled AUC implementation, the false positive rate is based on saliency values sampled uniformly from fixation locations on a random set of other images [3,22].

Distribution-Based Metrics. The similarity score (SIM) is a histogram intersection measure. Each distribution is scaled so that its sum is one. Similarity is the sum of the minimum value between the two scaled distributions at each point. When SIM equals one, the distributions are the same and when SIM equals zero, there is no overlap between the two distributions. The earth mover's distance (EMD)[18] is based on the minimal cost to transform one distribution (the saliency map) into the other distribution (the fixation map). Smaller values of EMD represent better agreement between the saliency map and the fixation map and when EMD equals zero, the two distributions are identical. The linear correlation coefficient (CC) is a measure of the linear relationship between a fixation map and a saliency map [2]. When CC is close to one, the linear relationship between the saliency map and the fixation map is nearly perfect. The Kullback Leibler divergence (KL)[10] is a measure of the information lost when the saliency map is used to approximate the fixation map. KL ranges from zero, when the two maps are identical, to infinity.

3   Experimental Results

Figure 3 shows the performance of the three models on the natural scenes and data visualizations. The results are displayed in the form of a percent difference score that is negative when the models performed better on natural scenes and positive when the models performed better on data visualizations. The corresponding numerical values are shown in Table 1. Table 2 shows the effect size, using Glass's delta across natural scenes and data visualization.

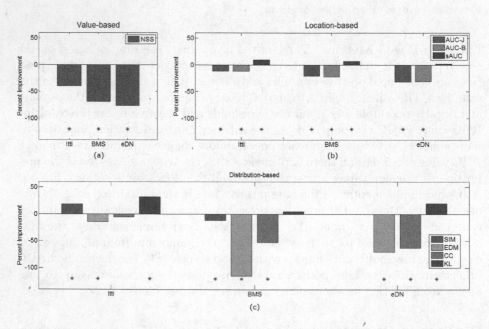

Fig. 3. Model Comparison Across Stimuli Type and Metric. (a) Value-based metric, (b) Location-based Metrics, (c) Distrbution-based Metrics. Results are displayed in the form of a difference score that is negative when the models performed better on natural scenes and positive when the models performed better on data visualizations.

Table 1. Model Comparison Across Stimulus Type. First value in each pair is sample mean; second value is standard error of the mean (SEM). Bold font indicates significant differences between mean values for natural scenes and visualizations ($p < 0.05$).

	Itti		BMS		eDN	
	Nat	Vis	Nat	Vis	Nat	Vis
AUC-J	**0.77 ± 0.002**	**0.68 ± 0.006**	**0.85 ± 0.001**	**0.67 ± 0.006**	**0.85 ± 0.001**	**0.58 ± 0.009**
SIM	**0.48 ± 0.002**	**0.57 ± 0.006**	**0.61 ± 0.002**	**0.54 ± 0.005**	0.52 ± 0.002	0.52 ± 0.005
EMD	**3.44 ± 0.016**	**3.92 ± 0.11**	**1.95 ± 0.013**	**4.19 ± 0.12**	**2.64 ± 0.013**	**4.48 ± 0.12**
AUC-B	**0.76 ± 0.002**	**0.67 ± 0.006**	**0.84 ± 0.001**	**0.65 ± 0.006**	**0.84 ± 0.001**	**0.58 ± 0.009**
sAUC	**0.59 ± 0.002**	**0.64 ± 0.007**	**0.59 ± 0.002**	**0.63 ± 0.006**	0.55 ± 0.002	0.56 ± 0.009
CC	0.42 ± 0.004	0.40 ± 0.017	**0.67 ± 0.002**	**0.32 ± 0.014**	**0.54 ± 0.002**	**0.20 ± 0.020**
NSS	**1.06 ± 0.012**	**0.64 ± 0.030**	**1.67 ± 0.012**	**0.52 ± 0.025**	**1.30 ± 0.006**	**0.30 ± 0.032**
KL	**0.92 ± 0.006**	**0.63 ± 0.019**	0.83 ± 0.012	0.79 ± 0.021	**0.97 ± 0.006**	**0.78 ± 0.018**

Table 2. Glass's Delta Effect Size for Model Comparison Across Stimulus Type. Bold font indicates significant differences between mean values for natural scenes and visualizations ($p < 0.05$). For normalization of Glass's delta, the natural scenes were treated as the control group.

	AUC-J.	SIM	EMD	AUC-B.	sAUC	CC	NSS	KL
Itti	**−0.98**	**1.23**	**0.66**	**−0.98**	**0.69**	−0.14	**−0.79**	**−1.16**
BMS	**−3.58**	**−1.00**	**3.79**	**−3.77**	**0.58**	**−3.21**	**−2.09**	−0.07
eDN	**−5.34**	−0.04	**3.07**	**−5.18**	0.14	**−4.22**	**−3.43**	−0.67

Generally, the models had poorer performance for data visualizations than for natural scenes. All three models performed worse on visualizations than on natural scenes as measured by four of the eight metrics: the value-based metric NSS, two location-based metrics, AUC-Judd and AUC-Borji, and the distribution-based metric EMD. For these metrics, the effect sizes were largest for the BMS and eDN models. The performance of the eDN model was not significantly different for visualizations and natural scenes when measured by the location-based metric sAUC and the distribution-based metric SIM. Similarly, the performance of the Itti model was not significantly different for visualizations and natural scenes when measured by the distribution-based metric CC. However, for the distribution-based metric KL, both the Itti and eDN models performed significantly better for data visualizations than natural scenes. This is consistent with the finding of Riche et al. [17] that the KL metric is quite different from the other metrics. Because the KL metric does not take absolute location into account, but considers only the statistical distribution of the map, two maps having similar distributions can have very different location properties. The performance of the BMS model was not significantly different for visualizations and natural scenes when assessed by the KL metric. For this metric, the effect size was largest for the Itti model followed by the eDN model, while the effect size for the BMS model was close to zero. Of note, for the metrics where the performance of all three models was significantly different between visualizations and natural scenes, the Itti model performed better on visualizations than either the BMS model or the eDN model. This is contrary to the general trend in performance on natural scenes for these metrics where eDN is the best performing saliency model.

4   Discussion and Conclusion

The visualizations used in this comparison study are all highly curated, employing text and graphic design principles to help viewers identify the most important results. The Itti model may perform best on these data visualizations because of its close ties to the human visual processing system, while other models have been designed and optimized for natural scenes, placing less emphasis on faithful representation of neural processes. The natural scene models may also under perform on data visualizations, since many graphical elements used in visualization have smaller spatial extent than objects that typically appear in natural scenes. The finer resolution graphical elements result in higher frequency components to which natural scene models maybe insensitive. Another factor that may limit the applicability of natural scene models is the use of text in data visualizations. Text plays a significant role in human attentional allocation and the resulting direction of eye movements. The process of reading text in a visualization would result in a higher density of fixations around text elements. Future work should leverage a taxonomy of visualization elements such as the one described in Munzner's book [13]. Our future research will focus on data visualization techniques for two-dimensional representation of high-dimensional data.

This comparison study has established a baseline that can be used to assess the performance of new saliency models for data visualizations. The current trend towards better model performance on natural scenes seems to come at the expense of performance on data visualizations. This inverse relationship between model performance on natural scenes and on data visualizations supports our position that new saliency models are needed to aid development of generalized theories of visual search for data visualizations. In future work, we will expand on existing models of visual saliency to address these issues and investigate the role of top-down visual attention in viewers' navigation of abstract data visualizations. Developing general models of top-down sense-making has proven to be quite difficult [14]. Knowledge elicitation techniques have been used to identify top-down goals and strategies and the resulting influence on eye movements. Other approaches have applied machine learning techniques to eye movement data collected as experts perform a given task. The resulting models can predict expert attention allocation for new stimuli, but it is often difficult to use these models to understand why experts allocate attention to certain content and not to other content. Because of this difficulty, we advocate the combination of computational models of bottom-up saliency with empirical studies of eye movements to identify tacit sense-making strategies.

As this work progresses, we will also explore the role of expertise in visual processing of data visualizations. Expertise is a crucial factor in top-down visual attention, and its impact may be even greater with abstract visualizations, where users cannot rely on their prior experience with real-world scenes to guide their search. Visual search tasks using abstract data visualizations can be contrasted with visual search tasks in complex decision making domains. For example, airport luggage screeners search x-ray imagery for prohibited items. In this domain, as in many abstract visualizations, the visual appearance of the target is often not known in advance and furthermore the target may be obscured by overlapping items. However, the users' knowledge about the image features may be quite different. Luggage screening personnel have extensive training and experience in how to search through images, but may have little expertise on the physics of the image formation process. In contrast, experts such as scientists and engineers who work with abstract data are likely to have very deep knowledge of the physical properties driving the content of visualizations. These differences should be considered as top-down factors are identified.

References

1. Borji, A., Itti, L.: State-of-the-art in visual attention modeling. IEEE Trans. Pattern Anal. Mach. Intell. **85**, 185–207 (2013)
2. Borji, A., Sihite, D.N., Itti, L.: Quantitative analysis of human-model agreement in visual saliency modeling: a comparative study. IEEE Trans. Image Process. **22**, 55–69 (2013)
3. Borji, A., Tavakoli, H.R., Sihite, D.N., Itti, L.: Analysis of scores, datasets, and models in visual saliency prediction. In: IEEE International Conference on Computer Vision (ICCV) (2013)
4. Borji, A., Itti, L.: Cat 2000: A large scale fixation dataset for boosting saliency research. In: CVPR 2015 Workshop on "Future of Datasets" (2015). arXiv:1505.03581
5. Borkin, M., Bylinskii, Z., Kim, N., Bainbridge, C.M., Yeh, C., Borkin, D., Pfister, H., Oliva, A.: Beyond memorability: visualization recognition and recall. IEEE Trans. Vis. Comput. Graph. **22**, 519–528 (2015). (Proceedings of InfoVis)
6. Borkin, M., Bylinskii, Z., Krzysztof, G., Kim, N., Oliva, A., Pfister, H.: Massachusetts (massive) visualization dataset. massvis.mit.edu
7. Bylinskii, Z., Judd, T., Borji, A., Itti, L., Durand, F., Oliva, A., Torralba, A.: Mit Saliency Benchmark
8. Connor, C.E., Egeth, H.E., Yantis, S.: Visual attention: bottom-up versus top-down. Curr. Biol. **14**(19), 850–852 (2004)
9. Green, T.M., Ribarsky, W., Fisher, B.: Building and applying a human cognition model for visual analytics. Inf. Vis. **8**, 1–13 (2009)
10. Itti, L., Baldi, P.: A principled approach to detecting surprising events in video. In: IEEE Computer Society Conference on Computer Vision and pattern Recognition (CVPR) (2005)
11. Itti, L., Koch, C., Niebur, E.: A model of saliency-based visual attention for rapid scene analysis. IEEE Trans. Pattern Anal. Mach. Intell. **20**, 1254–1259 (1998)
12. Matzen, L.E., Haass, M.J., Tran, J., McNamara, L.A.: Using eye tracking metrics and visual saliency maps to assess image utility. Paper Presented at the IS and T International Symposium on Electronic Imaging: Human Vision in Electronic Imaging, San Francisco, CA, USA (2016)

13. Munzner, T.: Visualization Analysis and Design. CRC Press, Boca Raton (2014)
14. Navalpakkam, V., Itti, L.: Modeling the influence of task on attention. Vis. Res. **45**, 205–231 (2005)
15. Peters, R.J., Itti, L.: Beyond bottom-up: incorporating task-dependent influences into a computational model of spatial attention. In: IEEE Conference on Computer Vision and Pattern Recognition (CVPR) (2007)
16. Pinto, Y., van der Leij, A.R., Sligte, I.G., Lamme, V.A.F., Scholte, H.S.: Bottom-up and top-down attention are independent. J. Vis. **13**(3) (2013)
17. Riche, N., Duvinage, M., Mancas, M., Gosselin, B., Dutoit, T.: Saliency and human fixations: state-of-the-art and study of comparison metrics. In: IEEE International Conference on Computer Vision (ICCV) (2013)
18. Rubner, Y., Tomasi, C., Guibas, L.J.: The earth mover's distance as a metric for image retrieval. Int. J. Comput. Vis. **40**, 99–121 (2000)
19. Vig, E., Dorr, M., Cox, D.: Large-scale optimization of hierarchical features for saliency prediction in natural images. In: IEEE Computer Vision and Pattern Recognition (CVPR) (2014)
20. Zhang, J., Sclaroff, S.: Saliency detection: a Boolean map approach. In: Proceedings of the IEEE International Conference on Computer Vision (ICCV) (2013)
21. Zhang, J., Sclaroff, S.: Exploiting surroundedness for saliency detection: a Boolean map approach. IEEE Trans. Pattern Anal. Mach. Intell. (TPAMI) **38**, 889–902 (2015)
22. Zhang, L., Tong, M.H., Marks, T.K., Shan, H., Cottrell, G.W.: Sun: a Bayesian framework for saliency using natural statistics. J. Vis. **16**, 1–20 (2008)

Auditory and Visual Properties in the Virtual Reality Using Haptic Device

Manabu Ishihara[✉] and Takafumi Komori

National Institute of Technology, Oyama College, Oyama-City, Tochigi 323-0806, Japan
ishihara@m.ieice.org

Abstract. The advantages of a system that uses virtual reality (VR) are that the software program can be changed to permit various types of technical training to be performed with a single device, and that the work environment can also be changed easily. Another advantage is that a network can be used to allow multiple users to train at different remote locations. An example of this phenomenon is the lag between video and sound in a network teleconference system. In an environment where latency exists, such a system cannot be said to be suitable as a technical training system, and this is a problem when using a VR system.

Keywords: Virtual Reality (VR) · Network · Visual · Auditory · Haptic

1 Introduction

The advantages of a system that uses virtual reality (VR) are that the software program can be changed to permit various types of technical training to be performed with a single device, and that the work environment can also be changed easily. Another advantage is that a network can be used to allow multiple users to train at different remote locations. With a standalone system, an independent device that does not interface with a network will experience no latency, and no time difference Δt will be generated for various sensory operations. However, with a VR space connected via the Internet or other network, as a result of network latency and packet loss, as well as differing amounts of information, the data transmission times for various sensory operations will not necessarily be the same. An example of this phenomenon is the lag between video and sound in a network teleconference system. In an environment where latency exists, such a system cannot be said to be suitable as a technical training system, and this is a problem when using a VR system.

Concurrent with these advances has been a wealth of research on haptic interface technology [1], and educators have begun exploring ways to incorporate teaching tools utilizing touch properties in their curriculums [2, 3]. This will make replacing familiar teaching tools with digital media incorporating VR seem more attractive. For example, various learning support systems that utilize virtually reality (VR) technology [4] are being studied. Examples include a system that utilizes a stereoscopic image and writing brush display to teach the brush strokes used in calligraphy [5, 6], the utilization of a robot arm with the same calligraphy learning system [7], a system that uses a "SPIDAR" haptic device to enable remote calligraphy instruction [8], and systems that analyze the

S. Lackey and R. Shumaker (Eds.): VAMR 2016, LNCS 9740, pp. 135–146, 2016.
DOI: 10.1007/978-3-319-39907-2_13

learning process involved in piano instruction [9] or in the use of virtual chopsticks [10]. However, with a VR space connected via the Internet or other network, as a result of network latency and packet loss [11, 12, 13], as well as differing amounts of information, the data transmission times for various sensory operations will not necessarily be the same.

In this study, we created a drum performance system in a VR space to investigate the effect of visual, auditory, and haptic sensation time differences generated while performing an operation in a VR space. As a result, we clarified the impact that delays of various information in a VR space have upon a user, and the impact of delays upon a user when that system is adjusted to more closely approximate an actual network.

2 Experiment Using Ball Striking Action (Preliminary Experiment)

2.1 Description of the Experiment

First, in order to investigate the linkage between cooperative characteristics of haptic, visual, and auditory senses in a VR space, we used PHANToM to create a program that will strike a ball within a VR space. Striking the ball causes a reaction force to be returned, and the user is thus able to sense the striking of the ball in the VR space.

In this study, we used a PHANToM Omni Device (Sensable Technologies) as our haptic device. It was attached to a control computer (CPU: Intel® Core™ i7-2600[3.00 GHz], RAM:4.00 GB, OS:Windows7Pro.,64bit) running Open-Haptics™ toolkit v3.0 as the control program. The participants were seven male   (17-20 years old).

The action of striking a ball with a pole causes a collision that returns a reaction force and exhibits basic characteristics. A sound is generated when the ball is struck, and the collision causes the ball to begin to move with respect to the pole. The sound of a billiard ball being hit was used as the sound generated when the ball is struck. A lag between the generation of sound and the start of motion imparted a feeling of sensory discomfort to test subjects when using this system. Therefore, we investigated human reactions and the acceptable range for deviation arising from differences in visual, auditory, and haptic operations occurring in the ball strike timing.

Figure 1 shows the execution screen. The blue sphere in the screen represents the tip of the pole, and PHANToM has been used to create a program in which the tip of the pole is moved to strike the white sphere in the center of the screen. As shown in the figure, by generating delays between the sound and haptic sense generated when striking the ball, and between the haptic sense and the video of the ball beginning to move, we tested the acceptable ranges of time difference for various senses.

The test subjects compared various measurement values for which the video and sound were delayed to a non-delayed reference of 0 ms, and selected one of three criteria corresponding to whether the generated video and sound seemed to be earlier than, later than, or simultaneous with the haptic reference.

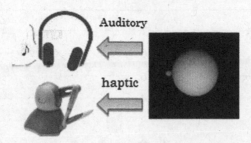

Fig. 1. Overview of the experiment

2.2 Experimental Results

Figures 2 and 3 show the experimental results of the visual and haptic characteristics and the auditory and haptic characteristics, respectively. The horizontal axes indicate the time difference until the respective video or sound is generated with respect to the haptic reference, and the vertical axes indicate the number of people who felt a delay with that time difference. The test subjects were men and women in their teens or twenties; 15 people participated in the visual–haptic experiment and 7 people participated in the auditory–haptic experiment. The time difference settings in these experiments ranged from 0 to ± 150 ms in 10 ms intervals (31 points) and ± 200 ms for a total of 33 points for the visual-haptic experiments and from 0 to ± 200 ms in 10 ms intervals for the auditory–haptic experiments for a total of 41 points.

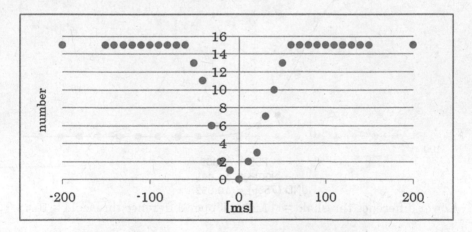

Fig. 2. Visual–haptic sense coordination characteristics

From Fig. 2 it can be seen, for example, that when a 30 ms time difference is generated between the video of the start of ball motion and the haptic reaction force when the ball is struck, 7 people were able to distinguish that difference.

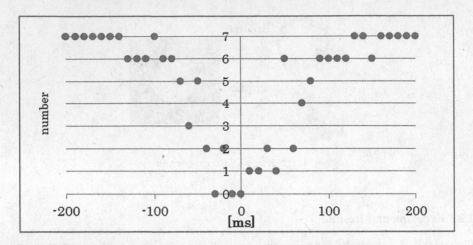

Fig. 3. Auditory–haptic sense coordination characteristics

From Figs. 2 and 3, it can be seen that as the delay time increases, the number of people capable of feeling a difference from the reference also increases. Furthermore, because the increase in people who can feel a difference occurs at a gentler rate in Fig. 3 than in Fig. 2, we can conclude that the effect of an auditory delay has less of an impact than the effect of a visual delay.

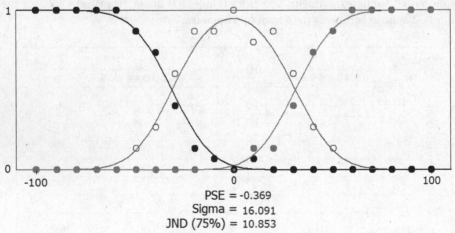

PSE = -0.369
Sigma = 16.091
JND (75%) = 10.853
Lower difference threshold = -11.222   Upper difference threshold = 10.48

Fig. 4. Visual–haptic sense characteristics

From Fig. 2, in comparing visual and haptic senses, it can be seen that at a time difference of ± 30 ms, approximately 50 % of the people began to feel a difference, and at about ± 50 ms and larger, nearly all the people could feel a difference. From Fig. 3, in comparing auditory and haptic senses, it can be seen that beyond a time difference of about ± 50 ms, more than 50 % of the total people began to feel a difference, and that from differences of about ± 80 ms, nearly all of the test subjects could feel a difference.

From the obtained results, the method of constant stimuli was used to analyze the time difference threshold, and Figs. 4 and 5 show those findings.

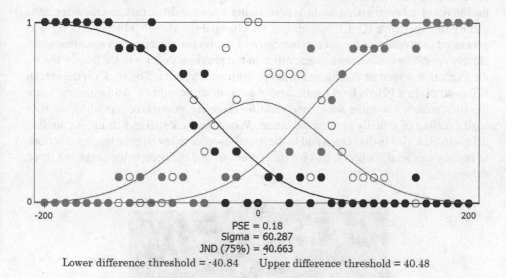

PSE = 0.18
Sigma = 60.287
JND (75%) = 40.663
Lower difference threshold = -40.84   Upper difference threshold = 40.48

Fig. 5. Auditory–haptic sense characteristics

From Fig. 4, in a comparison of auditory and haptic senses, with respect to a standard stimulus of 0 ms, an upper limen of 10.48 ms and a lower limen of −11.222 ms were obtained. This finding indicates that for time differences of up to approximately ± 10 ms, 75 % of the test subjects did not distinguish any difference from 0 ms. Similarly, from Fig. 5, with respect to a standard stimulus of 0 ms, an upper limen of 40.48 ms and a lower limen of −40.84 ms were obtained. This finding indicates that in a comparison of auditory and haptic senses, for time differences of up to approximately ± 40 ms, 75 % of the test subjects did not distinguish any difference from 0 ms.

It can be seen that the number of users who feel a difference in the program begins to increase when, due to delays, the haptic–visual data time difference begins to exceed 10 ms or the haptic–auditory data time difference begins to exceed 40 ms. Visual sense is said [14] to have a greater impact than auditory sense, and that statement is consistent with these findings. Moreover, for visual sense, there exists research showing that people begin to sense network latency when the delay reaches approximately 30 ms, and this is consistent with the finding that 50 % of the test subjects began to feel a difference at this level.

3   QoE Measurement with Drum Performance System in a VR Space

3.1   Drum Performance System

In this experiment, we created a drum performance system in a VR space to investigate the impact of delay on a person who is performing a more realistic task and the associated quality of experience (QoE). In addition, we changed the way in which the delay was generated to investigate the acceptable range of delays for a person in a state that more closely approximates network latency than in the previous experiment. Figure 6 shows the execution screen of the created drum performance system. The stick on the screen is moved using a PHANToM haptic device so as to strike a drum. At the timing when the stick strikes a drum, a sound and reaction force are generated, providing the user with a feeling of actually playing the drums. When the stick strikes a drum, we applied delays to the video in the screen and to the sound in order to investigate human reactions to latency in visual, auditory, and haptic operations and the acceptable ranges of those delays.

Fig. 6.   Program execution screen

3.2   Measurement with Constant Delay and Random Delay

In this experiment, we took measurements using two types of delays: constant and random. Each type is explained below.

3.2.1   Constant Delay
When a drum is struck, a predetermined single type of delay time only is generated. Since a constant delay will always be generated, this differs from an actual network environment, but it is thought that basic human responses to delays could be measured in this manner.

3.2.2   Random Delay

If the same delay time always occurred for all communication, then the delay could be predicted and managed accordingly, but delay times are not necessarily constant. Especially in the case of the Internet, since in principle, the location through which a packet will be transferred is not known, predicting the arrival time of a packet is extremely difficult. In consideration of the fluctuation in such a network, we conducted experiments in which random delays of two or more preset delay times would occur when a drum is struck. Accordingly, the delay format more closely resembled the state when using an actual network than in the case of a constant delay. For this experiment, two types of delays (Delay 1 and Delay 2) were preset in advance. We measured the rates of occurrence of the two delays and set them to occur with nearly equal probability.

3.3   QoE Measurement of Drum Performance System with Constant Delay

Video and sound delays were generated when a drum is struck, and we investigated the impact on people at that time. In the previous experiment, measurements were made using three criteria, but in this experiment, the users performed evaluations to rank each delay on a five-step scale from 1 to 5. The criteria for the five evaluations are shown in Table 1.

Table 1. Experimental evaluation ranking

evaluated value	quality	operability of system
5	Excellent	to have good operability
4	Good	v
3	Fair	v
2	Poor	v
1	Bad	to have not good operability

The experiment was conducted for both sound and video with measurements taken in the range of 0 to 150 ms in 10 ms intervals for a total of 16 measurement points. The delays were presented to the test subjects at random, without prior notification. The experiment was conducted multiple times for each test subject, and measurements were taken a total of 20 times for 7 test subjects.

Figure 7 shows the experimental results. From this figure, it can be seen that the users evaluated the delay at lower values as the delay time increased. It can also be seen that a video delay has a greater impact than a sound delay on the evaluation results.

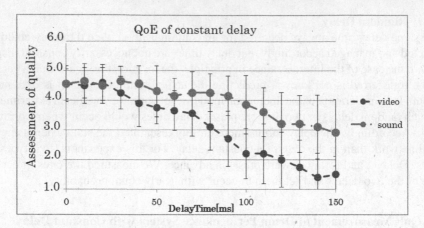

Fig. 7. QoE measurement results with constant delay

In addition, for sound delays greater than the standard deviation, the evaluation value increased gradually as the delay time increased. For video delays, however, it can be seen that the evaluation values became smaller if the delay time became excessively large. This is because users are thought to concentrate their evaluations at the "poor" level when the video delay time becomes large. On the other hand, for sound delays, there was a variety of evaluations even when the delay time was 150 ms. There is thought to be a delay time zone during which individual differences appear in the impact of a delay.

For video delays, evaluation values of 3 or below for "normal" or lower quality were recorded at 80 ms, but for sound delays, there were no evaluation values of 3 or less until 150 ms. From the results of the previous experiment in which the number of users who feel a difference in the program begin to increase when the haptic-visual data time difference begins to exceed 10 ms or the haptic-auditory data time difference begins to exceed 40 ms, there is thought to be a discrepancy between the time difference value at which a difference is felt due to delay and the time difference value at which quality is affected significantly.

3.4 QoE Measurement of Drum Performance System with Random Delay

The measurement range consists of Delay 1 fixed at a single value and Delay 2 varied from 0 to 150 ms in 10 ms intervals, for a total of 16 points. Here, the experiment was performed for two random delays, with the value of Delay 1 being fixed at 0 ms and fixed at 30 ms.

3.4.1 QoE Measurement with Random Delay (Delay 1 = 0 Ms)

Figure 8 shows the experimental results. From Fig. 8, it can be seen that for a random delay in which Delay 1 is fixed at 0 ms, the video quality is evaluated at an overall higher value than in the case of a constant delay, and the evaluation values have risen to a level comparable to those of a sound delay.

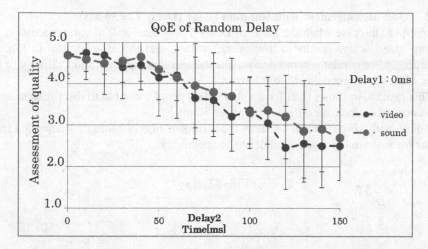

Fig. 8. QoE measurement results with random delay (Delay 1 = 0 ms)

When a video with a constant delay is evaluated, the quality drops below the "normal" level at evaluation value 3 in the vicinity of 80 ms, but with a random delay, the quality evaluation maintains a value of 3 or higher up to 110 ms. Therefore, we found that even if the delay time is not stable, as long as one of the delay times is short, QoE will be able to maintain a high value. Furthermore, in the case of a sound delay, no significant changes with respect to a constant delay were seen. As for the standard deviation, in contrast to a constant delay, we confirmed that the standard deviation would spread out as the delay time increased, even with a video delay. In the case of a sound delay, the spreading out of the standard deviation is more pronounced for a random delay than for a constant delay. From the above, we found that increasing the number of delays presented and more closely approximating the state of using a network causes the determination of quality by users to deviate even further.

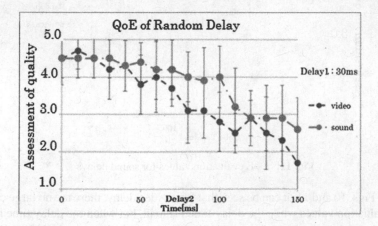

Fig. 9. QoE measurement results with random delay (Delay 1 = 30 ms)

3.4.2 QoE Measurement with Random Delay (Delay 1 = 30 Ms)

Compared to the case when the value of Delay 1 was fixed at 0 ms, the evaluation of random video delays results in low overall values, and this can be seen in Fig. 9. Accordingly, for similar random delays, it is thought that the evaluation values will be lower when the longer delay time is longer.

This result also shows that, for a video delay, people are able to discriminate time differences when the time difference is about 30 ms.

Additionally, Figs. 10 and 11 show the results of Figs. 7 through 9 compiled into graphs for video delays and sound delays, respectively.

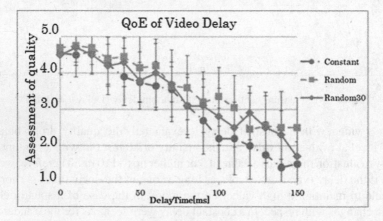

Fig. 10. QoE evaluation values with video delays

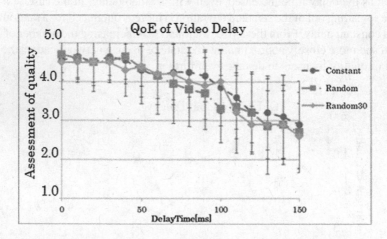

Fig. 11. QoE evaluation values for sound delays

From Figs. 10 and 11, it can be seen that for a video delay, there are no large changes in the evaluation values while the delay time is small, but when the delay time reaches about 80 ms, most evaluation values are in agreement with Constant Delay < Random

Delay (Delay 1 = 30 ms) < Random Delay (Delay 1 = 0 ms). For sound delays, no large change in QoE was observed for either constant delays or random delays.

4 Concluding Remarks

In this study, it can be seen that the number of users who feel a difference in the program begins to increase when, due to delays, the haptic–visual data time difference begins to exceed 10 ms or the haptic–auditory data time difference begins to exceed 40 ms. Visual sense is said to have a greater impact than auditory sense, and that statement is consistent with these findings. Moreover, for visual sense, there exists research showing that people begin to sense network latency when the delay reaches approximately 30 ms, and this is consistent with the finding that 50 % of the test subjects began to feel a difference at this level.

When a video with a constant delay is evaluated, the quality drops below the "normal" level at evaluation value 3 in the vicinity of 80 ms, but with a random de-lay, the quality evaluation maintains a value of 3 or higher up to 110 ms. Therefore, we found that even if the delay time is not stable, as long as one of the delay times is short, QoE will be able to maintain a high value. Furthermore, in the case of a sound delay, no significant changes with respect to a constant delay were seen. As for the standard deviation, in contrast to a constant delay, we confirmed that the standard deviation would spread out as the delay time increased, even with a video delay. In the case of a sound delay, the spreading out of the standard deviation is more pronounced for a random delay than for a constant delay. From the above, we found that increasing the number of delays presented and more closely approximating the state of using a network causes the determination of quality by users to deviate even further.

This result also shows that, for a video delay, people are able to discriminate time differences when the time difference is about 30 ms.

It can be seen that for a video delay, there are no large changes in the evaluation values while the delay time is small, but when the delay time reaches about 80 ms, most evaluation values are in agreement with Constant Delay < Random Delay (De-lay 1 = 30 ms) < Random Delay (Delay 1 = 0 ms). For sound delays, no large change in QoE was observed for either constant delays or random delays.

Acknowledgements. This work was supported by JSPS KAKENHI Grant Number 25350369.

References

1. Ohnishi, H., Mochizuki, K.: Effect of delay of feedback force on perception of elastic force: a psychophysical approach. IEICE Trans. Commun. **E90-B**(1), 12–20 (2007)
2. Ishihara, M.: On first impression of the teaching materials which used haptic display. IEEE J. Trans. Fundam. Mater. **129**(7), 490–491 (2009). (in Japanese)
3. Ishihara, M.: Haptic device using a soldering test system. In: Tino, A., Stephanidis, C. (eds.) HCII 2015 Posters. CCIS, vol. 528, pp. 190–195. Springer, Heidelberg (2015). doi: 10.1007/978-3-319-21380-4_34

4. Hirose, M., et al.: Virtual Reality, Sangyo Tosho (1993) (in Japanese)
5. Yoshida, T., Muranaka, N., Imanishi, S.: A construction of educational application system for calligrapy master based on virtual reality. IEEE J. Trans. Electron. Inf. Syst. **117-C**(11), 1629–1634 (1997). (in Japanese)
6. Yoshida, T., Yamamoto, T., Imanishi, S.: A calligraphy mastering support system using virtual reality technology and its learning effects. IEEE J. Trans. Fundam. Mater. **123-A**(12), 1206–1216 (2003). (in Japanese)
7. Henmi, K., Yoshikawa, T.: Virtual lesson and its application to virtual calligraphy system. TVRSJ **3**(1), 13–19 (1983). (in Japanese)
8. Sakuma, M., Masamori, S., Harada, T., Hirata,Y., Satou, M.: A Remote Lesson System for Japanese Calligraphy using SPIDAR, IEICE of Jpn., Technical Report, MVE99–52, pp. 27–32, Oct. 1999 (in Japanese)
9. Otsuka, G., Sodeyama, G., Muranaka, N., Imanishi, S.: A construction of a piano training system based on virtual reality. IEEE of J. Trans. Electron. Inf. Syst. **116-C**(11), 1288–1294 (1996). (in Japanese)
10. Yamaguchi, Y., Kitamura, Y., Kishino, F.: Analysis of learning process of virtual chopsticks. IEICE of Jpn., Technical Report, MVE2001-3, pp. 11–16, June 2001 (in Japanese)
11. Ishihara, M.: Empirical study regarding representing roughness with haptic devices. In: Proceedings of 2013 IEEE 2nd GCCE, pp. 471–473, Chiba, Japan, Oct. 2013
12. Sithu, M., Ishibashi, Y., Fukushima, N.: Effects of dynamic local lag control on sound synchronization and interactivity in joint musical performance. ITE Trans. Media Technol. Appl. **2**(4), 299–309 (2014)
13. Ishihara, M., Komori, T.: Characteristic evaluation of the audio and visual system of haptic device. In: Proceedings of 2014 IEEE 3nd GCCE, CFP14GCB-USB, pp. 356–357, Chiba, Japan, Oct. 2014
14. Ishihara, M., Negishi, N.: Effect of feedback force delays on the operation of haptic displays. IEEJ Trans. Electr. Electron. Eng. **3**(1), 151–153 (2008)

Exploring Behavioral Methods to Reduce Visually Induced Motion Sickness in Virtual Environments

Behrang Keshavarz[✉]

Toronto Rehabilitation Institute – University Health Network, Toronto, Canada
behrang.keshavarz@uhn.ca

Abstract. The use of Virtual Environments (VE) is continuously growing and is becoming more important for research, rehabilitation, and entertainment. Unfortunately, visually induced motion sickness (VIMS) is still a major issue and a common side-effect of VEs. The symptom cluster of VIMS is multifaceted and can include oculomotor issues, fatigue, disorientation, dizziness, and/or nausea. Over the past decades, several different remedies for VIMS have been introduced and tested with mixed results. The present paper will summarize some of the most promising countermeasures, with a particular focus on behavioral techniques. This will include a discussion of adaptation and training, postural stability, and factors that make a VE experience more pleasant. Despite the existence and the success of some of these methods, it is highly desirable to continue exploring techniques that will ultimately guarantee the well-being and safety of VE users in the future.

Keywords: Simulator sickness · Motion sickness · Vection · Prevention · Countermeasures · Sensory conflict · Postural stability

1 Introduction

Visually induced motion sickness (VIMS) is a specific form of traditional motion sickness and can occur in users of Virtual Environments (VEs), such as in driving or flight simulators or during video games (see [1], for an overview). Typical symptoms can range from pallor, fatigue, cold sweat, and oculomotor issues to disorientation, dizziness, nausea, and/or vomiting. In contrast to traditional motion sickness, physical movement is often absent or limited during VIMS, instead, symptoms are typically caused by visual stimulation.

The genesis of VIMS is not fully understood yet and several different theories try to explain this sensation. Two of the most prominent theories of VIMS involve sensory conflict and the role of postural control. The *sensory conflict theory* [2, 3] proposes that VIMS is caused by a mismatch between or within the visual, vestibular, and somatosensory senses. In other words, VIMS arises in situations when the information delivered by these senses is not in accordance with each other. In the case of VEs, the visual stimulation can—if it is compelling enough—generate the sensation of self-motion (so-called vection; for overviews see [4, 5]), although the VE user typically remains stationary. In contrast, the vestibular and somatosensory senses signal stasis, resulting

© Springer International Publishing Switzerland 2016
S. Lackey and R. Shumaker (Eds.): VAMR 2016, LNCS 9740, pp. 147–155, 2016.
DOI: 10.1007/978-3-319-39907-2_14

in a visual-vestibular/somatosensory conflict. According to the sensory conflict theory, this mismatch can result in VIMS if it is novel to the user and successful coping or adaptation strategies have not yet been established by the organism. In contrast, the *postural instability hypothesis* [6, 7] proposes that VIMS occurs in situations in which the ability to control ones posture is challenged and/or reduced. That is, visual stimulation in VEs can cause changes in postural sway (defined as small involuntary displacements of the body) which in turn has been shown to be linked to VIMS. For instance, Stoffregen and colleagues [8] have observed changes in postural sway in participants who later reported to be motion sick. However, both the sensory conflict theory and the postural instability theory have their strengths and weaknesses (see [1], for a discussion) and a final evaluation is, at this stage, not possible.

Despite the lack of theoretical understanding of VIMS as a whole, it is highly desirable to develop successful countermeasures to prevent (or at least minimize) VIMS. The prevalence of VIMS has been estimated to range from 5 % to 60 % of VE users [9], depending on the setup of the VE system and the task that is used. Given that VE systems are now easily accessible to everyone (e.g., through affordable head-mounted devices such as Oculus Rift, Google Cardboard, HTC Vive etc.) and are becoming more and more popular, even a small fraction of the above mentioned estimations might result in a substantial number of users who are at risk of suffering from VIMS. From a marketing point of view, this number is doubtlessly troublesome, as it might hamper the acceptance of VE systems at large. But more importantly, VE systems are not only used for entertainment purposes, but are gaining more importance in the context of rehabilitation and research. For instance, driving simulators are a highly valuable and commonly used tool to train and assess driving performance following serious illness or injuries (e.g., stroke, traumatic brain injury etc.), as these patient populations cannot be safely trained and tested with real on-road driving. Therefore, it is not tolerable that the application and success of driving simulators is jeopardized by the occurrence of VIMS.

In the past, a variety of techniques trying to reduce VIMS has been introduced (for overviews see [1, 10]). In the following sections, I will summarize some of these techniques, with a particular focus on *behavioral methods* that I have personally used to counteract VIMS. To begin with, however, I will briefly discuss the use of anti-motion sickness medication (and explain why they are not useful with respect to VIMS), before I will continue with a description of selected behavioral methods to reduce VIMS. Note that the present paper is not meant to be an exhaustive review of all existing countermeasures, but rather it focuses on those techniques that showed promising results within my own realm of research.

2   Medication and Naturopathic Approaches

Medical countermeasures are often the method of choice to cope with traditional motion sickness when travelling. Anti-sickness drugs are often available over-the-counter and typically offer rapid relief. Various drugs have been previously tested, including antihistamines (e.g., meclozine, cyclizine) and anti-cholinergics (e.g., scopolamine) (see [11, 12], for overviews). Although these drugs have been shown to successfully reduce traditional motion sickness and can also provide relief from VIMS to some extent [3, 13], most of these medications can lead to serious side-effects such as dizziness, fatigue, or impaired cognitive functions. Consequently, the applicability of medical drugs with respect to VIMS is highly limited. Drowsiness, for instance, may be a tolerable side-effect for passengers of long overnight flights, but not so for the pilots who are being trained in a flight simulator and for whom unimpaired mental capacities are a necessity. In most cases when VEs are used, the side-effects related with anti-sickness medication are unacceptable, making these drugs impractical for VEs.

In addition to classic anti-sickness medications, several ingestible, inhalable, or alternative medical approaches not classified as drugs have been investigated to counteract traditional motion sickness and VIMS. For instance, ginger is frequently referred to as being an effective anti-motion sickness agent and companies promise relief from VIMS after the intake of ginger-based pills. However, evidence for the efficacy of ginger during controlled experimentation is limited and the few studies that have been conducted revealed mixed findings [14, 15].

3   Behavioral Countermeasures

To prevent the undesirable side-effects caused by anti-sickness medications, a variety of behavioral countermeasures against VIMS has been introduced in the past. Among others, technical modifications can reduce the risk of VIMS, such as reducing the visual field-of-view [16, 17], minimizing the time-lag between actions performed in the VE and the visual and/or motion responses [18, 19], or reducing the use of Head Mounted Displays [20]. However, some of these modifications are not feasible. Reducing the field-of-view, for example, might be a reasonable solution at home (i.e., moving farther away from the TV or computer screen), but it is not an acceptable solution for driving or flight simulators that aim to provide an immersive virtual experience and want to create a strong sense of presence or vection. Consequently, other behavioral countermeasures that do not interfere with the technical aspects and the VE experience are needed. Some promising techniques have been already explored and will be discussed next.

3.1   Adaptation and Training

One of the most efficient techniques to minimize and prevent VIMS is arguably *adaptation*. As mentioned earlier, the sensory conflict theory of motion sickness proposes that VIMS is not only rooted in a sensory conflict, but rather occurs when the organism has not yet established coping strategies to deal with these sensory incongruences. Consequently, repeated exposure to the same stimulus that initially caused VIMS in the first place should result in reduced VIMS after a while. Indeed, several studies found that adaptation is a successful mechanism to minimize VIMS [21–23]. For instance, Hill and Howarth [24] had their participants play a 20-min video game over the course of five consecutive days and measured sickness severity. VIMS significantly decreased after each gaming session and was reduced to a minimum after the 5th experimental day. Although repeated exposure has been shown to be successful in preventing VIMS, it can be time-consuming, resource-intensive, and requires a high amount of dedication. Consequently, adaptation might not always be feasible as the method of choice to cope with VIMS despite its success.

Another coping strategy could potentially be *training*. As noted above, adaptation typically requires repeated exposure to the exact same nauseating stimulus to allow the organism to successfully adapt over time. Training, in contrast, does not underlie this restriction; a separate, different (and probably less complex) VE setup could be used to train VE users to cope with VIMS before they are exposed to the actual task-relevant VE. Supporting evidence for this assumption was found in one of my recent studies (in preparation), where a link between video game experience and VIMS was discovered. In that study, participants were asked to perform a simulated driving task using a commercial console video game on a large projection screen. None of the participants was familiar with the video game that was used. Interestingly, those participants who at least sometimes played video games at home (irrespective of the type of game), reported less sickness compared to those who never played video games at all (see [25] for similar findings). This suggests that video game experience might have a protective effect on the occurrence of VIMS and, consequently, that video games could be used as a training tool to reduce it. However, further systematic experimentation is needed to further elaborate on this initial finding.

3.2 Supporting Postural Stability

According to the postural instability theory of motion sickness [6], VIMS is not caused by a sensory conflict per se, but is primarily elicited in situations that challenge maintaining one's postural stability (with postural stability defined as minimizing uncontrolled body movements). Previous studies have shown that changes in postural stability (i.e., decreased or increased postural sway) are associated with or even precede VIMS [8, 26]. Consequently, increasing postural stability should result in a reduction of VIMS. In fact, several studies investigated the efficacy of passive restraint against VIMS (e.g., by fixating the participants' bodies to a rigid surface), unfortunately with mixed results [27–29]. In a study that demonstrated a positive effect of passive restraint, Chang et al. [30] asked standing participants to play a console video game that generated VIMS. Half of the participants were passively restrained using elastic straps, whereas the other half was not restrained and stood freely during gameplay. Results showed that those participants who were passively restrained reported significantly less VIMS compared to the unrestrained participants. Recently, Keshavarz et al. [31] exposed younger and older participants to a driving video game for 25 min in two test sessions. In one session, participants' torso and head were restricted to a back- and headrest using elastic straps. In the other session, participants were not restrained and the back- and headrest were removed. VIMS was continuously recorded in both tests sessions. An overall difference between the unrestrained and restrained condition did not emerge, however, some participants indeed benefited from passive restrained. That is, older adults who became sick when playing the driving game without restraint, reported less VIMS when their bodies were fixated with the straps. Interestingly, this effect was only observed in the older adults, who are known to have generally reduced postural stability due to age-related changes, but it did not show for younger adults. Thus, passive restraint can—under certain circumstances and in certain populations—indeed minimize VIMS. Nevertheless, note that passive restraint might bear issues that might limit its applicability, such as fostering anxiety in some users. Also, active and unrestricted movement can be essential for some VE applications and therefore preventing such movements is not an option.

3.3 Promoting a Pleasant Ambience

In a set of multiple studies, [32–34] demonstrated that VIMS can be successfully reduced by pleasant music, pleasant odors, and constant airflow. In all of these studies, participants were exposed to a 15 min long video on a large screen showing a bicycle ride that was shot from a first-person point of view. While watching the video, participants were continuously monitored and reported their level of VIMS using the Fast Motion Sickness Scale, a verbal self-rating scale particularly designed to measure VIMS [35].

In the first of the three studies [32], participants were randomly assigned to four groups: the first group was provided with relaxing music while watching the video, the second group listened to neutral pop music, the third group to stressful music, and the fourth group was not provided with any music. After stimulus presentation, participants were asked to rate the pleasantness of the music that they were exposed to. Results showed that music that was perceived as pleasant—regardless whether the music was of relaxing, neutral, or stressful nature—successfully alleviated VIMS. In other words, participants who perceived the music as being pleasant reported less VIMS compared to the control group and to the groups who rated the music as unpleasant. Currently, a follow-up study is being conducted to further investigate the mechanisms underlying this effect, aiming to determine the role of the music's valence and arousal level with respect to reducing VIMS (in preparation). In contrast to pleasant music, background sound matching the visual scene (i.e., street noise produced by pedestrians or cars) does typically not reduce VIMS [36, 37].

In the second study [33], two different odors (leather as aversive scent and rose as pleasing scent) were chosen and provided to the participant while they watched the same video of the bicycle ride. Similar results compared to the music study mentioned above were found. Again, the odor that was perceived as pleasant (regardless of whether it was leather or rose) significantly reduced VIMS, whereas the unpleasant odor did not affect the level of VIMS.

Finally, in the third study [34], one group of participants was provided with constant airflow that was produced by two stationary fans that were positioned alongside the large projection screen while being exposed to the bicycle video. A second group acted as control group and did not receive airflow. Results showed that the group that was provided with airflow reported significantly less VIMS compared to the control group, suggesting that keeping a laboratory air-conditioned and providing sufficient airflow can be an effective, simple, and affordable way to minimize VIMS.

In a nutshell, all treatments used in the three studies reduced VIMS to a similar extent. However, the reason for the positive effect of pleasant music, pleasant odors, and airflow remains speculative, as none of the current theories of VIMS can sufficiently explain why and how VIMS should be reduced by these countermeasures. Distraction might come to mind first, but if pure distraction was the key, then music and odors in general should reduce VIMS, and not only music and odors that were perceived as pleasant. An alternative explanation could be that creating a pleasant ambience might interfere and conflict with the negative sensation of VIMS, which in turn might not allow VIMS to fully unfold. If this is the case, other methods that further facilitate the pleasantness of the VE ambience should have similar (or even enhancing) effects.

3.4   Alternative Potential Remedies

Gaze stabilization. Adding a stable fixation point to the center of the visual screen has been demonstrated to reduce VIMS [38, 39]. In fact, developers of commercial video games now sometimes superimpose a small transparent circle on top of the visual screen to reduce VIMS (e.g., *Mirror's Edge* by EA Digital Illusions Creative Entertainment, see http://www.engadget.com/2008/07/17/how-mirrors-edge-fights-simulation-sickness/). This is particularly helpful in games that involve rapid and abrupt virtual camera turns (e.g., as in first-person shooting games). However, a fixation point might be an acceptable solution for video games that are designed to entertain, but it might not be for applications that are used for training, rehabilitation, and research purposes. For instance, simulated driving studies often measure natural gaze behavior using eye-tracking and a fixation point is not tolerable in this case.

Vestibular/Motion Cues. It has been noted in the past literature that providing vestibular cues in addition to visual stimulation should reduce VIMS by reducing a potential visual-vestibular conflict [40]. Unfortunately, the situation is more complex and adding vestibular/motion cues is per se not a guarantee that VIMS will diminish. As motion cues provided by any simulator are by definition not a perfect replica of real-world motion (e.g., due to limitations in motion range or due to imperfect motion algorithms), adding motion cues alone is not sufficient to decrease VIMS. Keshavarz et al. [41] recorded VIMS ratings for older and younger adults who performed a simulated driving task. Participants were assigned to two separate groups: in the first group, a fixed-base driving simulator with only visual cues was used (240° horizontal and 110° vertical curved field-of-view), whereas in the second group additional motion cues were provided (using a 6 degrees-of-freedom hexapod motion platform). Interestingly, VIMS did not significantly differ between the two groups.

In contrast, Bos [42] demonstrated that high-frequent vibration cues can reduce motion sickness. The author positioned blindfolded participants on a rotating chair and asked them to perform head movements while being rotated, a procedure known to quickly and reliably induce motion sickness. During chair rotation, participants were provided with high-frequent vibration to the head. As a result, head vibration reduced motion sickness severity by 25 %, potentially by adding noise to the vestibular system which reduced the sensory conflict. Following up on this finding, D'Amour et al. [34] tested vibration to the seat as a remedy against VIMS. While watching a VIMS-inducing video, one group of participants was provided with high-frequent seat vibration generated by a vibrating device that was attached to the bottom of the chair, whereas another group received no treatment. Although seat vibration reduced VIMS by approximately 35 %, the reduction of VIMS missed statistical significance. Nevertheless, it seems promising to further investigate the effect of vibration as a potential countermeasure against VIMS.

4   Conclusion

Visually induced motion sickness is a serious issue for the design and the use of virtual environments. To date, reliable techniques that can fully prevent VIMS are unfortunately missing, but several behavioral methods have emerged over the last decades that showed promising results. Adaptation is so far the arguably most reliable method to reduce VIMS, but it is often not feasible due to time and budget restrictions. Passively supporting postural stability can be effective for some people, but its application can be limited in some cases. Creating a pleasant ambience, on the other hand, is simple, affordable, and easily applicable, however, its reliability to reduce VIMS in different VE settings and scenarios is yet to be proven.

The decision which method is the most appropriate one to counteract VIMS should be made on a case-by-case basis, taking into account several different factors. For instance, the intended application of the VE often dictates which countermeasure is useful and which is not. In other words, some techniques such as introducing a fixation point or reducing the field-of-view can be proper methods to alleviate VIMS for video games and other entertainment devices, but they might not be in the context of research or rehabilitation. Other factors that should be taken into account often involve the available budget (e.g., is adaptation affordable?) or the targeted population (e.g., postural stability might be more effective for older users).

In sum, the technological progress over the last decades has yielded new and innovative VE trends, however, VIMS is still an issue that has not been fully solved. Optimizing existing techniques as well as exploring new options should be future goals to prevent VIMS and ultimately guarantee the well-being and safety of VE users.

References

1. Keshavarz, B., Hecht, H., Lawson, B.D.: Visually induced motion sickness: Characteristics, causes, and countermeasures. In: Hale, K.S., Stanney, K.M. (eds.) Handbook of Virtual Environments: Design, Implementation, and Applications, pp. 648–697. CRC Press, Boca Raton, FL (2014)
2. Oman, C.M.: Motion sickness: a synthesis and evaluation of the sensory conflict theory. Can. J. Physiol. Pharmacol. **68**, 294–303 (1990)
3. Reason, J.T., Brand, J.J.: Motion Sickness. Academic Press, New York (1975)
4. Hettinger, L.J., Schmidt, T., Jones, D.L., Keshavarz, B.: Illusory self-motion in virtual environments. In: Hale, K.S., Stanney, K.M. (eds.) Handbook of Virtual Environments: Design, Implementation, and Applications, pp. 435–466. CRC Press (2014)
5. Keshavarz, B., Riecke, B.E., Hettinger, L.J., Campos, J.L.: Vection and visually induced motion sickness: how are they related? Front Psychol. **6**, 472 (2015)

6. Riccio, G.E., Stoffregen, T.A.: An ecological theory of motion sickness and postural instability. Ecol. Psychol. **3**, 195–240 (1991)
7. Stoffregen, T.A., Riccio, G.E.: An ecological critique of the sensory conflict theory of motion sickness. Ecol. Psychol. **3**, 159–194 (1991)
8. Smart Jr, L.J., Stoffregen, T.A., Bardy, B.G.: Visually induced motion sickness predicted by postural instability. Hum. Factors **44**, 451–465 (2002)
9. Kennedy, R.S., Drexler, J., Kennedy, R.C.: Research in visually induced motion sickness. Appl. Ergon. **41**, 494–503 (2010)
10. Golding, J.F., Gresty, M.A.: Pathophysiology and treatment of motion sickness. Curr. Opin. Neurol. **28**, 83–88 (2015)
11. Sherman, C.R.: Motion sickness: review of causes and preventive strategies. J. Travel Med. **9**, 251–256 (2002)
12. Shupak, A., Gordon, C.R.: Motion sickness: advances in pathogenesis, prediction, prevention, and treatment. Aviat. Space Environ. Med. **77**, 1213–1223 (2006)
13. Regan, E.C., Ramsey, A.D.: The efficacy of hyoscine hydrobromide in reducing side-effects induced during immersion in virtual reality. Aviat. Space Environ. Med. **67**, 222–226 (1996)
14. Estrada, A., LeDuc, P.A., Curry, I.P., Phelps, S.E., Fuller, D.R.: Airsickness prevention in helicopter passengers. Aviat. Space Environ. Med. **78**, 408–413 (2007)
15. Lien, H.-C., Sun, W.M., Chen, Y.-H., Kim, H., Hasler, W., Owyang, C.: Effects of ginger on motion sickness and gastric slow-wave dysrhythmias induced by circular vection. Am. J. Physiol. Gastrointest. Liver Physiol. **284**, G481–G489 (2003)
16. Bos, J.E., de Vries, S.C., van Emmerik, M.L., Groen, E.L.: The effect of internal and external fields of view on visually induced motion sickness. Appl. Ergon. **41**, 516–521 (2010)
17. Keshavarz, B., Hecht, H., Zschutschke, L.: Intra-visual conflict in visually induced motion sickness. Displays **32**, 181–188 (2011)
18. Akizuki, H., Uno, A., Arai, K., Morioka, S., Ohyama, S., Nishiike, S., Tamura, K., Takeda, N.: Effects of immersion in virtual reality on postural control. Neurosci. Lett. **379**, 23–26 (2005)
19. Draper, M.H., Viirre, E.S., Furness, T.A., Gawron, V.J.: Effects of image scale and system time delay on simulator sickness within head-coupled virtual environments. Hum. Factors J. Hum. Factors Ergon Soc. **43**, 129–146 (2001)
20. Patterson, R., Winterbottom, M.D., Pierce, B.J.: Perceptual issues in the use of head-mounted visual displays. Hum. Factors **48**, 555–573 (2006)
21. Cheung, B., Hofer, K.: Desensitization to strong vestibular stimuli improves tolerance to simulated aircraft motion. Aviat. Space Environ. Med. **76**, 1099–1104 (2005)
22. Domeyer, J.E., Cassavaugh, N.D., Backs, R.W.: The use of adaptation to reduce simulator sickness in driving assessment and research. Accid. Anal. Prev. **53**, 127–132 (2013)
23. Hu, S.Q., Stern, R.M., Koch, K.L.: Effects of pre-exposures to a rotating optokinetic drum on adaptation to motion sickness. Aviat. Space Environ. Med. **62**, 53–56 (1991)
24. Hill, K., Howarth, P.: Habituation to the side effects of immersion in a virtual environment. Displays **21**, 25–30 (2000)
25. Ujike, H., Ukai, K., Nihei, K.: Survey on motion sickness-like symptoms provoked by viewing a video movie during junior high school class. Displays **29**, 81–89 (2008)
26. Stoffregen, T.A., Faugloire, E., Yoshida, K., Flanagan, M.B., Merhi, O.: Motion sickness and postural sway in console video games. Hum. Factors J. Hum. Factors Ergon. Soc. **50**, 322–331 (2008)
27. Bonnet, C.T., Faugloire, E., Riley, M.A., Bardy, B.G., Stoffregen, T.A.: Motion sickness preceded by unstable displacements of the center of pressure. Hum. Mov. Sci. **25**, 800–820 (2006)

28. Lackner, J.R., DiZio, P.: Decreased susceptibility to motion sickness during exposure to visual inversion in microgravity. Aviat. Space Environ. Med. **62**, 206–211 (1991)
29. Mills, K.L., Griffin, M.J.: Effect of seating, vision and direction of horizontal oscillation on motion sickness. Aviat. Space Environ. Med. **71**, 996–1002 (2000)
30. Chang, C.-H., Pan, W.-W., Chen, F.-C., Stoffregen, T.A.: Console video games, postural activity, and motion sickness during passive restraint. Exp. Brain Res. **229**, 235–242 (2013)
31. Keshavarz, B., Novak, A.C., Hettinger, L.J., Stoffregen, T.A., Campos, J.L.: The role of age and postural stability for visually induced motion sickness in a simulated driving task. Proc. Hum. Factors Ergon. Soc. Annu. Meet. 59, 770–770 (2015)
32. Keshavarz, B., Hecht, H.: Pleasant music as a countermeasure against visually induced motion sickness. Appl. Ergon. **45**, 521–527 (2014)
33. Keshavarz, B., Stelzmann, D., Paillard, A., Hecht, H.: Visually induced motion sickness can be alleviated by pleasant odors. Exp. Brain Res. **233**, 1353–1364 (2015)
34. D'Amour, S., Campos, J.L., Keshavarz, B.: The efficacy of airflow and seat vibration on reducing visually induced motion sickness. In: Lake Ontario Visionary Conference (L.O.V.E.), Niagara Falls, ON (2016)
35. Keshavarz, B., Hecht, H.: Validating an efficient method to quantify motion sickness. Hum. Factors J. Hum. Factors Ergon. Soc. **53**, 415–426 (2011)
36. Keshavarz, B., Hecht, H.: Stereoscopic viewing enhances visually induced motion sickness but sound does not. Presence **21**, 213–228 (2012)
37. Keshavarz, B., Hecht, H.: Visually induced motion sickness and presence in videogames: The role of sound. Proc. Hum. Factors Ergon Soc. Annu. Meet. **56**, 1763–1767 (2012)
38. Webb, N.A., Griffin, M.J.: Optokinetic stimuli: motion sickness, visual acuity, and eye movements. Aviat. Space Environ. Med. **73**, 351–358 (2002)
39. Yang, J.X., Guo, C.T., So, R.H.Y., Cheung, R.T.F.: Effects of eye fixation on visually induced motion sickness are they caused by changes in retinal slip velocity? proc. Hum. Factors Ergon. Soc. Annu. Meet. **55**, 1220–1224 (2011)
40. Curry, R., Artz, B., Cathey, L., Grant, P., Greenberg, J.: Kennedy SSQ results: fixed vs. motion-base ford simulators. In: Proceedings of the Driving Simulation Conference Europe 2002, pp. 289–300 (2002)
41. Keshavarz, B., Ramkhalawansingh, R., Haycock, B., Shahab, S., Campos, J.L.: The role of multisensory inputs on simulator sickness in younger and older adults during a simulated driving task. In: Proceedings of the Driving Simulation Conference Europe 2015, Tuebingen, Germany, pp. 239–240 (2015)
42. Bos, J.E.: Less sickness with more motion and/or mental distraction. J. Vestib. Res. Equilib. Orientat. **25**, 23–33 (2015)

Assessment of Kim's Game Strategy for Behavior Cue Detection: Engagement, Flow, & Performance Aspects

Crystal S. Maraj[1](✉), Stephanie J. Lackey[2],
Karla A. Badillo-Urquiola[1], and Irwin L. Hudson[3]

[1] Institute for Simulation and Training,
University of Central Florida, Orlando, FL, USA
{cmaraj,kbadillo}@ist.ucf.edu
[2] Design Interactive, Orlando, FL, USA
stephanie.lackey@designinteractive.net
[3] US Army Research Laboratory, Orlando, FL, USA
irwin.hudson@us.army.mil

Abstract. Psychological constructs, such as engagement and flow, can be used to determine an individual's involvement in a task and predict levels of performance during Simulation-Based Training (SBT) in military operations. This experiment used a virtual form of Kim's game (an observational training game that includes memorization of objects and later recall), to improve pattern recognition and behavior cue detection, during SBT. The purpose of this experiment was to assess participant engagement and flow between two conditions, Kim's game vs. the control. Seventy-five participants were randomly assigned to either condition, and completed a pre-test, training vignette, post-test, and multiple questionnaires which assessed the individuals' levels of engagement and flow. Experimental results show the control group reported higher levels of both engagement and flow in all subscales, and flow as a higher predictor of performance than engagement. This paper examines plausible explanations why the engagement questionnaire did not assess differences in performance. The lack of statistically significant findings may be a result of the engagement survey questions and the type of task (i.e., discrete or continuous). Finally, this paper provides future recommendations for examining the role of engagement and flow for simulation-based behavior cue detection training.

Keywords: Education · Training · Military · Behavior cue detection · Pattern recognition · Engagement · Flow

1 Introduction

Simulation-Based Training (SBT) supports specialized training and adaptability by employing simulated platforms [1]. Allowing a shift in "higher-order skills" (e.g., coordination and decision-making), SBT fills the gap between traditional, classroom-based learning and live training scenarios. Behavior cue detection is a central application of SBT in pattern recognition training, especially in the Military training

S. Lackey and R. Shumaker (Eds.): VAMR 2016, LNCS 9740, pp. 156–163, 2016.
DOI: 10.1007/978-3-319-39907-2_15

domain. Pattern recognition gives the ability to assess human behavior in complex combative environments by early identification of threatening actions via visual processing. This is achieved by a combination of bottom-up and top-down processing [2]. The bottom up process includes gathering pieces of information to create generalizations without previous knowledge on the subject, while the top-down process is taking the big picture and breaking it down to smaller pieces.

Current literature regarding pattern recognition training in the military reference techniques that may be inadequate for advancing threat detection skills in warfighters (i.e., fingerprint matching, facial and handwriting recognition, speech detection). According to Fischer and Geiwetz [3], there is no formal training for detecting patterns in Soldiers' environments, and most of their pattern recognition skills are due to years of field experience. A study regarding pattern recognition training, determined that soldiers who received formal training performed better than those trained in the traditional classroom [3].

Both the Marine Corps and the Army have developed training curriculums to improve soldiers' pattern recognition through observational games, as well as routine observations and reports [4, 5]. One of the observational training games used, Kim's game, calls for the individual to memorize several objects in an organized manner for recall at a later time (Sniper Sustainment Training, n.d.). Kim's game has been found to improve improvisation skills, responsiveness, and analytic thought process [6]. It allows individuals' to better their memory, and increase change blindness and change detection awareness. The utilization of Kim's game may help train Soldiers in behavior cue detection, as it enhances the skills necessary to observe an environment more critically, memorize rapidly, and deepen descriptive skills.

Two metrics that assists SBT experimentation include Engagement Measure and Flow State Short Scale. Engagement determines how involved a participant is in the task, as well as facilitates cognitive processes, achievement, higher order perceptual skills [7–9] and training transfer [10]. The point in which a participant becomes unaware of their surroundings is defined as Flow [11]. According to Csikszentmihalyi [12], high Flow scores should correlate with high performance level. The purpose of this experiment was to assess participant engagement and flow for a signal detection task amongst a Kim's game group and a control group.

2   Methods

2.1   Participants

There was a total of 75 (n = 37) participants, comprised of 41 females and 34 males. The Kim's game group had 36 participants, while the control group had 39. Restrictions for participation consisted of US citizenship and an age restriction of 18 to 40 years ($M = 22.72$, $SD = 3.75$). Participants were required to have normal or corrected to normal vision and were administered the Ishihara Colorblindness test. The constraints on visual ability were due to the critical involvement of discerning visual stimuli in the experimental task. Compensation for participation consisted of either a monetary reward ($10/hour) or class credit.

2.2   Experimental Design

This experiment followed a between-subjects design with two conditions, the control and the instructional strategy Kim's game. The dependent variables consisted of the Engagement, Flow, and performance measurements as the dependent variables.

2.3   Measures

Engagement. Charlton and Danforth's [13] engagement measure asks questions on how involved the participant felt (e.g., "I sometimes found myself to become so involved with the scenarios that I wanted to speak to the scenarios directly"). The measure has a total of seven questions rated on a scale from 1 (strongly disagree) to 5 (strongly agree).

Flow.   Flow was assessed using Jackson, Martin, and Eklund's [11] questionnaire, measuring the level of the participant's mental state during the task. A sample question from this measure is, "I was completely focused on the task at hand." Answers to each question were rated using a 1 (strongly disagree) to 5 (strongly agree) scale.

Post-test Detection Accuracy Scores.   Detection accuracy scores were calculated as a percentage based on the number of targets stimuli correctly identified within the vignette. The ratio was determined by the number of correctly identified targets divided by the total number of targets within each vignette.

Post-test False Positive Detection.   False positive detection identified a non-target model depicting a target behavior cue. Identification of false positive non-target cues and model types were calculated to determine any correlations between cue or model type and false positive detection.

Post-test Response.   Time Response time was determined by the amount of time a participant reacts to an event that appears on the screen, either clicking the target to detect a match or selecting the no change icon to indicate no match. The time was measured in seconds.

2.4   Experimental Testbed

Virtual Battlespace 2 (VBS2) was used as the experimental testbed. The experiment was conducted using a standard desktop computer with a 22-inch display monitor. For this experiment, there were four target cues (i.e., slap hands, clenched fists, wring hands, and check six) and four non-target cues (i.e., idle talking, check watch, cross arms, rub neck). Table 1 provides the descriptions of the behavior cues, as well as the corresponding classification for each of the target cues. All eight cues were modeled using 3D models of various skin tones.

Table 1. Target and non-target behavioral cues. Adapted from Salcedo [14].

	Kinesic behavior cue	Description	Classification
Target	Slap Hands	The back of one hand strikes the palm of the other hand.	Aggressiveness
	Clench Fists	Fingers are curled and squeezed into the palms.	Aggressiveness
	Wring Hands	Fingers and palm of one hand clasp the opposite hand and rub along the fingers.	Nervousness
	Check Six	The head turns to look over the shoulder followed by the body turning around 180°.	Nervousness
Non-Target	Idle Talking	Conversational behavior indicated by subtle hand and arm gestures.	N/A
	Check "watch"	Head angles down and one arm is raised slightly as if checking the time on a watch.	
	Cross Arms	Arms are bent at the elbows and overlap each other across the front of the body.	
	Rub Neck	Palm and fingers of one hand rubs the side of the neck.	

2.5   Procedure

Upon arriving, participants were randomly assigned to either the control or Kim's game condition. The experimenter and participant signed an informed consent describing the voluntary nature of the experiment and procedures. The experimenter proceeded by obtaining pre-experimental information from the participant, and by administering the Ishihara Test for Color Blindness [15]. Participants who failed were subject to dismissal; otherwise the experiment continued. After a demographics questionnaire was completed by the participant, an interface training lesson provided the user a chance to become familiar with the navigation and detection controls expected in the following scenarios.

Participants completed an interface training which required a passing score of over 75 %. Once completed they filled out a pre-test that gauged the user's initial ability to detect the target kinesic cues (i.e., nervousness and aggressiveness). A second interface training followed, this allowed users to note the color change, if any, among a group of barrels.

After training participants were given a five-minute break, followed by kinesic cue training slides which demonstrated the aggressive and nervous behaviors (e.g., clench fists classified as aggressive, wringing hands as nervous) via model icons. Proceeding a second break, a 17-minute practice vignette was delivered asking participants to identify any changes in the models (e.g., a change from a non-target cue behavior to a target cue behavior). Upon completion, the Engagement Measure and Flow State Short Scale were administered. After a final break, the last interface training was provided for the post-test scenario, followed by a 40-minute long post-test scenario. The experiment concluded with a debriefing, then participants were dismissed.

3 Results

A one-way between-groups ANOVA was conducted. No statistically significant difference in Engagement between Kim's game and the control groups. Another one-way between-groups ANOVA was conducted in order to determine the difference in Flow between Kim's game and the control group. It was found that the Acton Awareness Merging subscale was significant between Kim's game and the Control groups F (1, 73) = 4.92, p = .03, and participants in the control group (M = 3.44, SD = 1.10) reported higher Action Awareness Merging than the Kim's game group (M = 2.89, SD = 1.04). There was also a significant difference between the two groups in the Clear Goals subscale F (1, 73) = 4.11, p = .05. The control group (M = 4.08, SD = .70) had a higher understanding of the Clear Goals than the Kim's game group (M = 3.75, SD = .69). Finally, a significant difference was also found in Transformation of Time F (1, 73) = 6.28, p = .01, and was reported higher in the control (M = 3.69, SD = 1.00) than in Kim's game (M = 3.06, SD = 1.09) (Table 2).

Table 2. ANOVA's for flow between Kim's game and control groups

Flow	Kim's game group		Control group				
	M	SD	M	SD	$F(1, 73)$	p	η^2
Action Awareness Merging	2.89	1.04	3.44	1.10	4.92	.03*	.063
Clear Goals	3.75	.69	4.08	.70	4.11	.05*	.053
Transformation of Time	3.06	1.19	3.69	1.00	6.28	.01*	.079

*p < .05

Correlational data showed a weak, positive correlation between the Engagement survey for Total Engagement (r = .23), More time in the Virtual Environment (r = .28), Buzz of Excitement (r = .24), and post-test detection accuracy (Table 3).

Table 3. Correlation between Engagement and Post-Test Performance

Engagement	Post-test detection	Post-test false positive detection
Total	.23*	−.24*
More Time VE	.28*	−.21*
Buzz of Excitement	.24*	−.25*

*Correlation is significant at the 0.05 level (2-tailed)

There were also weak, negative correlations between the Engagement survey for Total Engagement (r = 1.24), Buzz of Excitement (r = −.25), and false positive detection. A moderate, positive correlation was found between Flow subscale Concentration Task at Hand and post-test detection accuracy, but all of the other subscales had no significant correlations.

Finally, neither Engagement nor Flow was found to be a statistically significant predictor of post-test performance. However, the results indicated that Flow had the largest contribution to post-test performance. More specifically, Concentration Task at Hand contributed largely to post-test detection accuracy, and Clear Goals to post-test false positive detection.

4 Discussion

Even though there were no significant results from the Engagement survey to explain practice performance or the post-test results, participants in both the Kim's game and control groups reported feeling some level of engagement. This could be due to the fact that the questionnaire focused more on engagement levels felt in relation to the VE, and less on the individual's perception of the engagement level. Another possibility is that the survey itself may not have been the most appropriate measure for the task at hand.

The weak, positive relationship between Engagement and post-test detection accuracy and also between More Time in the VE and post-test detection accuracy could be due to the fact that participants felt more comfortable with the task the more time that they spent in the VE, which resulted in higher levels of engagement and better performance. The weak, negative relationship between Total Engagement and false positive detection could be attributed to the fact that the more engaged a participant was, the more they were able to pay attention and had fewer false positives. Finally, the negative correlation between Buzz of Excitement and false positive detection could be due to practice in previous tasks during the experiment, which increased their confidence and led to fewer mistakes.

Participants in the control group reported higher levels in all the subscales of Flow (i.e., Action Awareness Merging, Clear Goals, and Transformation of time) than participants in the Kim's game group after completing the practice scenario. This could be due to the practice scenario test, as the control group received an uninterrupted, continuous series of events, while individuals in the Kim's game group received a more discrete task. This could have affected time perception, as the Control group received a more 'seamless' task, and could lead to losing track of time. The moderate, positive relationship between Concentration at Task and post-test detection accuracy may be explained by the idea that as the individuals concentrate on the task, the detection accuracy is greater. These results are also supported by the multiple linear regression conducted, as Concentration at Task was reportedly the largest contributor to post-test detection accuracy.

The control group also had shorter response times than the Kim's game group, which indicates the control group felt a higher level of flow during the post-test. This could be due to a lack of flash recognition within the Kim's game group, which is a technique used to improve visual memory recall [16]. In order for the brain to store visual information for later recall, it needs to quickly and accurately process incoming stimuli [17]. The length of the flashing time affects an individual's ability to recall information [18]. The Kim's game group received visual stimuli at a faster rate than the control group, which could attribute to these results.

5   Limitations

One limitation found in this experiment was the Engagement survey. Upon observing the results, it was concluded that the survey may not be an appropriate measurement for this task. The scale may need to be redesigned for future experiments to account for the lack of "sensitivity" it has for assessing performance of behavior cue detection.

6   Conclusion

Overall, the control group seemed to have higher reported levels of Engagement and Flow across all subscales. It is possible that the control group felt more comfortable as they received more repetition of the same practice, instead of a new task like the Kim's game group. Perhaps designing a new Engagement survey, or including physiological measures in future studies would yield different results.

Acknowledgements.   This research was sponsored by the U.S. Army Research Laboratory – Human Research Engineering Directorate Advanced Training & Simulation Division (ARL HRED ATSD), in collaboration with the Institute for Simulation and Training at the University of Central Florida. This work is supported in part by ARL HRED STTC contract W911NF-14-2-0021. The views and conclusions contained in this document are those of the authors and should not be interpreted as representing the official policies, either expressed or implied, of ARL HRED STTC or the U.S. Government. The U.S. Government is authorized to reproduce and distribute reprints for Government.

References

1. Martin, Hughes, C.E., Schatz, S., Nicholson, D.: The use of functional L-systems for scenario generation in serious games. In: Proceedings of the Workshop on Procedural Content Generation in Games (No. 6). ACM, New York (2010)
2. Connor, C.E., Egeth, H.E., Yantis, S.: Visual attention: bottom-up versus top-down. Curr. Biol. **14**(19) (2004)
3. Fischer, S.C., Geiwetz, J.: Training Strategies for Tactical Pattern Recognition. United States Army Research Institute for the Behavioral and Social Sciences, Alexandria (1996)
4. Robert, S., Baden-Powell, S.S.: Scouting Games. vol. 4. The Scout Library (1921)
5. Sniper Sustainment Training. (n.d.). Retrieved from Chapter 9
6. U.S. Army. Sniper Training. Washington, D.C.: Field Manual No. 23-10 (1994)
7. Brandimonte, M.A., Passolunghi, M.C.: The effect of cue-familiarity, cue-distinctiveness, and retention interval on prospective remembering. Q. J. Exp. Psychol. Hum. Exp. Psychol. **47**, 565–588 (1994)
8. Antonacci, D., Modaress, N.: Second life: the educational possibilities of a massively multiplayer virtual world. In: Proceedings of the EDUCASE Southwest Regional Conference, Austin, Texas (2005)
9. Lee, V.E., Smith, J.B.: Effects of high school restructuring and size on early gains in achievement and engagement. Sociol. Educ. **68**, 241–270 (1995)
10. Baddeley, A.: Working Memory. Science **255**, 556–559 (1992)

11. Jackson, S.A., Martin, A.J., Eklund, R.C.: Long and short measures of flow: The construct validity of the FSS-2, DFS-2, and new brief counterparts. J. Sport Exerc. Psychol. **30**(5), 561–587 (2008)

12. Csikszentmihalyi, M.: The flow experience and its significance for human psychology in optimal experience. pp. 15–35. Cambridge University Press, Cambridge (1988)

13. Charlton, J., Danforth, I.: Distinguishing addiction and high engagement in the context of online game playing. Comput. Hum. Behav. **23**(3), 1531–1548 (2005)

14. Salcedo, J.: Instructional Strategies for Scenario-Based Training of Human Behavior Cue Detection and Classification with Robot-Aided Intelligence, Surveillance, and Reconnaissance. Doctoral Dissertation, Orlando, Fl, U.S.A. (2014)

15. Ishihara, S.: Ishihara's Tests for Color Deficiency. Kanehara Trading, Tokyo (2013)

16. Godnig, E.C.: The Tachistoscope Its History & Uses. J. Behav. Optom. **14**, 39–42 (2003)

17. LaBerge, D., Samuels, S.J.: Toward a theory of automatic information processing in reading. Cogn. Psychol. **6**, 293–323 (1974)

18. Soule, R.L.: Flash recognition training in law enforcement work-next exposure ready now. J. Crim. Law Criminol. Police Sci. **49**, 590 (1958)

Olfactory Stimuli Increase Presence During Simulated Exposure

Benson G. Munyan[✉], Sandra M. Neer, Deborah C. Beidel,
and Florian Jentsch

University of Central Florida, Orlando, FL, USA
benson.munyan@knights.ucf.edu

Abstract. Exposure therapy (EXP) is an extensively studied and supported treatment for anxiety and trauma-related disorders. EXP works by exposing the patient to the feared object or situation in the absence of danger in order to overcome the related anxiety. Various technologies including head-mounted displays (HMDs), scent machines, and headphones have been used to augment the exposure therapy process by presenting multi-sensory cues (e.g., sights, smells, sounds) to increase the patient's sense of presence. Studies have shown that scents can elicit emotionally charged memories, but no prior research could be identified that examined the effect of olfactory stimuli upon the patient's sense of presence during simulated exposure tasks. **Methods:** 60 adult participants navigated a mildly anxiety-producing virtual environment (VE) similar to those used in the treatment of anxiety disorders. Participants were screened for olfactory dysfunction and history of seizures. Participants completed questionnaires pertaining to their (a) tendency to immerse themselves in activities and (b) current health. Visual exploration and presence ratings were collected throughout the experiment. **Results:** Linear Mixed Modeling showed statistically significant relationships between olfactory stimuli and presence as assessed by both the In group Presence Questionnaire (IPQ: $R2 = .85$, $(F(3,52) = 6.625$, $p = .0007)$ and a single item visual-analogue scale ($R2 = .85$, $(F(3,52) = 5.382$, $p = .0027)$.

Keywords: Exposure therapy · Presence · Augmented reality · Olfaction · Immersion

1 Introduction

Presence, when used to describe immersive feelings in virtual reality (VR), has been conceptualized and defined in different ways (for a review, see Lombard & Ditton1). Presence is most often described from the concept of transportation2, that is to say, people are usually considered "present" when they feel as if they are actually in the virtual world. Creative methods utilized for the purposes of increasing presence in virtual reality may include the use of tactile feedback, surround or 3D sound, and head mounted displays (HMDs) with high visual fidelity.

One benefit of elevated levels of presence is that when asked to recall, users remember the environment as if it was a real place instead of a simulated location [2]. Similarly, VR environments may produce the same emotions and physical reactions as

© Springer International Publishing Switzerland 2016
S. Lackey and R. Shumaker (Eds.): VAMR 2016, LNCS 9740, pp. 164–172, 2016.
DOI: 10.1007/978-3-319-39907-2_16

their real-world counterparts when the level of presence experienced by the user is sufficiently high [1]. The ability to evoke similar emotions and physical reactions is particularly useful for clinical applications. For example, Hodges et al. [3] found that participants with clinical diagnoses of acrophobia reported increased anxiety when presented VR that included great heights. This ability to evoke real emotions from artificial environments has presumably led to the use of VR for the treatment of numerous anxiety disorders [4–6], as well as PTSD [7–10].

Exposure therapy (EXP) is a treatment that involves repeated presentations of feared situations or stimuli to overcome the patient's anxiety. For example, those who are fearful of dogs can eliminate their fear by repeated exposures to dogs in which the feared outcome (being bitten, for example) does not occur. Gradually, the anxiety of being around dogs will decrease and the patient learns that not all dogs are dangerous. This decrease is called habituation [11], and is analogous in humans to extinction models used in animals [12]. When conducting exposure therapy, multiple cues associated with the feared situations or stimuli are often incorporated to enhance extinction [13–15].

It is generally believed that the more senses are utilized by a medium, the greater its ability to generate a sense of presence [16–20]. In fact, many studies have examined the effect of screen size [21–24], sound [15], and multi-speaker systems [19] on presence. Tactile stimuli also increase presence [25], and have been used in the treatment of combat-related PTSD [26, 27]. It has also been suggested that olfactory delivery systems be introduced to VR [28]. Given the substantial research supporting the relationship between olfaction and strong emotional memory [29–33], it seems logical to explore the effect of olfaction on presence during virtual-reality assisted exposure therapy, as virtual reality is increasingly utilized and has been shown to be efficacious in the treatment of anxiety and trauma-related disorders [34–37].

However, the utility of olfactory stimuli (OS) to increase presence during simulated exposure therapy tasks is not yet known. In this investigation, we examined whether OS were associated with changes in presence within a virtual environment. We hypothesized that participants would experience higher levels of presence when engaged in VE's while receiving OS.

2 Methods

2.1 Sample

The sample consisted of 60 participants between the ages of 18 and 31 years of age ($M = 20.48$, $SD = 3.13$). Sixty-five percent (65 %) were male ($n = 39$), while ethnicity varied, including 38 Caucasians, 11 Hispanics, 6 African Americans, 2 Asians, and 3 who identified as Other (e.g., of mixed ethnic background). To be included in the study, participants were required to achieve a passing score on a brief test of olfactory function (see below). A history of seizures, epilepsy, or current prescriptions for beta-blocking or anxiety medications excluded individual participants from participating in the study.

2.2   Assessment Instruments

The Quick Smell Identification Test (QSIT; Sensonics, Inc., Haddon Heights, NJ) is a three-item multiple-choice test consisting of three microencapsulated odorant strips. The QSIT has been shown to be highly reliable over time ($r = 0.87$) and highly sensitive to identifying olfactory loss, particularly in those with severe olfactory deficits [38].

. The Igroup Presence Questionnaire (IPQ) [39] is a 14-item self-report questionnaire designed to measure presence utilizing a 7-point Likert scale that loads onto three subscales; spatial presence (the sense of physically being in the VE), involvement (focus on the VE and involvement experienced), and experienced realism (subjective realism of the VE).

To determine presence during the experiment, participants were asked to rate their immersion on a visual-analogue scale (VAS). VASs have moderate to strong correlations with Likert based items [40]. VASs have superior metrical characteristics than discrete scales and can have a wider range of statistical methods applied to their measurements [41].

Participants were asked after scripted events to rate their presence during the exposure task. This rating was on a 7-point Likert scale to remain consistent with the Likert scale of the IPQ. The question, "How present do you feel?" was anchored at one (not at all) and seven (very much) prior to the start of each trial.

The Simulator Sickness Questionnaire (SSQ) [42] is a 16-item self-report scale used to rate common symptoms of simulator sickness on a 4-point scale. Such symptoms include general discomfort, headache, eyestrain, sweating, and vertigo. The SSQ was used for pre- and post-experimental assessment to assess symptoms commonly associated with VR use.

Visual Scanning (VS) was assessed as a behavioral index of presence as first hypothesized by Sheridan [43]. To assess VS, hidden "triggers" were anchored to the virtual avatar. When the participant explored the VE by turning their head or virtual body, a virtual beam swept across the trigger, resulting in a numerical score.

2.3   Procedure

Following consent, participants were asked to complete self-report measures (described above). Upon completion, each participant was assisted with the virtual reality equipment and encouraged to explore a virtual room in order to familiarize him/herself with the virtual reality controls and head mounted display (HMD). After a ten-minute familiarization period, participants were provided instructions regarding the upcoming task. Once questions had been addressed, the first exposure trial began. Participants were instructed to report problematic symptoms of simulator sickness at any point while in the VE.

During Trial 1 (T1), 50 % ($n = 30$) of participants received OS congruent with the VE; the other half of participants received no OS. After completion of T1, participants removed the HMD and headphones for a ten minute reset period, during which they completed additional self-report measures for T1. After the reset period concluded, experiment instructions were reiterated and Trial 2 (T2) began. During T2, 50 %

($n = 30$) of the sample reversed olfactory condition, while the remaining participants remained in their T1 condition, meaning they either continued receiving scents, or they again received no scents. Upon completion of T2, participants completed self-report measures for T2, at which point their participation in the study concluded.

2.4 Virtual Reality System

The OS were ceramic pellets impregnated with scented oil (Dreamreapers Inc., Melrose Park, IL) consistent with the scent of smoke, garbage, cotton candy, and popcorn. Stimuli were delivered via air dispersion by a USB controlled Scent Palette (Virtually Better Inc., Decatur, GA).

The VE was modeled in 3D and controlled with the Unity3D engine (Unity Technologies, San Francisco, CA) and approximated an abandoned carnival at night. Participants were asked to imagine that they had lost their keys within the carnival, and were directed to retrieve them. The VE was presented to the subject using the Oculus Development Kit II HMD (Oculus VR, Irvine, CA) and high-fidelity stereo headphones (Audio Technica ATH-M50x; Audio Technica, Stow, Ohio). The VE was generated by a PC with an Intel® i5-4670 3.4ghz CPU, 16 gigabytes of RAM, and an Nvidia® GTX 780 Ti GPU. Participants navigated through the environment at their own pace and had full control over their movement utilizing a wireless Xbox 360 controller (Microsoft Inc., Redmond, WA). The participant had access to a virtual flashlight allowing them to explore any unlighted areas should they choose to examine the VE in greater depth. Participants were guided through the VE via location-based prerecorded narration. Congruent ambient sounds accompanied the visuals of the VE. At various locations within the VE, scripted events were presented to add realism to the VE. For example, an audio sample of an unseen object bumping into a metal garbage can was played as the participant passed a 3D garbage can. For those in the OS condition, this was augmented with the smell of garbage.

3 Results

3.1 Data Screening

Of 122 adults recruited via community announcements and the University of Central Florida, 62 were not included in the final analyses. Reasons include simulator sickness and discontinuation ($n = 18$), subthreshold ability to smell ($n = 5$), technical malfunctions ($n = 38$) and noncompliance with the experimental task ($n = 1$). Chi-squares and ANOVAs were conducted to determine if those excluded from the final sample were different proportionally to those included. No significant differences were found with the exception of gender; females were more likely to report their desire to discontinue or suffer from simulator sickness than males ($p = 0.012$).

Jackknife distance measures were calculated to identify multivariate outliers utilizing the critical value formula recommended in Penny [44]. Seven such outliers were identified, but demonstrated a negligible effect on p-values. These outliers did not possess enough influence to alter the significance of any analyses. Thus, the outliers were included in the final sample.

3.2   Statistical Analyses

All analyses were conducted on the final sample of 60 participants using JMP Pro 11.2.0 (SAS Institute Inc., Cary NC) after screening for data normalcy. All analyses defined significance utilizing a p-value of < 0.05.

3.3   Presence Ratings

Linear Mixed Model (LMM) analyses were utilized to assess change between trials for continuous outcome variables and within- and between-subject effects. Group membership served as a between-subjects effect, while trial and sex was assigned as within-subjects factors. IPQ scores were examined utilizing LMM predicted by sex, trial, gender, and group. There was a significant main effect for trial, $R^2 = .85$, ($F(1,52) = 6.3669$, $p = .0147$) and the group*trial interaction, $R^2 = .85$, ($F(3,52) = 6.625$, $p = .0007$). With regard to the main effect for trial, participants felt significantly more present during T1 than T2 ($LSM_{T1}=61.68$ & $LSM_{T2}=59.26$). With regard to the interaction, the Scent-No Scent (S-NS) group showed a disproportionate decrease in presence in T2 compared to other groups, while the No Scent-Scent (NS-S) group reported an increase in presence. This increase and decrease in presence (respectively) indicated that participants felt more presence when OS were present. The control groups maintained relative stability across trials, as the Scent-Scent (S-S) group on average declined by just over a single point (1.37, $LSM_{T1}=60.37$ & $LSM_{T2}=59.00$) while the No Scent-No Scent (NS-NS) group declined less than one point (.7, $LSM_{T1}=57.44$ & $LSM_{T2}=56.74$).

Examination of the VAS showed a significant main effect for trial, $R^2 = .81$, ($F(1,52) = 7.955$, $p = .0068$), also indicating that participants felt more present during T1 ($LSM_{T1}=73.48$ & $LSM_{T2}=67.25$). The group*trial interaction, $R^2 = .85$, ($F(3,52) = 5.382$, $p = .0027$) showed a disproportionate decrease in presence between T1 and T2 ($LSM_{T1}=79.43$ & $LSM_{T2}=61.32$) in the S-NS group compared to other groups. The NS-S group saw a gain in VAS scores during T2 ($LSM_{T1}=74.81$ & $LSM_{T2}=79.74$) which suggests that introducing OS increased perceived presence, even after one trial experienced within the VE.

3.4   Discussion

The purpose of this study was to explore the effect of OS on presence during a simulated exposure task. Results indicated across two separate measures (IPQ & VAS) that OS positively influenced the amount of perceived presence when administered, and that perceived presence decreased when OS were withheld. This finding supports our original hypothesis, and suggests that (a) the addition of scents may increase presence for participants during an exposure task, and (b) the removal of scents, once presented, likely results in a reduction of presence. These findings are very important, as EXP is enhanced when the number of cues utilized increases [13–15]. The inclusion of scents not only increases the number of cues, but may also increase the degree to which patients "buy in" to treatment, which is important because treatment credibility has been shown to increase treatment initiation [45].

One potential benefit of including OS may be increased generalization post-treatment. For example, in combat-related PTSD the scent of smoke may serve as a specific trigger. While traditional EXP may effectively reduce physiological reactivity in a patient with PTSD, the inclusion of smoke during EXP may allow broader generalization. Without scents included, everyday activities like camping or cooking may remain avoided at greater frequency than if congruent scents (e.g. smoke) had been included during the treatment. Conversely, it may be that scents affect the therapeutic process by facilitating memory recall of otherwise difficult-to-remember situations [46]. These results indicate that OS are not a detriment to presence and as such, the use of OS during EXP for disorders like PTSD or specific phobias should be considered. However, it appears that OS should not be discontinued once the user has experienced them due to reductions in reported presence. Additionally, OS may assist with treatment acceptability or in other words, patient "buy in" as anecdotal accounts of OS's effectiveness has already been described in the memory literature [47].

A last consideration that came from this study is the strong correlation between IPQ and VAS scores. This finding may indicate that simple scales can accurately assess presence, which may be beneficial for researchers who need less disruptive ways to assess momentary presence as interrupting tasks to assess presence can actually diminish presence.

4 Limitations

This study has several limitations. First and foremost, this experiment was conducted with participants who were not inherently anxious about the VE being presented. For example, our participants did not possess fears specific to the VE that would have been present in a clinical population, such as warfighters who have experienced combat. Future research may wish to utilize a clinical population. For example, soldiers or veterans in a convoy VE may better illustrate the influence of scents (e.g., diesel fuel or exhaust) on presence.

Our groups were also not optimally balanced for gender, due to gender differences in experiencing simulator sickness [48]. Women were much more likely to voice their desire to discontinue. After careful deliberation, the decision was made to recruit males only due to disproportionate attrition.

Overall, this study demonstrates the potential of olfactory stimuli used in exposure therapy, and indicates that OS may be effective in increasing presence during scenarios similar to those used in EXP. The score patterns for the reversal groups (S-NS & NS-S) trended in the hypothesized directions. If OS directly increases presence during individual sessions of EXP, the effect on treatment outcome must also be examined. Given the escalating patient care costs of anxiety disorders, the utilization of scents may positively impact treatment efficacy, through increased patient acceptability or greater habituation in-session. More research in this area is required.

Acknowledgements. This research was supported by a Grant-In-Aid of Research from Sigma Xi, The Scientific Research Society. We wish to thank Fallen Planet Studios for VE consulting and creation.

Author disclosure statements.

No competing financial interests exist.

References

1. Lombard, M., Ditton, T.: At the heart of it all: The concept of presence. J. Comput. Mediated Commun. 3 (1997)
2. Slater, M., Pertaub, D.P., Steed, A.: Public speaking in virtual reality: Facing an audience of avatars. IEEE Comput. Graph. Appl. **19**, 6–9 (1999)
3. Hodges, L.F., Kooper, R., Meyer, T.C., De Graaff, J.J.H., Rothbaum, B.O., Opdyke, D., Williford, J.S., North, M.M.: Presence as the defining factor in a VR application (1994)
4. Parsons, T.D., Rizzo, A.A.: Affective outcomes of virtual reality exposure therapy for anxiety and specific phobias: a meta-analysis. J. Behav. Ther. Exp. Psychiatry **39**, 250–261 (2008)
5. Owens, M.E.: Does virtual reality elicit physiological arousal in social anxiety disorder. In: Psychology. University of Central Florida (2013)
6. Powers, M.B., Emmelkamp, P.M.G.: Virtual reality exposure therapy for anxiety disorders: A meta-analysis. J. Anxiety Disord. **22**, 561–569 (2008)
7. Rothbaum, B.O., Hodges, L.F., Ready, D., Graap, K., Alarcon, R.D.: Virtual reality exposure ther-apy for Vietnam veterans with posttraumatic stress disorder. J. Clin. Psychiatry **62**, 617–622 (2001)
8. Rothbaum, B.O., Hodges, L., Alarcon, R., Ready, D., Shahar, F., Graap, K., Pair, J., Hebert, P., Gotz, D., Wills, B.: Virtual reality exposure therapy for PTSD Vietnam veterans: A case study. J. Trauma. Stress **12**, 263–271 (1999)
9. Difede, J., Hoffman, H.G.: Virtual reality exposure therapy for World Trade Center post-traumatic stress disorder: A case report. Cyberpsychology Behav. **5**, 529–535 (2002)
10. Mclay, R.N., Wood, D.P., Webb-Murphy, J.A., Spira, J.L., Wiederhold, M.D., Pyne, J.M., Wiederhold, B.K.: A randomized, controlled trial of virtual reality-graded exposure therapy for post-traumatic stress disorder in active duty service members with combat-related post-traumatic stress disorder. Cyberpsychology Behav. Soc. Netw. **14**, 223–229 (2011)
11. Butler, A.C., Chapman, J.E., Forman, E.M., Beck, A.T.: The empirical status of cognitive-behavioral therapy: a review of meta-analyses. Clin. Psychol. Rev. **26**, 17–31 (2006)
12. Myers, K.M., Davis, M.: Mechanisms of fear extinction. Mol. Psychiatry **12**, 120–150 (2007)
13. Rescorla, R.A.: Extinction can be enhanced by a concurrent excitor. J. Exp. Psychol. Anim. Behav. Processes **26**, 251–260 (2000)
14. Thomas, B.L., Ayres, J.J.B.: Use of the ABA fear renewal paradigm to assess the effects of ex-tinction with co-present fear inhibitors or excitors: Implications for theories of extinction and for treating human fears and phobias. Learn. Motiv. **35**, 22–52 (2004)
15. Rescorla, R.A.: Deepened extinction from compound stimulus presentation. J. Exp. Psychol. Anim. Behav. Processes **32**, 135–144 (2006)
16. Anderson, D.B., Casey, M.A.: The sound dimension. IEEE Spectr. **34**, 46–51 (1997)
17. Barfield, W., Zeltzer, D., Sheridan, T., Slater, M.: Virtual Environments and A dvanced Interface Design Virtual Environments and Advanced Interface Design, pp. 473–513. Oxford University Press, New York (1995)
18. Kim, T.: Effects of presence on memory and persuasion. University of North Carolina: Chapel Hill, NC (1996)

19. Short, J., Williams, E., Christie, B.: The social psychology of telecommunications. Wiley, New York (1976)
20. Bouchard, S., Côté, S., St-Jacques, J., Robillard, G., Renaud, P.: Effectiveness of virtual reality exposure in the treatment of arachnophobia using 3D games. Technol. Health Care **14**, 19–27 (2006)
21. Welch, R.B., Blackmon, T.T., Liu, A., Mellers, B.A., Stark, L.W.: The effects of pictorial realism, delay of visual feedback, and observer interactivity on the subjective sense of presence. Presence Teleoperators Virtual Environ. **5**, 263–273 (1996)
22. Hendrix, C., Barfield, W.: Presence within virtual environments as a function of visual display parameters. Presence Teleoperators Virtual Environ. **5**, 274–289 (1996)
23. Freeman, J., Lessiter, J., Pugh, K., Keogh, E.: When presence and emotion are related, and when they are not. In: Paper presented at the 8th Annual International Workshop on Presence (2005)
24. Ijsselsteijn, W., De, Ridder H., Freeman, J., Avons, S.E., Bouwhuis, D.: Effects of stereoscopic presentation, image motion, and screen size on subjective and objective corroborative measures of presence. Presence Teleoperators Virtual Environ. **10**, 298–311 (2001)
25. Hoffman, H.G., Hollander, A., Schroder, K., Rousseau, S., Furness, T.: Physically touching and tasting virtual objects enhances the realism of virtual experiences. Virtual Reality **3**, 226–234 (1998)
26. Rizzo, A.A., Graap, K., Perlman, K., Mclay, R.N., Rothbaum, B.O., Reger, G., Parsons, T., Difede, J., Pair, J.: Virtual Iraq: Initial results from a VR exposure therapy application for combat-related PTSD. Stud. Health Technol. Inform. **132**, 420–425 (2008)
27. Rizzo, A.S., Difede, J., Rothbaum, B.O., Reger, G., Spitalnick, J., Cukor, J., Mclay, R.: Development and early evaluation of the Virtual Iraq/Afghanistan exposure therapy system for combat-related PTSD. Annal. NY Acad. Sci. **1208**, 114–125 (2010)
28. Chen, Y.: Olfactory display: development and application in virtual reality therapy. In: Paper Presented at the 16th International Conference on Artificial Reality and Telexistence (2006)
29. Herz, R.S., Engen, T.: Odor memory: Review and analysis. Psychon. Bull. Rev. **3**, 300–313 (1996)
30. Herz, R.S., Cupchik, G.C.: The emotional distinctiveness of odor-evoked memories. Chem. Senses **20**, 517–528 (1995)
31. Herz, R.S.: Are odors the best cues to memory? a cross-modal comparison of associative memory stimulia. Ann. NY Acad. Sci. **855**, 670 (1998)
32. Chu, S., Downes, J.J.: Proust nose best: Odors are better cues of autobiographical memory. Memory Cogn. **30**, 511–518 (2002)
33. Chu, S., Downes, J.: Odour-evoked autobiographical memories: Psychological investigations of proustian phenomena. Chem. Senses **25**, 111–116 (2000)
34. Powers, M.B., Emmelkamp, P.M.: Virtual reality exposure therapy for anxiety disorders: A meta-analysis. J. Anxiety Disord. **22**, 561–569 (2008)
35. Reger, G.M., Holloway, K.M., Candy, C., Rothbaum, B.O., Difede, J., Rizzo, A.A., Gahm, G.A.: Ef-fectiveness of virtual reality exposure therapy for active duty soldiers in a military mental health clinic. J. Trauma. Stress **24**, 93–96 (2011)
36. Gahm, G., Reger, G., Ingram, M.V., Reger, M., Rizzo, A.: A Multisite, Randomized Clinical Trial of Virtual Reality and Prolonged Exposure Therapy for Active Duty Soldiers with PTSD. DTIC Document (2015)
37. Opriş, D., Pintea, S., García-Palacios, A., Botella, C., Szamosközi, Ş., David, D.: Virtual reality exposure therapy in anxiety disorders: a quantitative meta-analysis. Depression Anxiety **29**, 85–93 (2012)

38. Jackman, A.H., Doty, R.L.: Utility of a Three-Item Smell Identification Test in Detecting Olfactory Dysfunction. Laryngoscope **115**, 2209–2212 (2005)
39. Schubert, T., Friedmann, F., Regenbrecht, H.: The Experience of Presence: Factor Analytic In-sights. Presence Teleoperators Virtual Environ. **10**, 266–281 (2001)
40. Hasson, D., Arnetz, B.B.: Validation and Findings Comparing VAS vs. likert Scales for Psychosocial Measurements. Int. Electron. J. Health Educ. **8**, 178–192 (2005)
41. Reips, U.D., Funke, F.: Interval-level measurement with visual analogue scales in Internet-based research: VAS Generator. Behav. Res. Methods **40**, 699–704 (2008)
42. Kennedy, R.S., Lane, N.E., Berbaum, K.S., Lilienthal, M.G.: Simulator sickness questionnaire: An enhanced method for quantifying simulator sickness. Int. J. Aviat. Psychol. **3**, 203–220 (1993)
43. Sheridan, T.B.: Musings on telepresence and virtual presence. Presence Teleoperators virtual Environ. **1**, 120–126 (1992)
44. Penny, K.I.: Appropriate critical values when testing for a single multivariate outlier by using the Mahalanobis distance. Appl. Stat. J. Royal Stat. Soc. Ser. C **45**, 73–81 (1996)
45. Spoont, M.R., Nelson, D.B., Murdoch, M., Rector, T., Sayer, N.A., Nugent, S., Westermeyer, J.: Im-pact of Treatment Beliefs and Social Network Encouragement on Initiation of Care by VA Service Users With PTSD. Psychiatr. Serv. **65**, 654–662 (2014)
46. Herz, R.S.: Scents of time. Sciences **40**, 34 (2000)
47. Vermetten, E., Bremner, J.D.: Olfaction as a traumatic reminder in posttraumatic stress disorder: case reports and review. J. Clin. Psychiatry **64**, 202–207 (2003)
48. Kolasinski, E.M.: Simulator Sickness in Virtual Environments. U.S. Army Research Institute (1995)

Depth Perception in Virtual Environment: The Effects of Immersive System and Freedom of Movement

Adrian K.T. Ng[✉], Leith K.Y. Chan, and Henry Y.K. Lau

Department of Industrial and Manufacturing Systems Engineering,
The University of Hong Kong, Hong Kong, China
{adriang,lkychan,hyklau}@hku.hk

Abstract. Concerns over the use of virtual reality (VR) systems in experimental psychological research exist. It is found that human egocentric depth perception in a virtual environment (VE) has significant errors compared to real physical environment. It is hypothesized that due to the presence of a human body as a size reference in a mixed reality CAVE-like system, the accuracy of depth estimation will improve. The second hypothesis proposes that when a participant is allowed to move around the VE, motion parallax will supplement the depth perception ability. Results showed that the features of an immersive system did not aid the estimation. Around 40 % underestimation of actual distance was observed above 15 m. By using a 3D-military jet instead of 2D-wall as the judgment object, a significant improvement in the accuracy is found. Pictorial cues were hence, suggested as the improvement basis for next part of the study.

Keywords: Depth perception · Distance estimation · imseCAVE · Perception · Virtual environment · Virtual reality

1 Introduction

The basic elements of virtual reality (VR) systems as defined by Burdea and Coiffet, "Immersion-Interaction-Imagination" (I^3) [1], are well developed as the technology of computer graphics and 3D displays advances. For example, at the Department of Industrial and Manufacturing Systems Engineering at the University of Hong Kong, an immersive, interactive VR system was developed called the imseCAVE based on the concept of the Cave Automatic Virtual Environment (CAVE™) [2]. The system with its automatic trackers and 3D image rendering can provide physical immersion projection to users. As for mental immersion, the success of such immersion depends on the design of the contents and the involvement of the users [3]. With the hardware and software readied, interaction and imagination in a virtual environment (VE) are endless upon creation of applications. MagicPad and MagicPen, build on top of imseCAVE, is a pen and paper like tangible user interface that allows users to interact and create things in VE, for example, drawing 2D and 3D objects, and playing physics game [4].

With the basic elements of immersive systems developed, many researches have started to look at practical applications of VR. In Psychology, VR tools have been used more frequently in psychological experiments and clinical applications for its ability to

© Springer International Publishing Switzerland 2016
S. Lackey and R. Shumaker (Eds.): VAMR 2016, LNCS 9740, pp. 173–183, 2016.
DOI: 10.1007/978-3-319-39907-2_17

present stimulus in environment with greater control over the variables [5]. For example, psychologists used VE to test the likelihood for people to help under different situations [6]. Variables of virtual bystanders and the virtual person that need helps can be experimentally manipulated easily. The bystander effect, a sophisticated high-level social behavior, is observed. VE is in fact, a useful interface compromising between experimental control and ecological validity. In Cognitive Science, VE technology could also be viewed as a unique asset, which provides the possibility of creating and presenting dynamic objects and environments for precise measurement of human cognition and interaction [7].

1.1   Depth Perception Error and Its Importance

Despite the usefulness of VR, some raised concerns over the use of VR systems as the tool in experimental psychological research. Increased attention had been brought to the aspect of human spatial perception. It is found that egocentric depth estimation (i.e. subjective distance perception to an object from the human subject) in VE have lower accuracy compare to real physical environment [8, 9].

Such error is worth investigating as depth perception is an important visual component for perceiving objects, navigating, reaching, and performing size judgments, to name but a few [10]. For experimental researchers, it is important to ensure that the VR systems could be used as an experimental tool in all aspects without any other adjustment. A useful experimental environment should provide an accurate measurement while containing minimum cues. In the above case, a VE should provide viewer an accurate depth perception, the ability to perceive object in three dimensions and the distance of the object; while containing minimum visual depth cues — anchors that assists perception [11].

If such error between VE and real environment differs significantly, researches may not be confident in using VE for many types of cognitive experiments, in particular those that require many spatial awareness, such as way-finding and visual perception. Researches may then investigate on the effects related to their particular cognitive aspect and whether there are any alleviation or improvement possible related to those kinds of cognition.

For Cognitive Scientists, such error is also worth investigating as such error maybe due to a different pathway of cognitive processes in human brain being simulated by VE, different from normal environment. The findings may help improve our understanding on cognition.

From Industrial Engineering (IE) perspective, simulation and visualization are the major uses of VR systems. For example, a container terminal quay crane simulation system in the imseCAVE allows users to simulate loading and unloading of containers [2]. It requires users' depth estimation to complete the tasks. Although previous literatures have not suggested any user-experience problem in simulation and visualization in VE reported attributes to the perception error, the user experience may still be able to improve if such error is improved or eliminated. Users will not know it is a problem until the error is adjusted and that they can compare the difference. To improve in the system perspective, the design of VE content and rendering matrix of VR software could be adjusted to be more effective and accurate [12].

The direction of the research is to explore the effects and possible improvements to the accuracy of human egocentric depth perception under CAVE-like immersive system in experimental psychology and IE perspective.

2 Background and Related Works

2.1 Overview

Since there are quite a number of previous researches on depth perception, Lin and Woldegiorgis, and Renner et al. carried out a comprehensive literature review respectively [8, 9]. Their analysis reveals that while egocentric distance estimation in real world is about 94 % accurate, it drops to around 80 % in VE on average, i.e. a 20 % underestimation or compression.

2.2 Comparing Immersive System with Other VR Systems

Although it is shown that the accuracy level in head-mounted displays (HMD) (73 %) and large screens (74 %) are similar [9], the underlying technologies, experiences, mechanism, and psychophysics are different. This paper does not wish to compare them exhaustively but to point out some points related to depth perception. First, a HMD mounts two-lens display in front of the eyes directly. The focus, screen distance and other psychophysical parameters of a HMD are completely different from an immersive system.

Second, as Milgram et al. proposed, the VR technologies fall into a reality-virtuality (RV) continuum, with real environment in one side and virtual environment on the other [13]. A normal HMD displays a complete virtual environment through the two-lens display, while a CAVE-like system, which is an immersive virtual reality system, displays a mixed reality (MR) through the 4-sides stereoscopic displays with the human body in the system. The person in the immersive system sees the virtual world and his body at the same time. This should provide body reference for visual perception of size.

It is true that as error occurs similarly in all hardware systems, it can be ruled out that such error is only limited to a certain system. However, owing to the differences between systems, separated efforts should be made to large screens and immersive systems in depth perception instead of merging it ambitiously with HMD as stereoscopic displays. In the following, immersive system will be focused.

2.3 Distance Perception

Distance estimation tasks require three essential mental processes in the viewer aspect: Perceiving, Analyzing and Reporting [8]. First, a person perceives and analyses to form a perception. A person employs his vision to perceive the distance of the target object from one's location by mental or physical reference point or object. The information is then processed with other considerations and strategies, for an adjustment to enhance the accuracy. Some previous studies had shown that many factors could affect a person's perception. For example, Naceri et al. found that subjects' performances are affected by the reliance of depth cues. Those that rely on different types of depth cues instead of relying heavily on the apparent size, only one type of depth cue, had more accurate estimation [14]. This is consistent with another study where underestimation was both found in poor and rich cue conditions but less in rich cue condition [15].

The perceptual spaces are generally divided into three egocentric regions [16]. Personal space which is immediately surrounding the observer is defined within 2 m. Action space where human could quickly walk to and interact with, is defined as 2 m to 30 m. Binocular disparity and motion parallax can be used in this space with movement in immersive system or in physical reality [17]. Although motion parallax is an important depth cue in depth perception in physical reality [18], there is no evidence showing that it could aid depth estimation in immersive system.

Vista space is defined as beyond 30 m where binocular disparity and motion perspective are not in use. Depth perception could only be derived from pictorial cues such as relative size and occlusion. The depth estimation error in this space has not been studied in immersive system.

2.4 Measurement Method

In the third phase, reporting, the person needs to decide how far the target is placed as obtained from the previous perception stage and tells the experimenter the estimation. There are a wide variety of protocols to measure a person's depth estimation. In researches related to VE, there are mainly 3 types: verbal estimation, visually imagined action, and perceptual matching [8, 9, 19].

Verbal estimation refers to directly stating the depth estimation in metric units such as meter. Visually imagined action refers to having the subject views the object and imagines walking to the object. Imagination time is recorded with their usual rate of walk for a depth judgment. Perceptual matching refers to having the subject to judge the distances with manipulating or judging an existing object in the screen.

Some suggested that verbal estimation is subjected to bias and noise [20]. However, as previous studies had shown that subjects are able to process depth perception with spatial relation well using perceptual matching [21], the problem of underestimation is not on the VR system itself but the bias and noise. Verbal estimation or other related numerical methods should be used to quantify the bias and noise. Klein et al. compared timed imagined walking, verbal estimation, and triangulated blind walking. They found very similar result in depth judgment in the three methods in both real physical environment and virtual environment [19].

2.5 Improvement Attempts

Some possible alleviative measures are being tested from varies aspects. Renner et al. and Ponto et al. proposed that current standard stereo-based physical measurements of eye position are not precise for proper viewing parameters [22, 23]. As an improvement attempt, users' inter-pupillary distance (IPD) is inputted into a geometric model to predict perceptual errors. Errors can then be inversely calibrated to provide a more accurate image. Improvements were found but such alleviative measures are complex and not optimum with individual differences.

From human experience aspect, manipulations in HMD settings related to learning and familiarization are found to improve the accuracy [21]. The interaction task designed to provide learning and familiarization process significantly reduces users' error to nearly veridical. However, such effects were not found in CAVE-like systems when tested with subject experience and environmental learning [15].

2.6   Aim of the Study

The aim of the study is to first explore the effects of immersive system for the accuracy of human egocentric depth perception under several environments. It is hypothesized that human depth estimation in VE is better when the person is in immersive system than viewing from a single screen stereoscopic display due to the presence of the human body in the MR, and such perception in action space will be even better when participants are allowed to move around since motion parallax should aid the estimation. Human depth estimation error in vista space and the effects of 2D and 3D object will also be investigated. In the later stage of the study, based on the results, measurement method changes and improvement attempts will be proposed and tested.

3   Method

As stated above, this study aims to measure human perception error of egocentric distance estimation in three different environments (single screen, imseCAVE without freedom of movement, imseCAVE with freedom of movement) (Figs. 1 and 2), using two different types of objects (2D- wall and 3D- military jet). Distances in action space (2–30 m) and vista space (> 30 m) were studied.

Fig. 1. Single screen stereoscopic display

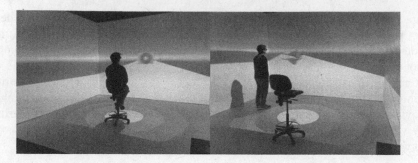

Fig. 2. imseCAVE (a) without freedom of movement (b) with freedom of movement

3.1 Experimental Setup

The experiment is carried in the imseCAVE, a VR system that facilitates the creation of an interactive immersive three-dimensional environment [2, 4]. It composited of three walls and a floor. The dimension is 4 m deep, by 3 m across and 3 m tall. All projectors use active 3D running at 120 Hz with XGA (1024 × 768 pixel) resolution. Images are displayed at 120 Hz, alternating between left and right image to create the three-dimension effect. Stereo image can be perceived with shutter glasses. The optical tracking system is used to track user position with 8 infrared cameras mounted at the ceiling to provide coverage. Markers are mounted on the 3D shuttle glass and handheld controller to enable the tracking systems to measure and calculate the 3D position and orientation of the user and the controller. The images could then be rendered to the viewer realistically.

For the first environment, only the front side is used as stereoscopic display. For the second and third environment, the full system will be used. The visual content is generated using Unity and MiddleVR, where dimension of the objects can be created and displayed in the system accurately.

The type of virtual environment in the study is chosen to be open space, which included a grey floor and a blue sky. The perception of infinity horizon is created by the impression of a horizon with vanishing point induced by the environment; while linear perspective was not available as a secondary depth cue. The texture of the background environment is chosen not to provide any texture gradient information. No metric aid and additional background object were provided.

The experimental condition is designed to be as simple as possible due to two reasons: First, as Armbrüster had tested in unicoloured background by verbal estimation with the type of environment (no space, open space vs. closed space) [11]. There were no significant differences between the environments. Second, the current study tries to represent a practical experimental environment with minimum visual depth cue that attempts to obtain an accurate measure in depth estimation. Hence, such open space with simple cues is selected.

The two different types of objects are drawn with clear and sharp features to be viewed from far away. The two-dimensional object is a wall with circles drawn reassemble a shooting target; while the three-dimensional object is a military jet colored in orange and blue. Both items are scaled for consistency. Both objects are not objects that could be seen in daily life, such manipulation prevented subjects to guess the object based on their daily experiences by the size.

3.2   Experimental Variables

The independent variables are the environment, type of object and distance of the target object. Three different environments were used: single screen stereoscopic display, immersive virtual reality system (CAVE) with and without freedom of movement. The two types of object were used: 2D flat wall and 3D military jet model. The primary dependent variable was the reported verbal depth estimation in meter by the participants. A percentage of error was then calculated by normalizing the result:

$$\% \ of \ Error \ = \ \frac{reported \ distance - actual \ distance}{actual \ distance} \times 100\% \qquad (1)$$

As human is found to have around 6 % of error in distance estimation in real world situation [8], an allowance is provided. An error near 0 is veridical, while a value $> .1$ shows overestimation, and a value $< -.1$ shows underestimation. The variables are analyzed in the Result session.

3.3   Participants

The research study recruited 40 subjects from the university community of University of Hong Kong; aged between 18 and 24 (with a mean age of 20.9); 20 were male and 20 were female. They volunteered to experience a virtual environment and were not given any payment, credit, or other compensation for their participation. We screened the participants for 20/20 vision of both eyes, either in natural or corrected, and usual normal stereopsis experience in 3D environment. Subjects that did not pass will not be invited to perform the test any further.

3.4   Experimental Task

Before collecting data, participants gave their consent on a form that explained the purpose of the study, and the confidentiality of individual's data sets are ensured. On the form, the subjects were advised that they might experience mild fatigue and discomforts such as motion and cyber-sickness during the procedure. Such fatigue and/or discomforts associated with the environment rendered were kept to a minimum and that should they experience any, they are free to take short breaks or quit at any time.

The visual acuity and stereopsis ability of subjects are checked so as to screen out those who normally do not perceive depth accurately even in physical reality. The subjects are then given a chance to familiar with a rich content VR environment and check if they perceive the rendered 3D content normally. The subjects were then listened to verbal description and demonstration of the task given by the experimenter in the test environment. Subjects were told that they would estimate distances in meters, where the numbers are random integer. They were also explicitly told that the numbers may not be multiple of 2 or 5. Subjects were informed and shown an object of egocentric distance of 2 m (the distance to wall of the immersive virtual reality system from the seat) as a dimensional reference of the system.

In the first two environments (single screen, imseCAVE without freedom of movement) (Figs. 1 and 2a), subjects are invited to sit in a fixed chair in the middle of the imseCAVE system (2 m from the front screen). The eye height is adjusted to be the same while standing and sitting. The subjects are required to give numerical verbal depth estimation of the object from their seat to the object in front of them in turn. In the third environment (imseCAVE with freedom of movement) (Fig. 2b), subjects are allowed to freely walk around the imseCAVE to view the virtual object and give numerical verbal depth estimation of the object from a designated location to the object. Two types of objects of random sequence were tested as independent variables in each environment. In each trial, the object is displayed in 7 distances ranging from 3 to 60 m. The distances presentation order is randomly permuted given that the same distances do not present twice in a row. After the total of 7 (distance) × 3 (environment) × 2 (object) = 42 data point collection, a debriefing was given. Object at some distances were displayed while revealing the true egocentric distances.

4   Results

Every participant made 42 estimations (7 × 3 × 2). On average, 29.98 ($SD = 11.1$) underestimated ($< -.1$), 5.87 ($SD = 3.6$) correctly estimated (between -.1 and .1), and 6.15 ($SD = 9.2$) overestimated ($> .1$) the distances over all the conditions and distances. Paired t-test results show that there is significant difference between underestimations and correct estimations ($t_{39} = 11.135, p < .001$), and underestimations and overestimations ($t_{39} = 7.503, p < .001$), while correct estimations and overestimations do not differ significantly ($t_{39} = -.206, p < .838$).

The numerical estimations were computed into percentage of error as stated in previous part for comparison. The results of a repeated measure ANOVA with factors of distance (7), environment (3) and object (2), and sex as between-subject factor revealed only a significant main effect for factor of distance ($F[6,228] = 79.801, p < .001$) and type of objects ($F[1,38] = 18.382, p < .001$).

Pairwise comparisons (t-tests) between the zero error and mean percentage error in estimated distances over all conditions show that the error in estimations of 3–7 m were not significant (see Table 1). Yet, for actual distance range above 15 m, the errors are significant. The signs and values indicate an underestimation of 34.6–44.5 % in actual range of 15–56 m (see Fig. 3). For the two types of object, 2D-wall yields -.351 % ($SD = .270$), while 3D-military jet yields -.214 % ($SD = .400$) error on average of estimated distance in all condition. Paired t-test results show that there is significant difference between them ($t_{39} = -4.323, p < .001$).

Table 1. Mean percentage error of estimated distance in all conditions

Actual distance range (meters)	Mean % error of estimated distance	Std. Deviation	t-Value	Sig.
3–4	0.063	0.216	1.836	.074
5–7	-0.034	0.318	-0.680	.500
15–17	-0.346	0.304	-7.201	.005
20–22	-0.393	0.357	-6.954	.005
30–32	-0.439	0.352	-7.886	.005
41–43	-0.384	0.446	-5.452	.005
55–57	-0.445	0.431	-6.533	.005

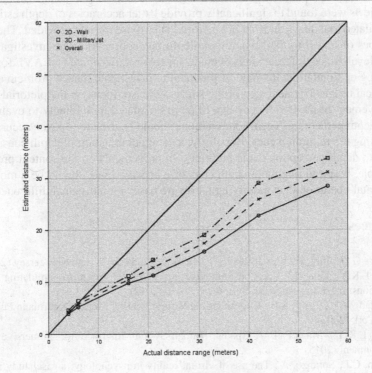

Fig. 3. Distance estimation against actual distance range

5 Discussion

The first part of the study was conducted to investigate the effects of immersive system on the accuracy of human egocentric depth perception by a simple VE that simulates a usual psychological experimental environment. Overall, virtual distances were under-estimated by participants.

CAVE-like immersive systems provide human body reference for size and freedom of movement for motion parallax. The hypothesis that these unique features may contribute to the depth perception and improve the accuracy of distance estimation was tested. The three environments had no differential effect on accuracy of depth perception. The features of immersive systems are not essential elements to depth estimation. Yet, since immersion is an important element in VR (the I^3), it should still be preserved when VR is used as an experimental tool to provide a total VR experience to the subjects.

Depth perception estimation in immersive system in such simple virtual environment was found to be inaccurate, including vista space. Researchers should take extra care when using VR systems as a cognitive experimental tool, especially if the tasks involve perception or navigation. One research direction could investigate if our visual system activates a different set of visual pathway in processing VR images.

The object types and distances in vista spaces were added as an exploration as there are no previous attempts. Compared to 2D objects and far away objects, 3D objects and closer objects were found to significantly provide better accuracies of depth estimation. It is speculated that this is due to more pictorial cues those objects provided. The effects of the types of object to the accuracy on depth perception could be investigated in a practical level. Since different kinds of objects were visualized in imseCAVE for virtual prototyping or simulation, it would be practical to investigate if such problem exists in the practical usage. The next step of the study will also, focus on the pictorial cues as an improvement basis. Depth cues should be first isolated individually to evaluate the effect to depth perception. Then, combinations should be tried to produce accurate estimation using the minimum cues. Hopefully, a clear combination of depth cues that are essential to depth perception could be found. Improvements on the content presented, for example, by providing more depth cues of a specific kind, should be a more ideal experimental operation than modifying hardware based on individual differences.

References

1. Burdea, G., Coiffet, P.: Virtual Reality Technology, 2nd edn. Wiley, New Jersey (2003)
2. Chan, L.K.Y., Lau, H.Y.K.: A cost effective virtual reality system for simulating logistics operations. Int. J. Logist. SCM. Syst. **6**(1), 71–76 (2012)
3. Sherman, W.R., Craig, A.B.: Understanding Virtual Reality. Morgan Kaufmann Publishers, New York (2003)
4. Chan, L.K.Y.: MagicPad: A Spatial Human-System Interface for Immersive Virtual Environment (2015)
5. Wilson, C.J., Soranzo, A.: The use of virtual reality in psychology: a case study in visual perception. Comput. Math. Methods Med. **2015**, 1–7 (2015)
6. Kozlov, M.D., Johansen, M.K.: Real behavior in virtual environments: psychology experiments in a simple virtual-reality paradigm using video games. Cyberpsychol. Behav. Soc. Netw. **13**(6), 711–714 (2010)
7. Rizzo, A.A., Bowerly, T., Buckwalter, J.G., Schultheis, M.T., Matheis, R., Shahabi, C., Sharifzadeh, M.: Virtual environments for the assessment of attention and memory processes: the virtual classroom and office. In: Sharkey, P., Sik Lányi, C., Standen, P.J. (eds.) 4th International Conference on Disability, Virtual Reality and Associated Technology, ICDVRAT 2002, pp. 3–11. University of Reading, England (2002)
8. Lin, C.J., Woldegiorgis, B.H.: Interaction and visual performance in stereoscopic displays: A review. J. Soc. Inf Disp. **23**(7), 319–332 (2015)

9. Renner, R.S., Velichkovsky, B.M., Helmert, J.R.: The perception of egocentric distances in virtual environments- A review. ACM Comput. Surv. **46**(2), 23 (2013)
10. Walk, R.D., Gibson, E.J.: A comparative and analytical study of visual depth perception. Psychol. Monogr. **75**(15), 1 (1961)
11. Armbrüster, C., Wolter, M., Kuhlen, T., Spijkers, W., Fimm, B.: Depth perception in virtual reality: distance estimations in peri-and extrapersonal space. Cyberpsychol. Behav. **11**(1), 9–15 (2008)
12. Saracini, C.: Spatial cognition in Virtual Environments (2011)
13. Milgram, P., Takemura, H., Utsumi, A., Kishino, F.: Augmented reality: a class of displays on the reality-virtuality continuum. In: Telemanipulator and Telepresence Technologies. SPIE, vol. 2351, pp. 282–292 (1995)
14. Naceri, A., Chellali, R., Dionnet, F., Toma, S.: Depth perception within virtual environments: comparison between two display technologies. Int. J. Adv. Intel. Syst. **3**, 51–64 (2010)
15. Murgia, A., Sharkey, P.M.: Estimation of distances in virtual environments using size constancy. Int. J. Virtual. Real. **8**(1), 67–74 (2009)
16. Cutting, J.E.: How the eye measures reality and virtual reality. Behav. Res. Methods. Instrum. Comput. **29**(1), 27–36 (1997)
17. Luo, X., Kenyon, R., Kamper, D., Sandin, D., DeFanti, T.: The effects of scene complexity, stereovision, and motion parallax on size constancy in a virtual environment. In: 2007 Virtual Reality Conference, VR 2007, pp. 59–66. IEEE (2007)
18. Rogers, B., Graham, M.: Motion parallax as an independent cue for depth perception. Perception **8**(2), 125–134 (1979)
19. Klein, E., Swan, J.E., Schmidt, G.S., Livingston, M., Staadt, O.G.: Measurement protocols for medium-field distance perception in large-screen immersive displays. In: 2009 IEEE Virtual Reality Conference, pp. 107–113. IEEE Computer Society (2009)
20. Thompson, W.K., Willemsen, P., Gooch, A., Creem-Regehr, S.H., Loomis, J.M., Beall, A.C.: Does the quality of the computer graphics matter when judging distances in visually immersive environments? Presence-Teleop. Virt. **13**(5), 560–571 (2004)
21. Richardson, A.R., Waller, D.: Interaction with an immersive virtual environment corrects users' distance estimates. Hum. Factors **49**(3), 507–517 (2007)
22. Renner, R.S., Velichkovsky, B.M., Helmert, J.R., Stelzer, R.H.: Measuring interpupillary distance might not be enough. In: ACM Symposium on Applied Perception, pp. 130–130. ACM (2013)
23. Ponto, K., Gleicher, M., Radwin, R.G., Shin, H.J.: Perceptual calibration for immersive display environments. IEEE Trans. Vis. Comput. Graph. **19**(4), 691–700 (2013)

Impact of Instructional Strategies on Workload, Stress, and Flow in Simulation-Based Training for Behavior Cue Analysis

Julie N. Salcedo[1(✉)], Stephanie J. Lackey[1], and Crystal Maraj[2]

[1] Design Interactive, Inc., Orlando, USA
{julie.salcedo,
stephanie.lackey}@designinteractive.net
[2] Institute for Simulation and Training,
University of Central Florida, Orlando, USA
cmaraj@ist.ucf.edu

Abstract. The U.S. Army desires to improve Intelligence, Surveillance, Reconnaissance (ISR) abilities by incorporating Unmanned Ground Systems (UGS) to aid in the identification of High Value Individuals (HVI) through the analysis of human behavior cues from safer distances. This requires analysts to employ perceptual skills indirectly via UGS video surveillance displays and will also require training platforms tailored to address the perceptual skill needs of these robot-aided ISR tasks. The U.S. Army identifies Simulation-Based Training (SBT) as a necessary training medium for UGS technologies. Instructional strategies that may increase the effectiveness of SBT for robot-aided ISR tasks include Highlighting and Massed Exposure. This study compared the impact of each strategy on trainee workload, stress, and flow during SBT for a behavior cue analysis task. Ultimately, the goal of this research effort is to provide instructional design recommendations that will improve SBT development to support effective training for emerging UGS capabilities.

Keywords: Virtual environments · Instructional design · Perceptual skills training · Simulation-based training

1 Introduction

In an effort to improve the safety and effectiveness of its Intelligence, Surveillance, Reconnaissance (ISR) patrol missions, the U.S. Army has engaged research and development endeavors to enhance and expand its remote ISR capabilities [1]. Increasingly, the settings of modern conflicts are occurring in more urbanized environments compared to conflicts of the recent past, which requires much closer contact ISR strategies such as identification of High Value Individuals (HVI) through behavior cue analysis, or the purposeful observation and interpretation of behavior in the environment [1]. Due to the remote surveillance capabilities, Unmanned Ground Systems (UGS) have been identified as necessary tools to support the execution of

© Springer International Publishing Switzerland 2016
S. Lackey and R. Shumaker (Eds.): VAMR 2016, LNCS 9740, pp. 184–195, 2016.
DOI: 10.1007/978-3-319-39907-2_18

behavior cue analysis tasks from a safe position [1]. Current development efforts to enhance fielded UGSs present an opportunity for the instructional design community to respond with recommendations for optimal training solutions in anticipation of the training requirement needs of these emerging Robot-Aided ISR (RAISR) systems.

1.1 Simulation-Based Training

The U.S. Army identifies Simulation-Based Training (SBT) as a necessary training component for emerging RAISR capabilities, such as the employment of UGSs to assist in HVI identification. SBT involves the training of targeted tasks and skills within a simulated version of the operational or task environment. Examples of SBT environments include live training simulations that physically replicate the character-istics of the operational environment, virtual simulations that utilize modern computing and display technologies to present 3D interactive training scenarios, and even mixed environments that combine elements of live and virtual simulation to fulfill training requirements. Possibly the most important benefit of SBT is the ability to train high-risk tasks in a safe, controlled environment. Also, depending on the task domain, SBT may contribute to more cost effective training measures. However, foundational SBT research has shown that implementation of simulations alone without appropriate instructional support risks contributing to negative training outcomes [2]. Therefore, effective SBT should incorporate instructional strategies and assistance tailored to the specific skill needs, training objectives, and desired performance outcomes of the task. In an ISR context, the identification of HVIs through behavior cue analysis involves monitoring the environment for behavioral anomalies, detecting suspicious behavior, and classifying those behaviors according to associated affective states and/or threat levels [3, 4]. Behavior cue analysis requires analysts to execute specific perceptual skills including: attentional weighting, search and scan, visual acuity, and pattern recognition [3, 4]. Effective instructional support solutions for SBT of behavior cue analysis must fulfill these perceptual skill requirements.

1.2 Instructional Strategies

Current instructional design literature identifies several instructional strategies that have shown to effectively support the development and improvement of perceptual skills required in the military training domain. The scope of this research effort investigates the application of two strategies—Highlighting and Massed Exposure—both identified as viable solutions to fulfill the perceptual skill needs of the behavior cue analysis task. Highlighting involves the explicit orientation of the trainee's attention to the presence of critical training content [5, 6]. In a simulated environment, this is often achieved through the use of a non-content related element such as a circle framing the stimulus to indicate its location [5]. Massed Exposure involves the presentation of a high volume of practice opportunities compared to what would be experienced in the operational environment [7]. In a previous study comparing the effects of Highlighting and Massed Exposure on performance outcomes, it was found that participants exposed to the Massed Exposure strategy during training had a tendency to detect critical targets earlier than participants who received the Highlighting strategy during training [3].

While the effect on performance outcomes may be a primary concern in instructional design research, the effect of the design, including the selected instructional strategies, on trainee perceptions has also shown to impact training effectiveness [8]. Therefore, to further extend the instructional design literature assessing the effectiveness of the Highlighting and Massed Exposure strategies for behavior cue analysis training, the objective of this experiment was to investigate the impact of these strategies on trainee perceptions related to workload, stress state, and flow experienced during training, which in turn my impact training effectiveness.

1.3   Workload, Stress State, and Flow

The workload, stress state, and flow constructs refer to the various types of demands that may be imposed on an individual while executing a given task. Workload comprises information-processing demands including: mental demand due to task complexity, physical demand due to strenuousness, temporal or time pressure demand, success and satisfaction in one's performance, the amount of mental or physical effort expended, and the degree of frustration [9, 10]. Stress state includes three overarching dimensions associated with task demand: task engagement, distress, and worry [11, 12]. Task engagement pertains to feelings of arousal, interest, motivation, and concentration during execution of a task. Distress pertains to an unpleasant state of tension characterized by low confidence and low perceived control. Worry pertains to feelings of task-induced self-consciousness, low self-esteem, and cognitive interference. Flow is defined as an optimal level of experience in which an individual becomes so highly involved in a task that awareness of the passage of time or events in the surrounding environment is often reduced [13, 14]. Flow addresses several unique dimensions of task demand including the level of challenge and skill balance, merging of one's actions and awareness during task execution, task goals and feedback, concentration, control, self-consciousness, awareness of the passage of time, and a sense of purpose.

A recurring ideal within instructional design research is to attain the proverbial *Zone of Proximal Development* (ZPD) during instruction. Theoretically, ZPD is achieved by providing instruction and practice opportunities that are neither too difficult nor too easy, in an attempt to facilitate an optimal level of learning [15]. ZPD aligns very well with the workload, stress state, and flow constructs. Negative levels of workload and stress state may indicate that the trainee's perceptual and cognitive resources are overtaxed by the method of instruction. Further, this may indicate that the challenge level of the training task is too strenuous, which may hinder appropriate skill acquisition. Likewise, instructional methods that offer a low degree of challenge may underutilize the trainee's resources and elicit boredom, thus, reducing flow [13].

1.4   Objectives/Hypotheses

The objective of this experiment was to assess the effect of the Highlighting and Massed Exposure instructional strategies on workload, stress state, and flow during SBT for a behavior cue analysis task. There was no precedent indicating any advantage of one strategy over the other for the given task. Therefore, the hypotheses tested in this experiment explored whether or not instructional strategy had a significant effect on workload, stress, and/or flow and whether or not a significant relationship exists between workload, stress, flow, and/or performance during behavior cue analysis training.

2 Method

2.1 Participants

Participation was restricted to U.S. citizens, ages 18 to 40 years, with normal or corrected to normal vision, and full color vision. Ninety volunteers (44 males, 46 females), aged 18 to 38 ($M = 21.57$, $SD = 3.25$) were recruited from the University of Central Florida (UCF) campus and UCF affiliated organizations. Participants were compensated at a rate of ten dollars per hour of participation. The experiment session was approximately one and a half hours in duration.

2.2 Experimental Testbed

A 22 inch (16:10 aspect ratio) computer monitor, desktop PC, and Virtual Battlespace 2 (VBS2) version 2.0 software comprised the experimental testbed equipment. The virtual environment was fully customized using the virtual character, object, and terrain assets provided in the VBS2 2.0 3D model library. The scenarios and vignettes simulated a video surveillance feed from an autonomous UGS traveling at 1.5 meters per second with a camera height of one meter. The UGS height and speed align with current research concerning the design of emerging surveillance robot systems [16]. Sixteen different virtual characters, ranging in skin tone from light to dark, portrayed selected target and non-target behavior cues. Target cues included two aggressive cues, slapping the hands and clenched fists, and two nervous cues, wringing the hands and check six, that were animated using the Autodesk® MotionBuilder® software. Seven non-target cues were selected from a library of animations provided with the VBS2 2.0 software. In an attempt to elicit a sufficient level of challenge, the event rate was set at 30 virtual characters per minute, which has shown to produce a moderate level of workload during threat detection tasks [17]. Presentation of the virtual characters and behavior cues was randomized and counterbalanced. The experimental task consisted of three procedures: monitoring, detecting, and classifying. Participants monitored the simulated UGS video surveillance feed, detected target behavior cues by clicking the virtual characters, and classified each target behavior cue detected as either *Aggressiveness* or *Nervousness* by selecting the appropriate classification button.

2.3 Conditions

For the training segment of the experiment, participants were randomly assigned to one of the three conditions: Control, Highlighting, or Massed Exposure. There was a 33 % target probability in the Control and Highlighting conditions, which is consistent with procedures in prior behavior and threat detection research [18]. This was doubled in the

Massed Exposure condition to a 66 % target probability, which has shown to increase visual acuity for threatening behavior cues [18]. The Highlighting condition had an added element of a non-content related feature to signal target cues, which consisted of a translucent blue box overlaid on virtual characters exhibiting target cues (Fig. 1).

Fig. 1. Example of the non-content related feature in the Highlighting condition

2.4   Measures

Performance Metric. The performance metric analyzed in this study was Detection Accuracy. Detection Accuracy scores were calculated as the percentage of correctly detected target behavior cues out of the total number of targets presented in each scenario or vignette. Performance scores were collected during each scenario or vignette using a data logging program customized for the experimental testbed.

Subjective Measures. Within the context of evaluating training effectiveness, trainee perception criteria are generally assessed using self-report subjective instruments such as surveys and questionnaires. This experiment utilized three well-validated questionnaires to assess participants' levels of workload, stress state, and flow experienced during training. Subjective measures included the short version of the NASA-Task Load Index (NASA-TLX), the short Dundee Stress State Questionnaire (DSSQ), and the short Flow State Scale (FSSS). The NASA-TLX assesses workload on six 0–100 point scales including: Mental Demand (task complexity), Physical Demand (strenuousness), Temporal Demand (time pressure), Performance (success and satisfaction), Effort (amount of mental/physical activity), and Frustration (irritation and stress) [10]. A Global Workload score may also be derived from the original six scales. The DSSQ measures participants' stress state using three 0–32 point scales including Engagement, Distress, and Worry [11]. The FSSS utilizes a 1–5 point scale to assess perceived levels of flow experienced during a task with items targeting the nine elements of flow including: Challenge and Skill Balance, Action-Awareness Merging, Clear Goals, Unambiguous Feedback, Concentration on the Task at Hand, Sense of Control, Loss of Self Consciousness, Transformation of Time, and Autotelic Experience [14].

2.5 Procedure

The experimental session was divided into pre-experiment, task familiarization, pre-test, training, and post-test segments. The total duration of each experimental session was approximately one and a half hours.

During the pre-experiment segment, the Ishihara's Tests for Colour Deficiency [19] was administered and participants who lacked full color vision were dismissed. Retained participants completed the informed consent procedures, a demographics survey, and an initial DSSQ. Next, to gain familiarity with the experimental task procedure and interface, participants viewed a narrated instructional slideshow and completed a task familiarization scenario to practice. To avoid priming effects, participants detected red and yellow barrels and classified each by color. Participants were provided up to two trials to achieve a 75 % Detection Accuracy for the barrel task before proceeding.

After demonstrating proficiency to complete the task procedure, participants completed a pre-test scenario which required detection and classification of target behaviors they perceived as aggressive or nervous. The pre-test scenario included a culturally agnostic urban and suburban terrain with 60 virtual characters exhibiting target cue types and 120 exhibiting non-target cue types. Culturally agnostic refers to settings and terrains that are non-geospecific and not exclusive to any single cultural group.

The training segment included a narrated slideshow explaining behavior cue analysis followed by four randomly ordered training vignettes. The slideshow consisted of descriptions, examples of the four target cue types, and a brief description of the instructional strategy applied in the following training vignettes. The training vignettes represented four terrains: Middle Eastern Urban, Middle Eastern Marketplace, Culturally Agnostic Urban, and Culturally Agnostic Suburban. Each training vignette included 60 virtual characters. The Control condition presented 20 virtual characters exhibiting target cues per vignette. The Highlighting condition presented 20 virtual characters exhibiting target cues per vignette that were highlighted by the specified non-content feature (Fig. 1). The Massed Exposure condition presented 40 virtual characters exhibiting target cues per vignette. After completing each training vignette, the participant responded to the NASA-TLX and the DSSQ. Upon completion of all training vignettes, the FSSS was administered. Finally, participants completed the post-test scenario in which targets were detected and classified according to the training provided. The post-test scenario presented a reversed route from the pre-test with 60 targets and 120 non-targets.

3   Results

3.1 Workload

One-way between subjects ANOVAs were conducted to compare the effect of instructional strategy on workload, measured by the NASA-TLX, in the Control, Highlighting, and Massed Exposure conditions. There was a significant effect of instructional strategy on the Temporal Demand scale for the three conditions [$F_{(2, 87)}$

= 4.71, p =.011]. Post hoc comparisons using the Tukey HSD test revealed that the mean score for Temporal Demand in the Highlighting condition was significantly less than the Control and Massed Exposure conditions (Table 1). This indicates that the level of perceived time pressure in the Highlighting condition was significantly less than that experienced in either the Control or Massed Exposure conditions. However, the Control and Massed Exposure conditions did not differ significantly. Overall, the mean Temporal Demand scores are fairly low indicating that none of the instructional strategies appeared to overload participants by causing excessive time pressure. Furthermore, there was not a significant effect of instructional strategy on the remaining subscales including: Mental Demand, Physical Demand, Effort, Frustration, Performance, and Global Workload.

Table 1. NASA-TLX Temporal Demand scale means and standard deviations per condition

	Control		Highlighting		Massed Exposure	
	Mean	*SD*	*Mean*	*SD*	*Mean*	*SD*
Temporal Demand	42.33	28.73	24.33	21.76	43.67	30.48

3.2   Stress State

The effect of instructional strategy on stress state, measured by the DSSQ, in the Control, Highlighting, and Massed Exposure conditions were compared with one-way between subjects ANOVAs. There was a significant effect of instructional strategy on the Distress scale for the three conditions [F (2, 87) = 4.86, p = .010]. Tukey HSD post hoc comparisons revealed that the mean score for Distress in the Massed Exposure condition was significantly greater than the Highlighting condition (Table 2) indicating that participants in the Massed condition experienced a significantly higher level of distress than participants in the Highlighting condition. The Control condition did not differ significantly from either the Highlighting or Massed Exposure conditions. Similar to the NASA-TLX, the mean Distress scores fall on the lower end of the scale suggesting that participants were not overly distressed in any of the conditions. Additionally, there was no significant effect of instructional strategy on the Engagement and Worry scales.

Table 2. DSSQ Distress scale means and standard deviations per condition

	Control		Highlighting		Massed Exposure	
	Mean	*SD*	*Mean*	*SD*	*Mean*	*SD*
Distress	16.53	4.92	15.47	5.85	19.47	4.58

3.3 Flow

One-way between subjects ANOVAs were also conducted to compare the effect of instructional strategy on flow state, measured by the FSSS, in the Control, Highlighting, and Massed Exposure conditions. There was a significant effect of instructional strategy on the Challenge-Skill Balance component of flow [F (2, 87) = 4.20, p = .018] with Tukey HSD post-hoc tests revealing a significantly greater mean score in the Highlighting versus Control condition (Table 3). The Unambiguous Feedback component showed a significant effect of instructional strategy [F (2, 87) = 6.52, p = .002] and post-hoc tests indicated that the mean score in the Control condition was significantly lower than Highlighting and Massed Exposure (Table 3). Instructional strategy also had a significant effect on the Concentration on the Task at Hand component [F (2, 87) = 3.59, p = .032] with post-hoc tests indicating a significantly greater mean score for Massed Exposure compared to the Highlighting condition (Table 3). Overall, high mean scores for the significant flow components suggests the instructional strategies did not inhibit the achievement of a sense of flow during the training vignettes.

Table 3. Selected short Flow State Scale means and standard deviations per condition.

	Control		Highlighting		Massed Exposure	
	Mean	SD	Mean	SD	Mean	SD
Challenge-Skill Balance	4.27	1.14	4.83	.379	4.67	.606
Unambiguous Feedback	3.70	1.06	4.40	.814	4.37	.615
Concentration of the Task at Hand	4.31	.712	4.17	1.02	4.70	.596

3.4 Correlations

The relationship between the measures of workload, stress state, and flow were assessed using Pearson's r correlations (Table 4). There was a weak positive correlation between Distress, measured by the DSSQ, and the Performance scale of the NASA-TLX indicating that increased levels of distress were associated with increases in performance satisfaction. Likewise, there were weak to moderate positive correlations between the NASA-TLX Performance scale and the Challenge-Skill Balance, Unambiguous Feedback, and Concentration of the Task at Hand components of the FSSS. This indicates that high levels of perceived task competence, how well one perceives he/she performed, and perceived task focus were associated with high performance satisfaction.

Interestingly, the DSSQ Distress scale had a weak positive correlation to the FSSS Unambiguous Feedback component and a stronger positive correlation to the Concentration on the Task at Hand component. This suggests that participants who felt they performed the task well and were highly focused on the task also reported a higher level of distress during the training vignettes.

Table 4. Pearson's r correlations between selected DSSQ, NASA-TLX, and FSSS variables

	Distress (DSSQ)	Performance (NASA-TLX)
Distress (DSSQ)	1	———
Performance (NASA-TLX)	.212*	1
Challenge Skill Balance (FSSS)	.165	.276**
Unambiguous Feedback (FSSS)	.258*	.371**
Concentration on Task at Hand (FSSS)	.523**	.353**

$* \, p < 0.05$ level, $** \, p < 0.01$ level

The relationships between Detection Accuracy during the post-test scenario and the subjective measures collected during the training vignettes were also assessed using Pearson's r correlations (Table 4). The weak positive correlation with the DSSQ Distress scale indicates that participants who experienced a greater degree of distress during the training vignettes had a slight tendency to score higher in Detection Accuracy during the post-test scenario. Likewise, the weak positive correlation with the NASA-TLX Performance scale reveals that participants who reported greater satisfaction in their training performance tended to have greater Detection Accuracy scores. Furthermore, as evidenced by the weak positive correlations to the FSSS Unambiguous Feedback and Concentration on the Task at Hand components, participants who had a better sense of their performance and had a greater focus on the task during the training vignettes were also slightly more likely to have higher post-test Detection Accuracy. Although these correlations are weak, they suggest that the levels of workload, stress, and flow experienced during the training phase of the experiment did not negatively impact participants' ability to accurately detect target behavior cues when the instructional support was removed (Table 5).

Table 5. Pearson's r correlations for Detection Accuracy

	Detection Accuracy
Distress (DSSQ)	.298**
Performance (NASA-TLX)	.246*
Unambiguous Feedback (FSSS)	.219*
Concentration on Task at Hand (FSSS)	.216*

$* \, p < 0.05$ level, $** \, p < 0.01$ level

4 Limitations

There was limited availability of functional UGS prototypes, actual fielded systems, or UGS design documents prior to the experimental testbed design. Therefore, the design of parameters for the simulated UGS and surveillance video-feed, including speed, camera height, and field-of-view, followed recommendations from current UGS research and development literature. There is no quantitative or anecdotal evidence from this experiment to suggest that the testbed design had a significant effect on the generalizability of the results to emerging UGS and RAISR training platforms.

Scenario development time was considerably reduced by leveraging the existing configuration of roadways and thoroughfares in each terrain when placing waypoints for the virtual UGS route. However, this method caused constraints with the proper placement, balance, and distribution of the virtual characters, animation triggers, and left versus right turns. In order to achieve greater experimental control, this limitation has been addressed in follow on experimentation by scripting a customized route planning program to generate properly balanced scenarios.

Utilizing the shortened version of the flow state measure (i.e., FSSS) may have reduced the sensitivity of the measure to fully assess the flow construct within this training task. An extended version may provide more robust results. There is limited research comparing the consistency and sensitivity of the short and extended versions of the flow measure within various task domains. Follow-on research should address this limitation to help explain the impact of the task domain on perceptions of flow.

5 Discussion

The hypotheses tested in this experiment predicted that the instructional strategies would have a significant effect on the level of workload, stress, and flow experienced during the behavior cue analysis training. Additionally, it was predicted that the subjective variables, (i.e., workload, stress, and flow) would be significantly related to each other and participants' behavior cue analysis performance. While all three hypotheses were at least partially supported by the results, the significant differences were minimal.

A particularly interesting result to acknowledge is the positive correlation between the DSSQ Distress scale and the FSSS Concentration on the Task at Hand component. Within this research effort, it is assumed that participants are more likely to become engaged in a task requiring detection of human targets versus non-human targets [20]. Accurate identification of HVIs is often vital to the success of ISR missions. Perhaps the emergence of this relationship between distress and the degree of task focus indicates that tasks involving the detection of human targets are rather distressing. Investigating this phenomena further within ISR and related task domains will assist in more accurately delineating the critical affective factors of performance in high-stress environments. Furthermore, identifying these factors will improve training objectives and instructional design of SBT to meet the affective requirements of high-stress tasks.

Ultimately, the practical significance of these results is that there is no apparent detriment to the training experience, in terms of workload, stress state, and flow, when either the Highlighting or Massed Exposure strategies are included in SBT for behavior cue analysis tasks. The decision-making involved in behavior cue analysis relies heavily on perceptual skills, such as, search and scan, visual discrimination, pattern recognition, and attentional weighting. Therefore, strategies aimed to improve these skills will likely improve the effectiveness of SBT for this and similar ISRtasks.

6 Conclusion

The results presented contribute to a larger research effort aimed at defining SBT design recommendations for RAISR tasks. This experiment sought to assess the impact of the Highlighting and Massed Exposure instructional strategies on levels of workload, stress, and flow during simulation-based behavior cue analysis training. Clearly, it may be concluded that the overall impact of the Highlighting and Massed Exposure instructional strategies had little consequence on workload, stress state, and flow during training. Either strategy has the capacity to support the development of critical perceptual skills for HVI identification without overloading trainees in the process.

Practically, it does not appear to matter which strategy is selected. However, if instructional designers desire to substantially reduce or even attempt to eliminate the demand and stress on the trainee, then the Highlighting strategy is the obvious choice. From a scenario development perspective, the Massed Exposure strategy may be faster to implement because it simply requires an adjustment of the input parameters to increase the number of targets versus non-targets and does not require the addition of a non-content highlighting feature. A likely solution is to combine these strategies to increase effectiveness of RAISR training systems. A combination of Highlighting and Massed Exposure elements may also be conducive to adaptive training systems by adjusting the support provided by each strategy to maintain a balanced level of task demand, trainee stress, and flow throughout a training session. The potential benefits afforded by these options present a prime opportunity for future instructional design and SBT investigations.

Acknowledgement. This research was sponsored by the U.S. Army Research Laboratory – Human Research Engineering Directorate Simulation and Training Technology Center (ARL HRED STTC), in collaboration with the Institute for Simulation and Training at the University of Central Florida. This work is supported in part by ARL HRED STTC contract W91CRB08D0015. The views and conclusions contained in this document are those of the authors and should not be interpreted as representing the official policies, either expressed or implied, of ARL HRED STTC or the U.S. Government. The U.S. Government is authorized to reproduce and distribute reprints for Government purposes notwithstanding any copyright notation hereon.

References

1. U.S. Army: TRADOC Pamphlet 525-7-9: The United States Army's Concept Capability Plan (CCP): Intelligence, Surveillance, and Reconnaissance. Department of the Army, Washington, D.C. (2008)
2. Oser, R.L., Gualtieri, J.W., Cannon-Bowers, J.A., Salas, E.: Training team problem solving skills: an event-based approach. Comp. Hum. Beh. **15**, 441–462 (1999)
3. Lackey, S.J., Salcedo, J.N.: Assessing instructional strategies for training robot-aided ISR tasks in simulated environments. In: Proceedings of Spring Simulation Multiconference, Tampa (2014)
4. Army, U.S.: ADRP 2-0: Intelligence. Department of the Army, Washington, DC (2012)

5. De Koning, B.B., Tabbers, H.K., Rikers, R.M., Paas, F.: Attention guidance in learning from a complex animation: seeing is understanding. Lrng. Inst. **20**(2), 111–122 (2010)
6. Underwood, G.: Visual attention and the transition from novice to advanced driver. Ergo **50** (8), 1235–1249 (2007)
7. Carroll, M., Milham, L., Champney, R.: Military observations: perceptual skills training strategies. In: Proceedings of Interservice/Industry Training, Simulation, and Education Conference (I/ITSEC), Orlando (2009)
8. Kirkpatrick, D.L., Kirkpatrick, J.D.: Evaluating Training Programs: The Four Levels, 3rd edn. Berrett-Koehler, San Francisco (2006)
9. Hart, S.G.: NASA-task load index (NASA-TLX): 20 years later. In: Proceedings of Human Factors and Ergonomics Society (HFES), San Francisco (2006)
10. Hart, S.G., Staveland, L.E.: Development of NASA-TLX (Task Load Index): results of empirical and theoretical research. In: Human Mental Workload. North Holland Press, Amsterdam (1988)
11. Matthews, G., Szalma, J., Panganiban, A.R., Neubauer, C., Warm, J.S.: Profiling task stress with the dundee stress state questionnaire. In: Cavalcanti, L., Azevedo, S. (eds.) Psychology of Stress: New Research, pp. 49–90. Nova Science, Hauppauge (2013)
12. Matthews, G., Campbell, S.E., Falconer, S., Joyner, L.A., Huggins, J., Gilliland, K., Grier, R., Warm, J.S.: Fundamental dimensions of subjective state in performance settings: task engagement, distress, and worry. Emotion **2**, 315–340 (2002)
13. Csikszentmihalyi, M.: Flow and the Foundations of Positive Psychology. Springer, Heidelberg (2014)
14. Jackson, S.A., Martin, A.J., Eklund, R.C.: Long and short measures of flow: the construct validity of the FSS-2, DFS-2, and New brief counterparts. J. Sport Exerc. Psy. **30**(5), 561–587 (2008)
15. Van de Pol, J., Volman, M., Beishuizen, J.: Scaffolding in teacher-student interaction: a decade of research. Ed. Psy. Rev. **17**, 89–100 (2010)
16. Mykoniatis, K., Angelopoulou, A., Soyler, A., Kincaid, P., Hancock, P.: Modeling and simulation of human robot interaction: face recognition implementations. In: IEEE Intel. System (2012)
17. Abich IV, J., Reinerman-Jones, L., Taylor, G.: Establishing workload manipulations utilizing a simulated environment. In: Shumaker, R. (ed.) VAMR 2013, Part II. LNCS, vol. 8022, pp. 211–220. Springer, Heidelberg (2013)
18. Mogg, K., Bradley, B.: Selective orienting of attention to masked threat faces in social anxiety. Beh. Res. and Ther. **40**(12), 1403–1414 (2002)
19. Ishihara, S.: Ishihara's Tests for Colour Deficiency. Kanehara Trading, Tokyo (2013)
20. Salcedo, J.N., Lackey, S.J., Maraj, C.: Impact of instructional strategies on motivation and engagement for simulation-based training of robot-aided ISR tasks. In: Proceedings of Human Factors and Ergonomics Society (HFES), Chicago (2014)

Multimodal Interaction in VAMR

Aspects of Voice Interaction on a Mobile Augmented Reality Application

Tiago Araújo[1]([⊠]), Carlos Santos[1], Brunelli Miranda[1], Nikolas Carneiro[1],
Anderson Marques[2], Marcelle Mota[1], Nelson Neto[1], and Bianchi Meiguins[1]

[1] Universidade Federal do Pará (UFPA), Belém, Brazil
tiagodavi70@gmail.com, gustavo.cbcc@gmail.com,
brunelli.miranda@gmail.com, nikolas.carneiro@gmail.com,
cellemota@gmail.com, dnelsonneto@gmail.com,
bianchi.serique@gmail.com
[2] Universidade Federal Rural da Amazônia, Capanema, Brazil
andmarques2006@gmail.com

Abstract. Mobile Augmented Reality has become more popular mainly because computational resources available in mobile devices, and in the enhanced view of real world that can be seen by the user. The interaction becomes an important point for success of these applications, featuring a natural and intuitive way for the user, and the chance of one, or two hands free for other interaction or activity. Therefore, this work presents the usability analysis of a Mobile Augmented Reality, the ARGuide, with the use of a voice service for interaction. The usability test analysis is based upon the most common interaction tasks of the users in this type of application. In the end, some good practices for the application interface building and speech interaction are shown.

Keywords: Mobile augmented reality · Voice interaction · Speech recognition · Arguide

1 Introduction

Technological development and the rising popularity of Mobile Augmented Reality (MAR) are reasons to widespread usage of this technology. Usability studies of MAR applications can help developers improve user experience, consolidating the use of these applications on several areas. Martínez et al. [1] shows some challenges for MAR application development, and among the presented challenges we can highlight the shortage of development patterns and little space for showing information. An alternative for present and organize information in MAR applications is using natural language.

Natural language interaction is the communication between human and machine using a language familiar for human [2]. This sort of interaction is important due to benefits provided to the user, among them, actions with higher intuitive interaction, minimizing cognitive effort and allowing the user concentrate in the task, instead of in the interaction [3]. Interaction by voice commands is an alternative for use with MAR applications, since tablets and smartphones have a built-in microphone.

S. Lackey and R. Shumaker (Eds.): VAMR 2016, LNCS 9740, pp. 199–210, 2016.
DOI: 10.1007/978-3-319-39907-2_19

It is common for mobile applications to offer many features to the user, reflecting on complex menus. These menus can hide some features, consuming user's time in the search of them. In this scenario, voice interaction can ease the search of some feature or set a shortcut for it [4].

The usage of voice in tablets and smartphones provides another advantage for the user. To hold the device with one hand and interact with the free one can be uncomfortable, as the device is bigger and heavier, like tablets. Interactions by voice commands can inhibit this problem, making the user interact with the application even holding the device with both hands.

In this work, a MAR application received a voice recognition service to help in navigation and content visualization using Points of Interest (POI). We analyze aspects of voice interaction and speech recognition based on a usability evaluation. We focus on task unit of the tests, like the navigation on a map and selection of Points of Interest in a MAR application. The application used for this work is the ARGuide [5].

2   Background

2.1   Voice Interaction

Speech is one of the most used form of communication of human being, standing between the three forms of communication (voice, gestures and facial expression) most used in everyday life [6]. The voice, when used in an application, is inserted in natural language concept.

Natural language interaction is the communication between human and machine using a familiar language for the human [2]. The Human Computer Interaction (HCI) field assigns an important role for this sort of interaction, due its benefits for the user, naming, actions that are more intuitive, minimizing cognitive effort and allowing the user to focus in the task, and not in the interaction [3].

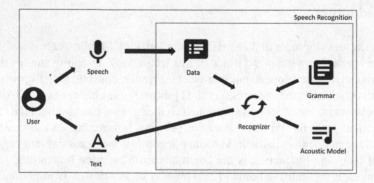

Fig. 1. Default model of a generic speech recognition service

Speech usage in smartphones and tablets also presents these advantages for the user. It is increasingly common that mobile applications developers offer more functionalities to the user, but this rise on functionalities requires more complex menus, which can hide some functions from the user, or demand a long time to the desired function to be found. In this scenario, voice interaction can ease the search of the user for a function, or even use it as a shortcut for the function [4]. Generally, speech recognizer has a default model, even varying little from application to application. Figure 1 has a diagram to show this model.

The recognizer starts when the user commands with the speech, this speech converts in data for interpretation, and is processed with the applications acoustic model, to interpret the signal, and with the grammar, to confirm if the speech is within the applications choose of words. Voice interaction presents practical use in various scenarios, but there few studies that use it with MAR.

2.2 Mobile Augmented Reality

MAR is the use of Augmented Reality (AR) concepts in mobile platforms, which blend merge the virtual content and real environment scenes in the mobile device screen [7]. This is done applying a layer of virtual information above a real scene.

Commonly the MAR applications show two main approaches to blend virtual content in the real scenes: markers or location. The marker approach uses recognition software of a particular pattern (such as QR Code) to select content, and the location approach uses the device's GPS and camera orientation to define what the user sees. The main characteristics of MAR are [8]:

- Presentation of augmented environment in mobile devices screen;
- Track technology: GPS, and pattern recognition of images;
- The graphical system is responsible for virtual objects rendering in augmented scenes;
- The worlds blend system mix real world and virtual objects.

The challenges in MAR application development are [9, 10]:

- Device sensors integration,
- Low precision in track technology;
- Limitations and divergent devices characteristics;
- User's interface variance;
- Lack of development patterns for MAR applications;
- Energy cost

Some guidelines must be followed to MAR applications development [11, 12]:

- Consider target user's profile, outdoor use, one or both hands and time of applications usage;
- Follow the good practices of AR usability and mobile applications. Leave the augmented scene clean, big icons and fonts, layers, 3D object interaction and consider real world;
- Consider devices limits, brightness, light reflection and low precision tracking;
- User's perception and cognition must be stimulated;

- Presentation of virtual information, consider information amount, information representation, information place and multiple visions;
- Evaluation: Adapt guidelines of usability evaluation for AR and mobile applications and evaluate a field at once using real users.

2.3 Related Applications

In order to support and construct the application's functionality in this paper, we selected three applications that based the choices of interaction and GUI design of the proposed application.

ARCity [13] is a MAR application that helps users to find a city's tourist attractions. This app has an integrated map and a classic RA browser of MAR applications. The ideas of do not leave the application to show the route in the map was well evaluated and is available in this article's application.

Immersive Tour Post [14] is a system that uses immersion with audio and video in an important or historic place of a city. The device is located in front of a POI and the tourists can know the history about the tourist attractions with an immersive video. The idea of the POI immersion is the great advantage of this technology, so the application proposed in this paper uses this concept in RA browser, although the user is not fully immersed in the application, this purpose is reached when user interact with the rotating POIs through its own axis.

Time Machine [15] is a MAR application that implements the panoramic image concept to make a list of tourist attractions in the current state and its past. The user can follow a visual timeline of these sights. The proposed application shows this timeline with historical photos of POIs. The images describe the story of these points with respect to what is depicted in the image.

3   ARGuide

ARGuide is a MAR application that uses georeferenced content as base for user navigation. The application allows the user to explore POI changing coordinated visions to access available content. The associated content of each POI can be multimedia, and the visions are different forms to visualize a POI. Coordinated visions means that the changes made in one vision reflects in all other, allowing that the user notices the same information with different perspectives. The available visions on application are:

- Map: Visualization of POIs application in a geographical map.
- RA Browser: Using the POI position, sets a marker in application camera correspondent to real world position
- POI List: Organizes POIs in a list.
- POI View: Shows POI content in a window, arranging text and media available.

The speech recognition service mainly affected two aspects of ARGuide, the GUI and architecture.

3.1 Graphical User Interface

The original ARGuide's GUI was changed to improve voice interaction, since previous ARGuide's interfaces were not developed for supporting voice interaction. The main changes of GUI are in Fig. 2.

Fig. 2. ARGuide's GUI in Map view, highlighting the main changes of the application

The changes seen in Fig. 2 includes:

- Use of text labels instead of visual representations. Labels in 2(a) inform the user the commandos available to the view in use, changing when the user changes the context (the view) in order to reflect controls of that view. Labels in 2(c) replaced icons in 2(b), in order to easy the interaction by suggesting to the user the commands that can be spoken.
- The POIs representation in the map were also changed to better suite voice interaction. In place of red markers, POIs are represented by text boxes with its name, allowing user to speak the POI name to open. POIView was adapted including a number for each media available for that POI, so the user can say the number of the media that should be opened.

3.2 Voice User Interface

To assess speech interaction, users should be able to navigate the ARGuide only using voice commands and with all the functionalities available by touch. The speech recognizer is always listening for user commands, starting and stopping with the application.

To allow speech interaction the ARGuide had gone through an architectural refactoring. A voice service has a link to a module of application as shown in Fig. 3. The application must set the actions to match the words recognized and execute them accordingly.

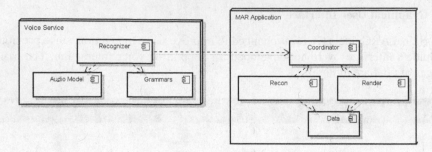

Fig. 3. Architecture for MAR application and voice recognition service

The Voice Service package are made of three components in order to process voice signals and extract action to the application. The Recognizer access the microphone and transforms its data to the useful information for the Audio Model, that process the signal and returns the recognized word (or sentence). The returned word is compared to the application grammar and if it is valid, the Recognizer sends it to the MAR Application package for processing the interaction. This package compares the received word with the active context in the application, and then execute the action (that depends both on the word and on the active context).

The grammar words are defined according to [4], the interaction follow guides from [11, 12] for MAR applications. Selected words should also be recognized by near variations, as plurals, synonyms and gender variations. Table 1 defines some interaction on the tool.

Table 1. Relations between voice commands, actions done by it and its GUI correspondent.

Voice commands	Action	GUI correspondent
esquerda, direita, cima, baixo (left, right, up, down)	Pan	Map /Image
aumentar, diminuir (zoom in, zoom out)	Zoom	Map /Image
aumentar, diminuir (zoom in, zoom out)	Ampliar ou diminuir raio de alcance.	AR Browser
subir, descer (move up, move down)	Scroll	List
qrcode, circuitos, ajuda, mapa, navegador ra, lista (qr code, circuits, help, map, ra browser, list)	Change between Menus & Views	QR Code reader, Circuits, Help and Views
<POI Name > [a]	Select POI	Map Marker I AR Marker I List Item

[a]This comand is dynamic and is dependable of the database items of the application.

The choice of the grammar words aimed to make possible that all the navigation are made using only the voice. For map navigation and image manipulation the same set of words were used due to they are analog to the actions they trigger. For the AR Browser the word set are the same as the zoom controller in map and image manipulation, due to the analog action are the same. The POI List only has scrolling controllers for going up and down.

Some commands recognized in every context, those are: menu selection, once the menus are always visible in the application; circuit exchange, that filter visible POIs in all views; help, that changes from view to view; view swap; POI selection, via POI name (except from the QR Code Reader).

4   Evaluation

Two evaluation methods were used to assess the interface and the voice commands in the application. One of those methods are based on tasks, which recorded interactions of each participant, and the other method is the usage of questionnaires, where the user answered questions about the application use and the user profile.

Table 2. List of tasks for the user test, divided by task units and classified by its complexity

Task number	Task	Task unit	Complexity
1.	Select a Circuit	a. Select circuit menu	2-Medium
		b. Select circuit	
2.	Find a POI using AR Browser	a. Select AR Browser view	3-Hard
		b. Fit AR view i) Apply zoom	
		c. Select POI	
3.	Find a POI using map	a. Select Map View	2-Medium
		b. (Optional) Fit Map view i) Use pan/zoom	
		c. Select POI	
4.	Find a POI using list	a. Select List View	2-Medium
		b. (Optional) Roll list	
		c. Select POI	
5.	Use QR Code Reader to find a POI	a. Select QR Code View	1-Easy
		b. Scan QRCode*	
6.	Navigate in a picture using pan and zoom	a. Select a picture	2-Medium
		b. Use pan/zoom	

4.1   Test Definition

Laboratory tests were conducted with 10 participants with low noise level (low air-conditioned noise). These users received training before using the app, through a showcase that presented app's functionalities available by touch and one POI selection via voice. The tasks used in this test are described in Table 2. The "Task" column defines the tasks proposed to the user and "Task Unit" defines the steps that compose each task.

We take complexity of a task by the minimum number of interactions (commands) needed in order to complete the task, one command is an easy task, two commands are medium and three commands make a hard task.

These tasks cover the main functionalities in the application for testing if the interface is proper for voice command interaction and if the chosen commands are meaningful and enough for the interaction. The following question were made to the user:

- How hard was the task?
- Have the application interface helped you completing the task?
- Was the speech recognition satisfactory for this task?

These questions allowed assess if the application interface helps the user completing tasks and if voice interaction helped in the same goal. The profile questionnaires contained the following questions:

- What is your age?
- How frequently do you use smartphones?
- Have you used speech recognition interaction in your smartphone before?
- Have you ever used a Mobile Augmented Reality application before?
- What have you liked in the application?
- What have you not liked in the application?
- Would you use the application if it were available for download in an app store?
- What would you point as positive and negative points in the application?
- In general, what is your evaluation of the application?

5   Results

The evaluation results made are based on questionnaire answers and tests video analysis. The data extracted from the videos is the number of errors related to speech recognition in each task unit and the number of errors related in which the GUI was not clear to the user and not lead him to end of the task. For the user profile, Fig. 4 binds two graphs with the users' answers of questionnaires.

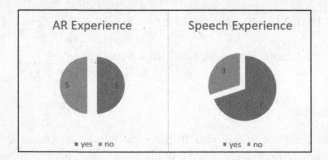

Fig. 4. Answers for user profiles, defining AR and speech experience

Most users has experience with voice interfaces e half of them used an AR application at least once. Age range of the users is between 22 and 42 years old and all of them use smartphone daily. The users' familiarity with the technology used can be an important factor to fulfillment of all tasks. There is not failure in any of them. Figure 5 shows the error average for the tasks of the users, divided by its respective task units.

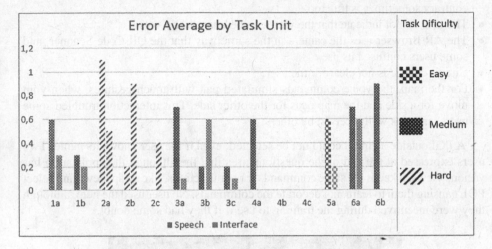

Fig. 5. Error average of user test, divided by task unit

The task with the higher error average for speech recognition is the task unit 2a, to select the AR Browser view from Map view. The word composition from this command ("Navegador RA"-"AR Browser") is divided by two, being the second word two spelled letters. The recognition system was not able to recognize this composition properly for all users, and most users opted to use the single word "navegador" ("browser"), supported as synonymous for the same action, as the voice command. Same difficulty can be seen in task 5a, swap to the QR Code Scanner view, that asks for a single voice command, but has a high error rate of speech recognition compared to error average of GUI.

The task with the higher error average for GUI is the task unit 2b, to extend the range radius of AR Browser. The users should apply zoom and extend the radius to see the marker of the POI. Most users had trouble to identify the widget to extend the range, and some had to remove all range from the AR Browser to understand that they should extend the range to see further POI.

Bugs found in the application by the users through the test, and one of them had influence in the map navigation. One of the words for pan the map was not being recognized ("acima"-"upward"), and the users had to use a synonymous ("cima"-"up") to do the navigation. A context bug, when changing POIView and QR Code Scanner, generated some confusion for the users, preventing them to navigate directly from the POIView to QR Code Scanner. Two users indicated another bug, they noticed that choosing a media in POIView after coming from the List view, the selection would choose the item list instead of the media. Problems reported by the users in questionnaire and the problems found analyzing the videos are listed below:

- Microphone icon in the subtitle looks like a button to start voice interaction (Fig. 2(a)).
- Some words on plural can not be recognized like the ones in the singular, and the contrary sometimes is true too.
- The tabs do not indicate that the view can be changed by voice.
- The AR Browser uses the camera in the same way that the QR Code Scanner, and some users confused its use.
- Circuit change is not clear for the user.
- For the map, the voice commands simulated pan with touch gestures, when yout move for a side and the map pans for the other side. This interaction troubled some users, and was well received by others.

A POI outside a circuit could not be selected, even if the user knows its name. Two users expressed at the end of the questionnaires that the although the application has various views, it keeps the same commands for some actions, like swap views and select POI, causing them to learn, not decorate the commands. No user used the help, although they were incentived during the training to use it if they had some doubt.

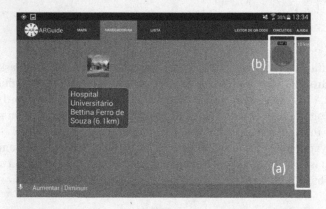

Fig. 6. AR browser view highlighting interface components

The units task 2c, 3c and 4c are the same (Select a POI), were the best received by the user. POI selection is a simple interaction, knowing the name of the POI the user can user it without the need to focus some marker in the screen, using the voice command as a shortcut. Two users highlighted speed reaction and visual feedback given by the application in POI selection. The suggestions of improvement for voice interaction can be listed as: Add more words for some commands, like the navigation ones.

- Give fail and success messages, with suggestions like: "Wanted to say:...?" in case of error.
- Clearly indicate what view between QR Code Scanner and AR Browser the user is using.

- Make the tab separator more visible and that tabs more separated from ARGuide logo.
- A customization option to select some commands before the user starts the usage of application.
- Redefine AR Browser layout. Figure 6(a) show the widget for manipulation of radius range and 6(b) the navigation radar, where each yellow dot is a POI of selected circuit. These points need more focus; most errors related to GUI could be avoided if these two widgets were clearer to the user.

6 Conclusion

Voice interaction allows a different user experience of an application. The MAR allows new types of exploration of a new place, or a new mode to explore old places. This work presented that is possible to unify this forms of interaction not overloading the user interaction. Efficient aspects of interaction was found, like the POI selection, as well as others can be improved, like the RA interaction. The results presented that a voice interaction in an RAM application are possible.

The selection of POI was the best solution to the interaction through voice interaction, therefore shortcuts interactions are feasible through voice interaction, (e.g. the user can speak the name of the POI if it is already known for the user, without search it in a vision). The RA browser's interface has some troubles in the voice interaction, and it will be redesigned next interaction. Based on the analysis of the results, a list of improvements was suggested. Among this improvements are the redesign of the RA browser' interface; to use more words in some commands; a custom interface to each user and error messages.

We expect that in the next application's iteration the improvements proposed in the session 5 may be made and a new test conducted, with a touch hybrid approach and voice to produce voice interactions guidelines to RAM applications.

References

1. Martínez, H., Skournetou, D., Hyppola, J., Laukkanen, S., Heikkila, A.: Drivers and bottlenecks in the adoption of augmented reality applications. J. Multimedia Theory Appl. 1(1), 27–44 (2014)
2. Shneiderman, B.: Designing the User Interface: Strategies for Effective Human-Computer Interaction, 3rd edn, pp. 293–295. Addison Wesley, Reading (1998)
3. Vidakis, N., Syntychakis, M., Triantafyllidis, G., Akoumianakis, D.: Multimodal natural user interaction for multiple applications: the gesture – voice example. In: International Conference on Telecommunications and Multimedia – TEMU (2012)
4. Xia, L., Kai, K., Xiaochun, W., Dan, W.: Research and Design of the "Voice-Touch-Vision" Multimodal Integrated Voice Interaction in the Mobile Phone (2010)
5. Lee, K.B.; Grice, R.A.: The design and development of user interfaces for voice application in mobile devices. In: 2006 IEEE International Professional Communication Conference, pp. 308–320, 23–25 Outubro 2006

6. Teixeira, A., et al.: Speech-centric multimodal interaction for easy-toaccess online services – A personal life assistant for the elderly. In: 5th International Conference on Software Development and Technologies for Enhancing Accessibility and Fighting Info-exclusion, DSAI 2013. Modeling and Simulation Design. AK Peters Ltd., Natick, MA (2013)

7. B.A. Delail, Weruaga, L., Jamal Zemerly, M.: CAViAR: Context aware visual indoor augmented reality for a university campus. In: Proceedings of the 2012 IEEE/WIC/ACM International Joint Conferences on Web Intelligence and Intelligent Agent Technology, (WI-IAT 2012), vol. 3, pp. 286–290. IEEE Computer Society, Washington, DC (2012)

8. Srinivasa, K.G., Jagannath, S., Akash Nidhi, P.S., Tejesh, S., Santhosh, K.: Augmented reality application: cloud based augmented reality android application to "know your world better". In: Proceedings of the 6th IBM Collaborative Academia Research Exchange Conference (I-CARE) on I-CARE 2014. ACM, New York (2014). Article 15

9. Markov-Vetter, D., Staadt, O.: A pilot study for augmented reality supported procedure guidance to operate payload racks on-board the international space station. In: IEEE International Symposium on Mixed and Augmented Reality (ISMAR), pp. 1–6, 1–4 October 2013

10. Doswell, J.T.: Augmented learning: context-aware mobile augmented reality architecture for learning. In: Sixth International Conference on Advanced Learning Technologies, pp. 1182–1183, 5–7 July 2006

11. Nielsen, J.: Usability Inspection Methods. In: Heuristic Evaluation. Katherine Schowalter, New York (1994)

12. Pyssysalo, T., Repo, T., Turunen, T., Lankila, T., Röning, J.: CyPhone—bringing augmented reality to next generation mobile phones. In: Proceedings of DARE 2000 on Designing augmented reality environments (DARE 2000), pp. 11–21. ACM, New York (2000)

13. de la Nube Aguirre Brito, C.: Augmented reality applied in tourism mobile applications. In: 2015 Second International Conference on eDemocracy & eGovernment (ICEDEG), pp. 120–125, 8–10 April 2015

14. Park, D., Nam, T.-J., Shi, C.-K.: Designing an immersive tour experience system for cultural tour sites. In: CHI 2006 Extended Abstracts on Human Factors in Computing Systems (CHI EA 2006), pp. 1193–1198. ACM, New York (2006). doi:http://dx.doi.org/10.1145/1125451.1125675

15. Feng, D., Meng, D., Zhang, Y., Weng, D.: Time machine: a mobile augmented reality system for tourism based on coded-aperture camera. In: 2013 IEEE 10th International Conference on Ubiquitous Intelligence and Computing and 10th International Conference on Autonomic and Trusted Computing (UIC/ATC), pp. 502–506, 18–21 December 2013

Gesture Interactions for Virtual Immersive Environments: Navigation, Selection and Manipulation

Paulo Dias[1,2(✉)], João Pinto[1], Sérgio Eliseu[3],
and Beatriz Sousa Santos[1,2]

[1] DETI/UA- Department of Electronics, Telecommunications and Informatics,
Aveiro, Portugal
{paulo.dias, jhpinto, bss}@ua.pt
[2] IEETA- Institute of Electronics and Informatics Engineering of Aveiro,
University of Aveiro, Portugal Campus Universitário de Santiago,
3810-193 Aveiro, Portugal
[3] 3iD + / I2ADS - Faculty of Fine Arts, University of Porto, Porto, Portugal
s.eliseu@ua.pt

Abstract. This paper presents an extension to a Platform for Setting-Up Virtual environments with the purpose of allowing gesture interaction. The proposed solution maintains the flexibility of the original framework as well as content association (PDF, Video, Text), but allows new interactions based on gestures. An important feature is the one to one navigational input based on Kinect skeleton tracking. The framework was used to configure a virtual museum art installation using a real museum room where the user can move freely and interact with virtual contents by adding and manipulating 3D models. Two user studies were performed to compare gestures against button-controlled interactions for navigation and 3D manipulation. Most users preferred the Kinect-based navigation and gesture-based interaction despite some learning difficulties and tracking problems. Regarding manipulation, the gesture-based method was significantly faster with similar accuracy when compared to the controller. On the other hand, when dealing with rotations, the controller-based method was faster.

Keywords: Virtual Reality · Navigation and manipulation in virtual environments · Gestural interaction · Kinect · 3duis · User study

1 Introduction and Motivation

This work aims to update a previously developed framework called pSIVE [1] to support recent hardware and allow gesture interaction in line with the Empty Museum concept [2]. One of the objectives was to create a setup where users can move freely inside an empty room, using a one to one position mapping from the real world to the virtual world, while viewing a virtual scene with the same spatial configuration. In this setup, besides navigation, the visitor had the possibility to interact with art-pieces, browsing contents (such as pdf files, images, textual information and videos), and even

© Springer International Publishing Switzerland 2016
S. Lackey and R. Shumaker (Eds.): VAMR 2016, LNCS 9740, pp. 211–221, 2016.
DOI: 10.1007/978-3-319-39907-2_20

modify the museum by adding and manipulating 3D models, therefore creating their own virtual museum. The final setup allows complete immersion of the user in an empty room using several Kinects for tracking and a head mounted display. A virtual museum prototype was developed where the user was able to navigate and modify the environment either hands-free (walking in a real empty room and using gestures), or standing still with a physical controller, while viewing the virtual museum through an Head Mounted Display (HMD). In what follows, we present some related work, and then discuss the framework's architecture, the interaction methods it supports and the virtual museum demonstration used to validate the framework. Finally, the results of two user studies comparing interactions with gestures and controllers are presented.

2 Related Work

The Empty Museum [2] is the application that most closely resembles ours. It is a multi-user immersive walkable and wireless system where users can navigate a virtual environment with content such as audio, text, images and video. The system includes a laptop computer in a backpack that renders the environment on a HMD according to the user perspective while connected to sensors that captures wireless movement. The only interaction provided is the user position update with no additional support for more complex interactions.

The training School developed for the DCNS group [3] is a virtual training environment, developed in OpenSpace3D, linked to a Learning Management System (LMS). This web solution provides access to training courses and pedagogical progress of students, as well as managing the content of the courses. Users can navigate in the environment, visualise training courses, media and products, check messages and chat with other users (students and teachers). The application allows interaction through a desktop environment, a web browser with mouse and keyboard or in an immersive environment with stereoscopic video projection supporting a Wiimote and kinect camera for content interaction.

The KidsRoom [4] explores computer vision technologies in an augmented reality interactive playspace for children by recreating a child's bedroom with two real walls and two large video projection screens, as well as ceiling mounted coloured lights, speakers, cameras and a microphone, all controlled by a six-computer cluster. Four cameras are pointing at the room, one for tracking, two for action recognition of people in the room, and one to provide a view of the room for spectators.

pSIVE [1] is a platform we previously developed that can be used to set up a virtual scene using a diversity of models associated to variety of content (pdf, video, text). It uses OpenSceneGraph [5] as graphical engine and VRJuggler [6] as a middleware to interpret input from trackers and controllers. Content can be accessed through a 2D linear menu that pops up when the user presses a button on the controller while looking at an object that has been configured with content.

None of the presented systems supports at the same time content presentation, one to one navigation and gesture interaction in the same framework as we propose in this work.

3   Framework

The developed framework took advantage of our previous work on pSIVE. The main features are still easy configuration, support for several contents (videos, pdf files, text and images), and hardware flexibility. However, in this work we have expanded and updated the framework to support recent hardware (Oculus Rift and Kinect) and abandoned the VRJuggler [6] library due to its difficult set-up and lack of recent development. The next sub-sections present details on the new version of the framework as well as a prototype developed to demonstrate its flexibility and illustrate the type of applications it can be used for.

3.1   Architecture

The architecture of the framework is presented in Fig. 1. The selected graphical engine is OpenSceneGraph (as used in pSIVE) to benefit of its VR libraries (namely osgOculusViewer for Oculus rift and osgVRPRN, a node kit to integrate the VRPN-Virtual Reality Peripheral Network providing access to a variety of VR devices). A PC based client-server architecture is used in which the client is responsible for all the rendering of the virtual world and handling of the (HMD orientation tracking. Several VRPN servers [7] communicate the hardware input, when using a physical controller, or the user skeleton information (positional data of head, hands and gripping gestures) to the client using one or several Microsoft Kinect devices. Skeleton data is collected with the Kinect SDK 1.8.

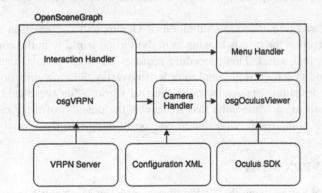

Fig. 1. Framework architecture

The framework is configured through several XML files, namely Config.xml (list of models, physical attributes (size, rotation, location) and available content), Kinect.xml (information to set-up the servers which read data from multiple Kinects) and Controls. xml (for the use and mapping of a physical controller). It receives input information from one or more VRPN Servers, which is interpreted by the osgVRPN library. That information is then handled in one of two ways: interaction with menus or content (Menu Handler), or navigation (Camera Handler). Finally, the scene is rendered for use with the Oculus Rift using the osgOculusViewer library.

3.2   Calibration

In order to calibrate the Kinect position regarding real world and allowing one to one navigation, a calibration tool was developed. The visualization Toolkit (VTK) [8] is used due to familiarity and easy access to the Iterative Closest Point (ICP) algorithm. The calibration process captures a depth image from the Kinect and allows the user roughly fit the point cloud within the 3D model using the keyboard. After the frame is positioned manually the user can adjust automatically the depth image with the model using VTK's ICP function (see Fig. 2). Finally, the transformation matrix is exported into a file ready to be used as input in our custom VRPN server for a given room with given Kinect positions.

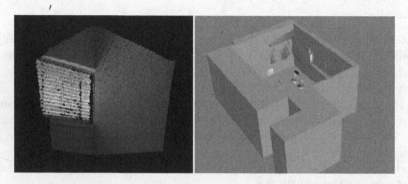

Fig. 2. A Kinect point cloud and final alignment with 3D model after ICP

Regarding head orientation, a calibration of Oculus Rift's orientation is necessary to match the direction the user is looking at in the virtual world with the corresponding direction in the real world. This procedure requires the user to stand facing the real world Kinect and grip their right hand in order to overlay the view direction of the 3D world with the direction they are facing in the real world. After these calibrations, the user should be facing a white cube that represents the position of the Kinect and can then freely walk in the room, with one to one positioning into the virtual room.

3.3   Custom VRPN Server

A custom VRPN Server using the VRPN library with the Microsoft Kinect library was developed to integrate Kinect information into our system. The Kinect 1.8 SDK was used to track the user skeleton and the grip gesture of both their hands. The coordinates are then transformed to real world coordinates using a transformation matrix computed during Kinect calibration. That information is communicated to the client by mapping Kinect information (user's left and right hands as well as global positions) through analogue channels. Left and right hand closing state are mapped as buttons. Head position is used by the client to define the camera position in the scene, while right and left hand positions are used to show visual aid (spheres) representing the user's hands. In a multiple Kinect setting additional information is sent to indicate which Kinect is detecting the user.

3.4 Virtual Museum

To validate our framework, we configured a virtual museum art installation: a virtual model of a real room of the museum of Aveiro was created and users were able to navigate and interact inside a virtual representation by just moving their body, while tracked by three Kinects covering most of the working area (Fig. 3). Besides visualization and navigation, users could also activate menus as well as select and manipulate 3D models of contents related to the museum (Fig. 4).

Fig. 3. Kinect setup in the virtual museum

Fig. 4. User manipulating a model in the virtual museum

4 Interaction

An important goal of the developed platform is flexibility in terms of hardware and interactions. In this section, we describe the interaction methods supported by the platform for navigation and manipulation.

4.1   Navigation

Three different methods of navigation are supported: the first one, and the main focus of our work, uses the Kinect skeleton information to position the user in the virtual scene, allowing to navigate the world by simply walking. As an alternative, when one to one tracking is not possible, a method based on a "Steering Wheel" metaphor [9] was implemented allowing the user to navigate the world as if driving a car and based on hands tracking. A physical button controller (Wiimote for example) can also be used to control user position and navigation. The forward and backward directions are determined by the user's viewing direction (gaze-directed), meaning s/he will always move towards or away from the direction s/he is looking at.

4.2   Manipulation

Regarding object manipulation, two different interaction modes are provided. One method uses a handle bar metaphor inspired in [9] to position, rotate and scale the objects (see Fig. 5). The original implementation was modified to allow positioning of the objects (the original proposal only coped with rotation and scaling).

Fig. 5. Handle bar metaphor for object rotation and scaling adapted from [9]

Using this metaphor, scale is updated according to the distance between the user's hands. Rotation is given by the angle between the vector calculated from the position of the user's hands and the horizontal/vertical planes. The object position is obtained by the midpoint between the user's hands in the world. Scale and rotation changes are accumulated during the manipulation, meaning that the user may combine rotations to make up for the fact that there is a missing DOF, and scale the object up or down without being limited by the length of their arms.

Manipulation can also be done with a controller. In our tests, a Wiimote was used, but any controller with buttons can be configured. In this case, manipulation is split into three modes that can be toggled using the controller: translation (x, y, and z axis), rotation (x, y, and z axis), and uniform scaling. The current mode is depicted by an icon on the display and manipulation takes effect with button presses.

5 User Studies

A preliminary study with 12 volunteers and a controlled experiment involving 28 participants have been performed to compare gestures and commands for navigation and manipulation. During both studies, execution times and accuracy of the movements were logged.

5.1 Preliminary Study

A preliminary study was performed with 12 volunteers participating in the University's summer academy (ages between 15 and 17) to compare the two methods of interaction and navigation in a virtual room. The input variables are the navigation and the menu selection methods. In one method, the user walks in the room to navigate, and is able to select an item by moving their hand and performing the grip gesture. In the other method, the user uses a controller with buttons to navigate in the room and interact with the menu. Both methods display radial menus and use an Oculus rift DK2 HMD.

The output variables were the time the participant took to get to the interaction position (interaction area shown as a sphere in Fig. 6) and activate the menu, the time necessary to select the correct option, and the number of incorrect selections.

Fig. 6. Experimental environment (green circle: interaction area) and user performing a gesture

The time differences to reach the interaction position are negligible between the two setups (35.25 s average for controller-based and 35.41 s for Kinect-based). Regarding interaction with the menu, users were faster to activate the correct option with the controller-based method (with an average 16.6 s) when compared with the Kinect-based method (30.3 s) that also presented more selection errors. Participants filled a questionnaire regarding navigation and interaction preferences and preferred Kinect interaction despite its worse performance for menu selection.

5.2 3D Manipulation Study

This study was used to compare the manipulation interaction styles. As such, we have gathered data regarding the manipulation times and accuracy, performing a comparison between gestures and a controller. Two different studies were performed. One regarding object position and the other regarding rotation/scale.

Method. This experiment aimed to verify if the two 3D manipulation methods were equally usable in our demonstration environment. Our experiment had two input variables, namely the two different manipulation methods: gestures or controller-based. The experiment was divided in two separate stages: the first consisted of a manipulation regarding the positioning of an object. In the gesture-based method, users performed a grip gesture with the two hands to start interaction and then move the hands to position the object. In the controller-based method, they used buttons to move the object. In both methods, the user's task was to position the object as such that it matched a ghost model of that object as closely as possible. The experiment continued to the next phase once the user verbally signalled that they were satisfied with their placement of the object. In the second stage, we evaluated the manipulation of the object's rotation and scale. Given some initial difficulties of the first users in this task, we decided to set two and a half minutes of training before starting the test and gathering data. Similarly to the manipulation, the users had an object centred inside the ghost model, with a different orientation and scale (Fig. 7), and they must use gestures or the controller's buttons to rotate and scale the object to match the ghost model as closely as possible. The experiment ended when the user verbally indicated that they were satisfied with the matching between the two models.

Fig. 7. Ghost model and rotated model used in the controlled experiment

In the positioning study, we logged three variables during user interaction: time elapsed until the objects was at a position below 0.002 units from the final position, time to the final position and final distance between the ghost and the final model in final position.

In the rotation/scale study, four key values were monitored: first time that the object reached our minimum requirement (a solid angle below $5°$ between the two models), time to the final position, and the angular and scale difference between the two models at the end of the interaction.

28 users participated in this experiment. All users performed the tasks with both experimental conditions (a within group experimental design was used). Half of the users performed the experiment using the Kinect first and the others using the controller first, in order to attenuate possible bias due to learning effects. The participants were observed while performing the experiment, and were asked to answer a questionnaire regarding their satisfaction, difficulties and preferred method.

Results. Table 1 presents the average results of the positioning tests. It shows that users take roughly half the time to achieve a distance below the threshold with the Kinect when compared with the controller. On the other hand, after achieving the minimum distance, the adjustments required until the best position were much faster with the controller. The accuracy in the final position was similar between both methods. Preferences were similar with 13 users preferring the Kinect, 14 preferring the controller and 1 having no preference.

Table 1. Positioning test results

	Kinect	Controller
Time to first position below threshold distance (s)	23.4 ± 13.0	48.1 ± 18.3
Best position time (s)	38.7 ± 29.0	54.8 ± 20.3
Best position (units)	0.00015	0.00013

Table 2 presents the average results of the rotation/scale tests. The scaling difference between models is not presented since its variation was negligible between both methods. Users achieved similar accuracy with both methods, with the Kinect-based method being 30 % slower than the controller-based method. However, despite being slower to reach a $< 5°$ error, the Kinect-based method was faster after that point in reaching the minimum angle error (17 s vs 22 s). This difference might be explained by the necessity to accumulate rotations in the Kinect-based method (only 2 degrees of freedom in rotation were available), where the controller-based method had 3 degrees of freedom in rotation. As previously, users' preferences were split between the two methods, with 12 users preferring the Kinect-based method, 13 users preferring the controller-based method and 3 having no preference. It is noteworthy that there were 11 failed attempts either with the controller-based (7) or the Kinect-based method (4), corresponding to users not able to reach an error below $5°$ within a reasonable time.

Table 2. Positioning test results

	Kinect	Controller
Time to first angle below threshold (s)	75.5 ± 53.6	53.5 ± 37.0
Time to best angle (s)	88.3 ± 57.3	75.8 ± 41.4
Angular difference (°)	1.19	1.03

6   Conclusions

The main goal of this work was to provide a framework that allows the creation of an interactive virtual world. The users can either interact with the environment by accessing content such as videos and pdf files within models in the scene, or by inserting and manipulating directly objects in the environment. The developed framework was tested in a live scenario, in the museum of the city of Aveiro. An art installation was created where users could navigate/move around a virtual/real room in the museum and experience virtual content, as well as setting up their own virtual exposition by adding models of monuments through a grid-like menu and manipulating them by positioning, rotating and scaling them in the virtual environment.

We adapted a previously developed framework to work with one or several Kinect cameras, tracking the user in a physical room and mapping their movements to the virtual scene. To do this we developed tools to calibrate the Kinect cameras with the real room and its virtual model. The use of a depth sensor also provided the opportunity to add gesture-based interaction for manipulating content.

Two user studies were performed, a preliminary one to compare input methods (controller *versus* gestures in a radial menu), and movement methods (tracked by the Kinect *versus* buttons on a controller). From this study, we concluded that users were interested in gesture-based controls and one-to-one mapped navigation, and while the navigation timings with the Kinect tracking method were comparable to the timings when using the controller, menu selection was not as good. We also performed a controlled experiment to compare gesture and controller-based manipulation. Both methods fare about the same when it comes to accuracy in the position, rotation and scale of the object, with the Kinect-based method being faster in positioning and the controller-based method faster when it comes to rotation.

From the results of these user studies, as well as the experience from developing and testing the framework, we consider that both controller-based and gesture-based methods have their place in interaction inside immersive virtual environments. Controller-based methods have the advantage of providing clearer and more accurate actuation when compared with gesture-based methods, where we found some cases of false-positives and false-negatives. On the other hand, gesture-based interaction methods provide us with a more natural type of interaction with the virtual environment, particularly in the case of object manipulation. We believe that a hybrid method of interaction could prove to be beneficial, where a physical controller might be used to activate menus and select options, while combined with depth and movement sensors to provide 6 degrees of freedom on manipulation tasks.

Acknowledgements.   The authors are grateful to all volunteer participants. This work was partially funded by National Funds through FCT - Foundation for Science and Technology, in the context of the projects UID/CEC/00127/2013 and Incentivo/EEI/UI0127/2014.

References

1. Souza, D., Dias, P., Sousa Santos, B.: Choosing a selection technique for a virtual environment. In: Shumaker, R., Lackey, S. (eds.) VAMR 2014, Part I. LNCS, vol. 8525, pp. 215–225. Springer, Heidelberg (2014)
2. Hernandez, L., Taibo, J., Seoane, A., López, R., López, R.: The empty museum. Multi-user interaction in an immersive and physically walkable VR space. In: Proceedings of International Conference on Cyberworlds, pp. 446–452. IEEE Computer Society (2003)
3. DCNS Training School - A virtual environment interfaced with an e-learning platform (2013). http://www.openspace3d.com/lang/en/2013/03/19/dcns-training-school
4. Bobick, A.B., Intille, S.S., Davis, J.W., Baird, F., Pinhanez, C.S., Lee, W., Campbell, L.W., Ivanov, Y.A., Schütte, A., Wilson, A.: The KidsRoom: a perceptually-based interactive and immersive story environment. Teleoperators Virtual Environ. 8(4), 367–391 (1999)
5. Wang, R., Qian, X.: OpenSceneGraph 3.0: Beginner's Guide. Packt Publishing, New York (2010)
6. Bierbaum, A., Just, C., Hartling, P., Meinert, K., Baker, A., Carolina Cruz-Neira., C.: Vr juggler: A virtual platform for virtual reality application development. In: Proceedings of the Virtual Reality 2001 Conference (VR 2001), VR 2001, p. 89, Washington, DC, USA. IEEE Computer Society (2001)
7. Taylor, R.M.II, Hudson, T.C., Seeger, A., Weber, H., Juliano, J., Helser, A.T.: Vrpn: A device-independent, network-transparent vr peripheral system. In: Proceedings of the ACM Symposium on Virtual Reality Software and Technology, VRST 2001, pp. 55–61. ACM, New York, NY, USA (2001)
8. Schroeder, W., Kenneth, M.M., Lorensen, W.E.: The Visualization Toolkit: An Object-oriented Approach to 3D Graphics, 2nd edn. Prentice-Hall, Upper Saddle River, NJ, USA (1998)
9. Cardoso, J.: 3D manipulation and navigation methods with gestures for large displays. Master thesis. Universidade de Aveiro, Portugal (2015)

Usability and Functionality Assessment of an Oculus Rift in Immersive and Interactive Systems Using Voice Commands

Valéria Farinazzo Martins[1], Paulo N.M. Sampaio[2],
Fernanda da S. Mendes[1], André Santos Lima[1],
and Marcelo de Paiva Guimarães[3(✉)]

[1] Computing and Informatics Program,
Mackenzie Prebisterian University, Sao Paulo, SP, Brazil
valfarinazzo@hotmail.com, nandayoko@hotmail.com,
andresantoslima@gmail.com
[2] Computing and Systems Graduate Program,
Salvador University (UNIFACS), Salvador, BA, Brazil
pnms.funchal@gmail.com
[3] Brazilian Open University(Federal University of São Paulo)/Master Program
of Faculty Campo Limpo Paulista, São Paulo, SP, Brazil
marcelodepaiva@gmail.com

Abstract. Virtual Reality has provided means to improve interface and user interaction with computational systems. This improvement has affected directly the degree of immersion and user interaction with computer-generated synthetic environments, through the utilization of human senses such sight, hearing, touch, smell and taste. This work aims to present a usability assessment and the functionalities of an interactive and immersive virtual reality system based on the utilization of the panoramic Oculus Rift device and interaction through voice commands. The virtual environment adopted to be integrated to the solution is the Google Street View through which user can visualize and navigate on. Besides assessment, this paper also introduces the hardware and software integration carried out, as the different phases of the development of the virtual environment.

Keywords: Virtual reality · Oculus rift · Voice commands · Immersion · Interaction

1 Introduction

Currently, the technologies applied in the development of application interfaces aim at turning users' experience to be as natural as possible [1–5]. For this purpose, the user's intuitive knowledge about the physical world has been considered in order to determine how this user interaction with the interface should be carried out. Virtual Reality (VR) is a relevant research area in the development of interfaces that explore users' experiences since it allows user interaction and their immersive participation with the simulation, either through visualization devices, touch or movement capture [6].

© Springer International Publishing Switzerland 2016
S. Lackey and R. Shumaker (Eds.): VAMR 2016, LNCS 9740, pp. 222–232, 2016.
DOI: 10.1007/978-3-319-39907-2_21

Indeed, VR does not constrain users only to simulation within real world, instead it amplifies the physical and temporal perception of users, enriching information and, thus, user's experience. For instance, it enables users to explore a volcano in eruption or navigate within a cell. VR has been a breakthrough within different knowledge areas: if we consider Engineering, for instance, reducing or avoiding the construction of mis-designed physical prototypes, or through the simulation of inaccessible or dangerous environments; when it comes to health environments, it is possible to provide realistic data analysis, patient monitoring and surgeries simulation. Clearly, the success of utilization of these environments depends on different factors, among them usability.

The goal of this paper is to assess usability and functionality of an Oculus Rift [7] in immersive and interactive environments using voice commands. For this purpose, an immersive application has been developed in order to provide navigation within Google Street View [8] – application that enables users to visualize streets and avenues. This application applies the user's head tracking in order to indicate which direction the user is visualizing, and user's voice to move around – a natural user interface.

Besides the usability assessment, this paper also presents the hardware and software integration carried out, as the development phase of the virtual environment. In order to achieve the proposed goals of this project the following activities were executed:

- Configuration, installation and deployment of the Oculus Rift device;
- Development of the voice-controlled immersive and interactive application;
- Execution of tests with the targeted audience, and;
- Analysis of the assessment results.

Some contributions related to the utilization of Oculus Rift can be found in the literature. Reiners [9] applied an Oculus Rift to have users immersed in an occupational health and safety learning environment. The experiments propose relevant activities and missions to be carried out by the user, focusing on his ability to identify high risk situations and react accordingly. Hoffman [10] applied this device as a support to help burn treatment. Once conventional methods (medication and therapies) are not effective for disinfecting wounds, for stretching burnt members and for stretching affected skin, which is painful for the patient. In this context, psychological intervention can also be helpful as a complement to standard analgesic medication prescribed. Therefore, patients can apply Oculus Rift in order to navigate within an ice customized environment while he is submitted to the painful procedures required. Since the patient's brain has been occupied navigating within virtual environment, he forgets the pain he is under. The paper presents an experiment carried out with an 11-year-old boy who had several electrical and flash burn injuries in his head, shoulders, arms and feet. He went through a 20 min session without VR in the first day, another VR session on the second day and a session without VR on the third day. On the day the patient had VR applied on the treatment he claimed the pain dropped from unbearable to mildly bearable.

The remaining of the paper is organized as follows: Sect. 2 describes the development phases of the application; Sect. 3 discusses the results obtained after running users tests; and, finally, Sect. 4 presents some final consideration of this work.

2 Development of a Voice-Controlled Immersive and Interactive Environment

The application adopted as basis for this implementation was Google Street View, which allows the panoramic visualization of a location in 360 degrees (horizontal) and 290 degrees (vertical), and also supports interaction using mouse and keyboard. The integration of this application with Oculus Rift and voice-commands provide users with an immersive interaction with any location anywhere in the world without leaving home. Therefore, it is also possible to visualize Google pictures of landscapes experiencing the immersive feeling of being there which is provided by the virtual environment. The voice commands were associated with action within the environment, such as go, back, back to search page.

The application has been developed using a prototyping technique [11, 12]. The development phases were iterative and in each development phase a new functionality was identified and aggregated to the system. Figure 1 depicts the development life cycle adopted:

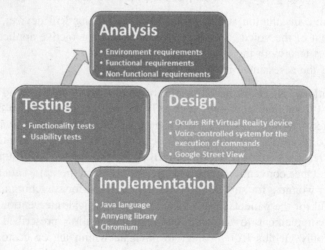

Fig. 1. The development life cycle

1. Analysis: definition of environment functional and non-functional requirements;
2. Design: definition of visualization and interaction device, and application design;
3. Implementation: the code is written and the hardware is configured;
4. Testing: testing functionality and usability.

2.1 Analysis

In order to specify the functionalities of the system (application and virtual environment) the following requirements were identified:

Environment Requirements: related to the physical environment where the application is being deployed:

– The environment should be kept in silence in order to ease voice capture by the microphone;
– User should be seat in a safe and steady place in order to avoid a possible fall since once the Oculus Rift is being deployed user loses sight and notion of the real physical space, and consequently loosing cognitive balance;
– The user cannot make sudden movements with his/her head in order to reduce sickness or dizziness.

• **Functional Requirements:** related to the functionalities of the system.

– The system should be executed on-line in order to access Google Street View;
– The addresses collected through voice-commands should be translated to a string which will be inserted in a text field;
– All the commands should be spoken in English.

• **Non-functional Requirements:** related to the response time when the application is executed. The interval in seconds should be as small as possible between the voice-command reception and the response presentation in order to provide a fast information retrieval and a straightforward presentation without interruptions, longer delays guaranteeing content integrity.

2.2 Design

Immersion is one of the important features of VR [6, 13], which can be provided by the deployment of a head mounted display. In this project the immersion is provided by the utilization of an Oculus Rift (Fig. 2). This device applies 360 degrees head motion tracking in order to allow users to look around as they would do in real life, providing a realistic experience.

Fig. 2. Oculus rift

The application was hosted on Web servers using technologies such as Java servlets and Javascript. The tools applied were:

- The Oculus Software Development Kit – SDK v0.3.2 [14];
- The version of Google Street View [8] applied was the Oculus Street View, which is a version designed for this device;
- The library Annyang [15] was applied for voice recognition. This Javascript library is oriented to web applications. Nevertheless, voice training is not applied in order to improve the degree of voice liability;
- The Google Chromium WebVR [16] was the Web browser applied, which is a version of Google Chrome oriented to the execution of Oculus Rift.

2.3 Implementation

This project was developed within 7 months, most of which was spent with studies on how to develop an application for Oculus Rift.

Figure 3 illustrates the operational flow for the developed application. Initially, the browser (in this case Chromium WebVR) presents a search page. In this page, there is a text field which will map voice commands into a text string. The commands are captured as voice through a microphone, as if user were typing it and clicking on the mouse. Thus, without the need to use hands to interact with the application, the user just pronounces the command and the local address, for instance, "Go to Wall Street New York". The voice command is captured by Annyang library and is sent to a servlet - a Java program that extends the capabilities of a server. This Annyang servlet processes information and presents it as an output text (string), which is then sent to another servlet that applies the Google Map's API called Geocode in order to map address into coordinates. At last, these coordinates are sent to Google Street View in order to present the required location on Oculus Rift. From this moment on, the user is free to navigate wherever he wants using voice commands. If user provides a non-specific address, for instance, "Go to Disney", then a pair of unknown coordinates is presented to the user.

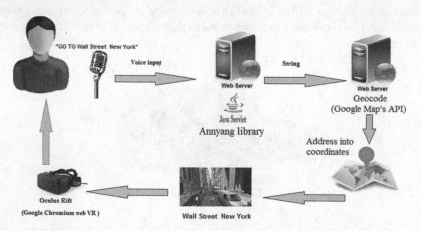

Fig. 3. Operational schema of the system

2.4   Testing

The functionality and usability tests were carried out with 15 users in three different locations: at the place where the group who developed the application lives, at the company one of the members of the group works and at the university where they study/work at. Initially, everyone filled out a pre-test questionnaire, which aimed at identifying the users' profile (age, sex, education attainment and technological literacy). In order to visualize the desired location, the user speaks some of the pre-defined commands, and the destination address. For instance, consider the command "go to" and the address "Wall Street New York". After this moment, the user navigated freely in the chosen street. In the end, all the users answered the post-testing questionnaire with questions related to functionalities and usability. The Likert scale [17] has been adopted (Strongly disagree, Disagree, Neither agree nor disagree, Agree, Strongly agree) in the questionnaire. Currently, it takes the application around 2 s from the moment the user triggers his request (he/she speaks the desired action) until its execution, which is acceptable, according to the user tests. If the physical location where the experiment is being carried out presents considerable noise from other sources, this duration may surpass 5 s and, thus, increases the probability of erroneous recognition of words by the application.

Table 1 depicts the post-testing questionnaire, which is applied for the application usability assessment, considering user experience, navigation dynamics, and potential execution errors. The questionnaire was filled out after the utilization of the application.

Table 1. Application usability assessment

System Utilization Experiences					
Evaluate the utilization of the system according to the criteria below marking with an X					
	Strongly disagree	Disagree	Neither agree nor disagree	Agree	Strongly agree
This application has a graphical interface pleasant and understandable					
It is easy to understand what we have to do within the application					
The interface is very intuitive					
It was easy to learn how to use the application					

(*Continued*)

Table 1. (*Continued*)

System Utilization Experiences					
Evaluate the utilization of the system according to the criteria below marking with an X					
	Strongly disagree	Disagree	Neither agree nor disagree	Agree	Strongly agree
The response time is enough (time between address recognition and The location rendering)					
The application works properly as for the recognition of my pronounciation					
When I hesitate (saying words like "mmmh", "aaahh"), the system ignores capturing only the words that define the address					
When I'm navigating on Street View the screen freezes					
When I turned my head the image gets blurred					
There are some color distortions when the 3D image is rendered					
It is not possible to visualize the image completely					
It is easy to navigate within the application using the Oculus Rift					
I would use the application to visit places before going there physically					
I felt dizzy when using the Oculus Rift					
Considerations about the application					
Positive aspects about the application:					
Negative aspects about the application:					
Suggestions about the application:					

3 Results

Through the results of the application of the pre-test questionnaire was possible to determine the users profile: people between 14 and 46 years old, within which most of the users were between 20 and 29 years old, representing half of the subjects. Most of them with undergraduate and graduate degree, using computers more than 15 h weekly and who already had experience with digital games. This profile also identified that the users already apply Google Maps and Street View to search addresses.

As for the obtained results of the application of the usability questionnaire (post-testing) it is possible to determine that:

- 54 % of the users strongly agree and 46 % of the users agree that the application has a pleasant and understandable graphical interface;
- 54 % of the users strongly agree, 33 % of the users agree and 13 % of the users were not sure if it was easy to understand what to do within the application;
- 47 % of the users strongly agree, 47 % of the users agree and 6 % of the users were not sure if the graphical interface is intuitive;
- 67 % of the users strongly agree, 20 % of the users agree, 6 % of the users disagree and 7 % of the users did not answer if it was easy to learn how to use the application;
- 34 % of the users strongly agree, 54 % of the users agree, 6 % were not sure and 6 % of the users strongly disagree that the performance of the system feedback is enough;
- 47 % of the users strongly agree, 6 % of the users agree and 34 % of the users were not sure if the application works properly in order to recognize the pronunciation;
- 27 % of the users strongly agree, 27 % of the users agree, 34 % were not sure and 12 % of the users did not answer if the system ignored correctly when they hesitated saying words like "mmmhh" and "Aaaah";
- 6 % of the users agree, 6 % of the users were not sure, 34 % of the users disagree, 41 % of the users strongly disagree and 12 % did not answer if when they are navigating on Street View the screen freezes;
- 2 % of the users agree, 12 % were not sure, 40 % of the users disagree and 36 % of the users strongly disagree that when they turn their head the image gets blurred;
- 6 % of the users strongly agree, 20 % of users were not sure, 37 % of the users disagree and 37 % of the users strongly disagree about having colors distortions when the 3D images are rendered;
- 12 % of the users agree, 12 % of them were not sure, 20 % of the users disagree and 40 % of them strongly disagree that they cannot visualize the images completely;
- 60 % of the users strongly agree, 34 % of the users agree and 6 % of the users were not sure if it was easy to get around within the virtual environment using the Oculus Rift;
- 60 % of the users strongly agree and 40 % of the users agree that they had the feeling of being physically present at the required location;

- 54 % of the users strongly agree, 20 % of the users agree, 20 % of the users were not sure and 6 % of the users disagree about using the application to visit places before going physically;
- 12 % of the users strongly agree, 27 % of the users agree, 6 % of the users not sure, 27 % of the users disagree and 28 % of them strongly disagree that they felt dizzy when using the device.

Through the previous information it is possible to conclude that for this group of users:

- The application has a pleasant and understandable graphical interface;
- It is easy to understand what it is possible to do with the application;
- The graphical interface if intuitive;
- It is easy to learn how to use the application;
- The response time of the application is enough;
- The voice recognition system works properly when the user hesitates saying words like "mmmhh" and "Aaaah" ignoring these words and capturing only important words such as the required address;
- The image does not freeze within Street View;
- When the user turns his head the image does not get blurred;
- There are no color distortions when the 3D image is rendered;
- It is always possible to visualize the image completely;
- It is easy to get around within the virtual environment using the device Oculus Rift;
- The system provides the feeling of immersion (being physically present) within the required location;
- Most of the users would use the system to visit the places before going there physically;
- The feeling of dizziness varies from person to person, some persons felt it other not.

4   Conclusions

The basic human senses (e.g., hearing, touch, taste, smell and sight) have been widely explored for the proposal of simulated virtual reality environments in order to provide immersion (where users feel integrated with the environment), interaction (user's actions affect the environment) and engagement (users feel engaged with the activities during simulation).

This work presented the development of the application that integrates the Oculus Rift with the Street View application. The application applies a voice recognition system to understand the required locations, contributing for a better human-computer interaction, since users' hands and body are free within the physical space to navigate within the virtual environment. Tests with 15 users were carried out and the results of this group were quite satisfactory.

According to the information collected from a group of users, it would be interesting the utilization of an audio software as for future works. Two options were proposed, the first one a pleasant background sound would be presented for relaxing the user navigates within the virtual environment with the required location; in the second one, the background noise of a large city (cars passing by honking and some persons talking) in order to simulate the physical presence.

It is clear the challenge of deploying new technologies for developers. Although being innovative, this project also presented some challenges and drawbacks, such as the lack of support of browsers.

References

1. Jain, J., Lund,A., Wixon, D.: The future of natural user interfaces. In: CHI 2011 Extended Abstracts on Human Factors in Computing Systems (CHI EA 2011), pp. 211–214. ACM, New York (2011). http://dx.doi.org/10.1145/1979742.1979527
2. Delimarschi, D., Swartzendruber, G., Kagdi, H.: Enabling integrated development environments with natural user interface interactions. In: Proceedings of the 22nd International Conference on Program Comprehension (ICPC 2014), pp. 126–129 (2014). ACM, New York. http://dx.doi.org/10.1145/2597008.2597791
3. Del Ra, W.: Brave NUI world: designing natural user interfaces for touch and gesture by Daniel Wigdor and Dennis Wixon. SIGSOFT Softw. Eng. Notes 36(6), 29–30 (2011). http://dx.doi.org/10.1145/2047414.2047439
4. Seow, S.C., Wixon, D., Morrison, A., Jacucci, G.: Natural user interfaces: the prospect and challenge of touch and gestural computing. In: CHI 2010 Extended Abstracts on Human Factors in Computing Systems (CHI EA 2010). ACM, New York, pp. 4453–4456 (2010). http://dx.doi.org/10.1145/1753846.1754172
5. Carter, M., Allison, F., Downs, J., Gibbs, M.: Player identity dissonance and voice interaction in games. In: Proceedings of the 2015 Annual Symposium on Computer-Human Interaction in Play (CHI PLAY 2015), pp. 265–269. ACM, New York. http://dx.doi.org/10.1145/2793107.2793144
6. Azuma, R.T.: A survey of augmented reality. Presence Teleoperators Virtual Environ. 6(4), 355–385 (1997). Earlier version appeared in Course Notes #9: Developing Advanced Virtual Reality Applications, ACM SIGGRAPH 1995 (Los Angeles, 6–11 August 1995), 20-1 to 20-38
7. Davis, B.A., Bryla, K., Benton, P.A.: Oculus Rift in Action, 1st edn, p. 440. Manning Publications, Greenwich (2015)
8. Google Street View. https://www.google.com/maps/streetview/. Accessed 02 July 2016
9. Reiners, T., Teras, H., Chang, V., Wood, L.C., Gregory, S., Gibson, D., Teras, M.: Authentic, immersive, and emotional experience in virtual learning environments: the fear of dying as an important learning experience in a simulation. In: 23rd Annual Teaching and Learning Forum, Perth, Australia, pp. 1–14, 30–31 January 2014
10. Hoffman, H.G., Meyer III, W.J., Ramirez, M., Roberts, L., Seibel, E.J., Atzori, B., Patterson, D.R.: Feasibility of articulated arm mounted oculus rift virtual reality goggles for adjunctive pain control during occupational therapy in pediatric burn patients. Cyberpsychol. Behav. Soc. Netw. 17(6), 397–401 (2014)
11. Smith, M.F.: Software Prototyping: Adoption, Practice and Management, p. 216. McGraw-Hill, London (1991)
12. Sommerville, I.: Software Engineering, p. 816. Pearson, New York (2015)

13. Sherman, W.R., Craig, A.B.: Understanding Virtual Reality: Interface, Application, and Design. The Morgan Kaufmann Series in Computer Graphic, 1st edn, p. 608. Morgan Kaufmann, San Francisco (2002)
14. Developer Center (2016). https://developer.oculus.com/. Accessed 02 July 2016
15. Annyang! Speech Recognition that just works (2016). https://www.talater.com/annyang/. Accessed 01 Oct 2016
16. WebVR: Bringing Virtual Reality to the Web (2016). http://webvr.info/. Accessed 02 Mar 2016
17. Likert, R.: A technique for the measurement of attitudes. Arch. Psychol. **140**, 1–55 (1932)

Research on Motion Model for Technique Movements of Competitive Swimming in Virtual Interactive Environment

Mao Jie[⊠]

College of Sports Engineering and Information Technology,
Wuhan Sports University, Wuhan 430079, China
Jiem027@163.com

Abstract. With the constant improvement of technologies for virtual interaction, it has gradually become a fashion to have virtual interactions about sports. For virtual interaction, unity 3D isn't only effective for presenting a 3A-rated vivid virtual environment, but may also perfectly interact with Motion Sensing equipment. As brand new and cutting-edge technologies in current field of 3D digital interactive multimedia, virtual interaction and Motion Sensing technologies have broad prospects for development and great space for applied research, so they may contribute to more research and applications in terms of sports. Based on literature consultation, interview, experiment and mathematical analysis, sports forms and environment are simulated by virtual reality technologies, to create a lifelike virtual 3D environment for sports. Virtual interaction is made possible for swimming to create a brand new sports pattern. Different movement orbits of human actions are acquired from virtual environment with Kinect Motion Sensing equipment, in order that 3D human body models could move in virtual swimming scenes. Suggestions are made to further improve the creation of virtual reality environment and add virtual equipment, so that virtual realities may be more vivid. With the use of Motion Sensing technologies, the application of more sports in virtual Motion Sensing interaction will be promoted.

Keywords: Motion Sensing · Virtual interaction · Kinect · Unity 3D

1 Introduction

As pioneer of Motion Sensing technologies, "motion capture" has originated from Max Fleischer's Rotoscope in 1915, and up till now, has been successfully applied in many fields such as virtual reality technologies, gaming platforms, research on ergonomics, simulations and biomechanical research [1]. Motion Sensing technologies may not only capture skeletal movements of human body on a real-time basis, but may also interact with surrounding equipment or environment. Involving several fields like games, medicine, commerce and smart home, they have huge space for development and imagination. In April 2013, the Perfect World released Motion Sensing videos of "Swordsman" produced by SharpNow, which launched the prototype of 3D sensing technologies based on gesture recognition technologies.

© Springer International Publishing Switzerland 2016
S. Lackey and R. Shumaker (Eds.): VAMR 2016, LNCS 9740, pp. 233–242, 2016.
DOI: 10.1007/978-3-319-39907-2_22

Nowadays, Motion Sensing technologies are fairly widely used in design. For instance, adequately investigated in the game industry, Kinect also takes the lead in other fields, including clinical medicine, remote operation, medical education and medical data survey. In the field of commerce, AR Door, a technology company in Russia, utilized the "virtual fitting mirror" invented with Kinect Motion Sensing peripherals. Then, shoppers could stand in front of virtual fitting mirrors and their 3D images of trying on new clothes could be automatically displayed. Concerning applied research on technological aids for the handicapped, Michael Zollner of the University of Konstanz developed the Navigational Aids for the Visually Impaired (NAVI) to help with the navigation of the blind. In addition, Motion Sensing technologies are used for robots and smart homes and so on [4].

In this paper, Unity3D is integrated with Kinect Motion Sensing technologies, and a virtual interactive Motion Sensing design based on Unity3D engine is completed for swimming by Kinect optical sensing.

2 Purposes

With the development of intelligent computer technologies, virtual interaction technology that can pass interactive equipment and software of Motion Sensing interactive system based on 3D digital content have emerged. Today, Motion Sensing technology isn't only an advanced 3D digital interactive multimedia technology, but also a brand new research interest in the field of human-computer interaction. Their application has been popular in fields of medicine, education, rehabilitation, e-commerce, competitive sports, animation and game production. With pretty broad prospect of application, this technology can realize new-generation human-computer interaction, 3D human modeling and skeleton tracking in terms of motion, gesture and language recognition. Its application is widespread from deep data to robot vision and control. In the future, it will be used more potentially, and there will be quite great market demands for designed virtual interactive Motion Sensing products.

3 Methods

(1) **Literature Consultation**
    Foreign and domestic literature about means for exploring Motion Sensing technologies, 3D human models and construction of virtual reality environment is consulted, to determine content and methods for studying Motion Sensing technologies.
(2) **Interview**
    By carrying out research about Chinese sports information technology and sports training and conducting structured and unstructured interviews of experts, opinions on research feasibility and effectiveness are summed up, to lay a foundation for surveys and empirical research.

(3) **Experiment**

Virtual interactive models are built for swimming with computer numerical simulation technology.

(4) **Mathematical analysis**

A data analysis is performed on research content of Motion Sensing technologies, including deep data flow and skeleton tracking.

4 Results

4.1 Motion Sensing Technologies

As current brand new and advanced technologies of 3D digital interactive multimedia, Motion Sensing technologies have a broad prospect of development and tremendous space for applied research, contributing to more studies and applications in the field of sports. Represented by Motion Sensing technologies, Kinect is a 3D Motion Sensing camera, as shown in Fig. 1 as follows. The emergence of Kinect hardware shall be attributed to combined use of technologies related to multiple aspects such as sound, light, electricity and machinery [3]. With a function for immediate dynamic capture, it may capture motions of human limbs to autonomously recognize, memorize, analyze and handle these motions. With this technology, people may have different movements and interact with each other in virtual scenes, but also share their pictures and information, etc through the internet, to make it possible that "the body is a controller".

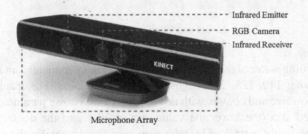

Fig. 1. Kinect for Xbox one Windows

As regards Kinect, key technologies are mainly characterized by skeleton tracking, motion recognition, facial recognition and speech recognition. Kinect acquires depth images and recognizes human skeletons by an infrared camera, to separate human body from background. It often recognizes skeletons by looking for the Chinese character "大". In the mean time, the skeleton acquisition is somewhat interfered by dark-colored clothes, so it is more favorable for acquiring skeletons if the background is white. Concerning spatial coordinate of skeletons, it is noteworthy that it is inadvisable to read skeletons from the right left or right, or else the skeletons will be overlaid and thereby impact intended explorations.

4.2   Construction of Virtual Environment

4.2.1   Scenario and Human Body Modeling

(1) **Model of swimming stadium**

The model of swimming stadium is made up of different parts, and the scenario model may be built as follows: The bottom of the swimming pool is modified by a built-in cubic model. Parameters such as "length", "width" and "height" are set to be 500 cm, 400 cm and 350 cm respectively. First of all, the top surface of the cuboid is cut into four sides which are intersected. Next, the cut middle large rectangle is intruded into the cuboid by "extrusion" to form a pool shape, as shown in Fig. 2.

Fig. 2. 3D model of swimming pool

Concerning water of the swimming pool, material parameters are set as follows: diffuse colors: 149, 178, 222; high gloss: 80; glossiness: 80; opacity: 40. VRay maps are concave and convex with noises. As regards noise parameters, ripple size is controlled at 5 (the lower the value, the smaller and the denser is the ripple. Besides, the ripple is tracked by reflection mapping in combination with light.

(2) **Human body modeling**

Human body modeling shall be based on physical attractiveness and physiology. Built model of human body is a polygonal model. Three inbuilt models of 3Dsmax are considered as head, upper part of body and breech respectively. Then, they are bridged after simple modification. Subsequently, the parts where human arms are and legs at the crotch form a section where arms and legs can be made. Arms and legs are extruded according to body proportions, to form the initial shape of human body. Next, basic structure of people (including hands and feet) is drawn according to orders like cutting, connection, disconnection, collapse and bridging. A "turbo smooth" modifier is added to an "editable polygon", in order to add planes to human body and make them smooth. At last, the planes may be modified by repeatedly using orders within the "Paint Deformation", so that the structure of human body could be more vivid and lively. Once the body is well made, efforts shall focus on hands, head and five organs as well as more detailed processing. In the process of making, it is necessary to ensure each plane has four sides as far as possible, whereas there can be some five-sided planes at turns. For instance, the turns are made by vertexes of five sides at the zygomatic bone. Lines shall be pulled in line with actual orientation of human muscle. For the muscle at arms and legs, there shall be lines perpendicular to their skeletons, so as to be helpful for producing animation of skeleton models. Attention shall be paid to check if there are more points. If yes, extra points shall be promptly eliminated, or else subsequent skinning will be impacted, as shown in Fig. 3.

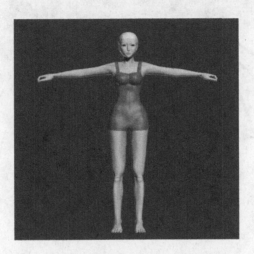

Fig. 3. Rendered model of swimming stadium

4.2.2   Construction of Unity Virtual Environment

DirectX11 is supported by Unity, which can realize lifelike 3A-rated virtual simulation scenarios in combination with optimized illumination system and ShaderLab, to make the virtual environment more real and vivid by efficiently simulating physical effects such as collision of rigid bodies and gravitation in a lifelike manner [12, 16].

In the entire design process, it is necessary to build a big environment like blue sky in scenarios apart from the earth. Required big environment may be created with the Skybox in Unity. The environment set up by the Skybox may be more realistic. The system itself is equipped with a resource pack of the Skybox, inside which there are six different materials of sky. In addition, materials of the Skybox necessary for design may be drawn according to mapping laws of the Skybox. Here, it is noteworthy that the sky can't be rendered unless the Skybox through "Render Settings". It may be rendered by clicking Edit→Render Settings to set options of Skybox Material.

In designing required Skybox, a new material sphere may be created by opening files Assets→Materials on the panel of Project, and the Shader properties inside the properties viewer are changed into Skybox. Import successive pictures that have been drawn pursuant to cube rules into the pic by opening the file titled Assets. Change their property from Wrap Mode into Clamp and then put them in the Materials based on pertinent orientations to render special environment [17, 23].

In Unity 4.x, water effects are created with a water resource pack known as Water (Pro). In this resource pack, there are two instances in Water4, including daylight and nighttime water, among which the latter appears to be darker. Drag water into the Hierarchy Panel and change the Scale of the Transform in the properties viewer to get required water size. Then, drag it to the desired place by a move tool, as shown in Fig. 4 as follows.

Fig. 4. A running scenario

4.3   Realization of Motion Sensing Effects for Games

After lots of literature and online materials, current Motion Sensing technologies are mostly realized by integrating Unity software with Kinect hardware, while the Kinect hardware mainly transmits data by following methods [24]:

1. KinectWrapper.unitypackage (Carnegie Mellon) plug-in;
2. OpenNI_Unity_Toolkit-0.9.7.4.unitypackage plug-in;
3. Zigfu plug-in;
4. Adevine1618 plug-in;
5. .dll plug-ins written and packaged in C#, C++ or Java.

After advantages and disadvantages of above plug-ins are analyzed, data of Unity software environment and Kinect equipment are transmitted by KinectWrapper. unitypackage plug-in and user-defined packaging plug-ins in this paper.

This paper focuses on illustrating Unity and Kinect data transmission processes of KinectWrapper.unitypackage plug-in. Other software environment includes Kinect SDK 1.7 and Unity 4.5.1.

4.3.1   Key Motion Sensing Technologies

KinectWrapper.unitypackage plug-in contains multiple scripts, which play different roles in data transmissions of Kinect equipment and Unity software, as shown in Table 1 as follows.

Table 1. A List of KinectWrapper.unitypackage Plug-in Scripts

Name of Scripts	Functions
KinectModelControllerV2	Control models, match human skeleton models with skeletal variables exposed by scripts (global variables) and bind 3D skeleton models with human skeletons recognized by Kinect hardware.
KinectPointController	Control points of body parts, which are set as exposure variables of scripts (global variables) for convenient control by Kinect equipment.
DeviceOrEmulator	Judge if Kinect physical equipment or Kinect simulation equipment is to be used.
DepthWrapper	Acquire people's data about depth images.
SkeletonWrapper	Acquire data about skeletons and obtain two persons' skeletons at most.
KinectInterop	Acquire data from Microsoft Kinect SDK; this is critical for data transmissions of Kinect and Unity3D.
DisplayDepth	Obtain people's depth images.
DisplayColor	Obtain people's RGB images.
KinectRecorder	Record motions, generate replay documents with Kinect emulator and only used when emulators are used.
KinectEmulator	Simulate Kinect equipment and run together with replay documents generated by KinectRecorder.
KinectSensor	Acquire data from Kinect by KinectInterop.

Apart from scripts, Kinect Prefab is critical for data transmissions of Unity3D software and Kinect equipment. In utilizing KinectPointController and KinectModel ControllerV2, the prefab shall be put inside the exposure variable Skeleton Wrapper (Sw).

4.3.2   Discussion of Model Movement

In this design, an interactive function is realized that "matchstick man" (prefab KinectAvatar) of KinectWrapper.unitypackage follows the Kinect equipment to acquire information about people's movements. All points on the Hierarchy panel are put to match with corresponding variables exposed by KinectPointController. Pertinent script "man.cs" is written to control the movement of the "matchstick man". Modify KinectPointController, and grant the vel value of "man.cs" to be "1", so as to modify "goTransform.position" of "man.cs". The "matchstick man" may move according to the value of "goTransform.position" of "man.cs" for realizing the interactive function that the "matchstick man" moves with people.

4.3.3 Motion Sensing Design of Swimming

The Kinect Prefab shall be placed inside the Hierarchy panel and the KinectModelControllerV2 needs to be put at the parent hierarchy. Place skeletons of this model corresponding to variables in exposed skeleton variables and drag the Kinect Prefab into the exposure variable Sw of KinectModelControllerV2 on the human model. Here, it is noteworthy that only 20 skeletons are controlled by Kinect, but more than 20 are under the control of KinectModelControllerV2. Therefore, variables of wrists, hands and fingers are supposed to be put inside skeletons of hands. It will be better for movement when variables of ankles and feet are placed inside such models. To control two models of human body, Player variable shall be set. Mask variable may be set if not all skeletons are expected to be controlled. The model may play its original animations as long as "Animated" is chosen, and BlendWeight (0 ~ 1) shall be set. The value of BlendWeight may be used for determining effects of synthetic motions achieved by animation and Kinect-driven motions, as shown in Fig. 5.

Fig. 5. Values of exposure variables of KinectModelControllerV2

After skeletons are bound, they shall be operated in combination with Kinect. In this way, the model can move with people.

5 Conclusions and Suggestions

5.1 Conclusions

(1) Virtual reality technologies are used for creating lifelike 3D environment or atmosphere for swimming that people can feel as if they are personally on the scene according to sports forms and swimming environment.
(2) In combination with Motion Sensing interactive technologies, virtual interactive interaction is made possible for swimming, to create a brand new sports pattern.
(3) Various movement orbits of human motions are acquired from virtual environment with Kinect equipment, in order that three-dimensional models of human body can move in virtual body-building scenes.

5.2 Suggestions

(1) Further improvements need to be made in creating virtual reality environment, and virtual equipment shall be added, so as to develop more vivid virtual realities.
(2) Motion Sensing technologies are utilized, in order that virtual Motion Sensing interactions may be realized in more sports.

Acknowledgment. We thank Wei Tian, Lu Qi and Du Yunyun for helpful discussions and the referees for greatly improving the manuscript. The research was supported by The National Social Science Fund of China.

References

1. Wang, G.J.: The Interactive Intelligent Control and Virtual Simulation Based On the Motion Capture Data. ANQING Normal Unicersity (2013)
2. Bai, D.: Motion Sensing Technologies. http://baike.baidu.com/view/5338106.html,2013-06-01
3. Yu, T.: Kinect Application Development in The Most Natural Way with The Machine Dialogue. Publishing House of Electronics Industry, Beijing (2012)
4. smile_979.:Kinect interactive technology of modern communication theory and advanced technology. http://wenku.baidu.com/link?url=q-kdTjuSLi7oIdXR7hZIMmZ60AsjPqleTe2yrKqI_9ukTurSd_S5L-kNRSCo3uJJME_1MpYGWzi6F-1PzYF5Wl4FMHZEeL-Hoy8lRQa_vjK.2014-11-06
5. Zai, X.F., Zhu, J.J., Pan, Z.G.: 3dsMAX modeling and its application in virtual reality. Comput. Simulation. **4**, 94–97+86 (2004)
6. Li, H.: 3DSMAX modeling technology analysis. J. Xingtai Univ. **4**, 106–107 (2009)
7. Huang, J., Zhang, H.Z.: The application of 3DSMAX in virtual reality. Geomatics Spat. Inf. Technol. **2**, 124–126 (2013)
8. Yang, D.C., Xu, K., Liu, L.: Using 3DSMAX to realize the animation simulation of humanoid robot. Mach. Des. Manuf. **2**, 48–49 (2002)

9. Cheng, J.H.: Virtual reality modeling technology based on 3DSMAX. J. Zhangzhou Normal Univ. (Nat. Sci.) **3**, 18–22 (2002)
10. Liu, B.W.: Modeling characteristics and effect of virtual reality scene. Comput. Eng. Appl. **5**, 137–141 (2014)
11. Liu, G.D.: Intuitive interaction interface and virtual reality. J. Wuhan Univ. Technol. **1**, 132–136 (2014)
12. Lan, J., Sun, J., Yang, Y.B.: Research on control method of skeletal tracking based on Kinect. **8**, 20–22+27 (2014)
13. Luo, Q.: Study on three dimensions body reconstruction and measurement by using kinect. In: Duffy, V.G. (ed.) DHM 2014. LNCS, vol. 8529, pp. 35–42. Springer, Heidelberg (2014)
14. Luo, Q., Yang, G.: Research and simulation on virtual movement based on kinect. In: Shumaker, R., Lackey, S. (eds.) VAMR 2014, Part I. LNCS, vol. 8525, pp. 85–92. Springer, Heidelberg (2014)
15. Wu, Z.D.: Research and implementation of a game engine based on Unity3d. In: ZhongShan University (2012)
16. Chen, Z.H.: With Unity3D Kinect game development of a summary of ideas, 11 March 2012. http://diandian.chenzhehuai.com/post/2012-11-03/40042962742
17. Han, J.D.D.: For Windows SDK Kinect development introduction(3): basic knowledge. http://www.cnblogs.com/yangecnu/archive/2012/04/02/KinectSDK_Application_Fundamentals_Part2.html,2012-04-02
18. HackerSaillen: Some studies on the use of Kinect in Unity3D. http://blog.csdn.net/hackersaillen/article/details/8780719,2013-04-10
19. Duncan, G.: ZDK = Zigfu Development Kit = Commercial Kinect Developent library for Unity3D and JavaScript [EB/OL]. https://channel9.msdn.com/coding4fun/kinect/ZDK–Zigfu-Development-Kit–Commercial-Kinect-Development-library-for-Unity3D-and-JavaScript,2012-03-19
20. Advine1618. KinectSDK-Unity3D_Interface_Plugin[EB/OL], 17 August 2013. https://gthub.com/adevine1618/KinectSDK-Unity3D_Interface_Plugin
21. Da, H.H.: Matrix4x4 matrix transformation of Unity3D development. http://sygame.lofter.com/post/117105_3b843c,2013-01-09
22. Chong, Q.: unity3d: Unity3D Water- Real water setting technique, 12 March 2013. http://cl314413.blog.163.com/blog/static/190507976201321211943837/
23. Yu, T.: The combination of Kinect and Unity. http://game.ceeger.com/forum/read. -Php?tid=2142, 2012-06-10
24. Kinect for Windows 1.7 .1.7 SDK and Developer Toolkit Known Issues[EB/OL]. https://msdn.microsoft.com/en-us/library/dn188692.aspx,2013-01-07

Ultrafast Facial Tracker Using Generic Cameras with Applications in Intelligent Lifestyle

Yung-Hui Li[1(✉)], Yuan-Ting Hu[1], Jethro Shen[1], Mihai Preda[2], Andrei Drexler[2], Carmen Sosoiu[2], Dragos Florin Stanculescu[2], Paul Liu[1], and Joe Ye[1]

[1] ULSee Inc., 3F., No. 28, Ln. 128, Jingye 1st Rd., Zhongshan Dist., Taipei, Taiwan
{li,yuanhu,jethro,paul,joe}@ulsee.com
[2] Holotech Studios, Str Emanoil Porumbaru 77, 4'th Floor, Sector 1, 011424 Bucharest, Romania
{mihai,andrei,carmen.sosoiu,florin}@facerig.com

Abstract. The core of Human-Computer Interaction (HCI) is to analyze and understand the user's intension, which can be mostly manifested from the facial movement and expression of the user. Hence, the stage facial detection and tracking is extremely important in an user-friendly interface between human and computer. In ULSee, we developed an ultrafast markerless facial tracking system which is robust to variation in environmental lighting, pose and occlusion. It can be run at a speed of 10 ms/frame on an iPhone 6S system. With such accuracy and speed, it can be used to support many intelligent HCI applications. In this work, we envision an intelligent lifestyle in the future that can be built upon the basis of the ULSee's ultrafast markerless facial tracker, ranging from virtual reality, augmented reality, real-time facial recognition and driver drowsiness detection. We believe, that through the joint force between ULSee's world-class tracker and our clients, more user-awareness HCI application will be invented and a new lifestyle will arise.

Keywords: Markerless facial tracking · Real-time avatar animation · Facial recognition · Driver drowsiness detection

1 Introduction

The core of HCI (Human-Computer-Interaction) system lies in its ability to understand user's intention and give an appropriate reaction based on the current environmental condition and context. To understand user's intention, most systems rely on the vision-based solution, which is to process the images/videos captured from the camera, locate the user's head, and further analyze the user's face image. There are multiple user attributes that an intelligent HCI system can infer based on vision-based solution, for example: user's emotion, age, sex, and expression variation. Those user's attributes together with dialog context can further be used as input for an intelligent HCI system. Therefore, how to locate user's face with high accuracy and analyze it is one of the most important functions in a vision-based and face-centric HCI system.

Face tracking has received a lot of attentions in research communities in recent years [1–7]. Traditional face tracking is to locate the rectangular area where the face appears

© Springer International Publishing Switzerland 2016
S. Lackey and R. Shumaker (Eds.): VAMR 2016, LNCS 9740, pp. 243–254, 2016.
DOI: 10.1007/978-3-319-39907-2_23

in a given input image. However, in order to further analyze user's attributes mentioned in the previous paragraph, detailed localization information about each local part of a face (e.g., eyes, nose and mouth) is also needed. Such detailed localization information can be trained and modeled by so-called "shape models", for example, active shape models and its variants [8–16]. A shape model, if constructed with robust machine learning algorithms and trained with large amount of data, can be used to track local part of a face very accurately and very efficiently (in real time). In ULSee, we implemented an ultrafast and very robust face tracker which can run in real time, and it works with generic consumer-level camera (i.e., no special camera needed). Besides facial tracking, there is a 3D face model built inside our tracker which can estimate the pitch, yaw and roll angle of the input face image in real time. The system flowchart of ULSee's facial tracker is described in Fig. 1.

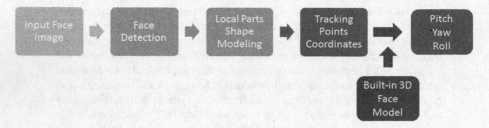

Fig. 1. The system flowchart of ULSee's facial tracker.

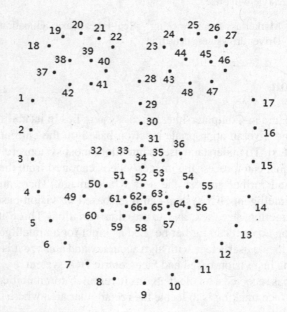

Fig. 2. The 66 tracking points for a face defined by ULSee facial tracker.

The number of tracking points returned by ULSee's tracker is 66. Those 66 points represent the location of lines that define the face contour (jaw line), eyebrows, eyes, nose and mouth accordingly. The numbering of these 66 points is illustrated in Fig. 2.

The output of ULSee's facial tracker (the coordinates of the 66 points, as well as the pitch, yaw and roll angles) can be further fed into other intelligent system for different applications. So far, ULSee's face tracker has been integrated with clients' system and many interesting and useful applications have been created, ranging from markerless real-time avatar animation, augmented reality (in the form of virtual glasses and jewelry try-on), face recognition and driver drowsiness detection. In the following sections, we will illustrate these applications one by one.

2   Real-Time Avatar Animation

One of the important clients to ULSee is Holotech Studios, the creator of FaceRig, which is a software that allows anyone to embody and animate outstanding real time CG character portraits via motion capture from a webcam. In FaceRig there are two distinct ways of translating tracking data to a 3D model movement.

2.1   Two Methods for Avatar Animation

One way is by interpreting tracking data as presence of certain landmark configurations which in turn should underlie actual human expressions, or more exactly human face postures. In this method, certain tracking data represents, for instance, a lifted eyebrow, or an eye squint, because respective landmarks change their relation in a specific way. For each distinct identifiable landmark configuration, a specific meaning can be attributed and this interpretation can be passed on to a system that establish correlations between these configurations and 3D animations states. We refer to this method as "animation retargeting" (or animation atomics retargeting).

Another way of transferring tracking data to a 3D model is by translating landmark movement to 3D object movement. Because the landmarks evolve in 2D space and because their inherent spatial relation is determined by the human face image on which those landmarks were identified, certain corrections and approximations must be done in order to function on a 3D model that not only moves in an extra dimension (depth) but very likely has different proportions between its inner features that the tracked human face. In this method the tracking data is not interpreted and thus does not use corresponding animations, but rather amplifies or diminishes position deltas in order to produce similar spatial relations in the 3D model components. In addition to these movement modifications, the depth placement and movement is approximated. This way the landmark movement is retargeted on the 3D model. We call this "free-form retargeting".

2.2   Animation Retargeting

Animation based retargeting, doesn't set 3D transformations (position, orientation, scale) directly to 3D objects. Tracking data is really a signal that certain landmark configurations are present. The configurations are relative to a neutral reference state and thus can be expressed in a normalized way, with their presence (actualization) having values between 0 (none) and 1 (maximum certainty that landmarks are different in a specific way). For each trackable feature a correspondent 3D spatial relation between 3D objects is made, carrying the same meaning, but the spatial relation between landmarks and 3D objects is arbitrary. They don't even have to correspond one to one. What mirrors the trackable features are 3D configurations not 3D objects. If the inner left eyebrow being raised is identifiable as such by the tracker, then there is a 3D configuration that mirrors this state, and the actualization of this expression state determines the actualization of the corresponding 3D configuration.

This 3D configurations, or spatial relations, represent the maximum tracking value. Because each trackable feature can have values between 0 and 1, and because the values are expressed relative to a tracking reference, the way correspondant 3D configurations behave must mirror this characteristic. They have to be expressed as an offset and this offset must be weighted, also between 0 and 1, just as the tracking feature.

In 3D graphics, the data storing attributes that vary their values over time are called animations. Thus, the additive 3D configurations with variable actualization are named additive animations. Neutral reference states are called base animations, because they serve as a 3D matrix base for final 3D space representation. While this neutral states could be static, and thus not really animations, it's probable that this neutral states to augment what is being tracked by additional movement, becoming actual animations.

The base animations are tracking independent, while the additive animations simply represent the trackable features in 3D space. Because the 3D models don't usually consist just in a collection of discrete objects, but rather mimic the appearance of real or realistic objects, the necessity of another approximation appears. The translation is from animated 3D objects and rendered 3D objects. The animated 3D objects serve as a base of translating tracking data in 3D data. 3D render objects depict real or realistic objects and they get to be drawn by the 3D render.

FaceRig tracking data analysis is based on the Facial Action Coding System (FACS) developed by anatomist Carl-Herman Hjortsjö and later updated by Ekman, Friesen and Joseph C. Hager. Facial movements are encoded by FACS in basic actions of individual muscles or groups of muscles called Action Units (AU). Some of the Action Units recognized by FaceRig are the following:

- Inner Brow Raiser
- Outer Brow Raiser
- Lid Tightener
- Nose Wrinkler
- Upper Lip Raiser
- Lip Corner Depressor
- Lip Pucker
- Jaw Drop

- Mouth Stretch
- Eyes Closed
- Head Turn Left/Right
- Head Up/Down
- Head Tilt Left/Right

For each Action Unit weight or intensity of the corresponding facial movement is computed. The weight is generally computed as a deviation of a specific group of land-marks' transformations from a default neutral pose.

In the Fig. 3 we are illustrating groups of landmarks that contribute to Action Units computation as follow:

- The red group of landmarks contribute on Lid Tightener and Eyes Closed AUs
- The orange group of landmarks contribute on Inner Brow Raiser and Outer Brow Raiser AUs
- The yellow group of landmarks contribute on Nose Wrinkler and Upper Lip Raiser AUs
- The blue group of landmarks contribute on Nose Wrinkler, Upper Lip Raiser, Jaw Drop, Lip Corner Depressor and Lip Pucker AUs
- The green group of landmarks contribute on Mouth Stretch, Lip Pucker, Lip Corner Depressor and Mouth Stretch AUs

Fig. 3. The correspondent relation between the groups of landmarks and Action Units (AU) (Color figure online)

The next step in the Animation Atomics Method is to map each Action Unit weight to a keyframe of the corresponding atomic animation of the avatar. After each animation is set to the correct keyframe they are blended together with the help of an Animation Tree.

2.3 Free-Form Retargeting

Free-form retargeting, at its core, is a system that translates image-space landmark movement (relative to a user-calibrated neutral pose) to 3D bone movement (relative to an artist-defined neutral pose). In its current incarnation in the FaceRig application, free-form retargeting can drive the bones corresponding to the avatar's mouth and eyebrows directly from tracking information. For aesthetic reasons a set of secondary bones, for which no tracking information is available, can also be driven by analyzing the current pose as defined by the primary bones and choosing the best matches from a set of artist-defined frames, enhancing expressivity (e.g. by simulating the thickening and rounding off of the cheeks when smiling). Since free-form retargeting only affects a few specific areas and not the entire bone hierarchy of the avatar it is only used in addition to Animation Atomics, overriding its output for the controlled regions.

The system relies on naming conventions for bone identification. For the mouth region a supplementary UV-mapped support mesh is used to define the area of movement for the affected bones. Secondary bone movement requires special animations, where each frame is interpreted as a specific pose to be identified and applied dynamically.

During avatar initialization, the neutral matrix in the idle pose for each controlled bone is recorded. For the mouth bones, the corresponding 2D location in the UV-space of the support mesh is also computed and stored. The 3 directly controlled regions (mouth, left and right eyebrows) are measured, allowing the system to drive avatars with different proportions from the user's.

Two examples of real-time avatar animation using FaceRig and ULSee's tracker are given in Fig. 4.

Fig. 4. Example images of real-time avatar animation using FaceRig with ULSee's facial tracker.

3   Virtual Try-on

3.1   Goal

Virtual try-on has attracted great attentions in recent years because of its commercial value in on-line shopping. A virtual try-on system with 2D cameras is much more favorable than using 3D sensors due to the availability of 2D cameras. However, estimating the 3D geometry via 2D images has many ambiguities and the inserted virtual objects are hardly fit to the real scenes, which degrades the user experience of the virtual try-on system. To this end, we develop a robust real-time virtual try-on system, the ULSee VTO system, based on our accurate facial tracker using only 2D consumer cameras. Our virtual try-on system consists of virtual glasses try-on, virtual cosmetics try-on, virtual jewelry try-on and other related face/head virtual try-on. The ULSee VTO system provides a practical 2D solution for virtual try-on and demonstrates its superior effects on the aforementioned try-on tasks.

3.2 Literature Review

Methods for real-time virtual try-on can be separated into two categories with respect to the two different image capturing devices, namely the 2D RGB cameras [18, 19, 21] and the 3D RGBD sensors [17, 20, 22]. Using the 3D sensors can get more accurate estimation than using the 2D cameras as it contains depth information, while the availability of the 3D sensors and its fragility to sunlight makes the 3D virtual try-on system less accessible. Despite the difference of the type of sensors, both 2D and 3D solutions rely on accurate tracking to capture the motion in real scene and reflect to the user in real-time. A fast and accurate facial tracker is an essential component in a virtual try-on application because it provides accurate head pose and landmark location estimation.

3.3 Tracking for Virtual Try-on

The ULSee VTO system contains virtual glasses try-on, virtual cosmetics try-on, virtual jewelry try-on and other related face/head virtual try-on. The virtual try-on system uses RGB images as input so that the system can run on devices such as mobiles and pads.

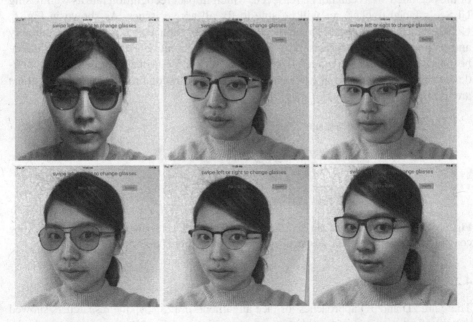

Fig. 5. The results of 6 different pairs of glasses try-on in the ULSee VTO system.

At the core of the ULSee VTO system is the ULSee facial tracker and the system uses the head tracker and head pose estimation to transform the virtual objects to fit the user's pose. To avoid jitters of the inserted objects, a further smooth pose will be calculated based on the temporal information. Then virtual objects, such as glasses, jewelries and masks, can be placed into the 2D image with respect to the landmark location given by the tracker.

The ULSee VTO system provides a much more convenient solution to reduce the efforts of try-on in physical stores. The examples of virtual glasses try-on using our system are shown in Fig. 5. The realistic try-on results demonstrate the effectiveness of the ULSee tracker.

4 Face Recognition

4.1 Difficulties in Face Recognition

In facial analysis, including face recognition, emotion recognition, and face demographics, three key issues need to be considered. The first is the pose of the face. If the faces are not frontal, no matter what methods are used, the face recognition rate will be seriously degraded. This is called pose alignment issue. The second issue is how to align gallery and probe face images correctly. For any given face, a few anchor points can always be retrieved. If the anchor points of each face image did not align to some specific positions, the feature extracted in local region will not match to each other, which in turn, degrades the recognition rate. This is called 2D alignment issue. The third issue is the occlusion due to sunglasses, eyeglass, and scarf. In such cases, the image features of the occluded areas can not be retrieved, which impact recognition rate as well. Using ULSee's facial tracker, we will be able to fix all above issues. As shown in Fig. 6, ULSee's facial tracker is able to predict the position of each anchor point very accurately and estimate face pose precisely to help pose alignment. For the case of occlusion, because ULSee's tracker can return confidence scores for each anchor points, the confidence scores can be used as a weighted coefficient if recognition-by-parts algorithms are used.

Fig. 6. ULSee's face tracker can estimate precise facial points locations in dark, strong lighting condition, and wear sunglass. Above images are acquired from internet.

4.2 Related Works

There are 2D and 3D approaches for face alignment. In [23, 24], the researchers showed that the effective alignment could improve recognition rate. For 2D alignment methods, the objective focus on aligning several anchor points of each face image to some specific positions. This process will enhance the discriminability of face image. In 3D alignment methods, the general objective focuses on changing non-frontal face images to frontal face images. In this transformation, it needs accurate estimations for the angle of face pose. If the estimated face pose is not accurate enough, the transferred face image may be broken.

4.3   ULSee's Approach

In ULSee, our face recognition system can achieve 97.41 % recognition rate in Labeled Faces in the Wild (LFW) view2 dataset [26] by using the advantages of our tracker. The advantages lie in that the tracker can detect and track 66 fiducial points precisely in real-time with estimated confident values of 66 points. For example, if users wear sunglass, the confident values of points on eye region may drop to 0.3. When using recognition-by-parts method with these confident values we can get better recognition performance.

5   Driver Drowsiness Detection

5.1   Goal

When driving a car, it is very easy for the driver to be distracted or get tired. Sensor-based technology has been developed specifically to help the driver avoid such situation, as shown in Fig. 7. This kind of technique needs constantly analyze the driver's face pose to tell if it is frontal or not. If the driver does not look straight ahead or her eyes are constantly closed up, it is highly likely that she is falling asleep [25]. This mechanism minimizes the risk due to driver's distraction or fatigue. Such application needs robust facial tracking and accurate pose estimation under different environmental illuminations, such as extremely weak or strong lighting condition.

Fig. 7. The illustration of the concept of driver drowsiness detection system, which is borrowed from [25].

5.2   Related Works

There are many facial tracking techniques in the literature. Some methods focus on fast point's detection. Some methods focus on fast point's tracking. Most of them can not handle the problem due to different lighting conditions.

5.3   ULSee's Approach

In ULSee, our facial tracker can deal with various illumination variations and estimate the head pose in real-time (more than 30 fps). Our tracker is able to operate in a wide range of environmental illumination, from 0.02 to 60,000 lx, as shown in Fig. 8. Besides the pose, our tracker is also able to return the precise location for eyes and eyebrow. Such robustness enables our tracker to be the core of the technology for the driver drowsiness detection. The final system is able to send out loud alarm when the driver seems to doze (through eyes contour analysis) or distracted (by analyzing the head pose). It is currently under internal testing with our client, who is one of the major automakers in Europe.

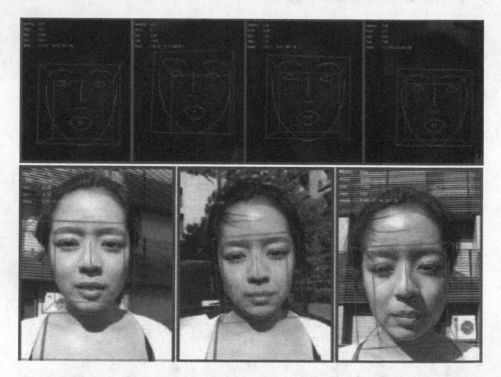

Fig. 8. The facial tracking result under extremely lighting variation (provided by ULSee). Top row: tracking result taken at 0.02 lx. Bottom row: tracking result taken at 46,000-60,000 lx.

6   Conclusion

Imagine a new future era driven by computer vision technology. When you drive, the intelligent system in car automatically monitors your status and alert you when you are distracted or drowsy. When you get home, the surveillance system automatically recognizes you are the owner of the house and open the door. When you get inside the living room, the air conditioner automatically turns on and the temperature is set to what you usually want. The TV is also turned on and tuned to your favorite sport channel. After dinner, when you play an online game with your friend, you can choose Yoda as your avatar, and Yoda will demonstrate exactly the same facial expression as you squint your eye or laugh widely.

With an ultrafast and robust facial tracking technology (for example, ULSee's facial tracker), all of the above applications are on their way and will be happening in the near future. User-friendly applications will make the future home and office become user-aware, and user-oriented intelligent lifestyle will become a mainstream.

References

1. Saxena, V.; Grover, S.; Joshi, S.: A real time face tracking system using rank deficient face detection and motion estimation. In: 7th IEEE International Conference on Cybernetic Intelligent Systems, 2008 (CIS 2008), pp. 1–6, 9–10 September 2008. doi:10.1109/UKRICIS. 2008.4798956

2. Harguess, J.; Changbo Hu; Aggarwal, J.K.: Occlusion robust multi-camera face tracking. In: 2011 IEEE Computer Society Conference on Computer Vision and Pattern Recognition Workshops (CVPRW), pp. 31–38, 20–25 June 2011. doi:10.1109/CVPRW.2011.5981790

3. Yoder, J., Medeiros, H., Park, J., Kak, A.C.: Cluster-Based Distributed Face Tracking in Camera Networks. IEEE Trans. Image Process. 19(10), 2551–2563 (2010). doi:10.1109/TIP. 2010.2049179

4. Faux, F., Luthon, F.: Robust face tracking using colour Dempster-Shafer fusion and particle filter. In: 2006 9th International Conference on Information Fusion, pp. 1–7, 10–13 July 2006. doi:10.1109/ICIF.2006.301713

5. Wang, P., Ji, Q.: Robust face tracking via collaboration of generic and specific models. IEEE Trans. Image Process. 17(7), 1189–1199 (2008). doi:10.1109/TIP.2008.924287

6. Painkras, E., Charoensak, C.: FaceProcessor: a framework for hardware design and implementation of a dynamic face tracking system. In: 2005 Fifth International Conference on Information, Communications and Signal Processing, pp. 172–176 (2005). doi:10.1109/ ICICS.2005.1689028

7. Shi, L., Zhu, Y.: Robust face tracking-by-detection via sparse representation. In: 2015 IEEE International Conference on Signal Processing, Communications and Computing (ICSPCC), pp. 1–4, 19–22 September 2015. doi:10.1109/ICSPCC.2015.7338846

8. Cootes, T.F., Taylor, C.J.: Using grey-level models to improve active shape model search. In: Proceedings of the 12th IAPR International Conference on Pattern Recognition, 1994. Vol. 1 - Conference A: Computer Vision & Image Processing, pp. 63–67, 9–13 October 1994. doi:10.1109/ICPR.1994.576227

9. Sugawara, Y., Lee, D.S., Kawanaka, A.: 3-D shape model retrieval using multi range image phase correlation method. In: 2012 IEEE International Symposium on Signal Processing and Information Technology (ISSPIT), pp. 000061–000066, 12–15 December 2012. doi:10.1109/ ISSPIT.2012.6621261

10. Davies, R.H., Twining, C.J., Cootes, T.F., Taylor, C.J.: Building 3-D statistical shape models by direct optimization. IEEE Trans. Med. Imaging 29(4), 961–981 (2010). doi:10.1109/TMI. 2009.2035048

11. Luo, S., Li,: Accurate object segmentation using novel active shape and appearance models based on support vector machine learning. In: 2014 International Conference on Audio, Language and Image Processing (ICALIP), pp. 347–351, 7–9 July 2014. doi:10.1109/ICALIP.2014.7009813

12. Cootes, T.F., Taylor, C.J., Lanitis, A.: Multi-resolution search with active shape models. In: Proceedings of the 12th IAPR International Conference on Pattern Recognition, 1994. Vol. 1 - Conference A: Computer Vision & Image Processing, pp. 610–612, 9–13 October 1994. doi:10.1109/ICPR.1994.576375

13. Baloch, S.H., Krim, H.: Flexible Skew-Symmetric Shape Model for Shape Representation, Classification, and Sampling. IEEE Trans. Image Process. 16(2), 317–328 (2007). doi:10.1109/TIP.2006.888348

14. Neumann, A.: Graphical Gaussian shape models and their application to image segmentation. IEEE Trans. Pattern Anal. Mach. Intell. 25(3), 316–329 (2003). doi:10.1109/TPAMI.2003.1182095

15. Huang, H., Makedon, F., McColl, R.: High dimensional statistical shape model for medical image analysis. In: 5th IEEE International Symposium on Biomedical Imaging: From Nano to Macro, 2008. ISBI 2008, pp. 1541–1544, 14–17 May 2008. doi:10.1109/ISBI.2008.4541303

16. Igual, L., De la Torre, F.: Continuous procrustes analysis to learn 2D shape models from 3D objects. In: IEEE Computer Society Conference on Computer Vision and Pattern Recognition Workshops (CVPRW), pp. 17–22, 13–18 June 2010. doi:10.1109/CVPRW.2010.5543280

17. Giovanni, S., Choi, Y.C., Huang, J., Khoo, E.T., Yin, K.: Virtual try-on using kinect and HD camera. In: Kallmann, M., Bekris, K. (eds.) MIG 2012. LNCS, vol. 7660, pp. 55–65. Springer, Heidelberg (2012)

18. Huang, S.H., Yang, Y.I., Chu, C.H.: Human-centric design personalization of 3D glasses frame in markerless augmented reality. Adv. Eng. Inf. 26(1), 35–45 (2012)

19. Saragih, J.M., Lucey, S., Cohn, J.F.: Real-time avatar animation from a single image. In: IEEE International Conference on Automatic Face and Gesture Recognition and Workshops (2011)

20. Tang, D., Zhang, J., Tang, K., Xu, L., Fang, L.: Making 3D eyeglasses try-on practical. In: IEEE International Conference on Multimedia and Expo Workshops (2014)

21. Yuan, M., Khan, I.R., Farbiz, F., Niswar, A., Huang, Z.: A mixed reality system for virtual glasses try-on. In: Proceedings of the 10th International Conference on Virtual Reality Continuum and Its Applications in Industry (2011)

22. Zhu, X., Qin, S., Yu, H., Ge, S., Yang, Y., Jiang, Y.: Interactive virtual try-on based on real-time motion capture. In: Advances in Multimedia Information Processing (2012)

23. Chen, D., Cao, X., Wen, F., Sun, J.: Blessing of dimensionality: high-dimensional feature and its efficient compression for face verification. In: Computer Vision and Pattern Recognition (CVPR) (2013)

24. Hassner, T., Harel, S., Paz, E., Enbar, R.: Effective face frontalization in unconstrained images. In: Computer Vision and Pattern Recognition (CVPR) (2015)

25. http://www.paneuropeannetworks.com/special-reports/eyealert-driver-fatigue-detection/

26. Huang, G.B., Learned-Miller, E.: Labeled Faces in the Wild: Updates and New Reporting Procedures. Technical Report UM-CS-2014-003, University of Massachusetts, Amherst, May 2014

Evaluation of Information Visualization Interaction Techniques Using Gestures and Widgets in 3D Environments

Brunelli Miranda[1(✉)], Carlos Santos[1], Nikolas Carneiro[1],
Tiago Araújo[1], Anderson Marques[2], Marcelle Mota[1],
Nelson Neto[1], and Bianchi Meiguins[1]

[1] Universidade Federal do Pará (UFPA), Belém, Brazil
brunelli.miranda@gmail.com, gustavo.cbcc@gmail.com,
nikolas.carneiro@gmail.com, tiagodavi70@gmail.com,
cellemota@gmail.com, dnelsonneto@gmail.com,
bianchi.serique@gmail.com
[2] Universidade Federal Rural da Amazônia, Capanema, Brazil
andmarques2006@gmail.com

Abstract. This paper presents the results of usability evaluation of an Information Visualization tool with touchless gestural commands. The tool has well-known visualizations tasks implemented in itself, allowing users to interact on a 3D scatterplot visualization technique. The chosen usability evaluation was the Think Aloud protocol, together with questionnaires conducted by an interviewer, both of them performed with five participants in a controlled environment.

Keywords: Information visualization · 3D interactions · Gestural commands · Usability evaluation

1 Introduction

During the last decades, the Information Visualization (InfoVis) area has been researched and improved, to the point that visualization are already used in several sectors of industry, government and non-governmental organizations, among others [1].

When extracting information directly from raw amounts of data, humans present difficulties to analyze and extract patterns [2]. Due to this reason, visual representations (such as shape, size, color and spatial location) are used to communicate abstract data attributes, thus forming an image that permits the user to view patterns and outliers or to create many analysis scenarios, improving the user understanding about the data [4]. The user's actions on the generated images are called interactions. Generally, users do these interactions by desktop input devices, such as keyboard and mouse.

The data can have multiples dimensions and the use of 3D environments allows a better spatial representation of the different dimensions in the data and its relationships. In a 3D environment, the interaction using desktop input devices will probably need additional interactions from users, since these interactions are meant for 2D environments.

© Springer International Publishing Switzerland 2016
S. Lackey and R. Shumaker (Eds.): VAMR 2016, LNCS 9740, pp. 255–265, 2016.
DOI: 10.1007/978-3-319-39907-2_24

This work aims to explore gesture tracking based interaction techniques n 3D InfoVis environments and present the results of a preliminary usability evaluation.

Section 2 presents the background of the studies fields explored in this work (InfoVis and Gesture Recognition) and the technologies used in the prototype's development. Section 3 describes the developed prototype, along with its functionalities; Sect. 4 explore the setup and results of the performed usability evaluation, and Sect. 5 is about the considerations reached after analysis of results and future works.

2   Background

This section summarizes the main concepts for the research fields approached in this work and the technologies used in the prototype's development.

2.1   Information Visualization

InfoVis aims to provide information to the user, from a graphical data representation, using an interactive computational environment and extending the user cognition [3]. Extended cognition, through data visualization and interaction, augment the user's ability to understand more easily data and its relationship.

In this work, we selected four 3D InfoVis tasks: overview, navigation (zoom, pan and rotation), filter and detail-on-demand. These tasks are well-known in InfoVis, appearing in many other studies, as showed by [5]. For the Visualization technique, we selected the 3D scatterplot visualization technique, due to the advantages of three dimensions over two dimensions, such as a greater number of items in the view [6] and improvement of user's spatial memory [7].

2.2   Gesture Recognition

Gesture is the use of limbs or the whole body motions to emphasize or express an idea or attitude [8]. According to the proposed taxonomy [9], the gestures used in the developed prototype are labeled as manipulative gestures. Manipulative gestures are used to interact with objects in an environment, for example, to move or rotate an item.

Manipulatives gestures were selected for this work, because they are better suited for interaction in InfoVis. The gestures defined for each tool functionality were selected based on two aspects: the user's ease to perform a gesture and the tracking device's capability to identify that same gesture.

2.3   Technologies

Unity. The Unity 3D [Unity] is a game engine with support to multiplatform, allowing the development of both desktop and mobile applications. In this work, it was used Unity 3D version 5.2.1, due to the sense of depth provided by three dimensional environment. The performance of the engine was another relevant factor considered during the implementation of the prototype. When compared to applications developed in other engines, Unity' applications presented a better performance [10].

Leap Motion. The Leap Motion device [11] is a vision-based gesture tracking device [12], as it spread an infrared pattern projection to identify user's hands. Unlike Kinect, Leap Motion detects only hands and some objects [13]. To detect the hands and gestures, the Leap Motion defines an area above itself, called hover zone, where user should place his hands, allowing them to be recognized. Leap Motion was selected as device for the development of this work, because it doesn't need the user to wear any kind of hand or finger accessory to perform the tracking.

3   Prototype

The developed prototype shows a visual representation of data arranged by predefined attributes in a 3D scatterplot. Figure 1D shows the main area of the visualization where visual items will be plotted. In Fig. 1A, we can see the name of the attribute set to each axis and its related color. Figure 1B presents the relation the visual item color and its corresponding value in data, in this scenario, the country where the car was made. Figure 1C, in a similar way to Fig. 1B, presents the relation between a visual item shape and the shape meaning.

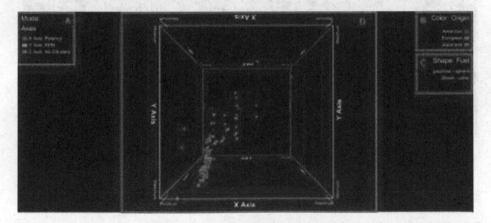

Fig. 1. InfoVis tool initial interface. Highlighted areas A, B and C shows information about the represented items, while area D is where items are plotted.

3.1   Functionalities

Menu. To access any other functionality, users must first call the menu and select an option, as showed in Fig. 2. To call the menu, the user extends his thumb and index fingers, making a gesture similar to an 'L' letter. In the menu, each option represents a different functionality.

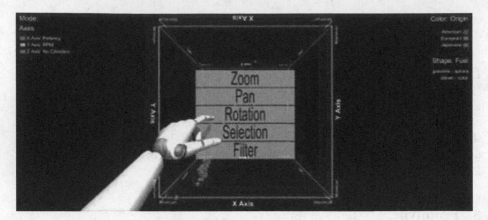

Fig. 2. Functionalities Menu appearing in the screen

Zoom. This functionality permits the user to apply zoom in and zoom out in the visualization. To do it, user must extend both index fingers, increasing or decreasing the distance between them (Fig. 3).

Fig. 3. User applying zoom in the visualization

Pan. To navigate inside the visualization, user must close one hand and open the other one (Fig. 4). While doing this, the user can move the opened hand in four directions (up, down, left and right), resulting in the visualization moving in the same direction.

Rotation. User can rotate the visualization in any of the three axes (x, y and z). To do this, the user can do a swipe gesture with on hand, moving an axis in the same direction of the gesture (example: from right to left). This gesture van be applied in the x and y axes, while in the z-axis, user must do a circle gesture, a circular motion of one finger in mid-air (Fig. 5).

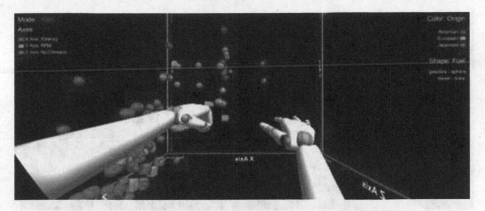

Fig. 4. User navigating in the visualization, using the pan functionality

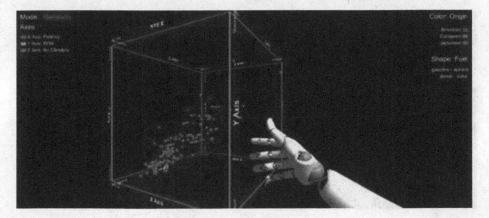

Fig. 5. User applying a rotation in the y-axis, from the right to left direction

Selection. In this functionality, user can select one item to see is details (detail-on-demand). The gesture of selection consists of the user touching a desired item in the visualization(Fig. 6B). The detail of the selected item are displayed on the left side of the interface (Fig. 6A).

Filter. This functionality allows user to filter the visualization by attribute. When this functionality is selected, it calls a new menu containing all the existing attributes in the database. After selecting one attribute, the user must select which values of this attribute he wishes to see in the visualization. Enabled values are present as blue buttons, while disabled values are presented as grey buttons in the interface (Fig. 7).

4 Usability Evaluation

This section describes the usability evaluation, showing its setup and obtained results.

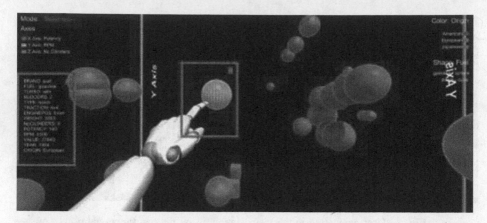

Fig. 6. A – Details of the selected item. B – User selecting one item from the visualization

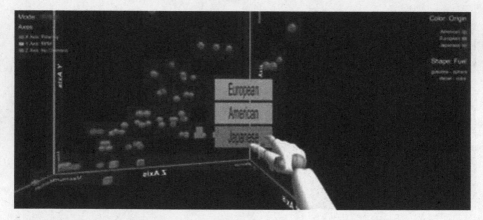

Fig. 7. User applying filter. The blue buttons represent enabled items in the visualization, while grey buttons are disabled items.

4.1   Evaluation Setup

For the usability evaluation, the Think Aloud Protocol [14] was chosen, as it allows to analyze user factors [15]. The evaluation was performed with five participants, three of the having already has experience with InfoVis and gesture-based applications.

Tasks were performed in a controlled environment, with video and audio recordings focusing on the screen and the participants' hands, allowing later analysis of participants' verbalizations and interactions.

Evaluation consisted of five tasks, each one with a time limit of five minutes, a set of required functionalities, a minimum amount of interactions for task completion, an objective to obtain information about the user interactions or interface aspects, and a specific complexity defined by the evaluator, as showed in Table 1. The complexity was determined based on the minimum number of interactions, task with 1 to 5 interactions were considered of low complexity, 6 to 10 were medium and more than 10 interactions was defined as high complexity.

Table 1. Description of tasks for user test

Task Number	Task	Required Functionalities	Minimum number of Interactions	Objective	Complexity
1	Identify cars moved by gasoline, using filter	Filter	4	Evaluate filter interaction	Low
2	Identify cars with high number of cylinders, using rotation, pan and zoom.	Rotation Pan Zoom	19	Evaluate interaction in 3D space	High
3	Identify which countries made cars with high potency.	User choice	8	Evaluate interaction in 3D space	Medium
4	Select the car with highest RPM.	Selection	11	Evaluate selection	High
5	Reset visualization	Reset	1		Low

The minimum number of interactions took in consideration the required steps inside the tool to achieve the desired result, an example is presented in Table 2.

Table 2. Example of step-by-step interaction to complete a task

Task	Step 1	Step 2	Step 3	Step 4
1	Call menu	Select "Filter"	Select "Fuel"	Select "Diesel"

Tests were performed on a Core I7 notebook, with 16Gbyte RAM, dedicated graphic processor with 2Gbytes RAM and 15" screen size, connected to a Leap Motion device. Tests were performed individually with a briefing of 3 to 5 min to present the tool features and interactions for each functionality.

4.2 Evaluation Results

All users completed the five tasks, with the average time for each task been presented in Fig. 8. However, during tasks execution some problems were observed with interactions and interfaces components.

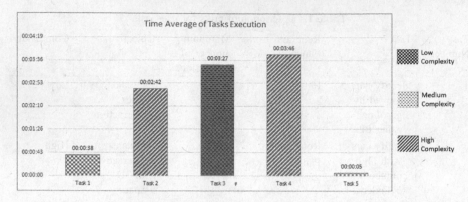

Fig. 8. Average time for each task completion with its defined complexity

Analyzing the hit and misses for each interaction and carrying out an average of all values, we observed a hit rate of 61 % and a miss rate of 39 % in the performance of an interaction (Fig. 9). These results demonstrate that the chance of an incorrect interaction was too high, affecting in user performance and his feelings, as discovered in the think aloud protocol.

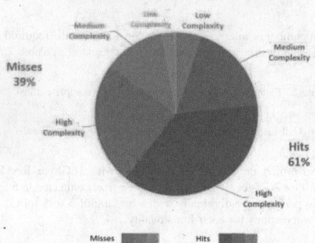

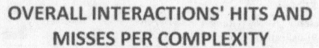

Fig. 9. The average users' performance in tasks. Blue indicates correctly performed interactions while orange indicated errors in interactions.

The reason behind the high miss rate lies in two factors: the leap motion's error rate and the selected gestures for each interaction. During tests, we observed problems related to the device's gesture tracking, resulting in wrong outcomes for user's interaction. Another observed problem was the mistaken recognition of gestures. For functionalities as rotation, which used similar gestures for different rotations, the chance of a wrong recognition was higher than for those functionalities with different gestures for each interaction.

For the think aloud protocol, the recorded videos and audios, of participants performing the tasks, were analyzed to extract the most relevant verbalizations. Classifying the verbalizations based on user's reactions while interacting resulted in four categories of feelings, namely: "Confused", "Finding", "Frustrated" and "Engaged".

"Confused" refers to situations where users received an unexpected outcome while interacting, resulting in a momentary state of user not knowing how to proceed to complete the task. "Finding" is when user discovers or perceives a new information in the interface, for example, the outcome of an interaction in the visualization. "Frustrated" generally occurs when an user is unsuccessful repeating the interaction; and in "Engaged", users are determined to perform an interaction no matter how many times they have to repeat it. The relation of user feelings per functionality is showed in Fig. 10.

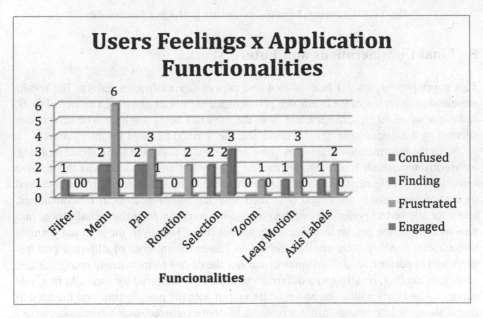

Fig. 10. The relation between users feelings and applications functionalities

After finishing all tasks, users were asked to answer a questionnaire about their experience with the InfoVis tool. The questions asked for the users' impressions on the tool through the rating of the main functionalities and users' thoughts about the good and bad aspects of the tool. The users' average grade for each functionality is showed in Fig. 11.

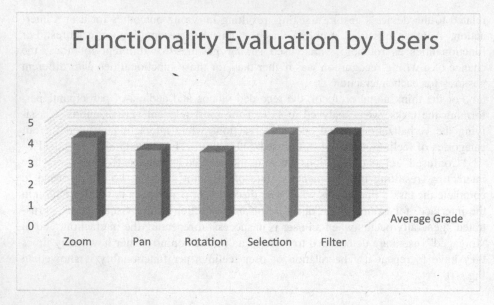

Fig. 11. The average of users' evaluation grades per functionality

5   Final Considerations and Future Works

This paper presented a 3D InfoVis tool and its usability evaluation results. The results presented an overview of the interaction performance in the tool, showing a hit rate of 61 % and miss rate of 39 % per interaction, with the miss rate being too high. The miss rate is affected by the device's recognition errors and the selected gestures for interactions.

With the information obtained in video analysis and using the think aloud protocol, we discovered which functionalities caused more problems for users and the reasons behind these problems. The reason why functionalities such as pan and rotation caused frustration on users is associated with their selected gestures. In both functionalities, users are allowed to perform more than one action to navigate in the visualization, and thus more than one gesture was implemented for them. However, the selected gestures in each functionality were similar, aiming to lessen the number of different gestures users had to perform, and this similarity caused the device to mistakenly recognize one gesture as another, resulting in a different outcome than expected by users. At first, this pattern caused only a little confusion on users, but with the passing time and the need to repeat the same interaction until it was successfully recognized, user's confusion turned into frustration.

The same is applied to menu functionality, as among the functionalities, menu had the highest frustration counter of all. Again, the reasons for this are associated with the device's recognition and the selected gesture. Interactions whose gestures involved the use of open hands and/or extended fingers were frequently mistaken as a menu calling, due to the "L" gesture, used to call menu, be easily recognized.

Even though there was difficulties, we observed that, for a small number of users, the different complexities per task did not exert great influence in users' performance, so although the number of interactions increased in each complexity, the users' hit and miss rate stayed uniform.

One of the users' most appreciated interactions was the reset visualization gesture. This gesture consisted of users' clapping hands twice and almost all users made a verbalization complementing the gesture and its interaction.

For future works, we will improve the tool, mainly the components that caused more difficulties for the users. It is necessary to review some of the selected interactions, particularly their gestures, to determine non-conflicting gestures. Another usability evaluation will be performed, with more participants, along with a heuristic evaluation. According to the results of these evaluations, we will propose guidelines for InfoVis tools based on gesture interactions.

References

1. Pinto, M., Raposo, R., Ramos, F.: Comparison of emerging information visualization tools for higher education. In: 16th International Conference on Information Visualization (IV) (2012)
2. Chen, M., et al.: Data, information, and knowledge in visualization. IEEE Comput. Graph. Appl. **29**(1), 12–19 (2009)
3. Card, S., Mackinlay, J., Shneiderman, B.: Readings in Information Visualization - Using Vision to Think. Morgan Kaufmann, San Francisco (1999)
4. Spence, R.: Information Visualization: Design for Interaction. Prentice Hall, Saddle River (2007)
5. Figueiras, A.: Towards the understanding of interaction in information visualization. In: 19th International Conference on Information Visualization (2015)
6. Ark, W., et al.: Representation matters: the effect of 3D objects and a spatial metaphor in a graphical user interface. In: Johnson, H., Nigay, L., Roast, C. (eds.) People and Computers XIII, Proceedings of HCI 1998, pp. 209–219. Springer, Heidelberg (1998)
7. Tavanti, M., Lind, M.: 2D vs 3D, implications on spatial memory. In: Proceedings of the IEEE Symposium on Information Visualization 2001 (INFOVIS 2001) (2001)
8. Turk, M.: Gesture recognition. In: Stanney, K.M. (ed.) Handbook of Virtual Environments: Design, Implementation, and Applications, Lawrence Erlbaum Associates, Hillsdale, N.J, pp. 223–238 (2002)
9. Pavlovic, V.I., Sharma, R., Huang, T.S.: Visual interpretation of hand gestures for human-computer interaction: a review. IEEE Trans. Pattern Anal. Mach. Intell. **19**, 677–695 (1997). IEEE Computer Society, Washington
10. Johansson, E., et al.: A closer look and comparison of cross-platform development environment for smartphones. Malardalen University (2014)
11. Leap Motion.: LeapMotion (2015). <https://www.leapmotion.com/>
12. Kaäniche, M.B.: Human Gesture Recognition (2009)
13. Spiegelmock, M.: Leap Motion Development Essentials. 1st ed. Packt Publishing Ltd. (2013)
14. Lewis, C.: Using the "thinking Aloud" Method in Cognitive Interface Design. IBM T. J. Watson Research Center. (Research report) (1982)
15. Mahrin, M.N., Strooper, P., Carrington, D.: Selecting usability evaluation methods for software process descriptions. In: Proceedings of the 16th Asia-Pacific Software Engineering Conference. Penang, pp. 523–529 (2009)

Novel Devices and Technologies in VAMR

Immersion in Cardboard VR Compared to a Traditional Head-Mounted Display

Ashfaq Amin[✉], Diane Gromala, Xin Tong, and Chris Shaw

Simon Fraser University, Burnaby, BC, Canada
{aamin,gromala,tongxint,shaw}@sfu.ca

Abstract. This paper describes a study that aims at finding the difference in levels of immersion between a Cardboard VR and a traditional Head-mounted Display (HMD)—the Oculus Rift DK2. Three groups of participants—the experimental group for Cardboard VR, and two control groups for Oculus Rift and a Desktop display—played *Cryoblast* in the same experimental setups for this study. Jennett et al.'s Immersive Experience Questionnaire was used to measure immersion for all the groups. The results indicate that the Cardboard VR, despite its simplicity and small screen size, is capable of providing an acceptable level of immersion compared to Oculus Rift's larger screen size. Since 'immersion' plays an important role in VR pain distraction, knowing the level of immersion for Cardboard VR may help determine its potential as an accessible VR device for chronic pain self-management.

Keywords: Mobile virtual reality · Cardboard VR · Oculus rift · Head-mounted display · Measuring immersion · VR for pain distraction · Pain management

1 Introduction

Virtual Reality (VR) – defined as three-dimensional, stereoscopic, interactive computer graphics – is a computer-generated environment that can simulate physical presence in virtual worlds by engaging human sensory experiences. In health research, VR has been demonstrated as a successful method for mitigating pain in numerous small research studies [7]. The VR simulation, typically designed as a game, helps distract patients from their physical pain and thereby reduces their perceived pain, and in some cases related anxiety. To make the distraction effective, it is thought that the more immersive an experience the patients have, the more distracted they will be from their pain [3, 4]. Moreover, researchers in a study by Hoffman et al. [5] found that the more sophisticated the VR technology, the greater the reported level of pain mitigation. Although the researchers admitted confounding variables, no other comparisons of HMDs for pain distraction had existed. Their assumption is nevertheless important, particularly because Cardboard VR does not merely present lower resolution or a smaller field of view than the Oculus Rift, but achieves VR through a fundamentally different technological approach.

Studies of the use of VR as acute pain distraction initially involved burn injuries among veterans. SnowWorld [1], for example, was a desktop VR simulation developed

© Springer International Publishing Switzerland 2016
S. Lackey and R. Shumaker (Eds.): VAMR 2016, LNCS 9740, pp. 269–276, 2016.
DOI: 10.1007/978-3-319-39907-2_25

by Hunter Hoffman et al. As the researchers described it, the VE drew patients' attention away from their pain experience and redirected it into the immersive 3D environment. Others, such as Steele et al. [2], used an HMD with a tracking device that controlled the movement of the gun inside 3D game. In a study of two adults undergoing painful dental procedures, Hoffman, Garcia-Palacios, et al. [3] demonstrated that an immersive VE resulted in lower subjective pain ratings during painful dental procedures than watching a movie without VR technology. Carlin et al. [4] also found that immersive VR distraction using SpiderWorld resulted in lower subjective pain ratings in two adolescents undergoing wound care for severe burns, compared to trials in which they played Mario Kart or Wave Race on a Nintendo without VR. More recently, VR combined with biofeedback and mindfulness-based stress reduction (MBSR), proved effective in reducing pain over short periods [6].

However, all of the VR simulations in these examples were based on older desktop platforms and traditional head-mounted displays that required professional technical operations and expensive VR equipment in medical settings. Considering the relative expense of HMDs, these factors together make VR inaccessible for patients' everyday interactions and varying needs. Compared to higher-end VR devices like the Oculus Rift, Google's Cardboard VR, which is cut out of pieces of cardboard and folded into a 3D viewer for smartphones, is significantly less expensive.

Given that VR pain distraction is an effective non-pharmacological analgesic, and Cardboard VR is more accessible because of its affordability and ease of use, it has the potential to act as a means to more accessible pain management which patients will be able to use themselves. Therefore, in order to discover if and to what degree Cardboard viewers may be effective for pain management, it is important to study the level of immersion that the Cardboard is capable of, compared to a traditional HMD. To this end, a research study was designed to compare immersion in three displays: a Cardboard VR, a desktop display, and a "traditional" HMD – an Oculus Rift. Because of its hardware limitations, the Cardboard VR was not expected to perform better in any way than the Oculus Rift. However, the Cardboard was predicted to provide a significantly better sense of immersion than the desktop display, despite its smaller size as a handheld device that relies on a user's smartphone. A comparatively higher level of immersion would suggest that Cardboard has the potential to become a VR self pain-management tool that many chronic pain patients could easily access. In the following sections, the method of measuring immersion, design of the study and results are described. Findings of studies such as the one reported in this paper may prove beneficial in designing more effective and immersive experiences on mobile VR platforms, particularly for patients who need to manage their on-going, long-term pain.

2   Traditional HMDs vs. Cardboard VR

Immersive VR, developed primarily in research labs and popularized by the media in the 1990 s, built upon a number of technologies and approaches to computer graphics that were initially described and tested in Ivan Sutherland's Sword of Damocles. At that time, VR was often described as a version of Star Trek's Holodeck [9] and as a "consensual hallucination" [10]. However, because the hardware for VR was extremely expensive and limited, and because 3D software and programming VR was so complex, it didn't become commercially viable in the 1990 s. Therefore, VR's popularity was eclipsed by the advent of the worldwide web and a number of other more accessible computational devices, networks and software.

After decades of commercially failed products and unfulfilled promises, Oculus Rift [12] is credited with bringing life back to the VR industry, and people again became excited about immersing themselves in a computer-generated world. Advanced HMDs like Samsung's GrarVR [13] are also now in the VR market. Although these devices are significantly cheaper than HMDs were a few years ago, they possibly are still not inexpensive enough for large-scale mass consumption, since their prices range from $350 to $1,500. The concept of do-it-yourself (DIY) VR, e.g., Google Cardboard VR, aims at closing this gap. Since the number of smartphone consumers are increasing at a geometric rate, the potential for DIY VR devices are tremendous (Fig. 1).

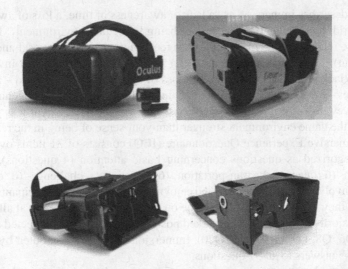

Fig. 1. The Oculus Rift DK2 (top left), Samsung Gear VR (top right), ARCHOS mobile HMD (bottom left), and Do-It-Yourself Cardboard VR (bottom right).

Although the Oculus Rift and Sumsung Gear VR quickly became commercially viable VR displays, other approaches to VR displays have also begun to emerge. One example is Google's Cardboard VR, which is cardboard that the consumer folds up into a viewer and includes plastic lenses. Another example is the plastic VR HMD designed for mobile phones like Archos Mobile VR. These are less expensive than Samsung Gear VR, but still provide a sense of immersion for VR applications.

Cardboard VR is a do-it-yourself (DIY) kit that utilizes a piece of cardboard with a magnet, a rubber band and a couple of pieces of plastic lenses. It has been manufactured by various companies and is priced from $3 to $30, according to material quality and design of the device. Although these cardboard or DIY VR displays are described as inexpensive alternatives to more traditional immersive VR HMDs, they differ from traditional HMDs in their design, construction materials, optics and reliance on smart-phones. Moreover, their methods of interaction are quite different from more traditional VR HMDs since those rely on handheld input devices (joysticks, mice, data-gloves) and desktop or laptop computers.

Despite limitations, the Cardboard-like DYI VR systems have an immense potential of getting a larger consumer base than the traditional HMDs since these are affordable and easy to carry. With a large user base, it has the possibility of becoming a regular device, which promises to give a taste of VR to users in their everyday lives. In cases of pain patients who have acute or chronic pain, and a percentage of who are disabled, expense is a considerable factor that determines whether or not an HMD is viable for home use.

3   Measuring Immersion

Jennett [8] describes immersion as "a lack of awareness of time, a loss of awareness of the real world, involvement and a sense of being in the task environment". Immersion in this sense relates to how present the user feels in the simulated world and how real (or engaging) the virtual environment (VE) seems. Jennett's definition involves two negatives – lack of awareness of time and loss of awareness of real world – along with two positives – involvement and a sense of being in the task environment. Jennett's likert type of survey instrument includes questions such as: "To what extent was your sense of being in the game environment stronger than your sense of being in the real world?"

The Immersive Experience Questionnaire (IEQ) consists of 31 items overall; they can be categorized as questions concerning basic attention (4 questions), temporal dissociation (6 questions), transportation (6 questions), challenge (6 questions), emotional involvement (5 questions) and enjoyment (4 questions). Participants are asked to rate how they felt at the end of the game on a scale of 1 to 5 (1 = not at all and 5 = a lot). The majority of questions are marked positively; while 6 are subjected to negated marking (Q6, Q8, Q9, Q10, Q18, Q20). Immersion scores are computed by summing participants' answers to all 31 questions.

This questionnaire was deemed appropriate since it was developed to measure immersion in video games and this study used a game that was played on three different platforms. Moreover, the questionnaire brings forward insights about attention, disso-ciation, transportation, challenge, emotional involvement and enjoyment that may be associated with each type of display.

4   Study Details

This section includes the study design, demographics of the participants and a brief description of the game used for this study. In the next section, findings from the study are described, followed by discussion and analysis.

4.1 Study Design and Method

The study was a between-subjects comparison of immersion across three platforms — Cardboard VR, Oculus Rift and a desktop display. There were three groups of participants. Participants in the experimental group used Cardboard VR, control group-1 used the Oculus Rift and control group-2 used the desktop display. Each participant played *Cryoblast* [15], a game designed for pain-management, on his or her respective display type for 10–15 min. Thereafter, the participant filled out the Immersive Experience Questionnaire based on the experience of playing the game on their display.

4.2 Participants

Aged between 22 and 19, thirty participants in total participated in this study. The participants were randomly assigned to one of the three groups—the experimental group (for Cardboard VR), control group-1 (for the Oculus Rift) and control group-2 (for the desktop). All participants had previous experiences of playing games on smartphones.

4.3 Apparatus

For the experimental group, a Google LG Nexus 5 smartphone and a *Dodocase* Virtual Reality Kit 1.2 [11], a standard version 1 of Cardboard VR commercially manufactured and sold by *Dodocase*, was used. An elastic head strap, attachable to the Cardboard viewer with Velcro, was used for mounting it to the head. For the control groups, Oculus Rift's Development Kit 2 (DK2) and an Alienware desktop PC (Alienware_X51_R2) was used. The desktop PC had an Acer GD235 Hz HDMI LCD display. For sound, Koss UR29 Full Size Headphones were used in all the three groups.

4.4 *Cryoblast* – the Game

Cryoblast [15] was developed for pain distraction using Unity3D for VR platforms. In this First Person Shooter (FPS) game, the player needs to shoot at "enemy" characters,

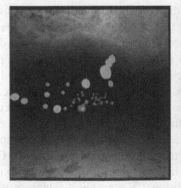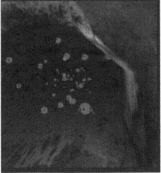

Fig. 2. Screenshots of *Cryoblast* on a smartphone in two different caves

and earn points by collecting as many coins as possible during the journey through six different caves. In *Cryoblast*, the enemies were designed as metaphors for the biological processes of pain, and the ammunition as a metaphor for pain-killing analgesics. The idea is to shoot analgesics at the agitated enemies (dysfunctional glial cells) to calm them down (Fig. 2).

5 Results

Immersion in the different displays was analyzed using one-way between-subjects ANOVA. The analysis revealed a significant effect of immersion for the three different displays at $p<0.05$ [$F(2, 27)=8.7824$, $p=0.0012$]. Post hoc analysis using the Tukey HSD indicated the mean scores for the Oculus Rift ($M = 115.5$, $SD = 18.08$) and the Cardboard VR ($M = 109$, $SD = 21.48$) were significantly different than that of the Desktop display ($M = 85.6$, $SD = 7.51$). However, the Cardboard VR did not significantly differ from the Oculus Rift ($p = 0.6658$) in this study.

5.1 Discussion and Future Studies

The difference in resolution and size of display play an important role with regard to immersive experiences. Compared to the smaller mobile screen used with the Cardboard VR, the Oculus Rift and Desktop PC have larger displays, with resolutions of 960×1080 and 1920×1080 respectively. The LG Nexus 5 also has the same resolution of 1920×1080 as the desktop monitor, but, while the screen size of the monitor is 23.60 inches, the Nexus 5 display is only 4.95 inches. These factors indicate an important finding: the Cardboard, despite having a small screen size, low power and graphics, performs well in delivering an immersive experience. It was quite extraordinary that the mean immersion scores of Cardboard VR ($M=109$) and Oculus Rift ($M=115.5$) were very close. It needs to be mentioned that in order for the game to be optimized for a smartphone, the graphics needed to be tuned down. The Rift is capable of handling very high quality 3D graphics, which *Cryoblast* was not designed for. Therefore, it may be argued that with high quality graphics and better game design, the Rift may have had a significantly higher mean score than the Cardboard VR.

However, the Oculus Rift's handling of high quality graphics has the drawbacks of being a comparatively expensive and heavy HMD, compared to the Cardboard. Moreover, the Cardboard has the potential to become a more common or everyday object with applications for alleviating pain, the efficacy of VR pain distraction may be enhanced since patients would be able to use their VR viewer beyond clinical contexts. Finally, although the design of the game is beyond the scope of this experiment, is very important too because without providing an engaging experience, it is difficult to manage and maintain a user's attention. The game that was used for this study is a prototype. Future developments include building a better, more polished version for smoother and more engaging gameplay. The next phase of this study, clinical testing of the Cardboard VR with chronic pain patients, is the most important since it is planned to determine Cardboard's performance compared to traditional VR systems, which recent studies suggest is problematic in terms of tolerance [14]. While this, of course, is a small study, it marks the beginning of examining the feasibility of Cardboard VR in the context of pain alleviation for patients who are suffering from long-term chronic pain.

6 Conclusion

Combined with an Android smartphone, Cardboard VR works as a more accessible albeit new kind of virtual reality gaming platform. Though the concept of "DIY VR" is very new, it has the potential to grow a large consumer base because of its low cost. More importantly, it can potentially be used for the large numbers of patients who might use it to alleviate their pain. The simplicity of Cardboard VR, if coupled with a carefully designed pain management game, can ensure the ease of use for chronic pain patients. For this reason, the next phase of the study aims at finding if and how Cardboard VR may be effectively used for pain management. Despite the limitations of the study described in this paper it gives a more solid grounding for the next phase of this study, which will repeat the experiment with acute and chronic pain patients to find out how effective Cardboard VR may be as a method of VR pain distraction. Findings from this study suggests that, for playing a small 3D VR pain-management game, the Cardboard VR can perform significantly well compared to the high end Oculus Rift HMD. The game used in this study was a small prototype and required the participants to play around 10-15 min to complete it. So, for a short time period Cardboard VR is capable of providing an acceptable amount of immersive experience. The performance of the Cardboard depends a lot on the users' smartphones. With the advancement in smart-phone technology it can be predicted that Cardboard-like DYI VR systems will be capable of providing better, more engaging and longer immersive experiences in near future.

References

1. Hoffman, H.G., Chambers, G.T., Meyer III, W.J., Arceneaux, L.L., Russell, W.J., Seibel, E.J., Patterson, D.R.: Virtual reality as an adjunctive non-pharmacologic analgesic for acute burn pain during medical procedures. Anna. Behav. Med. **41**(2), 183–191 (2011)
2. Steele, E., Grimmer, K., Thomas, B., Mulley, B., Fulton, I., Hoffman, H.: Virtual reality as a pediatric pain modulation technique: a case study. Cyberpsychology Behav. **6**(6), 633–638 (2003)
3. Hoffman, H.G., Garcia-Palacios, A., Patterson, D.R., Jensen, M., Furness III, T., Ammons Jr., W.F.: The effectiveness of virtual reality for dental pain control: a case study. CyberPsychology Behav. **4**(4), 527–535 (2001)
4. Carlin, A.S., Hoffman, H.G., Weghorst, S.: Virtual reality and tactile augmentation in the treatment of spider phobia: a case report. Behav. Res. Ther. **35**(2), 153–158 (1997)
5. Gromala, D., Tong, X., Choo, A., Karamnejad, M., Shaw, C.D.: The virtual meditative walk: Virtual reality therapy for chronic pain management. In: Proceedings of the 33rd Annual ACM Conference on Human Factors in Computing Systems, pp. 521–524. ACM, April 2015

6. Choo, A., Tong, X., Gromala, D., Hollander, A.: Virtual reality and mobius floe: cognitive distraction as non-pharmacological analgesic for pain management. In: Schouten, B., Fedtke, S., Schijven, M., Vosmeer, M., Gekker, A. (eds.) Games for Health 2014, pp. 8–12. Springer, Heidelberg (2014)

7. Garrett, B., Taverner, T., Masinde, W., Gromala, D., Shaw, C., Negraeff, M.: A rapid evidence assessment of immersive virtual reality as an adjunct therapy in acute pain management in clinical practice. Clin. J. Pain 30(12), 1089–1098 (2014)

8. Jennett, C., Cox, A.L., Cairns, P., Dhoparee, S., Epps, A., Tijs, T., Walton, A.: Measuring and defining the experience of immersion in games. Int. J. Hum Comput Stud. 66(9), 641–661 (2008)

9. Rheingold, H.: Virtual reality, the revolutionary technology of computer-generated artificial worlds-and how it promises and threatens to transform business and society. Nueva York: Simon Schuster 16, 23 (1991)

10. Gibson, J.J.: The senses considered as perceptual systems (1966)

11. Dodocase VR Kit 1.2. www.dodocase.com/products/virtual-reality-viewer-diyvr-hat-hat-mounted-display-bundle

12. Oculus Rift. https://www.oculus.com/en-us/rift/

13. Samsung Gear VR. https://www.oculus.com/en-us/gear-vr/

14. Tong, X., Gromala, D., Gupta, D., Squire, P.: Usability comparisons of head-mounted vs. Steriscopic desktop displays in a virtual reality environment with pain patients. In: Proceedings of the 22nd Medicine Meets Virtual Reality Conference (2016)

15. Tong, X., Gromala, D., Choo, A., Amin, A.: The design of an immersive mobile virtual reality serious game in cardboard head-mounted display for pain management. In: Proceedings of the 5th EAI International Symposium on Pervasive Computing Paradigms for Mental Health (2016)

2D and 3D Iconography on Augmented Reality Interfaces

Luiz Henrique Cavalcanti[(✉)]

Indiana University School of Informatics and Computing, Indianapolis,
IN 46202-3103, USA
{Faiola,presrini,luccaval}@iupui.edu

Abstract. Given the increasing amount of studies about augmented reality environments and interface construction for this type of applications, the adequate use of icons in this context is gaining more and more relevance. The new forms of interaction used in augmented reality originate changes on the maneuver of digital elements, among them the iconic ones. This paper aims studying the use of icons in digital environments and discussing their correct use in augmented reality environments.

Keywords: Augmented reality · Iconography · Interface development

1 Introduction

This work aims to discuss the relation between the use of two and three dimensional (2D and 3D) icons in highly realistic environment interfaces, and the consequent factors of the choice for any of these alternatives. Beyond, the possibility of hybrid 2D/3D interfaces construction is analyzed.

The use of icons in digital interfaces is certainly a vastly studied research field. There are methods of construction and analysis directly developed to test interface efficiency and functional appropriateness [1, 2]. However, in augmented reality (AR) environments, the real world image is overlapped with digital information, which causes a change on the perception and manipulation of icons [3, 4]. This becomes even more evident at the moment that non-traditional types of visualization and interaction interfaces are used, like HMDs (Head-Mounted Displays), data gloves and others found in mobile platforms [5, 6]. To comprehend the impact of iconography in this mixed interfaces is necessary to analyze the functions and relations that these icons will be representing.

Nowadays, studies about interaction in AR environments have shown that those ambient present some differences when compared to the methods used in virtual reality (VR) applications. These differences cause some variations on the criteria used to construct an adequate iconography for these interfaces and on how they are noticed by the user [7]. To better comprehend these differences and how they affect the icon definition process and its use in augmented reality is the main objective of this paper. Based on the research performed by the authors, this work outstands due to its focus on iconography in AR, which has not been largely explored until now.

© Springer International Publishing Switzerland 2016
S. Lackey and R. Shumaker (Eds.): VAMR 2016, LNCS 9740, pp. 277–286, 2016.
DOI: 10.1007/978-3-319-39907-2_26

2   Background

2.1   Theory of Icons

Icons are widely interpreted as images that have a relationship of similarity (an abstraction) to something known, and possessing at least one detail in common with the represented object. This concept makes icons the key to transmit information successfully [1].

Pierce [8] defines icons in his second tricotomy, relative to representamem, as the most basic way of representing metaphorically the reality, being directly related to what is defined by him as the firstness of the information transmission process. As stated by Pierce, icons bring with themselves characteristics similar to the object or information they symbolize.

The term icon, however, is generally used to represent any reality or information metaphorically. This term's generalization is even more used when the main focus is the use of icons on digital interfaces [9].

2.2   Icons on Digital Interfaces

The ISO/IEC standard, specifically the ISO/IEC 11581-1:1995, specifies a definition of icons and their use on digital interfaces. Based on this definition, icons are elements of a distinct language supported by a metaphorical representation through pictograms. The icons differ from other screen elements because of the fact they can represent objects, markers, tools and controls in order to allow their manipulation by users. Icons also have the communicative function of giving the status or performance of activities, transmitting the information necessary to the ideal fulfillment of the task [2].

The most common ways of utilizing icons on digital interfaces is their use with buttons, alert signals and object representation (e.g., icons representing files and folders) [9], as shown in Fig. 1.

Fig. 1.   Examples of icon representation: (a) action; (b) object; (c) status

Icon conception is based on heuristic parameters related to legibility, clarity and level of understanding. Since it is a kind of illustration, its construction is oriented by some graphic elements such as style, color, contrast, texture, luminosity and volume, taking into consideration the type of function it is wished to represent and the interface's project context: targeted audience, functionality and historical precedents [1].

3   Icons on AR and VR Environments

In AR the interfaces construction process becomes more complex, because of the possibility of physical and virtual manipulation, icon reaction and multiple user interaction with the virtual environment. All of these elements must be considered in this type of interface [10, 11].

3.1 Adequacy

Skogen [12], in her pilot studies, performed an experiment in order to define the ideal level of complexity to be used in the creation of a digital interface icon, maximizing its comprehension. As a result, it became clear that the use of aesthetically more elaborated icons that have a higher number of familiarities to the desired objects or actions presented better performance during task's realization. This proved that the higher the abstraction, the less efficient will be the communication provided by icons.

As shown in Fig. 2, Skogen positioned a set of icons in four different quadrants over a board, according to their level of complexity and familiarity. On this board, miniatures of the icons evaluated by Skogen were also placed in one of the four quadrants in order to verify which of them obtained the best results on a user based research realized earlier.

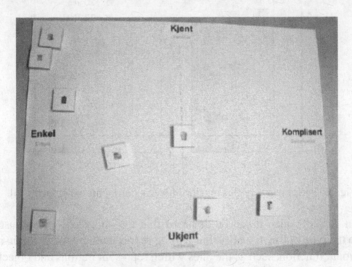

Fig. 2. Example of icon qualification by Skogen [4]

The methodology used in this study allows evaluating the ideal level of abstraction that should be used in the construction of more adequate iconographic projects. However, the work developed by Skogen deals only with the association between icons and corresponding represented objects, not taking into consideration the complete interface and aspects such as circumstances and user motivations for icon manipulation. From this point of view, Skogen's evaluation is essential for icon construction, but must be extended with further actions in order to succeed when using these techniques on complex interface systems like the AR ones. Concepts related to user needs and motivations must be demonstrated and will be discussed later.

3.2 Activity

Ark [13] shows in his experiments the relationship established between the use of 3D and 2D icons in digital interfaces, and also in his "ecological" interfaces. He has defined this kind of interface as being interfaces prepared to simulate environments or specific situations. In his conclusions, the choice of the icon type affected directly user's search and reaction time, and the 3D icons were perceived by the system's operator with more difficulty. However, the 2D icons' level of understanding and comprehension were revealed smaller when compared to 3D ones, as illustrated in Fig. 3. In this figure can be observed that even when the results on the second day are smaller than the ones on the first day (thanks to the familiarization obtained with the interface), the relation among the types of icons stays the same.

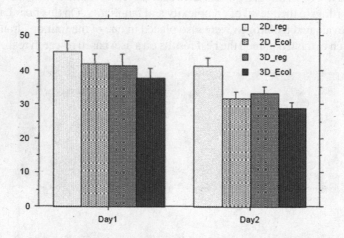

Fig. 3. Performance results obtained by Ark during his experiments [6]

Based on Ark's results, it can be deduced that the choice of icons must be done according to the type of functionality that will be represented by them. Static icons that have operational function, such as the ones which represent buttons and objects, can be used in their 3D form, since they do not require a significant small response time. However, icons indicating alerts or some information must be perceived as fast as possible by the user, and for this reason the 2D representation is more adequate.

3.3 Manipulation

Smallman [14] also presents in his studies results similar to the ones found by Ark. However, he presents some new arguments in favor of the capabilities inherent to 3D icons when it comes to represent a greater amount of information, since they can assume a higher number of functions or object characteristics. Besides the fact that 2D icons' search time is smaller than 3D ones, the communication level of a 3D representation works better when the goal is to transmit a higher amount of information, like the example illustrated in Fig. 4 where the icon itself has information related to direction, orientation, behavior, and airplane model.

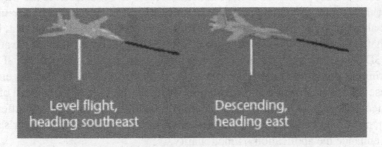

Fig. 4. Icon model presented by Smallman

In the same way that concepts like user needs and motivations were highlighted in Skogen's work, it is fundamental to point out in Ark's and Smallman's work the importance they gave to iconographic system suitability to the task of the application interface at hand. In the case of AR interfaces, to understand this suitability requires comprehending the environment's behavior as well as the data that will be digitally inserted on it.

4 AR Interaction and the Use of Icons

Different from what occurs in VR, AR has not yet its interaction techniques completely explained and classified. One of the reasons that justify this lack of classification could be the fact that the majority of VR interaction techniques can be used in AR applications without problems.

Broll and his colleagues [8] recently proposed a new classification of interaction techniques specifically for AR environments. They have stated that 3D or VR interaction techniques cannot be directly applied to AR. Therefore, they have subdivided different interaction techniques into spatial interaction, command-based interaction, virtual control interaction and physical control interaction.

Despite this classification includes a great part of interaction techniques used in AR, it shows itself insufficient and is not widely accepted by scientific community.

The construction of AR interfaces presents some important questions related to the use of an adequate iconography. Many authors have studied and debated these questions in wider contexts. In this section, it will be discussed questions targeting perception in a 3D environment, suitability in ecological environments, like the variations presented in Ark's ecological interfaces and the possibility of using real icons.

At first, interaction in 3D immersive environments already adds to icon construction a variety of possibilities not applicable to 2D environments. For example, volume and perspective are two characteristics that considerably alter the perception of the constructed icon. This type of ambient allows direct interaction to the iconic objects, since the user does not need to click on the icon anymore; now, he/she can press, activate by direct looking or simply walking near the icon.

This variation in icon manipulation enables the icon to have not just one function, but a series of them, since the function can vary according to the way the manipulation occurs [15]. The next point that deserves attention in both VR and AR is the way icons can adapt themselves to the augmented environment and be perceived by the user. In his study about icons in virtual environment interfaces, Ark [13] presents that, beside the fact that 3D icons are more suitable when applied to an ecological interface ambient having a 3D basis, they suffer from a low search response time, if compared to 2D ones.

By bringing this problem to the context of AR environments, a question emerges about these icons visualization and adaptation in the world. It is clear the need of highlighting icons presence in the virtual environment through the use of differential rendering, positioning or shape and volume variations. This could decrease user's search time and enhance the application's functionality.

According to the interaction technique used, there is a variation in icon manipulation and its functionality, as shown in that exemplifies the mivaDesk application (see Sect. 4). The interaction techniques followed the classification suggested by Bowman. Each one of the interfaces adopts different types of iconography depending on the interaction technique used (Fig. 5).

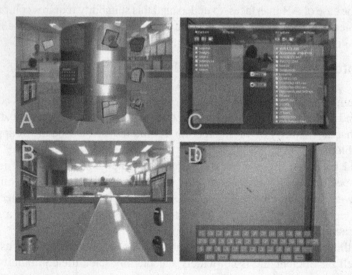

Fig. 5. Examples of AR interaction techniques and the presence of icons on each interface: (a) gesture manipulation and 3D widgets (mivaDesk menu); (b) walking navigation (mivaDesk idle interface); (c) system control (mivaDesk file transfer interface); (d) symbolic input (mivaDesk soft keyboard)

At last, the use of an AR ambient focuses the attention to a brand new possibility related to information representation: the use of real icons. As explained in Sect. 2, basically, icons are representations of real objects or information familiar to users. Because of that, it is hard to a user that is already accustomed to some specific system or culture to comprehend some new interface constructed. In AR, however, it is possible to link information or even activities to an object or real phenomena: a real object from an AR interface can become the iconic reference to some system's action (e.g., a product can be turned into a shortcut to an ingredient sheet and its nutrients table or stock management). These possibilities are based on recent researches and studies, like 3D reconstruction from 2D images and markerless AR. The last one is a relative new concept. It utilizes many computer vision algorithms to extract image characteristics, which could be transformed into 3D reference points. A set of these points gives origin to a mapping of the real scene, and can be used to position the desired virtual objects through a previously chosen viewpoint.

5 Discussions

Based on iconography construction and functionality principles defined in previous sections, related to generic interfaces and specific AR ones, some considerations can be made. Based on the studies shown, it is possible to enumerate three important points about the use of 2D and 3D icons in AR environments: manipulation, activity and adequacy.

The first of them, manipulation, helps to evaluate the ways of interaction that each interface must support, how the user can interact with the environment and its elements, how visualization occurs, and what are the available possibilities of element control by the user. Section 3.3 highlighted the importance of user necessities and task objectives in an iconography project. This stage provides essential information to be used during icon creation in order to easily control the interface. The creation of application scenarios through the use of history boards and watched simulations allows highlighting specific interface manipulation cases and some iconography needs. Through these procedures, it is possible to list all the necessary iconography related to the type of interaction available to system users.

In sequence, activity is related to the function icons will perform. It is necessary to define adequately which functions and under which circumstances each one of them will be used (equipment used and interaction techniques adopted), and what is needed for their ideal performance. Response time, visibility and importance factors will be the start for iconographic planning of each interface used. Through them it will be possible to make decisions and to define methods for evaluation and later icon performance check. In order to optimize this process, it is recommended the construction of a table containing each icon function and technical characteristics needed, based on interface objectives and flowcharts.

At last, the icons adequacy to the targeted applicable environment and AR ambient must be verified, in order to better adapt them to their functions and usage methods. After this verification for a specific interface, it is possible to elaborate graphical aspects for icon construction: if the icon must have 2 or 3 dimensions, which shape is indicated, color, style, contrast, volume etc. Also referred to adequacy, it is necessary to observe the set of experiences of potential system users to select the most efficient graphical iconic language that communicates to these individuals.

By using these highlighted points on icon utilization in AR interfaces, a solid base of procedures for obtaining data related to their construction can be established. These procedures are summarized in Fig. 6, which shows an example of methods table for evaluation of distinct interface aspects.

construction aspects	activity	manipulation	adequacy
function	checklist	simulation	
visual aspects (color, contrast, shape...)	heuristically evaluation	history board	heuristically evaluation
performance aspects	flowcharts		checklist
usability aspects	users tests	users tests	benchmark
results	list of icons	development guidelines	visual parameters

Fig. 6. Example of a group of procedures to be used for icons development, based on manipulation, adequacy and activity aspects.

This procedure of the methodological definition of data acquisition can be applied to any type of digital interface. However, in case of AR interfaces, in order to minimize the number of problems related to user interaction, this action becomes vital for the project success. In Fig. 7, it is possible to observe the general scheme of procedures that recover data supporting interface iconographic projects.

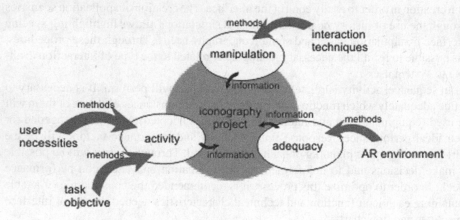

Fig. 7. General diagram showing relations between manipulation, activity and adequacy

The selection of which aspects must be evaluated and the choice of methods and techniques which will be used in data acquisition should vary from case to case, hence providing the project team with a major amount of relevant information. The methods and techniques listed in Fig. 6 can be found in Baxter [16], as well as in other works related to this research area [6, 17, 18].

Through the use of this methodology, an optimization on the construction of iconographic systems for AR interfaces is expected. The retained methodology considers project orientations based on a more complete comprehension about the usage circumstances of these interfaces: "Who will use it?", "Where are they used?", "What are they used for?", "In which way are they used?".

6 Conclusions

The use of the methodology and concepts detailed in this paper proved to be relevant during all design processes and lead to important decisions about the application interface regarding the 2D and 3D icons used. The understanding of the impacts of wrong iconography in VR and AR enviroments can bring to the community more control over the experience provided and allow better results in cognitive and functional perception from the users.

As future work, a case Study based on VR interfaces will implemented. Some usability and performance tests should validate the final product an check the benefits of methodology.

References

1. Santaella, L.: A Teoria Geral dos Signos: Semiose e Autogeração. Ática, São Paulo (1995)
2. Barr, P., Noble, J., Biddle, R.: Icons R icons. In: Proceedings of the Fourth Australasian user Interface Conference on User Interfaces 2003, vol. 18, pp. 25–32. Australian Computer Society, Inc. (2003)
3. Broll, W., Lindt, I., Ohlenburg, J., Herbst, I., Wittkämper, M., Novotny, T.: An infrastructure for realizing custom - tailored augmented reality user interfaces. IEEE Trans. Vis. Comput. Graph. **11**, 722–733 (2005)
4. Bowman, D., Kruijff, E., LaViola Jr., J., Poupyrev, I.: 3D User Interfaces: Theory and Practice. Addison-Wesley, Boston (2004)
5. Lewis, R.C., Mandyam, G.D., Dickens, M.C.: Multiple actions and icons for mobile advertising. U.S. Patent 9,111,286, issued 18 August 2015
6. Bowman, D., Hodges, L.: Travel in immersive virtual environments: an evaluation of viewpoint motion control techniques. In: IEEE Virtual Reality Annual International Symposium, pp. 45–52 (1997)
7. Azuma, R., Baillot, Y., Behringer, R., Feiner, S., Julier, S., MacIntyre, B.: Recent advances in augmented reality. In: IEEE Computer Graphics and Applications, pp. 34–47 (2001)
8. Peirce, C.: Collected Papers of Charles Sanders Peirce. In: Hartshorne, C., Weiss, P. (eds.) Harvard University Press, pp. 1931–35
9. Wang, H.F., Hung, S.H., Liao, C.C.: A survey of icon taxonomy used in the interface design. In: Proceedings of the 14th European Conference on Cognitive Ergonomics: Invent! Explore!, pp. 203–206. ACM (2007)
10. Poupyrev, I., Tan, D., Billinghurst, M., Kato, H., Regenbrecht, H., Tetsutani, N.: Developing a generic augmented-reality interface. IEEE Comput. **35**, 44–49 (2002)
11. Mine, M.: Virtual Environment Interaction Techniques, UNC Chapel Hill CS Dept.: Technical report TR95-018. 1995
12. Skogen, M. An Investigation into the Subjective Experience of Icons: A Pilot Study, Information Visualization (2006)

13. Ark, W., Dryer, C., Selker, T., Zhai, S.: Representation matters: the effect of 3D objects and a spatial metaphor in a graphical user interface. In: Johnson, H., Lawrence, N., Roast, C. (eds.) People and Computers XIII, Proceedings of HCI 1998, pp. 209–219. Springer, London (1998)
14. Smallman, H., John, M., Oonk, H., Cowen, M.: Information availability in 2D and 3D displays. IEEE Comput. Graph. Appl. (2001)
15. Datcu, D., Lukosch, S., Brazier, F.: On the usability and effectiveness of different interaction types in augmented reality. Int. J. Hum.-Comput. Interact. **31**(3), 193–209 (2015)
16. Baxter, M.: Projeto de Produto. Edgard Blücher, São Paulo (2000)
17. Eisen, H.A.: ICONER: A tool for evaluating icons. ACM SIGCHI Bull. **21**(3), 23–26 (1990)
18. Brookshire Conner, D., Snibbe, S., Herndon, K., Robbins, D., Zeleznik, R.: Three-dimensional Widgets, Interactive 3D Graphics Symposium, pp. 183–188 (1992)

Optimizing 3D Object Visualization
on the Web

João Victor de Figueiredo Leite[1],
João Marcelo Xavier Natário Teixeira[1,2(✉)], and Veronica Teichrieb[1]

[1] Voxar Labs, CIn, Universidade Federal de Pernambuco, Recife, Brazil
{jvfl, vt}@cin.ufpe.br
[2] DEINFO, Universidade Federal Rural de Pernambuco, Recife, Brazil
jmxnt@cin.ufrpe.br

Abstract. With the rise of new technologies for visualizing 3D information in the browser, a trend can be observed concerning the growing use of such technologies in web-based applications, due to browsers being present in virtually every device. Also, a growth can be observed in the 3D printing field, since the printers are becoming cheaper as the technology evolves. This study aims to develop a loader and a web visualizer for the 3MF format, and test its performance across desktop and mobile devices, searching for an optimized way of displaying 3D printing data in browsers. To test the validity of the loader, a 3D printing simulator was also implemented and tested across platforms. It was discovered that 3MF is better than STL for visualizing 3D content on the web, due to its greater capabilities, extensibility, and even a smaller loading time given the right optimizations.

Keywords: 3D visualization · 3MF · Three.js · Web

1 Introduction

Lately, new web technologies in the field of 3D graphics have been developed, such as WebGL [1], "Three.js" [10] and Babylon [4], which are enabling a pervasive cross-browser form of processing and displaying graphical data without most of the portability concerns traditional technologies have, leaving only typical cross-browser API differences as a possible problem. These new technologies have already enabled powerful new tools to be developed [23], and their performance can be fine-tuned to work well both on desktop and mobile platforms [24].

Currently, those visualization technologies are being explored widely and a myriad of examples are available. Many of them are now related to a field that has been gaining attention in the last years: 3D printing.

3D printing, or additive manufacturing, is the process of transforming information contained in a digital three-dimensional object into a physical object. It achieves such feat by extracting horizontal cross-sections of the virtual objects, which are then printed and laid down until the whole object is created [12].

Throughout the last couple of years, 3D printing technology has risen in popularity, even further than what was expected according to experts [2]. This gave spawn to a

© Springer International Publishing Switzerland 2016
S. Lackey and R. Shumaker (Eds.): VAMR 2016, LNCS 9740, pp. 287–298, 2016.
DOI: 10.1007/978-3-319-39907-2_27

series of very differentiated applications ranging from manufacturing composite elements [17] to printing biomaterials [15].

However, the file format considered as the de facto standard, STL (Standard Triangulation Language) [19, 21, 22], is falling behind since it is limited in its representational capabilities in regard to the constantly evolving technological scenario. Therefore, new initiatives were founded in order to find a suitable format that can be extended as needed, providing support to emerging technologies, such as AMF (Additive Manufacturing Format) [20] and 3MF (3D Manufacturing Format) [13].

2   ThreeMF Loader

The loader proposed in this work was implemented through the use of the "Three.js" library to parse 3MF files in accordance with the specifications [3]. This section discusses the "Three.js" library and the loader's architecture.

According to its specification [3], a 3MF file is in fact a zip file that obeys the Open Packaging Conventions [18]. For this work, the main files observed inside the zip are the 3Dmodel.model, which stores 3D models as triangular meshes, and the image textures files, because both contain the core of what is necessary to fully display the 3D model that the 3MF file represents. It is noteworthy that the 3Dmodel.model file is, in fact, an XML file.

2.1   Three.Js

"Three.js" is a lightweight 3D library that simplifies 3D graphics usage inside a browser [10]. It features a simple API and has different options of rendering engines, with the default engines being: HTML5 canvas and SVG elements, CSS3D and WebGL. For the purposes of this work, the WebGL renderer was used together with the HTML5 canvas element, so the models could be rendered to the screen. The following classes were utilized in this work to fully represent a 3MF model:

- **Scene:** Manages the rendering of several models on the screen. Each model must be constructed and added to the scene separately by using one of the provided classes in "Three.js".
- **Geometry:** Contains all the information about the objects vertices, faces, colors and texture UVs, and also includes positional information.
- **Face3:** Represents a triangle shaped face in space by referencing vertices previously added to a Geometry. As an added bonus, this class also stores which color or texture used.
- **Mesh:** Related to Geometry and the Material which will be used to display it.
- **MeshPhongMaterial:** The material utilized for this work, defining that the Phong shader will be used to represent the objects after they are loaded.

By utilizing such classes, one can fully describe a triangular mesh, regardless of size, even if such mesh contains more complex information such as color and textures. For a concrete example about the library's initialization and object construction, please refer to the source code of this project [11], and also to the examples at the "Three.js" website.

2.2   Architecture

For the definition of the loader's architecture, current loaders at the "Three.js" base code were studied, and a general structure was identified. As a result, a new class called ThreeMFLoader was created as per the needs of the structure.

The primary function of "Three.js" loaders is the load function, which receives a url and returns a model. But, despite having a similar signature, some loaders differed about the function return type, which was defined either as Mesh or Geometry objects depending on the loader. Considering that the function of a loader should not affect how the loaded model is displayed, it was decided that the ThreeMFLoader should just return a Geometry and a list of the accompanying textures, leaving the materials choice to the final user.

Since the 3MF is a zip file, libraries regarding the use of zip files in Javascript had to be found, because no other "Three.js" loader had to deal with a zipped file at the time this work was done. So, the "zip.js" library [14] was chosen as a means to do so, and functions were defined to load the "3Dmodel.model" file and the related texture image files from the 3MF zip file.

However, the "zip.js" library uses Web Workers, which are essentially an implementation of threads in the Javascript environment, implying in the files being extracted from the zip file in an asynchronous manner. A simple synchronization control was then devised through counting all the files that needed to be extracted, and then subtracting such counter by one each time a file was fully extracted.

With all the files available for parsing after extracting, new functions were defined to parse the "3Dmodel.model" file. Given that such file is an XML file, the default Javascript's DOM parser was utilized to navigate through it, with several new functions being created to modularize each of the XML file nodes concerns.

The root function for XML processing, called processXML, is responsible for separating and storing the information of tags that can later be referenced by other elements, such as the texture2d, colorgroup and texture2dgroup tags.

Besides the processXML function, the parseObjects function can be defined as being fundamental in the parsing process. It extracts all the vertex and triangle tags from an object node and inserts them onto a Geometry as Face3 objects. Each triangle node can also hold a reference to either a colorgroup or a texture2dgroup, and thanks to the pre-processing done by the processXML function, such information is available to be used and inserted in the Face3 object, or inside the Geometry object, as it happens in the UV mappings case.

Most of the functions besides the processXML and parseObjects can be classified as helper functions, since they only take care of simpler details, like extracting the coordinates of a vertex. In such way, they are not discussed here, but are available for consultation at the source code of the project [11].

3   Printing Simulator

In order to validate the loader usefulness in a real web application, a basic 3D printing simulator was implemented. This section will present the basic implementation details of the Simulator, describing the libraries.

3.1   Implementation

After the model is in the appropriate structure, to simulate the additive manufacturing process one has to divide it into layers, effectively slicing it. To achieve slicing, a CSG (Constructive Solid Geometry) library was utilized, namely the "CSG.js" library [6].

The "CSG.js" library implements CSG Boolean operations by using BSP (Binary Space Partitioning) trees, but at the time of implementation of this work it was severely outdated [6]. A suitable updated version was found inside the source code of the OpenJSCad project [8], which enabled the implementation of the slicing feature through the use of CSG's intersection operation.

Despite being an updated version, the "CSG.js" basic data structures differ from the ones found in "Three.js", and as such a third component was needed in order to enable interoperability between the libraries; the "ThreeCSG.js" [5] was used to do so. However, the new component was also outdated. Thus, the "ThreeCSG.js" library had to be updated, which presented a need to better understand the "CSG.js" data structures.

Similarly to "Three.js", "CSG.js" has a set of classes designed to represent 3D models, from which some were selected based on their likeness to "Three.js" data structures. Those are the CSG, Polygon, Vertex and Vector3D classes, described as follows:

- **CSG:** Represents a 3D model and contains a list of Polygons. Its chosen counterpart in the "Three.js" library is the Geometry class.
- **Polygon:** A 3D polygon represented by a list of vertices. Since it describes a face in the high level CSG object, this class was used to be the equivalent of a Face3 object, despite being more general.
- **Vertex:** Represents a single 3D point and can be directly correlated to a "Three.js" vertex.
- **Vector3D:** Require for the construction of a CSG Vertex. It represents a vector or a point in 3D space.

After updating the "ThreeCSG.js" library, the objects could be easily con- verted between CSG and Geometry objects, giving "Three.js" full access to the "CSG.js" capabilities. The intersection operation was available to "Three.js" Geometry objects, and a parallelepiped could be defined in a way that slices varying heights by intersecting it with an arbitrary Geometry, given that the parallelepiped has depth and width equal to the geometry (Fig. 1).

Fig. 1. The defined parallelepiped intersecting a tetrahedron.

As result, two functions were defined in a separate file called "3DPrinterSimulator.js":

- **generateSlices:** Receives a mesh and a slice height, and then produces the sliced mesh as Geometry objects.
- **displaySlices:** Receives the "Three.js" scene, a list of mesh slices, a delay time and feedback function. It renders each slice in the scene according to the delay set by the user, then executes the feedback function so the user may know that the simulation has ended.

By using such functions, one can effectively simulate the 3D printing process on a "Three.js" geometry by first generating the slices with the desired height, and then displaying them (Fig. 2).

Fig. 2. Intermediary simulation results of the 3D printing process.

4   Results

To confirm the pervasiveness and effectiveness of the technologies utilized, the loading process was tested both on mobile and desktop platforms. This section describes the tests performed in this work, which were executed in four models: Tetrahedron, Rhombicuboctahedron, Dodecahedron chain and Heartgears (Fig. 3).

Fig. 3. Loaded 3MF models.

4.1   File Format Comparison

Although the STL format has been the *de facto* standard for printing over the past two decades, it is severely limited and fail to address the evolving needs for 3D printing [19, 21, 22]. Some extensions have been proposed, but they were not widely accepted [16, 25]. As a side-effect of the lack of extensions, nowadays the STL file format is only able to save and load simple 3D meshes based on triangles, and has no support for texture, color, and materials. It is important to notice that an STL file can be represented in either ASCII or Binary, with the only difference between them being their file size in bytes, since the Binary format is considerably smaller than the plain ASCII file.

As for the 3MF file format, it proposes to fix some of the STL problems, offering a specification with flexible rules for extensions. In such way, although it still only supports triangular models, it can be easily extended in order to support more complex representations. Additionally, texture, color, and materials are already supported out of the box [3]. It also comes with only one representation, (i.e., a zip file).

An in-depth comparison between file sizes is shown as follows (Table 1), where files containing exactly the same information were compared in order to ascertain which is better suited for web visualization given the file size taken to represent the same object.

Table 1. File format sizes (in KB).

Model	Number of Triangles	STL Size	Binary STL Size	3MF Size
Tetrahedron	4	2	1	2
Rhombicuboctahedron	44	12	3	2
Dodecahedron chain	7680	1323	376	62
Heartgears	30636	6363	1502	326

Thus, it can be observed that the size of a 3MF file grows slower than STL files, even the binary one. Also, since the smaller file size makes downloading faster, the 3MF file is better suited for web visualization in regard to file size.

4.2   Loading Time

The file size only affects the download speed of the model; its effect can be nullified if parsing takes too long. Hence, tests gauging was conducted to learn whether the unzipping and parsing of the 3MF file will negate the file size benefits. The tables in sequence (Tables 2, 3, 4 and 5) describe the loading times of the STL and 3MF formats. In the tests, three types of devices were used: PC, smart phone, and tablet. Each model was loaded 100 times on each device, and the average times and their standard deviations were recorded.

The devices specifications are listed as follows:

PC ASUS N56JR-EH71
    Processor 2.4GHz Intel I7 4700HQ
    Video Card NVIDIA Geforce GTX 760M with 2GB of memory
    RAM 12GB
    Browser Chrome 47
    OS Windows 8.1
Phone iPhone 5S
    Processor 1.3GHz Apple A7
    Video Card PowerVR G6430 RAM 1GB
    Browser Safari 9
    OS iOS 9.2
Tablet Samsung Galaxy Note 2014 Edition
    Processor 1.3GHz quad-core Exynos 5420
    Video Card Mali-T628
    RAM 3GB
    Browser Android Native Browser
    OS Android 4.3

Table 2. STL file parsing time (average time in ms).

Model	PC (Standard Deviation)	Phone (Standard Deviation)	Tablet (Standard Deviation)
Tetrahedron	0.185 (0.164)	1.022 (1.468)	0.994 (0.958)
Rhombicuboctahedron	1.085 (0.336)	4.435 (2.268)	11.816 (3.130)
Dodecahedron chain	239.523 (29.469)	581.258 (56.211)	856.718 (102.663)
Heartgears	1185.450 (106.550)	5879.429 (187.686)	4614.742 (1177.846)

Table 3. Binary STL file parsing time (average time in ms).

Model	PC (Standard Deviation)	Phone (Standard Deviation)	Tablet (Standard Deviation)
Tetrahedron	0.085 (0.136)	0.185 (0.398)	0.371 (1.219)
Rhombicuboctahedron	0.090 (0.047)	0.128 (0.068)	0.711 (0.307)
Dodecahedron chain	7.329 (2.486)	9.244 (2.034)	33.484 (17.117)
Heartgears	36.959 (7.898)	47.643 (4.248)	122.044 (12.729)

Table 4. 3MF unzipping times (average time in ms).

Model	PC (Standard Deviation)	Phone (Standard Deviation)	Tablet (Standard Deviation)
Tetrahedron	133.605 (15.447)	61.501 (29.877)	140.397 (12.603)
Rhombicuboctahedron	134.651 (50.706)	62.273 (27.945)	148.852 (13.751)
Dodecahedron chain	199.252 (104.746)	242.116 (43.144)	806.121 (190.775)
Heartgears	313.421 (62.440)	716.328 (221.484)	2482.954 (98.507)

Table 5. 3MF parsing times (average time in ms).

Model	PC (Standard Deviation)	Phone (Standard Deviation)	Tablet (Standard Deviation)
Tetrahedron	0.171 (0.137)	0.579 (0.166)	2.413 (4.560)
Rhombicuboctahedron	0.423 (0.175)	1.314 (1.075)	4.070 (2.546)
Dodecahedron chain	42.404 (17.966)	56.067 (12.799)	438.604 (165.474)
Heartgears	308.822 (73.671)	392.871 (725.502)	2230.832 (161.264)

The binary STL file format seems more advantageous in loading times, especially when the 3MF unzipping time is factored in. Nonetheless, it is important to notice that the unzipping time can still be compensated by the smaller file size on larger models, since unzipping files has a relatively short time and is not prone to variations given the users access to a fast Internet connection.

4.3   Loaders Comparison

During the development of this work, one of the objectives was to contribute to the "Three.js" source code by the addition of a 3MF loader. However, a third party loader was submitted before, and a comparison between the one previously submitted (current Three.js' 3MF loader) [10] and the one developed here was drawn in regards to capabilities and loading times.

As far as capabilities go, the loader present at the "Three.js" code parses some minor tags from 3MF that the loader proposed here does not, such as the metadata tag, which contains information such as the file author, creation date, among others. As for the loader here proposed, it provides support to textures and colors as extra features.

Architecture-wise, it is important to notice that the libraries utilized to unzip files were different. While the proposed loader uses the "zip.js" library, the "Three.js" loader uses the "jszip.js" library [7]. When tested in regards to unzipping time, "jszip.js" proved to be much faster than "zip.js" (Table 6). However, it did not work on the tested phone and tablet, even when changing browsers. The browsers tested were Safari, Chrome, Opera, Firefox and the Native Android Browser.

Table 6. Time taken by each loader to unzip files in PC (average time in ms).

Model	"Three.js loader PC Average (Standard Deviation)	Our loader PC Average (Standard Deviation)
Tetrahedron	0.208 (0.364)	133.605 (15.447)
Rhombicuboctahedron	0.277 (0.906)	134.651 (50.706)
Dodecahedron chain	5.189 (2.071)	199.252 (104.746)
Heartgears	20.799 (2.621)	313.421 (62.440)

When compared regarding parsing times, the "Three.js" loader also outperformed the one presented in this work (Table 7). By analyzing the parsing functions of each work, it was discovered that the bottleneck of this work's loader was the need for computing the normals when each face of the geometry was created. In "Three.js" loader, this apparently is already done automatically by the data structures utilized.

Table 7. Time taken by each loader to parse models in PC (average time in ms).

Model	"Three.js" loader PC Average (Standard Deviation)	Our loader PC Average (Standard Deviation)
Tetrahedron	0.119 (0.069)	0.171 (0.137)
Rhombicuboctahedron	0.287 (0.132)	0.423 (0.175)
Dodecahedron chain	24.834 (11.513)	42.404 (17.966)
Heartgears	127.893 (28.460)	308.822 (73.671)

It is important to notice that, during tests, it was discovered that the "Three.js" loader uses a Javascript API called TextDecoder, does not working on all Desktop browsers [9], and by the tests performed, it does not work on mobile devices as well. However, it is a problem that can be fixed, since there are libraries which implement API and give support to such browsers. While there is a loader already in the "Three.js" source code which is more efficient, some opportunities to improve such loader were identified while it was analyzed. It can be further optimized if a different function is used to separate the XML nodes, and support to textures and colors can also be added.

4.4   Printing Simulator Analysis

Since the objective of the final product of the simulation was to run both on mobile and PC, tests were conducted to assert that it could effectively run on those platforms. That is, besides loading and displaying the models, the device where the simulator runs must be able to simulate slicing in a timely fashion, so the user can use it without waiting for results.

In such a way, tests were conducted to determine the speed in which the devices could calculate each slice. Table 8 shows the time it takes for each slice to be computed; each average and standard deviation were taken from 100 samples, except for the Heartgears model which were tested on the mobile devices. For this model, in both phone and tablet, only 10 samples were run due to the long time it took to compute each slice, and the fact that, sometimes, the browser froze while computations were being made.

Table 8. Slicing times (average time in ms).

Model	PC (Standard Deviation)	Phone (Standard Deviation)	Tablet (Standard Deviation)
Tetrahedron	1.248 (0.878)	3.115 (3.337)	7.220 (6.766)
Rhombicuboctahedron	1.836 (0.914)	6.745 (5.894)	11.899 (5.584)
Dodecahedron chain	637.616 (129.334)	1002.773 (234.394)	3360.233 (872.014)
Heartgears	2677.336 (546.256)	8075.494 (2468.433)	19855.443 (2078.619)

Given that the most complex models take too long for the slices to be computed, a strategy was devised to minimize such effects. Each slice is only computed once when the application is used, and a cache is established, so if the user so desires, the simulation can be viewed smoothly after its first execution. Nevertheless, the caching strategy did not solve one problem: complex models cannot be easily simulated through the use of the CSG intersection operation, especially on mobile devices which sometimes froze when the simulation was running. This leaves two options for the simulations to be effective on mobile devices: either optimize the used functions, or precompute the simulation and leave it available as a source file that the final user will use without noticing.

From these two options, the latter is considered to be a better option for incrementing this work on the future, given that it would also make the voxelization of the models possible regardless of the time that would take for the simulation to run, and the results would be available in a fast manner both on PC and mobile.

5   Conclusion

The 3MF model file loader and visualizer were successfully developed and validated through the implemented printing simulator. Meanwhile, the tests conducted were important for properly comparing the STL format and the new 3MF format, not only for their capabilities, but also regarding their possible use in a web application.

When considering file sizes and capabilities, the 3MF is better suited because it has improved scalability, extensibility, and support for textures and colors. For instance, the Heartgears binary STL model is 4.6 times bigger than its 3MF counterpart, and it only contains a triangulated model.

Nonetheless, one can argue that, due to greater loading times, the binary STL file is preferable when considering mobile devices, since in worst case it can take approximately 38.6 times more to load a complex 3MF model than it takes to load the same model in binary STL (as the Heartgears model in the tablet). However, the analysis made when comparing our loader versus the "Three.js" loader showed some points where our loader can be substantially optimized, and as such the loading times for the 3MF format can be greatly reduced, effectively nullifying this argument in the future.

As for the mobile uses for the simulator, it is clear that more optimized approaches will be needed in the future, since the gap between mobile and desktop is still enough to make some applications instances, as in the simulator when working with large models, impractical. The tests showed that a model can take up to almost 20 s for just one slice to be produced in mobile, and in some cases the tab simply crashed without the simulation running.

Regarding the open source contributions of this work, the fact that a more efficient loader already exists at the "Three.js" source code does not mean that there will not be any contribution. Support to texture and color can be added to it, and opportunities for improving it were also identified while its code was being analyzed. Therefore, a contribution to the open source community is still possible.

Acknowledgments. The research results reported in this paper have been partly funded by a R&D project between HP Brazil R&D division and UFPE originated from tax exemption (IPI-Law number 8.248, of 1991 and later updates).

References

1. WebGL: OpenGL ES 2.0 for the Web. Khronos Group, https://www.khronos.org/webgl/. Accessed 16 Oct 2015
2. 3D Printing Has Expanded Faster Than Expected, http://bit.ly/1LmQUI2. Accessed 16 Oct 2015
3. 3MF Specification, http://3mf.io/what-is-3mf/3mf-specification. Accessed 16 Oct 2015
4. Babylon.js, http://www.babylonjs.com/. Accessed 14 Jan 2016
5. Constructive Solid Geometry with CSG.js, http://learningthreejs.com/blog/2011/12/10/constructive-solid-geometry-with-csg-js/. Accessed 16 Oct 2015
6. CSG.js. https://github.com/evanw/csg.js/. Accessed 16 Oct 2015
7. JSzip, https://github.com/Stuk/jszip. Accessed 1 July 2016

8. OpenJSCad, http://openjscad.org/. Accessed 16 Oct 2016
9. TextDecoder,   https://developer.mozilla.org/en-US/docs/Web/API/TextDecoder/decode. Accessed 14 Jan 2016
10. Three.js, A Javascript 3D library, http://threejs.org/. Accessed 16 Oct 2015
11. ThreeMFViewer. https://github.com/jvfl/ThreeMFViewer. Accessed 15 Jan 2016
12. What is 3D printing? http://3dprinting.com/what-is-3d-printing/. Accessed 16 Oct 2015
13. What is 3MF? http://3mf.io/what-is-3mf/. Accessed 16 Oct 2015
14. zip.js A JavaScript library to zip and unzip files, https://gildaslormeau.github.io/zip.js/. Accessed 15 Jan 2016
15. Bandyopadhyay, A., Bose, S., Das, S.: 3D printing of biomaterials. MRS Bull. **40**(02), 108–115 (2015)
16. Chiu, W., Tan, S.: Multiple material objects: from cad representation to data format for rapid prototyping. Comput.-Aid. Des. **32**(12), 707–717 (2000)
17. Dudek, P.: Fdm 3D printing technology in manufacturing composite elements. Arch. Metall. Mater. **58**(4), 1415–1418 (2013)
18. Ecma, T.: Office open xml (2006)
19. Hague, R., Reeves, P.: Rapid prototyping, tooling and manufacturing, vol. 117. iSmithers Rapra Publishing (2000)
20. Hiller, J.D., Lipson, H.: Stl 2.0: a proposal for a universal multi-material additive manufacturing file format. In: Proceedings of the Solid Freeform Fabrication Symposium, pp. 266–278. No. 1, Citeseer (2009)
21. Jurrens, K.K.: Standards for the rapid prototyping industry. Rapid Prototyping J. **5**(4), 169–178 (1999)
22. Kumar, V., Dutta, D.: An assessment of data formats for layered manufacturing. Adv. Eng. Softw. **28**(3), 151–164 (1997)
23. Rego, N., Koes, D.: 3dmol. js: molecular visualization with webgl. Bioinformatics **31**(8), 1322–1324 (2015)
24. Sawicki, B., Chaber, B.: Efficient visualization of 3D models by web browser. Computing **95**(1), 661–673 (2013)
25. Stroud, I., Xirouchakis, P.: Stl and extensions. Adv. Eng. Softw. **31**(2), 83–95 (2000)

Holographic Humans

Alexiei Dingli$^{(\boxtimes)}$ and Nicholas Mifsud

Department of Intelligent Computer Systems, Faculty of ICT,
University of Malta, Msida, Malta
alexiei.dingli@um.edu.mt, nicholas.mifsud.12@um.edu.mt

Abstract. Over the last few years, holographic technology has been
made readily available. This modern technology may have various applications ranging from medical, cultural, educational and communication
industries. Focusing on the three latter industries, the main aim of this
project is to create virtual agents to behave in a believable manner and
display them within a three dimensional model of local megalithic temple
'Hagar Qim' in a museum context. These holographic humans are not
only visually appealing with clear animations but also behave in a psy-
chologically sound and autonomous manner, matching our expectations
of what life was like in those times. Believability is a cornerstone within
Artificial Intelligence and consequently, in order to achieve such a high
degree of autonomy and believability, the holographic humans developed
in this work are self-determined with their own reactive plan of actions to
organise their daily routines. In order to produce such believable behaviour, computational motivation models based on psychological theories
from natural intelligence are explored. Furthermore, visitors are able to
interact with the holographic humans in order to get a clearer picture of
life in prehistoric times and witness the diverse personalities and interests
of the humans. Finally, the system was tested empirically by a number
of people and questionnaires were filled in order to test the subjective
concept of believability of the system as a whole. Highly positive feedback was generated with a 96 % believability rate and an 80 % agreement
that this platform would be suitable in a museum context. The designed
system manifested believable daily routines which visitors were able to
relate to as the humans planned their activities just like any ordinary
person would having time to be productive and make the most of a day
whilst also adhering to biological needs such as thirst and hunger as well
as sleeping when dusk falls upon the virtual environment. Therefore,
artificially intelligent holographic humans were created to serve as an
interactive educational platform.

1 Introduction and Background

Museums are rich cultural hubs which serve the purpose of retaining and/or
restoring various cultural aspects as well as educating citizens on the various
cultural aspects pertaining to the specific display. Locally, museum experiences
are presently static and non engaging. With the use of cutting edge technology

S. Lackey and R. Shumaker (Eds.): VAMR 2016, LNCS 9740, pp. 299–307, 2016.
DOI: 10.1007/978-3-319-39907-2_28

and virtual agents enhancing the user experience of museum exhibits, museums may once again become a prime attraction [1].

The computing industry has an increasing concern when it comes to developing sophisticated virtual agents. Many commercial game developers implement traditional techniques such as finite state machines, rule-based systems and genetic algorithm to express intelligent behaviour. However, these approaches all depend on user interaction. Therefore if this interaction is not present, the agents will remain idle creating a non intelligent zombie effect [2]. Additionally, with today's highly detailed reconstructions of the real world in virtual worlds, having these agents rely on user interaction would not suffice to crate a believable platform. Therefore, virtual agents must be self-sustaining and able to follow their own agenda, living their own lives as their own human beings, altering their plans only when a user interacts with them [3].

Consequently, it may be noted that autonomy within the agents is a prerequisite and is sometimes seen as a trivial matter when it is confused with automation of an agent where goals are defined during the design phase [4].

Behaviour believability of virtual agents is argued to be a complex concept within the field of Artificial Intelligence. Multiple researchers all define the term "believable behaviour" in different ways, ranging from modelling different human psychological traits such as coping with emotions [5] or modelling anticipation [6] to having different simulation levels of detail defined in order to keep believable consistency within systems [7]. Others model different emotions and emotional models based on the changes in the environment in order to change the internal emotional state of the agent and consequently produce human-like behaviour [8].

Avradinis et al. argue that believability is not to be confused with realism even though the two are closely related. Realism, they argue has to do with the reconstruction and visual effects of the real world whilst believability is concerned with the actions of the virtual agent being consistent and sound with the environment the agent is in [3].

Therefore believability is concerned with the generation of behaviour that would be consistent to the agents' internal states and personality. This according to De Rosis et al. is how a believable agent should act in order to be consistent and coherent with the unwritten laws that govern the virtual world [9]. Furthermore, Ortony [10] and Dautenhahn [11] elaborate that believability does not necessarily imply complex behaviours but rather the agent's behaviour must match what would be expected of it from the user to allow users to easier relate to the agents.

This calls upon a motivational approach which mimics natural intelligence. Through different psychological models, it is noted that humans have basic biological needs that constantly need to be satisfied and they react according to the current situation of the world and their internal state as defined in Maslow's theory of Needs [12]. Many respected researchers base their work on this approach such as Avradinis et al. [3], Liu et al. [13], Krümpelmann et al. [14], and Chen et al. [15]. These develop motivational architectures where internal numerical scales are updated through the environment. Once these levels dip under a certain threshold, the agent temporarily differs from their current agendas to satisfy their needs. This produces believable daily routines as it would result in the same daily patterns as those of natural humans, hence matching the expectations that the human users would have.

This motivational model is implemented and extended through this work to include the social aspect of prehistoric virtual humans through an interface which allows the user to communicate with the humans that would be acting out their daily routine. Additionally, these believable virtual humans would be portrayed through a holographic device and set in a prehistoric world. This holographic platform is used to act as a museum exhibition in order to use the holographic humans as an informative and educational platform.

2   Aims and Objectives

The main research question this project seeks to achieve is whether holographic agents in a persistent holographic environment can be perceived as believable entities displaying routines, personalities and interests found in natural intelligence. Essentially, capturing the meaning of what it is to be human. Additionally, the project investigates the applicability of these holographic agents to museum exhibitions to educate visitors in a new interactive manner.

The project seeks to address the research question by achieving the following aims:

- Create a sufficient computational architecture for the virtual agents in order to be perceived as believable agents who perform natural daily routines and allow users to relate to the agents.
- Encompass the social aspect of the agents through the development of an interface for the viewer to communicate with the virtual humans. This further contributes to the believability aspect as it would generate more respect the visitors would have for the virtual agents.
- Create a sufficient virtual world to be projected as a holographic overlay on a physical model to mimic a museum exhibit and evaluate its educational aspect. This is achieved through the projection of a pre historic environment on a model, as well as through the creation of a virtual environment together with sophisticated human animations. This would serve as the virtual world for the virtual agents to live in.

3   Implementation

3.1   Motivational Architecture

The first step in implementing the system was to acquire a computational model of Hagar Qim's layout. Once this was modelled, it was three dimensionally printed to obtain the physical model. The same model was also imported into the Unity game engine to further develop the virtual world. The temple model was coloured black so as to not show on the holographic display and allow the physical model to be seen. However it was still kept in the environment to block the lower parts of the humans when they are standing behind stones to improve realism of the overlay. It was also needed to create an appropriate navigational mesh for the humans to explore the world appropriately.

Next a terrain object was used to create the flooring and was painted in accordingly. Additionally a directional light was used to mimic the effect of the sun and provide light to the scene. Additionally, a layout of activities was decided upon as well as the different activities that each agent would perform.

With these in place, coding of the synthetic behaviour could begin. Since the humans were designed to select activities that were not being performed by anybody at that particular point in time, the first thing that was implemented is this social aspect in which the humans keep track of the current states of the other humans. Before the human would select an activity, an array list is updated to store the current states of all the different humans in the environment. The different humans are looked up and the current state class variable is copied into a local array list.

Once the human has an idea of what the other humans are doing, he or she may select a free activity. However, before the human is allowed to select a job, different checks are performed to check the well-being of the person. The different internal levels are checked and if these are below a certain threshold then the humans would be motivated to satisfy the specific need rather than select a job. However, if these internal levels are satisfied then the human moves on to select a prehistoric job from the assigned jobs. Therefore in order to take an informed decision, the array list of all the current states of the other humans is consulted for a particular state and if it is found it means someone is currently performing that action and therefore the job must be skipped for now. Another layer of checks also serves as a form of memory so that the human does not choose the same action twice in a row. This process is highlighted in Fig. 1.

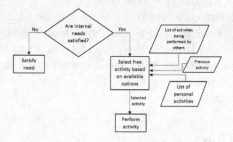

Fig. 1. Intelligent selection of activities. Source: [16]

Once a job is selected, the state of the human is set and the levels begin to decrease at the appropriate rate. At the same time, the human walks to the appropriate destination and upon arrival the animation of the activity is played. Upon arrival the boredom level begins to decrease.

In parallel to all these computations, the humans' internal levels are constantly being updated. The levels are updated through a function which is fired at every frame of the game. Each job affects the internal scales at different rates as manual labour is more tiring than arts and crafts. Therefore, by checking the current job of the human, the internal scales would be decremented appropriately. The reactive motivational architecture methods that command the logic of when the internal needs have to be satisfied, follow the same reasoning of the other jobs. They update the current state of the human and they start a path to the locations of where food and drink are found. However, once the human arrives at the destination, in addition to decrementing the boredom level, the energy, thirst and hunger levels are incremented (depending on the need that is being satisfied at that time). The internal levels are constantly monitored. This is due to the fact that the level of a need may hit zero whilst an action is being performed. Consequently, it would need immediate attention and not wait until the human gets bored of the current job. Therefore, as soon as the scale reaches zero, indicating the human's deficiency from a basic biological need, it would be picked up by the framework, interrupt the current activity and fire the method to satisfy the need instead.

3.2   Interface

The mobile interface was created using the Brass Monkey software development kit [17]. The dynamic controller in the framework allowed for the creation of the interface the way it was designed. That is, having a main menu screen to select the different humans, which once selected, a textual paragraph explaining what they are doing in the environment, as well as buttons at the bottom of the screen to allow the user to select different activities are displayed.

The interface is not a sequence of different screens, but rather one static screen that has changes in a texture field which shows the different textual paragraphs and buttons that are displayed and hidden at the appropriate times. Therefore each button on the interface, besides manipulating the behaviour of the humans, also updates the interface accordingly.

When a human is selected through the interface, the current state is checked and the appropriate texture is selected. It also checks the state of the world and whether the two previously interacted before.

The interface also calls upon methods from the motivational architecture through the activity buttons as once these are pressed the appropriate methods are fired so that the agent moves to the location and the levels are updated accordingly. Additionally, it not only manipulates the agent it is currently communicating with, but when the buttons are pressed, it also searches for any agents that are performing the current activity and forces it to select a new activity, repeating the whole intelligent activity selection defined in the previous subsection.

Finally, if the human is in a state where he or she is satisfying a need, then the interface does not display the default text and buttons, but rather a simple line excusing the agent and removes the buttons. This disables the choice of forcing the agents to perform different activities, which in turn, increases believability as the interface respects the fact that the agents are their own human beings with their own needs.

3.3   Animations

The animations were all created in the images of prehistoric men and women. Each agent was fitted with a boolean modifiers. When these boolean values are set to true, the animation plays. Therefore an invisible box was placed at each location of each activity. Once the agent comes into contact with this box, the appropriate boolean is modified and the animation is played. It is played in a continuous manner whilst the human is in that area. As soon as the human leaves the area, the boolean is set to false and walking animations are played instead.

The walking animations do not make use of these boxes but rather take into consideration the direction the agent is moving in to play the appropriate animation.

4   Evaluation

Due to the subjective nature of believability that this project seeks to aim, evaluation could not be done through any computational means. Consequently, the involvement of empirical testing through a questionnaire is essential. Various users had to use and interact with the system themselves, after which they were requested to fill in a questionnaire. This method of evaluation is suggested and carried out by other researches such as Martinho et al. [6] and Alfonso [18] whose work also involved the creation of a believable agent. To truly test if their system achieved their aims, they too had a number of different users from all walks of life use their system and after respond to a questionnaire.

Following the footsteps of these respected researchers, thirty test subjects viewed and interacted with the system for around ten minutes, after which a questionnaire was filled in. These encompassed varying ages, the youngest being ten years old whilst the eldest was sixty six.

The designed questionnaire focused on five main topics; the believability of the behaviour the humans displayed, the usefulness and value of the created interface, the realism of the world and animations, the effect of the holographic overlay and lastly, the educational aspect and the system's applicability for a museum. By testing for these, the three main aims of the project may be determined whether they were achieved or not. The tabulated results could be found in Table 1.

Starting off with the believability of the system, most identified that the agents within the system behaved in a believable manner as they all performed different typical activities essential for their survival but also had their own needs and emotions. They added that the needs is what completed the system as without them the humans would have autonomously and repetitively done

Table 1. Intelligent selection of activities. Source: [16]

	Statements	No. of Agreements	%	No. of Disagreements	%
Believability	Agents behaved in a believable	29	96	1	4
	Agents were social beings	30	100	0	0
	Agents walked along believable paths	25	83	5	17
	Internal levels contributed to believability	30	100	0	0
	Agents were reactive	30	100	0	0
	Agents had believable daily routines	30	100	0	0
Clarity	System was clear and easy to follow	30	100	0	0
Interface	Interface was user-friendly	30	100	0	0
	Interface enhanced experience	30	100	0	0
	Agents displayed different personalities	24	80	6	20
Holographic Display	Physical model came to life	30	100	0	0
	Coherent system was created	30	100	0	0
Realism	Environment hacks improved system	22	73	8	27
	Animations were realistic enough	15	50	15	50
	Animations were necessary to consider the agents as humans	21	70	9	30
Museum	System applicable for museums	24	80	6	20
	System has an educational value	30	100	0	0

jobs without achieving any visible aims. One criticism was faced in this aspect in the fact that it did not totally encompass all the aspects of pre historic life as the humans did not age, reproduce or adhere to nature's callings such as voiding the bladder which are also natural human behaviours. The finished product matched the expectations the users had on prehistoric life and therefore was considered to be believable with a high percentage.

The interface was well received across all the ages and added value to the system as all enjoyed communicating with the sophisticated holographic humans. However, some had problems identifying the different personalities of the humans. This is not vital for the system however it is an additional design factor that would add to the whole experience. The personalities presented through the interface may not have been adequate enough for some people to relate to them completely or they felt that the natural language was too scripted and had a negative impact on the believability of the personalities. Better sophistication on the model that drives the text produced could have been implemented to enhance the variations in the text produced.

The holographic display received positive feedback when asked if the overlay added value and life to the static three dimensional model of the temple. The exact mapping of the overlay with the physical model created one whole coherent system as the activity of the stone work seemed to directly interact with the stones of the actual physical model whilst the walking animations would also be blocked by the physical stones in the model.

However, some heavy criticism was directed towards the realism of the world created and the animations of the humans. Some of the animations, while managing to capture the image of prehistoric men, were not realistic enough as they were either not very detailed or were lacking in variety. Additionally, many agreed that the environmental effects such as the lighting of the torches and the dimming of the light at night time were not all that noticeable. Moreover, most testers felt that the animations were necessary in order for the humans to actually be identified as humans. Although there was a mixed feeling, the majority stated that it was not enough that they only behave like humans, they must also look like them in order to relate to the humans and perceive them as believable humans.

Lastly, from the statistical data gathered users would appreciate the system in a museum setting. They were also able to get a better understanding of how life in those days actually was thereby verifying the educational aspect of the project.

5   Conclusion and Future Work

In conclusion, the main aim of creating a sophisticated computational model to manifest believable behaviour was achieved with satisfactory results. The reactive motivational architecture developed manifested behavioural patterns that were perceived as believable and relatable by 96 % of the thirty people who used the system. The agents matched the expectations of the users and they were able to relate to and interact with the holographic humans on an intellectual level.

Additionally, the second aim of this project was achieved through the development of the mobile interface. This provided a basis to develop the social aspect of the agents as different personalities with their interests are shown through it. This further improved the narrative concept of the system to help educate viewers and provide a better insight on the daily routine of prehistoric men and the hardships tribes in those times had to face without the luxury of contemporary technologies. Again this interface achieved satisfactory results as there was a 100 % agreement that the interface added value to the project and allowed the humans to be interpreted as more social. However, a lower percentage, 80 %, perceived this interface as a platform to manifest agent personalities. It may be concluded that although it was beneficial to the system, further research should be put into developing better sophisticated interfaces to bring out the personalities of the humans more efficiently.

Although the visual appeal of the system faced some criticism, study was, for the most part, successful as the main aims this work sought to achieve had a lowest scoring of 80 %. The graphical world only served as a base to manifest believable behaviour on and the aims and objectives focused mainly on the generation of believable social agents rather than creating detailed reconstructions of the world. Therefore, it may be concluded that by achieving the aims presented in this work, virtual agents may be perceived as believable humans and may serve as a platform to educate people in a new innovative way. The agents' daily patterns matched the expectations of the viewers and even surpassed them by educating every visitor and giving them a better understanding of what life was like in those days simply by observing and interacting with these intelligent agents.

However, besides extending the framework to include more activities, there is still room for further research into how virtual agent behaviour could be improved to encompass complex long term aspects of natural intelligence and catering for higher levels of Maslow's theory. Moreover, the literature covered in this project together with the results achieved, indicate that further research needs to be put into the generation of interfaces to develop sophisticated enough interfaces to reflect the intelligence and personalities of the agents.

References

1. Johnston, S.F.: Representing holography in museum collections. In: Illuminating Instruments, pp. 97–116 (2009)
2. de Sevin, E., Thalmann, D.: A motivational model of action selection for virtual humans. In: Computer Graphics International 2005, pp. 213–220. IEEE (2005)
3. Avradinis, N., Panayiotopoulos, T., Anastassakis, G.: Behavior believability in virtual worlds: agents acting when they need to. SpringerPlus **2**(1), 246 (2013)
4. Luck, M., d'Inverno, M., et al.: A formal framework for agency and autonomy. ICMAS **95**, 254–260 (1995)
5. Marsella, S., Gratch, J.: Modeling coping behavior in virtual humans: don't worry, be happy. In: Proceedings of the Second International Joint Conference on Autonomous Agents and Multiagent Systems, pp. 313–320. ACM (2003)
6. Martinho, C., Paiva, A.: Using anticipation to create believable behaviour. In: Proceedings of the national conference on Artificial Intelligence, vol. 21, p. 175. AAAI Press, MIT Press, Menlo Park, Cambridge, London (1999, 2006)
7. Brom, C., Šerý, O., Poch, T.: Simulation level of detail for virtual humans. In: Pelachaud, C., Martin, J.-C., André, E., Chollet, G., Karpouzis, K., Pelé, D. (eds.) IVA 2007. LNCS (LNAI), vol. 4722, pp. 1–14. Springer, Heidelberg (2007)
8. Mehta, M., Mishra, K., Corradini, A.: Dynamic relationship management for personality rich character presentations in interactive games. In Proceedings of the 5th Conference on Speech Technology and Human-Computer Dialogue, SpeD 2009, pp. 1–6. IEEE (2009)
9. De Rosis, F., Pelachaud, C., Poggi, I.: Transcultural believability in embodied agents: a matter of consistent adaptation. In: Agent Culture: Human-Agent Interaction in a Multicultural World, pp. 75–106 (2004)
10. Ortony, A: On making believable emotional agents believable. In: Emotions in Humans and Artifacts, pp. 189–211
11. Dautenhahn, K.: The art of designing socially intelligent agents: science, fiction, and the human in the loop. Appl. Artif. Intell. **12**(7–8), 573–617 (1998)
12. Maslow, A.H., Frager, R., Fadiman, J., McReynolds, C., Cox, R.: Motivation and Personality, vol. 2. Harper & Row, New York (1970)
13. Liu, Z., Hong, Y., Liu, Q., Chai, Y.J.: An emotion model for virtual agents with evolvable motivation. In: Pan, Z., Cheok, A.D., Müller, W. (eds.) Transactions on Edutainment VI. LNCS, vol. 6758, pp. 154–163. Springer, Heidelberg (2011)
14. Krümpelmann, P., Thimm, M., Kern-Isberner, G., Fritsch, R.: Motivating agents in unreliable environments: a computational model. In: Klügl, F., Ossowski, S. (eds.) MATES 2011. LNCS, vol. 6973, pp. 65–76. Springer, Heidelberg (2011)
15. Chen, L., Bechkoum, K., Clapworthy, G.J.: Equipping a lifelike animated agent with a mind. In: de Antonio, A., Aylett, R.S., Ballin, D. (eds.) IVA 2001. LNCS (LNAI), vol. 2190, p. 72. Springer, Heidelberg (2001)
16. Mifsud, N.: Holographic humans. Undergraduate honors thesis, University of Malta (2015)
17. Brassmonkey software development kit. http://playbrassmonkey.com/developers. Accessed 24 May 2015
18. Afonso, N., Prada, R.: Agents that relate: improving the social believability of non-player characters in role-playing games. In: Stevens, S.M., Saldamarco, S.J. (eds.) ICEC 2008. LNCS, vol. 5309, pp. 34–45. Springer, Heidelberg (2008)

Screen Space Cone Tracing
for Glossy Reflections

Lukas Hermanns[1], Tobias Franke[2], and Arjan Kuijper[1,2(✉)]

[1] Technische Universität Darmstadt, Darmstadt, Germany
[2] Fraunhofer IGD, Darmstadt, Germany
arjan.kuijper@igd.fraunhofer.de

Abstract. Indirect lighting (also Global Illumination (GI)) is an important part of photo-realistic imagery and has become a widely used method in real-time graphics applications, such as Computer Aided Design (CAD), Augmented Reality (AR) and video games. Path tracing can already achieve photo-realism by shooting thousands or millions of rays into a 3D scene for every pixel, which results in computational overhead exceeding real-time budgets. However, with modern programmable shader pipelines, a fusion of ray-casting algorithms and rasterization is possible, i.e. methods, which are similar to testing rays against geometry, can be performed on the GPU within a fragment (or rather pixel-) shader. Nevertheless, many implementations for real-time GI still trace perfect specular reflections only. In this work the advantages and disadvantages of different reflection methods are exposed and a combination of some of these is presented, which circumvents artifacts in the rendering and provides a stable, temporally coherent image enhancement. The benefits and failings of this new method are clearly separated as well. Moreover the developed algorithm can be implemented as pure post-process, which can easily be integrated into an existing rendering pipeline.

1 Introduction and Motivation

In this work a novel method for real-time glossy reflections is presented. This method can be implemented as a pure post-process, which simplifies the effort, of integrating it into an existing graphics application, considerably. Similar algorithms are already implemented, not only in video games, but also in CAD and AR applications [2,4,16] and reflections for indirect lighting are essential in GI simulations [14]. These reflections increase the photo-realism of Computer Generated Imagery (CGI) drastically.

Indirect lighting is implemented in a broad range of GI applications since many years, particularly in film productions such as Terminator 2 (1991), Avatar (2009), and the first feature-length computer animated motion picture Toy Story (1995) [5]. From the very beginning, developers are striving to reduce the calculation overhead or rather to accelerate the rendering process. This is because accurate rendering can take several hours or days even on high performance computer systems, depending on the scene and shading complexity. Therefore the

© Springer International Publishing Switzerland 2016
S. Lackey and R. Shumaker (Eds.): VAMR 2016, LNCS 9740, pp. 308–318, 2016.
DOI: 10.1007/978-3-319-39907-2_29

costs and duration to produce photo-realistic imagery can be very high. To solve
this, there are many algorithms to achieve photo-realism by approximating the
influence of indirect light, for both real-time and non real-time rendering [12].
Some of these simulate the indirect light by distributing many small direct light
emitters throughout the scene, called Virtual Point Light (VPL), but which
then requires new optimizations or rather hierarchies of spatial data structures
[10,14]. Still others store and propagate the indirect light through the scene
within a volume, called Light Propagation Volume (LPV), which then causes a
large memory footprint for large scenes and high resolution volumes. However,
methods like VPL and LPV lack an important part of indirect light, which will
be discussed in this work and is shown in the above image. Our novel approach
for real-time reflections is a rough approximation but still produces plausible
effects of indirect lighting. It is fast, fully dynamic, and can easily be integrated
into an existing rendering pipeline, because it is a pure post-process. Hence,
the result of an intermediate render pass is the only input for this effect. No
information about the scene is required.

2   Related Work

In this section we will analyze several approaches for real-time reflections and
then make a comparison to summarize their benefits and failings.

2.1   Analytical Area Lights

We start out with a simple method for glossy reflections which deals with
direct lighting only: Analytical Area Light (AAL). The three basic models of
light shapes are: Directional-, Point-, and Spot light. In classical fixed function
pipelines these are the usual lighting primitives to shade geometry. All of them
only have a position and optionally a direction, but neither an area nor volume. This makes it very easy and fast to determine the light intensity for each
pixel, because only a scalar product and the distance between that pixel and
the respective light source must be computed. However, every light source in
reality has a volume. This can be simulated more plausible with AALs, which
cover a specific area on the screen. The formulas for these light models resemble
the basics of ray tracing. Ray intersection tests are performed against all AALs
for every pixel, otherwise the nearest distance between the current pixel and
the primitive light geometry is computed. Since these light models require more
complex and more flexible calculations, they became popular with the advances
of programmable shader units in modern hardware, but the research around
them has begun long before [3]. In addition, glossy reflections can be simulated
easily by adding a further light attenuation depending on the surface roughness. Contrariwise, they only allow direct lighting, since with indirect lighting
everything is treated as a light source, but AALs only provide limited shapes,
such as cuboids, spheres, cylinders, and capsules. Although there are more complex AALs, such as fractals, these shapes are not enough to represent an entire
reflectable scene. Therefore, one can use them only as direct light emitters.

Advantages: (1) accurate calculation for incident radiance and (2) easy to implement. Disadvantage: direct lighting only.

2.2 Planar Reflections

We continue with one of the oldest methods for reflections of indirect lighting, which is still used in modern 3D engines: Planar Reflections. For planar reflections there are two major methods: the first one is to use a stencil buffer and the second one is to use a render target (also framebuffer). With the first method, the stencil buffer operates as the name implies like a stencil. It allows to reject pixels outside the stencil pattern. The reflected scene should only be visible inside this pattern, and to generate it, the reflective geometry is rendered with certain render states enabled. We can divided this algorithm into the following steps: 1. Clear frame- and stencil buffers. 2. Render scene with default settings but without reflective geometry. 3. Render reflective geometry into stencil buffer. 4. Render scene inside the stencil pattern with mirrored view transformation. In the second method, the steps of rendering the actual and the mirrored scene are in the reverse order. We first have to render the mirrored scene into the render target. Then the render target serves as the source of the texture (and also of the reflective light color), which is mapped onto the reflective geometry, when the actual scene is rendered. In some cases this method may be used but it has a larger memory footprint. This is a very simple method which allows perfect specular reflections with correct geometry reconstruction. The correct reconstruction originates from the fact that the scene is rendered a second time, which can be very time consuming. This also means that the performance depends on the scene complexity. Another disadvantage is that this only works for planar reflectors such as mirrors or flat water puddles, because the mirroring is due to a mirrored matrix transformation, which does not allow any distortions. Note that this method has nothing to do with ray tracing or something similar. It is just a secondary rasterization pass. However, there are also hybrid approaches which combine geometry- and image-based rendering, such as Forward Mapped Planar Mirror Reflections [1]. Such a technique is used in the idTech 3 game engine (1999) and even older ones.

Advantages: (1) perfect reconstruction of reflected geometry and (2) Easy to implement. Disadvantages: (1) Depends on scene complexity and (2) Planar reflectors only.

2.3 Environment Maps

Another still widely used method are (localized-) Environment Maps (also Cube Maps). In this case the scene is rendered from six view angles into a cube map at a localized position. A cube map internally consists of six texture layers, one for each cube face. This captures a 360 degree view in a single texture. These cube maps are typically placed by an artist within a world editor and generated during the world building process this process is also called baking. Such a cube map stores the entire light influence for the point where the cube map was rendered. Usually the cube maps are additionally pre-filtered (or blurred) to efficiently simulate a basic glossiness for all surfaces [8]. The blurring simulates a wider distribution of reflection rays, which causes a glossy appearance. As already mentioned: the reflections from each cube map are only correct for a single 3D point. Whenever a cube map is used for other points, the reflections are only correct for infinitely distant light. Such a candidate is the (nearly) infinitely distant sun. To overcome this restriction several cube maps are generated in a scene, between which the application must choose at runtime. To avoid the popping effect (discrete switching between textures), some applications interpolate between the N nearest cube maps (the popping effect is visible in games like Half-Life 2 and Portal using the Source Engine). A further improvement are parallax corrected cube maps [13], which can adjust the singular location to a cubic environment. However, even this method is severely limited due to its cubic nature and needs further adaptation by artists. This technique is used in the game Remember Me (2013) and the Source Engine (2004).

Advantages: (1) Easy to implement and (2) Very fast. Disadvantages: (1) Must be placed by artist, (2) Limited to fixed count, and (3) Only correct for infinitely distant light.

2.4   Image Based Reflections

We now continue with ray tracing like methods: Image Based Reflections (IBR). In this method several IBR proxies are placed by an artist in the world editor, whereat an IBR proxy is a box which captures a small volume in the scene which is then rendered into a 2D texture. For each reflection ray an intersection test against the plane, which is spanned by that box, is computed. These ray against plane tests are very fast but this reflection model is only useful for nearly planar reflectors such as building facades or streets for instance. Although a single plane intersection test is fast some form of hierarchy is required if many IBR proxies are used (e.g. 50+) to avoid testing against all planes for every pixel. In addition the method is inappropriate for perfect specular reflections since the geometry inside an IBR box is approximated by a plane. For glossy reflections the results are reasonable because the distorted planar reflector can not be perceived exactly by the viewer. This technique is used in the game Thief 4 (2014) from 2014 and the Unreal Engine 3 (UE3) (2006).

Advantages: (1) Good visual approximation and (2) Very fast. Disadvantages: (1) Must be placed by artist and (2) Nearly planar reflectors only.

2.5   Screen Space Local Reflections

Finally we look at a pixel based ray tracing method: Screen Space Local Reflections (SSLR). In a nutshell: we transform the reflection ray from view space into screen space, and then move along this ray until we step through the depth buffer. By this algorithm, we hope to find the intersection of a ray against the scene geometry, which is stored in form of the depth buffer. That means, in particular, we can only find intersections with geometry, which is already visible on the screen. This is why it is called a screen space effect. Many SSLR implementations perform this simple ray hit search only, which is commonly called a linear ray march. Once the first hit is found, a binary search for refinement can be done. To simulate glossy reflections most applications apply subsequent blur passes to the reflection color buffer. But there are also alternatives where several rays are casted and the average color forms the result. A frequently used optimization, to find the ray intersections, is to render this pass only at half resolution, which yields to acceptable results when a blur pass is applied anyway. The advantage of SSLR is that it allows reflections of arbitrary geometry (assumed the geometry is visible on screen). It can additionally be implemented as a pure post-process or a set of consecutive post-processes, which alleviates the effort to integrate it into a present 3D engine. It is moreover independent of the scene complexity because the reflections are fetched from the color buffer of a previous render pass. The calculations are computed for every pixel which makes the algorithms effort proportional to the number of pixels on the screen. Disadvantages are primarily the limitations of the screen boundary and the hidden geometry problem. This technique is used in UE3 and the game Killzone Shadow Fall (2013). Such ray tracing approximations are state of the art in the field of post-processing [7,11].

Advantages: (1) Reflection of arbitrary geometry and (2) Pure post process. Disadvantages: (1) Hiden geometry problem and (2) Limited to screen space.

2.6   Screen Space Cone Tracing

Based on local reflections in screen space, we move on to a method which traces cones instead of rays: SSCT [6]. Again, the cone is an approximation for many reflection rays. The process is very similar to SSLR but in each iteration of the ray march we sample from a certain MIPmap of the depth texture, which is a further approximation of the actual cone. By relying on MIP-maps certain integration errors are unavoidable. This is due to solid angles that can subtend either flat spaces or multiple pieces of geometry. It can manifest as alias or temporal inconsistency when moving the camera view. Such errors will increase notably as the cone angle size increases to simulate more glossy appearances. Thus for SSCT using a proper texture filter is crucial. Next to nave MIP-mapping, manual filtering by using slices of a 3D texture, where each slice is a Gaussian blurred version of the original texture [9], has also been tested. The results are significantly better in quality but loose the fast texture accesses since we sample from a high resolution 3D texture.

Advantages: (1) Reflection of arbitrary geometry, (2) Pure post process, and (3) Glossy reflections with arbitrary roughness. Disadvantages: (1) Hiden geometry problem, (2) Limited to screen space, and (3) Artifact avoidance is very slow.

2.7   Hi-Z Cone Tracing

The last presented method is from the book GPU Pro 5: HZCT [15]. The remarkable concept with this method is on the one hand that the ray tracing and cone tracing parts are clearly separated and on the other hand that the ray tracing process is accelerated with hierarchical buffers. These hierarchical buffers will be generated during the post-process in each frame and allow a faster, stable, and precise ray tracing in screen space. While SSLR and SSCT use a binary search to refine the intersection point, HZCT is much more target-oriented. However, a disadvantage is that HZCT does not allow tracing rays which point towards the camera. This is due to the ray setup in combination with the hierarchical buffers. As soon as an intersection has been detected, the cone tracing pass integrates all incident radiance from the intersection point to the ray origin using the visibility buffer. The cone approximation is quite similar to that in SSCT but it is combined with a visibility buffer to circumvent invalid integration over a large solid cone angle.

Advantages: (1) Reflection of arbitrary geometry, (2) Pure post process, (3) Glossy reflections with arbitrary roughness, (4) High stability and precision, and (5) Acceleration with hierarchical buffers. Disadvantages: (1) Hiden geometry problem, (2) Limited to screen space, (3) Unable to ray trace towards the camera, and (4) Complex to implement.

2.8   Comparison

The only method which provides perfect reconstruction of reflected geometry here are planar reflections. All the other techniques merely approximate the reflections in a more or less coarse manner. Unfortunately, planar reflections are inappropriate for every reflective geometry which has not a planar shape. Moreover the necessity of re-rendering the scene makes it unfeasible for post-processing. Nevertheless, planar reflection is still a valuable fallback method, especially when others fail with receiving scene information. A very efficient method here are environment maps, which is at least beneficial as fallback, too. Primarily because they can be pre-computed. But either with or without parallax correction, using environment maps requires some adaptation by artists, i.e. the reflections can not be computed as a pure post-process. At least the localization within the scene must be managed with a world editor. This also applies to IBR. From the screen space ray- and cone tracing methods, HZCT seems to be the most advanced technique. The major benefits over SSLR and SSCT are the stability, the precision, and the acceleration. However, like most ray tracing algorithms in screen space, it is limited to the screen boundary and we have the hidden geometry problem. Even HZCT does not solve these restrictions, but this is where fallback methods are considered.

3   Screen Space Cone Tracing

The core idea of this work is based on SSCT [6]. However, the implementation is based on HZCT and will be slightly augmented with a fallback for rays pointing towards the camera, to maximize the extent of reflection rays in screen space. We will then provide a quality comparison to the original HZCT and a method from the field of SSLR. The previous section presented benefits and failings of related work. The most advanced technique for screen space reflections seems to be HZCT. However, it does not cover the maximum extent of the screen space, because rays pointing towards the camera can not be gathered. Fortunately, this method separates ray tracing and cone tracing, thus the ray tracing part can be augmented with linear ray marching for exceptional cases. After we review the algorithm in detail we will take a closer look at a couple of SSLR methods. One of them is a technique used in Killzone Shadow Fall, in which a mask buffer is generated alongside the ray tracing process. This is later used to enhance the blurring of the ray trace color buffer, which is required for glossy reflections in this SSLR method. The blurred variants are stored inside the MIP-chain.

3.1   Overview of HZCT

Since the method is based on HZCT we continue with an overview of the different passes as proposed in GPU Pro 5. The core algorithm can be divided into five steps: **Hi-Z Pass**: Generates the entire MIP chain of the Hi-Z buffer. This hierarchical buffer is required to accelerate the ray tracing. **Pre-Integration Pass**: Generates the entire MIP chain of visibility buffer. This hierarchical buffer is required for accurate radiance integration during cone tracing. **Pre-Convolution Pass**: Pre-filters the color buffer. A blur pass of the default MIP-map generation can be used here. **Ray-Tracing Pass**: Finds the ray intersections. This pass requires the Hi-Z buffer. **Cone-Tracing Pass**: Integrates incident radiance for a solid cone angle. This pass requires the Hi-Z-, the color-, and the visibility buffers.

The last two steps can be combined into a single shader. It is also possible to split them up, but this should only be taken into account when it really matters, because particularly state changes to the framebuffer binding are very time consuming and it would also increase the memory footprint.

3.2   Competitor: SSLR

Before we compare SSCT with SSLR methods we first take a closer look at glossy reflections in SSLR, such as Killzone (- Shadow Fall). Although SSLR only uses ray tracing there are several methods to implement glossiness. The nave approach is to cast multiple rays and take the mean value of the color samples. A smarter approach is to split the algorithm into multiple passes again and blur the ray trace color buffer. This is how it is done in Killzone. A mask buffer is used to enhance the blurring of the ray trace color buffer. We can divide this algorithm into the following three steps: 1. **The Ray-Tracing Pass** generates the ray trace color buffer and mask buffer. 2. **The Blur Pass** generates the MIP levels for both the color- and mask buffer with a Gaussian blur. 3. **The Reflection Pass** draws final reflections on the screen.

3.3 Optimizations

There are many ways for optimizations in post-processing effects. Particular for ray tracing effects with multiple stages. As already mentioned, a frequently used optimization is to render the respective effects only at half resolution. However, this is usually only justifiable when blur passes are involved, which hide the lower texture quality. Another issue is memory efficiency. Incoherent memory access stalls the graphics pipeline, due to wasted memory bursts (larger blocks of data for better cache utilization). The game Thief 4 approximates the normal vectors with $(0, 0, 1)T$ for better memory coalescing. The bump mapping (effect to enhance shading appearance on textures) is implemented supplementary as a post-process, i.e. the normal deviation is applied after the ray tracing. Furthermore gradient-based texture operations should be avoided within dynamic branching, or they should be at least moved out of flow control to prevent divergence. They may force the pipeline to load texture data for program paths where they are not needed, due to the massive parallelism on GPUs. In practice, this means that the intrinsics textureLod/textureGrad should be preferred over texture (in GLSL) and SampleLevel/SampleGrad should be preferred over Sample (in DirectX High Level Shading Language (HLSL)) respectively.

4   Results and Discussion

The example images compare our method SSCT with the original method HZCT, then with the related method SSLR. All rendering times are determined with a hardware timer query, which is very precise and they only reflect the rendering duration of the effect, excluding the scene rendering. Figure 1 compares SSCT with HZCT on a wooden cylinder on the floor which reflects the surrounding tiles. In Fig. 2 the outside of a window is reflected on the floor. Here, HZCT only captures a small amount of that window, but SSCT extends the range of the reflective area. Moreover HZCT ignores the reflections on the front wall completely, whereas SSCT additionally reflects the floor underneath the window.

In Fig. 3 glossy reflections are visible on the floor and the walls of the Sponza Atrium. The scene itself is rendered neither with shadow mapping nor complex BRDF models. Only a single directional light source is embedded and only the stone floor reflects indirect light. Here, SSCT produces much better results than SSLR for long ray traversals. Artifacts in SSLR are visible on the walls, due to a constant step size in the ray marching. See also Table 1. The roughness factor is also used for the normal deviation, to increase the rough appearance.

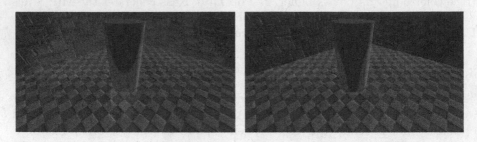

Fig. 1. Looking down to the floor at a cylinder, which reflects the tiles (960 × 540 resolution. Left: SSCT rendering time ≈ 3.49 ms Right: HZCT rendering time ≈ 1.04 ms

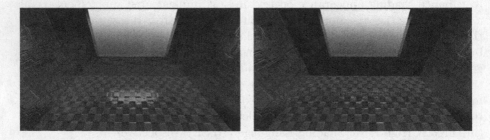

Fig. 2. Looking down to the floor, which reflects the outside of a window (960 × 540 resolution). Top: SSCT rendering time ≈ 2.25 ms. HZCT rendering time ≈ 1.12 ms

Table 1. Performance results for various resolutions and roughness factors.

Resolution	Roughness	SSCT performance	HZCT performance	SSLR performance
640 × 480	0.0	0.76 ms	0.69 ms	1.14 ms
640 × 480	0.1	0.81 ms	0.74 ms	0.68 ms
800 × 600	0.0	1.12 ms	1.02 ms	1.69 ms
800 × 600	0.1	1.17 ms	1.10 ms	0.99 ms
960 × 540	0.0	1.50 ms	1.10 ms	1.86 ms
960 × 540	0.1	1.54 ms	1.19 ms	1.09 ms
1280 × 768	0.0	2.45 ms	1.92 ms	3.31 ms
1280 × 768	0.1	2.66 ms	2.07 ms	1.95 ms
1920 × 1080	0.0	4.92 ms	4.07 ms	6.09 ms
1920 × 1080	0.1	5.30 ms	4.49 ms	4.02 ms

Fig. 3. Glossy reflections are visible on the floor and the walls of the Sponza Atrium (1920 × 1080 resolution). Top: SSCT rendering time ≈ 5.30 ms, enlarged image detail ≈. Bottom: SSLR rendering time ≈ 5.19 ms, enlarged image detail

5 Conclusion

We have seen a novel method for local glossy reflections called SSCT. The implementation has been presented in detail and a comparison to other state of the art methods has been shown as well. Our method is based on HZCT and is augmented with a fallback for special cases. The advantages of our method over other SSLR methods are, that the cone tracing produces more plausible looking glossy reflections and it can be clearly separated from the ray tracing process. Additionally the input parameters for SSCT are more correlated with the material configuration of a BRDF. This is due to the cone tracing, which is derived from multiple ray samples. That makes it much easy for artists to create plausible effects in 3D scenes. In contrast, most SSLR implementations merely blur the entire ray trace color buffer, which is out of proportion to BRDF and material parameters. Moreover the cone tracing in SSCT considers the amount of cone intersection with the scene and takes several texture samples, while glossiness in SSLR is usually based on a single and unweighted texture sample from the blurred ray trace color buffer. We can, though, make use of ideas implemented in SSLR: because of the modular nature of SSCT, we can further enhance the image quality by using a mask buffer in the blur pass for the color buffer. However, our method still lacks solutions for the hidden geometry problem and the screen boundary limitations. Only workarounds do exist to circumvent these restrictions. We can summarize, therefore, local reflections in pure screen space effects are still an unsolved area of indirect lighting. Nevertheless, in prepared scenes and in combination with other reflection techniques it can be very useful with satisfying frame rates.

References

1. Bastos, R., Stürzlinger., W.: Forward mapped planar mirror reflections. Technical report, University of North Carolina at Chapel Hill (1998)
2. Bauer, F., Knuth, M., Kuijper, A., Bender, J.: Screen-space ambient occlusion using a-buffer techniques. In: Computer-Aided Design and Computer Graphics, CAD/Graphics 2013, pp. 140–147. IEEE (2013)
3. Campbell, III, A.T., Fussell, D.S.: An analytic approach to illumination with area light sources. Technical report, University of Texas at Austin, Austin, TX, USA (1991)
4. Engelke, T., Becker, M., Wuest, H., Keil, J., Kuijper, A.: MobileAR browser - a generic architecture for rapid AR-multi-level development. Expert Syst. Appl. **40**(7), 2704–2714 (2013)
5. Henne, M., Hickel, H.: The making of "toy story". In: Proceedings of the 41st IEEE International Computer Conference, COMPCON 1996, pp. 463–468 (1996)
6. Hermanns, L., Franke, T.A.: Screen space cone tracing for glossy reflections. In: ACM SIGGRAPH 2014 Posters, SIGGRAPH 2014, p. 102:1 (2014)
7. Johnsson, M.: Approximating ray traced reflections using screen-space data (2012)
8. Kautz, J., McCool, M.D.: Approximation of glossy reflection with prefiltered environment maps. In: Proceedings of the Graphics Interface 2000 Conference, pp. 119–126 (2000)
9. Kuijper, A., Florack, L.: The relevance of non-generic events in scale space models. Int. J. Comput. Vis. **1**(57), 67–84 (2004)
10. Limper, M., Jung, Y., Behr, J., Sturm, T., Franke, T.A., Schwenk, K., Kuijper, A.: Fast, progressive loading of binary-encoded declarative-3D web content. IEEE Comput. Graphics Appl. **33**(5), 26–36 (2013)
11. McGuire, M., Mara, M.: Efficient GPU screen-space ray tracing. J. Comput. Graphics Tech. (JCGT) **3**(4), 73–85 (2014)
12. Schwenk, K., Voß, G., Behr, J., Jung, Y., Limper, M., Herzig, P., Kuijper, A.: Extending a distributed virtual reality system with exchangeable rendering backends - techniques, applications, experiences. Vis. Comput. **29**(10), 1039–1049 (2013)
13. Sébastien, L., Zanuttini, A.: Local image-based lighting with parallax-corrected cubemaps. In: ACM SIGGRAPH 2012 Talks, SIGGRAPH 2012, p. 36:1 (2012)
14. Stein, C., Limper, M., Kuijper, A.: Spatial data structures to accelerate the visibility determination for large model visualization on the web. In: Web3D14, pp. 53–61 (2014)
15. Uludag, Y.: Hi-Z screen-space cone-traced reflections. In: Engel, W. (ed.) GPU Pro 5, Chap. 4, pp. 149–192. CRC Press (2014)
16. Wientapper, F., Wuest, H., Kuijper, A.: Reconstruction and accurate alignment of feature maps for augmented reality. In: 3DIMPVT 2011: The First Joint 3DIM/3DPVT Conference, pp. 140–147. IEEE (2011)

Lifetime and Deployment Limits for Mobile, 3D-Perceptual Applications

Yan Liu[1(✉)], Yun Li[1], Lennart Johnsson[1,2], and Andrew A. Chien[1,3]

[1] University of Chicago, Chicago, IL 60637, USA
{joey2005,yunli}@uchicago.edu, achien@cs.uchicago.edu
[2] University of Houston, Houston, TX 77004, USA
johnsson@cs.uh.edu
[3] Argonne National Laboratory, Lemont, IL 60439, USA

Abstract. Low-cost image and depth sensors (RGBD) promise a wealth of new applications as mobile computing devices become aware of the 3D structure of their environs. However, while sensors are now cheap and readily available, the computational demands for even basic 3D services such as model-building and tracking are significant. We assess these requirements of a basic 3D service that would be required to support many proposed 3D applications, building an analytical model calibrated with detailed empirical measurements. Our results show that both cooperative use of ensembles of mobile devices and adaptive 3D sensor data processing are important to bring compute requirements into feasible ranges.

1 Introduction and Objectives

The advent of low-cost IR sensors with real-time RGBD (depth) data is stimulating new applications that use 3D knowledge to create new user experiences. Such 3D sensing and computation is demanding for mobile devices. We perform a rigorous study of a 3D tracking service to support mobile 3D applications, characterizing feasible battery life with ensembles of todays wearables, smartphones, tablets, and laptops. First, using a combined metric (lifetime-speed), we compare ensemble capability. Second, using a lifetime metric, we bound realistic application times on a variety of ensembles. Most are quite short, even at low frame rates, lifetimes of a few hours, and at 30 fps, a few minutes. Third, we explore cloud support, showing that Wifi-based support is possible, LTE-based support is not – communication consumes too much energy. Finally, we assess the opportunity to improve lifetime by adapting resolution and frame rate, showing a 6-fold potential improvement.

2 Application and Performance Model, Data Comparison

2.1 SLAMBench: A 3D Perception Service

We describe an analytical model for SLAM [5,10] computation and compare it to real-time system measurements. SLAM includes three major steps: de-noising

S. Lackey and R. Shumaker (Eds.): VAMR 2016, LNCS 9740, pp. 319–329, 2016.
DOI: 10.1007/978-3-319-39907-2_30

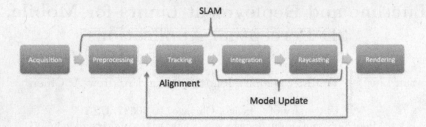

Fig. 1. Acquisition + SLAM + Rendering Pipeline

sensor depth data, frame alignment with the scene model, and model update. In SLAMBench [13], used in our experiments, de-noising use a bilateral filter with Gaussian weights, alignment an ICP [1] algorithm using point-to-plane matching [3,14] and projective mapping [2], and frame integration with the model using a Truncated Signed Distance Function [4] then raycasting to generate the updated model point-cloud. Our analytical model estimates for the SLAMBench stages are summarized in Table 1 (Fig. 1).

Table 1. A model for simultaneous localization and mapping (floating-point operations/frame)

Phase	Complexity (FP operations)
Preprocessing	$1050 \times N_p + O(1)$
Frame alignment[a] ("tracking")	$152 \times N_{it} \times N_p + O(1) \approx 1130 N_p$
Integration[b] (TSDF update)	$\approx (20 + 180 \times FOV_f \times TSDF_f) \times N_V + O(1)$
Model update (Raycasting)	$\approx (250 + 44 \times N_{steps}) \times N_p + O(1)$

[a]For the estimates below $N_{it} = 7.44$ representing the average for 80 test cases.
[b]FOV_f: fraction of voxels in field of view. $FOV_f = 0.1$ in the estimates. $TSDF_f$: fraction of voxels in FOV subject to update. $TSDF_f = 0.5$ for the Far-Fast case, and 0.15 for the Near-Slow case. N_p = number of pixels, N_{it} = ICP iterations scaled to full resolution, N_V = number of voxels, N_{steps} = number of steps in raycasting to find ray hit with surface. $N_{steps} = 45$ for the Far-Fast case, 28 for the Near-Slow case.

Many scene-dependent factors can affect the precise computation count for 3D modelling. For example, the number of model voxels in the field of view determines the number of voxels that need to be updated for model integration and raycasting, and thus affecting the integration and raycasting computation counts. While full analysis of such scene dependence is beyond the scope of this paper, we provide a simple approximation that uses simple factors for the major element (see subpoint 2 in Table 1). These factors are based on offline analysis for the specific experiments used in this paper; an online method is a good area for future work.

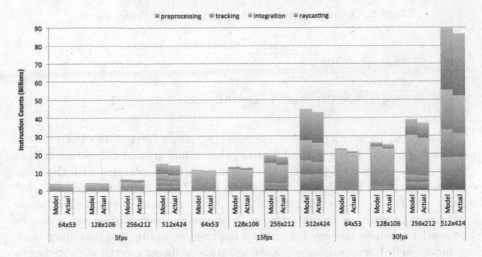

Fig. 2. Model and measured instruction counts (Far-Fast)

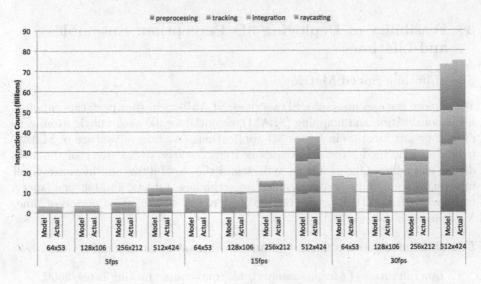

Fig. 3. Model and measured instruction counts (Near-Slow)

2.2 Basic Characterization and Data Comparison

In this section, we present measurements from a range of experiments, comparing them to our analytical model. We collected 512×424 depth images at 30 fps using the Microsoft Kinect V2 sensor that is moving along a 2-meter track. To explore a key dimension of computational challenge, we vary the distance (sensor to scene) from 1.5 m (Near) to 2 m (Far) as well as the rate of camera movement from 0.06 m/s (Slow) to 0.2 m/s (Fast).

Table 2. Compute, battery and weight specs for device classes

	Wearable	Smartphone	Tablet	Laptop
Compute (GIPS)	2	5	10	20
Battery (WH)	0.75	11	20	75
Weight (pounds)	0.06 (1 oz)	0.31 (5 oz)	1	2

Timing and instruction counts are collected on an Intel i5-3350P CPU. We use downrezing (reducing the remove/depth resolution) and subsetting frames we use can compare a range of frame rates and sensor resolutions with the same experimental data. This data is presented in Figs. 2 and 3. To compare measured results with the model, we convert our floating-point counts from the model are to instructions with an average ratio of 2:1 based on overall observed averages. The model captures the key features of required computation, matching measurements well. For example, key features, such as linear growth with increases in pixels/frame and frame rate are captured clearly (see Figs. 2 and 3).

3   Feasibility of Deploying 3D Perception: Ensembles and Lifetimes

3.1   Lifetime-Speed Metric

We explore the execution of a 3D services, SLAMbench, that performs simultaneous localization and mapping (SLAM), essential for 3D aware navigation, rendering, or just location in future 3D applications. We take advantage of SLAMbench's partitioned structure, mapping its six stages to a variety of different device ensembles. Our goal is to understand the capabilities and lifetimes of all interesting combinations of wearables, smartphones, tablets, and laptops (specifications see Table 2). To assess the usability of the service over a period of time, we define two metrics:

$$LS = \text{Lifetime-Speed product} = \#\text{frames computable} \times \text{maximum tracking rate}$$

$$L = \text{Lifetime} = (\#\text{frames computable}/\text{maximum tracking rate})/3600$$

3.2   Single Devices and Ensembles

We compare devices and ensembles, using the LS metric. First Fig. 4 compares single device for two sensing resolutions. As expected, using lower resolution significantly increases lifetime, and the largest devices have the longest lifetimes.

Next we consider two device ensembles in Fig. 5. With two devices, the decomposition of SLAMbench across the devices is important. Our results show that lifetime is greatest for those deployments that put the computationally intense stages on the larger devices, and for lower sensing resolution. Three device ensemble data is presented in Fig. 6, and the results show that decomposition is even

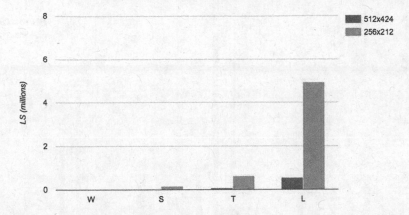

Fig. 4. LS metrics for single device ensembles (wearable, smartphone, tablet, and laptop), several blue bars are too small to see.

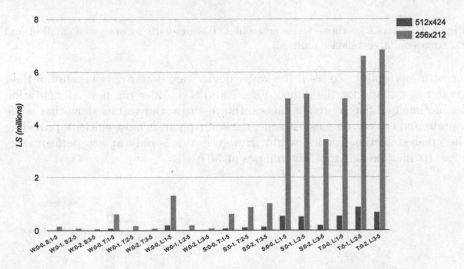

Fig. 5. LS metrics for two-device ensembles (Configs with <2 stages on largest device omitted)

more complex, but the best configurations have the same property – the computationally intense stages on the largest devices.

Overall, Figs. 4, 5, and 6 show that for appropriate computation mapping, LS is mostly determined by the largest device. For example, at resolution 512×424 in Fig. 5, maximum LS values achieved are 10,000 for smartphone, 70,000 for tablet, and 200,000 for laptops. Best LS is achieved when computation maps to the largest device (heaviest).

3.3   Lifetimes for Weight-Comparable Ensembles

For mobile users, the dominant issue on whether to take a device along may be its weight. Our results show that larger devices have greater capability, but at

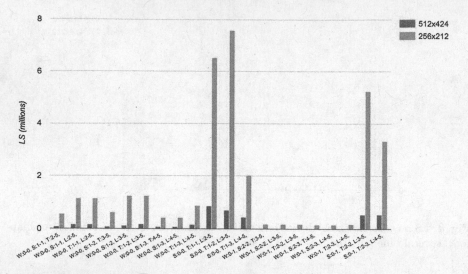

Fig. 6. LS metrics for three-device ensembles (Configs with >2 stages on smallest and <2 stages on largest device omitted)

a cost in portability. To see if the larger devices are better only because of their greater size (bang for the gram), Figs. 7 and 8 consider the best configuration for lifetime in different weight classes. Interestingly, our results show that while laptops and tablets are most capable, the smartphone is most efficient, providing the greatest lifetime for its weight. However, this is only at low performance, 1 fps. Its lifetime falls to a few minutes at 30 fps.

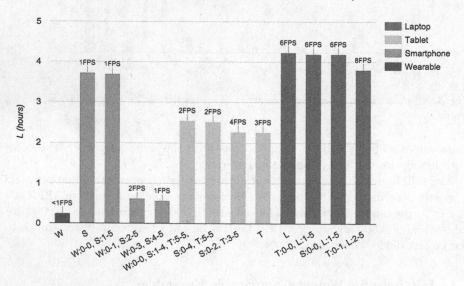

Fig. 7. Lifetime at Best frame rate. Achieved Best frame rates labels at top

Table 3. Energy/bit for various network technologies [6,9]

	WiFiw (nJ/bit)	Bluetooth (nJ/bit)	LTE (nJ/bit)
Transmission energy	500	250	100×10^3

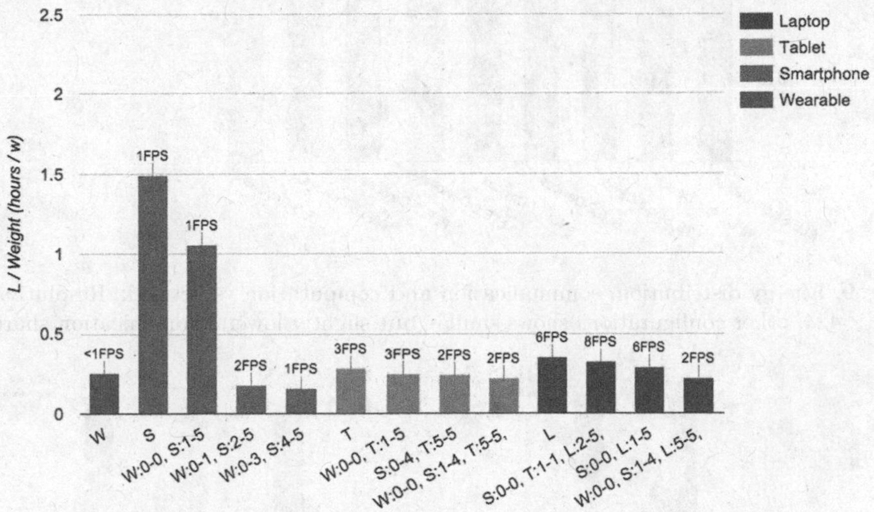

Fig. 8. Lifetime normalized by weight at Best frame rate. Achieved Best frame rates labels at top

3.4 Communication Limits

For ensembles, distributing the 3D service computation means that data must be transmitted between devices. Here we examine the energy cost of that communication within an ensemble, comparing it to energy expended on computation (Fig. 9). In nearly all cases, the computation energy dominates; communication energy manageable for Bluetooth and WiFi. However, LTE is too expensive to use in ensemble 3D service, requiring over 90 % of energy required for communication. This suggests that even with advances in LTE efficiency cloud-based SLAM or even partial cloud-based SLAM is unlikely to be viable (Table 3).

4 Adaptive Control to Reduce Computation

4.1 Single Frame Rate and Resolution

Others have explored novel and customized data structures to reduce the computation cost of 3D model building and tracking [7,8,11,12,15,16]. Typically, point-cloud based reconstruction has high levels of redundancy, enabling robust reconstruction. The ICP algorithm can support SLA with lower resolutions and frame rates. As a baseline, we consider the highest resolution frames (512×424)

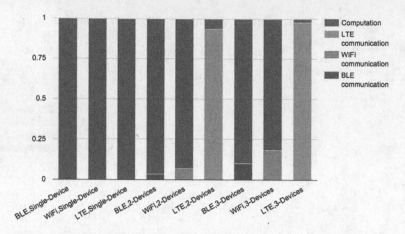

Fig. 9. Energy distribution, communication and computation vs network. Resolution: 512×424, other configurations shows similar but slightly lower communication share.

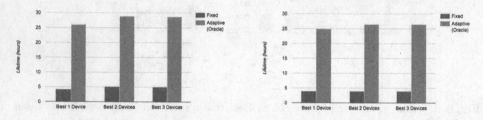

Fig. 10. Potential benefit for a best single Frame Rate and Resolution (Oracle), Near-Slow (left) and Far-Far (right). Resolution is reduced 16x and 64x and frame rate slightly, keeping mean tracking error within 10 %. Ensembles are the best for that number of devices ($L, T : 0 - 1, L : 2 - 5$ and $S : 0 - 0, T : 1 - 1, L : 2 - 5$ for Near-Slow, $L, T : 0 - 2, L : 3 - 5$ and $S : 0 - 0, T :! - 2, L : 3 - 5$ for Far-Fast)

and maximum frame rate can be achieved to create the baseline for both computation and accuracy. We assumed that the mean absolute Trajectory error (ATE) must be kept within 10 % of the best possible, and show results for the lifetime improvement in Fig. 10. By picking the best rate and resolution, our study shows that the lifetime for a range of ensembles can be increased by up to 6-fold.

Interesting, these results appear to be consistent over a range of movement speeds and scene distances. Even in Far-Fast, 6-fold improvements are possible by using low resolution. In fact, the results are nearly as good as for Near-Slow.

4.2   Best Collection of Frames – Rate and Resolution

While the previous comparison assumed a single fixed, optimal choice, there is much opportunity to adapt at a finer temporal scale. To understand the potential of per frame adaptive resolution and frame rate adaptive control, we search exhaustively for the best combinations of resolution and frame rate in a

3-segment movement pattern. We first collect the depth images with Microsoft Kinect V2 camera moving at 0.5 m/s (Superfast) for a 4-second movement experiment. Second we split the collected depth images into the three segments, dividing equally by distance along the movement track. Finally we consider all possible resolution and frame rate combinations for each segment and compute the mean ATE. Each set of choices produces both a total data volume, and an ATE. Each becomes a point in the 2D scatterplots shown in Figs. 11 and 12. Our results show a remarkable dynamic range of over 300-fold at close to the same ATE.

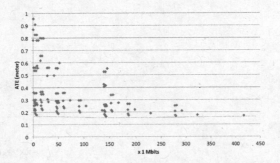

Fig. 11. Minimum mean ATE achieved at given data rate for Far-Superfast with adaptive control. Optimal adaptive control can be a big win (400 Mbits/1.2 Mbits = 333-fold).

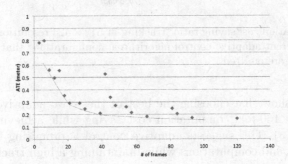

Fig. 12. Minimum mean ATE achieved at given total frames for Far-Superfast with adaptive control

Our results show that choices in adaptation matter a great deal as low data size adaptive control can achieve both very high and low mean ATE. But, the results are encouraging for adaptation because there are low data size adaptive control that matches the best mean ATE (see Figs. 11 and 12. For example, 1,200 kbits over the 4 s experiment is only 40 KB/s, but delivers close to best mean ATE. Likewise, a small fraction of the frames (40 out of 120) or 10 fps achieves close to best mean ATE even for this high speed motion. In short, if some intelligent adaptive control can choose close to the optimal, a remarkably small amount of data is required while producing near lowest mean ATE.

The smaller data – resolution and frame rate – also dramatically reduces the computation required. To assess the potential benefit, we compute the computation cost savings with two simple adaptive control algorithms: (1) Fixed frame rate, adapt resolution based on mean depth of point cloud, and (2) Fixed resolution, adapt frame rate based on tracked sensor velocity. These results are shown in Fig. 13.

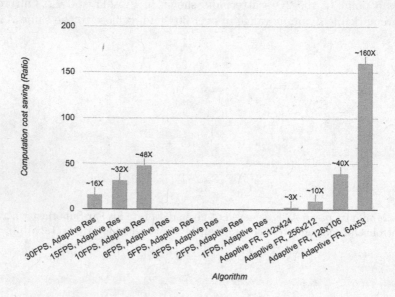

Fig. 13. Computation cost saving ratio (tracking at 512 × 424 resolution and 30 FPS as baseline) for different adaptive control algorithms, configurations that do not achieve competitive ATE are omitted.

Our results show that choosing the best of these two adaptive control algorithm, enables a 160-fold computation cost saving while achieving near lowest ATE. (see Fig. 13). This suggests adaptive control is promising to save energy (communication and computation) while maintaining a high tracking accuracy.

5   Summary and Future Work

Our study of a 3D perception service sheds insights into viable ensembles. At low frame rates, smartphones can support simple applications today. For fast motion, larger devices are required for peak compute speed and lifetime. Cloud support is not feasible. Adaptive frame rate and resolution is a promising approach to save energy. Future efforts should consider a broader range of devices, and movement.

Acknowledgements. This work was supported in part by the National Science Foundation under Award CNS-1405959. We also gratefully acknowledge generous support from Intel, HP, and the Seymour Goodman Foundation.

References

1. Besl, P.J., Mckay, H.D.: A method for registration of 3-D shapes. IEEE Trans. Pattern Anal. Mach. Intell. **14**(2), 239–256 (1992)
2. Blais, G., Levine, M.D.: Registering multiview range data to create 3D computer objects. IEEE Trans. Pattern Anal. Mach. Intell. **17**(8), 820–824 (1995)
3. Chen, Y., Medioni, G.: Object modeling by registration of multiple range images. In: Proceedings of IEEE Conference on Robotics and Automations, Sacremento, pp. 2724–2729 (1991)
4. Curless, B.: A volumetric method for building complex models from range images. In: Proceedings of the SIGGRAPH, pp. 303–312 (1996)
5. Dissanayake, G., Clark, S., Newman, P., Durrant-Whyte, H., Csorba, M.: Estimating uncertain spatial relationships in robotics. IEEE Trans. Rob. Autom. **17**(3), 229–241 (2001)
6. Huang, J., Qian, F., Alexandre Gerber, Z., Mao, M., Sen, S., Spatscheck, O.: A close examination of performance and power characteristics of 4G LTE networks. In: International Conference on Mobile Systems, pp. 225–238 (2012)
7. Klingensmith, M., Dryanovski, I., Srinivasa, S., Xiao, J.: Chisel: real time large scale 3D reconstruction onboard a mobile device. In: Robotics Science and Systems 2015, July 2015
8. Kottas, Dimitrios G., Hesch, Joel A., Bowman, Sean L., Roumeliotis, Stergios I.: On the consistency of vision-aided inertial navigation. In: Desai, Jaydev P., Dudek, Gregory, Khatib, Oussama, Kumar, Vijay (eds.) Experimental Robotics. STAR, vol. 88, pp. 303–317. Springer, Heidelberg (2013)
9. Lauridsen, M., Nol, L., Srensen, T.B., Mogensen, P.: An empirical LTE smartphone power model with a view to energy efficiency evolution. Intel Technol. J. **18**(1), 172–193 (2014)
10. Leonard, J.J., Durrant-Whyte, H.F.: Mobile robot localization by tracking geometric beacons. IEEE Trans. Rob. Autom. **7**(3), 376–382 (1991)
11. Montemerlo, M., Thrun, S., Koller, D., Wegbreit, B.: FastSLAM: a factored solution to the simultaneous localization and mapping problem. In: AAAI National Conference on Artificial Intelligence, pp. 593–598 (2003)
12. Mourikis, A.I., Roumeliotis, S.I.: A multi-state constraint kalman filter for vision-aided inertial navigation. In: Proceedings - IEEE International Conference on Robotics and Automation, pp. 3565–3572 (2007)
13. Nardi, L., Bodin, B., Zia, M.Z., Mawer, J.: Introducing slambench, a performance and accuracy benchmarking methodology for SLAM. Eprint Arxiv (2014)
14. Rusinkiewicz, S., Levoy, M.: Efficient variants of the ICP algorithm. In: 3DIM, pp. 145–152 (2001)
15. Schops, T., Engel, J., Cremers, D.: Semi-dense visual odometry for ar on a smartphone. In: 2014 IEEE International Symposium on Mixed and Augmented Reality (ISMAR), pp. 145–150 (2014)
16. Schöps, T., Sattler, T., Häne, C., Pollefeys, M.: 3D Modeling on the go: interactive 3D reconstruction of large-scale scenes on mobile devices. In: 2015 International Conference on 3D Vision (3DV), pp. 291–299, 19–22 October 2015

Study of a Virtual Conference in a Mirror World with Avatars and HMD

Evelyne Lombardo[1(✉)], Christophe Guion[2], and Joaquin Keller[2]

[1] Laboratory of Science of Information and Systems, Kedge Business School LSIS,
CNRS, Toulon, France
evelyne.lombardo@kedgebs.com, eve_lombardo@hotmail.com
[2] Orange Lab, Issy-les-Moulineaux, France
{Christophe.guion,Joaquin.keller}@orange.com

Abstract. We propose in this paper to conduct an experiment in a virtual conference with avatars in a mirror world with HMD, with a particular study of the sense of presence (or psychological immersion) in this virtual conference. For this, we first describe our theoretical framework, then we expose our experiment, we give our results, the limits of our research and our future research prospects.

Keywords: Mirror world · Avatars · HMD · Virtual conference with HMD

1 Introduction

Virtual conferences have already been tested on the 3D platform "second life", however, an immersive conference in a mixed reality in a mirror world has never been experienced.

To meet the challenges of the city of tomorrow, especially in expanding digital urban services and create value, it seems important to test this kind of new technologies for conference. The purpose of our experiment is to test the ability to hybridize physical reality and virtual reality in these mirror worlds for mixed use offered two types of lecturers present and distant, to understand the prospects of tomorrow's uses.

In the literature, there is a gap in the study of sense of presence in a mirror world, it's the reason why, we want to look this problem more precisely. So we will study the sense of presence and communication with avatars in our experiment of testing a virtual conference with other participants present and absent and represented by avatars in a mirror world. We first present our theoretical framework, then we write our experiment, and we then give our methodology and results.

2 Framework

2.1 Mirror Worlds

The concept of mirror world was invented by David Gelernter computer scientist at the University of Yale. He speaks for the first time of a hypothetical mirror world in 1991 in his book "Mirror worlds".

© Springer International Publishing Switzerland 2016
S. Lackey and R. Shumaker (Eds.): VAMR 2016, LNCS 9740, pp. 330–338, 2016.
DOI: 10.1007/978-3-319-39907-2_31

A mirror world is a representation of the real world in a digital form. It allows to map the real-world structures in an accurate and geographically. The mirror worlds offer a software model of real human environments.

The concept of "mirror worlds" differs from that of "virtual worlds" because they are not in direct connection with real models and are described as fictions, while the mirrors worlds are connected to real models and range closer to reality. A mirror world is closely related to augmented reality, but a mirror world can also be seen as an autonomous manifestation of the digital reality and may contain virtual items or other forms in which information will be integrated. For example, programs like Google Earth, Microsoft Virtual Earth or Google Street View are mirrors in 3D worlds (Fig. 1).

Fig. 1. Dive Real, the mirror world of our experiment. The picture below shows avatars immersed in a "mirror world" Google Street View kind; these avatars are superimposed on the space that is a real mirror of the world photographed beforehand.

2.2 Immersion and Sense of Presence

In the literature, there are two types of immersion: the technological immersion and the psychological immersion.

The technological immersion (Cadoz 1994) made possible by the device and caused particularly by 360 degrees. In this school of thought, immersion would strongly linked to technology. (Bystrom et al. 1999; Draper et al. 1998; Slater and Wilber 1997).

The psychological immersion (Slater et al. 2001) is independent of the device (for example, a book, projecting us in a virtual world, we can provoke a psychological immersion, without technological and physical immersion). This type of immersion is called "sense of presence" and approaches the concept of "flow" (Csikszent-mihalyi 1990) which wastes the user's sense of time and space. We explain in our article the exploration of our experiment, questioning us on this issue of immersion and sense of presence.

Witmer and Singer (1998) considers immersion as a psychological condition, like perception of "being in", of "being surrounded by", immersion suppose for these authors:

1. The insulation of the physical environment
2. The perception of feel "included" in the virtual environment
3. The "natural" state of interactions and perception of control
4. The perception of movement in a virtual environment.

In our study we will take the first definition of Witmer and Singer (1998) to describe the sense of presence studied.

There are 7 factors identified in the literature that affect this type of sense of presence:

1. Ease of interaction: interaction correlates with the sense of presence felt in the virtual environment and (Billinhurst Weghorst (1995))
2. The user control class: the sense of presence increases with the sense of control and shares in the virtual environment (Witmer and Singer 1998)
3. Realism of the image: the more realistic virtual environment is, the more the sense of presence is strong (Witmer and Singer 1998; Welch et al. (1996).)
4. Duration of the exhibition: prolonged exposure beyond 15 min with the virtual environment does not give the best result for the sense of presence (Stanney (2000)) and there is even a negative correlation between the prolonged exposure in the virtual environment and the sense of presence (Witmer and Singer 1998), which is explained by discomfort associated with prolonged use of a head-mounted display (nausea, headache, dizziness), experimentation advocated was therefore of maximum 15 min with HMD.
5. Social presence and social presence factors: the social presence of other individuals (real or avatars), and the ability to interact with these individuals increases the sense of presence (Heeter 1992).
6. Individual perception factors of information and entertainment systems: individual differences in terms of perception and representation of information between individuals are key factors in the sense of presence: Slater and Usoh (1993) shown by example that people regarded as visuals were more likely to have a high sense of presence that individuals kinesthetic or auditory individuals.
7. Quality of the virtual environment: quality, realism, the ability of the environment to be fluid, to create interaction are key factors in the sense of presence of the user (Slater and Usoh 1993; Hendrix and Barfield 1996). These factors affecting the sense of presence are considered in the presence of two questionnaires that we used (Fig. 2).

Fig. 2. During our experiment

3 Experiment

Experiment in partnership with the city of Antibes and the company Orange will take place at the Convention Palace, it aims to:

- test during a virtual conference with Dive Real in mirror world will include analysis of:
- meetings between avatars in the mirror world Exhibition Centre,

- meetings between avatars in the mirror world Exhibition Centre during the virtual conference,
- meetings mixing avatars present in the mirror world Exhibition Centre and people actually on site at the Congress Centre;
- evaluate the user experience in the proposed course and to deduce the areas of progress, or targeting scenarios uses. This analysis will be performed by measuring inter alia the sense of presence (psychological immersion) for the various combinations of situations and devices available to users.

A first step of our experiment was to test the first version of our device during the Science Festival in October 2015 (in parallel to the site of Valencia and Antibes), we used the head-mounted immersive DK2 allowing a 360 degrees in the virtual environment to test the sense of presence (psychological immersion).

4   Methodology

We will present in our article the results of this first experiment. Our first experiment was to present the Dive Real, which is a platform in a mirror world at the Science Festival at the Valencia site and on the site of Antibes (congress). We describe first the Dive Real platform. Dive Real is a platform where users can:

1. choose their avatar (male/female versus, with the choice between several types of men and women (ethnicity/age/style clothing
2. communicate through avatars chat
3. move in the virtual environment: walk, run, go right, left, turn, turn
4. teleport from one city to another one and from a city street at other. The experiment consisted of study the sense of psychological presence among users:
5. on the platform Dive Real, without the HMD
6. on the platform Dive Real, with HMD, and to compare the two groups.
7. We have devised the following typical scenario:

- Five minutes to explain the operation of the interface Dive Real
- Ten minutes where users had the task to teleport where they wanted to explore the environment and possibly communicate with the avatars around them, or join them in a specific location.
- Ten minutes of questionnaires.

To test the psychological sense of presence, we used two canonical questionnaires that have been tested several times in other research and are statistically significant:

– First, the canonical test of presence of Witmer and Singer (1994). This Questionnaire on the sense of presence, which tests the sense of presence by 24 questions on a 7-point scale (0–7), ranging from "not at strongly disagree" to "strongly agree".

This test determines the degree of perceived presence and measure its effects depending on factors determining the sense of presence,

1. control and response of the virtual environment (sample question: "To what extent were you able to control the virtual environment?"),
2. interaction with the virtual environment (sample question: "to what extent the environment he was responsive to the actions you were doing there"),
3. locomotion in the virtual environment (sample question: "up how the movement sensation within the virtual environment he was realistic")
4. and details of the interface (sample question: "to what extent the visual quality of the graphics equipment you she was inconvenienced in performing the required tasks?"). This test of presence therefore holds 6 subscales: **realism, ability to act, interface quality, opportunity to review, self-assessment of performance, hearing and sense haptic**. This first test measures the sense of presence, after experimentation. Second, Bouchard Canon test et al. 2014. The questionnaire consists of two parts: the first part, consisting of 6 items testing the sense of presence after the experiment, the second part, consisting of 38 items, testing sense of presence during the experiment. For each item, there are 5 scales ranging from "strongly disagree" to "strongly agree". There are 4 factors that affect the sense of presence included in the questionnaire:

- the spatial presence,
- the feeling of being engaged,
- the realistic aspect of the environment,
- the negative effects of the environment.

19 items test the spatial presence (sample items: "I felt I was able to interact with the virtual environment", 13 items testing the feeling of being committed by users (sample item: "I felt involved in the virtual environment", five items test the natural and realistic environment (sample item: "the content seemed realistic", 6 items test negative effects of the environment (sample item: "I felt disoriented", "I felt tired").

5 Results

We present in this article the results for the group with HMD.

5.1 Results of the First Test: Witmer and Singer (1998)

Results with Oculus, present test of Witmer and Singer (1998).
General results of all subjects (average).

- Realism: 4, 3 on 7
- Ability to act: 4, 7 on 7
- Interface quality: 4, 6 (inverse items) on 7
- Opportunity to review: 5, 2 on 7
- Self-assessment of performance: 4, 2 on 7

We have not tested the haptic and sound dimensions because it was not relevant to our experiment (no sound or haptic sense solicited).

5.2   Results of the Second Test, Test of Bouchard et al. (2014)

General results of all subjects (average).

Spatial presence, 1, 9 on 5
Feeling of being engaged, 2, 9 on 5
Realistic aspect of the environment, 2, 3 on 5
Negative effects of the environment. 1, 4 on 5

Discussions: Factors in favor of the sense of presence in the virtual environment in the mirror world. After the experience in the virtual environment, all users surveyed felt moderately sad that the experience is over, all would have liked the experience continues, all clearly remembered parts of the experience, most recommend experience to their friends. Some had the impression of a return trip

During their experience in any virtual environment felt "absorbed", all of the subjects felt involved in the virtual environment, all had fun in the virtual environment, all have felt to visit places in the virtual environment, not one felt tired. The content seemed realistic to fifty cents topics. All felt they were not just looking at something. No subject felt dizzy by experimentation. Most of the subjects were given the impression that the virtual environment was part of real life. All subjects felt that visited scenes could actually exist in the real world. No subject experienced eye strain, none felt nausea, felt none of headache. All the subjects had the impression that the characters were aware of their presence. All subjects responded emotionally to the virtual world. The content has pleased the majority of subjects. Most of the subjects felt able to change the course of events in the virtual environment. Most of the subjects had the impression of being in the same space as the characters and/or objects. Most of the subjects felt that some parts of the virtual environment (for example, the characters or objects) met their shares. Three quarters of the subjects had the impression that it was participating in life in the virtual environment.

Discussions: Factors working against the sense of presence during their experience in the virtual environment in a mirror world. No subject has lost track of time, very few subject has felt able to interact with the virtual environment, very few subject perceived the virtual environment as natural, none felt that the characters and/or objects could almost touch them. Very few have had the impression of being really "there" as if they were in real life. Very few have had the impression of moving in response to certain parts of the virtual environment (low interaction with the virtual environment). The experience in the virtual environment was moderately intense for half the subjects and very few have focused more attention on the virtual environment and their own thoughts (personal concerns, dreams, etc.). Very few have had the impression of being present (e) in the visited scenes. Half the subjects had the impression to be able to move objects in the virtual environment (low interactivity of the virtual environment). None felt the different characteristics of the virtual environment. Very few subjects felt wrapped by the virtual environment. No subjects felt that the people and objects were solid and real. Very few have had the impression that he could reach or touch objects.

6   Conclusion

We proposed in this paper to conduct an experiment in a virtual conference with avatars in a mirror world with HMD, in particular studying the sense of presence (psychological immersion) in this virtual community of avatars. For this, we first describe our theoretical framework, then we have exposed our experiment conducted in collaboration with Orange and Congress Centre d'Antibes, we gave the results of our first experiment, which took place during the festival of Science at the conference hall of Antibes and Talence.

We can now conclude that a large search site remains open on the study of virtual conference in a mirror world, which not only allow avatars to share knowledge and practices, but also to users to teleport from one world real to the virtual world and vice versa, for the moment only with real places and not images recorded in real time. We can also attach ourselves to the prospects opened such research when opportunities for avatars (and therefore to the real people behind the screens) will be multiplied when the user can, for example, is no longer teleport into a mirror mode already existing in the real world but in the real world in real time with their avatar. Analysis of the psychological sense of presence or immersion in these new contexts seems necessary, even indispensable, and opens new fields in the social, psychological and in the field of human interaction communication.

References

Bell, M.W.: Indiana University. J. Virtual Worlds Res. Past Present Future, **1**(1) (2008)

Badot, O., Cova, B.: Communauté et consommation: perspective pour un "marketing tribal". Revue Française du Marketing **1**(151), 5–17 (1995)

Cadoz, C.: Les réalités virtuelles. Dominos-Flammarion, Paris (1994)

Csíkszentmihályi, M.: Flow: the Psychology of Optimal Experience, 1st edn. Harper and Row, New York (1990). poche

Azuma, R., Baillot, Y., Behringer, R., Feiner, S., Julier, S., MacIntyre, B.: Recent advances in augmented reality. IEEE Comput. Graph. Appl. **21**(6), 34–47 (2001)

Caudel, T., Mizell, D.: Augmented reality: an application of heads-up display technology to manual manufacturing processes. In: Hawaii International Conference on System Sciences (1992)

Deleuze, G.: L'Image Mouvement. Editions de Minuit, Paris (1983)

Deleuze, G.: L'Image Temps. Editions de Minuit, Paris (1985)

Kollock, P., Smith, M.: Introduction: communities in cyberspace. In: Smith, M., Kollock, P. (eds.) Communities in Cyberspace, pp. 3–25. Routledge Press, London (1999)

Roush, W.: Second earth. Technol. Rev. **110**(4), 10 (2007)

Gelernter, D.: Mirror Worlds: The Day Software Puts the Universe In a Shoebox… How it Will Happen and What It Will Mean?. Oxford University Press, New York (1991)

Slater, M., Linakis, V., Usoh, M., Kooper, R., Street, G.: Immersion, presence, and performance in virtual environments: an experiment with Tri-Dimensional Chess. In: ACM Virtual Reality Software and Technology (VRST), pp. 163–172 (2001)

Turkle, S.: Cyberspace and Identity. Contemp. Sociol. **28**(6), 643–648 (1999)

Wenger, É.: Communities of Practice: Learning Meaning and Identity. University of Cambridge Press, Cambridge (1999)

Wenger, É., McDermott, R.A., Snyder, W.: Cultivating Communities of Practice: A Guide to Managing Knowledge. Harvard Business School Press, Cambridge (2002)

Weissberg, J.L.: Présences à Distance. L'Harmattan, Paris (1999)

Bystrom, K.-E., Barfield, W., Hendrix, C.: A conceptual model of sense of presence in virtual environments. Presence: Teleoperators Virtual Environ. 5(1), 109–121 (1999)

Draper, J.V., Kaber, D.B., Usher, J.M.: Telepresence. Hum. Factors, 40(3), 354–375 (1998)

Slater, M., Wilbur, S.: A framework for immersive virtual environments (FIVE): speculations on the role of presence in virtual environments. Presence: Teleoperators Virtual Environ. 6(6), 603–616 (1997)

Witmer, B.G., Singer. M.J.: Measuring presence in virtual environments: apresence questionnaire. Presence: Teleoperators Virtual Environ. 7(3), 225–240 (1998)

Billinhurst, M., Weghorst, S.: The use of sketch maps to measure cognitive maps virtual of environments. In: Proceeding of Virtual Reality Annual International Symposium (VRAIS '95), pp. 40–47 (1995)

Welch, R., Blackmon, T., Liu, A., Mellers, B., Stark, L.: The effects of pictural realism, delay of visual feedback, and observer interactivity on the subjective sense of presence. Presence: Teleoperators Virtual Environ. 5(3), 263–273 (1996)

Stanney, K.M.: Unpublished research data. University of Central Florida (2000)

Heeter, C.: Being there: the subjective experience of presence. Presence: Teleoperators Virtual Environ. 1(2), 262–271 (1992)

Slater, M., Usoh, M.: Representations systems, perceptual position, and presence in virtual environments. Presence: Teleoperators Virtual Environ. 2(3), 221–233 (1993)

Hendrix, C., Barfield, W.: Presence within virtual environments as a function of visual display parameters. Presence: Teleoperators Virtual Environ. 5(3), 274–289 (1996)

Witmer, B.G., Singer, M. J.: Measuring immersion in virtual environments. ARI Technical Report 1014. U.S. Army Research Institute for the Behavioral and Social Sciences, Alexandria, VA (1994)

Bouchard, S., Robillard, G., St-Jacques, J., Dumoulin, S., Patry, M.J., Renaud, P.: Reliability and Validity of a Single-Item Measure of Presence in VR (2014)

Using iBeacons for Location-Based Tracking in Alternate Reality Games: A Pilot Study

Alexia Mandeville$^{(\boxtimes)}$ and Carrie Crossley

E2i Creative Studio, Institute for Simulation and Training, Orlando, FL, USA
{amandevi,ccrossle}@ist.ucf.edu

Abstract. iBeacons provide location-based tracking that can act as a powerful tool in data collection as well as design for alternate reality gaming. Using beacons to incorporate location-based tracking in a museum environment, E2i Creative Studio conducted a pilot study using a mobile event application in order to test the feasibility of using an alternate reality game to collect data on the visitors in the physical space. Four hundred users engaged in the app and game, providing researchers with valuable timing and tracking data. From the data collected, this paper informs and provides insights for engaging players in virtual reality through location-based gaming using iBeacons.

Keywords: Alternate reality · Location-based gaming · Location data · iBeacons · Game design · Bluetooth low energy devices · Gamification · Positional data · Indoor-positioning systems · Museums

1 Introduction

Alternate reality games (ARGs) represent the next generation in mobile and social gaming, where a player can be integrated into the game with every step they take in the real world. ARGs combine digital interactions with experiences in the real world, allowing players to participate in a variety of competitive and collaborative activities (Kim et al. 2008). With the growth in presence of Global Positioning System (GPS) tracking and mobile devices, ARGs are becoming increasingly common in the gaming world. For example, games like Pokémon Go (The Pokémon Company 2015) and Ingress (ref) provide large player bases with a virtual world that's capable of being explored through the physical world. ARGs keep players involved over time through their dynamic nature; game content is constantly changed or updated as players all over the world solve puzzles, tell stories, and launch attacks (Kim et al. 2008).

2 Background

iBeacon is a protocol developed by Apple, used in various iBeacon-compatible Bluetooth Low Energy (BLE) devices, typically called beacons. Beacons are commonly small devices, about one to two inches in diameter. When these devices come into the general area of a user's phone or Bluetooth-enabled device (assuming the user has given the app permission to use iBeacons), they prompt a notification to the user's

© Springer International Publishing Switzerland 2016
S. Lackey and R. Shumaker (Eds.): VAMR 2016, LNCS 9740, pp. 339–347, 2016.
DOI: 10.1007/978-3-319-39907-2_32

mobile device. This looks like a basic notification on someone's phone that may be tailored to the specific application. iBeacons are currently being used for a variety of applications, including gaming, data collection, and increasing engagement of visitors in public spaces such as libraries and museums (Eng 2015).

Despite the effectiveness of GPS in alternate reality games for worldwide gameplay, GPS cannot provide gameplay in micro-environments such as a specific room, building, or area. Instead, beacons can provide the ability for an indoor-positioning system in smaller environments such as these. Developers have the ability to place a beacon anywhere considering their small size and wireless portability and adjust their transmission range programmatically. For example, Estimote, a popular beacon manufacturer, states that range of their transmission is up to 70 meters, with four possible proximity zones ranging from 0.5 meters to 70 meters in diameter (Estimote 2014). Game developers and other content creators can utilize this flexibility in their designs to trigger events at specific locations in the physical world through mobile applications. According to the Internet of Things, the world of mobile devices, sensors, and connected hardware is ever growing, with 9 billion interconnected devices in 2013 and an expected forecast of 24 billion interconnected devices by 2020 (Gubbi et al. 2013), allowing for an expansion of a mobile audience and gaming consumers.

The design for ARG location-based games has dual layers, involving a virtual environment laid on top of a physical environment. Between location-based gameplay and the networked capability of mobile devices, ARGs can encourage social interactions through community events or player-versus-player (PvP) interactions. For example, Pokémon GO affords player's interactions through battling and trading Pokémon that they have collected through their exploration of the real world (The Pokémon Company 2015). Developers for ARGs must take into account how their virtual environment will affect physical gameplay, especially in a micro-environment such as a building. Will an influx of users to one physical area create chaos, comprising a player's safety? While this can create less-than-ideal situations, it can also be used as a tool to drive physical exploration through virtual reality.

3 Deep Sea Discovery Game

In a partnership with the Orlando Science Center (OSC), E2i Creative Studio piloted a mobile AR game in 2016 at Otronicon, an annual technology convention. The project was designed to meet the science center's need for a mobile event application; OSC wanted to provide convention visitors with scheduling information through both Android and iPhone platforms. Additionally, E2i's goal was to automate timing and tracking collection through gameplay. In order to achieve these goals, an event application was developed that contained an alternate reality game. The purpose of the application was not only to provide visitors with information, but also to test the feasibility of driving visitors through the physical environment with an indoor-positioning system built on beacons while collecting timing and tracking data.

Science centers and museums typically collect timing and tracking data on visitors manually, recording quantitative data on where the visitors traveled, as well as how long they remained in the area (Yalowitz and Bronnenkant 2009). Automating the data collection process can allow for the capture of exponentially more data, and assist live observers to delve deeper into emerging patterns, and allow for more efficient data visualizations and mapping based on the accuracy of beacons inside the building. With over 15,000 visitors to the science center during the event, and over 560 users downloading the pilot application, %3.7 of users downloaded the application during the weekend long event. With the application not being marketed or publicized before the event, the pilot of the event application was proven to be a viable tool for data collection based on the amount of downloads.

Deep Sea Discovery utilizes a RadBeacon Dot, a beacon created by Radius networks (Radius Networks 2016). These specific beacons were chosen based on their price, and the ability to replace the battery inside. The size of the beacons allow for flexibility when installing, with the diameter of the beacon being about the size of a quarter (Fig. 1).

Fig. 1. The RadBeacon Dot by radius networks

3.1   Design Overview

Deep Sea Discovery, the alternate reality game developed and piloted within the event application by E2i, is a monster collection game that utilizes beacon technology. The game allows players to use the Orlando Science Center as a physical platform for exploration of different aquatic zones with the goal to document, collect, and learn about a variety of sea creatures (Fig. 3).

Players discover real-world aquatic creatures with respect to their scientifically accurate aquatic zone. In order to encourage players to explore the area, a unique aquatic zone was assigned to each of the four floors in the OSC building, mimicking the structure of real world aquatic zones:

Six to twelve beacons were installed on each level to notify players of a creature encounter. At each encounter, players have the ability to document a creature, but their effectiveness relies on their level and experience points, in conjunction with the creature's level, rarity, and sensitivity. Players increase their skills and stats by exploring and documenting various creatures throughout the building.

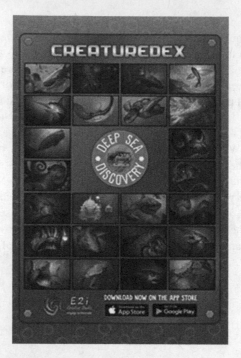

Fig. 2. A poster showing all creatures capable of being documented in Deep Sea Discovery

Physical Building Level	Corresponding Aquatic Level
1	Epipelagic (Sunlight Zone)
2	Mesopelagic (Twilight Zone)
3	Bathypelagic (Midnight Zone)
4	Abyssopelagic (Abyss)

Fig. 3. Physical and virtual levels in Deep Sea Discovery

3.2   Systems, Creatures, and Player Statistics

This section outlines specific mechanics in Deep Sea Discovery in relation to metrics and screen states.

Encountering and Moving Closer to a Creature: Once a player encounters a creature by physically coming into the range of a beacon, a notification shows up on their phone. They can click on that notification, and a screen shows the creature and what proximity of the player to the creature. The player can move closer to the creature (in a hot or cold fashion), but the creature may flee if the player does not have the proper stats in relation to the creature.

Documenting a Creature: If the player encounters a creature they may opt to immediately document it, or move closer to it. The closer the player gets to the creature, the more percentage documentation they can gain, as well as "experience", raising their skills. A creature may need to be documented multiple times in order to obtain %100 documentation (Fig. 4).

Screen Descriptions

Screen	Description
Character/Creature-Dex Screen	Shows player stats and list of creatures that have been found/have not been found
Creature specific screen	Shows stats on specific character
Creature encounter screen	Player encounters a character- shows stats of character, proximity of player to creature

Fig. 4. Screens in Deep Sea Discovery

CreatureDex: This element acts as a library of what creatures the player has documented. The player starts with an empty CreatureDex, and throughout their exploration and documentation, they collect each creature until they have successfully documented every creature in the game (Fig. 5).

Player Stats: Upon first starting the game, the player starts with an initial Level rating of 1. Document and Approach begin with random values equaling 20 when added.

Level: This stat gives players an overall understanding on how skilled their character is, and how well he/she can fair when attempting to document certain creature. This number is raised when enough Experience Points are gained, which in turn raises the player's stats. When documenting a creature, this equation is used: Player (Level/Creature's Rarity*10) + 2+iBeacon Range. Also, when getting close to a creature, the player's Level will come into play when trying to determine whether the creature has noticed the player. The formula for this is as follows: Distance(limited from 0–100) + Creature's Sensitivity-Player's Level.

Experience Points (shown as experience bar): For every successful documentation the player will receive some of these points. When certain milestones are reached, the player's level will rise. The formula for calculating experience gained is as follows: ((30*Animal's Level)/5)*((2*Animal's Level + 10)2.5/(Animal's Level + Player's Level + 10)2.5) + 1. On gaining experience, if the player's total experience reaches this number: (Player's Level)3 + 7, then the player will increase in level.

Fig. 5. Screenshot of the main screen of Deep Sea Discovery, showing the CreatureDex

Creature stats:

Zone: This indicates on what level the creature can be found in (Epipelagic, Mesopelagic, Bathypelagic and Abyssopelagic).

Level: This is meant to be used as a basic understanding of the creature's difficulty in relation to the player's level. To calculate this number, find the average between the creature's Rarity and Sensitivity.

Rarity: This represents the creature's anatomical complexity, and basically how hard it is for the player to document it. This stat is tested against the player's Level stat (as mentioned below).

Sensitivity: This represents the creature's ability to notice the player. This stat is contested against the player's Level.

4 Data Collection

The data collected from the game and application proved to be important to both the developers and the Orlando science center by providing insights for future applications and exhibits. Data was collected from over 560 visitors, plotting their travel through the Orlando Science Center.

Types of Data Collected from Visitors:

Player ID: This data is based on a date-time stamp of when the user started the application. This allows data analysis of how many total people used the application, as well as allowing analysis of how many people used the app per day or during a specific time of day

Beacons Visited: This data is recorded based on the beacons that contacted the user's device. They are recorded in sequential order of when the user visited them. This is used to track where the player moved in the physical space of the science center by mapping it to a diagram (See Fig. 2.) This allows for analysis of timing and tracking throughout the Orlando Science Center

In order to track player movement, the beacons were labeled and installed throughout the science center, and were mapped out by beacon ID, shown in Fig. 6.

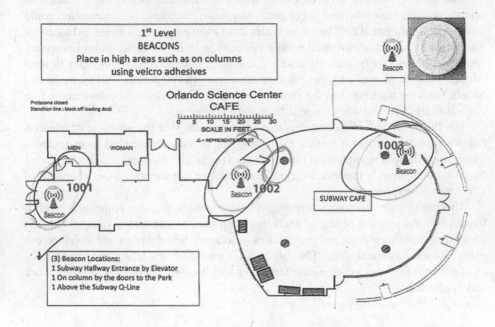

Fig. 6. A map showing a section of the first level of the Orlando Science Center. Three beacons are labeled on the map corresponding to the ID they send to the database.

4.1 Map Data

The data collected can be analyzed by plotting the data points corresponding to each beacon on the prepared maps. This gives a visual representation of visitor tracking. Analysis for this type of visualization can be completed at a glance, seeing where exactly traffic patterns exist based on the clusters of data points as well as the congestion of lines of travel.

This timing and tracking data is important not only to inform design choice in alternate reality gameplay, but for museum management to analyze which exhibits are being visited and how long visitors are engaged in the exhibit. The analysis of timing and tracking data makes it possible to streamline and better design engaging visitor experience, and informs the design of efficient and popular exhibits that maximize not only the amount of visitors, but the engagement of each person visiting.

5 Conclusions

This application allowed E2i Creative Studio to pilot an effective design tool using an emerging technology, but there is still a lot of exploration available in location-based gaming using iBeacons. Beacons are not widely known throughout gaming and simulation, and companies like The Pokemon Company and Niantic are just recently beginning to produce games in the ARG realm.

The data is valuable to a variety of different stakeholders, not only limited to science centers, museums, and developers. Any entity, building, or organization could utilize indoor positional data based on visitor's, or even employee's travel and location. Theme parks have started implementing beacons in order to create more immersive applications and experiences. Holland's Tulpenland utilizes beacons in order to send educational data to user's phones on their attractions (RFID Journal 2015). Parks can benefit from the tracking data the same way museums and science centers can, while also allowing their visitors to benefit from the experience.

The minor amount of games available and the infancy of the adoption of iBeacon hardware allows for much further exploration to be completed. One facet includes game or application manipulation through data. Design and mechanics could be altered based on one player's input or location. How can we use the data from yesterday to affect today's experience?

This emerging technology is a powerful tool for design and data collection, and E2i Creative Studio sees the benefit of analyzing positional data to inform design. There is a world of experimentation and possibilities in location-based design and development using indoor positional data. The lab looks forward to exploring the capabilities of alternate reality and location-based tracking with beacon technology in future work and applications.

References

Kim, J.Y., Allen, J.P., Lee, E.: Alternate reality gaming. Commun. ACM **51**(2), 36–42 (2008)

Gubbi, J., Buyya, R., Marusic, S., Palaniswami, M.: Internet of things (IoT): a vision, architectural elements, and future directions. Future Gener. Comput. Syst. **29**(7), 1645–1660 (2013)

Yalowitz, S.S., Bronnenkant, K.: Timing and tracking: unlocking visitor behavior. Visitor Stud. **12**(1), 47–64 (2009)

The Pokémon Company, I.: Pokémon GO Allows Players to Catch 'em All in the Real World. Business Wire (English), October 2015

Eng, S.: Connection, not collection: using iBeacons to engage library users. Comput. Libr. **10**, 12 (2015)

Estimote, Inc. Beacon Tech Overview (2014). developer.estimote.com

Niantic, Inc. Where Virtual Meets Real. The New York Times, July 2014

Radius networks. RadBeacon Dot (2016). http://store.radiusnetworks.com/products/radbeacon-dot

Swedberg, C.: Harvard museum, Remy Martin and Tulip Theme Park adopt LabWerk's Beacon solution. RFID Journal, June 2015. http://www.rfidjournal.com/articles/view?13154/

Augmenting Reality Through Wearable Devices

Peter A. Smith[✉]

University of Central Florida, Orlando FL, USA
Peter.smith@ucf.edu

Abstract. Wearable devices such as smart watches, fitness bands, and other easily concealable sensors are become ever more ubiquitous in today's society. People are often checking their steps, heart rate, or text messages, with the same ease in which they would check the time only a few years ago. With all the data being collected and shared there is a new opportunity to leverage this information to better inform augmented reality. With wearable devices, there is the ability to create a fully personal augmented reality experience, tailored to the user's preferences, abilities and bio-metrics. This includes the ability to track things like heart rate and skin temperature, and inform runners when they are overheating, or suggest to sedentary workers that they perform exercise, and take the stairs, but when combined with rich interactive narrative, rules, and goals the feedback from these devices become an augmented reality game.

The ability for wearables to support augmented reality experiences is already in place. Users often already own the devices and they already interact with their own phones, or computers. It is possible to both leverage a single user's data, but also aggregate data across users and provide an even more immersive experience. This research discusses the use of wearable sensors in a framework of more complicated augmented experiences with design examples user analysis from a smart watch game for pedestrian safety (Crime Watch), and the wearable technology infrastructure that supports it.

Keywords: Smart watches · Wearable technology · Augmented reality · Ubiquitous computing · Gamification

1 Introduction

Wearable devices are increasingly becoming ubiquitous technologies. Large numbers of people are wearing smart watches and fitness bands. These are influencing how the users interact with the world. Sometimes this influence can' be motivating. For example a fitness band can encourage more walking or exercise. Other times this can be a distraction, like a text message taking the users attention from a conversation. No matter how these devices are normally used, they can also be used as portals to augmented reality experiences. The ability for wearables to support augmented reality experiences is already in place. Users often already own the devices and they already interact with their own phones, or computers. It is possible to both leverage a single user's data, but also aggregate data across users and provide an even more immersive experience.

© Springer International Publishing Switzerland 2016
S. Lackey and R. Shumaker (Eds.): VAMR 2016, LNCS 9740, pp. 348–355, 2016.
DOI: 10.1007/978-3-319-39907-2_33

This research discusses the use of wearable sensors in a framework of more complicated augmented experiences with design examples from a smart watch game for pedestrian safety (Crime Watch), and the wearable technology infrastructure that supports it.

2 Background

Smart watches are a relatively new phenomenon that is growing in popularity. Smart watches sync with smart phones (i.e. iPhone, Android) allowing wearers to engage with their phone's information without taking the phones out of their pockets. One popular use is controlling music in a car without having to go through the complicated process of taking out a phone, unlocking it, opening the music app, and selecting a song. This can all be done with a few clicks on the buttons on the side of the watch.

Sensors in Smart Watch AR are usually leveraged from a cell phone. This provides a certain limitation on the type of input that can be leveraged, unless the design incorporates both a phone and watch component. Allowing all available sensors in both devices to be used in applications. Table 1 shows the appropriate technologies for device based AR found in phones.

Table 1. Comparison of available AR sensor tech, modified from [1]

Technology	iBeacon	NFC	Markers
Hardware Requirements	Requires a handheld device that supports Bluetooth Low Energy.	Requires a handheld device that supports Near Field Communication (Not iOS)	Requires a device that has a camera installed.
Range	Up to 250 feet away and as close as a few inches.	A few inches away at most. The ability to touch handheld preferred.	Needs a direct line of sight, but could work across varied distances depending upon camera resolution.
App Requirements	Apps must know about specific beacons in advance and know what to do when those beacons are detected	App does not need to know about specific NFC chips though they can. Information can be stored and shared directly from the chip.	Apps may know about specific markers, but some standard format markers can contain information (QR Codes) and could use general purpose apps.
Setup Required by User	The user only needs to install the app and possibly enable	The user needs to install the app and enable NFC on	The user may have a general purpose app or might need

(Continued)

Table 1. (*Continued*)

Technology	iBeacon	NFC	Markers
	Bluetooth through the phones settings. This can be done through the app as well.	their phones. They will also need to physically touch sensors.	to install a specific app. No other functions need to be modified.
Setup Required by app developer	iBeacons need to be placed in specific locations by the developer. Finding the best location can be difficult.	NFC tags are placed in specific places. Generally easier to place than iBeacons, but may require specific information written to them.	Unique markers must be developed with visual variation.
Benefit	Can determine locations in and around buildings with high accuracy and no physical connection from the user. Can be used for long and short distances. Can be completely hidden	Can contain information. Can record information for user. Inexpensive Easily Hidden from view	Low cost solution Supports most devices
Issues	Higher cost than other solutions Proximity is directionless Requires Bluetooth on the device	Needs magnetic shielding on metal Short Range No iOS support	Needs line of sight Cannot be hidden Often considered unsightly

Additional sensors that can be leveraged on a cell phone are GPS, accelerometer, and compass sensors. Watches often also provide access to additional accelerometers, pulse sensors, buttons, galvanic skin response, and other sensors depending upon the device. Leveraging these sensors along with strong narrative and a gamification layer can provide an augmented experience without the use of traditional AR hardware.

3 Wearable Device Games

In the past there have been many attempts to make wearable device games. This includes games that leverage the Nintendo Game Boy Advance to add pedometer support. The gamified Striive device provided a FitBit style interface with an imbedded game.

Nintendo made a walking game that included sensors for both the player and their dog. All of these systems attempted to combine both movement and games. Newer devices such as watches have opened a new area of wearable device AR.

4   Technology Supporting Wearable Device AR

As the watch market matures there are now three leading types of watches, there are also many common sensors. These sensors find themselves in each type of watch or fitness sensor.

4.1   Common Wearable Sensors

The common sensors found in these devices are: Accelerometers, pedometers, pulse rate sensors, galvanic skin response sensors, and leveraged device sensors.

4.2   Major Wearable Categories

There are three major types of watches.

Apple Watch. The Apple Watch is developed by Apple and in only compatible with iPhone devices. The apple watch includes accelerometers, pulse rate sensor, and touch screen. These watches cost $300 and up and all work the same. Watches last about a day on single charge.

Android Wear. Android Wear is a category of smart watch designed by Google, but implemented by a large number of manufacturers. This means that the watches are often customized and it is not possible to know exactly what features will be available. Costs range from $80–$400 and up. Also, they come in both round and square screens. Watches last about a day on a single charge.

Pebble Watch. Pebble has three models of watch. One has a round screen. The other two are square, and are very similar except one is black and white, while the other has a color screen. They work equally well on both iPhone and Android phones. These watches range about $99 though prices vary. The screens are e-ink so the phones last almost a week on a single charge.

Fitness Bands. Fitness bands come in many shapes and sizes. The most capable of these bands currently is the Microsoft Band. This band includes skin temperature, pulse, galvanic skin response, and more. Costs are about $200.

5   Common Wearable Device Applications

The common applications on wearable devices are light in functionality. There are many reasons for this including the need to conserve battery power, the need to be unobtrusive to the users, and the small size of the screen. So, it may seem inconceivable that augmented reality applications could run on such a device, but watches have been augmenting our reality for centuries, if only to provide the date and time to the wearer. Common applications extend this by providing real time weather, health, and other information to the user. Games for watches had traditionally been bland or simple remakes of Atari or other older games, but watch based AR is possible.

6 Crime Watch Case Study

In a recent study conducted by the National Complete Streets Coalition found that the top 4 most unsafe cities in the United State were in Florida, and the top city was Orlando with over 200 pedestrian deaths last year. Further, there have been over ten pedestrian deaths on Alafaya Trail in front of the University of Central Florida in the last seven years. Authorities have cited large six lane roads, fast moving traffic, and a large pedestrian population as causes of these problems. However, it is difficult to assess where these issues are occurring, and even harder to capture the focus of drivers on pedestrians when they are already focused on getting to where they are going and the huge number of vehicles that seem like a more prominent threat.

In an effort to help bring driver focus to pedestrians, and to identify problem intersections within the city, a smart watch based game that will increase awareness of drivers on pedestrians was designed. This project is an innovative approach to pedestrian safety, which could lead to many other types of games for pedestrian safety, as well as crowd sourced data collection.

The benefit to the University is that there is a real possibility that the game could lead to impactful change on campus and throughout the city. Safety on campus for both pedestrians and drivers is important. Even playing the mental game of finding people breaking traffic rules has an immediate change in a driver's mindfulness of their surroundings. With motivation added through games there will be an increased awareness in players.

6.1 Split Design

The design of Crime Watch is split between the phone and the wearable. Each side is used when most appropriate to the user. For reporting data the watch is used. For exploring the data the phone.

Watch Side. The watch side of Crime Watch runs on Pebble watches. The interface on the watch originally had a much more complex design, allowing the player to report multiple types of violations for both vehicles and pedestrians. It also allowed the player to view their statistics (Fig. 1).

Realizing that these extra options made running the game more difficult the design was changed to only allow for the reporting of generic pedestrian or automobile violation. When reporting the watch leverages the phones GPS and reports both the type of violation and its location.

Fig. 1. Crime watch running on a pebble watch

Mobile Device Side. The game provides a mobile app as an entry point that will describe the games narrative and engage the players in acting as a Dick Tracy style detective, helping to track a particular population that does not follow traffic laws. Tracking of this population will be done at traffic lights when the driver is stopped, through their smart watch. The watch app will harness GPS data from their phones and allow the driver to report pedestrians that are crossing inappropriately, cars that are running lights, and other common violations. On the phone app players will be able to see maps or areas others have reported, track their own reports, and will be given points for and achievements through a gamification layer in the app. More active players will be promoted to higher levels and will earn more points on a leader board though a rich gamification layer (Fig. 2).

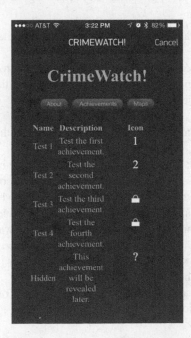

Fig. 2. Crime watch achievements

Gamification, or the act of adding gaming elements to real world situations, is a growing field with many recorded successes. Applying that to pedestrian safety is the logical next step. Smart watch research is in its infancy, but as we are on the precipice of Apple releasing their first watch in 2015, it is time to begin this type of research.

6.2   Leveraging the Crowd

More importantly, once drivers are asked to observe others committing traffic violations, and are engaged in the game they will begin to notice these violations even when they are not playing the game. They will spend more time thinking about the points they could earn in their current drive, then in the activities they would engage in when they arrive at their destination, and they will create a safer environment for pedestrians.

The results of players reporting traffic violations of both cars and pedestrians will be maps tracking various violations around intersections. These maps can then be used to determine issues with various intersections. For example, if cars are running the light, maybe the light isn't long enough, or if pedestrians are walking out in traffic, maybe there isn't enough time or clear visibility of all the traffic. Visits to these intersections combined with the types of reports collected can help shed some light into the urban design of the city.

7   Design Considerations for Wearable Device Applications

In the development of this application the following design considerations were developed.

- Battery Life: This is at a premium on watches. It is important to use as little battery as possible
- Attention: Watch applications can easily take attention from the user. There needs to be special attention paid to not taking too much attention.
- Appropriateness: Applications need to be appropriately scaled for use on small devices
- Distracted Driving: Watch use can also lead to distracted driving. Reducing text can help this.
- Distracting all the time: Watches can also be distracting in other settings.
- Small text on screen: Screens are small. If the text is also small it will be hard to read which can lead to more time spent looking at the watch than needed.
- Social interaction issues: Watches can distract the user and when the user looks at them they will look impatient because of centuries of watch use. This might not however be the case. Only ping the user when necessary.
- Fragmentation: Not all watch apps can run on all watches. With a small install base it is important to cast the widest net possible.
- Nothing complex: No applications should be complex on the watch. Shift complexity to the host device.

8   Conclusions

Most smart watch games are poorly converted Atari 2600 style arcade games, or passive play games similar to Farmville or Cookie Clicker. This will be one of the first games to actually leverage smart watch technology. The data collected can be used to identify problem intersections for both vehicles and pedestrians. Other variations of this game could find other dangerous urban design issues. Possibly more impactful, the same technology could be applied in other fields. For example, soldiers could identify possible IED locations, or crowd source enemy locations and armaments. These watches also include accelerometers; some even include heart rate and other sensors, and can be used as pedometers to track healthy activity in their wearers.

Reference

1. Scramboo. iBeacons, NFC, Augmented Realty, QR Codes – What's best for engaging users? Part 3. Scramboo Blog. http://www.scramboo.com/ibeacons-nfc-augmented-reality-qr-codes-what-is-best-for-engaging-mobile-users-part-3

Virtual Humans as Centaurs: Melding Real and Virtual

William R. Swartout[✉]

USC Institute for Creative Technologies, 12015 Waterfront Drive, Los Angeles,
CA 90094, USA
swartout@ict.usc.edu

Abstract. Centaurs are man-machine teams that can work together on problems and can out-perform, either people or computers working alone in domains as varied as chess-playing and protein folding. But the centaur of Greek mythology was not a team, but rather a hybrid of man and horse with some of the characteristics of each. In this paper, we outline our efforts to build virtual humans, which might be considered hybrid centaurs, combining features of both people and machines. We discuss experimental evidence that shows that these virtual human hybrids can outperform both people and inanimate processes in some tasks such as medical interviewing.

Keywords: Artificial intelligence · Virtual humans · Intelligent agents · Virtual reality · Centaurs

1 Introduction

In computer science, *centaur* has come to refer to human-computer teams that collaborate on tasks and can often out-perform either humans or computers alone. This approach has been used successfully in domains such as chess [1] and protein-folding with the FoldIt system [2]. In the teamed view of centaur, both humans and computers remain distinct, but join together to solve problems. However, if we go back to Greek mythology, a centaur is not a team, but rather a distinct and unique entity that is a hybrid of a man and a horse, blending characteristics of both. If we think of things from that perspective, then we could broaden the notion of centaur in computer science to not only concern the nature of human-computer teams, but also confront what it might be like to create hybrid entities that combine aspects of both people and computers.

2 Virtual Humans as Centaurs

At the USC Institute for Creative Technologies, our work on virtual humans [3, 4] may suggest one possible approach to creating such hybrids. Virtual humans are embodied, autonomous computer agents that look and behave as much as possible like real people. They use verbal and non-verbal communication to interact naturally with real people. They perceive humans using computer vision. They model and exhibit emotions, and represent their own belief, desires and intentions as well as those of others. Studies have

© Springer International Publishing Switzerland 2016
S. Lackey and R. Shumaker (Eds.): VAMR 2016, LNCS 9740, pp. 356–359, 2016.
DOI: 10.1007/978-3-319-39907-2_34

shown that people respond to virtual humans much like real people [5–7]. We have used virtual humans in a variety of roles as role-players in simulations, as guides in educational settings, and as coaches in medical applications.

3   Simsei and MultiSense

Recently, we have seen ways in which a virtual human may outperform either real people or inanimate systems alone. *Simsensei* [8] is a virtual human designed to act like an intake nurse, interviewing patients about PTSD and depression. The Simsensei virtual human, Ellie (shown in Fig. 1), uses language and non-verbal gestures such as head nods, mirroring gestures and body posture to engage and build rapport with the patient. Simsensei uses the MultiSense framework [8] which employs machine learing to form hypotheses about the patient's condition by integrating information from multiple data streams, such as data about the patient's facial expression, body posture and activity, voice prosody and speech content.

Fig. 1. Virtual interviewer Ellie

The MultiSense dashboard, shown in Fig. 2, indicates various inputs that go into MultiSense such as body position, facial tracking, and eye gaze, as well as some of MultiSense's outputs such as levels of body activity and gaze attention.

The hypotheses MultiSense forms about the patient are used to guide the interview and create an assessment about the patient's condition. For example, if the patient seems to be disturbed by a particular question (which might be indicated by agitated body movements) Simsensei will inquire whether talking about the topic makes the patient uncomfortable. Similarly, if MultiSense detects that a patient seems to be avoiding a question (which might be indicated by eye gaze avoidance, among other things) Simsensei will probe deeper.

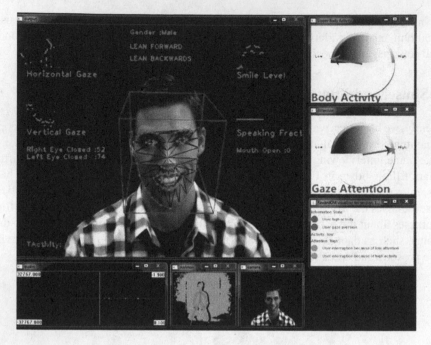

Fig. 2. MultiSense perception dashboard

4   Results and Conclusions

Early on, we found that subjects reported they felt more comfortable and willing to disclose sensitive information to Ellie than to a real human because they did not fear being judged. A follow-up study [9] confirmed this effect: people will disclose more to a computer-based virtual agent. In another study with veterans returning from Afghanistan [10], we found that the soldiers disclosed more symptoms of PTSD and depression to Ellie than they did to a standard paper form, even if the form was anonymous.

Two factors seem to lead to these results. On one hand, people recognize that they are interacting with a computer, which removes the fear of judgment. But on the other hand, the virtual human uses gestures and conversation to build rapport and make the subject more comfortable. Thus, the computer and human aspects of a virtual human work together to produce a better performance than either alone could produce.

Thus, virtual humans may represent a new metaphor for how we interact with computers. At one level, adopting this metaphor means that the human-computer interface disappears because interacting with a computer becomes much like interacting with another person. At a perhaps deeper level adopting this metaphor can bring social elements to the interaction, as outlined above, which has been difficult to do with traditional interfaces. Adding social elements makes it possible to create new kinds of applications addressing new issues.

Acknowledgements. The effort described here is supported by DARPA under contract W911NF-04-D-0005 and the U.S. Army. Any opinion, content or information presented does not necessarily reflect the position or the policy of the United States Government, and no official endorsement should be inferred.

References

1. Cassidy, M.: Centaur Chess Shows Power of Teaming Human and Machine, Huffpost Technology (2015)
2. Khatib, F., et al.: Algorithm discovery by protein folding game players. Proc. Nat. Acad. Sci. **108**(47), 18949–18953 (2011)
3. Swartout, W., et al.: Toward virtual humans. AI Mag. **27**(1), 96 (2006)
4. Swartout, W.: Lessons learned from virtual humans. AI Mag. **31**(1), 9–20 (2010)
5. Reeves, B., Nass, C.: The Media Equation. Cambridge University Press, Cambridge (1996)
6. Krämer, N.C., Tietz, B., Bente, G.: Effects of embodied interface agents and their gestural activity. In: Rist, T., Aylett, R.S., Ballin, D., Rickel, J. (eds.) IVA 2003. LNCS (LNAI), vol. 2792, pp. 292–300. Springer, Heidelberg (2003)
7. Gratch, J., et al.: Can virtual humans be more engaging than real ones? In: 12th International Conference on Human-Computer Interaction, Beijing, China (2007)
8. DeVault, D., et al.: SimSensei Kiosk: a virtual human interviewer for healthcare decision support. In: Proceedings of the 2014 International Conference on Autonomous Agents and Multi-agent Systems. International Foundation for Autonomous Agents and Multiagent Systems (2014)
9. Lucas, G.M., et al.: It's only a computer: virtual humans increase willingness to disclose. Comput. Hum. Behav. **37**, 94–100 (2014)
10. Rizzo, A., et al.: Automatic behavior analysis during a clinical interview with a virtual human. Stud. Healthc. Technol. **220**, 316 (2016). (in press)

VAMR Applications in Aviation, Space and the Military

Mixed Reality Training of Military Tasks: Comparison of Two Approaches Through Reactions from Subject Matter Experts

Roberto Champney[1(✉)], Julie N. Salcedo[1], Stephanie J. Lackey[1], Stephen Serge[2], and Michelle Sinagra[1]

[1] Design Interactive, Inc., Orlando, USA
{roberto,julie.salcedo,stephanie.lackey,
michelle.sinagra}@designinteractive.net
[2] Institute for Simulation and Training,
University of Central Florida, Orlando, USA
sserge@ist.ucf.edu

Abstract. This paper discusses a training-based comparison of two mixed reality military trainers utilizing simulation elements that are categorized on different areas of the virtuality continuum. The comparison encompassed exposing subject matter experts (SMEs) to the training systems. Independent groups of SMEs interacted with each system through conducting expert system evaluations. Independent groups of military officers experienced each system for call for fire/close air support training. Following these exposures, participants were queried on the constructs of simulator sickness, training utility, simulator fidelity, usability, and immersion. The results are contrasted and discussed. The outcomes of this comparison serve to promote discussion among the scientific community concerning the training tradeoffs affected by the virtuality continuum.

Keywords: Augmented reality · Training · Learning · Immersive training · Virtual reality · Wearable technology · Mixed reality · Training systems · Augmented virtuality · Simulation-based training · Joint forward observer · Call for fire · Close air support · Simulator fidelity

1 Introduction

The use of mixed reality in simulation-based training has gained popularity due to its ability to blend real and virtual elements of an experience which may increase the effectiveness of instruction. One particular aspect contributing to the value of mixed reality is its ability to present a compelling contextual experience without the complete artificiality of virtual reality or the risks or costs involved with a completely real experience. Within the realm of mixed reality, there is a continuum of virtuality that ranges from a fully real environment to a completely virtual environment (Milgram et al. 1994). A variety of training systems spanning across the mixed reality spectrum have been prototyped and developed for military fire support task domains including Call for Fire and Close Air Support (CFF/CAS). However, there is presently limited

© Springer International Publishing Switzerland 2016
S. Lackey and R. Shumaker (Eds.): VAMR 2016, LNCS 9740, pp. 363–374, 2016.
DOI: 10.1007/978-3-319-39907-2_35

empirical evidence to inform how much exposure and what type of "reality" or "virtuality" is necessary for training purposes. Current approaches to address this issue primarily focus on optimizing the amount of fidelity (e.g., the amount of realism) in the simulation (e.g., Milham et al. 2008a,b). These methods seek to characterize the necessary sensory, psychological, and functional cues necessary to successfully execute a task in an operational environment in order to prescribe what elements must be provided within a simulation trainer. Given that it is unlikely to replicate 100 % of the cues, one may optimize the amount of fidelity provided based on the criticality of these cues for successful task execution. Even with such methods, decision-makers must determine how to implement the cues and select an appropriate intervention along the virtuality continuum. Stakeholders and decision-makers may weigh risk and cost variables when deciding which elements should be virtual (e.g., military ordnance, aircraft / vehicles, damage), but other aspects may not be as straight forward to decide (e.g., on site location versus virtual location). While the training capabilities of systems may be similar, other aspects of the user experience may be impacted by the approaches taken to provide the simulation. This paper seeks to explore some of these factors by comparing the impressions of subject matter experts after interacting with these systems during operational training exercises.

2 Background

The emergence of virtual reality (VR), and later mixed reality (MR), has sparked the development of a broad range of training systems given its ability to provide a viable pedagogical venue for the training of a variety of domains. In particular there seems to be value in merging elements of the physical real-world environment with virtual computer generated imagery to provide an "authentic" participatory experience which can increase the effectiveness of instruction, while improving trainee attention, engagement, and motivation (Kamarainen et al. 2013); particularly in supporting situated and constructivist learning theories involving authentic inquiry and active observation (Dunleavy and Dede 2014). The current study sought to examine the learning reactions and user experience reactions from subject matter experts (SME) from distinct training approaches to the same operational domain. This study consisted of a formative evaluation of two Call for Fire (CFF)/Close Air Support (CAS) simulators. Model A was a portable-outdoor capability augmented reality (AR) system incorporating a head-mounted video-see through display, accompanying backpack hardware and fully functional simulated Binocular tool. Model B was an augmented virtuality (AV) indoor system incorporating an optical-see through display inside a darkened enclosure and representative props for Binoculars and Compass tools. Both systems utilized a real map, pen and notepad for manual tasks within the training. Of interest in the different approaches was the perceived usability of the systems, the presence and magnitude of any simulation sickness, and the impact on immersion while training with the systems.

2.1   Operational Domain

Ground Warfighters often employ artillery or mortars in support of missions. A CFF is the process by which a request is made to execute an attack on a target (U.S. Army 1991a,b; Stensrund et al. 2013). These requests are usually initiated by an expert Warfighter (e.g., Joint Fires Observer, Forward Observer, Joint Tactical Air Controller) who is the communication link between Warfighters in the field and those providing the attack (e.g., artillery, mortars). This observer is usually located away from the fight but in a position enabling visual access to locate and identify targets and the effects of attacks on those targets. As part of this process the observer must identify, determine the location of the target, and develop an attack plan while exercising careful decision-making given the dynamic nature of the environment and the likelihood of friendly forces nearby. The attack itself is executed through a series of communications between the observer and a Fire Direction Center (FDC). The communications determine the availability of assets to support the requested attack and relay the command to attack to the firing units (e.g., artillery, mortars). Given the complexity and risks involved with the execution of the attacks in this domain, training for CFF is multi-faceted. Traditional training for this domain involves classroom training, followed by practical exercises, simulation and finally live fire exercises to demonstrate proficiency in knowledge and skills (US Army 2013).

2.2   Mixed Reality Continuum

To better understand the differences offered by the two systems evaluated in this study it is necessary to review the continuum of mixed reality. Conceptually one could define mixed reality as a continuum between the real world and a completely virtual world. Milgram and Kishino (1994) proposed such a continuum in their Taxonomy of Mixed Reality Visual Displays (see Fig. 1). While this represented visual displays the same continuum could be utilized to represent the various types of simulator fidelity (physical, functional and psychological). Augmented Reality (AR) which is utilized in Model A lies closer to the real world given the use of superimposed simulation onto a largely real environment. Augmented Virtuality (AV) which is utilized in Model B lies closer to the virtual world given the use of a primarily virtual/synthetic environment augmented by select real elements.

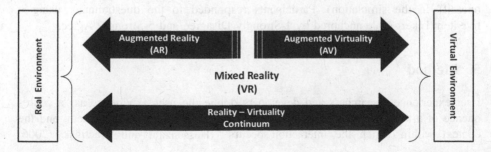

Fig. 1. Taxonomy of mixed reality visual displays (Adapted from Milgram and Kishino 1994)

3 Participants

The study was divided into two separate data collection events-one for each system. For Model A – AR, the participants were comprised of five (5) U.S. Marines with prior training and field experience in the CFF/CAS domain. Participants had an average of 8.15 (SD: 2.36) number of years of military service and reported their current role as Forward Observer, EWS Student, or Joint Tactical Air Controller (JTAC). All participants were male and ranged in age from 24 to 38 years old (M = 31, SD = 6.8).

For Model B – AV, the participants were comprised of three males with prior Reserves training and field experience in the CAS domain. Participants had an average of 10.25 (SD: 2.84) of experience military service and reported their current role as a Joint Terminal Attack Controller (JTAC), Tactical Air Control Party (TACP) specialist, and Forward Air Controller for both the U.S. Marine Corps (USMC) and the U.S. Air Force (USAF). All participants were make and ranged in age from 27–32 years old (M = 29.67; SD = 2.52).

4 Materials

The following tools were used to gather data during the study.

System Usability Scale (SUS): The systems' global usability was evaluated using the SUS (Brooke 1996), a 10-item Likert scale anchored by 1-Strongly Disagree and 5-Strongly Agree (providing a total score ranging from 0–1–00).

Simulator Sickness Questionnaire (SSQ). The SSQ (Kennedy et al. 1993) was used to assess the incidence and severity of adverse symptoms associated with using the training simulation systems. The SSQ consists of a checklist of 16 symptoms, each of which is related in terms of degree of severity (none, slight, moderate, severe), with the highest possible total score (most severe) being 300. A global score reflecting the overall discomfort level known as the Total Severity (TS) score is obtained through a weighted scoring procedure; three subscales representing dimensions of simulator sickness were also calculated (i.e., Nausea [N], Oculomotor Disturbances [O], and Disorientation [D]).

Immersion Questionnaire: A subset of items selected from Jennett et al. (2008) was used to assess the level of cognitive absorption and flow (i.e., the sense of "loosing oneself" in the simulation). Participants responded to the questionnaire using a five-item Likert scale anchored by 1-Strongly Disagree and 5-Strongly Agree.

5 Method

User experience researchers and developers define the user experience as "a consequence of a user's internal state, the characteristics of the designed system, and the context within which the interaction occurs" (Hassenzahl and Tractinsky 2006;

Law et al. 2009). Under this definition, it is recommended that user experience evaluation focus on the impact of the system characteristics and context of the user's psychological state or well-being (Law et al. 2009). In the present evaluation, user experience was evaluated subjectively along several constructs identified to have a potential impact on the effectiveness of simulation-based training platforms including: simulation sickness, usability, and immersion.

The data collection conditions differed slightly across the two systems in order to maintain their operational usecase conditions (i.e., how they would be utilized in a real world application; outdoors versus indoors), yet the methods were kept as similar as possible.

The experimental procedure consisted of pre-exposure, system familiarization, usage, and post-exposure phases. In the pre-exposure phase, participants were provided a brief of the experiment purpose, potential risks and benefits, and experimental tasks. Participants signed the informed consent document if they agreed to participate, and completed the Demographics Questionnaire, as well as a pre-exposure SSQ. Next, in the system familiarization phase, an experimenter assisted the participant with attaching the HMD and then explained the features, tools, and controls to be used during the scenario. The participant was given the opportunity to adjust the HMD for comfort and to gain familiarity with the system's environment and interactions within the system. During the usage phase participants were able to experience a training scenario by observing a target, interacting with simulation tools and observing an attack on a target. Following this, the participant completed the post-exposure questionnaires including: post-exposure SSQ, Subjective Usability Scale, Immersion Measure, and additional questionnaires (these additional questionnaires were varied across the two conditions and thus not included in this manuscript) (Figs. 2 and 3).

Fig. 2. Model A – Augmented Reality (AR) system

Fig. 3. Model B – Augmented Virtuality (AV) system

6 Results and Discussion

6.1 Usability

The SUS was used as a global measure of usability perceived by the participants when interacting with the system. Adequate usability may have training implications as incidences of confusion or frustration with the technology may detract from the learning experience. The results indicated that Model A had an average score of 54 (SD: 17.01) and Model B an average score of 82 (SD: 5) which was significantly higher than Model A. A score of 54 corresponds with an objective measure of "OK" usability (Bangor et al. 2009) and a score of 82 corresponds with "Good-Excellent" usability (see Table 1).

Table 1. Subjective usability scale results

	Model A		Model B		Independent samples T-Test	
	M	SD	M	SD	t	p (2-tailed)
SUS Score	54.00	17.01	82.50	5.00	−2.75	0.033*

Based on responses from the individual questions in the SUS it can be determined that for both Models the detractors from usability were the perceived complexity of setting up the system for use (e.g., "I think I would need the support of a technical person to be able to use this system, Model A M: 2.2, SD: 1.1 and Model B M: 3.67, SD: 0.58, t: −2.48, p: 0.048; and "I need to learn a lot of things before I could get going with this system" Model A M: 1.60, SD: 1.34 and Model B M: 3.00, SD: 0, t: –2.33, p: 0.080). Both systems were prototypes and as such, additional refinement to ensure a high level of usability would be beneficial. Key differences were observed between the two models with regards to specific statements. Specifically, participants believed Model B was significantly more unnecessarily complex than Model A. Yet, participants found Model B (M: 2.6, SD: 0.55) to be better integrated than Model A (M: 4.00, SD, 0.00; t: –5.72, p:0.005) (Table 2).

Table 2. Subjective usability adjective ratings

Adjective	Adjective rating	
	M	SD
Worst Imaginable	12.5	13.1
Awful	20.3	11.3
Poor	35.7	12.6
OK	50.9	13.8
Good	71.4	11.6
Excellent	85.5	10.4
Best Imaginable	90.9	13.4

6.2   Simulator Sickness

Participants interacting with the training systems were assessed for simulator sickness symptoms before and after exposure. It is a common practice in simulator sickness studies to limit exposure to participants demonstrating pre-existing symptoms (i.e., SSQ > 7.48; for example see Champney et al. 2007), however, this was not viable under the current study as it would not be representative of the operational conditions (i.e., Warfighers would need to the utilize the system regardless of any pre-existing discomfort such as fatigue, a headache, etc.). While no participants were excluded from

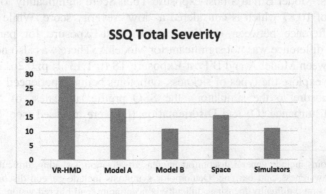

Fig. 4. Simulator sickness results in comparison with other similar VR systems (Stanney et al. 1998).

participation based on their pre exposure SSQ score, the data were analyzed for both participants having an SSQ score of 7.48 or less, and all participants regardless of their pre-existing symptoms (Fig. 4).

Table 3. SSQ total score before and after training

Model	Pre-exposure		Post-exposure		Paired sample T-Test	
	M	SD	M	SD	t	p (one-tailed)
A	10.15	8.00	18.17	15.83	1.1963	0.2547
B	8.00	13.00	10.87	15.74	−3.85	< 0.001*

*p ≤ .025

Table 4. Virtual reality stimulus dose (Source: Stanney et al. 2015)

VR stimulus dose	SSQ percentile	SSQ score
Low	25th	< 15.5
Moderate	50th	< 20.1
Medium	75th	< 27.9
High	95th	< 33.3
Extreme	99th	< 53.1

The amount of time participants were in the training systems ranged from 29 to 45 min. Given that the likelihood and intensity of simulation sickness is influenced by exposure time, the amount of exposure to the simulated environment should be taken into account. Ideally the amount of exposure would not produce problematic simulator sickness (i.e., a SSQ Total Severity [TS] score < 20.1 based on Kennedy et al. 2003; Stanney 2001). The results indicated that Model A showed an average post exposure TS SSQ score of 18.17 (SD = 15.63) which is considered a "moderate" dose spectrum as compared to VR systems (see Table 3) and thus even susceptible individuals would be expected to be able to tolerate a single live fire exercise without problematic simulator sickness. Model B had a post-exposure Total Score significantly lower than 20 with a mean of 10.87 which is considered a "low" severity score. While there was a significant difference between Pre-Exposure to Post-Exposure for participants in Model B, this difference was not significant for Model A. There was also no significant difference between Model A and B Post-Exposure TS (t: 1.1371; p: 0.2611) (Table 4).

To further explore the types of sickness symptoms being experienced immediately following exposure to the simulators, the SSQ profile subscales[1] of Nausea (N), Oculomotor disturbance (O) and Disorientation (D) were assessed (see Table 5). As

---

[1] Nausea symptoms include general discomfort, increased salivation, sweating, difficulty concentrating, stomach awareness, and burping. Oculomotor symptoms include general discomfort, fatigue, headache, eye strain, difficulty focusing, difficulty concentrating, and blurred vision. Disorientation symptoms include difficulty focusing, nausea, fullness of the head, blurred vision, dizziness with eyes open or closed, and vertigo.

shown in Table 5, Model A had an O > N > D SSQ profile. This profile is similar to that observed in other military simulators (O > N > D) and is different from traditional virtual reality profiles (N > O > D) (Kennedy et al. 2003). Model B had a different profile where the Oculomotor subscale had the highest severity score followed by Disorientation and then Nausea. This pattern (O > D > N) is different from other military simulators (O > N > D) and VE profiles (N > O > D) (Kennedy et al. 2003). Given that the oculomotor SSQ subscale score is highest for both systems than those of the Nausea and Disorientation subscales, this indicates that the visual display charac-teristics of Model A and B system may be responsible for the reported sickness symptoms (i.e., headache, difficulty focusing).

Table 5. Simulation sickness profile

Groups	Simulator Profile
Model A	O > N > D
Model B	O > D > N

While the profile patterns were reversed for N and D subscales, it is challenging to determine the implications of the results of these two subscales. This is because Model A is an outdoor system whose N scale symptomology may be influenced by the local climate or location (i.e., sweating, difficulty concentrating) and was likely driven higher by the operational environment (e.g., hot summer day in direct sunlight). Nonetheless, the fact that oculomotor-related symptoms produced the highest subscale results implies that the training system had a greater impact over the operational environment (whether indoors or outdoors).

6.3 Immersion

The results of Immersion assessment showed that in general participants were able to be absorbed by the simulation. This is observed by an average immersion score that is different from the neutral response in the scale (i.e., 3 in a 5 point Likert scale; Model A t: 2.9397, I: 0.0260 and Model B I: 28.9013, p: 0.0001). The results also indicate that the average immersion rating was significantly higher for Model B than for Model A (see Table 6).

Table 6. Immersion rating

	Model A		Model B		Ind. Samples T-Test	
	M	SD	M	SD	t	p (2-tailed)
Immersion	3.40	0.36	4.19	0.27	−2.76	0.04*

7 Discussion

The usability results (e.g., relatively high SUS scores) to indicate generally good acceptance by participants. Model B ratings were higher than those of Model A which may be attributed to what participants observed in terms of technical glitches or complexities experienced while interacting with the system. The fact that Model A is a wearable system makes the nature of the prototype more evident as cables and glitches are more directly experienced by the user. In contrast, Model B seemed more robust and glitches were less apparent to the participant, but could be maintained through the operator/instructor interface (away from the participant). This is evidenced by participants' rating of unnecessary complexity and integration of system functions, in both of which Model B was rated better. Other relatively low ratings seemed to be related to intimidation by the technology. Participants' lowest ratings for both systems were recorded for the question "I think I would need the support of a technical person to be able to use this system". Given that participants did not have to setup or activate the system itself but rather just use the system to execute CFF tasks, it is believed these ratings stem from technical intimidation given the highly technical setup required for use of the systems based on what they observed from the operators.

With regards to Simulator Sickness, both systems rated very well given the amount of severity of the reported symptoms. Both post-exposure average SSQ Total Scores were below the 20.1 threshold for Moderate sickness. Given that the likelihood and intensity of simulation sickness is tied to the amount of exposure (Nelson et al. 2000) it is necessary to ensure that exposure times are related to the expected amount of time in an operational training exercise. The amount of time used in this study was not based on training expectations and thus, care should be taken when making inferences regarding simulation sickness expectations under training conditions. Similarly, care should be taken with participants' after-exposure handling given the unknown timeline of symptom progression. Past studies have found symptoms and after-effects remain for one hour or longer (Champney et al. 2007). In particular oculomotor disruption (e.g., eyestrain, inability to focus) should be further studied given the operational domain under which Warfighters operate and the circumstances in which they depend on visual capabilities to operate safely and effectively.

In general, participants felt more immersed in Model B than in the Model A system. Although the observations taken showed that all participants were able to successfully execute and train on the operational tasks, participants indicated that Model B produced a more immersive experience. These findings are not surprising given the approach used. Model B produced an experience where participants were moderately shielded from the surrounding environment and "transported" to an operational virtual world. In contrast, Model A moderately relied on the real environment onto which virtual content was superimposed through a limited field of view apparatus. The differences between the real and virtual world were much more evident in Model A given this approach where real stimuli (e.g., ordnance, aircraft, people) and events surrounded the participant. For instance, while the visual detail of virtual artifacts in the environment were of high quality they possessed artificial characteristics compared to the real objects. The same could be said of sound and other physical elements of a higher intensity (e.g., real explosive ordnance versus artificial ordnance through wearable speaker). Model B in contrast provided a more isolated experience which may have contributed to the higher level of immersion. During the scenario, the participant interacted with the system within the 7' × 7' × 7' enclosure. Although the participant was separated from the SME instructor/role player by a partition, he still interacted with the SME via two-way radio communication.

Acknowledgements. This material is based upon work supported in part by the Office of Naval Research (ONR) under contract N00014-12-C-0216 and the Army Research Laboratory (ARL) under contract W911QX-13-C-0052. Any opinions, findings and conclusions or recommendations expressed in this material are those of the authors and do not necessarily reflect the views or the endorsement of the ONR or ARL.

References

Bangor, A., Kortum, P., Miller, J.: Determining what individual SUS scores mean: adding an adjective rating scale. J. Usability **4**(3), 114–123 (2009)

Brooke, J.: SUS: a "quick and dirty" usability scale. In: Jordan, P.W., Thomas, B., Weerdmeester, B.A., McClelland, A.L. (eds.) Usability Evaluation in Industry. Taylor and Francis, London (1996)

Champney, R.K., Stanney, K.M., Kennedy, R.S., Hash, P., Malone, L., Compton, D.: Recovery from virtual environment exposure: expected time-course of symptoms and potential readaptation strategies. Hum. Factors **3**(49), 491–506 (2007)

Dunleavy, M., Dede, C.: Augmented reality teaching and learning. In: Spector, J.M., Merrill, M. D., Elen, J., Bishop, M.J. (eds.) The Handbook of Research for Educational Communications and Technology, 4th edn, pp. 735–745. Springer, New York (2014)

Jennett, C., Cox, A.L., Cairns, P., Dhoparee, S., Epps, A., Tijs, T., Walton, A.: Measuring and defining the experience of immersion in games. Int. J. Hum. Comput. Stud. **66**(9), 641–661 (2008)

Johnson, L.,

Kamarainen, A.M., Metcalf, S., Grotzer, T., Browne, A., Mazzuca, D., Tutwiler, M.S., Dede, C.: EcoMOBILE: Integrating augmented reality and probeware with environmental education field trips. Comput. Educ. **68**, 545–556 (2013)

Kennedy, R.S., Lane, N.E., Berbaum, K.S., Lilienthal, M.G.: Simulator sickness questionnaire: an enhanced method for quantifying simulator sickness. Int. J. Aviat. Psychol. **3**(3), 203–220 (1993)

Milgram, P., Kishino, F.: A taxonomy of mixed reality visual displays. IEICE Trans. Inf. Syst. **E77-D**(12), 1321–1329 (1994)

Milgram, P., Takemura, H., Utsumi, A., Kishino, F.: Augmented Reality: A class of displays on the reality-virtuality continuum. In: SPIE 2351 Telemanipulator and Telepresence Technologies, p. 282 (1994)

Nelson, W.T., Roe, M.M., Bolia, R.S., Morley, R.M.: Assessing simulator sickness in a see-through HMD: Effects of time delay, time on task, and task complexity (ADA: 430344). Air Force Research Laboratory, Wright-Patterson Air Force Base (2000)

Milham, L.M., Carroll, M.B., Jones, D.L., Dean, S.E., Chang, D.: Cue fidelity evaluation: a requirements-driven approach to training effectiveness evaluation. In: Proceedings of the Interservice/Industry Training, Simulation, and Education Conference (I/ITSEC) Annual Meeting, Orlando, FL (2008a)

Milham, L.M., Carroll, M.B., Stanney, K.M., Becker, W.: Training requirements analysis. In: Schmorrow, D., Cohn, J., Nicholson, D. (eds.) The Handbook of Virtual Environment Training: Understanding, Predicting and Implementing Effective Training Solutions for Accelerated and Experiential Learning. Ashgate Publishing, Aldershot (2008b)

Stanney, K.M., et al.: Aftereffects and sense of presence in virtual environments: Formulation of a research and development agenda. Int. J. Hum. Comput. Interact. **10**(2), 135–187 (1998). Report sponsored by the Life Sciences Division at NASA Headquarters

Stanney, K.M., Kennedy, R.S., Hale, K.S.: Virtual environment usage protocols. In: Hale, K.S., Stanney, K.M. (eds) Handbook of Virtual Environments: Design, Implementation and Applications, pp. 797–810 (2015)

U.S. Army: FM 6-30: Tactics, Techniques, and Procedures for Observed Fire. Department of the Army, Washington (1991a)

U.S. Army: FM 6-30: Tactics, Techniques, and Procedures for Observed Fire, U.S. Army, Washington (1991b)

Stensrund, B., Fragomeni, G., Garrity, P.: Autonomy requirements for virtual JFO training. Proceedings in Interservice/Industry Training, Simulation and Education Conference, Orlando (2013)

U.S. Army: JCAS Memorandum of Agreement: Joint Fires Observer. U.S. Army, Washington (2013)

Augmented Reality for the US Air Force

Amber Gilbert[(⊠)]

Air Force Research Lab, Materials and Manufacturing Directorate,
Manufacturing and Industrial Technologies Division, Dayton, Ohio, USA
amber.gilbert.1@us.af.mil

Abstract. Increasing weapon system manufacturing complexity, combined with decreasing United States Department of Defense budgets and an aging manufacturing workforce, require a paradigm shift in how the US Air Force provides training and work instructions in manufacturing and maintenance environments. The Air Force Research Lab's Manufacturing and Industrial Technologies group seeks to develop and demonstrate industrial applications leveraging wearable technologies and augmented reality to achieve this shift and enable the Air Force's vision of the "Factory of the Future." This paper will describe the steps already taken and expected future efforts in this area.

Keywords: Augmented reality · Mixed reality · Wearables · US air force · Digital work instructions · Manufacturing

1 Introduction

Performance requirements for US Air Force (USAF) weapon systems increasingly drive needs for higher precision and quality manufacturing on the first build. For example, complex composite aircraft assemblies require meticulous, exact work to meet performance requirements. Emerging complex materials, manufacturing methods, and assembly processes bring increased opportunities for errors on the production floor. These errors necessitate rework, repairs, or sometimes even scrap of the non-conforming materiel. The costs and time involved in correcting errors consume resources that the Air Force cannot afford, particularly as the culture of "doing more with less" continues to grow across the US Department of Defense (DoD) [1].

The Air Force is interested in moving toward production of weapon systems in smaller lot sizes and tailoring each lot to address specific mission requirements, which increases production variability and the need for getting things right on the first try. When building small lot sizes, the production workforce does not have the same opportunity to learn on the job and improve quality with repetition as they do in current production settings where lot sizes include hundreds of the same item. The Air Force and its supporting contractors need to flatten the learning curve so that the quality of the first aircraft is the same as the twentieth. Efficient training and interactive, in-process instructions can help the workforce adapt more quickly to new tasks. As older workers retire, a way is needed to transfer their expertise and guidance more efficiently to a new generation. This is even more important considering that the DoD does not have twenty years to train new workers to the same skill and knowledge levels existing in the

S. Lackey and R. Shumaker (Eds.): VAMR 2016, LNCS 9740, pp. 375–385, 2016.
DOI: 10.1007/978-3-319-39907-2_36

current manufacturing workforce. Younger members of the workforce in particular are accustomed to using electronic devices in everyday life, but when they reach a manufacturing floor, particularly within the defense industrial base, they must rely on antiquated systems—many still paper-based—to obtain necessary training, work instructions, and quality requirements. Even when electronic instructions are available, they are often text-based and include only two-dimensional representations of the parts.

The Air Force Research Lab (AFRL) Manufacturing and Industrial Technologies (AF ManTech) Division seeks to address these and other factors to modernize the Air Force's manufacturing capabilities and processes. Envisioned is a "Factory of the Future" integrating humans and technology on the production floor to enable agile manufacturing and to improve quality, efficiency, and safety [2]. To achieve this vision, AF ManTech strives to invest in emerging and developing state-of-the-art technologies and to incorporate those technologies into USAF operations, both those performed directly by the Air Force and those contracted to supporting companies.

Technologies that show promise for improving manufacturing and maintenance workforce effectiveness include digital work instructions and, in particular, presentation thereof through augmented reality. Major aerospace OEMs such as Airbus and Boeing are investing heavily in augmented/mixed reality (A/MR) solutions, and they are developing rapidly [3, 4].

To gain the maximum advantages of digital work instructions, interactive, context-specific instructions should walk workers through tasks step by step, and feedback should let workers know whether tasks have been accomplished correctly. Task completion information should be collected and returned automatically to factory management and aircraft data repositories as needed to provide actionable, real-time factory awareness and as-built information for individual aircraft. These technologies should be unobtrusive and simple to navigate. An industrial setting for providing digital work instructions provides a particular challenge—but also a ripe opportunity space—for A/MR. The Air Force is beginning to explore this space and seeks to determine what applications of wearable technologies and augmented reality may be best suited for USAF-related manufacturing environments.

2   Augmented Reality for Industrial Settings and the DoD

To clarify further discussions in this paper, a few definitions will be given regarding terms that are often heard in discussions of augmented reality, particularly for industrial environments.

Digital work instructions are simply work instructions which are presented electronically to the worker at their *point of use (POU)* on the production or depot floor. Even a simple move from paper work instructions to a digital representation of the same instructions—same text and images, perhaps with related information appropriately hyperlinked to each other—provides benefits on the shop floor. The paper trail of printed instructions can be greatly reduced, and foot traffic to obtain the instructions may be minimized if the instructions are presented on a portable device.

Using electronic work instructions also helps keep the instructions up to date with engineering changes in real time, reducing rework by ensuring that workers are always utilizing the most recent version.

When 3D image capabilities replace 2D images in electronic work instructions, even greater benefits are seen. Directions may include much clearer visual information, making task completion or component placement more intuitive. Interactivity with the 3D images is particularly helpful, since workers may manipulate the images to gain better understanding of the task. Errors due to complexity of the parts being assembled are thus decreased, and work accomplished shows greater fidelity to the product design [5]. If as-manufactured, as-built data is incorporated, work instructions may even be tailored to be specific to the tail or serial number being produced.

Digital, 3D display of instructions can be improved further by presenting information and instructions to workers through augmented reality. *Augmented reality* (AR, and used interchangeably with the term "*mixed reality*" in this writing) overlays digital information on the real world. This may be achieved through a number of technologies, and a few examples are as follows:

- A tablet that simultaneously uses its camera function to show the user an assembly in front of them while displaying visual and/or audible information about and 3D models of the parts
- A projection system which displays step-by-step work instructions directly onto a fuselage while skin sections are being attached, with color coding for different types of fasteners
- Glasses (or a helmet with a transparent visor) that allow the user to look through them and see both the real world and information that is placed in the user's field of view and related to the objects which the user is seeing

Augmented/mixed reality (A/MR) should not be confused with virtual reality. *Virtual reality* is a fully immersive experience, often achieved by means of a headset which encapsulates the wearer's field of vision [6]. Virtual reality is not seen as a viable option for manufacturing settings. Workers cannot walk around a factory floor while wearing something which impedes their entire field of vision! Needless to say, this would cause an unacceptable safety concern.

Whatever technologies are used, AR combines the physical and digital worlds, endeavoring to use information from the latter to help the user make better sense of the former.

2.1 Initial AFRL Study

To understand the current state of AR for manufacturing, AF ManTech sponsored an industry study [5] which performed the steps described below and was completed in April 2015:

- Reviewed recent literature on augmented reality, especially for industrial applications
- Assessed current and developing state-of-the-art POU technologies by visiting major technology providers (Google, Sony, Epson, etc.)

- Defined the DoD's baseline of needs and capabilities by tours and discussions at multiple DoD locations and industrial base partners (such as Boeing Defense Systems, Lockheed Martin, Oklahoma City Air Logistics Center, Portsmouth Naval Shipyard, and others)

Four major technologies were studied—tablets, projection, glasses, and VR visors. Because of the previously-mentioned safety issues found for VR visors, they will not be discussed further in this paper. The goals of the study were to identify and prioritize manufacturing and sustainment user requirements, common enabling technologies, and technology gaps for production and depot maintenance environments. The study team was comprised of AF ManTech, Universal Technologies Corporation, and Schaefer Marketing Solutions. Their findings formed a discussion (summarized in the following sections) of the advantages of each POU technology studied, challenges observed for industrial A/MR overall, and recommendations for further AF ManTech investments.

2.1.1   Tablets

Tablets have been found to greatly reduce or eliminate paperwork on the shop floor. They deliver more accurate instructions to the worker, since they are kept up-to-date with engineering changes in real time. Additional time savings are seen when workers do not have to wait for lengthy instructions to print on paper. Users gain a better perspective with the ability to manipulate and zoom in and out of images to understand the part or assembly in question. New ideas or best practices are very easy to capture, as well, using a tablet's photography and videography tools; these can then be incorporated into training or instructions as appropriate to transfer skills and knowledge to younger workers. Other advantages noticed through use of tablets during production were (1) immediate documentation of non-conformances, which saved workers' time since they did not have to document it on paper, then wait till the end of their shift to enter it into a computer, and (2) reduced miscommunication that was simply due to poor handwriting!

During the visit to Portsmouth Naval Shipyard, a Navy project was discussed which had investigated tablet usage in ship production at Portsmouth and three other Naval shipyards and maintenance sites. Parallel work was performed with one group using the old paper-based system and the other group utilizing a pilot POU system. The demonstration's extrapolated cost savings were $61M a year by 2018—for a total project cost of $27M. A similar case study by Iowa State University and a major DoD industry partner found an 800% improvement in quality and a 30% productivity improvement. The industry partner was "blown away by the quality improvement," which they considered to be a bigger business case than the cost improvement [5].

Tablet applications for use in industrial settings are fairly mature and were the most widely available of the four technologies studied. Users are often already familiar with tablet usage, as many have their own tablets at home, so that training is easier than with some other technologies.

2.1.2   Projection

Projection has major advantages in that it induces the least burden on IT infrastructure and has gained worker acceptance due to its ease of use. It is scalable from a relatively small area to much larger areas. Since projectors are typically anchored well above the working area, they do not impede movement of people, materiel, and equipment into the work area. Projectors are fairly easy to install, after which they are also low-maintenance; other than the occasional bulb needing to be replaced, they do not require much care. Projection is the most mature technology of the three for industrial settings, but it has limited adoption throughout the DoD thus far, primarily because of lack of awareness.

Previous AF ManTech investment successfully developed a projection application which is currently in use for several different USAF weapon systems [7]. It was developed to assist with composite skin fastener installation. Because of variations in composite skin thicknesses, each fastener hole is measured and the correct fastener grip length for that hole is recorded. Previously, this process was entirely manual; holes were measured with a handheld tool, while the appropriate fastener grip lengths were recorded on sticky notes and masking tape near the holes. The fasteners were then manually selected, prepared, placed in the corresponding holes, and installed. As one might imagine, this was very time-intensive and resulted in numerous incorrectly located fasteners (which then led to rework, repair, or scrap of the affected assemblies). With the new projection system, a wireless grip gun is used to identify and digitally record the fastener sizes needed for the different holes. This information is automatically sent to supply, which creates a fastener kit accordingly. Fastener sizes and locations are projected directly onto the assembly, with color-coding for different fastener sizes. Installation instructions are projected onto the assembly to guide workers step by step through assembly of the different components. One of the Air Force Original Equipment Manufacturers (OEMs) has found several hundred hours of labor reduction per aircraft from using this projection system, as well as an unquantified amount of error reduction and rework, for an estimated total savings of $111M on one weapon system alone (after total development and installation costs around $8M for several weapon system production lines). Further developments of this capability could include job progress tracking and feedback to the user throughout the process.

2.1.3 Glasses

Glasses are seen as the ultimate ideal for manufacturing settings since they provide truly hands-free capability. Because they overlay instructions and 3D models over real objects directly in the user's field of view, the worker does not have to move their line of sight from work in progress to view needed information. They provide the ability to record as well as to transmit, which may be particularly helpful when paired with image recognition to provide job tracking and feedback to the workers on the successful completion of their tasks.

Numerous technology companies are working to develop augmented reality glasses, and this momentum has only increased since AFRL's baseline study. While many of them focus mostly on gaming and home life applications, some are delving into AR glasses for industrial use, as well. Some safety glass and helmet versions [8, 9] are in development, which is especially positive because many manufacturing workers are already required to wear safety glasses and hard hats. Rather than introducing yet another thing for the workers to wear and keep track of during their shift, AR safety glasses would simply provide additional utility for something to which workers are already accustomed.

2.1.4   Challenges

As with most things, these technologies are not perfect, and each has its own unique challenges to overcome for optimal effectiveness on the production line. Tablets are not hands-free, so workers may have difficulty performing their tasks while using one. Many of the electronic work instructions used with tablets are still focused on 2D, text-based instructions, rather than moving to more updated presentations which provide additional benefits. Projection requires a fairly fixed, open space with multiple projectors for each location. It also suffers from line of sight issues, so it does not work well for a dynamic environment or for enclosed spaces. Glasses experience issues with correctly adjusting to the depth of the user's field of vision and fidelity of the data presented. Major concerns are the power requirements and data bandwidth required, as well.

Other challenges are common to all of these digital work instruction technologies. Augmented reality is only as good as the data that drives it. To be of use on a factory floor, good technical data packages and translation to useful information for the worker will be crucial. A healthy connection with the Digital Thread must be arranged so that Point of Use technologies both provide input to and feed from the information contained therein. *Digital Thread* refers to the DoD's goal of modern data management, linking, and analysis to enable informed decision-making with as-manufactured, as-built, as-flown, and as-maintained information for each unique item or aircraft [10]. This is especially difficult for legacy aircraft, which often lack complete technical data packages (deficient or absent process and property definitions, as well as design intent), 3D data, and other important digital information. The DoD struggles to balance modern IT infrastructure with security needs, usually to the detriment of their internet and network capabilities. Between DoD network policies and cybersecurity concerns inherent to live wireless internet connections, security of the data and data feeds will be a large obstacle to work through before implementation of any A/MR solutions in DoD facilities. Ownership of the data being recorded must stay with the DoD and/or its partners, as appropriate, rather than being owned by the technology provider of any augmented reality solution. One final DoD-specific consideration: different processes, needs, and policies amongst the Services (or even at different locations within a single Service) may impede the fullest extent of advancement available through joint problem-solving and technology improvements.

2.1.5   Findings

The initial case study improved AF ManTech's understanding of user requirements and technology gaps across multiple domains. A formal analysis of technological alternatives provided a prioritized list of available technologies and potential solutions. Estimated returns on investment were compared, and ideas were provided for implementation in both production and sustainment environments. An important thing to note is that the breadth of user requirements and operational environments will likely negate a "one size fits all" solution. While technology development will reap greater benefits from multi-organization and -Service cooperation, it is expected that some locations will benefit more from some technologies than others. Also, using different technologies for different personnel or functions at any given location may prove more beneficial than using the same solution for every employee there. For example, inspectors and quality assurance personnel might find tablets to be most useful, while glasses may be ideal for the technicians assembling components.

An interesting finding of the study highlighted when it makes economic sense to implement an augmented reality or POU solution. As can be seen in Fig. 1, the best value of AR seems to be found for tasks of relatively high complexity and high repetition—but not quite so much repetition as to justify automating the task.

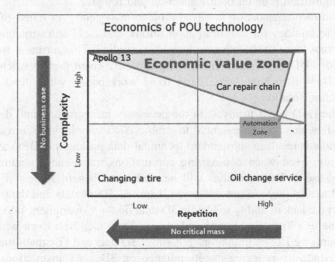

Fig. 1. Economics for POU Technology [5]

Several benefits were found from POU implementation. Work instructions and 3D models were provided to the user at the location of work accomplishment. Users could more easily track their own job progress and identify and fix errors very quickly after they occurred. The paper trail and foot traffic to obtain work instructions was eliminated. Training efforts were eased greatly, and corporate knowledge could be more easily transferred. In addition, as-built, as-manufactured data could then be used to make work instructions individualized to each job or aircraft tail number. An example of when this would be beneficial is during depot maintenance on legacy aircraft; cyclical loading on the aircraft over time may mean its components no longer exactly match the nominal dimensions of their original drawings, or repairs may exist on part of the skin or structure that affect how a worker must access inspection areas. Tailoring a task's instructions to accommodate the actual dimensions of the aircraft components or the repair in place could save time and mistakes due to conflicts between the as-is and as-designed states of the aircraft.

2.1.6   Baseline Study's Recommendations

Several recommendations were made in the final report for this study based on the information learned. The first recommendation was to combine wearable image recognition technology with POU work instructions to improve quality through automated real-time error-proofing. For instance, this would enable continuous, automatic aircraft panel seam inspection throughout assembly and repair. All seams are currently inspected 100 % more than once (between steps and after each assembly). If the seams are found to be out of specification, rework must be accomplished to remedy the issue. With the recommended improvement, however, the computer could scan and record the seams while workers assemble the parts. The system could then alert the workers if pieces are being misassembled. The error could be resolved immediately, rather than disassembling the component to redo several steps upon finding the error later. This would save significant time on both inspection and rework.

The second recommendation involved projection systems. As stated earlier, it is a fairly mature technology for industrial applications, and its IT infrastructure burden is much lower than those of the other technologies studied. This means it might be the best option for DoD depot maintenance applications, given their restricted network capabilities. They often have large, fairly fixed workspaces, which lend themselves well to projection solutions.

Finally, the DoD needs to invest in the necessary infrastructure and data procurement standards which will be essential to enable AR technologies. Current data procurement standards result in substandard technical data packages (TDPs) available for government use, even when considering applications much more mature than AR. Mixed reality use in DoD facilities will be of limited benefit at best if TDP completeness and availability are not addressed. Limited 3D models and data are used in the DoD now; the lack of ability to handle 3D data on the Government side will restrict or preclude the usability of tablets and glasses in DoD facilities. Even without taking AR into account, the DoD's limitations regarding 3D data and IT capabilities must still be addressed. Industry is increasing its reliance on 3D work instructions. Although these are often presented on a computer workstation and driven by nominal CAD model data, rather than being presented at the worker's POU with as-manufactured information, they are still a step in the right direction. Innovation in the DoD will be limited at best if the DoD does not move toward more modern standards regarding TDPs, 3D data, and IT infrastructure and capabilities.

3   Next Steps for Air Force ManTech

After the initial AFRL study, AF ManTech has continued to monitor industrial A/MR technology developments. There is much work being done to improve AR applications for manufacturing and maintenance environments, as well [3, 4, 8, 9, 11–13]. AF ManTech is in the process of defining appropriate AR technology topics on which to focus, selecting specific application areas, and determining demonstration and use case opportunities. Potential interest areas include the following:

- Real-time training during actual task completion
  - On-the-job training—work done during training is part of the production line
  - Increased production with more experienced workers continuing to provide value-added work on production rather than training less experienced personnel
  - Reduction in quality differences from personal learning styles—worker capabilities depend on directly following visual instructions, rather than being dependent on correctly interpreting text instructions and 2D drawings

- Work instructions
  - Quantify benefits of work instruction presentation through POU applications
  - Compare POU benefits to the costs to implement—including installation, training to use the POU technology, preparation of work instruction packages for POU vs. conventional methods
  - Understand maintenance needs for POU tools and the methods and personnel needed to keep them up to date
- Improved tracking and verification of task completion
- Instant communication with SMEs who are not on the production floor or maintenance line
  - Description of non-conformances with actual images (video, photographs, and/or 3D model annotation)
  - Explanation and clarification of instructions
  - Coordination of repair design and installation, even if the user and SME are on opposite sides of the globe
- Business intelligence for factory awareness—more accurate, real-time information for plant management, as well as providing information for value stream analyses and process improvements
- Quality improvement through in-situ quality inspections and immediate notification and resolution of errors

A number of considerations must be addressed during these AF ManTech efforts. For starters, mixed reality development should coincide and have a natural symbiosis with Digital Thread efforts. POU technologies should help populate the Digital Thread with data gathered during task completion, such as job tracking and quality assessment. Conversely, AR technologies will be useless for manufacturing settings without input from a well-constructed, healthy Digital Thread.

Another consideration will be to balance the standardization of AR usage across the DoD with location- and Service-unique requirements. More standardization than is currently in place would likely be beneficial, but a single solution will not address all the needs of every location—at least not without becoming so unwieldy that it ceases to be a solution and turns into a another, more technologically advanced problem. A case in point would be the infamous Expeditionary Combat Support System (ECSS) in which the Air Force spent over a billion dollars attempting to develop an over-arching enterprise resource planning program which ultimately failed [14]. In a related vein, one POU technology will likely not solve every problem on the shop floor; combinations of technologies are expected to provide the eventual solution. To illustrate the advantage of a smartly connected federated system as opposed to having one large system which addresses all information needs, consider the sharing of information amongst smart devices. One might have a smart watch, a cell phone, and a tablet, each of which contains its own version of a particular fitness tracking app. One would not expect the smart watch to perform all the same functions as the tablet—but it does not need to, either. The smart watch unobtrusively tracks the specific fitness items for which it has been programmed, and the information is stored in the cloud. The cloud maintains the authoritative records of the fitness information, but it also disseminates the data to each device with the fitness tracking program and that user's account so that the data on each device is identical. One device may serve better than another for recording that data, while a difference device may serve better for displaying information derived from that data. Finding the combination of AR technologies that works best for all involved parties will present its own challenge, and developers will need to make sure that information is shared easily between different locations and types of technology with minimal human involvement.

While many electronic work instructions are still focused on 2D images and text-based instructions, AR may provide more intuitive ways to communicate directions. The process to assemble components may be made much clearer with 3D animations and step-by-step guides. For instance, IKEA® and LEGO® directions contain very few, if any, words and are on paper rather than being animated, but they are still able to effectively communicate to their users what needs to be done. Of course, any solution(s) must be user-friendly, reduce human error, and maintain end-user safety. Developing these technologies is pointless unless they provide faster, easier production and maintenance and lead to higher asset availability, reliability, and quality.

Finally, while initial demonstrations and use cases are expected to take place in production environments, AF ManTech would like to structure these demonstrations so that they will also provide as much useful information as possible for implementation in sustainment environments. Guiding developments and demonstrations to be scalable from one environment to another may meet with limited success, though, due to the differences in requirements and capabilities already in place.

4 Conclusions

The economic arguments for advancing and adopting Point of Use technologies are clearly favorable. There is still work to be done to improve them, especially for manufacturing settings, but it *is* being done and will become increasingly more widespread in the next several years. This is a vital time for the United States Department of Defense to be involved and to take a leadership position to guide development of these industrial AR solutions. Otherwise, they will not be positioned to take greatest advantage of the benefits these advancements have to offer. Providing safe, working equipment to our warfighters in a timely manner is a worthy goal. Indeed, it is and must be the end goal of any technological improvements brought about through DoD ManTech efforts. Augmented reality can help us achieve it.

References

1. Department of Defense: Better Buying Power. http://bbp.dau.mil/
2. Air Force ManTech—Factory of the Future Vision and Strategic Thrust Plan (presentation) (2012). https://www.dodmantech.com/ManTechPrograms/Files/AirForce/Cleared_Factory_of_the_Future_Dist_A_ITI_Short_Presentation.pdf
3. Airbus Factory of the Future. http://www.airbusgroup.com/int/en/story-overview/factory-of-the-future.html

4. Boeing Says Augmented Reality Can Make Workers Better, Faster. http://recode.net/2015/06/08/boeing-says-augmented-reality-can-make-workers-better-faster/
5. Poindexter, J.W., Schaefer, M.: Manufacturing Technology II (MATES II), Task Order 0010: Point of Use Digital Work Instruction, Requirements Study and Analysis of Alternatives. Technical report, Schaefer Marketing Solutions (2015)
6. McKalin, V.: Tech Times—Augmented Reality vs. Virtual Reality: What are the differences and similarities? (6 April 2015). http://www.techtimes.com/articles/5078/20140406/augmented-reality-vs-virtual-reality-what-are-the-differences-and-similarities.htm
7. US DoD confers 2012 ManTech award on FILLS development team. http://www.compositesworld.com/news/us-dod-confers-2012-mantech-award-on-fills-development-team
8. Epson Moverio BT-2000 safety eyeglasses. http://www.epson.com/cgi-bin/Store/jsp/Landing/moverio-smart-eyewear-bt-300-bt-200-bt-2000.do
9. DAQRI Smart Helmet—the world's first wearable human machine interface. http://industrial.daqri.com/?utm_source=daqri&utm_medium=button&utm_content=nav&utm_campaign=industrial
10. Air Force ManTech—Cradle to Cradle Digital Thread for Manufacturing (presentation). https://www.dodmantech.com/ManTechPrograms/Files/AirForce/Cleared_DT_for_Website.pdf (2014)
11. Digital Manufacturing and Design Innovation Institute. http://dmdii.uilabs.org/
12. NGRAIN: See Beyond Reality. http://www.ngrain.com/products/industrial-applications/
13. Scope Instructional AR. http://www.scopear.com/instructiona-ar
14. The US Air Force Explains Its $1 Billion ECSS Bonfire. http://spectrum.ieee.org/riskfactor/aerospace/military/the-us-air-force-explains-its-billion-ecss-bonfire

Research on the Use of Puppeteering to Improve Realism in Army Simulations and Training Games

Tami Griffith[1], Tabitha Dwyer[2], Corey Kinard[2(✉)],
Jeremy R. Flynn[3], and Vic Kirazian[2]

[1] U.S. Army Research Lab, Human Research & Engineering Directorate,
Advanced Training & Simulation Division, Orlando, USA
tamara.s.griffith.civ@mail.mil
[2] Cole Engineering Services, Inc., Orlando, FL, USA
{tabitha.dwyer,corey.kinard,
vic.kirazian}@cesicorp.com
[3] University of Central Florida, Institute for Simulation and Training,
Orlando, FL, USA
jflynn@ist.ucf.edu

Abstract. Virtual environments are increasingly used to provide training in military applications. These virtual spaces can represent large complex operational environments or simply a simple room. In either case the realism of the interpersonal interactions can be an important factor that influences the trainee's decisions. Interactions may include micro-expressions, small-motor movements, eye movement and voice intonation. This paper describes research conducted by the U.S. Army Research Lab, Human Research & Engineering Directorate, Advanced Training & Simulation Division along with Cole Engineering Services, Inc. and University of Central Florida, Institute for Simulation and Training on the use of tools that allow an individual to take ownership of an avatar in the Unreal 4 game engine. This is being described as puppeteering and is expected to improve realism and engagement. Potential uses for this technology are also described.

Keywords: Puppeteering · Virtual realism · Real-time interactions

1 Introduction

Neil Stevenson's *The Diamond Age: Or, a Young Lady's Illustrated Primer* [1] describes a future where a young girl receives an interactive book capable of providing her vast knowledge. The book provides instruction through allegories and simulations. Unfortunately, not everything can be taught in that way. Some learning must take place through interactions. In the book, interactive movies evolved because artificial intelligence was unable to meet the interactive needs of entertainment. "Ractors" are actors in those movies because they react directly to the participant, creating realistic interpersonal experiences from anywhere in the world. It was through this technology that the young girl continued to gain learning. A common theme in the book is the vast difference

© Springer International Publishing Switzerland 2016
S. Lackey and R. Shumaker (Eds.): VAMR 2016, LNCS 9740, pp. 386–396, 2016.
DOI: 10.1007/978-3-319-39907-2_37

between Artificial Intelligence (AI), which is renamed "pseudo-intelligence" in the book, and human intelligence. Interactive movies are expensive but highly valued because people are willing to pay for human intelligence and can quickly identify pseudo intelligence. The Turing Test – which is used to distinguish human from machine – is alluded to throughout the story. This concept resonated with the teams at the U.S. Army Research Lab, Human Research & Engineering Directorate, Advanced Training & Simulation Division along with Cole Engineering Services, Inc. and University of Central Florida, Institute for Simulation and Training, and drove them to explore ways to improve the realism of human interactions within games and simulations.

Virtual environments are becoming more realistic, with textures and lighting that can make you feel like you're actually in a desert or trudging through a cave. Virtual characters are also increasing in realism. Characters have scars, skin imperfections and asymmetry that makes them relatable. Cut-scenes and pre-canned animations look more life-like. The technology described in this paper explores ways to improve realism when interacting with game or simulated characters.

The team explored various off-the-shelf tools that would allow an individual to take ownership of a virtual character using the Unreal 4 (UE4) game engine. Facial micro-expressions, such as wincing, avoiding eye-contact, frowning or smirking have the potential to be important in deciding how you will respond to an individual. Additionally, gestures such as shrugging, pointing or shifting weight could potentially make a case for an individual's frame of mind or intentions. Having the ability to replicate these movements in real-time can greatly increase the level of realism in a virtual environment. Characters must react realistically to actions or verbalizations of the player character or trainee. This goes far to suspend disbelief and immerse the trainee in the scenario in an evocative way.

This paper will explore the topic of puppeteering in simulated environments. For the purpose of this paper, this includes simulators, games and virtual environments. As such, the term simulation is intended to be inclusive and synonymous with game and virtual environment. The focus of this paper is on the use of puppeteering to support various types of training in virtual environments.

2 The Importance of Realism

2.1 The Role of Fidelity

Fidelity can be described as the level of realism displayed in a simulation [2]. Improved computer graphics cards and processing speed has made it possible to render virtual environments that appear very life-like. However realism still comes at a cost. Creating realistic environments takes a large amount of artist time and building realistic character behaviors takes a great amount of developer time. Increased realism also comes at a higher processing cost. Each effort within a virtual or simulated environment must include a trade-off analysis between the level of realism and performance [3].

Research [4] indicates that greater fidelity is associated with improved engagement and sense of presence. Higher fidelity can influence the extent to which users are able to suspend disbelief that the virtual environment is real and that what happens within it is meaningful with respect to the learning goals of the developer. In fact, research [5] has shown that if the simulation cannot provide the appropriate level of fidelity in relation to real-world cues, the result can influence training by providing negative training transfer or negative training.

Despite arguments supporting the value of higher fidelity environment to support training, there are also training goals that can be met without a high-fidelity simulation. For example, Norman, Dore and Grierson [6] showed that a low-fidelity simulation of heart sounds functioned as well, and in some cases better, than higher cost and higher-fidelity simulators. The important take-away from that research is that "the relationship between simulation fidelity and learning is not unidimensional and linear" [6].

One compelling argument for improved fidelity comes from Vice et al. [7]. The research was focused on the US Marine Corps Combat Hunter training program which is focused on battlefield situational awareness and observation skills. They found that subject matter experts may be proficient at a task, but may not be able to articulate the cues necessary to support decision making. Using eye-tracking, electroencephalogram (EEG), cognitive workload and attention allocation, the researchers were able to explore event-related potentials (ERPs) based on slight variations that occurred, in some cases outside of the participant's awareness. Performance was varied, but higher amplitude ERP waveforms were detected in the virtual condition which indicated higher levels of processing taking place.

Based on the previous discussion, simulation fidelity is important in association with cues that may stimulate action on the part of a simulation, such a defensive driving. However, fidelity should also be considered in association with its role in immersing a trainee in the training scenario, or establishing presence, and the associated level of engagement in the scenario.

2.2   The Role of Presence, Immersion and Engagement

Presence is a concept that can be defined as the "extent to which a person's cognitive and perceptual system are tricked into believing they are somewhere other than their physical location" [8]. Brown & Cairns [9] make the argument that presence is the same as total immersion. They describe examples where gamers create distraction-free environments, low-light and high game-volume, that enable them to suspend disbelief in the game world. Researchers in learning and psychology may consider this state cognitive engagement [10]. Cognitive engagement involves "seeking, interpreting, analyzing and summarizing information, critiquing and reasoning through various opinions and arguments; and making decisions" [11]. Engagement has long been correlated with positive student outcomes [12, 13]. But it is important to ensure that students engage with the learning material rather than the mechanism for providing the learning material [14].

2.3   The Role of Experiential Learning

Simulations allow students to experience situations before being faced with them in the real-world. Learning that is grounded in experience is the concept behind experiential learning. Kolb [15] described how learning transformation takes the form of internal reflection or through active manipulation of the external world. Knowledge gained through experiential learning, and understood at a deep, conceptual level, would be expected to be transferred and generalized more readily [16].

Puppeteering applied to simulated training events provides an opportunity for learners to experience a wide range of experiential training scenarios. Changing the scenario is simply a matter of changing the activities of the puppeteers.

One concern with using puppeteering in simulated training is that live actors increase the support burden of training events. This is an important and valid concern. However, there are live training events that occur in the Army where entire villages of people are paid to support week-long live training activities. Employing puppeteering would allow a much smaller group of actors to support the training. These puppeteers could be anywhere in the world while they support the training events. This greatly reduces the overall support costs of this type of event.

3 Technical Solutions

3.1 Art and Animation

Facial performance motion capture, or "mocap," has been used extensively in both the visual effects and game industries for over a decade. While there are many different types of capture systems, ranging from marker-based to marker-less, most of them do not offer a real-time solution for driving an avatar, or what we're calling "virtual puppeteering." This isn't a shortcoming of the technology; rather, it is a realization that most end-users of facial animation systems are not using the technology in real-time, but applying it to use-cases that allow post-processing. In a traditional production an actor's or actresses' facial performance is captured, then a team of animators will take that raw data and polish it into a believable facial animation to be used in the film or video game [17]. If the capture system offers any real-time capabilities, it generally is used for previewing and not for final animation. The need for real-time tracking narrows the field of software solutions to only a few.

Our chosen development environment is Epic Game's Unreal Engine 4® (UE4). The team conducted market research and found two different facial tracking software systems of varied tracking quality and total cost to the end-user. The two systems used different methods for tracking a target face. One used a depth camera, such as a Kinect 1.0 or a Primesense Carmine, to scan a person's face and track facial expressions. This method required each person to go through a set of 24 calibration expressions before facial tracking could begin. Calibration success was determined by how well the person could make the required expression shapes. The second software solution used a standard off-the-shelf web camera and required no calibration. The actor simply oriented themselves in view of the camera and the system began tracking. It is worth mentioning that in both cases, it was best to have a camera that performed well in low lighting conditions.

Character's faces were animated via morph targets rather than via joint-based deformation. The team created 51 morph targets representing various facial positions during the production of phonemes and facial expressions in a content-creation package such as Maya, which were used to control a character in real-time. This could be accomplished through multiple methods such as modeling the facial expressions by hand or by utilizing scan data and photogrammetry. The 51 morph targets developed, along with neutral expression and 4 eye movements (up, down, left and right), are shown in Fig. 1.

The expressions were imported as morph targets and mapped to the skeletal mesh in UE4 to prepare the assets for the software team. The range of each shape goes from zero to one, with zero being the neutral, default face, and one being the full extent of the expression. Each shape is named in the game engine so they can be referenced and driven by the game code.

Another focus area for the team was to combine real-time face tracking with real-time, full-body motion capture in order to achieve a holistic natural performance. This allows the actor to express emotion through body language, which is critical in a training exercise. We chose a new-to-market, 32-sensor motion capture system to captured full-body motion for a few reasons. The wearable sensors and accompanying software is very low-cost at only $1,500, whereas some of the competitors range up to ten times that amount. This cost makes it possible to field multiple suits if a training exercise requires

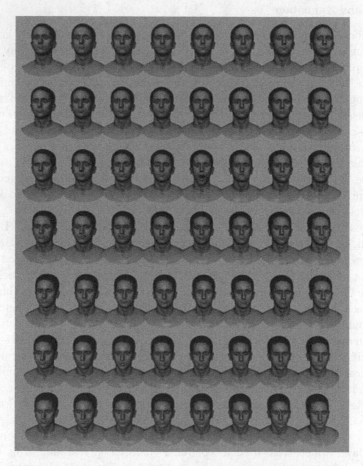

Fig. 1. Morph Targets generated

more than one role-player. The system is marker-less, which means cameras aren't needed to capture the motion. This is important because it allows for more flexibility and portability to the capture process, and you are not limited to a small area to do the performance. The software package already works with the UE4 skeleton for animation. This means when using UE4 to rig characters there is no additional art or animation necessary to apply the technology. Lastly the full body motion capture set captures and streams in real-time, enabling us to send animations to UE4 via community created plugin.

Fig. 2. Wearable markers for full body virtual puppeteering

3.2   Software Development

As the team conducted market research, a clear technical division emerged. It was necessary to combine two separate technical solutions, one for the face and another for the body. With current technology, any real-time facial animation solution needed the camera to be too close to the face to also detect the body, and anything that could handle detailed body movements would not be able to process the facial expressions with high enough fidelity.

First the team focused on facial tracking. The goal was to reach high fidelity facial expressions to improve simulated training for the US Army. After working with several commercial products, it became clear that two of the products allowed us to stream live facial micro-expressions to the gaming engine. As described in the previous section on art and animation, real-time puppeteering in a game engine is an emerging technology. Unfortunately neither real-time facial tracking solution had a direct pipeline for controlling an avatar inside of UE4. The candidate software packages came with network interface specifications and had examples running in Maya, but a native plugin needed to be developed for UE4 to read the network data and drive the facial animations.

Thanks to thorough documentation, the team was able to create a plugin for UE4 within a couple of weeks. The plugin handles the receipt of network packets from the facial tracking software and translates it into data that are usable within the engine. A packet is sent from the tracking software to the engine once per frame. The packet includes an array of values between 0 and 1 for each face shape. It also includes eye rotation information as well as head rotation and translation. The eyes and head are skeletal movements, while the rest are applied to morph targets in the engine [18].

On the UE4 software side, a single idle animation is applied to the puppet avatar. Then a single animation is manipulated by changing each of the over-fifty values of the morph targets and skeletal joints. The frame rate is based on the camera in our case, which captures data at 30 frames per second. Since the morph target values come every frame, there is no interpolation. In each frame, the value (between 0 and 1) of each morph target is set to the value of each of the corresponding morph targets on the character. The correct bones are identified for head and eyes, and the incoming rotation and translation values are used for the animation. The currently playing animation is asked to update every frame, so we essentially create a real-time animation based on human input with nothing more in game than a single idle animation. Figure 3 shows a sample of the 51 data points being displayed on a character at one point in time. Each value is represented by the vertical lines. The teal line that is highlighted shows the brows upper center (BrowsU_C) value as 0.71 (Fig. 4).

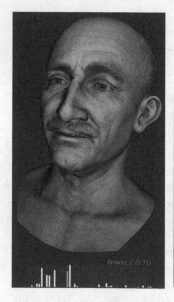
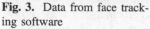

Fig. 3. Data from face tracking software

Fig. 4. Resulting animation within UE4

After implementing the real-time facial puppeteering solution we confirmed our suspicions, that without a moving body the level of immersion and suspension of disbelief was compromised. As a short-term solution we applied pre-defined gesture animations the puppeteer could call upon with on-screen visual cues using a gamepad. This is a similar approach to many commercial video games that allow the player to "emote" using series of predefined animations. Although this may work in a scripted scenario, it was very limited in terms of the number of gestures, it took longer to train the puppeteer, and it didn't look natural.

Using the newly released motion capture sensor set described in the art section, the team took a similar approach to accomplish full body implementation in UE4. The human-worn sensors send their location translation and rotation data across the network each frame. In this case, the data is collected at between 60 to 120 frames per second. The plugin handles the packet consumption and translation into software objects. Once again, a single animation is played on the avatar in-game and manipulated by setting the skeletal bone translations and rotations every frame. This gives the actor natural motions, such as shrugging, pointing, bending over laughing, kicking, or even dancing, and translates it one to one onto the in-game avatar. The display is at 30 frames per second to maintain realism and manage data throughput. The current limitation is a lack of higher level calibration and collision, such as crossing your arms or clapping. These issues may be mitigated in a software update to the motion capture software [19], and may potentially be overcome with an inverse kinematics implementation within UE4. Figure 5 shows the sensor system being applied to the UE4 skeleton system.

The challenge, then, is to bring these technologies together; facial expressions, body motion capture, and game controls to navigate the game environment. The solution must allow the actor to move and talk at the same time, so the camera must

Fig. 5. Real-time motion capture sensor system applied to UE4 skeleton

move with the actor. Various camera mounting strategies are being explored to allow this, such as a chest harness (as seen in Fig. 2) and helmet mount. Navigation is controlled using an analog navigation controller such as the Playstation® Move Navigation Controller (Fig. 6). It is hung at the side of the actor to be grabbed and dropped as needed so as not to interfere with hand and arm motions.

Fig. 6. Playstation® move navigation controller [20]

4 Applications

There are many potential applications for this technology. They fall into two basic, overlapping themes: direct, potentially emotional, interpersonal interactions; and breathing life into a virtual landscape. Interpersonal interactions have been applied to a wide range of leadership training. For example, a simulation can train leaders to recognize the signs of sexual harassment/assault, drug or alcohol abuse or Post-Traumatic Stress Disorder (PTSD), to name a few. In addition, avatars can be controlled through AI within an urban environment. Trainees can approach an AI character sweeping their front porch. A puppeteer takes ownership of that character, so that they are able to engage in a meaningful discussion, answer questions, act as a threat, or request assistance. This mirrors a true tactical environment where anything can happen and the trainee experiences the immediate and long-term consequences of their choices. As soon as the trainee disengages with that character, the AI would take over the behaviors and the puppeteer could step into the role of the next character the trainee encounters. One person could play many roles. This can provide the sense that the town is teeming with life with extremely low costs to support.

There are many more applications, such as PTSD therapy, exposure therapy, entertainment and the list goes on in areas this team has not even considered.

5   Discussion/Conclusions

The real-time connection between facial tracking software and body motion tracking linked to UE4 that is controlled through natural motions by an actor, is now a reality. So, how well does the system work in practice? It functions well, but there is room for improvement. While there is great power in the ability to drive character performance in real-time in a way that is completely unscripted, the downside is that there isn't an artist in the loop to clean up the peculiarities that may appear in the data. Real-time puppeteering can quickly enter the "uncanny valley." The uncanny valley is a theory used in reference to a sense of unease or revulsion caused when a computer-generated figure or humanoid robot bears a near-identical resemblance to a human being, then perceiving an indication that it isn't human [21, 22]. There is little actual data to support the theory, however the idea is widely supported. Virtual puppets that express complex emotions, such as talking and laughing at the same time, can bring about unusual results such as odd mouth shapes and showing far too much of their teeth. The uncanniness can be reduced by either visually stylizing the character or by training the actor on how to keep their performance within behaviors that appear more realistic.

There is a need for realistic human characters in virtual environments for various applications. The focus of this paper is on US Army training, however, the process can be applied to a wide range of uses. The process for integrating various technologies to provide real-time puppeteering have been described along with their strengths and weaknesses. The technology is in its infancy, but the expectation is that, with more investments in virtual and augmented reality, the need for puppeteering technology will increase.

References

1. Stephenson, N.: The Diamond Age: Or, a Young Lady's Illustrated Primer. Bantam Spectra Book, New York (2000)
2. Feinstein, A.H., Cannon, H.M.: Fidelity, verifiability, and validity of simulation: constructs for evaluation. Dev. Bus. Simul. Experiential Learn. **28**, 58–67 (2014)
3. Breslau, L., Estrin, D., Fall, K., Floyd, S., Heidermann, J., Helmy, A.: Advances in network simulation. Computer **33**(5), 59–67 (2000)
4. McMahan, R., Bowman, D., Zielinski, D., Brady, R.B.: Evaluating display fidelity and interaction fidelity in a virtual reality game. IEEE Trans. Vis. Comput. Graph. **18**, 626–633 (2012)
5. Summers, J.E.: Simulation-based military training: an engineering approach to better addressing competing environmental, fiscal and security concerns. J. Wash. Acad. Sci. **98**, 9–22 (2012)
6. Norman, G., Dore, K., Grierson, L.: The minimal relationship between simulation fidelity and transfer of learning. Medical Education, Blackwell Publishing, Ltd (2012)
7. Vice, J., Skinner, A., Berka, C., Reinerman-Jones, L., Barber, D., Pojman, N., Tan, V., Sebrechts, M., Lathan, C.: Use of neurophysiological metrics within a real and virtual perceptual skills task to determine optimal simulation fidelity requirements. In: Shumaker, R. (ed.) Virtual and Mixed Reality, HCII 2011, Part I. LNCS, vol. 6773, pp. 387–399. Springer, Heidelberg (2011)

8. Patrick, E., Cosgrove, D., Slavkovic, A., Rode, J.A., Verratti, T., Chiselko, G.: Using a large projection screen as an alternative to head-mounted displays for virtual environments. In: CHI Letters (2000)
9. Brown, E., Cairns, P.: A Grounded investigation of game immersion. In: CHI 2004 Late Breaking Results, London, UK (2004)
10. Li, M., Jiang, Q., Tan, C.-H., Wei, K.-K.: Enhancing user-game engagement through software gaming elements. J. Manage. Inf. Syst. **30**, 115–150 (2014)
11. Zhu, E.: Interaction and cognitive engagement: An analysis of four asynchronous online discussions. In: Instructional Science, pp. 451–480 (2006)
12. Kuh, G.D., Kinzie, J., Schuh, J.H., Whitt, E.J.: Never let it rest: lessons about student success from high-performing colleges and universities. Change Mag. High. Learn. **37**(4), 44–51 (2005)
13. Pascarella, E.T., Terenzini, P.T.: How College Affects Students: A Third Decade of Research (Volume 2). Jossey-Bass, San Francisco (2005)
14. Ke, F.: A case study of computer gaming for math: Engaged learning from gameplay? Comput. Educ. **51**, 1609–1620 (2008)
15. Kolb, D.A.: Experiential Learning: Experience as the Source of Learning and Development (Second Edition), Upper Saddle River. Pearson Education Inc., NJ (2015)
16. Molanis, C., Burns, D., Assudani, R., Chinta, R.: Assessing experiential learning styles: A methodological reconstruction and validation of the Kolb Learning Style Inventory,". Learning and Individual Differences **23**, 44–52 (2013)
17. Lowther, J., Shene, C.-K.: Rendering + modeling + animation + postprocessing = computer graphics. J. Comput. Small Coll. **16**(1), 20–28 (2000)
18. Faceshift, Interfacing with Other Applications (2014)
19. Perception Neuron, Perception Neuron Axis Forum (2016)
20. Playstation, Playstation Move Navigation Controller (2016)
21. Tinwell, A.: The Uncanny Valley in Games and Animation, pp. 165–170. CRC Press, Boca Raton (2014)
22. Mori, M.: The Uncanny Valley. IEEE **19**(2), 98–100 (2012)
23. Summers, J.E.: Simulation-based military training: an engineering approach to better addressing competing environmental, fiscal and security concerns. J. Wash. Acad. Sci. **98**, 9–22 (2012)
24. McMahan, R.P., Bowman, D.A., Zielinski, D.J., Brady, R.B.: Evaluating display fidelity and interaction fidelity in a virtual reality game. Trans. Vis. Comput. Graph. **18**, 626–633 (2013)

Tasking Teams: Supervisory Control and Task Management of Autonomous Unmanned Systems

Robert S. Gutzwiller[✉] and Douglas S. Lange

Space and Naval Warfare Systems Center Pacific (SPAWAR), San Diego, CA, USA
{robert.s.gutzwiller1,doug.lange}@navy.mil

Abstract. How does one collaborate with and supervise a team? Here, we discuss a novel interface for managing tasks, developed as part of a multi-heterogeneous unmanned systems testbed, that aids cognitive operations and teaming. Existing models of team effectiveness among humans can frame cooperative teaming of computer agents and human supervisors. We use the three main characteristics of the input – process – output model to frame discussions of the task manager interface as a potential teaming facilitator, finding it should facilitate effectiveness on several elements. We conclude with the expectation of examination and support from future experiments.

Keywords: Teams · Autonomous systems · Supervisory control · Task management

1 Introduction

Automation is inherent in the future of unmanned system command and control (C2). Future capabilities may demand an inversion of the human-robot control scheme, where a single person or small team can control vast numbers of unmanned systems. This is the claim of the very near future, according to Defense Department unmanned systems roadmaps and scientific advisory boards [1, 2]. The advent of unmanned systems and advanced algorithmic techniques push human-automation interaction issues into the forefront of the news, and our scientific pursuits.

The increase in complexity required to realize these visions both in the laboratory and in the real world is daunting. While 50 vehicles can be controlled by a single person [3] we are a long way from flexibly intelligent autonomy. Although robots may be useful for dull, dirty and dangerous tasks, they must also become our colleagues, and share in the work as part of a team.

In the past, developers have tried and many times failed to integrate automation and the human. Approaches that focus on machines and their capabilities alone are unlikely to succeed, *unless* they consider the human's role in depth as part of user-centric design. Without it, many have observed conditions where the human does not properly understand what an autonomous agent was doing, or what it would do next. These are problems

This work was prepared by an employee of the United States government as part of the employee's official duties and is not subject to United States copyright. Foreign copyrights may apply.

© Springer International Publishing Switzerland 2016
S. Lackey and R. Shumaker (Eds.): VAMR 2016, LNCS 9740, pp. 397–405, 2016.
DOI: 10.1007/978-3-319-39907-2_38

even with relatively simple automated systems when poorly understood; the problems compound as complex, artificial neuro-evolutionary algorithms are used to determine autonomy behaviors.

The spread of cognitive engineering methods and the results of increased study of humans attempting to operate more complex autonomy [4–7], lend themselves to these team perspectives. Though these levels of interaction have been studied with small teams and within 1:1 human-to-robot ratios, less is known about how to effectively team in a supervisory context (though see [8] on mixed-initiative adaptive systems in search and rescue).

In this paper, we explain our perspective on creating human-autonomy teaming in supervision through a task-manager interface using the Input, Process, Output (IPO) model [11, 12]. The task manager is part of teaming interfaces available within a multiple unmanned system simulation and testbed (IMPACT; see also Lange & Gutzwiller, 2016, this conference). We discuss how this novel task-manager interface could facilitate human-agent teaming and the study of human-automation interaction.

2   Human-Agent Teaming for Task-Centric Operation

The use of a task manager (TM) interface serves as a task-based communication and cooperation point between the human operator and the autonomous agents that IMPACT employs. The TM tracks and organizes the myriad of high-level cognitive tasks a supervisor must manage (see Fig. 1).

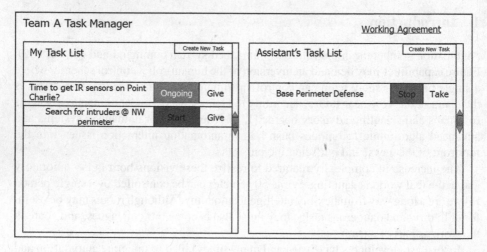

Fig. 1. The conceptual task manager interface. Two columns of "tasks" represent the task queues of the human user (left column) and an autonomous assistant (right column) in this case. Tasks are created by pulling orders from a chat service that picks up orders and critical information.

The TM facilitates task execution by priming and linking to interface elements in the testbed, sometimes pre-configuring them for the particular task when the user starts the task. Users can give and take tasks, allowing for more control of autonomy. Indications for basic task progression (such as *start*; *ongoing*; and *stop*) are included for each task. As we do not presume to capture all possible tasks, the users themselves can also create tasks. Not shown is our approach to prioritize tasks within the queues, which is still under development.

The task manager is thus designed as a cognitive aid to mitigate the known costs to memory for goals resulting from cognitive overload and interruptions [9, 10]. Even without its integration as an aid for managing and collaborating with autonomy, it is likely to provide performance and awareness benefits as situations approach cognitive overload.

The TM is also useful from a teaming perspective, which is the focus here. A standard team model, the Input, Process, and Outcome (IPO) model [11, 12] can be used to understand the factors that influence human team effectiveness. We examined each major attribute of this model in reference to task-based teaming with unmanned systems in mixed-initiative supervision. Whether the TM is likely to improve each element and potential effects or consequences of implementation are discussed.

2.1 Inputs

Input variables influence team interactions as part of the properties of the team, even before work has begun. As related to the IPO model, these are elements such as individual *motivation, expertise*, and team characteristics such as *composition*, and *team mental models*. Because a team in our system is comprised of humans and the autonomy, each has a role in enhancing the ability to engage collaboratively. It is also agreed that trust and transparency influence team properties. The TM may improve upon both of these facets (e.g. [13]).

Motivation reflects the willingness to act and do some task. Most team activity can be broken into tasks. While computer agents do not have traditional motivation, humans may still impute such characteristics [14]. In the current TM interface, the communication of motivation is multifaceted. Presumably, motivation is whether any agent "picks" a task and begins doing it. In our concept, this choice is made far earlier than at the moment of task arrival for the automation. Instead as part of building a team mental model, a working agreement – a set of rules and expectancies that govern which tasks and under what conditions agents take responsibility for task performance – is instantiated. The user can partially dictate motivation through working agreements to restrict conditions when agents will handle tasks. In this view, by default motivation to perform tasks becomes a first-in-first-out method since all motivation appears equal.

Motivation will also factor in for the human component of these team interactions. Humans face a variety of motivational challenges to their work. While we do not aim to explore them all, challenges seem to arise when there is no sense of *accomplishment* or a lack of a clear *goal*. Articulating tasks through the TM interface is one method to motivate operators by improving both of these antecedents. Displaying tasks in a task queue helps identify the work remaining to be done, which may motivate operators to "clear their plate" of items. Displaying task completion may improve the sense of accomplishment (especially if a history of recently completed tasks is provided in the system).

We are also considering a mechanism to display frequently reoccurring tasks, such as perimeter defense and base of operations patrols. These are inactive tasks, but can be populated or primed via the queue so that a user could have more awareness of upcoming tasks and demands. Motivation to "clear" items may increase based on the anticipation of incoming future tasking, and improvement related to clarifying goals and reducing reliance on memory.

The TM could also be an effective mechanism for wrapping mission-essential tasks together. Presumably, one could set a given mission as prioritized for the human or the autonomy, or any combination thereof. Priority, still under exploration in IMPACT, is a piece of motivational teaming. Members must decide and collaborate on how important tasks are as part of distributing the tasks between queues and for each agent within the queue. Priority expression could ultimately reflect the motivation of an autonomous member, as mirrored in the TM interface. Naturally, this changes the prior default of first-in-first-out. Determining which is optimal is a different consideration not yet addressed.

Team composition and agent expertise relates in part to the origin of the team. Often autonomy teams are created in an ad-hoc manner based on asset positioning, capabilities, and strategic relevance. Command and control algorithms may drive the creation of ad-hoc teams. In collaboration, then, the TM may reduce load on the supervisor in creating or sourcing an effective team, allowing them to focus on completing relevant tasks at the proper level of abstraction. In other words, a task may help create a proper team of vehicles.

A task manager should succeed for ad-hoc teams by clearly defining task assignments (e.g., [15]) reducing or removing the ambiguity of responsibility. Though in the current TM we only show one human and one agent queue, it is likely that in the near future there will be many humans, and many agents. Thus considerable composition elements can be integrated, addressing the expected expansion to the number of needed agents and humans.

Team mental models for command and control teams are particularly amenable to task-based representation [16]. Toward that notion, the TM is a good candidate for improving collaboration, as collaboration will naturally take place around tasks. Collaboration requires some shared understanding of information from the environment, along with rationale for interpreting, or acting upon it [17]. Shared understanding or "common ground" [18], is provided through the TM queue view which creates the ability to standardize communication to tasks, via ownership, initiation, progress and completion, can establish some common ground.

No matter what the tasks-based elements allow, trust is a key input to any human-autonomy teaming. Trust can be defined as "the attitude that an agent will help achieve an individual's goals in a situation characterized by uncertainty and vulnerability" [19]. In the context of the task manager, the operator must trust that the autonomous agent will (a) pick up their tasks as established in the working agreement, and (b) can execute them well enough to fulfill mission requirements. Uncertainty arises concerning the tasks population of the queues because not all tasks can be determined *a priori*, leaving the human to identify and perform new ones as they emerge. We assume that the human is more flexible than the autonomy.

Uncertainty is also present in all forms of information from the environment. To the extent that the system is using that information, in this case pulling information from chat to populate a task queue, there will sometimes be mistakes. However, with access to both the task queues and the chat window, an operator should be able to reconcile these immediate differences.

It is important to note that, unlike other efforts on this project, the TM interface does not take the extra steps of expanding on the full reasoning process of an algorithm or agent (but see [20]).

2.2 Processes

Processes, the "P" in the IPO model, refer to the individual and team activities that turn the inputs of the team into outputs. These are facets of teaming like *communication*, *cooperation*, *coordination* of execution and *shared awareness*. The TM could facilitate two types of teaming processes: **taskwork** (the processes and methods for goal-based performance) and **teamwork** (interactions needed between members of a team) [21]. By combating memory failures and attention problems, the TM may enhance human taskwork.

The TM may also enhance teamwork. **Coordination** and **communication** form the core teamwork processes. Coordination is the process of sharing foundational information that guides actions in the team. The process can often be aided with information displays to easily identify agent-task pairs, and timelines for mission execution (see for example the interface in [22]). These help assign roles and identify collaborative points. Since the teaming here is oriented around tasks, the TM is a natural facilitator. Issuing orders through a delegation interface becomes an example of coordination for providing each vehicle in a heterogeneous team with their role and actions toward a higher task. IMPACT is already using a playbook-style interface for unmanned vehicle teams [6]. Sharing expectations and knowledge between agents and the supervisor facilitated by the TM lays a foundation for good coordination [23, 24]. Coordination suffers as communication degrades, because the shared understanding of roles and functions declines [25]. The TM interface may improve coordination with clear task assignment in the queues, and in the formulation of the working agreements that guide action.

Communications, as the second of these teamwork processes, refers to how (and whether) agents share information during team activity. Agents may attempt different methods to share intent, rationale, and information past, present and future [16]. There is an underlying assumption of the ability to formulate a comprehensible statement about each of those aspects. Humans often understand intentions through the observation of activities and make initial sense of communications by understanding others' mental models [26]. In teaming with autonomy in task-centric environments, tasks are within operator view; our queue display and tracking facilitate a small part of the communication process.

Task-centricity allows the human to observe the behavior of the autonomy itself. For example, selecting an ongoing task in the autonomous agents queue could retrieve all of the necessary information it would take a human to perform the task as well, allowing the human to be "on" the loop if they choose. But the same interface provides **shared awareness** of what the human members are doing to the system and the autonomy.

2.3 Output

The final component of the IPO model, Output, is the result and byproduct of team process execution. Outputs are most commonly assessed via performance of the team [16], including quality, quantity, and safety measures. How well the team did at the tasks, how many products were created (and/or the avoidance of critical errors) are typical measures. Note in these assessments, if joint human-autonomy teaming improves, the measurement of output will indicate the improvement.

Outcomes are measures that are easily comparable between the operation of only human or only autonomous agents in isolation and the mix of both. Whether the task manager supports collaboration is very testable as related to mission outputs. Manipulations to elements of the TM that may affect Input and Process can be evaluated against output criteria.

In the iterative, multi-mission domain of unmanned system operations, there will be many opportunities to evaluate use of the TM. And with each evaluation, there is the capability to provide feedback to the autonomy, and to the human agents. Both feed into learning capabilities of each agent. We have incorporated various measures into our plans to learn from operations which rely on use of the TM interface [27]. The TM is important in capturing unique output measures, such as task throughput– the amount of tasks assigned to queues, performance times, and how many are exiting the queue. Throughput may be more operationally relevant than any one tasks success with its elements of quantity and quality.

3 Summary

Task management is a central concern in command and control, as described here. Whereas many previous systems operate with function-centric design, tasks align agents both human and computer toward understandable discrete pieces of overall mission performance. The TM interface tracks and provides the necessary controls to delegate responsibility between multiple agents performing tasks.

A task-centric conceptualization has been promoted for unmanned system C2 [28], and we take this basic notion and apply it within task management. However, we also conceptualize an autonomous agent that manages these tasks and chooses, within the constraints of working agreements, how and who should execute. The management interface itself serves as a team-collaboration tracking tool, in which the interplay between humans and the system is visible, grounded in tasks that matter to mission viability, and provides agents with useful information about each other. We used the IPO framework to outline the applications through input, process, and outputs. In each aspect of team effectiveness, expected benefits were outlined for the TM.

Motivation is not a standard aspect of an autonomous systems design. Here it was linked with task responsibility and prioritization, two key components of system performance. By providing a manager for tasks, clearly displayed attributes are communicated between agents. The mechanisms of the TM using queues and tasks also should reduce or remove ambiguity in assignments, a problem for ad-hoc teams and a method for improving team mental models.

We expect the TM to improve the taskwork of the human members of a team by reducing the cost of memory failures and interruption. However, is also helps display the behavior of the autonomous agent in terms of tasks, improving the communication process.

In summary, we believe that team methods can be applied to supervisory control and aided by a task management interface which integrates human performance knowledge in this domain (e.g., [27]). We also note a similar effort to develop templates for teaming (Lange & Gutzwiller, HCII 2016) providing useful "plans" for when certain team configurations and communication patterns may be needed. We will be exploring how to develop these plans within the context of the task management system used here.

We believe the next logical step is to demonstrate experimentally how the task manager supports cognition, human automation interaction and in general, human-automation teaming. Our plans include investigations of each of the major areas of potential benefit outlined here as part of the IMPACT project.

Acknowledgements. This work was supported by the Space and Naval Warfare Systems Center Pacific *Naval Innovative Science and Engineering* Program. The US Department of Defense Autonomy Research Pilot Initiative under the project entitled "Realizing Autonomy via Intelligent Adaptive Hybrid Control" also supported this work.

This manuscript is submitted with the understanding that it is the work of a U.S. government employee done as part of his/her official duties and may not be copyrighted. We request that the publication of this work include a notice to this effect.

References

1. DoD, Unmanned Systems Integrated Roadmap FY2013-2038 (2013)
2. Department of Defense Science Board, "The role of autonomy in DoD systems", Off. Undersecretary Def. Acquis. Technol. Logist., July 2012
3. Bishop, R.: Record-breaking drone swarm sees 50 UAVs controlled by a single person, Popular Mechanics, p. 2 (2015)
4. Squire, P.N., Parasuraman, R.: Effects of automation and task load on task switching during human supervision of multiple semi-autonomous robots in a dynamic environment. Ergonomics 53(8), 951–961 (2010)
5. Ruff, H.A., Calhoun, G., Draper, M., Fontejon, J.V., Guilfoos, B.J.: Exploring automation issues in supervisory control of multiple UAVs. In: Proceedings of Human Performance, Situation Awareness, Automaion Technology Conference, pp. 218–222 (2004)
6. Miller, C.A., Parasuraman, R.: Designing for flexible interaction between humans and automation: delegation interfaces for supervisory control. Hum. Factors 49(1), 57–75 (2007)
7. Chen, J.Y.C., Barnes, M.J.: Human–agent teaming for multirobot control: a review of human factors issues. IEEE Trans. Hum. Mach. Syst. 44(1), 13–29 (2014)

8. Hardin, B., Goodrich, M.: On using mixed-initiative control: a perspective for managing large-scale robotic teams. In: Proceedings of ACM/IEEE International Conference on Human Robot Interaction, pp. 165–172 (2009)
9. Dismukes, R.: Remembrance of things future: prospective memory in laboratory, workplace, and everyday settings. Rev. Hum. factors Ergon. **6**, 1–86 (2010)
10. Altmann, E.M., Trafton, J.G., Hambrick, D.Z.: Momentary interruptions can derail the train of thought. J. Exp. Psychol. Gen. **142**(1), 1–12 (2013)
11. Ilgen, D.R., Hollenbeck, J.R., Johnson, M., Jundt, D.: Teams in organizations: from input-process-output models to IMOI models. Annu. Rev. Psychol. **56**, 517–543 (2005)
12. Mathieu, J.E., Maynard, M.T., Rapp, T., Gilson, L.: Team effectiveness 1997–2007: a review of recent advancements and a glimpse into the future. J. Manage. **34**(3), 410–476 (2008)
13. Chen, J.Y.C., Procci, K., Boyce, M., Wright, J., Garcia, A., Barnes, M.: Situation awareness–based agent transparency, ARL Technical report 6905 (2014)
14. Waytz, A., Cacioppo, J., Epley, N.: Who sees human?: the stability and importance of individual differences in anthropomorphism. Perspect. Psychol. Sci. **5**(3), 219–232 (2010)
15. Kolbe, M., Künzle, B., Enikö, Z., Wacker, J., Grote, G.: Measuring coordination behaviour in anaesthesia teams during induction of general anaesthetics. In: Flin, R., Mitchell, L. (eds.) Safer Surgery: Analysing Behaviour in the Operating Theatre, pp. 203–221. Ashgate Publishing Ltd., Aldershot (2009)
16. Burtscher, M.J., Manser, T.: Team mental models and their potential to improve teamwork and safety: a review and implications for future research in healthcare. Saf. Sci. **50**(5), 1344–1354 (2012)
17. Malin, J.T., Schreckenghost, D.L., Woods, D.D., Potter, S.S., Johannesen, L., Holloway, M., Forbus, K.D.: Making intelligent systems team players: Case studies and design issues. volume 1: human-computer interaction design. NASA Technol. Memo. **104738**, 1–276 (1991)
18. Klein, G., Bradshaw, J.M., Feltovich, J.M., Woods, D.D.: Common ground and coordination in joint activity. In: Rouse, W.B., Boff, K.R. (eds.) Organizational Simulation, pp. 139–184. John Wiley & Sons, New York (2005)
19. Lee, J.D., See, K.A.: Trust in automation: Designing for appropriate reliance. Hum. Factors **46**(1), 50–80 (2004)
20. Chen, J.Y.C., Barnes, M.J.: Agent transparency for human-agent teaming effectiveness. In: IEEE International Conference on System Man and Cybernetics, pp. 1381–1385 (2015)
21. McIntyre, R., Salas, E.: Measuring and managing for team performance: emerging principles from complex environments. In: Guzzo, R., Salas, E. (eds.) Team Effectiveness and Decision Making in Organizations, pp. 9–45. Jossey-Bass, San Francisco (1995)
22. Cummings, M.L., How, J., Whitten, A., Toupet, O.: The impact of human-automation collaboration in decentralized multiple unmanned vehicle control. In: Proceedings of IEEE (2011)
23. Patterson, E.S., Watts-Perotti, J., Woods, D.D.: Voice loops as coordination aids in space shuttle mission control. Comput. Support. Coop. Work **8**(4), 353–371 (1999)
24. Schuster, D., Ososky, S., Phillips, E., Lebiere, C., Evans, A.W.: A research approach to shared mental models and situation assessment in future robot teams. In: Proceedings of the Human Factors and Ergonomics Society Annual Meeting, pp. 456–460 (2011)
25. Fiore, S.M., Jentsch, F., Becerra-fernandez, I., Salas, E., Finkelstein, N.: Integrating field data with laboratory training research to improve the understanding of expert human-agent teamwork. In: Proceedings of Hawaii International Conference on System Science, pp. 1–10 (2005)

26. Klein, G.: Streetlights and Shadows: Searching for the Keys to Adaptive Decision Making. MIT Press, Cambridge (2009)
27. Gutzwiller, R.S., Lange, D.S., Reeder, J., Morris, R.L., Rodas, O.: Human-computer collaboration in adaptive supervisory control and function allocation of autonomous system teams. In: Shumaker, R., Lackey, S. (eds.) VAMR 2015. LNCS, vol. 9179, pp. 447–456. Springer, Heidelberg (2015)
28. Cummings, M., Bertucelli, L., Macbeth, J., Surana, A.: Task versus vehicle-based control paradigms in multiple unmanned vehicle supervision by a single operator. IEEE Trans. Hum. Mach. Syst. 44(3), 353–361 (2014)

From Inter*face* to Inter*space* Conceptual Framework for Multimodal Flight Deck Controls

Daniela Kratchounova[✉]

Flight Deck Human Factors Research Laboratory, Civil Aerospace Medical Institute,
Federal Aviation Administration, 6500 S. MacArthur Blvd., Oklahoma City,
OK 73169, USA
Daniela.Kratchounova@faa.gov

Abstract. Pilots' awareness of the flight deck as a shared space is intrinsic and they interact with each other freely and naturally in it. However, these pilot-to-pilot interactions bear little resemblance to the pilot-aircraft interactions which are constrained within instrument panel areas where the majority of pilot interfaces currently reside. The inherent spatial characteristics of the flight deck afford the notion of an interspace. The interspace can be an environment where: (a) the pilots interact with technology in a multimodal fashion such that the actions in one modality complement, and collaborate the input from the others, producing a well-choreographed user experience; and (b) the spatial organization, temporal synchronization, and semantic collaboration of control input devices reflect the integration patterns characterizing people's use of different modalities. Thus, the key to an effective design paradigm shift is contingent on successfully emulating these naturally occurring modality communication and cooperation patterns within the intended interspace.

Keywords: Multimodal input controls · Flight deck human factors · Flight crew interface

1 Introduction

In recent years, multimodal systems have gained considerable interest, and research in this area is expanding rapidly. Most research in the area of human-computer interaction has treated system input and output as separate domains. As a result of this division, two major groups of interfaces have emerged: multimodal input (e.g., touch, gestures, voice, and conventional input devices) and multimedia output (e.g., computer-based interactive audio-video presentations) [1, 6]. Furthermore, a knowledge gap still exists between the domain of system output research (i.e., users' performance with multimedia presentations) and user performance research with multimodal input devices in the context of human–computer interaction [18]. Specifically, while conventional input devices are ubiquitous, familiar, and well established, they can quickly become an interaction

The rights of this work are transferred to the extent transferable according to title 17 U.S.C. 105.

© Springer International Publishing Switzerland 2016
S. Lackey and R. Shumaker (Eds.): VAMR 2016, LNCS 9740, pp. 406–415, 2016.
DOI: 10.1007/978-3-319-39907-2_39

impediment, especially when users need to interact with environments rich in sophisticated multimedia output. Therefore, to successfully integrate multimodal control input devices into a complete and well-balanced system (i.e., equivalent input–output capabilities), a clearly-defined conceptual framework is required. The intent behind the framework presented here is twofold. First, a conceptual framework is essential to identifying the theoretical constructs that could provide an insight into the natural integration patterns characterizing people's use of different input modalities. Second, such a framework is also critical to identifying the means of successfully engineering these patterns into a system.

Pilots' awareness of the flight deck as an interaction *space* is intrinsic. However, the pilot-aircraft interaction flow, especially with respect to aircraft system control inputs, consists of series of unintuitive, discrete actions pilots need to perform using conventional physical controls (e.g., knobs, buttons, and cursor control devices). This applies to even the most sophisticated flight decks to date. Furthermore, these pilot-aircraft control input interactions are also very much constrained within numerous "flat" surface areas in the flight deck where the majority of pilot interfaces are currently located (e.g., instrument panels, displays, side consoles, and overhead panels). However, the inherent *spatial* characteristics of this interaction environment support the notion of expanding the inter*face* to what could effectively become one continuous interaction space—a virtual, multilayered "bubble"—an inter*space*. In the most general sense, the inter*space* can be an environment where people interact with technology freely and naturally in a multimodal fashion so that the actions in one modality complement, collaborate, and corroborate the input from the others, producing a well-choreographed and more organic user experience. Furthermore, the inter*space* can be an environment that is flexible, where an optimal blend of cooperating modalities can be used to overcome the weaknesses and capitalize upon the strengths of each individual modality. Hence, the key to an effective paradigm shift in designing multimodal control systems is contingent on the successful integration of the naturally occurring modality communication and cooperation patterns [14] within the intended inter*space*.

2   Background

The need to optimize pilot-aircraft interactions motivated the aviation research community to focus on researching new and novel control input technologies [10, 16, 19]. For example, Leger [10] identified a need for alternative control input technologies (e.g., voice, gaze, gesture controls) as these improvements would allow the integration of more features into aircraft while the pilots need to keep eyes focused on flying remains high. He further highlighted multimodal integration of two or more of these novel technologies as a method that would allow the user to operate the system under natural logic (as opposed to system-imposed logic). Implementing modality redundancy and complementarity would reduce the risk of error due to short-term memory failure and would also simplify the flight deck layout. This would offer more space for displays and important information. Finally, the author concluded that capitalizing on multimodal interactions with aircraft systems may require less training than complex conventional physical input devices.

Merchant and Schnell [16] reported on the development of a simulator that combined voice and gaze control. This combined approach was selected in order to overcome some of the limitations of gaze control and voice control when either method was used alone. Combining the two modalities was deemed by the researchers as the most appropriate way to alleviate the limitations of each individual modality.

Rood [19] introduced some general considerations related to the integration of alternative control technologies into flight decks from both a human factors and an engineering perspective. The author purported that from a human factors perspective, it was important to avoid a bottleneck to ensure that the potential for human input and system capability was not hindered by the interface. Alternative control technologies could reduce this bottleneck. Rood [19] also identified important recommendations for designing a multimodal interface such as task modeling, prototyping, context of task, and task loading, with modeling error and error correction being especially important.

Furthermore, considerable research has been conducted in the aviation domain regarding speech recognition and voice control: touch screens, touchless gesture recognizers and controllers, and eye tracking and gaze control systems [4, 5, 7, 13]. However, no unifying conceptual framework exists for the synergistic integration of conventional [2] and nonconventional [15] control input modalities into the flight deck. The conceptual framework outlined in this paper is inspired by four theoretical constructs:

- Communication [20],
- Complementarity of people and technology [11],
- Distributed cognition [8, 9], and
- Modality cooperation [14].

Furthermore, this framework is motivated in part by the recent significant maturation of control input technologies including touch screens, voice recognition, eye tracking, and touchless gesture recognition, among others.

3   Communication

The most well-known and influential model of communication [20] consists of five basic elements: an information source, a transmitter, a channel, a receiver, and a destination. The model also includes a sixth element— noise— a factor that may lead to the signal received being different from the one sent. Shannon and Weaver's [20] seminal work led to very valuable research on redundancy in language and in making information measurable. It also gave birth to the mathematical study of information theory. The model may seem more information-centered than meaning-centered. However, the opening paragraph of Weaver's introduction essay, "The Mathematical Theory of Communication," suggests a very broad application of the fundamental principles of communication theory [20]. Namely, communication is described to include all of the ways by which one mind may affect another. This includes not only written and oral speech, but all human behavior. Yet a broader definition of communication also includes the means by which one mechanism affects another. Additionally, Shannon and Weaver [20] defined the following terms:

- Information entropy as the measure for the uncertainty in a message,
- Redundancy as the degree to which information is not unique in the system,
- Noise as the measure of information not related to the message, and
- Channel capacity as the measure of the maximum amount of information a channel could carry.

They also addressed three main challenges to communication:

- Technical: how accurately a message can be transmitted,
- Semantic: how precisely the desired meaning is conveyed, and
- Effectiveness: how the conveyed meaning affects behavior in a predictable way.

In the context of this framework, the meaning of the sixth element (noise) of Shannon and Weaver's [20] model is expanded to include all the factors that affect the received signal and make it different from the one sent. That is, all the factors (e.g., context) that implicitly modify the message and reduce the information entropy, as well as those factors (e.g., noise) that explicitly increase the information entropy in a message, are also included.

In summary, the first theoretical construct of this conceptual framework encompasses the broadest view of communications, which entails all the means by which people and technologies interact. While communication theory is the most theoretical of all the four elements considered, it establishes the outermost boundaries of the conceptual framework. Its applicability to (a) identifying the natural communication patterns that characterize flight crews' interactions with technology on the flight deck, and (b) successfully engineering those interactions into a system by emulating their temporal, spatial, and semantic features becomes more distinct with the introduction of the rest of the framework elements.

4   Complementarity of People and Technology

Jordan [11] postulated that people and technology are not comparable but instead complementary, and that because they possess different capabilities, limitations, strengths, and weaknesses in order to successfully accomplish a task, people and technology require mutual dependency. Jordan identified several basic guidelines for implementing complementarity. One is that technology serves people in two ways: as tools and as production machines. The key notion behind complementarity of tools is that people perform best under conditions of optimum difficulty (i.e., if the job is too easy people get bored, and if the job is too hard they get fatigued). Therefore, tools should be used to bring the perceptual, cognitive, and motor requirements of a task to the optimal levels for human performance. The author reiterated that it is in managing contingencies that people are irreplaceable by technology, and that people degrade gracefully, whereas machines can either do the job or they fail. Jordan [11] challenged the human factors engineering community to develop systems where the motivation for the human element is embedded within the task itself. That is, unless there is a challenge to the human operators in every task, activity, and responsibility assigned to them, they will not complement the machines. They will quickly realize that they are used unproductively and will resist and rebel against it. Nothing could be more wasteful than developing systems that cause the human elements to rebel against the system. Consequently, in the context of a flight deck, if safety and efficiency of flight are to be maximized, the focus must be on ways to develop and support the complementary nature of the flight crew and flight deck systems, especially controls.

In summary, the value of Jordan's work to this conceptual framework is in its positive affirmation that control functions, or functions in general, are not to be allocated to either humans or technology [11]. Rather, the interactions of humans and technology are to be carefully tailored, taking into account the mutual dependencies between task components and the ways they are performed by humans and technology.

5 Distributed Cognition

The original theory of distributed cognition was developed by Hutchins [8] and further advanced by Hutchins and Klausen [9]. The notion that cognition is fundamentally distributed is the underpinning of the theory, and its unit of analysis is a functional group rather than an individual mind. This unit of analysis was termed "a system of distributed cognition" [9]. Specifically, to provide an insight to the performance of the flight deck as a system, the authors discussed a much larger unit of cognitive analysis that included both the crew and the information environment (e.g., aircraft systems, voice communications with air traffic control and between air traffic control and other aircraft in the vicinity). This approach afforded a more thorough description of the cognitive processes by tracing the movement of information through the system and the mechanisms that carry out performance, both of the individual and of the system as a whole. The analyses revealed a pattern of cooperation and coordination of actions among crew members which, on one level, could be seen as a structure for propagating and processing information within the crew, and on another, as a system in which shared cognition evolved as a system-level property. The relationship between the cognitive properties of the system, as determined by the movement of representations and the cognitive properties of the individual components, identified a set of possible pathways for information to take through the system. Some of the observed pathways were anticipated by the design while others not intended in the design were, nonetheless, contributing to its performance characteristics. Pathways deemed redundant contributed to the higher of robustness of the system.

In summary, according to Hutchins and Klausen [9], the system's cognitive properties are determined in part by:

- The cognitive properties of the individual pilots,
- The properties of the representational structures through which a task relevant representational state was transmitted,
- The specific organization of the representations supported in those structures,

- The interactions of the higher level representations held by the members of the crew, and
- The shared characteristics of knowledge and access to task relevant information between the crew members.

In the context of this conceptual framework, the central theme of distributed cognition theory (i.e., the rejection of the traditional assumption that cognitive processes were limited to the internal mental states of an individual) offers a more holistic view of cognitive processes on a flight deck. Specifically, these processes are not only distributed across individual crew members engaged in collaborative tasks, but also between the crew and the artifacts they employ, and between the crew and the features of the environment surrounding them. The distributed cognition approach aims to demonstrate how intelligent processes in human activity surpass the boundaries of the individual. They transcend into the realm of multiple human contributors using multiple modalities to interact with each other and with multiple technological devices in order to reduce the information entropy. This, in turn, enables them to cooperate and ultimately complete a given task successfully.

6 Modality Cooperation

Martin, Veldman, and Béroule's [14] theoretical framework was premised on a question regarding the appropriateness of using multimodality. They suggested that multimodality should be used only if it helped achieve usability criteria including (a) fast interaction; (b) robustness to system recognition errors, unexpected events, and user errors; (c) intuitiveness; (d) ease of linking presented information to more inclusive contextual knowledge; and (e) good transfer of information from one modality to another. To accomplish this, Martin et al. proposed six basic types of cooperation between modalities:

- Equivalence: information is processed by any available modality best suited at that moment for a specific task;
- Specialization: specific kind of information is always processed by the same modality;
- Redundancy: the same information is processed by all modalities;
- Complementarity: different chunks of information are processed by different modalities and then merged;
- Transfer: information is produced by one modality and used by another (e.g., transfer between two input modalities, two output modalities, or an input and an output modality); and
- Concurrency: different chunks of information are processed by several modalities at the same time but not merged (parallel use of several modalities).

In summary, Martin, Veldman, and Béroule [14] identified the usability goals of multimodal systems and further elaborated on how six basic types of modality cooperation could be used to best meet those goals. Here, the understanding of how to combine modalities and why a specific combination of modalities may improve the pilot–aircraft interactions is vital for the successful integration of multimodal control input devices into the flight deck.

7 Synthesis

The theoretical constructs that can provide an insight into the natural integration patterns characterizing people's use of different input modalities and help recognize the means of successfully engineering these patterns into an inter*space* system described so far are:

- Communication as defined by Shannon and Weaver [20];
- Complementarity of people and technology as recommended by Jordan [11];
- Distributed cognition as defined by Hutchins [8]; and
- Modality cooperation as proposed by Martin, Veldman, and Béroule [14].

These components echo one shared notion. That is, in today's information society people interact with and through technology; and therefore people and technology can be seen as the elements of one entity (e.g., a system). These elements continuously communicate and cooperate throughout the lifecycle of the system. Cooperation requires communication in order to successfully exchange information and to show and interpret the intent of present and future actions. Communication also requires cooperation in order to ensure a successful outcome. This includes integration of shared knowledge coming through the different communication channels and from all of the distributed elements of the system. However, successful continuous communication and cooperation within a system is a multifaceted phenomenon that depends on how prudently the results from the research into the natural temporal synchronization, spatial organization, and semantic cooperation between those elements are reflected in the design process.

One system that could benefit from optimizing the temporal, spatial, and semantic facets of the interactions within it is the flight deck. For example, in establishing the spatial aspects of the inter*space*, several interaction strata, or zones, could be defined within the inter*space* by using an approach similar to the creation of reach isorating surfaces[1] [21]. Reed et al.'s integrated approach to measuring and modeling reach difficulty and capability was based on the assumption that maximum reach is a probabilistic concept and should be modeled as such and that a maximum reach is a maximum difficulty reach. Figure 1 provides a notional illustration of a crew inter*space*[2] including:

- Inner inter*space* stratum: pilot's immediate surroundings that are within easy reach without torso movement (e.g., location of physical controls–control yoke, side stick);
- Intermediate inter*space* stratum: the zone with medium to high difficulty reach without torso movement (e.g., location of heads-down visual displays, instrument panels); and

---

[1] Surfaces with uniform reach difficulty rating level.
[2] Centered at the left seat pilot to minimize clutter

- Outer inter*space* stratum: the area confined by the perimeter of the physical flight deck enclosure that is not reachable without torso movement or reachable with higher degree of difficulty and with torso movement (e.g., windshield).

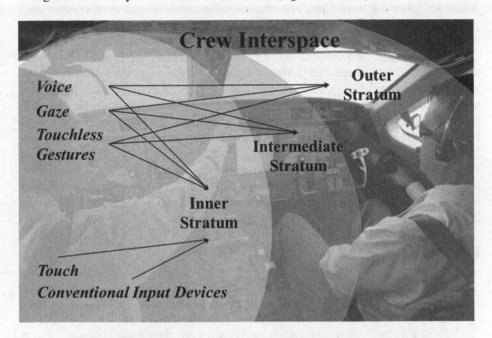

Fig. 1. Notional control input modality allocation into the crew inter*space*

Furthermore, a set of control input modalities is "mapped" to each stratum as a hypothetical inter*space* modality allocation. That is, based on their inherent spatial properties (e.g., reach envelope), conventional physical controls [2, 11], and touch-based controls [3] are allocated to the Inner inter*space* stratum, while voice, eye gaze, and touchless gesture controls [4, 5, 7, 13] are allocated to all three strata of the inter*space*. The ultimate goal of this notional arrangement is that the actions in one modality complement, collaborate, and corroborate the input from the others, producing a well-choreographed and more organic inter*space* on the flight deck.

8   Discussion and Conclusion

Control inputs on today's aircraft flight decks are mostly completed by using a multitude of rotary knobs, push-buttons, cursor control devices, etc. The need to optimize the pilot-aircraft interaction flow motivated the aviation research community to focus on researching new and novel control input technologies. Considerable research has also been conducted in the aviation domain regarding the implementation of speech recognition and voice control, touch screens, touchless gesture recognizers and controllers, and eye tracking and gaze control systems. Such nonconventional control input technologies have been researched as both standalone nonconventional control input methods and in combination with conventional physical interfaces. However, only recently have some of these control technologies reached the required level of maturity for aviation application. Now, they have the potential to help simplify flight deck operations and allow for more direct and intuitive interactions with aircraft systems via a properly engineered and contextually suitable selection of a control modality or a combination of modalities [13, 17].

In the context of the conceptual framework presented here, and founded on rigorous analyses of pilot tasks across all phases of flight, research conducted within the framework will focus on the examination of new and novel control input modality combinations within the flight deck interspace. Furthermore, in the research and development process, the naturally-occurring, mutual disambiguation between modalities will be leveraged to mimic the more intuitive collaboration in human-to-human interactions. Such an approach is deemed essential to the successful shift toward well-balanced system input-output capabilities and better management of uncertainty in interpreting users' intent. The research goals include crew workload optimization, minimization of the potential for human error, and aiding error detection and recovery, thus improving the user experience and ultimately improving the safety of flight.

References

1. Bourdot, P., Krus, M., Gherbi, R.: Management of non-standard devices for multimodal user interfaces under UNIX/X11. In: Proceedings of the International Conference on Cooperative Multimodal Communication (CMC/95). Part I, (pp. 49–62), May 1995
2. Buxton, W.: There's more to interaction than meets the eye: some issues in manual input. In: Norman, D.A., Draper, S.W. (eds.) User Centered System Design: New Perspectives on Human-Computer Interaction, pp. 319–337. Lawrence Erlbaum Associates, Hillsdale (1986)
3. Buxton, W., Hill, R., Rowley, P.: Issues and techniques in touch-sensitive tablet input. ACM SIGGRAPH Comput. Graph. 19(3), 215–224 (1985)
4. Calhoun, G.L., Arbak, C.J., Boff, K. R.: Eye-controlled switching for crew station design. In: Proceedings of the Human Factors and Ergonomics Society Annual Meeting, vol. 28(3), pp. 258–262). SAGE Publications, October 1984
5. Calhoun, G.L., Janson, W. P., Arbak, C.J.: Use of eye control to select switches. In: Proceedings of the Human Factors and Ergonomics Society 30th Annual Meeting, vol. 30, pp. 154–158 (1986)
6. Coutaz, J., Caelen, J.: A taxonomy for multimedia and multimodal user interfaces. In: Proceedings of the 1st ERCIM Workshop on Multimodal HCI, pp. 143–148, November 1991
7. Hatfield, F., Jenkins, E.A., Jennings, M.W.: Eye/Voice Mission Planning Interface (EVMPI), (No. TR-J103-1). Synthetic Environments Inc., McLean, VA (1995)
8. Hutchins, E.: The technology of team navigation. In: Galegher, J., Kraut, R., Egido, C. (eds.) Intellectual Teamwork: Social and Technical Bases of Collaborative Work. Lawrence Erlbaum Assoc., Hillsdale (1990)
9. Hutchins, E., Klausen, T.: Distributed cognition in an airline cockpit. In: Engström, Y., Middleton, D. (eds.) Cognition and Communication at Work, pp. 15–34. Cambridge University Press, New York (1996)
10. Leger, A.: Synthesis-and expected benefits analysis. RTO Lecture Series 215 Alternative Control Technologies: Human Factors Issues, 9-1, 9-10 (1998)

11. Jordan, N.: Allocation of functions between man and machines in automated systems. J. Appl. Psychol. **47**(3), 161 (1963)
12. Mackinlay, J., Card, S.K., Robertson, G.G.: A semantic analysis of the design space of input devices. Hum. Comput. Inter. **5**(2), 145–190 (1990)
13. Majaranta, P., Bulling, A.: Eye tracking and eye-based human-computer interaction. In: Fairclough, S.H., Gilleade, K. (eds.) Advances in Physiological Computing, pp. 39–65. Springer-Verlag, London (2014)
14. Martin, J.-C., Veldman, R., Béroule, D.: Developing multimodal interfaces: a theoretical framework and guided propagation networks. In: Bunt, H., Beun, R.-J., Borghuis, T. (eds.) CMC 1995. LNCS (LNAI), vol. 1374, pp. 158–187. Springer, Heidelberg (1998)
15. McMillan, G.R., Eggleston, R.G., Anderson, T.R.: Nonconventional controls. In: Salvendy, G. (ed.) Handbook of Human Factors and Ergonomics, 2nd edn, pp. 729–771. Wiley, Hoboken (1997)
16. Merchant, S., Schnell, T.: Applying eye tracking as an alternative approach for activation of controls and functions in aircraft. In: Proceedings of the 19th Digital Avionics Systems Conference, pp. 5A5/1–5A5/9. IEEE Computer Society, New York, NY (2000)
17. Oviatt, S., Cohen, P.: Multimodal interfaces that process what comes naturally. Commun. ACM **43**(3), 45–53 (2000). doi:10.1145/330534.330538
18. Oviatt, S., Coulston, R., Lunsford, R.: When do we interact multimodally: cognitive load and multimodal communication patterns. In: Proceedings of the 6th International Conference on Multimodal Interfaces, pp. 129–136. ACM, October 2004
19. Rood, G.M.: Human factors issues for the integration of alternative control technologies. RTO Lecture Series 215 Alternative Control Technologies: Human Factors Issues, 8-1, 1-7 (1998)
20. Shannon, C.E., Weaver, W.: The Mathematical Theory of Communication. University of Illinois press, Chicago (1963)
21. Reed, M.P., Parkinson, M., Chaffin, D.B.: A new approach to modeling driver reach. (SAE Technical Paper 2003-01-0587). PA, SAE International World Congress, Warrendale (2003)

Virtual Reality Based Navigation Training for Astronaut Moving in a Simulated Space Station

Xiang Liu[⊠], Yuqing Liu, Xiuqing Zhu, Ming An, and Fuchao Hu

National Key Laboratory of Human Factors Engineering,
China Astronaut Research and Training Center, Beijing 100094, China
lx9177xiang@163.com

Abstract. Spatial disorientation and navigation problems have a critical impact on crews' work schedule and safety in spacecraft. To help astronauts have an adaptation practice and gain navigation skills when moving in space station, we employed virtual reality techniques to establish a navigation training system and conducted experiments on the system in order to obtain optimal training strategies. The paper firstly describes the architecture of the VR based navigation training system, and then presents the experiment design for investigating the influence of different training strategies on navigation performance. Experiment results verified the system feasibility and proposed some suggestions for navigation training.

Keywords: Spatial orientation · Virtual reality · Simulation · Navigation · Training

1 Introduction

In manned spaceflight, astronauts have often encountered spatial disorientation and navigation problems, especially in spacecraft with complex three-dimensional architectures such as space station [1]. Gravity makes it effortless for us to maintain spatial orientation on the ground, but in space, astronauts must rely more on visual information to orient because proprioceptive cues like inner ear organ and muscles are not that liable in weightlessness [2]. Thus, Astronauts tend to orient by recognizing familiar objects though they floated into an arbitrary body orientation and had difficulty recognizing objects when viewed from different perspectives. It is reported that "visual reorientation illusions" and navigation problems occurred frequently [3–6]. Crew members could not define a typical reference frame because "floors" "ceilings" and "walls" were constantly changing. Furthermore, they have difficulty visualizing the spatial relationships between landmarks on the interiors of the two modules for the bound of walls. To establish a sense of direction, they would need a complex mental rotation, which made it more difficult to get a mental relationship between adjacent modules. Especially when they transferred to a novel module with a different local visual vertical, astronauts could lose their sense of direction instantaneously. Without the assistance of landmarks or waypoints, astronauts could not instinctively know which way to turn or find their way back. Spatial disorientation and navigation problems have a critical impact on crews' work schedule and safety in spacecraft.

S. Lackey and R. Shumaker (Eds.): VAMR 2016, LNCS 9740, pp. 416–423, 2016.
DOI: 10.1007/978-3-319-39907-2_40

Compared with traditional spacecraft, space station expanded their scale greatly and had a more complex construction. Astronauts were no longer restricted in tight living spaces, their tasks frequently asked them to work in various orientations relative to the spacecraft interior and transit from one module to another, which required an integrated skill of spatial orientation, fast moving and judgement of the relationship between two modules. These features come up with new challenge on astronauts training. Traditional ground trainer mockups have some limitations in navigation training. Firstly, simulated modules are separate or not physically connected in the same way as they are in the actual vehicle, which makes it difficult to develop a "cognitive map" of the space station. Secondly, it is physically impossible to experience different body orientations and views in simulators.

It is proved that preflight training in virtual reality devices might reduce the incidence of spatial disorientation and help astronauts develop an integrated cognitive mental map of spacecraft so that their performance in orientation and navigation tasks is improved [7–9]. VR technology provides a vivid visual scene to train astronauts orient and navigate on visual cues. In a virtual weightless environment, astronauts experience observing modules in different perspectives and their navigation skills were studied to find an optimal training strategy.

2 VR Based Navigation Training System

To help astronauts have an adaptation practice and gain navigation skills when moving in space station, we employed virtual reality techniques to establish a navigation training system and conducted experiments on the system in order to obtain optimal training strategies. The VR based navigation training system consists of a simulated space station, human-computer interactive devices, computer simulation module and faculty processing module, as shown in Fig. 1.

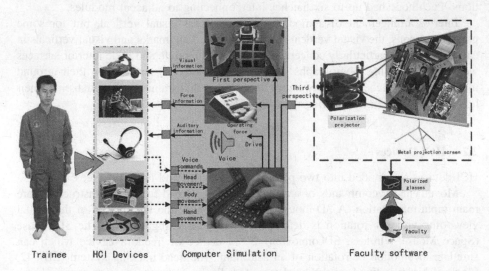

Fig. 1. The architecture of VR based navigation training system

2.1 Simulated Space Station

As the foundation of spatial orientation and navigation training, a virtual scene of orientation practice for intra-space station activities was build. Trainees were immersed in the virtual environment and encouraged to look around and interact with panels and equipment. On the reference of MIR and International Space Station, a model of simulated space station was established, as shown in Fig. 2.

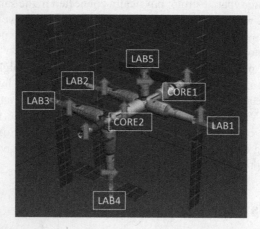

Fig. 2. Simulated space station used in the navigation training system. Green arrows represent visual verticals. (Color figure online)

The architecture of the simulated space station consisted of eleven modules in total, two core modules, five labs, two manned spacecraft and two nodes. Core modules, labs and manned spacecraft are large rectangular modules differed by their interior functions. Each node had up to six hatches interconnecting to adjacent modules.

Interior arrangement of a module defines a local visual vertical, but for some practical reasons, the visual verticals are not aligned. Landmarks and visual verticals in each module are particularly concerned. Most of the module and node interior surfaces were textured using photographs of actual ISS interior surfaces or their ground mockups. The hatches in each module too narrow and trainees must first pitch their head naturally when transferring a hatch.

2.2 HCI Devices

HCI devices are divided into two parts – input devices and output devices.

Movements or commands of a trainee's viewpoint and functional instructions are main input information. A 3D-mouse is used to control the locomotion of the virtual viewpoint while its rotation is detected by a head-tracking system. The 3D-mouse (Space Mouse Wireless, 3Dconnexion) is six degree of freedom device which can simulate locomotion or rotation of an astronaut. The head-tracking system (FB-042, Flock of birds) is fixed on the head-mounted display, when trainees turn their head, views in the head-mounted display changes at the same time. Instruction controls are achieved by voice or keyboard.

Vision and hearing are main outputs. When training, trainees wear a high-resolution head-mounted display (self-designed) with a wide field of view, audio aids are provided through earphones as well.

2.3 Software Function

The basic functionality of computer simulation software is to drive and manage the virtual training scene above, create an actual environment with a high visual and physical quality in which trainees have a natural manipulation experience. The software is composed of interactive programs, collision detection programs, sound effects simulation programs, voice processing programs, virtual scene generation and management programs, etc.

Faculty software is a significant part of the navigation training platform. It puts forward training commands and deals with training data. Data processing part consists of data recording module and integrated evaluation module. The former collects key behavior and performance data while training including the position and orientation of the astronaut, time consuming, pointing errors, etc. The latter deals with the selected data and gives an integrated evaluation of the performance by a well-trained neural network.

When using the VR based navigation training system, faculty firstly initializes training task and trainees wear HCI devices to interact. The motion of trainees' head and body, voice instruction are collected by client and then sent to simulation server

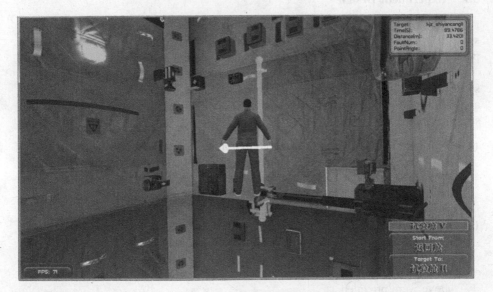

Fig. 3. A training scene in simulated space station in the first view. Virtual astronaut (not the actual size) and white arrow are assistance only in training phase

through network. The server manages the virtual training scene, realizes collision detection and information processing, etc. The signal of virtual scene is sent to head-mounted display.

Figure 3 shows a training scene in simulated space station in the first view. Each tour starts from any point of the start cabin with a random orientation. Trainees must find the hatch first and design a route to the target cabin in mind. When transfer a node, they use their spatial knowledge or assistance to find the right direction. In training phase, a small virtual astronaut and a white arrow are provided. The astronaut represents the trainee's orientation and the arrow represents local visual vertical. Trainees adjust their directions relative to the arrow (local visual vertical) and learn the structure of the module from different perspectives. Task description and performance are shown in the corner.

3   Experiment

Due to constraints on gravity, we obtain spatial knowledge in a single body orientation on earth and prefer to remember routes as a sequence of landmarks. But in space station, astronauts can float into any body orientation and the local visual verticals of adjacent modules are not always consistently aligned. Thus the "cognition map" seems more important. Both landmarks and sense of direction are significant in navigation, but is it better to navigate in a familiar view with variable body orientations or in a constant body orientation guided by a world reference frame? We conducted an experiment to find optimal navigation strategies for astronaut training.

3.1   Experiment Design

An experiment was performed (n=30) to investigate the effect of three training strategies on task performance in VR based navigation training system. All subjects passed the Cube Comparison Test and accomplished the experiment.

At the beginning of training phase, subjects have no cognition of the simulated space station. To get a better understanding of the entire space station, each subject was assigned to one of three groups balanced by individual abilities with different training strategies:

(1) Constant group. Subjects were forced to maintain a constant orientation relative to the entire space station. The strategy resembles underwater creatures moving. When the target is above, trainees must just float up with no pitch. We locked two degree of freedom (roll and pitch) of the 3D-Mouse actually. Navigation aids above were provided.
(2) Inconstant group. Subjects were allowed to maintain an orientation aligned with the visual vertical of the module stayed in. when they arrive at a novel cabin, they must adjust their body orientation aligned with local visual vertical, in other words, get the virtual astronaut and the white arrow aligned. Navigation aids above were provided.

(3) Control group. Subjects were not provided any navigation aids and float in a random orientation.

In training phase, each subject has 18 routes to get familiar with interior layouts of the simulated space station. After that 12 sequential routes were conducted in test phase. Subjects found the hatch first and reached the target cabin as soon as possible. When arrived they were then instructed to turn around and point back to the start cabin (pointing backward task) as quickly and accurately as possible. All subjects were in good visibility in the first six tests while smoke was introduced in the following six tests. Time consuming, locomotion distance, pointing errors and turning errors were measured in each test. Spatial knowledge and the configuration of the simulated space station are investigated in the interview after all tests.

3.2   Experimental Results

Time consuming and pointing errors are key performance measures. Results are shown in Figs. 4 and 5.

Subjects of constant group have lower pointing errors and get a better performance with smoke while inconstant-trainees complete the task faster in good visibility conditions. Results of ANOVA show that main effect of visibility is significant [$F(1, 27) = 4.3$, $p=0.043$] on time consuming and training strategy [$F(2, 27) = 5.8$, $p=0.005$] has a significant effect on pointing errors. Strategy×visibility effect is not significant on performance indicators.

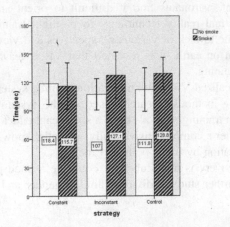

Fig. 4. Time consuming for no smoke and smoke in simulated space station, grouped by training strategy. Error bars represent±1 SEM.

It is revealed that inconstant-trainees use the strategy we orientate on earth and get more familiar with landmark and route knowledge, constant training facilitates sense of direction and helps develop an integrated cognitive mental map. We draw the conclusion that both constant and inconstant strategies result in better performance

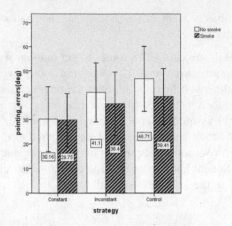

Fig. 5. Pointing errors for no somke and smoke in simulated space station, grouped by training strategy. Error bars represent±1 SEM.

compared with control group. The optimal training strategy we recommend is a mixed strategy. Astronauts should master a comprehensive study of spatial knowledge and orientation skills on visual information by using both two methods.

4 Conclusion

Due to complex structures of large spacecraft and human physiological changes in weightless environment, astronauts find it difficult to orient and navigate in space station, we applied virtual reality technology to preflight training, reducing spatial perceptual problems due to lack of various perspectives and views when trained in a single body orientation on earth. It is revealed that VR is feasible and effective for astronaut navigation training.

We designed and realized VR based navigation training system. Our present study and navigation training methods research based on the system draw the following conclusions: navigation training methods have a significant effect on task performance. Astronauts should master a comprehensive study of spatial knowledge and orientation skills on visual information by using both two methods.

An interesting discovery is that Cube test could be a good predictor of trainees' performance. In our further study, individual ability, gender and human behavior are principally concerned.

References

1. Oman, C.M.: Spatial orientation and navigation in microgravity. In: Mast, F., Jancke, L. (eds.) Spatial Processing in Navigation, pp. 209–247. Imagery and Perception, Springer, New York (2007)
2. Richards, J.T., Oman, C.M., Shebilske, W.L., et al.: Training, transfer, and retention of three-dimensional spatial memory in virtual environments. J. Vestib. Res. **12**, 223–238 (2002)

3. Oman, C.M.: Human visual orientation in weightlessness. In: Harris, L., Jenkin, M. (eds.) Levels of Perception, pp. 375–398. Springer-Verlag, New York (2003)
4. Aoki, H., Ohno, R., Yamaguchi, T.: The effect of the configuration and the interior design of a virtual weightless space station on human spatial orientation. Acta Astronaut. **56**, 1005–1016 (2005)
5. Oman, C.M., Benveniste, D., Aoki, H., et al.: Spacecraft module visual verticals and training affect spatial task performance. Habitation **10**, 202–203 (2006)
6. Oman, C.M., Shebilske, W.L., Richards, J.T., et al.: Three dimensional spatial memory and learning in real and virtual environments. Spat. Cogn. Comput. **2**(4), 355–372 (2000)
7. Harm, D.L., Parker, D.E.: Preflight adaptation training for spatial orientation and space motion sickness. J. Clin. Pharmacol. **34**, 618–627 (1994)
8. Harm, D.L., Parker, D.E.: Perceived self-orientation and self-motion in microgravity, after landing and during preflight adaptation training. J. Vestib. Res. **3**, 297–305 (1993)
9. Stroud, K.J., Harm, D.L., Klaus, D.M.: Preflight virtual reality training as a countermeasure for space motion sickness and disorientation. Aviat. Space Environ. Med. **76**, 352–356 (2005)

Application of Virtual Environments for Infantry Soldier Skills Training: We are Doing it Wrong

Douglas B. Maxwell[✉]

Advanced Training and Simulation Division, U.S. Army Research Laboratory,
Orlando, FL, USA
douglas.maxwell3.civ@mail.mil

Abstract. Simulation based training (SBT) technology has been shown to be effective in a number of domains such as for pilot training and ground vehicle operator training. In the dismounted infantry soldier skills domain, the low hanging fruit for effective use of SBT is equipment operations training. However, the complexities of the operational environment are often too difficult to replicate in current virtual environments to present an accurate or effective training for the skills requiring identification of enemy activity or reacting to enemy contact. The U.S. Army Research Laboratory and the University of Central Florida have been conducting studies using large numbers of soldiers to determine how effective virtual training methods are in comparison to traditional training methods for dismounted infantry soldier skills. This paper will discuss recommendations for changes in the employment of virtual training systems that could have a meaningful impact on the performance of soldiers.

Keywords: Simulation based training · Leadership training · Collective training · Virtual environments · Infantry soldier skills training

1 Introduction

As of the writing of this paper, the U.S. Army is entering a new acquisition cycle to replace the current virtual training program of record, the Virtual Battle Spaces 3 (VBS3). The VBS3 is based on a commercial gaming engine called ARMA3 owned by Bohemia Interactive. The VBS3 is widely used within the U.S. Army for various simulation based training activities, including but not limited to infantry soldier skills training. The VBS3 is often criticized for being difficult to deploy and use, however actual usage data is difficult to acquire. The information contained in this paper is derived from field observations and data collection activities from March through December of 2015 at the 211th Florida Army National Guard Regional Training Institute's Warrior Leader Course. The purpose of the data collection activities was to determine baseline training effectiveness comparison of simulation based training methods versus traditional classroom and physical walkthrough means.

A research team composed of U.S. Army Research Laboratory (ARL) and University of Central Florida Institute for Simulation Technology (IST) personnel conducted ten data collection activities by folding into the monthly Warrior Leader Course training

© Springer International Publishing Switzerland 2016
S. Lackey and R. Shumaker (Eds.): VAMR 2016, LNCS 9740, pp. 424–432, 2016.
DOI: 10.1007/978-3-319-39907-2_41

cycle. Each month the team would travel to Camp Blanding, Florida and collect questionnaire and performance evaluations from the course managers. By combining the team member's observations, the questionnaire data, and the performance evaluations, certain conclusions backed by statistically relevant data could be drawn.

It is a natural reaction of the acquisition community to attempt to improve a product by replacing it with another material solution. Without understanding why the VBS3 adoption and usage was less than expected, there is a danger that the replacement system may have the same issues. In the following sections, there will be discussion of the applicability of the simulators to infantry soldier skills training, issues surrounding distributed training, understanding and leveraging the strengths of the medium.

2   Source Data and Field Observation

Observations in this paper derived from data collection events performed over a two year period from January 2014 to December 2015 at various Florida Army National Guard sites. The WLC managers worked closely with the ARL/UCF research team to determine how best to use it for a comparison study. This study was extremely fortunate to find an accommodating unit to allow for observation and even adopt suggested adjustments to the course.

A between-treatments experiment was designed to compare the training effectiveness of soldiers provided a virtual training method versus traditional training means. The period of instruction for this course is 20 days, with days one through 17 consisting of all soldiers provided the same classroom training with slides and instruction subject matter experts. Normally, day 18 is reserved for practical exercises and four hours is provided for simulator time. The practical exercises are provided in the form of virtual "walkthroughs" where the four major tasks are posed to the soldiers and they practice reacting to the situational stimulus. The simulation can pose situations such as indirect fire, improvised explosive device detection, land navigation to rally points, and more. The 211th RTI uses the U.S. Army's VBS3 product for this simulation.

The formal assessment of the squad's performance is done on days 19 and 20 using on-site situational training exercise (STX) lanes. For this experiment, and adjustment was made to the POI such that the class was separated into two groups and provided with different walkthrough training treatments. The control group was sent to a wooded areas and an instructor provided practical exercises with guided instruction (Fig. 1). This control group represents a traditional method of providing the practical instruction.

The experimental group was provided a training treatment that included simulation based training in a classroom setting and used the VBS3 suite (Fig. 2). Although the experimental design of the data collection activity treated the virtual treatment as a generic technology, the VBS3 was chosen as the target simulator and use existing training material for the course. The scenario provided within the VBS3 was created by onsite contractors and was an approximation of the STX lanes the soldiers would encounter the following day during their performance evaluations.

Fig. 1. Small group leader providing guided instruction

Fig. 2. Screenshot of virtual battle spaces 3 application in-use

The ARL/UCF research team was allowed unrestricted access to the course managers, classrooms, battle training center, practices areas, and STX lanes. The accomodations made by the 211th allowed for a deep examination of the course and the affect a simulation based training system had on the performance of infantry soldiers. The course managers were provided with periodic updates and briefed regularly on the progress of the data collection. The course managers also solicited advice from the research team on how to improve the use of the VBS3 system and played an integral role in the experimental design of the follow on study scheduled to start in the Spring of 2016.

3 Are Simulation Based Trainers Applicable to Infantry Soldier Skills Development?

The assumption to the question posed above is "yes". Is this assumption valid? Currently, infantry soldier tasks are not properly identified as candidates for simulation based training applications (Whitney et al. 2013). Since very little guidance is provided in the employment of the simulation based training, the ad-hoc nature of the training presents a number of challenges. Onsite simulator support (often consisting of contractors) is directed by the course managers to create scenarios aligned to the course material without much thought put into whether the tasks *should* be taught in the simulator. Applicability should be an early stage of the training design (Arthur et al. 2003), not an afterthought.

Virtual environments are not a substitute for instructor led training, rather they can be treated as proxies for the live environments. The need for guidance and feedback from instructors or intelligent tutors is still required (Vogel-Walcutt et al. 2013). Further, the guidance needs to be timely and directly applicable to the student's immediate situational awareness (Kirschner et al. 2006).

For the dismounted light infantry, three main activities they need to perform is shoot, move, and communicate (*FM 3-21.8 The Infantry Rifle Platoon and Squad* 2007). Any simulated activity, whether live or virtual, must have some value in the training to one or more of those activities. Shooting is a kinetic activity and it does not make sense to attempt to use a technology such as VBS3 to teach marksmanship, that is why the U.S. Army has other dedicated virtual trainers for that activity and physical ranges. However, the virtual environments could be leveraged to teach mission planning, or *when* to shoot.

The limitations of the technology must be identified and recognized as factors for what is trained by the simulation. The activities created to support the learning objectives inside the virtual environment must be based on validated learning theory (Landers and Callan 2012).

There is a pervasive belief that is supported by some in literature that serious games need high end graphics quality, or put another way high fidelity graphics equate to quality training and education (Chalmers and Debattista 2009). Graphics fidelity is a moving target with technological advances made continuously. Further, research into virtual environment instructional design suggests that factors such as scenario interactivity and functional alignment with the tasks to be trained have an impact on knowledge transfer as well (Hamstra et al. 2014).

4 Leverage Strengths of Medium

Relating the medium to dismounted infantry soldier skills, consider environments that allow for team coordination, particularly in a distributed manner. Distributed simulation based training can be performed in the barracks or at home station for pre-deployment acclimation of concepts and skills maintenance. Distributed training is key to the next generation of infantry soldier skills training, as even current technology allows for collective skills development. Since most tasks infantry soldiers are trained for are collective in nature, a simulation technology that allows for remote participation coupled with task coordination may be a more appropriate medium to use.

Time spent in the simulators will allow for the soldiers to gain tool expertise as well as provide opportunity for self-paced learning. Allowing soldiers to access the simulators from home station offers a cost effective means for training by allowing collective activities without the need for physical co-location at a battle training center (Fig. 3).

Fig. 3. WLC Students working through react-to-contact simulations in VBS3

Distributed training can be done safely. In the U.S. military, a significant barrier to adoption is information assurance policy. For next generation systems, decoupling data from the simulator such that the sensitive portions of the training can be performed behind a firewall, but critical issues such as tool training can be done safely on open networks using benign unclassified or generic scenarios. End-to-end encryption on modern platforms is becoming feasible on the near-term horizon. Additionally, encryption within the various content and terrain databases is also feasible and would add an extra layer of protection to the training networks. Assuming the firewalls are compromised, if the data is harvests from the databases or midstream through man-in-the-middle attacks, the data would be useless to the attacker.

A technology development lesson learned with current simulation based training environments is that information assurance and encryption cannot be treated as an afterthought. Careful design considerations and requirements specifications must be defined during the initial stages of systems engineering for new synthetic training environments. Caution is strongly urged to avoid commercial entertainment solutions or products that have no hope of accreditation due to licensing restrictions.

5   Common Soldier Feedback

The ARL/UCF research team was rewarded with a wealth of feedback from the soldiers during the months of data collection. Common themes began to emerge from the feedback and a few of the issues are discussed here.

In this case study, leadership training stands out as an appropriate candidate application of the technology. The soldiers reported they were comfortable with the communications mechanisms within the VBS3 and were able to communicate with each other and squad leaders effectively. The squad leaders were observed directing the fire team leaders for effective response coordination. Radio discipline and correct communication skills with the tactical operations center was positive, allowing the soldiers to adequately communicate coordinates and timing of various contact situations as well as correctly call in medical evacuation (Fig. 4) and improvised explosive device disposal requests.

Fig. 4. VBS3 Successful call for medical evacuation

The soldiers reported difficulty with the user interfaces. The VBS3 was described as confusing and required too much time to gain proficiency in its use. To put into context, the control group of the WLC study was able to start task training immediately upon arriving at the live training area, normally at 0800 on Day 18 of the POI. In contrast, the soldiers in the virtual training group received approximately 90 min of VBS tool training and acclimation exercises before WLC task training began after a brief break at 0945. Much less time was devoted to task training and walkthrough rehearsals than the control group. The consequence was that practical exercise time for the virtual group either reduced the number of tasks that were trained or the amount of time for each task was truncated.

The soldiers reported the locomotion interface into the virtual system was not natural given the kinds of tasks they were asked to perform and that it was difficult to discriminate between team members. Further, they had difficulty discerning direction of fire in the simulation as naturally as in a live training exercise.

Game mechanics for the entertainment industry are different than in an infantry soldier training context. For example, pulling 360 security is not entertaining, glamorous, or fun. Many of the tasks the soldiers are trained for are performed collectively and not entertaining. To relieve the tedium of some of the tasks, it is suggest that a narrative be included in the scenario. For example, if the tasks are to react to contact of some kind, then it would be beneficial to set the stage of the scenario with a back-brief to include some local politics, situational awareness of any known insurgent activity, perhaps some dossier information on major personalities in the area, etc....

6   The Applicability Continuum

The findings from the observations described in this paper underline the importance of understanding which tasks are most appropriate for use with simulation based training technology. There is likely a sliding scale of applicability, a continuum, along which tasks fall. Since major factors such as performance, time, and cost are measures of the return on investment of the simulation technology, it is critical the training community understands how best to apply the new systems in the most appropriate way possible.

Figure 5 shows a graphical representation of the proposed continuum. The center of the continuum, or $< 0, 0, 0 >$, represents the current traditional (non-simulation based) training methods. We have a clear understanding through decades of live training with infantry soldiers to be able to look at historical records for baseline data. It is understood how much time (period of instruction) is takes for a given class, such as the Warrior Leader Course mentioned previously. Costs are understood for travel, lodging, instruction, and site usage. Lastly, performance expectations for the course are also understood. It is important to note that the continuum must be populated by data gathered from different tasks and genericizing assumptions that simulation based training is applicable to one task based on the data from a different task must be done with caution.

Let's examine a hypothetical example and apply it to the continuum in Fig. 5. A particular task such "react to ambush" may yield from a sample of 20 squads that soldiers trained with a simulation on this task are able to demonstrate significant performance gains at low cost and at the same amount of time (Fig. 5). This is represented by the diamond glyph.

Over time, as more and more tasks are examined and added to this continuum, it is anticipated that certain trends my present. The "clumping" of data may indicate that certain tasks may yield common applicability characteristics that will allow future decision makers to plan for the inclusion of simulation based training in the courses. For example, if the goal of the class is to reduce as much time as possible but maintain baseline proficiency, then selecting only the tasks that lie on the negative side of the time axis will satisfy the requirement.

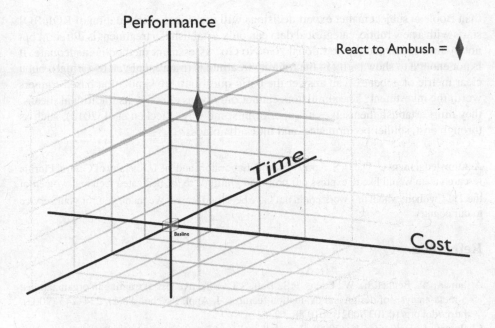

Fig. 5. Applicability continuum with performance, Time, and Cost axes

7 Conclusions

A number of key observations and lessons learned can be derived from this study. For example, a common user interface for synthetic training environment using simulation based training for infantry must be considered. If the U.S. Army is adopting a virtual environment program of record, then it makes sense to teach it in basic training. This common user interface needs to be introduced early and reinforced often throughout the soldier's career. A possible solution may be to make the user interfaces reconfigurable, recognizing that "one-size" does not fit all.

A material solution is not the entire answer. Replacing the current trainer with a new training system without changing usage behavior will likely result in similar disappointment. The Army is motivated to address gaps with material solutions, but a thorough study of the applicability of this technology to the skills required by the soldier is critical. A call for caution not to rush to a new acquisition cycle without trying modified approaches first.

Although there is room for improvement for the VBS3 application, the data suggests changes in the deployment and usage of the VBS3 could greatly increase its adoption and training effectiveness. It is hoped the acquisition community will examine the research performed in this area and adopt not just a material solution but also a change in the way the technology is used.

The U.S. Army needs to establish a firm return on investment (ROI). By formalizing methodologies for assessment (Pickup 2013) and creating rubrics based on scales rather than Boolean subject matter expert decisions will assist in the formulation of ROI. ROI starts with a new rubric, categorical data can only establish if a treatment is different but not by how much and the traditional "Go/No Go" assessment method is inadequate. It is not enough to show parity in the training treatments (traditional versus virtual), but a clear metric of goodness can answer the basic question: Are simulation based trainers worth the investment? The simulators cannot only be as effective as traditional means, they must establish themselves as superior in some way (Riecken et al. 2013), such as through cost, soldier performance, and time advantages.

Acknowledgements. The U. S. Army Research Laboratory and the University of Central Florida research team would like to express our profound gratitude to the dedicated men and women of the 211th without whom this work could not have been performed. We thank you for your service to our country.

References

Arthur Jr., W., Bennett Jr., W., Edens, P.S., Bell, S.T.: Effectiveness of training in organizations: a meta-analysis of design and evaluation features. J. Appl. Psychol. **88**(2), 234–245 (2003). http://doi.org/10.1037/0021-9010.88.2.234

Chalmers, A., Debattista, K. (2009).: Level of realism for serious games. In: Proceedings of the 2009 Conference in Games and Virtual Worlds for Serious Applications, VS-GAMES 2009, pp. 225–232 (2009). http://doi.org/10.1109/VS-GAMES.2009.43

FM 3-21.8 The Infantry Rifle Platoon and Squad, vol. 8, Washington, D.C. (2007). http://armypubs.army.mil/doctrine/DR_pubs/dr_a/pdf/fm3_21x8.pdf

Hamstra, S.J., Brydges, R., Hatala, R., Zendejas, B., Cook, D.A.: Reconsidering fidelity in simulation-based training. Acad. Med. J. Assoc. Am. Med. Coll. **89**(3), 387–392 (2014). http://doi.org/10.1097/ACM.0000000000000130

Kirschner, P., Sweller, J., Clark, R.: Why minimal guidance during instruction does not work. Educ. Psychol. **41**(2), 75–86 (2006). http://doi.org/10.1207/s15326985ep4102

Landers, R.N., Callan, R.C.: Training evaluation in virtual worlds: development of a model. J. Virtual Worlds Res. **5**(3), 1–22 (2012). http://journals.tdl.org/jvwr/index.php/jvwr/article/view/6335/6300

Pickup, S. (2013).: ARMY AND MARINE Better Performance and Cost Data Needed to More Fully Assess Efforts (2013). http://www.gao.gov/assets/660/657115.pdf

Riecken, M., Powers, L.T.C.J., Janisz, C., Kierzewski, M.: The Value of Simulation in Army Training (13073), 1–16 (2013)

Vogel-Walcutt, J.J., Fiorella, L., Malone, N.: Instructional strategies framework for military training systems. Comput. Hum. Behav. **29**(4), 1490–1498 (2013). http://doi.org/10.1016/j.chb.2013.01.038

Whitney, S.J., Temby, P., Stephens, A.: Evaluating the Effectiveness of Game-Based Training: A Controlled Study with Dismounted Infantry Teams. Edinburgh (2013)

Test-Bed for Integrated Ground Control Station Experimentation and Rehearsal: Crew Performance and Authority Pathway Concept Development

Derek McColl[1](✉), Simon Banbury[2], and Ming Hou[1]

[1] Human-Systems Integration Section,
Defence Research and Development Canada, Toronto Centre, Toronto, Canada
{derek.mccoll,ming.hou}@drdc-rddc.gc.ca
[2] C3 Human Factors Consulting Inc., Montréal, Canada
simon.banbury@c3hf.com

Abstract. Canada's Joint Unmanned Surveillance and Target Acquisition System program for acquiring an uninhabited aircraft system requires an interim ground control station for developing operator interface technologies and investigate training needs for the future aircraft. Defence Research and Development Canada is developing the Test-bed for Integrated Ground Control Station Experimentation and Rehearsal for this purpose. The test-bed consists of six workstations for the uninhabited aircraft system crew and five researcher and trainer workstations. A human factors engineering trial was performed on the test-bed with two crews performing a simulated mission scenario. The operator performance results from the trial indicated that both crews performed reasonably well at the individual level, with one crew exhibiting poor teamwork behaviors. Specifically, one crew did not follow rules of engagement and standard operating procedures when engaging a target. Subject matter expert observations determined that the crews had insufficient doctrinal knowledge, crew coordination, and situational awareness. Participant feedback indicated that the simulated scenario could be made more detailed, and they made suggestions to improve the test-bed interface. To support following rules of engagement and standard operating procedures and participant recommendations, this paper presents the development of the Authority Pathway Concept, an intelligent human-machine interface for a ground control station that presents the status of each of the steps required for engaging an enemy target.

Keywords: Uninhabited aircraft system · Ground control station · Human-machine interface · Operator performance

1 Introduction

The Canadian Armed Forces (CAF) initiated the Joint Unmanned Surveillance and Target Acquisition System (JUSTAS) program to procure and field a mature Medium Altitude Lone Endurance (MALE) Uninhabited Aircraft System (UAS) to provide mandatory capabilities for domestic and international operations [1]. The JUSTAS UAS

© Her Majesty the Queen in Right of Canada 2016
S. Lackey and R. Shumaker (Eds.): VAMR 2016, LNCS 9740, pp. 433–445, 2016.
DOI: 10.1007/978-3-319-39907-2_42

will complement existing reconnaissance, surveillance, and target acquisition capabilities as well as increase Canada's maritime and artic domain awareness [1]. The UAS is also required to have precision strike capability to support Land and Special Operations forces [1].

The Royal Canadian Air Force, working on JUSTAS, needs an interim ground control station (GCS) to train Canada's legacy Heron crews and new UAS crews to prepare for the JUSTAS UAS GCS. Defence Research and Development Canada (DRDC) has been tasked with assessing the required training needs and operator interface technologies in order to make recommendations for UAS GCS design and training. DRDC is also developing recommendations for Directorate – Technical Airworthiness and Engineering Support (DTAES) on the airworthiness certification process for the UAS GCS. DTAES currently does not have any airworthiness standards for UAS GCSs. DRDC is developing an experimental UAS GCS to complete these tasks.

UAS crews can face high-workload conditions by having multiple sensor views, large amounts of data for analysis, and the teleoperation nature of UAS missions. UAS crews have indicated that new GCS HMIs would allow for substantial improvements to system effectiveness and performance, including better UAS control, more efficient data management and the dissemination of that information [2]. DRDC is performing trials on the experimental JUSTAS UAS GCS to determine what components/parts of the GCS can be effectively improved by new HMIs.

This paper presents the operator performance and participant feedback results of a human factors engineering (HFE) trial on an experimental UAS GCS. Additionally, a new HMI concept designed is presented to support the UAS crew based on the results of the HFE trial. The rest of this paper is organized as follows. Section 2 describes DRDC's UAS GCS simulator. Section 3 summarizes the HFE trail. Section 4 presents a novel intelligent HMI based on the results of the HFE trial. Concluding remarks are presented in Sect. 5.

2   Test-Bed for Integrated Ground Control Station Experimentation and Rehearsal - TIGER

DRDC and the Warfighter Readiness Research Division of the US Air Force Research Laboratory (AFRL) (711HPW/RHA) are expanding AFRL's PRINCE UAS GCS simulator for use as an experimental UAS GCS [3]. This new GCS simulator, called Test-bed for Integrated GCS Experimentation and Rehearsal (TIGER), will be used by DRDC for the development of new UAS GCS capabilities, (i.e., HMIs, perform learning and training studies for different crew complements, and investigate manning requirements, GCS certification requirements, and new GCS workstation layouts). The current TIGER layout is shown in Fig. 1.

TIGER is comprised of six crew workstations for UAS operators. These workstations include the Air Vehicle Operator (AVO), Payload Operator (PO), Image Analyst (IMA-A), Image Reporter (IMA-R), Electronic Warfare Analyst (EW-A), and Electronic Warfare Reporter (EW-R). Although the intelligence stations, IMA and EW, could be placed in a separate location from the AVO and PO, they are included as a part of TIGER to encourage effective crew collaboration and effectiveness. Previous

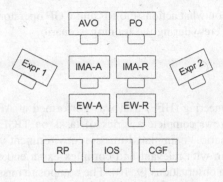

Fig. 1. TIGER workstation layout

research has shown that, in general, distributed teams have difficulties developing and maintain cohesion [4–6] and collaborative technologies have not eliminated these issues [7, 8]. The AVO and PO stations control the flight, weapons, and sensor operation of the simulated MALE UAS using the same software as AFRL's PRINCE. The IMA-A and IMA-R monitor, analyze, and report any important events identified in the UAS's video sensor stream. The IMA-A and IMA-R workstations use the Multi-Intelligence Analysis and Archive System software made by General Dynamics. The EW-A and EW-R monitor, analyze and report on important radio communications intercepted via the UAS radio. The EW-A and EW-R stations use simulation radio software custom made for TIGER. All six crew stations have a standard communication software suite consisting of a chat client and a voice radio. All the workstations have Situational Awareness (SA) displays showing sensor imagery and tactical maps. Each workstation also has Command and Control (C2) planning software consisting of Portable Flight Planning Software and Microsoft Office. The hardware at each workstation includes a desk, chair, 3 monitors, keyboard and mouse, radio headset and push to talk pedal. In addition, the AVO and PO stations have joystick and throttle flight/sensor controls.

TIGER also includes five researcher and trainer workstations. These workstations include the Instructor Operating Station (IOS), Computer Generated Forces (CGF) station, a Role Player (RP) station, and two Experimenter (Expr) stations. The experimenters monitor and record crew actions and behaviors. Experimenters have access to the Live Virtual Constructive Networked Control Suite for recording and making notes on events occurring in the simulated environment and Coalition- Performance Evaluation and Tracking Software that automatically identifies significant events occurring in the simulated environment. The CGF operator utilizes Modern Air Combat Environment (MACE) software by Battlespace Simulations Inc. to create and control any virtual entities in the simulated scenario. The RP uses a stealth viewer client of the image generator software that allows him/her to view the simulated environment from any perspective during the scenario. The RP also uses the radio and chat communication tools on TIGER to communicate with the crew as any external team member or person that has been incorporated into the training scenario, e.g., mission manager or Joint Terminal Attack Controller (JTAC). The IOS operator oversees the crew training, deciding on what actions the RP and CGF operator should take based on the performance of the crew during the training scenario.

3   TIGER Trial

A Human Factors Engineering (HFE) trial was performed at AFRL in January 2015. The trial had 2 UAS crews complete a series of tasks on TIGER during a simulated composite mission scenario. A simulated mission environment was selected to ensure an event-based approach with relevant and complex experiences that would result in rich individual and team observations [9, 10]. The composite mission scenario was also designed to be representative of a JUSTAS mission. This trial was performed to establish baseline individual and team performance levels for TIGER crews completing a simulated composite mission scenario, get UAS crew feedback, and provide specific guidance for the development of customized TIGER HMIs.

3.1   Participants

The participants included 10 CAF personnel experienced in the UAS crew roles included in TIGER. The participants' backgrounds included time as a part of the Canadian Heron UAS Detachment, experience on the CP-140 Maritime Patrol Aircraft, and ground based analysis and reporting roles.

The participants included two personnel familiar with the AVO role, two familiar with the PO role, three familiar with image analysis and reporting, and three familiar with electronic warfare analysis and reporting. These 10 participants were divided into 2 TIGER crews, crews A and B. One of the personnel familiar with image analysis and reporting filled the role of IMA-A on crew A and IMA-R on crew B. One of the personnel familiar with electronic warfare analysis and reporting filled the role of EW-A for both crews A and B. All participants had a year or more operational experience with their corresponding UAS crew roles.

3.2   Methods

Training. All the participants received one day of training on TIGER before performing the evaluation mission. Training involved familiarization with the hardware and software components, system functions and HMI operation for each participant at his/her corresponding TIGER workstation. This was followed by each crew participating in a training scenario so that the participants could practice mission tasks on TIGER. An example of one of the TIGER crews operating TIGER is shown in Fig. 2.

As part of the training, a general project briefing was given to the participants so that they understood the limitations of TIGER and the scenario in order to manage their expectations. This was done to minimize participant feedback on known issues and encourage the participants to be involved in the evaluation of TIGER.

Fig. 2. TIGER during trial at AFRL

Mission Scenario. A simulated composite scenario, called "Objective Titan," was used for the TIGER evaluation. The goal of this scenario was to have a realistic series of vignettes (simulation events) linked into a narrative that stimulated all crew members.

The Objective Titan composite scenario takes place in a coastal city. Human and Signals Intelligence confirmed that enemy forces are threating a Canadian consulate and are coordinating an attack from a nearby residential area. If the UAS crew can locate and identify the leader of the insurgents, a ground-based task force, including a JTAC, will deploy by small boat and armored SUV convey to kill or capture the insurgent leader. The TIGER crew is tasked with observing the convoy route and surrounding area for threats. If threats are observed eyes should be maintained on the contacts and the task force must be notified. The JTAC may use the UAS crew for strike plans and/or in coordination with other assets. Given the urban location, collateral damage estimate is high.

Prior to performing the Objective Titan composite scenario, participants were given a briefing on the scenario including materials that would be expected for a real mission, including geographic locations, times, weather, rules of engagement, and intelligence regarding the threats and contacts of interest.

To successfully complete the scenario, the TIGER crew must complete 4 vignettes: (i) *pattern of life* – the TIGER crew must collect intelligence, via radio frequency transmissions and UAS sensor imagery, over areas of interest, and determine that the ground-based task force should be deployed; (ii) *convoy over-watch* – TIGER crew must monitor the convoy route for signs of threats, in this case potential improvised explosive devices; (iii) *call for direct fire* - the TIGER crew must respond to a direct fire request from the JTAC on board the convoy; (iv) *call for in-direct fire* – the convoy is ambushed and the JTAC calls for the UAS to provide a targeting solution for a CF-18.

Observations and Metrics. A variety of measures and observations were taken during the TIGER evaluation mission, including: operator performance, SA, workload, and participant feedback. This paper focuses on the results of monitoring operator performance and participant feedback. It should be noted that during the pre-mission briefing, it was also explained to the participants that the experimenters would periodically administer questionnaires to them while they performed the Objective Titan composite scenario.

Operator Performance. TIGER crew performance was measured by a UAS subject matter expert (SME) using a behavioral marker checklist with 10 items. The checklist was created as a list of appropriate behavioral responses to preprogrammed simulation events during the composite scenario. The SME rated the participants on 5-point scales (1 being "very poor" to 5 being "very good") of competence for each behavioral marker in the checklist. Additionally the same 5-point scale was used to measure 5 team behavioral markers, based on [11], to determine the effectiveness of essential teamwork processes: (i) communication, (ii) monitoring, (iii) coordination and prioritisation, (iv) cross-checking, (v) conflict resolution. The SME also took observational notes on crew performance.

Participant Feedback. TIGER crew feedback on TIGER and the scenario was collected throughout the evaluation and afterwards during the de-briefing. The de-briefing was also used by the researchers to examine questionnaire results on topics such as: which periods of the scenario were crew members over- or underloaded, periods of teamwork breakdown and recovery, losses of individual and shared SA, poor usability and utility ratings, poor operator performance measures.

3.3   Results

Operator Performance. The 10 items of the behavioral markers checklist followed by the 5 team behavioral markers, and the average results for each marker are shown in Fig. 3. Crew A was rated at "fair" (3) or "good" (4) levels by the SME for all the task specific behavioral markers except in "use of EW tools to provide useful targeting information (IMA)" and "accuracy of reporting combat assessment and collateral effects," for which they were rated as "poor" (2). Crew A struggled with respect to the team behavioral markers, receiving a "very poor" or "poor" rating in "crew monitoring," "crew's coordination and prioritization," and "crew's conflict resolution."

Crew B was rated at "fair" or "good" levels by the SME for all the markers except in "accuracy of targeting solution to JTAC," and "crew's conflict resolution" for which they received "very good" ratings and "UAS positioning to optimize weapon performance" and "timeliness of providing targeting solution to JTAC" for which they received "poor" ratings.

Overall both crews performed reasonably well on the individual task markers, and Crew B has good team behaviors. However Crew A suffered from poor teamwork behaviors, which likely resulted in difficulties performing the other tasks rated on the checklist. The SME observer recommended that TIGER training include UAS doctrine, tactics techniques and procedures (TTPs), and crew concepts be developed for future TIGER trials.

SME Observations. The SME made detailed accounts of various aspects of the crews performance, including doctrinal knowledge, leadership and crew coordination, and situational awareness.

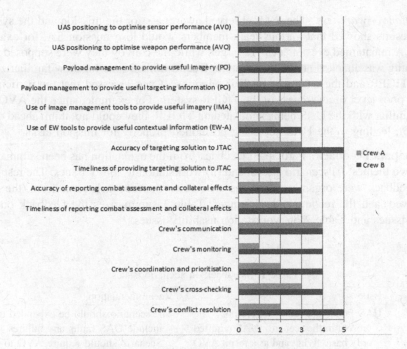

Fig. 3. Average operator performance ratings for both crews

Doctrinal Knowledge. The various TIGER crew members did not have the same level of UAS doctrinal knowledge. There were also gaps in basic doctrinal knowledge, for example Crew A did not consider Rules of Engagement (ROEs) and the Law of Armed Conflict, which resulted striking a target without following standard operating procedures (e.g., not checking for collateral damage and not performing battle damage assessment). These gaps had a direct influence on crew SA and performance during the evaluation mission.

Leadership and Crew Coordination. The AVO role is assigned as the crew commander for UAS operations. However, since the AVO participants came from a non-combat unit that did not require crew command experience, they did not take lead of the crew during the mission and were left out of important crew member discussions, missing important mission information. This resulted in poor SA and decision making.

Overall crew coordination was also limited, especially for Crew A, with the majority of coordination happening in each of the TIGER sub-teams (AVO and PO, IMA-A and IMA-R, and EW-A and EW-R). This also resulted in poor crew SA, with certain crew members missing important mission information that was critical for making decisions during the mission. Crew B had better overall crew coordination and had better overall mission success. The SME noted that the training did not include standardized tactical communication which led the crew into confusing situations and to act on artificially perceived priorities.

Situational Awareness. The SME observed awareness for the mission and the system. The results showed that various team members would lose mission SA, for example Crew A maintained eyes on a CF-18 target, while the convoy they were supposed to be watching was attacked at another location. Due to limited time for crew familiarization with TIGER and the outcomes of their missions, it was assessed that the participants had a poor level of awareness of the TIGER system. For example, since the AVO was not familiar with the UAS being simulated on TIGER, they could not think ahead of the aircraft, leading to the UAS not being positioned properly for mission tasks.

Participant Feedback. Participant feedback from the evaluation has been summarized into two themes: (i) scenario issues, and (ii) workstation usability issues. The results of the feedback were organized in to the crew roles the feedback came from, the issue observed, and the recommended changes. Table 1 summarizes the feedback on scenario issues and Table 2 on workstation usability issues.

Table 1. Feedback on scenario issues

Role	Issue	Recommendation
AVO	UAS faults and failures were not present in the scenario. UAS required only basic flying and as a result AVO did not get fully accustomed to flight capabilities.	The scenario should be expanded to include UAS faults and failures. Scenario should require AVO to perform advanced UAS handling (e.g., quickly change speed and heading to maintain visual contact in urban setting)
EW-A	Scenario EW intercepts are not realistic	EW intercepts should not be a synthetic voice (removes emotion) and should contain static. Messages should be longer and more repetitive. Non-threat EW intercepts should be included to increase realism.
IMA and EW	Scenario did not require production of intelligence products, only reporting of POL using chat.	IMA-R and EW-R should be briefed to develop intelligence products on completion of the scenario.
All	All operators reported experiencing mostly optimal and underload levels of workload. Rarely did they experience periods of overload.	The complexity and temporal demands of the mission should be increased in order to explore the effects of overload on individual and crew performance and the implementation of automation technologies.
All	Simulated forces could be made more realisitic in terms of actions and movements.	Complexity and realism of the scenario should be increased by creating more detailed patterns of life for civilian and enemy entities.

(Continued)

Table 1. (*Continued*)

Role	Issue	Recommendation
All	No briefing or general awareness of ROEs and C2 structure.	Crew briefing should include ROEs and C2 structure for the mission. It is recommended that a GUI concept be developed to represent the required (and currently obtained) permissions in order to engage a target.

Table 2. Feedback on workstation usability issues

Role	Issue	Recommendation
AVO	Sensor field of view not present on map.	Implement
AVO	No support of future position of UAS.	Anticipatory display should show location of UAS in one minute on map. This would support future positioning of UAS and payload by AVO and PO.
PO	Sensor zoom controller is difficult to operate.	Zoom control should be implemented on a the joystick hat button, with one press equivalent to changing the zoom one level.
PO	Found it difficult to locate mouse cursor on screens.	Adjust size of cursor or provide a shortcut key to move cursor to a home position.
IMA	IMA operators not familiar with Sensor Command and Control Planning Suite.	Implement Multi-Intellgence Analysis and Archive System.
IMA	Both IMA-A and IMA-R roles are flexible and both should have access to the same software.	Implement
EW-A	Missing a frequency skipping function on the scanners in order to avoid civilian communications.	Implement
EW-A	Direction finding Line of Bearings are missing.	Implement and operator should be able to interact with line of bearings in order to refine the ellipse.
EW-A	EW-A and EW-R should have their own chat room.	Implement
IMA-R and EW-R	IMA-R and EW-R would benefit from reporting templates.	To expedite the creation of chat reports, it is recommended that a chat graphical user interfaces

(*Continued*)

Table 2. (*Continued*)

Role	Issue	Recommendation
		(GUI) concept be developed to allow the operator to quickly create chat reports and updates.
All	Crews had issues with placement of menu items, icons, and arrangement of interface, system prompts, and error messages.	GUI for each workstation should be reviewed by HFE expert to identify issues and recommendations for improvement. Re-design should be reviewed by SMEs.

4 Authority Pathway Concept

One of the main issues the SME observer noted was that both crews had gaps in doctrinal knowledge, particularly with respect to the ROEs and Law of Armed Conflict. One of the crews did not follow standard operating procedures for striking a target. This issue was echoed in the participant feedback that recommended a shared screen GUI concept be developed to represent the required and currently obtained permissions in order to engage a target. An intelligent adaptive interface, called the Authority Pathway concept, has been developed to ensure TIGER operators follow ROEs, the Law of Armed Conflict, and standard operating procedures for engaging a target. An intelligent adaptive interface dynamically changes the interface display of a human-machine system to adaptively react to external events [12]. For TIGER, the Authority Pathway concept intelligently changes a GUI based on the input from the TIGER crew, UAS controlling authority, and software agents.

The Authority Pathway concept supports the UAS crew by displaying and updating the status of the steps required to release a weapon on the basis of a Positive Identification (PID). Discussions with the UAS SME led to the development of a decision tree in which the steps for firing a weapon are outlined, Fig. 4. The figure describes the sequences of activities required by the crew (dashed outlines) and the permissions required from the UAS' controlling authority (solid lines) in order to engage a target following a PID.

The Authority Pathway concept was developed from this decision tree so that the steps for firing a weapon are visualized and the confirmation for each step presented, Fig. 5. Within such a concept, the system will not be able to fire unless the necessary confirmations are in place.

In this concept, each confirmation step is presented as either green (ready or completed) or red (awaiting action or permission). In addition, the last step completed or authorized is presented in green/blue and 'pulsed' so that observers can quickly ascertain which step needs to be completed next. Finally, when completed, each step in the pathway time is stamped so that it can be cross-referenced with chat-based reporting and other mission data (e.g., captured imagery of EW intercepts received).

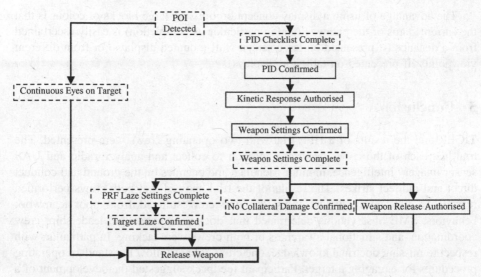

Fig. 4. Steps required to release a weapon on the basis of PID. Steps requiring authorisation external to TIGER have a solid border, steps performed by TIGER crew have a dashed border.

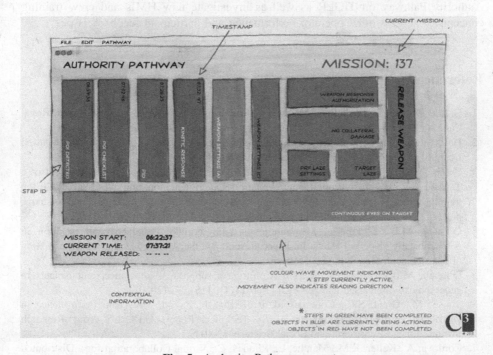

Fig. 5. Authority Pathway concept

The advantage of using a display concept comprising large blocks of colour is that the current status of the pathway (and in particular its completion) is easily ascertained from a distance (if presented on large screen wall-mounted displays) or from different viewpoints (if presented on table-top displays).

5 Conclusions

TIGER and the results of a HFE trial with two operating crews were presented. The trial had each of the crews perform a mission to collect and analyze radio and UAS sensor imagery intelligence, monitor friendlies and enemies on the ground and conduct direct and indirect strikes. The results of the trial showed that both crews performed reasonably well on individual tasks, but one crew suffered from poor teamwork behaviors. SME observations determined that doctrinal knowledge, leadership, crew coordination, and situational awareness of both crews were lacking. In particular, with respect to missing doctrinal knowledge, one crew did not follow the standard operating procedures for engaging a target. Participant feedback suggested the development of a GUI to support the crew in following the proper steps for engaging an enemy. These issues prompted the development of a new intelligent HMI concept called the Authority Pathway. The Authority Pathway concept visualizes the steps required, and the progress being made, for TIGER operators to follow the ROEs and Law of Armed Conflict to legally engage a target. Future work will continue the development and testing of Authority Pathway on TIGER as well as investigate new HMIs and crew training concepts to address other operator performance and participant feedback issues.

References

1. Garrett-Rempel, D.: Will JUSTAS Prevail? Procuring a UAS capability for Canada. Royal Can. Air Force J. **4**(1), 19–31 (2015)
2. Hou, M., Banbury, S., Burns, C.: Intelligent Adaptive Systems: An Interaction-Centred Design Perspective. CRC Press, Boca Raton (2015)
3. Covas-Smith, M., Grant, S.C., Hou, M., Joralmon, D.Q., Banbury, S.: Development of a Testbed for integrated ground control station experimentation and rehearsal (TIGER): training remotely piloted aircraft operations and data exploitation. In: Unmanned Systems, pp. 1–11. Association for Unmanned Vehicle Systems International (AUVSI) (2015)
4. O'Leary, M.B., Mortensen, M.: Subgroups with attitude: imbalance and isolation in geographically dispersed teams. In: Paper presented at the Annual Meeting of the Academy of Management, Honolulu (2005)
5. O'Leary, M.B., Mortensen, M.: Go (Con)figure: subgroups, imbalance, and isolates in geographically dispersed teams. Organ. Sci. **21**(1), 115–131 (2010)
6. Singer, M., Grant, S.C., Commarford, P., Kring, J., Zavod, M.: Team Performance in Distributed Virtual Environments, p. 70. Technical Report 1118, US Army Research Institute for the Behavioral and Social Sciences (2001)
7. Cordova, A., Keller, K.M., Menthe, L., Rhodes, C.: Virtual Collaboration for a Distributed Enterprise, Technical Report, RAND Corporation (2013)

8. Driskell, J.E., Radtke, P.H., Salas, E.: Virtual teams: effects of technological mediation on team performance. Group Dyn. Theor. Res. Pract. **7**(4), 297–323 (2003)
9. Fowlkes, D.J., Oser, R.L., Salas, E.: Event-based approach to training (EBAT). Int. J. Aviat. Psychol. **8**(3), 209–221 (1998)
10. Fowlkes, D.J., Burke, C.S.: Event-based approach to training (EBAT). In: Stanton, N., Hedge, A., Brookhuis, K., Salas, E., Hendrik, H. (eds.) Handbook of Human Factors and Ergonomic Methods. CRC Press, Boca Raton (2005)
11. Baker, K., Banbury, S.: Force Level Tactical Command & Control in a Littoral Environment. Report I: Literature Review and Mission Analysis. DRDC Contract Report CR2008-999 (2008)
12. Hou, M., Zhu, H., Zhou, M.C., Arrabito, R.: Optimizing operator-agent interaction in intelligent adaptive interface design: a conceptual framework. IEEE Trans. Syst. Man Cybern. Part C Appl. Rev. **41**(2), 161–178 (2011)

Object Manipulation by Virtual Menu Interaction Using Free-Hand Input in a Desktop Virtual Reality Maritime Situation Display

Ronald Meyer[1]([⊠]), Alexander Mertens[1], Jeronimo Dzaack[2], and Christopher M. Schlick[1]

[1] Institute of Industrial Engineering and Ergonomics, RWTH Aachen University, Aachen, Germany
{r.meyer,a.mertens,c.schlick}@iaw.rwth-aachen.de
[2] Atlas Elektronik GmbH, Sebaldsbrücker Heerstr. 235, 28309 Bremen, Germany
jeronimo.dzaack@atlas-elektronik.com
http://www.iaw.rwth-aachen.de
http://www.atlas-elektronik.com

Abstract. Marine situation displays or digital sea charts are an essential tool and the basis for marine safety and security applications and define the core element for providing human operators with situational awareness while performing surveillance tasks and to support them in anticipating dangerous situations.

1 Introduction

Marine situation displays or digital sea charts are an essential tool and the basis for marine safety and security applications and define the core element for providing human operators with situational awareness while performing surveillance tasks and to support them in anticipating dangerous situations. They provide essential information by showing collected data and fused information to give the operator a preferably clear picture of a current situation to support in taking appropriate actions. Their usage are both common in the military sector as well as in civil applications such as coastal guard scenarios or for surveillance purposes for critical offshore infrastructures. State of the art digital sea charts used in on- and offshore applications are usually held two-dimensional with planar top-view showing the sea floor as shaded areas indicating sea depth. A planar visualization of the digital sea chart is currently predominant but lacks of providing the operator with spatial relationships among items and objects being shown in the digital map as soon as spatial data has to be reduced by one spatial dimension to match the standard two-dimensional data model which is predominantly used. Object placements in the real world are asynchronous in their altitude positioning especially when ground and air targets are visualized concurrently, e.g. in a rescue situation where sea and aircraft vehicles are deployed simultaneously. Modern sensor technology output such as processed data of sonars or radar provides three-dimensional data sets which has to be

S. Lackey and R. Shumaker (Eds.): VAMR 2016, LNCS 9740, pp. 446–453, 2016.
DOI: 10.1007/978-3-319-39907-2_43

projected for being displayed in a 2D or 2.5D environment. Three-dimensional display systems such as stereoscopic displays or full immersive virtual reality display systems as the "Oculus Rift" or the "Samsung Gear VR" provide the user with virtual depth perception and facilitate the representation of data under maintaining their spatial dimension. Recent developments in spatial input technology, such as the "Microsoft Kinect 2" or the "Leap Motion Controller" make 3D interaction technology available to the consumer market.

We developed a prototype using a stereoscopic display to implement a maritime situation display showing a digital sea chart with vessel tracking data with a freehand pointing technique using the "Leap Motion".

2 State of the Art

Zlatanova et al. [18] see a need of 3D information in geographical information systems (GIS) rapidly increasing and summarize practical applications of 3D GIS in areas that are relevant for marine and submarine data representation which are environmental monitoring, public rescue operations, geological and mining operations, transportation monitoring, hydrographical activities and military applications. The demanded consensus of functionality for a 3D GIS remains the same over 2D GIS and should imply the same functionality as data capture, data structuring, data manipulation, data analysis and data representation. Marine or maritime GIS systems hence are a strong tool where huge data sets are merged together and provide operators with requisite information. Burkle and Essendorfer [3] describe their concept of a system where data of short-range, medium-range and long-range surveillance systems are merged in a "universal ground station", where operators observe fused data from all kinds of aerial and underwater sensors, cameras, land and underwater vehicles to ensure the operator to have a preferably broad view of a maritime area of interest. Prototypes of stereoscopic visualizations of GIS were developed and evaluated by Wartell et al. [16] and implemented as a head tracked stereoscopic environment but did not cover the aspect of interacting with the stereoscopic environment. Wittman et al. analyzed a stereoscopic visualization of an air-traffic controller work station in comparison to a classical 2D representation of data on a group of experts and non-experts. Their research indicates advantages in stereoscopic visualizations of spatial data in surveillance scenarios and give a clear recommendation for non-trained personnel using a stereoscopic visualization system as they had had a benefit in identifying conflicts in air traffic over the 2D representation [17].

The application of a stereoscopic visualization environment requires rethinking classical interaction paradigms conducted via mouse and keyboard and considering a spatial interaction method which provides a more natural and intuitive way to interact with a virtual spatial environment. Complex interaction tasks in a 3D stereoscopic environment require at least three translational and three rotatory degrees of freedom hence a stereoscopic visualization disqualifies the classical interaction paradigm of mouse and keyboard. Prototypes of three-dimensional digital sea chart applications have been described in previous work indicating positive results. Most prototypes work on a small set of sea chart data and use devices supporting two-dimensional input. Gold et al. [7] concluded that the three-dimensional visualization of digital sea chart data has the potential to reduce navigational risks and developed "The Marine GIS", a 3D prototypical visualization system of a digital sea chart with two dimensional input using mouse and keyboard on a 2D display.

The use of 3D displays to visualize three-dimensional information suggests to extend input to three dimensions as suggested by Bowman [2]. Three-dimensional visualizations implicate challenges on the interaction side of a chosen interaction paradigm. Ren & O'Neill [13] evaluated marking menus optimized for 3D environments in a freehand selection scenario and point out that the selection of the menu has to be designed carefully since freehand pointing in virtual environments excludes physical touch of an interface or button clicking. Research conducted by Callahan et al. found pie menu structures reduce selection time and achieve a lower error rate in selection over linear menus [4]. Ni et al. [12] describe their concept of a pie menu being controlled by freehand input in a 2D large screen setting using their so-called "rotate and pinch" method. Selection of a pie menu button is conducted by rotation of the user's wrist which highlights one of the pie menu buttons which is followed by a pinch-click of one of the user's fingers to the thumb to activate a pie menu button. A similar setting is given in a stereoscopic desktop environment where physical feedback is not given when interacting with virtual entities. Hence, the combination of free hand input using a pie menu structure in a stereoscopic desktop environment indicates promising results.

3   Prototype Development

We developed a workflow to convert two-dimensional high resolution digital sea chart material into three dimensional elevation data which we use as a basis to visualize a geo-referenced three-dimensional model of the seabed and render it in a stereoscopic desktop environment. The conversed seabed data guarantees a high recognition value for marine operators since we plan to evaluate our system with end users from the domain of maritime security. The current state of our prototype collects live marine traffic data from a web service which is displayed geo-referenced in the virtual environment. Map objects collected from the web service are shown as two-dimensional track symbols based on the military standard 2525 (cf. Fig. 1 [14]. We subject to replace the two-dimensional symbology with 3D symbols in a consequent study. The menu interaction task is based on a scenario that has previously been assessed in the scope of this research where an operators task is to classify vessels that indicate malicious behavior [10]. The operator achieves the task by navigating through the menu structure choosing appropriate indications.

We use the Leap Motion as an input device to track the users hand to provide a virtual model of her/his hand to be visualized in the virtual environment using a minimalistic visualization. A previous study conducted in the scope of this research on visualization of virtual hand model recommends modeling the virtual hand as a point cloud with interconnected lines to keep the visualization of the

Fig. 1. Digital sea chart in stereoscopic environment showing positions of vessel traffic

hand model minimalistic 2 [11]. This type of visualization of the virtual hand minimizes the effect of occluding data or interactive elements while interacting with the virtual environment.

3.1   Menu Interaction Development

On the basis of using the virtual hand model as a pointing device in the virtual environment we developed an interaction paradigm that utilizes direct pointing interactions on virtual entities with a successional menu interaction to manipulate classification properties that are shown on the three-dimensional digital sea chart.

Our virtual menu is based on different free hand gestural input method approaches which all follow the principle of the so-called pie menu structure. We defined different activation methods of the pie menu buttons which were partly derived from observations from studies previously conducted in the scope of this research and combined with evaluated concepts from the literature. The interaction process consists of two steps: First the operator chooses the interactive entity in the virtual environment by a directed pointing movement on the virtual entity which activates the virtual pie menu either by proximity close to the object in either egocentric mode, where the menu orientation is adapted to the moving direction of the pointing finger, or in allocentric mode, where the menu is aligned perpendicular to the map basis (cf. figures 7 and 6). In a second step the user will choose actions from the activated pie menu structure. We will test three different activation methods for a pie menu button:

1. The finger tip of the operator must have a minimum velocity to activate a menu button when conducting a push gesture on the button (cf. 3). The user must conduct the pointing movement rapidly to evoke the menu button

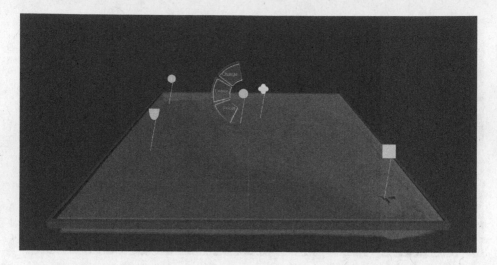

Fig. 2. Virtual translucent menu shown in egocentric orientation

while the virtual finger is moved towards the virtual depth. Rigid postures are avoided by rapid movement. In a previous study we observed participants being challenged by directed pointing movements towards the display volume [11]

2. Two-layer-activation: The menu button is activated when two layers of the virtual button are penetrated in a certain order (cf. 4). This action must be conducted slowly and evokes controlled movements by the user. We expect a comparatively lower error rate for this activation method but increased muscular tension.

3. The finger has to be pulled beyond the radius of the pie menu structure to activate the menu button with a minimum velocity (cf. 5). We expect this activation method to enable the user to be quickly enabled to handle the selection task on the pie menu since there is no necessity correcting the virtual finger in depth. We expect even better results in performance times between activation and selection with the egocentric orientation of the menu since the trajectory correction is expected to be smaller in comparison to the allocentric orientation (cf. 7 and 6). The illustration also shows the difference of angle between the correction task in the allocentric and egocentric menu. Hence, we expect less muscular activity for the egocentric orientation resulting from a bigger angle which we will measure during our experimental task.

4   Experimental Design

We currently conduct an experiment using a factorial design with untrained users where the three described menu activation methods are defined as independent variables. We use an electromyographical measuring device to measure physical

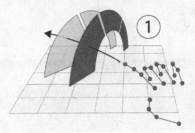

Fig. 3. Virtual finger tip trajectory for fast penetration of button with velocity activation of menu button

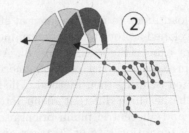

Fig. 4. Virtual finger tip trajectory for penetrating two layers of the virtual button slowly for menu activation

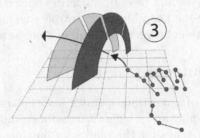

Fig. 5. Virtual finger tip trajectory for radial high velocity swipe-out movement for menu activation

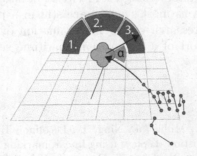

Fig. 6. Illustration of virtual hand movement for menu activation in allocentric orientation

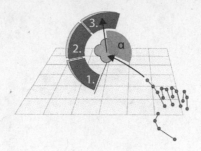

Fig. 7. Illustration of virtual hand movement for menu activation in egocentric orientation

stress and a NASA task load index to measure mental effort as dependent variables. Gramann et al. developed a procedure to determine a user's orientation to prefer either allocentric or egocentric orientations [8]. A successive comparison of the user's individual preference to the performance in each allocentric and egocentric can be conducted by using their method. The main task is conducted as a factorial design with the three different menu interaction types and the distinction of egocentric and allocentric menu orientation which results in six factors. Each factor has a repetition rate of 30 trials and include the independent variables which are activation of the menu to pie menu button selection time and error rate. Our prototype consists of a 27 stereoscopic display with passive stereoscopic glasses and pixel line altering polarization filters in a single user work place. We use the Leap Motion Controller as input device to converse a minimalist virtual representation of the human hand as a direct pointing input.

5   Anticipated Outcomes

Our menu design is part of a maritime operator's workplace using a hybrid visualization of a small 2D display and a bigger three-dimensional stereoscopic screen. The different activation types for the pie menu buttons are designed to evoke different intensities of physical strain. Not much research about the ergonomic aspects of freehand interaction is currently found and influences of different trajectory movement in an interaction task in virtual desktop environment has not received much attention as most systems are still in a prototypical condition. The final state of our research covers the evaluation of ergonomic aspects in physical and mental effort of a stereoscopic maritime situation display for an operator's workplace.

References

1. Bailly, G., Walter, R., Müller, J., Ning, T., Lecolinet, E.: Comparing free hand menu techniques for distant displays using linear, marking and finger-count menus. In: Campos, P., Graham, N., Jorge, J., Nunes, N., Palanque, P., Winckler, M. (eds.) INTERACT 2011, Part II. LNCS, vol. 6947, pp. 248–262. Springer, Heidelberg (2011)

2. Bowman, D.A.: 3D User Interfaces : Theory and Practice. Addison-Wesley, Boston (2005)
3. Burkle, A., Essendorfer, B.: Maritime surveillance with integrated systems. In: 2010 International Waterside Security Conference (WSS), pp. 1–8, November 2010
4. Callahan, J., Hopkins, D., Weiser, M., Shneiderman, B.: An empirical comparison of pie vs. linear menus. In: Proceedings of the SIGCHI Conference on Human Factors in Computing Systems, pp. 95–100. ACM (1988)
5. Chattopadhyay, D., Bolchini, D.: Touchless circular menus: toward an intuitive UI for touchless interactions with large displays. In: Proceedings of the 2014 International Working Conference on Advanced Visual Interfaces, pp. 33–40. ACM (2014)
6. Das, K., Borst, C.W.: An evaluation of menu properties and pointing techniques in a projection-based VR environment. In: 2010 IEEE Symposium on 3D User Interfaces (3DUI), pp. 47–50, March 2010
7. Gold, C., Chau, M., Dzieszko, M., Goralski, R.: 3D geographic visualization: the Marine GIS. In: Fisher, P.F. (ed.) Developments in Spatial Data Handling, pp. 17–28. Springer, Heidelberg (2005)
8. Gramann, K., Onton, J., Riccobon, D., Mueller, H.J., Bardins, S., Makeig, S.: Human brain dynamics accompanying use of egocentric and allocentric reference frames during navigation. J. Cogn. Neurosci. **22**(12), 2836–2849 (2010)
9. Kockro, R.A., Reisch, R., Serra, L., Goh, L.C., Lee, E., Stadie, A.T.: Image-guided neurosurgery with 3-dimensional multimodal imaging data on a stereoscopic monitor. Neurosurgery **72**, A78–A88 (2013)
10. Meyer, R., Bützler, J., Dzaack, J., Schlick, C.M.: Development of interaction concepts for touchless human-computer interaction with geographic information systems. In: Kurosu, M. (ed.) HCI 2014, Part II. LNCS, vol. 8511, pp. 589–599. Springer, Heidelberg (2014)
11. Meyer, R., Btzler, J., Dzaack, J., Schlick, C.M.: Ergonomic design and evaluation of a free-hand pointing technique for a stereoscopic desktop environment. In: Proceedings 19th Triennial Congress of the IEA (2015)
12. Ni, T., McMahan, R.P., Bowman, D.: Tech-note: rapMenu: remote menu selection using freehand gestural input. In: IEEE Symposium on 3D User Interfaces, 3DUI 2008, pp. 55–58. IEEE (2008)
13. Ren, G., O'Neill, E.: 3D Marking menu selection with freehand gestures. In: 2012 IEEE Symposium on 3D User Interfaces (3DUI), pp. 61–68, March 2012
14. Smallman, H.S., St John, M., Oonk, H.M., Cowen, M.B.: Track recognition using two-dimensional symbols or three-dimensional realistic icons. Technical report, DTIC Document (2000)
15. Wacharamanotham, C., Hurtmanns, J., Mertens, A., Kronenbuerger, M., Schlick, C., Borchers, J.: Evaluating swabbing: a touchscreen input method for elderly users with tremor. In: Proceedings of the SIGCHI Conference on Human Factors in Computing Systems, pp. 623–626. ACM (2011)
16. Wartell, Z., Ribarsky, W., Hodges, L.: Third-person navigation of whole-planet terrain in a head-tracked stereoscopic environment. In: Proceedings of Virtual Reality, pp. 141–148. IEEE (1999)
17. Wittmann, D., Baier, A., Neujahr, H., Petermeier, B., Sandl, P., Vernaleken, C., Vogelmeier, L.: Development and Evaluation of Stereoscopic Situation Displays for Air Traffic Control. Universittsbibliothek, Ilmenau (2011)
18. Zlatanova, S., Rahman, A., Pilouk, M.: 3D GIS: current status and perspectives. Int. Arch. Photogram. Remote Sens. Spat. Inf. Sci. **34**(4), 66–71 (2002)

A Performance-Based Training Evaluation for an Augmented Virtuality Call for Fire Training System

Stephen R. Serge[1](✉), Julie N. Salcedo[2], Roberto Champney[2],
Stephanie J. Lackey[2], and Gino Fragomeni[3]

[1] University of Central Florida Institute for Simulation and Training,
Orlando, USA
sserge@ist.ucf.edu
[2] Design Interactive, Inc., Orlando, USA
{julie.salcedo,roberto,
stephanie.lackey}@designinteractive.net
[3] US Army Research Laboratory, Orlando, USA
gino.f.fragomeni@mail.mil

Abstract. A Call for Fire is a complex task requiring specialized training and is performed by a Joint Forward Observer (JFO). As newer technologies become available, innovative ways of incorporating mixed reality into simulation-based training becomes possible. One such approach is through augmented virtuality (AV). AV mixes a heavily virtual environment with interactive objects in the real world, which differs from augmented reality in that the latter overlays virtual elements into a representation of the real world. An AV Call for Fire Simulator was developed in order to assess the efficacy of AV technology for simulation-based training in the JFO training course. This paper describes a training effectiveness evaluation conducted to assess the overall effectiveness of AV integration into current training standards and methodologies.

Keywords: Augmented virtuality · Mixed reality · Simulation-Based training · Head-Mounted displays · Performance

1 Introduction

There exists a keen interest in the utilization of virtual and mixed reality training applications, specifically in the military domain. Increasing availability of technologies capable of integration into current training programs have made realizing these interests increasingly feasible recently. One particular domain area of focus in the present research is Call for Fire (CFF). CFF is a highly complex task required for requesting and directing artillery fire and close air support (CAS) over a specific target area, initiated by a Joint Forward Observer [1]. The CFF task is highly multidimensional, requiring a number of skillsets and proper communication between multiple personnel in order to execute a request effectively.

Current CFF training utilizes classroom and simulated components. Existing simulation hardware allows JFO trainees to learn the proper procedures for executing a

© Springer International Publishing Switzerland 2016
S. Lackey and R. Shumaker (Eds.): VAMR 2016, LNCS 9740, pp. 454–464, 2016.
DOI: 10.1007/978-3-319-39907-2_44

CFF in a safe and repeatable environment. JFO training also requires that individuals maintain currency in their training by recertifying every six months. However, the current simulation technologies are difficult to relocate, are cost prohibitive, and lack a sense of engagement and immersion that can benefit training outcomes [2, 3]. One approach for simulation development has utilized Augmented Virtuality (AV) to help mitigate some of the prohibitive factors existing in typical training, as well as provide adequate training outcomes for CFF training programs.

The present research sought to examine the efficacy of training a CFF-CAS task that utilized AV technology for the simulation portion of training. This effort was undertaken in order to assess the overall effectiveness of an AV system for CFF training, as well as to determine the potential value of a more compact and visually immersive virtual environment for CFF training. The evaluation of the system's training effectiveness followed the Kirkpatrick 4-level model [4, 5]. This model suggests that training may be evaluated along the constructs of learning, reactions, transfer, and impact. While the Kirkpatrick model supported the overall approach to the presented evaluation, the focus of this effort was to assess the viability of an AV-integrated version of a CFF trainer to train a CAS task. Therefore, a complete 4-level assessment was not conducted. Rather, the present evaluation focused on the learning (i.e., task performance) and trainee reaction (i.e., satisfaction) aspects of this model in an effort to address the following research questions:

- Does AV provide an effective training environment for students undergoing CFF training (i.e., does the simulator promote learning measured by passing grades during a training scenario)?
- Does AV technology promote high levels of satisfaction as a result of interaction with the simulator?

2 Background

2.1 Call for Fire and Close Air Support Training

A CFF typically requires a JFO to identify, transmit, and coordinate information between multiple parties in order to effectively guide indirect or close air support fires onto a given target. A JFO is a specialized soldier who receives training necessary to request such fires on a particular target within their target area [6]. During a typical mission, a JFO will obtain visual contact on a target or group of targets within a designated area from a nearby observation point. During a CAS mission, the JFO will acquire target information and communicate that information to a Joint Terminal Attack Controller (JTAC). The JTAC will verify the information passed by the JFO and, in turn, handle communication with aircraft pilots on station. During a CAS request, the JFO is responsible for obtaining target location, elevation, orientation, and providing information on the type of mark (e.g., laser designator, talk-on, etc.) for the aircraft to locate and verify targets. They are also responsible for providing feedback regarding the results of ordnance effects and making adjustments for reattacks, if necessary.

Executing a CAS request requires high levels of efficiency and accuracy from the JFO. In order to execute a CAS request, a JFO in the field must first obtain their position and location, identify any targets for CAS, and observe the immediate area for any threats to possible CAS aircraft. The JFO must communicate this information to his or her fires direction center or JTAC. After coordinating information in the previous step, the JFO must collect specific target or target set information, including a target description, elevation, and grid location, as well as direction and distance of friendly forces from targets and any flight restrictions (e.g., final attack heading and no-fly areas). The JFO must then relay this information to the JTAC. Unless the JFO has specialized equipment for marking the desired target, they must conduct a target talk-on with the pilot. This involves communicating directly with the aircraft pilot and guiding them visually to the target's location. Once the pilot and JFO reach target correlation, the JTAC with authorize the pilot to begin their attack run and the pilot will drop ordnance on the target while the JFO observes and communicates any necessary corrections to munition targeting. Once the CAS mission is completed, the JFO relays battle damage assessment information and continues on the mission.

2.2   Current JFO Training

The Army requires one JFO per maneuver platoon [7]. Through training, the JFO trainee receives the necessary knowledge and skills to request surface-to-surface fires, naval CFFs, AC-130 CFFs, and CAS CFFs with a JTAC. JFO certification requires classroom, live, and simulated training exercises, as well as prior experience in a fires role (e.g., forward observer) before enrolling. Official JFO certification training takes place over two weeks and consists of a mixture of classroom and simulation exercises. Once certified, a JFO must maintain currency by accomplishing 13 live or simulated CFF events every six months. Current pass rate for JFO certification is approximately 75 % of individuals enrolled in the course [8].

Currently, the U.S. Army incorporates Simulation-Based Training (SBT) into the JFO course curriculum. The SBT systems can provide an immersive and engaging mission rehearsal space in a virtual environment. The current simulation system consists of a virtual CFF scenario typically projected onto a screen in front of a classroom. Students sit at a station that consists of equipment used during a CFF mission (e.g., binoculars, compass, map, etc.). Trainees are able to interact with this equipment in conjunction with the virtually projected environment in front of them.

However, this interaction requires the trainee to view a secondary monitor to observe how manipulation of the provided equipment alters the view of the environment. This action sometimes leads to incorrect handling and usage of the JFO's equipment, as well as serve as a potential distractor from the actual training exercise. While the simulation may provide some level of immersion, the system as a whole lacks realism in terms of equipment usage and expectations [9].

2.3   Augmented Virtuality

While current training systems are able to produce effective JFO personnel, there are a number of potential ways to increase both the perceived realism and immersion of the simulated portion of CFF training. One method of promoting more realism throughout training and authentic interaction with the tools and equipment is to incorporate an AV approach to the SBT portion of training.

Milgram and Kishino [10] provide a reality-virtuality continuum that helps identify different types of mixed reality. At one end of the continuum lies reality, while at the other lies virtuality, consisting of a completely virtual environment; AV lies closer to the virtuality side. AV, by definition, is a type of mixed reality that includes a predominately virtual environment that maintains some form of interactive elements or objects in the real world. For example, a virtual surgical trainer may utilize real-life surgical tools in order for a trainee to interact with a virtual patient in a simulated environment [11]. The goal of such an approach is to both increase presence of the trainee during SBT and increase the realism of actions within a virtual environment (Fig. 1).

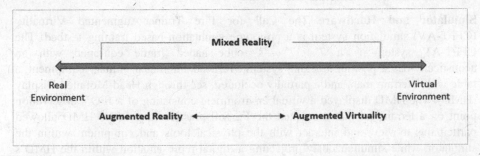

Fig. 1. A simplified representation of Milgram and Kishino's (1994) Reality-Virtuality Continuum.

One method of incorporating AV into current CFF training is by utilizing see-through head-mounted display (HMD) technology. The projection of the virtual environment within the HMD and incorporation of real-world, physical equipment (e.g., compass, binoculars, etc.) that map and correlate to movements in the VE should provide for higher feelings of realism and immersion during training. However, the effectiveness of such training within the CFF domain is uncertain. The present research sought to examine the viability of AV as implemented into CFF simulation training during an actual fires officer training course to obtain a more robust dataset to determine if the use of AV technology is effective for positive outcomes in task performance.

It was hypothesized that (1) performance scores for the CFF task would be significantly higher than the cutoff score for receiving a passing grade and (2) satisfaction ratings would be significantly higher than a neutral response on a subjective Training Satisfaction Survey (TSS).

3   Method

3.1   Participants

A total of 42 U.S. Army officers (32 male) undergoing the Basic Officer Leadership Course (BOLC) for Artillery Field Officers at Ft. Sill, OK were recruited for participation. The average age of these officers was 23.67 years (SD = 2.08). Additionally, participants had served an average of 22.19 months (SD = 24.19) in the military. Thirty-seven participants (88.1 %) indicated having experience on the CFF task either through simulation-based training or live training in the field. Additionally, participant data were collected during week 15 of their 18 week Field Artillery BOLC course, which included classroom instruction of the basic CFF and CAS principles. These participants were selected because they were considered a highly representative sample for this experiment as they were currently undergoing field artillery training, which the AV simulator was able to accommodate. Participation was restricted to U.S. citizens between the ages of 18-40 with normal or corrected-to-normal vision.

3.2   Experimental Materials and Design

Simulator and Hardware. The Call for Fire Trainer-Augmented Virtuality (CFFT-AV) simulation system is a prototype simulation-based training testbed. The CFFT-AV system is a 7' × 7' × 7' cube-shaped frame equipped with an acoustically-based position tracking system overhead, simulated military equipment, a table with a terrain map, and a partially occluded, see-through Head-Mounted Display (HMD). The HMD displayed a virtual environment consisting of a JFO's observation point on a terrain set that mimicked the Ft. Sill practice range. The HMD allowed participants to view and interact with the physical tools and equipment within the simulator, while simultaneously projecting a digital representation within the HMD's virtual overlay of the environment. While wearing the HMD, participants had the ability to turn their heads and body around in order to view an entire 360° virtual environment. The view within the HMD updated in real time based on the direction in which the participant was looking.

The equipment inside the simulator consisted of a terrain map, compass, binoculars, laser range finder, map pens, and a radio. Participants were able to physically interact with all objects in the real world. When the participants picked up and held either the compass, binoculars, or laser range finder close to the front of the HMD, as though they were using an actual device, virtual representations populated within the viewable area of the HMD, changing the image relative to the tool being used. Other tools were placed in clear view on top of the table (Fig. 2).

Scenario and Task. The CFF scenario consisted of a Type 2 CAS request. The virtual environment took place in a large, open field with numerous targets blocking main roadways. The scenario took place under clear weather conditions and optimal visibility with no direct enemy fire. The objective was to clear the roadways of targets to allow freedom of movement on the main surface roads. This scenario mimicked one used for the simulation portion of BOLC training.

Fig. 2. CFFT-AV hardware and trainee interaction tools for the CAS task

Dependent variables included performance metrics for the completion of the CFF/CAS task. Performance was evaluated using the official scoring methods and scorecards for BOLC simulation training, which provided a score of out of 50 possible points. A score of 40 was required to receive a "Go" (i.e., pass). Scores were broken down on the scoresheet into smaller subtasks, allowing students to earn partial points based on the subtask completed successfully. There were a total of 6 subtasks with 1-8 components each for a total of 18 items, ranging between 1-5 points each.

Task completion time was also collected via audio recordings of radio transmissions. Timing metrics included completing the task within 20 min of identifying a target or target set, time to provide the JFO target brief, and duration of the target talk-on with the pilot.

The Training Satisfaction Survey (TSS) consisted of 44 items. Participants rated the degree to which they agreed or disagreed with each item on a 5-point scale (i.e., 1 = Strongly disagree; 5 = Strongly agree). The items on the survey provide subscale measurements related to individual satisfaction with the way the training provides or supports information regarding objectives, support for learning, problem solving, feedback, fidelity, and utility [12].

Procedure. Participation took place within a block of approximately 1 h, with each participant completing the task individually. Participants first reviewed an informed consent for their participation and were given an opportunity to ask any questions regarding the experiment. After providing consent, participants completed an initial set of questionnaires to provide information about themselves, including demographics, military experience, and familiarity with the CFF task. Once completed, participants were briefed by a Subject Matter Expert (SME) regarding the situation and scenario, as well as the objective of each participant acting as the JFO within the simulation. The SME was one of three certified JTACs and highly familiar with the CAS procedures used in the scenario (Appendix A).

Once briefed, participants were provided with a functional overview of the HMD and AV environment, as well as instructed on how to interact with the equipment within the simulator and communicate with the instructor during the experimental session. After becoming familiarized with the simulation equipment, participants began completing the JFO CAS request with the instructor over the radio.

Participants were given approximately 30 min to complete the entire simulation task. Once completed, they were asked to complete a set of post-exposure questionnaires including the TSS. After completion of the final questionnaires, participants were debriefed on their performance in the simulator and the nature of the research, provided with an opportunity to ask questions, and were dismissed.

4 Results

Preliminary data checks were conducted to ensure no extreme outliers were present in the data. Results revealed no extreme outliers present in the data. However, one participant's data was excluded from the final analysis due to their nominal skills in the area of land navigation and being unable to complete a significant portion of the scenario in the allotted time. Additionally, since multiple SME also served as graders, consistency between ratings was examined to ensure scores between graders were consistent. Results from this comparison revealed no significant differences between graders on task performance scores ($t(40) = -.493$, $p = .625$).

4.1 Performance on the Call for Fire Task Scenario

Results for overall simulation scenario performance were compared to the minimum BOLC simulation passing score of 40. Thirty-five out of 42 participants were able to achieve passing scores (83.3 %). The average score for all participants ($M = 43.98$, $SD = 5.29$) was significantly higher than the minimum passing score of 40 ($t(41) = 4.88$, $p < .001$).

Prior experience with CAS training, either virtually or live, was examined to determine whether this factor had any effect on performance scores. Results showed that 88.1 % of participants had some prior training with CAS. However, this training did not have a significant effect on performance results between groups (Mann-Whitney U = 79.5, $p = .612$).

4.2 Time Performance

Participants had 20 min from the time they identified a target for CAS to guide ordnance on the target from the aircraft. Per BOLC standards, failure to complete this task within the given 20 min resulted in an automatic failure. A One-Sample t-test revealed that average time from target identification to contact of ordnance on a target ($M = 17:18$, $SD = 4:31$) was significantly lower than the BOLC standard ($t(41) = -3.88$, $p < .001$).

However, further examination of the data revealed that only 31 out of the 42 participants were able to complete the task within the given 20 min time limit, meaning that 73.8 % were eligible to receive a passing mark on their performance based on the time allotted for scenario completion. Those who completed the simulation within the allotted time also had higher scores on their overall performance within the simulator than those who did not complete the scenario in time. In addition, other time measurements (i.e., Target brief and Talk-on) were also completed significantly faster by those scoring higher on the simulation performance metric. The descriptive data and statistical results are presented in Tables 1 and 2, respectively.

Table 1. Means and SDs for task perfomance measures

Performance Metric	Go (time)	No-Go (time)
Total Score	45.26 (4.54)	40.36 (5.77)
Target Brief Time	156.13 (74.81)	257.10 (126.77)
Talk-On	210.84 (97.25)	293.82 (94.69)
ID-to-Ordnance	918.61 (201.79)	1374.18 (102.05)

Note: Time measured in seconds

Table 2. T-test results between groups on time performance

Performance Metric	Mean Diff.	Std. Error	t(df)	p
Total Score	4.89	1.71	2.86(40)	.007
Target Brief Time[*]	−100.97	42.35	−2.38(11.16)	.036
Talk-On	−82.98	33.91	−2.45(40)	.019
ID-to-Ordnance	−455.57	47.54	−9.58(34.72)	< .001

[*] indicates equal variances not assumed.

4.3 Subjective Satisfaction with Training

Results from the six TSS subscales were compared to a neutral scale score (i.e., 3 = neutral). One-Sample t-tests were conducted to compare scores. All TSS subscale scores were significantly higher than the neutral score, indicating that participants were generally satisfied with the training they received from the CFFT-AV (Table 3).

5 Discussion

The goal of the present experiment was to determine the overall effectiveness of a CFF trainer that incorporated AV simulation training technology. The CFFT-AV system relies on AV to provide increased realism while training by incorporating an HMD to present a 360-degree virtual world around the trainee rather than using a projector or monitor screen. Preliminary research exploring AV technology has outlined how the technology provides both high immersion and increased realism in procedural training

Table 3. Results from One-Sample *t*-tests on the TSS Survey

Sub-Scale	M	SD	t
Objectives & Information	4.71	0.419	26.49*
Support	4.71	0.465	23.65*
Problem-Solving	4.48	0.649	14.74*
Feedback & Guided Reflection	4.82	0.381	31.01*
Fidelity	4.27	0.580	14.22*
Utility	4.60	0.521	19.91*

Note: All means compared to neutral scale value of '3.'
* indicates $p < .001$

of CFF-related tasks [12]. The findings of this evaluation add to that literature by providing insight into the relationship between incorporating AV into SBT with an HMD and performance outcomes.

It was predicted that the CFFT-AV would provide adequate training for the CFF-CAS request scenario, as well as result in a generally positive reaction from the participants. Performance results indicated that the majority of participants were able to achieve a passing grade on their CAS scenario. Additionally, approximately three-quarters of participants were able to achieve a passing grade within the acceptable time-to-completion from target identification to ordnance on target. Considering that this was the first time many of the participants performed a CAS request with a JTAC, whether live or simulated, these numbers indicate that the CFFT-AV system is an effective training medium for the BOLC course and JFO training. Despite the system being in a prototype stage, trainees were still able to obtain positive performance scores using the system.

Participants responded to the training in a generally positive way, supporting the second hypothesis. BOLC students reported highly on all satisfaction subscales, indicating that they felt as though the CFFT-AV system provides an adequate amount of information and/or support to individuals training the CFF task. In its current form, the integration of the CFFT-AV simulator into CFF-CAS training for BLOC students led to an effective and positive training experience. Increased satisfaction during SBT and learning are linked to increased levels of motivation [14], which are both related to increased levels of training performance and learning outcomes [15]. As such, future iterations of the CFFT-AV system should adhere to a similar functional design as the current system in order to maintain or improve upon current levels of learner satisfaction.

The CFFT-AV simulator was able to evoke high levels of performance and satisfaction ratings from participants. While this supports the overall effectiveness of the system in general, this effort was unable to attain performance scores and subjective satisfaction from the current CFFT program of record simulator for comparison.

Based on available literature, the student pass rate appears to be on par with that of the CFFT-AV [7]. Still, future research that examines the two systems independently may yield findings that better define the differences between the overall effectiveness of the CFFT-AV and the current CFFT training systems.

Acknowledgements. This research was sponsored by the U.S. Army Research Laboratory – Human Research Engineering Directorate, Advanced Training and Simulation Division (ARL/HRED/ATSD), in collaboration with the Institute for Simulation and Training at the University of Central Florida. This work is supported in part by ARL/HRED/ATSD contract W911QX-13-C-0052. The views and conclusions contained in this document are those of the authors and should not be interpreted as representing the official policies, either expressed or implied, of ARL/HRED/ATSD or the U.S. Government. The U.S. Government is authorized to reproduce and distribute reprints for Government purposes notwithstanding any copyright notation hereon.

Appendix

Grouping	Procedure	Description
CAS Request	Send SALT Report	- Includes size, activity, location (grid, altitude, distance, direction) and time within 10 minutes of occupying OP
	Observer Lineup	- String of information relayed from JFO to JTAC to help identify JFO location and any specialized equipment to assist in CAS
	Situation Update	- Threat activity, enemy grid vicinity, friendly location (distance and cardinal direction from target), artillery activity, remarks and restrictions for aircraft
JFO Target Brief (9-line)	Elevation	- Target elevation within 25m (82ft)
	Target Description	- Accurate and descriptive target description
	Target Location	- Target location within 50m
	MarkType	- Supply mark type, if applicable
	Friendly Force Location	- Closest friendlies from target (cardinal direction & distance)
	Flight Restrictions	- Ingress/Egress directions; NFAs
	(Check for Bad Read Backs)	- Request and confirm read back of lines 4 & 6
Talk On	Target Talk On	- Describe terrain to visually guide pilot to target(s)
	Target Correlation	- Provide enough information to ID correct target(s)
Execution	Observer Instructions	- Confirm and request attack/abort
	Munition Corrections	- Relay ordinance correction if needed
Battle Damage Assessment	Report success or failure	- Briefed final success/failure mission details to pilot or JTAC

References

1. Army, U.S.: FM 6-30: Tactics, Techniques, and Procedures for Observed Fire. U.S. Army, Washington (1991)
2. U.S Army PEO STRI: Call for Fire Training (CFFT II Plus). http://www.peostri.army.mil/PRODUCTS/CFFT+/
3. Hamari, J., Shernoff, D.J., Rowe, E., Collier, B., Asbell-Clarke, J., Edwards, T.: Challenging games help students learn: an empirical study on engagement, flow, and immersion in game-based training. Comput. Hum. Behav. **54**, 170–179 (2016)
4. Kirkpatrick, D.L., Kirkpatrick, J.D.: Evaluating Training Programs: The Four Levels, 3rd edn. Berrett-Koehler Publishers Inc, San Francisco (2006)
5. Kirkpatrick, D.L., Kirkpatrick, J.D.: Implementing the Four Levels: A Practical Guide for Effective Evaluation of Training Programs. Berrett-Koehler Publishers, San Francisco (2007)
6. Strensrud, B.S., Fragomeni, G., Garrity, P.: Autonomy requirements for virtual JFO training. In: Proceedings of the Interservice/Industry Training, Simulation, and Education Conference. Arlington (2013)
7. Lang, G.T.: JFO Sustainment: A Critical Requirement. Fires Bulletin, Ft. Sill (2009)
8. Joint Fires Observer Pre-Course: Building the Foundation. Redleg Update Newsletter, Ft. Sill (2015)
9. Fragomeni, G., Lackey, S.J., Champney, R., Salcedo, J.N., Serge, S.: Training effectiveness evaluation: call for fire trainer – augmented virtuality (CFFT-AV). In: Shumaker, R., Lackey, S. (eds.) VAMR 2015. LNCS, vol. 9179, pp. 263–272. Springer, Heidelberg (2015)
10. Milgram, P., Kishino, F.: A Taxonomy of Mixed Reality Visual displays. IEICE Trans. Inf. and Syst. **E77-D**(12), 1321–1329 (1994)
11. Samur, E.: Performance metrics for haptic interfaces. Springer Science + Business Media, New York (2012)
12. Jefferies, P.R.: A framework for designing, implementing and evaluating simulations used as teaching strategies in nursing. Nurs. Educ. Perspect. **26**(2), 96–103 (2005)
13. Salcedo, J.N., Serge, S.R., Lackey, S.J., Hurter, J., Champney, R., Fragomeni, G.: Training Effectiveness Evaluation of Augmented Virtuality for Call for Fire Training
14. Koh, C., Tan, H.S., Tan, K.C., Fang, L., Fong, F.M., Kan, D., Lye, S.L., Wee, M.L.: Investigating the effect of 3d simulation-based learning on the motivation and performance of engineering students. J. Eng. Educ. **99**(3), 237–251 (2010)
15. Salas, E., Wildman, J.L., Piccolo, R.F.: Using simulation-based training to enhance management education. Acad. Learn. Educ. **8**(4), 559–573 (2009)

The Effect of Agent Reasoning Transparency on Automation Bias: An Analysis of Response Performance

Julia L. Wright[1(✉)], Jessie Y.C. Chen[1],
Michael J. Barnes[2], and P.A. Hancock[3]

[1] US Army Research Laboratory, Orlando, FL, USA
{Julia.l.wright8.civ,Yun-sheng.c.chen.civ}@mail.mil
[2] US Army Research Laboratory, Ft. Huachuca, Sierra Vista, AZ, USA
michael.j.barnes.civ@mail.mil
[3] University of Central Florida, Orlando, FL, USA
Peter.Hancock@ucf.edu

Abstract. We examined how the transparency of an agent's reasoning affected the human operator's complacent behavior in a military route selection task. Participants guided a three-vehicle convoy through a simulated environment in which they had a limited amount of information about their surroundings, all this while maintaining communication with command and monitoring their surroundings for threats. The intelligent route-planning agent, RoboLeader, assessed potential threats and offered changes to the planned route as necessary. RoboLeader reliability was 66 %, and the participant had to correctly reject RoboLeader's suggestion when incorrect. Access to RoboLeader's reasoning was varied across three conditions (no reasoning, reasoning present, and increased reasoning transparency), and each participant was assigned to one of the three conditions. Access to agent reasoning improved performance and decreased automation bias. However, when reasoning transparency increased, performance decreased while automation bias increased. Implications for presentation of reasoning information in operational settings are discussed in light of these findings.

Keywords: Human-agent teaming · Automation bias · Agent transparency · Complacency

1 Introduction

Soldiers interact with a wide variety of automated and robotic assets, both as part of their normal duties as well as to expand their scope of influence. Employing robotic assets to assist in their duties allows the Soldier to manage multiple tasks of increasing complexity. Such aids permit more effective multitasking and enhance performance on secondary tasks [1]. This is accomplished by reducing their workload and freeing cognitive resources [2]. These benefits are especially important when a Soldier is managing a team of robotic assets. Research has shown that a single operator managing multiple robotic assets can suffer performance decrements such as reduced situation

© Springer International Publishing Switzerland 2016
S. Lackey and R. Shumaker (Eds.): VAMR 2016, LNCS 9740, pp. 465–477, 2016.
DOI: 10.1007/978-3-319-39907-2_45

awareness (SA) and increased workload [3–5]. As the number of robots increase, so do these performance decrements [6]. To assist an operator managing a team of robots, an intelligent agent, RoboLeader (RL), has been developed [7]. RL acts as a mediator between the human operator and the team of subordinate robots. This gives the operator a single point of contact for such robotic assets. Several studies with RL have shown that using such an intelligent agent as a mediator for the robotic team improves both the operators' SA and task performance, while decreasing their perceived workload [8–10].

However, the use of an intelligent agent as a mediator between the operator and robotic team is not without problems. Supervisory control issues such as reduced SA and increased complacency [11] become apparent as the operator is further removed from the inner 'loop' of control [2, 12]. Previous RL studies have indicated that while the operator benefitted from reduced workload, their task performance or SA did not always improve concomitantly [8]. Indeed, increasing RL's level of assistance resulted in decreased performance for certain individuals [10]. While the addition of the intelligent agent can be a boon to an operator managing multiple tasks, it also creates the distance that makes effective supervision of the team more difficult. Often this "distance" results in the operator displaying automation bias in favor of agent recommendations. It remains unknown whether this bias is a result of the operator recognizing they do not have enough information to confidently override the agent suggestions when appropriate, or whether complacency is due to an operator's out-of-the-loop (OOTL) role. Increasing the transparency of the agent has been recommended as one way to reduce this distance, pulling the operator back into the inner loop of control [13]. One way to do this is to increase the operator's understanding of the agent's reasoning (i.e., why is the agent making this recommendation). As the users' understanding of the rationale behind a systems' behavior grows, the more accurate the users' calibration of their trust and reliance is expected to be [14–16].

1.1 Current Study

In order to distinguish between the latter two propositions, we engaged in the present study. Participants guided a convoy of robotic vehicles (an unmanned aerial vehicle [UAV], an unmanned ground vehicle [UGV], and a manned ground vehicle [MGV]) through a simulated environment with an intelligent agent (RoboLeader) assisting with the route planning task. As the convoy progressed, events would occur that would necessitate re-routing the convoy, and RL would recommend changes to the route as these events occurred. The participant had information from a variety of sources regarding the events, and had to either accept or reject RL's recommendation. In each scenario, RoboLeader suggested route changes 6 times, 4 times of which RL's suggestion was the correct choice. The participant was required to recognize and correctly reject an incorrect suggestions. In addition to the route selection task, participants maintained communications with command and monitored the area for threats. Operator complacency and trust across differing agent transparency conditions (explained below) were evaluated via performance and response time measures.

Agent transparency was manipulated by varying participants' access to RL's reasoning; participants were randomly assigned to one of three agent reasoning transparency

(ART) conditions. ART 1 was the Baseline—the agent notified the operator that a route revision was recommended, however, no reasoning for the suggestion was given (i.e., 'Change to convoy path recommended'). ART 2 had the same notification process as in ART 1, but RL also explained its reason for the suggested route change (e.g., 'Change to convoy path recommended. Activity in area: Dense Fog'). ART 3 had the same information as in ART 2, but RL also provided the time of report (TOR) (e.g., 'Change to convoy path recommended. Activity in area: Dense Fog. TOR: 1 [h]').

We hypothesized that access to agent reasoning would improve operator performance, reduce complacent behavior, and increase trust in the agent—but only to a degree, beyond which increased transparency of agent reasoning would negatively impact operator performance, increase complacent behavior, and reduce trust in the agent (i.e., ART 1 < ART 2 > ART 3). This hypothesis recapitulates an inverted [extended] U-shaped function often observed in operators in stressful conditions [22, 23]. Performance on the route planning task was evaluated using the number of correct acceptances and rejections of RL's suggestions. Automation bias was evaluated by the number of incorrect acceptances. Distrust was evaluated objectively via incorrect rejections of RL's suggestions, and subjectively via scores on a usability and trust survey. Decision time was expected to increase as access to agent reasoning increased: ART 1 < ART 2 < ART 3. Although RL's messages were slightly longer in ARTs 2 and 3 than in ART 1, additional time was not expected to be required for reading the messages. Participants were expected to take longer to process the information and reach their decision, resulting in a longer decision time. Shorter response times may indicate less deliberation on the part of the operator before accepting or rejecting the agent recommendation. This could mean either positive automation bias or reduced task difficulty.

2 Method

2.1 Participants

Sixty participants (26 males, 33 females, 1 unreported, Min_{age} = 18 years, Max_{age} = 32 years, M_{age} = 21.4 years) from a large southern US university participated for either class credit or cash compensation.

2.2 Materials

Simulator. The simulator in this experiment was a modified version of the Mixed Initiative Experimental (MIX) Testbed [17], a distributed simulation environment developed for investigating how unmanned systems are used and how automation affects human operator performance. The RoboLeader algorithm was implemented on the MIX Testbed and had the capability of collecting information from subordinate robots, making tactical decisions, and then coordinating the activities of subordinate robots [7]. The Operator Control Unit (OCU) of the MIX Testbed (Fig. 1) was modeled after the Tactical Control Unit developed under the ARL Robotics Collaborative Technology Alliance. The simulation was delivered via a commercial desktop computer system, 22-inch monitor, standard keyboard, and three-button mouse.

1. Map and Route Overview

7. UAV Camera Feed

2. RoboLeader Communications Window

3. Command Communications Window

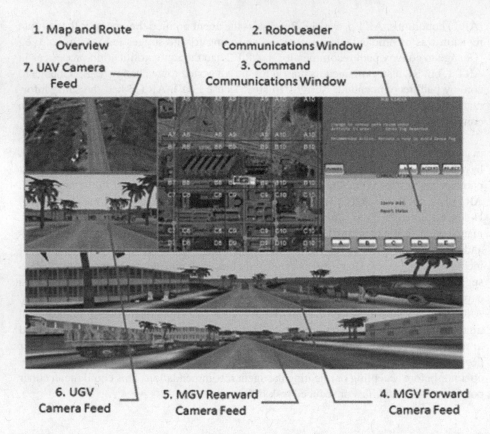

6. UGV Camera Feed

5. MGV Rearward Camera Feed

4. MGV Forward Camera Feed

Fig. 1. Operator Control Unit (OCU), the user interface for convoy management. OCU windows are (clockwise from the upper center): 1. Map and Route overview, 2. RoboLeader communications window, 3. Command communications window, 4. MGV Forward 180° Camera Feed, 5. MGV Rearward 180° Camera Feed, 6. UGV Forward Camera Feed and 7. UAV Camera Feed.

Demographics. A demographics questionnaire was administered at the beginning of the training session and information on participant's age, gender, education level, computer familiarity, and gaming experience was collected.

2.3 Procedure

After signing the informed consent, participants completed a demographics questionnaire, a reading comprehension test, and a brief Ishihara Color Vision Test to screen for eligibility to participate in the experiment. Participants then received practice on their tasks. This training was self-paced and delivered by PowerPoint® slides. Participants were trained on the elements of the OCU, identifying map icons and their meanings, steps for completing various tasks, and completed several mini-exercises for practice. The training session lasted approximately 1.5 h. Participants were assessed on their proficiency on the required tasks before proceeding to the experimental session, and those that did not achieve at least 90 % on the assessments were dismissed.

The experimental session lasted about 2 h and began immediately after the training session. Participants were randomly assigned to an Agent Reasoning Transparency (ART) condition (ART 1, ART 2, or ART 3). Each experimental session had three scenarios, each lasting approximately 30 min. The scenario order and ART were counterbalanced across participants.

Participants guided a convoy of three vehicles (their MGV, a UAV, and a UGV) along a predetermined route through a simulated urban environment. As the convoy proceeded, events occurred which may have necessitated altering the route. Events and their associated area of influence were displayed on the map. The operator either accepted the suggestion or rejected it and kept the convoy on its original path. RoboLeader (RL) suggested a potential route revision six times per session. Two of these suggestions were incorrect, requiring the participant to correctly reject the suggestion. Once RL suggested a route revision, participants had 15 s to acknowledge the suggested change before RL automatically continued along the original route. Once acknowledged, the vehicles paused until the participant either agreed with or rejected RL's suggestion.

Participants maintained communication with 'command' via a text feed directly below RL's communication window. Incoming messages (from either source) appeared approximately every 30 s. Communications from command included messages directed at other units, which the participant should disregard, and requests for information, which required a response. Each mission contained 12 information updates, two of which would result in the need to override RL's route recommendation.

While moving through the environment participants' maintained local security surrounding their MGV by monitoring the MGV and UGV indirect-vision displays and detect threats (armed civilians) in the immediate environment. Participants identified threats by clicking on the threat in the window using the mouse, and received no feedback on this task. There were unarmed civilians and friendly dismounted soldiers in the simulated environment to increase the visual noise present in the threat detection tasks. Following completion of all three scenarios participants were debriefed and any questions they had were answered by the experimenter.

2.4 Experiment Design and Performance Measures

The study was a between-subject experiment with Agent Reasoning Transparency (ART) as the independent variable. Dependent measures were route selection performance score, automation bias score, distrust score, and decision time.

Data was analyzed using planned comparisons ($\alpha = .05$). Specifically, ART 1 was compared to ART 2, ART 2 to ART 3, and ART 1 to ART 2 + 3, unless otherwise noted. Omnibus ANOVAs ($\alpha = .05$) are also reported.

Performance Score. Total correct acceptances and rejections were summed across all missions. The range for this score is 0 (no correct rejects or accepts) to 18 (all suggestions correctly accepted or rejected).

Automation Bias. Twice each mission RoboLeader made a suggestion that should be rejected. Participants scored 1 point for each incorrect acceptance and these were summed across all missions. Higher scores indicate higher automation bias. The score range for this measure is 0 – 6.

Distrust. Four times each mission RoboLeader made a suggestion that should have been correctly accepted. Participants scored 1 point for each incorrect rejection and these were summed across all missions. Higher scores indicate greater distrust. The score range for this measure is 0 – 12.

Decision Time. Decision time was measured as time between alert acknowledgment and route selection, and averaged across missions.

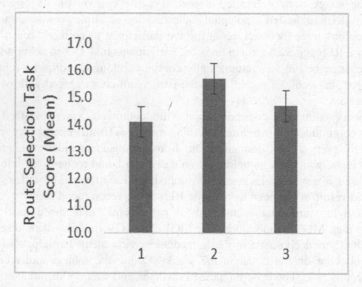

Fig. 2. Average Route selection task score by agent reasoning transparency level. Bars denote SE.

3 Results

3.1 Route Selection Task Performance

There was no significant effect of ART on the route selection task scores, $F(2,57) = 2.00$, $p = .145$, $\omega^2 = .03$ (Fig. 2). Planned comparisons revealed mean performance scores were slightly higher in ART 2 ($M = 15.70$, $SD = 2.23$) than in ART 1 ($M = 14.10$, $SD = 2.59$), $t(57) = 1.98$, $p = .053$, $r_c = 0.25$. There was no significant difference in performance between ART 2 and ART 3 ($M = 14.70$, $SD = 2.81$), $t(57) = -1.24$, $p = .221$, $r_c = 0.16$. The hypothesis was partially supported, as the medium-large effect size between ARTs 1 and 2 indicates that the addition of agent reasoning did improve route selection. Scores in ART 3 were lower than those in ART 2, however this difference was not significant, indicating that performance in these two conditions was essentially the same.

3.2   Automation Bias

Evaluating Automation Bias scores between ART conditions, there was a violation of the homogeneity of variance assumption. As such, Welch's correction has been reported, and contrast tests did not assume equal variance between conditions. There was a significant effect of ART on automation bias, $F(2,34.8) = 7.96$, $p = .001$, $\omega^2 = .14$ (Fig. 3). Mean automation bias scores were lower in ART 2 ($M = 1.14$, $SD = 1.28$) than in ART 1 ($M = 3.25$, $SD = 2.27$), $t(57) = -3.63$, $p = .001$, $r_c = 0.55$, and ART 3 ($M = 2.65$, $SD = 2.32$), $t(57) = 2.55$, $p = .016$, $r_c = 0.43$. Overall, automation bias scores were significantly lower when agent reasoning was provided, t $(57) = -2.31$, $p = .028$, $r_c = 0.38$. The hypothesis was supported, since access to agent reasoning did reduce automation bias in a low information environment, and increased transparency of agent reasoning began to overwhelm participants, resulting in increased automation bias.

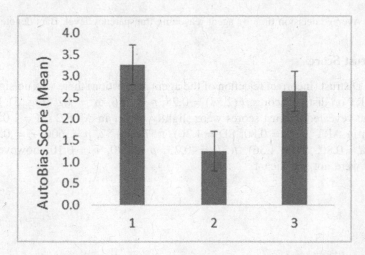

Fig. 3. Average Automation bias scores by agent reasoning transparency level. Bars denote SE.

Automation bias could also be indicated by reduced decision time on the route selection task. We hypothesized that decision time would increase as agent reasoning transparency increased, as participants should require additional time to process the extra information. Thus, reduced time could indicate less time spent in deliberation, which could be an indication of automation bias.

There was not a significant effect of ART on elapsed decision time, $F(2,57) = 1.51$ $p = .230$, $\omega^2 = .02$ (Fig. 4). Mean automation bias scores were lower in ART 2 ($M = 2787.58$, $SD = 1055.09$) than in ART 1 ($M = 3530.32$, $SD = 1567.98$), $t(57) = -1.74$, $p = .088$, $r_c = 0.22$, and ART 3 ($M = 3176.34$, $SD = 1383.57$), $t(57) = 0.91$, $p = .367$, $r_c = 0.12$. Overall, decision times were lower when agent reasoning was provided, but not significantly so, $t(57) = -1.49$, $p = .144$, $r_c = 0.19$.

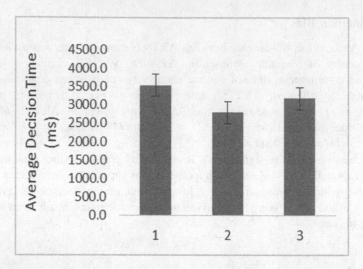

Fig. 4. Average decision time by agent reasoning transparency level. Bars denote SE.

3.3   Distrust Score

Evaluating Distrust (incorrect rejection of the agent suggestion) there was no significant effect of ART on distrust scores, $F(2,57) = 0.28$, $p = .756$, $\omega^2 = .02$, (Fig. 5). Planned comparisons revealed distrust scores were slightly higher in ART 2 ($M = 1.05$, SD = 1.15) than in ART 1 ($M = 0.80$, SD = 1.36), $t(57) = 0.52$, $p = .606$, $r_c = 0.07$, and ART 3 ($M = 0.80$, SD = 1.36), $t(57) = -0.73$, $p = .470$, $r_c = 0.10$, however these differences were not significant.

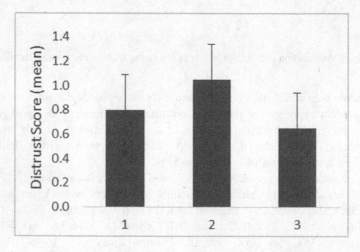

Fig. 5. Average Distrust scores by agent reasoning transparency level. Bars denote SE.

3.4 Usability and Trust Survey

There was not a significant effect of ART on Trust score, $F(2,57) = 2.52$, $p = .089$, $\omega^2 = .05$, (Fig. 6). There was also a significant curvilinear trend to the data, $F(1,57) = 4.15$, $p = .046$, $\omega^2 = .05$. Planned comparisons revealed that trust scores in ART 2 ($M = 54.40$, SD $= 10.23$) were slightly lower than in ART 1 ($M = 58.55$, SD $= 8.28$), $t(57) = -1.29$, $p = .202$, $r_c = 0.17$, and significantly lower than ART 3 scores ($M = 61.60$, SD $= 11.72$), $t(57) = 2.24$, $p = .029$, $r_c = 0.28$. These findings did not support the hypothesis, as ART 2 had the lowest Trust scores while ART 3 had the highest.

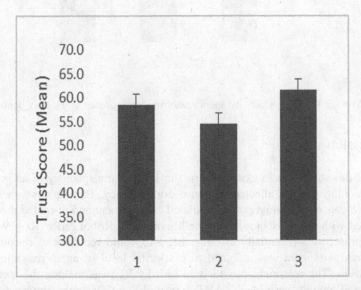

Fig. 6. Average Trust scores by agent reasoning transparency level. Bars denote SE.

There was a significant effect of ART on Usability scores, $F(2,57) = 5.11$, $p = .009$, $\omega^2 = .12$, (Fig. 7). There was also a significant curvilinear trend to the data, $F(1,57) = 9.96$, $p = .003$, $\omega^2 = .13$. Pairwise comparisons showed that Usability scores in ART 2 ($M = 40.75$, SD $= 6.60$) were significantly lower than those in either ART 1 ($M = 46.75$, SD $= 5.33$), $t(57) = -2.98$, $p = .004$, $r_c = 0.37$, or ART 3 ($M = 45.75$, SD $= 7.03$), $t(57) = 2.49$, $p = .049$, $r_c = 0.31$. Overall, Usability scores were significantly lower when agent reasoning was present than when it was not, $t(57) = -2.01$, $p = .049$, $r_c = 0.26$.

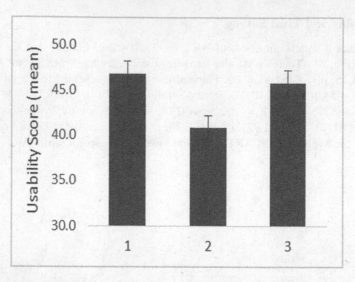

Fig. 7. Average Usability scores by agent reasoning transparency level. Bars denote SE.

4 Discussion

The goal of this study was to examine how the level of transparency of an intelligent agent's reasoning process affected response complacency. Participants supervised a three-vehicle convoy as it traversed a simulated environment and re-routed the convoy when needed with the assistance of an intelligent agent, RoboLeader (RL). When the convoy approached a potentially unsafe area, RL would recommend re-routing the convoy. Each participant was assigned to a specific level of agent reasoning transparency (ART). The reasoning provided as to why RL was making the recommendation differed among these levels. ART 1 provided no reasoning information—RL notified that a change was recommended without explanation. The type of information the agent supplied varied slightly between ARTs 2 and 3. This additional information did not convey any confidence level or uncertainty but was designed to encourage the operator to actively evaluate the quality of the information rather than simply respond. Therefore, not only was access to agent reasoning available, but the impact of the type of information the agent supplied could be examined also.

Performance on the route selection task was evaluated via correct rejections and acceptances of the agent suggestion. An increased number of correct acceptances and rejections, and reduced response times were all indicative of improved performance. Route selection performance was hypothesized to improve with access to agent reasoning and then decline as agent reasoning transparency increased, and this hypothesis was partially supported. Performance did improve when access to agent reasoning was provided. However, increased transparency of agent reasoning did not result in a performance decrement.

Complacent behavior was examined via primary (route selection) task response, in the form of automation bias (i.e., incorrect acceptances of RL suggestions). As predicted, access to agent reasoning reduced incorrect acceptances, and increased reasoning transparency increased incorrect acceptances. Complacent behavior was highest when no agent reasoning was available. When the transparency of agent reasoning was increased to its highest level, complacent behavior increased to nearly the same level as in the no-reasoning condition. This pattern of results indicated that while access to agent reasoning in a decision-supporting agent can counter automation bias, too much information results in an out-of-the-loop (OOTL) situation and increased complacent behavior.

Similar to previous findings [16], access to agent reasoning did not increase response time. In fact, decision times were reduced in the agent reasoning conditions, even though the agent messages in the reasoning conditions were slightly longer than in the no reasoning condition and required slightly more time to process. Similar studies have suggested that a reduction in accuracy with consistent response times could be attributed to a speed-accuracy trade-off [18]. However, the present findings indicated that may not be the case. We saw an increase in accuracy with no accompanying increase in response time (hence no trade-off). What appears to be more likely is that not only does the access to agent reasoning assist the operator in determining the correct course of action, but the type of information the operator receives also influences their behavior.

The objective measure of operator trust indicated no difference in trust due to agent reasoning transparency. Subjective measures indicated agent reasoning had no effect on operator trust and reduced the usability evaluation. Increased transparency of agent reasoning resulted in increased trust and usability ratings, however there was no associated improvement in performance. Interestingly, operators reported highest trust and usability in the conditions that also had the highest complacency, and lowest in the condition that had the highest performance.

In all conditions, the operator received all information needed to correctly route the convoy without the agent's suggestion. In the Baseline condition, the operators demonstrated a clear bias for the agent suggestion. With a moderate amount of information regarding the agent reasoning, the operators were more confident in overriding erroneous suggestions. In the highest reasoning transparency condition, operators were also given information regarding when the agent had received the information (i.e. its recency), and while this information did not imply any confidence or uncertainty on the part of the agent, such additional information appeared to create ambiguity for the operator. This encouraged them to defer to the agent's suggestion.

5 Conclusion

The findings of the present study are important for the design of intelligent recommender and decision-aid systems. Keeping the operator engaged and in-the-loop is important for reducing complacency, which could allow lapses in system reliability to go unnoticed. To that end, we examined how agent transparency affected operator complacent behavior, as well as task performance, and trust. Access to agent reasoning was found to be an effective deterrent to complacent behavior when the operator has limited information about their task environment. Contrary to the position adopted by Paradis et al. [19], operators do accept agent recommendations even when they do not know the rationale behind the suggestions. In fact, the absence of agent reasoning appears to encourage automation bias. Access to the agent's reasoning appears to allow the operator to calibrate effectively their trust in the system, reducing automation bias and improving performance. This outcome is similar to findings previously reported by Helldin et al. [20] and Mercado et al. [16]. However, the addition of information that created ambiguity for the operator again encouraged complacency, resulting in reduced performance and poorer trust calibration. Prior work has shown that irrelevant or ambiguous information can increase workload and encourage complacent behavior [11, 21], and these findings align with those. As such, caution should be exercised when considering how transparent to make agent reasoning and what information should be included.

References

1. Parasuraman, R., Molloy, R., Singh, I.L.: Performance consequences of automation–induced complacency. Int. J. Aviat. Psychol. **3**(1), 1–23 (1993)
2. Parasuraman, R., Sheridan, T.B., Wickens, C.D.: A model for types and levels of human interaction with automation. IEEE Trans. Syst. Man Cybern. Part A Syst. Hum. **30**(3), 286–297 (2000)
3. Chen, J.Y.C., Durlach, P.J., Sloan, J.A., Bowens, L.D.: Human robot interaction in the context of simulated route reconnaissance missions. Mil. Psychol. **20**(3), 135–149 (2008)
4. Wang H, Lewis M, Velagapudi P, Scerri P, Sycara K.: How search and its subtasks scale in N robots. In: Proceedings of the 4th ACM/IEEE International Conference on Human Robot Interaction, pp. 141–148. ACM Press, 9–13 March 2009, La Jolla, CA, New York (NY) (2009)
5. Wang J, Wang, H, Lewis M.: Assessing cooperation in human control of heterogeneous robots. In: Proceedings of the 3rd ACM/IEEE International Conference on Human Robot Interaction, pp. 9–15. ACM Press, 12–15 March 2008, Amsterdam (The Netherlands). New York (NY) (2008)
6. Lewis, M.: Human interaction with multiple remote robots. Rev. Hum. Factors Ergon. **9**(1), 131–174 (2013)
7. Chen, J.Y.C., Barnes, M.J., Qu, Z.: RoboLeader: A surrogate for enhancing the human control of a team of robots. Aberdeen Proving Ground (MD): Army Research Laboratory (US), Report No.: ARL–MR–0735, January 2010. http://www.dtic.mil/get-tr-doc/pdf?AD=ADA514855
8. Chen, J.Y.C., Barnes, M.J.: Supervisory control of multiple robots: effects of imperfect automation and individual differences. Hum. Factors **54**(2), 157–174 (2012)
9. Chen, J.Y.C., Barnes, M.J.: Supervisory control of multiple robots in dynamic tasking environments. Ergonomics **55**, 1043–1058 (2012)
10. Wright, J.L., Chen, J.Y.C., Quinn, S.A., Barnes, M.J.: The effects of level of autonomy on human–agent teaming for multi–robot control and local security maintenance. Aberdeen Proving Grounds (MD): Army Research Laboratory (US), Report No.: ARL–TR–6724, November 2013. www.dtic.mil/cgi-bin/GetTRDoc?AD=ADA595105
11. Chen, J.Y.C., Barnes, M.J.: Human–agent teaming for multirobot control: A review of human factors issues. IEEE Trans. Hum. Mach. Syst. **44**(1), 13–29 (2014)

12. Wickens, C.D.: Designing for situation awareness and trust in automation. In: Proceedings of the International Federation of Automatic Control (IFAC) Conference, Baden–Baden, Germany. Amsterdam (The Netherlands), Elsevier Ltd., pp. 174–179, 27–29 September 1994

13. Chen, J.Y.C., Procci, K., Boyce, M., Wright, J., Garcia, A., Barnes, M.J.: Situation awareness–based agent transparency. Aberdeen Proving Ground (MD): Army Research Laboratory (US), Report No.: ARL–TR–6905, April 2014. http://www.arl.army.mil/www/default.cfm?technical_report=7066

14. Lee, J.D., See, K.A.: Trust in automation: designing for appropriate reliance. Hum. Factors **46**(1), 50–80 (2004)

15. Lyons, J.B.: Being transparent about transparency: a model for human–robot interaction. Papers from the 2013 AAAI Spring Symposium Series, 25–27 March 2013, Stanford, CA. Palo Alto (CA). The AAAI Press, pp. 48–53 (2013)

16. Mercado, J.E., Rupp, M., Chen, J.Y.C., Barber, D., Procci, K., Barnes, M.J.: Intelligent agent transparency in human-agent teaming for multi-UxV management. Hum. Factors **58**, 401–415 (2016). (in press)

17. Barber, D., Davis, L., Nicholson, D., Finkelstein, N., Chen, J.Y.C.: The Mixed Initiative Experimental (MIX) testbed for human robot interactions with varied levels of automation. In: Proceedings of the 26th Army Science Conference, ASC 2008, Orlando, FL, 1–4 December 2008, U.S. Dept. of Army, Washington, DC (2008)

18. Wickens, C.D., Clegg, B.A., Vieane, A.Z., Sebok, A.L.: Complacency and automation bias in the use of imperfect automation. Hum. Factors **57**(5), 728–739 (2015)

19. Paradis, S., Benaskeur, A., Oxenham, M., Cutler, P.: Threat evaluation and weapons allocation in network-centric warfare. In: 8th International Conference on Information Fusion, vol. 2, pp. 1078–1085. IEEE, 25 July 2005

20. Helldin, T., Ohlander, U., Falkman, G., Riveiro, M.: Transparency of automated combat classification. In: Harris, D. (ed.) EPCE 2014. LNCS, vol. 8532, pp. 22–33. Springer, Heidelberg (2014)

21. Westerbeek, H., Maes, A.: Route-external and route-internal landmarks in route descriptions: Effects of route length and map design. Appl. Cogn. Psychol. **27**(3), 297–305 (2013)

22. Hancock, P.A., Warm, J.S.: A dynamic model of stress and sustained attention. Hum. Factors: J. Hum. Factors Ergon. Soc. **31**(5), 519–537 (1989)

23. Yerkes, R.M., Dodson, J.D.: The relation of strength of stimulus to rapidity of habit-formation. J. Comp. Neurol. Psychol. **18**, 459–482 (1908)

Medicine, Health and Well-Being Applications of VAMR

Utilizing Digital Game Environments
for Training Prosthetic Use

Matt Dombrowski, Peter A. Smith, and Ryan Buyssens[✉]

University of Central Florida, Orlando, FL, USA
{mattd,Peter.smith,Ryan.Buyssens}@ucf.edu

Abstract. When the children receive their prosthetic, many of them still need to learn or, in many cases, relearn elements such as grabbing, squeezing and other range of movement with their newly fitted prosthetic. In this case, electromyogram or EMG sensors control the arms. The EMG is worn on an existing muscle and detects muscle movement as input. The EMG data feeds into the prosthetic device to stimulate movement in the hand. New users of this device are often confused over how to control the motion at first. Limibitless solutions, the creators of this device, approached the team at the University of Central Florida's School of Visual Art & Design, about the possibility of developing videogames to train the use of the prosthetic prior to children receiving them, in hopes of reducing the time it takes to become proficient with the device.

Keywords: Games for health · Game based training · Augmented reality · Game design · Gamification

1 Introduction

Over the past few years the rise of the 3D printing industry has taken the consumer market by storm. Various companies including researchers at Limbitless Solutions and the Open Hand Project have printing and developed EMG controlled limbs for children.

The inclusion of 3D printing balances rising costs and helps give a wider community access to previously expensive technology. Based on the previous research, the goal of the present study is to create a game that address the complex issues of children's rehabilitation process pertaining to their 3D printed appendages. The University of Central Florida's School of Visual Arts & Design have partnered with Limbitless Solutions to take their 3D printed prosthetics and address challenges that the recipients of the limbs are facing.

UCF SVAD researchers are using the actual hardware in the prosthetics to interface with games built by University students. Leveraging the newest in Serious Game design and development techniques to help interactively train the prosthetic recipient to utilize their new addition. The games utilize this EMG data to create an alternative interactive experience to help train the child in an enjoyable and stress free virtual environment. The research team is made up of a game designer, digital maker, and digital artist. Utilizing their individual expertise they have developed an interface for training the use of these arms through video games built in Unity3D. Various games are also being

© Springer International Publishing Switzerland 2016
S. Lackey and R. Shumaker (Eds.): VAMR 2016, LNCS 9740, pp. 481–489, 2016.
DOI: 10.1007/978-3-319-39907-2_46

designed in an effort to create gameplay that would help the child achieve various benchmarks in rehabilitation. This paper discusses the challenges that the researchers faced in, not only, developing the hardware for the game but also the need for a very specific visual gameplay experiences for the device.

2   Background

This Emerging technology allows for the development for alternative solutions for rehabilitation for those who have disabilities. The current need is for a game to assist in the rehabilitation process and training of those learning to use their newly acquired prosthetic limbs. This section explores the rising awareness of accessibility within video games as well as the solutions that are being offered to level the playing field between the typical user and those who are disabled. In addition, it will delve into the use of custom hardware and software developments to benefit in rehabilitation and training.

2.1   History of Accessibility in Digital Media

The idea of game accessibility issues for the disabled is not a new issue in the field of digital media. In the late 1990's the World Wide Web addressed accessibility issues requiring federal websites to be accessible to the disabled. In Section 508, which focuses primarily on federal websites, prompted the World Wide Web Consortium to develop universal standards to better unify the interaction of websites with their visitors. This is an early occurrence in the effort to make digital technologies more available to those who previously could not interact with them. In addition it sets the stage for later accessibility awareness and accommodations in the video game industry.

In the video game industry the same lacking accessibility challenges occur. Disabled gamers face many challenges and frustrations that their non-disabled counter parts do not encounter. Disabled gamers face challenges through various types of visual, auditory, mobility and cognitive disorders. In 1997, the US Census states that 25.5 % of the US population suffers from these types of disabilities [1]. There was a need for accessibility in video games. The International Game Developers Association (IGDA) forms the Game Accessibility Special Interest Group (SIG). The goals of this group are to define the needs of the disabled and to develop and support the creation of technology to help aid in equality for disabled gamers [1].

2.2   Addressing Accessibility Solutions

According to Huynh [2] accessibility for games can be categorized into two groups. Specially developed software and equipment that can assist the user with commercial games and, games that are designed specifically for disability rehabilitation. Today, some games are designed to be accessible, while others are not. Developments on the software side came in the form of screen readers, magnifiers and speech recognition. The hardware side focused on specialized, custom controllers. Though not all accessibly concerns are always met, the awareness of these concerns aides in the development of new interactive technologies that can be enjoyed by all.

2.3 Rehabilitation Benefits from Gaming

What if this newly developed interactive accessible technology could be not only used for entertainment, but also be used for rehabilitation in those who are disabled? The idea of using digital media as a form of rehabilitation is not new. In a study completed in 2009, researchers complied a literature search of 11 electronic databases to identify articles on the effects interactive computer play (ICP) in correlation to children with sensorimotor disorders. [3] The search was for research published between January 1995 and May 2008. In their findings, they narrowed their results to 13 out of 16 studies that found positive results with the use of interactive computer play in children who had disabilities. Nine of these studies focused on movement quality. Only two studies showed no improvement while the other seven showed positive results. [3] Not only did the findings conclude that the children found the interactive rehabilitation techniques fun, but also the children found the rehab motivating. According to their findings, the use of ICP in rehabilitation was a "highly promising area" in which further research was encouraged. [3] In the process section of this article we will address how we plan to follow their recommendation for further research.

In 2012 researchers studied the use of commercially developed video games to aid in rehabilitation of balance in lower limb amputees. The study was aimed to examine both the safety and the benefits of balance therapy in conjunction with a commercially developed video game balance board. In this 4-week study, amputation participants gained greater balance. Furthermore, the amputees' center of pressure was decreased and they performed closer to those of typically developing children of their age [4]. This study proved that through the use of balance training with commercial video game systems that video game therapy techniques can benefit those with limb amputation. One issue that remains is that commercial entertainment games are not specifically designed for rehab. Through our research we will further explore the development of rehab specific gaming in conjunction with specialized hardware.

Custom rehabilitation game design is an area of interest to many researchers. Dawson et al. [5] recommend that future research focus on increasing measuring and recording of performances throughout training and investigating how these training tools are impacting treatment. Their study focuses on Myoelectric training systems over the past few years.

3 Limbitless Prosthetic Arm

In 2014 the team at Limbitless Solutions met a young man named Alex. Alex was born without most of his right arm. Unfortunately, the cost of a typical prosthetic was too high for Alex's family. The team at Limbitless built a low cost prosthetic in only 8 weeks. The arm was created in the UCF Manufacturing Lab, and was powered by low cost electromyography (EMG) sensors. The total cost of the arm was $350.00, but it was provided to Alex's family free of charge [6].

The team at Limbitless went a step further and open sourced their arm's design and software, so others can build their own arm as well. The design for this is available on 3D printable object sharing site Thingiverse [7]. The idea being anyone who needs these prosthetics could download and build their own.

The Limbitless prosthetic arm has a fixed elbow and a hand that opens and closes. The arms are 3D printed in the UCF Manufacturing Lab 3D printers. They have a sturdy plastic feel. New models borrow designs from Marvel super heroes, like Iron Man, and Spider-Man. Designs for girls include Disney's Frozen.

It works through a small embedded Arduino chipset that takes in signals from the user's muscles using EMG (as seen in Fig. 1) and then moves a small servo motor to open and close the hand. The control is similar to a garage door, where the user flexes a muscle to open the hand and flexes again to close the hand. The strength and duration of these movements does not affect the motion of the hand.

Fig. 1. Limbitless arm in use

The garage door style control, as compared to a squeeze to close, release to open system is to reduce fatigue in the user. Having to hold a flexed muscle to maintain grip, could quickly become tiring. Unfortunately, this motion is not naturally intuitive to new users. In an effort to train kids this control scheme, prior to them receiving their prosthetics, the system was integrated into videogames designed to train how to utilize the controls before the arm is in the hands of a new user.

3.1 The Training Interface

The prosthetic training interface is made up of two parts. The first is the actual hardware found inside the Limbitless Prosthetic Arm. The other is a custom built interface, also powered by Arduino, that takes the input from the Limbitless hardware and interfaces into the computer game developed using Unity3D, a popular game engine.

Prosthetic Interface. The prosthetic interface side of the training hardware is identical to the hardware found in the Limbitless prosthetic arm. The internals can be seen in Fig. 2 below. This interface includes the same Arduino chip, interfaced with the same battery, servo, and EMG interface. The only difference being, that the actual prosthetic enclosure is replaced with a small hardware enclosure.

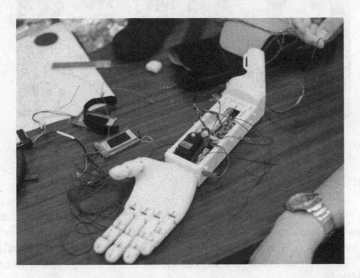

Fig. 2. Internals of the arm [7]

The reason for using the exact hardware is to exactly simulate all the delays in the operational arm. Given the desire to train users to use the real arm, representing the interface accurately is of the utmost importance. Any changes in the reaction from the arm could result in negative training.

The output from this side of the controller is the signal that is usually sent to a servo motor. The Servo motor in this case is replaced by the game interface. Games can then be designed by any number of development teams, reusing the same interface.

Game Interface. The game side of the interface, while also Arduino based hardware, is completely agnostic to the Limbitless side of the hardware. The reason for doing this is, to ensure that the Limbitless side works exactly like the real arm hardware. The delay of the second Arduino is negligible, as no additional hardware or sensors get in the way, and there is no additional load on the Limbitless hardware (Fig. 3).

The game interface is based primarily on an Arduino Uno and a Unity3D plugin called Uniduino. Uniduino allows for interaction between the Arduino hardware and Unity3D [8]. This allows the Limbitless signals to be input directly into a game.

Fig. 3. Arduino interface to Unity3D game using Uniduino [8]

4   Game Design Methodology

In an effort to design a variety of games and test out as many design concepts as possible within the games. The Limbitless Prosthetic arm interface was implemented in 14 games developed for the course Casual Games Production in the University of Central Florida's School of Visual Art and Design's Digital Media Game Design track, in the Spring Semester of 2016.

Each game was designed by a group of four students on average, with a reasonable mix of both artists and programmers. In some cases it might weigh more heavily to one side or the other. The games started by selecting an Atari 2600 game to base their core mechanics on, and then changed a mechanic and added a mechanic. This exercise leaves the games having the simple controls of an old school Atari game, but also made something uniquely different from what others had played before.

An example of one of these games is Time Tilt. This is a game based loosely on the game Joust, but with power-ups, guns, and a time travel motif. While the game is reminiscent of the classic game, it still feel original. This game is an especially good example, as the flappy bird like control is well suited to the prosthetic interface.

After designing and creating the games, the students were provided code to allow them to interact with the prosthetic interface. This interface was easily implemented and the EMG replaced a button in the game. The games still maintained other controls, like directions, that could be input by the other arm of the participants. This provided the ability to not only practice with the EMG interface, but coordinating that practice with their other limb.

5   Design Consideration

Through the development process 14 games were developed. Of the 14 games created some worked extremely well with the technology and some did not. While developing these games we have discovered some issue that need to be taken into account in order to develop optimally for the prosthetic interface. These are described in more detail below.

5.1   Gameplay Should Match Task

When designing a game to train a task it is important to consider the transferability of the task. In the case of designing games for prosthetic use there is a propensity in some designers to include the controls as a simple replacement for an existing button in any game. The issue is, the prosthetic is used in a very specific way. Games that simulate the act of grabbing or closing will have a larger impact on the training outcomes.

5.2   Perception vs. Functionality

The prosthetic arm uses a garage door like control scheme. This means you trigger it once to open the hand you trigger it again to close it. These messages can be interrupted but holding the command does not increase the power or produce any extra response. Unfortunately, game designers are used to programming functions around holding a button down. This is commonly used to charge an attack, or increase the height of a jump. Fighting back against this design pattern can be hard for game designers.

5.3   Number of Controls

Ideally games would only use the prosthetic controller. This limits the control input down to only one button, but it would allow the user to concentrate on learning the control. This, however, limits the types of games that could be made. Given the user most likely has an existing hand they can use. The control can be mapped to both the prosthetic control and the buttons available to a single hand on a standard controller, a keyboard or a mouse. It is recommended that this be limited to direction buttons.

5.4   Input Speed

The EMG can produce responses every 16th of a second but it can take half a second to see reaction in the arm. So, controls cannot be fast twitch even though that is generally considered fun. The controls should react in the time that the actual hand can respond, even if the hardware can take in the information at a faster rate. This delay can be simulated in hardware, but the games still need to be designed to take that into account during game play.

5.5   Complexity of Game Activities

The activities in the games should be fast enough to allow for as many opportunities to practice as possible. This means the game should be fast paced and easy to understand.

While Role Playing Games are popular they often have long periods of unraveling story or exploring environments and not fighting enemies, or flapping wings on a bird, etc. These games are not well suited to this type of training. Casual or Arcade style games on the other hand are good examples of what could be made for this type of training.

5.6   Design with Interface in Mind

The previous design lessons lead to the conclusion that games should be made specifically for the prosthetic arm interface, and existing games should not be shoehorned into working with the interface. The reason for this is, games that do not take the previous concerns into account may have issues that will lead to negative training. There are, however, lots of opportunities to redesign existing games to bring them in line with the requirements of the interface.

5.7   Art Should Appeal to Target Audience

The visual appeal of the games need to be audience appropriate. In an effort to ensure that these games would appeal to young individuals, the art styles for the game built were based on existing picture books. These books provide example art styles that are appealing to a young audience and have a simple design language to make it easy to audiences to understand them, and relatively easy for developers to implement.

5.8   Games Should Be Fun

When designing games for kids, the games absolutely need to be fun. While there will be motivation to learn how to use their prosthetics, kids still have access to so much more interesting media and games, and these games need to be able to hold their attention. In an effort to accomplish this, game mechanics were borrowed from existing great games. Great effort was put into making the games fun. This includes applying the design patterns above, but also through user testing, and focus group testing, with users. It is hard to make a fun game, and making one that is fun that is also useful is so much more difficult.

6   Conclusions

As expected when designing a game for training, matching the training domain and accurately simulating the environment were incredibly important. Further designing for children is another challenge that needed to be overcome. Making games that work, train, are appealing to the audience, and fun to play is a demanding challenge. At the same time, designing games for use to train prosthetics has been a great experience. Not all the games designed for this worked out, but we still learned some design patterns that can be applied to future games.

As the Limbitless prosthetic arm reaches more children, the games developed here can be used as pre-training. Thus helping children get up and running more quickly.

6.1 Future Work

The interface should be released to the public, and be available to download for free from the Thingiverse webpage next to the Limbitless Arm design. This would allow for the greatest number of people to benefit from this work. The games could also be used with other prosthetic systems. Like those controlled by the Myo Band [9, 10]. Integrating that same technology should be a relatively low challenge, with a high impact.

The interface could also be used for non-prosthetic VR applications. Anything that could use input from EMG. This might include exercise in meditation, or more tangible tasks, like controlling robots. Now that the system is built the applications are Limbitless (pun intended).

Acknowledgments. We would like to thank Limbitless Solutions for their support on this project. We are honored to be able to support the amazing work they are doing to bring cost effective prosthetics to children in this small way.

References

1. Bierre, K., Chetwynd, J., Ellis, B., Hinn, D.M., Ludi, S., Westin, T.: Game not over: accessibility issues in video games. In: Proceedings of the 3rd International Conference on Universal Access in Human-Computer Interaction, pp. 22–27 (2005)
2. Huynh, L.K.: Low-cost solutions for making hands-free video games. Doctoral dissertation, Texas A&M University–Corpus Christi (2010)
3. Sandlund, M., McDonough, S., Häger-Ross, C.: Interactive computer play in rehabilitation of children with sensorimotor disorders: a systematic review. Dev. Med. Child Neurol. **51**(3), 173–179 (2009)
4. Andrysek, J., Klejman, S., Steinnagel, B., Torres-Moreno, R., Zabjek, K.F., Salbach, N.M., Moody, K.: Preliminary evaluation of a commercially available videogame system as an adjunct therapeutic intervention for improving balance among children and adolescents with lower limb amputations. Arch. Phys. Med. Rehabil. **93**(2), 358–366 (2012)
5. Dawson, M.R., Carey, J.P., Fahimi, F.: Myoelectric training systems. Expert Rev. Med. Devices **8**(5), 581–589 (2011). Griffiths, M.: The educational benefits of videogames. Educ. Health **20**(3), 47–51 (2002)
6. Limbitless Solutions: Meet Alex Pring (2015). http://limbitless-solutions.org/index.php/2015/07/01/alex/
7. Limbitless Solutions: Limbitless Arm for Alex (V1) (2015). http://www.thingiverse.com/thing:408641
8. Uniduino: Uniduino Home Page (2016). http://www.uniduino.com/
9. Thalmic Labs: Myo Site (2016). https://www.myo.com/
10. Sorrel, C.: This High-Tech Prosthetic Works With A Game-Controller Sold On Amazon. Co.Exist (2016). http://www.fastcoexist.com/3055732/this-high-tech-prosthetic-works-with-a-game-controller-sold-on-amazon

Full-Body Portable Virtual Reality
for Personal Protective Equipment Training

James Coleman Eubanks[1](✉), Veena Somareddy[1],
Ryan P. McMahan[1], and Alfonso A. Lopez[2]

[1] University of Texas at Dallas, Richardson, TX, USA
{j.coleman.eubanks,vxs124730,rymcmaha}@utdallas.edu
[2] Raytheon Company, Richardson, TX, USA
Alfonso.A.Lopez@raytheon.com

Abstract. This paper presents a full-body, portable virtual reality prototype for training personal protective equipment procedures to surgical staff. The system consists of a head-mounted display for viewing the virtual world, inertial measurement units that track the user's full-body movements, and handheld controllers for bimanual interactions. With these capabilities, our system affords the development of gross psychomotor skills, in addition to knowledge-based cognitive skills. The system hardware is designed to be portable and does not require a dedicated space for usage. The system software includes two training modules. An instructional module uses an error-avoidant training approach to teach trainees correct actions. A practice module uses an error-management approach that allows trainees to rehearse their skills while receiving automated assessments on their mistakes. Future work includes an evaluation of the prototype with medical subject-matter experts.

Keywords: Virtual reality · Training · Personal protective equipment

1 Introduction

Personal protective equipment (PPE) is an important aspect of medical procedures that protects healthcare workers and patients from infectious diseases [1]. PPE protects against droplet, contact, and airborne transmissions of pathogens [2]. When used consistently, PPE reduces transmissions and protects both the healthcare workers and patients [3]. However, PPE must be correctly donned and doffed to minimize the risk of exposure. It has been shown that failure to adhere to PPE protocols provide opportunities for infections to be transmitted [1].

Despite its importance, researchers have observed that PPE compliance is modest and practiced procedures vary greatly among healthcare workers. Mitchell et al. [1] observed that only 34 % of healthcare workers donned all required PPE. Using eye protection was particularly an issue, with only 37 % of workers complying. In another study, Zellmer et al. [2] observed that less than half (43 %) of healthcare workers removed PPE in the correct order. In their meta-analysis of many studies, Erasmus et al. [4] found that only 40 % of healthcare workers complied with hand hygiene protocols,

© Springer International Publishing Switzerland 2016
S. Lackey and R. Shumaker (Eds.): VAMR 2016, LNCS 9740, pp. 490–501, 2016.
DOI: 10.1007/978-3-319-39907-2_47

including glove use. Similarly, Manian and Ponzillo [5] observed that only 41 % of surgical healthcare workers properly complied with gown use.

Considering these issues, training interventions are needed to improve PPE use and compliance with protocols [1]. In fact, 9 % of healthcare workers have reported never receiving formal training on PPE [6]. However, there are some challenges for such interventions. First, different institutions and educators use heterogeneous methods and curriculums, which result in education and training experiences of variable quality and content [7]. To further complicate varying interventions, Puro and Nicastri [8] have revealed that separate medical organizations recommend conflicting PPE protocols. Another challenge for training interventions is the need for periodic refreshers, in order to maintain knowledge and competence [9]. Some hospitals have developed eLearning modules to address these challenges [10], but research indicates that these eLearning interventions might only be effective for healthcare workers with less than one year of experience [11]. Furthermore, most psychomotor skills cannot be learned from online interventions, only from physical practice [12].

Virtual reality (VR) provides the opportunity to develop unique interventions that overcome the challenges of training. Like eLearning modules, VR can provide consistent computer-based lessons that do not vary in quality or content [13] and afford automated assessments [14]. However, unlike other computer-based interventions, VR provides the opportunity to practice gross psychomotor skills [15], and with force-feedback devices, fine-motor skills [16]. Additionally, by leveraging the sense of "being there" (i.e., presence [17]), VR has been used to arouse greater levels of fear [18], which afford better memory recall [19]. This could be beneficial to experienced healthcare workers receiving periodic refreshers. Finally, VR also provides benefits compared to real-world simulations, such as more training opportunities due to the ability to instantly reset a training simulation and negligible recurring costs, as virtual supplies are free compared to real-world ones.

Considering the benefits of VR, we have developed a prototype of a VR system for training surgical PPE protocols. The system hardware consists of an Oculus Rift head-mounted display (HMD), a full-body portable tracking system comprised of inertial measurement units (IMUs), two Nintendo Wii Remotes for bimanual interactions, and a high-performance laptop worn in a backpack. Together, these hardware components make the system completely portable and easy to store, which are important requirements for hospitals with limited space [14]. The prototype's software consists of an instructional module and a practice module; both focused on hand hygiene and the donning of PPE. The instructional module employs error-avoidant training techniques that ensure trainees are only exposed to correct actions [20]. However, the practice module employs an error-management approach, which uses errors as opportunities to learn and encourages experimentation [21]. The practice module also supports automated assessments based on the actions of the trainee.

After discussing related interventions, we discuss the requirements that we identified for using VR as a training intervention for PPE. We then describe how the system hardware and software for our initial prototype addresses these requirements. We conclude with our plans to evaluate the prototype with subject-matter experts and how the prototype can be extended to become a viable training intervention for PPE.

2 Related Work

Two types of interventions have been used for training PPE use and its importance. In situ simulations, which involve replicating real-world events through simulated scenarios, have been used to assess the use of PPE by hospital staff. Phin et al. [22] conducted an in situ simulation of an influenza pandemic and observed the PPE use of the hospital staff. While they concluded that the simulation increased the confidence and preparedness of the staff, they noted that it required large quantities of PPE and generated a large amount of clinical waste. As mentioned, VR would avoid such issues.

A second type of intervention has been the use of eLearning modules. These modules often focus on the cognitive skills associated with donning and doffing PPE, such as identifying the correct sequence. In one example [23], trainees use a mouse to click and drag available PPE to the appropriate body parts of a virtual avatar while the simulation monitored incorrect placements and sequences. However, prior research indicates that these eLearning modules may only benefit healthcare workers with little experience [11]. Furthermore, psychomotor skills cannot be learned this way [12].

3 Intervention Requirements

The goal of our research was to develop a prototype of a VR system for training PPE protocols. As different healthcare professions have different PPE protocols [5], we decided to limit the scope of our prototype to surgical technologists. Surgical technologists are responsible for preparing operating rooms (ORs) for surgery, managing supplies and equipment during operations, and cleaning up the OR [24]. The Association of Surgical Technologists (AST) has clearly defined standards for PPE, including surgical attire [24] and surgical scrub (i.e., the process of removing microorganisms from the nails, hands, and forearms) [25]. Using the AST standards as a requirements document, we identified the donning and scrub training tasks seen in Table 1.

Table 1. Donning and surgical task requirements based on AST standards

Task	Details	Location
1. Don head cover	• Cover all head and facial hair	Changing room
2. Don scrub suit	• Tuck shirt into pants • Completely cover undershirts	Changing room
3. Don shoe covers	• Disposable shoe covers should be worn if contact with body fluids is anticipated	Changing room
4. Don surgical mask	• Completely cover nose and mouth • Contour pliable noseband to fit nose	Scrub room
5. Don safety eyewear	• Tape top of mask to prevent fogging	Scrub room
6. Perform surgical scrub	• Prewash the hands and forearms with non-antimicrobial soap	Scrub room

(*Continued*)

Table 1. (*Continued*)

Task	Details	Location
	• Clean nails with disposable nail cleaner under running water • Scrub all four sides of one hand and forearm from the fingertips to 2 inches above elbow, including between fingers • Hold hand higher than elbow so that water runs from fingertips to elbow • Repeat for other hand and forearm • Completely dry hands and arms	
7. Don sterile gown	• Open gown package on the prep table • Face the sterile field • Hand circulator tag to tie gown in back	Operating room
8. Don sterile gloves	• Use the cuffs of the sterile gown to keep the hands covered • Open gloves package on the prep table • Insert cuff-covered hand in one glove • Insert cuff-covered hand in other glove • Pull cuffs of gloves over the gown cuffs	Operating room

In addition to training-task requirements, there are several logistical requirements for making a VR intervention feasible and practical to use. First, the VR system must be affordable and not cost-prohibitive [26]. Second, the VR system should be located within or near the hospital's skills lab for accessibility [27]. Third, the system should be compact or easy to store, considering the limited space that most hospitals struggle with [14]. Finally, it should be easy to operate and require little maintenance [28].

4 System Hardware

After considering the identified intervention requirements, we decided to use a full-body, portable VR system similar to the one described in [29]. The system consists of four major components. An Oculus Rift Development Kit 2 (DK2) HMD provides an immersive visual display for the user to view the virtual world. IMU sensors strapped to the user's major body segments provide full-body tracking capabilities. Two Nintendo Wii Remotes allow for bimanual interactions. Finally, a high-performance laptop runs the training modules and renders the graphics to the HMD. Together, these components provide a full-body VR system that is portable and affordable.

4.1 Head-Mounted Display

Our original portable VR system used an Oculus Rift DK1 as an HMD [29]. Since then, Oculus released the DK2, which uses a low-persistence display to reduce simulator sickness [30]. The DK2 provides a 100° diagonal field of view (FOV) with a display resolution of 960 × 1080 pixels per eye. It also has a goggle-like form factor

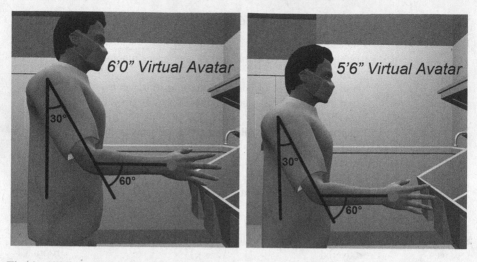

Fig. 1. While our system uses forward kinematics to track relative movements, anthropometrics are used to ensure absolute movements that match the user's real-world movements.

with elastic straps and weighs approximately 440 g. In addition to being the visual display, we use the DK2's internal IMU to track the orientation of the user's head.

4.2 Full-Body, Portable Tracking System

The full-body, portable tracking system uses 16 wireless YEI 3-Space IMUs strapped to the user's hands, arms, upper arms, shoulders, feet, calves, thighs, waist, and chest. Again, head tracking is provided by the DK2's internal IMU. Each IMU includes a 3-axis accelerometer, a 3-axis gyroscope, and a 3-axis magnetometer. Using sensor fusion, the accelerometer's gravity vector and the magnetometer's compass vector are used to correct most of the drift (i.e., error accumulation) incurred by the gyroscope's angular velocity readings. This allows each IMU to accurately report the orientation of the body segment that it is attached to.

Because the IMUs can only report acceleration and not accurate translations, we use a rigid-body skeleton to track the relative movements of the user's limbs. By applying the reported orientations of the user's body segments to the corresponding joints, the rigid-body skeleton mimics the relative motions of the user due to forward kinematics. However, this does not provide an absolute position for the skeleton.

As explained in [29], we use an algorithm based on the kinematics of the heels during gait to provide absolute tracking of the skeleton's position. Whenever a heel joint strikes the ground, we identify it as the new anchor for the rigid-body skeleton. As the user moves, the skeleton's segments move relative to the pelvis, which serves as the origin of the tracking hierarchy. This results in the anchor no longer being in the same position, as the heels are constantly moving relative to the pelvis during gait. By translating the skeleton's pelvis to restore the heel to its original position when it became the anchor, the skeleton is propelled through the virtual world in the same manner that the user is moving in the real world.

Another important aspect to our full-body tracking system is the use of anthropometrics (i.e., the study of human measurements) to improve the accuracy of the absolute tracking. As seen in Fig. 1, the lengths of the avatar's body segments have a large impact on the overall position of the limbs, despite having the same joint orientations. Hence, in order for the avatar's movements to absolutely match the user's physical movements, the body segments of the avatar must be scaled to match the lengths of the user's actual body segments. To avoid measuring each of the user's body segments, we use anthropometric proportions identified by Drillis et al. [31] to estimate the segment lengths given only the user's total height and hip height. This improves the accuracy of the tracking system without lengthening the setup time.

4.3 Bimanual Handheld Controllers

While our full-body tracking system reports the positions of the user's hands, it is not capable of determining if the user is grasping or interacting with a virtual object. To afford bimanual interactions, the system includes two Nintendo Wii Remotes. These wireless handheld controllers provide discrete button inputs via Bluetooth for creating 3D interaction techniques. While pressing a button to grab an object is not as realistic as closing one's fist, we have found that discrete button events are much more usable than noisy input streams, such as electromyography devices (e.g., the Myo armband) and computer vision techniques (e.g., the Leap Motion). However, to mimic the biomechanics of making a fist, we require both the thumb and index finger buttons are pressed to grab and hold a virtual object.

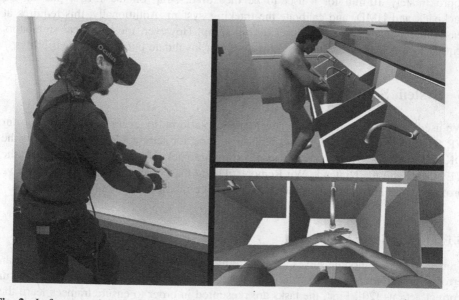

Fig. 2. Left: user using the full-body tracking system to interact with the virtual world. Top right: a third-person perspective of the user's avatar. Bottom right: the user's first-person perspective of the virtual world and avatar.

4.4   High-Performance Laptop

We use an Alienware 15 laptop for computing power in our VR system. In addition to running our training applications, the laptop processes the input data of the DK2, YEI IMUs, and Wii Remotes. It also renders the graphics for the DK2. To keep the system portable, we place the 3.2 kg laptop in a mesh backpack that the user wears.

4.5   Advantages and Limitations

Our VR system hardware offers several advantages in consideration of the intervention requirements. The DK2 allows users to immersively view the virtual world, PPE, and their avatar, which should afford greater presence [32]. The full-body tracking system and Wii Remotes provide opportunities to practice gross psychomotor skills, such as prewashing the hands (see Fig. 2). Altogether, the components cost less than $7.5K, which is attractive compared to many medical simulators [7]. The system is also self-contained and wireless, which makes it portable and easy to store.

However, there are limitations to our current system. Foremost is the inability to practice fine-motor skills, such as scrubbing between the fingers and using the cuffs of the gown while donning the sterile gloves. In many cases, we have been able to design interactions for simulating these fine-motor skills, such as grabbing near the top of the mask to simulate contouring the pliable noseband. But the lack of precise finger tracking and accurate haptic feedback is prohibitive to developing some psychomotor skills, such as using the cuffs to don gloves.

Another limitation of our system is a lengthy setup time. Altogether, it takes approximately 10 min for a user to be measured, strap on the IMUs, put on the backpack and HMD, and calibrate the tracking system. Additionally, this requires at least one technician to aid the user during setup. However, most medical simulators require technicians to facilitate, so this does not invalidate our system's feasibility.

5   System Software

We used Unity 5, a game engine development platform, to create the software for our VR training prototype. Unity 5 has built-in support for certain VR devices, such as the DK2. However, we had to create custom software packages to integrate data from the YEI IMUs and the Nintendo Wii Remotes. Using these packages and Unity, we have prototyped an instructional module and a practice module for training interventions.

5.1   Instructional Module

Our instructional module serves as an introduction to the training tasks. It employs an error-avoidant training approach, in which the trainee is only allowed to perform correct actions [20]. First, the tasks are presented in order to ensure trainees learn the proper sequence of PPE. For each task, a series of steps is presented to the trainee via textual popup windows and corresponding audio (see Fig. 3). The trainee must properly complete each step before the module will move onto the next step. Additionally, interactions not involved with the current step are disabled. For example, the trainee cannot prewash the hands and forearms before donning the safety eyewear. This ensures introductory trainees are not exposed to incorrect actions.

5.2   Practice Module

After completing the instructional module, the practice module provides the trainee opportunities to rehearse the sequence and donning of PPE and performing the surgical scrub. It uses an error-management approach, in which trainees are permitted to experiment with their decisions and actions, in order to actively learn from their mistakes [21]. Unlike the instructional module, the practice module does not proactively provide task information to the trainee. Additionally, all of the task interactions are available at all times. Hence, the trainee can prewash the hands and forearms before donning the safety eyewear. Meanwhile, the system software records the actions of the trainee, including their sequence. This tracked information is used at the end of the module to provide an automated assessment (see Fig. 4). This assessment includes feedback on incorrect or missed actions so that the trainee may correct them.

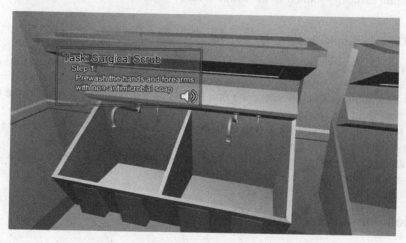

Fig. 3. The instructional module uses textual popup windows and audio to explain the tasks

5.3   Trigger-Based Interactions

As mentioned, both the instructional module and the practice module provide numerous interactions, such as prewashing the hands and forearms or donning the safety eyewear. During development, we had to choose between using physics-based and trigger-based interactions. For example, in a physics-based implementation, donning the safety eyewear would require precisely positioning the eyewear to rest on the ears and nose of the avatar. While easier to implement, as a developer can rely on Unity's physics engine, these types of interactions are difficult to accomplish and are usually unrealistic, despite being based on physics. Instead, we developed a series of

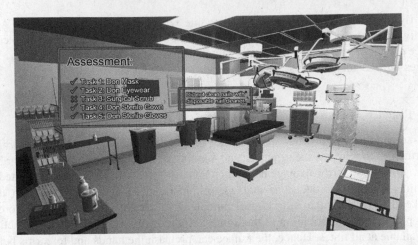

Fig. 4. The practice module uses tracked actions to provide an automated assessment

triggered actions and joint-based deformations for each PPE. For instance, if the trainee grabs one end of the surgical mask and releases it near the avatar's ear, the mask end will be automatically jointed to the avatar's ear.

5.4   Current Limitations

As a prototype, the system's current software has limitations. Due to limited resources and time, we have not prototyped all of the tasks, PPE, and locations identified in the intervention requirements. Because the first three training tasks (i.e., donning the head cover, scrub suit, and shoe covers) usually occur only once a day, we decided to focus on the remaining tasks that should occur each time the healthcare worker enters the OR. This avoided having to model a third environment (i.e., the changing room) and eliminated some of the more complex trigger-based interactions (e.g., tucking the scrub shirt into the pants).

6   Refining the Prototype

In the near future, we are planning to use the Rapid Iterative Testing and Evaluation (RITE) method [33], with medical subject-matter experts, to evaluate the potential usefulness of such a VR training intervention and to improve upon our prototype. We have identified a local hospital and medical center to collaborate with on the RITE process. We will be recruiting medical students, residents, and surgical staff for it.

7   Conclusions and Future Work

PPE protocols are important, as they protect both healthcare workers and patients. However, research indicates that PPE compliance is modest and that training interventions are needed. In situ and eLearning interventions have been investigated, but

VR provides new opportunities and advantages over these prior methods. To explore these potential benefits, we have developed a full-body, portable VR prototype for training PPE protocols to surgical staff. We first used standards defined by the Association of Surgical Technologists as intervention requirements, and then developed system hardware and software components to address those requirements. The hardware includes an HMD, an IMU-based tracking system, handheld controllers for bimanual interactions, and a high-performance laptop for portable computing power. The software includes an instructional module for introducing the training tasks and a practice module for rehearsing skills and learning from mistakes. In the near future, we will use the RITE approach to evaluate and improve upon the prototype using subject-matter expert feedback.

Acknowledgements. This research has been partially supported by an award from the I/UCRC iPerform Industry Fund associated with NSF award IIP-1439718.

References

1. Mitchell, R., Roth, V., Gravel, D., Astrakianakis, G., Bryce, E., Forgie, S., Johnston, L., Taylor, G., Vearncombe, M., C.N.I.S. Program: Are health care workers protected? An observational study of selection and removal of personal protective equipment in Canadian acute care hospitals. Am. J. Infect. Control **41**, 240–244 (2013)
2. Zellmer, C., Van Hoof, S., Safdar, N.: Variation in health care worker removal of personal protective equipment. Am. J. Infect. Control **43**, 750–751 (2015)
3. Fijter, S.D., DiOrio, M., Carmean, J., Schaffzin, J., Quinn, M., Musser, K., Nazarian, E., Moore, M., Beall, B., Gertz Jr., R., Kallen, A., Kim, C., Duffy, J.: Bacterial meningitis after intrapartum spinal anesthesia - New York and Ohio, 2008–2009. Morb. Mortal. Wkly. Rep. **59**, 65–69 (2010)
4. Erasmus, V., Daha, T.J., Brug, H., Richardus, J.H., Behrendt, M.D., Vos, M.C., van Beeck, E.F.: Systematic review of studies on compliance with hand hygiene guidelines in hospital care. Infect. Control Hosp. Epidemiol. **31**, 283–294 (2010)
5. Manian, F.A., Ponzillo, J.J.: Compliance with routine use of gowns by healthcare workers (HCWs) and non-HCW visitors on entry into the rooms of patients under contact precautions. Infect. Control Hosp. Epidemiol. **28**, 337–340 (2007)
6. John, A., Tomas, M., Cadnum, J., Mana, T.S.C., Jencson, A., Shaikh, A., Donskey, C.J.: Are healthcare personnel trained in correct use of personal protective equipment? In: IDWeek 2015, p. 332. IDSA (2015)
7. Kulaylat, A.N., McKinley, S.K., Kenning, E.M., Zheng, F.: Surgical education and training at the crossroads between medical school and residency. Bull. Am. Coll. Surg. **99**, 24–29 (2014)
8. Puro, V., Nicastri, E.: SARS and the removal of personal protective equipment. Can. Med. Assoc. J. **170**, 930 (2004)
9. Niles, D., Sutton, R.M., Donoghue, A., Kalsi, M.S., Roberts, K., Boyle, L., Nishisaki, A., Arbogast, K.B., Helfaer, M., Nadkarni, V.: "Rolling Refreshers": a novel approach to maintain CPR psychomotor skill competence. Resuscitation **80**, 909–912 (2009)
10. Desai, N., Philpott-Howard, J., Wade, J., Casewell, M.: Infection control training: evaluation of a computer-assisted learning package. J. Hosp. Infect. **44**, 193–199 (2000)

11. Hon, C.-Y., Gamage, B., Bryce, E.A., LoChang, J., Yassi, A., Maultsaid, D., Yu, S.: Personal protective equipment in health care: can online infection control courses transfer knowledge and improve proper selection and use? Am. J. Infect. Control **36**, e33–e37 (2008)

12. Choules, A.P.: The use of elearning in medical education: a review of the current situation. Postgrad. Med. J. **83**, 212–216 (2007)

13. Clarke, A.: Designing Computer-Based Learning Materials. Gower Publishing, Ltd., Brookfield (2001)

14. Ruiz, J.G., Mintzer, M.J., Leipzig, R.M.: The impact of e-learning in medical education. Acad. Med. **81**, 207–212 (2006)

15. Saposnik, G., Teasell, R., Mamdani, M., Hall, J., McIlroy, W., Cheung, D., Thorpe, K.E., Cohen, L.G., Bayley, M., S.O.R.C. SORCan: Effectiveness of virtual reality using Wii gaming technology in stroke rehabilitation a pilot randomized clinical trial and proof of principle. Stroke **41**, 1477–1484 (2010)

16. Grantcharov, T.P., Kristiansen, V.B., Bendix, J., Bardram, L., Rosenberg, J., Funch-Jensen, P.: Randomized clinical trial of virtual reality simulation for laparoscopic skills training. Br. J. Surg. **91**, 146–150 (2004)

17. Slater, M., Usoh, M., Steed, A.: Taking steps: the influence of a walking technique on presence in virtual reality. ACM Trans. Comput. Hum. Interact. (TOCHI) **2**, 201–219 (1995)

18. Chittaro, L., Buttussi, F., Zangrando, N.: Desktop virtual reality for emergency preparedness: user evaluation of an aircraft ditching experience under different fear arousal conditions. In: 20th ACM Symposium on Virtual Reality Software and Technology (VRST), pp. 141–150 (2014)

19. Finn, B., Roediger, H.L.: Enhancing retention through reconsolidation negative emotional arousal following retrieval enhances later recall. Psychol. Sci. **22**, 781–786 (2011)

20. Heimbeck, D., Frese, M., Sonnentag, S., Keith, N.: Integrating errors into the training process: the function of error management instructions and the role of goal orientation. Pers. Psychol. **56**, 333–361 (2003)

21. Van Dyck, C., Frese, M., Baer, M., Sonnentag, S.: Organizational error management culture and its impact on performance: a two-study replication. J. Appl. Psychol. **90**, 1228–1240 (2005)

22. Phin, N.F., Rylands, A.J., Allan, J., Edwards, C., Enstone, J.E., Nguyen-Van-Tam, J.S.: Personal protective equipment in an influenza pandemic: a UK simulation exercise. J. Hosp. Infect. **71**, 15–21 (2009)

23. Hung, P.-P., Choi, K.-S., Chiang, V.C.-L.: Using interactive computer simulation for teaching the proper use of personal protective equipment. Comput. Inf. Nurs. **33**, 49–57 (2015)

24. Association of Surgical Technologists: Standards of Practice for Gowning and Gloving. http://www.ast.org/uploadedFiles/Main_Site/Content/About_Us/Standard_Gowning_and_Gloving.pdf

25. Association of Surgical Technologists: Standards of Practice for Surgical Attire, Surgical Scrub, Hand Hygiene and Hand Washing. http://www.ast.org/uploadedFiles/Main_Site/Content/About_Us/Standard_Surgical_Attire_Surgical_Scrub.pdf

26. Brooks Jr, F.P.: What's real about virtual reality? IEEE Comput. Graph. Appl. **19**, 16–27 (1999)

27. Mantovani, F., Castelnuovo, G., Gaggioli, A., Riva, G.: Virtual reality training for health-care professionals. CyberPsychol. Behav. **6**, 389–395 (2003)

28. Munz, Y., Kumar, B.D., Moorthy, K., Bann, S., Darzi, A.: Laparoscopic virtual reality and box trainers: is one superior to the other? Surg. Endosc. Intervent. Tech. **18**, 485–494 (2004)

29. Eubanks, J.C., Lai, C., McMahan, R.P.: Portable virtual reality: inertial measurements and biomechanics. In: 1st Workshop on Everyday Virtual Reality (WEVR), pp. 1–4 (2015)

30. Zielinski, D.J., Rao, H.M., Sommer, M.A., Kopper, R.: Exploring the effects of image persistence in low frame rate virtual environments. In: IEEE Virtual Reality (VR), pp. 19–26 (2015)
31. Drillis, R., Contini, R., Bluestein, M.: Body segment parameters. Artif. Limbs **8**, 44–66 (1964)
32. McMahan, R.P., Bowman, D.A., Zielinski, D.J., Brady, R.B.: Evaluating display fidelity and interaction fidelity in a virtual reality game. IEEE Trans. Visual. Comput. Graph. (TVCG) **18**, 626–633 (2012)
33. Medlock, M.C., Wixon, D., Terrano, M., Romero, R., Fulton, B.: Using the RITE method to improve products: a definition and a case study. In: Usability Professionals Association, Orlando, FL (2002)

New Emergency Medicine Paradigm via Augmented Telemedicine

Gregorij Kurillo[1], Allen Y. Yang[1(✉)], Victor Shia[1], Aaron Bair[2], and Ruzena Bajcsy[1]

[1] University of California at Berkeley, Berkeley, CA, USA
{gregorij,yang,vshia,bajcsy}@eecs.berkeley.edu
[2] University of California Davis Medical Center, Sacramento, CA, USA
aebair@ucdavis.edu

Abstract. In many emergency scenarios, medical care is initially provided by first responders in the field and later by physicians at designated centers. In the setting of traumatic injury, the so-called "golden hour," the efficiency of patient triage and medical transport may greatly affect the outcomes of emergency treatment. In current practice, the initial communication and interaction between physician and first responders is limited to voice or, in rare instances, video conferencing, while the attending physicians cannot receive other more comprehensive, critical patient information. This paper proposes to address these fundamental technology gaps and information bottlenecks by leveraging the state-of-the-art 3D teleimmersion and augmented reality (AR) technologies.

Keywords: Telemedicine · Virtual reality · Augmented reality · Collaboration · Remote interaction · Emergency medicine

1 Introduction

Telemedicine refers to clinical and healthcare services that are provided at a distance via the use of telecommunication and information technologies. To date, telemedicine has been applied in many areas of medical care, such as emergency medicine, remote diagnosis, surgery, rehabilitation, and many others. It has been well documented that telemedicine can improve access to medical services and their quality for rural or poor communities [1]. Telemedicine is also being used in critical care to connect patients in the field with medical professionals at trauma centers. Based on the means of interaction between providers or provider and patient, the telemedicine systems can be roughly divided into two categories: (1) synchronous or real-time systems and (2) asynchronous or store-and-forward systems [2]. The advantage of the synchronous approach is in its ability to immediately address the care and provide support for time-critical clinical decisions. The asynchronous approach on the other hand entails of exchanging relevant information over the network, analyzing it offline, and then providing a medical decision. This approach most often does not entail direct interaction with the patient but is rather focused on interpretation of medical data (e.g. radiology imaging, ultrasound, EKG, etc.). In the remainder of this paper we therefore focus on the synchronous or real-time telemedicine.

S. Lackey and R. Shumaker (Eds.): VAMR 2016, LNCS 9740, pp. 502–511, 2016.
DOI: 10.1007/978-3-319-39907-2_48

Real-time telemedicine systems have only in recent years been adopted in emergency medicine. In civilian and military scenarios, remote support is particularly critical in the so-called "golden hour" of trauma, where the efficiency of care greatly affects the outcome. Telemedicine can be applied at various stages of emergency care from triage and transport to consultation with specialists in the hospital. Typical solutions include two-way videoconferencing with single or multiscale views of the room and patient, alongside vital signs, medical imaging, and interviews with all participants, including the patient and family [2]. This vast information space, however, can be overwhelming and can limit critical decision-making due to the information bottlenecks and technology-imposed limitations on communication between specialist and patient-side care provider. Although the video information and vital signs are helpful, the feedback information provided to the emergency responders is typically only conveyed verbally, limiting the capacity of provided remote support. There is a need to deliver the information more concisely while minimizing the effort to retrieve relevant information generated locally or remotely at any given moment. In this paper, we propose a novel augmented telemedicine platform based on the emerging technologies of 3D teleimmersion, virtual reality (VR) and augmented reality (AR) that will address some of these issues and introduce disruptive capabilities in all the stages of collection, representation, transmission, and user interaction.

2   Background

Telemedicine technology began in the late 1960's and early 1970's in the NASA space program to monitor biometric data and provide guided medical treatment by non-physicians for astronauts during space flights [3]. This technology was subsequently applied to deliver healthcare to remote Indian Papago Tribe in Arizona as part of the project called STARPAHC (Space Technology Applied to Rural Papago Advanced Health Care) in the 1970's [4]. Telemedicine was first deployed in a disaster in the aftermath of 1985 earthquake in Mexico City and later on during several other events around the world, such as 1988 earthquake in Armenia [5, 6]. This technology was early on embraced also by the United States Department of Defense (DoD) during 1980's and 1990's to provide support during global military missions. Although many bases had on-site clinics, the telemedicine made much broader range of physicians and specialists available to deployed soldiers. During the Persian Gulf War, telecommunication technologies were integrated into mobile health units providing transmission of CT images via satellite and international telephone network. Similar technology was also used during the military interventions in Somalia and Bosnia, where commercially available technology was used to transmit x-rays, ultrasound, CT scans, and other medical imaging data, and full-motion videos to remote field hospitals for diagnostic support [5]. Despite the advances in communication and video technology, wider use of telemedicine in subsequent wars in Iraq and Afghanistan was hindered by the lack of satellite bandwidth [7]. Instead, medical personnel used email to send pictures of casualties, wounds, and medical records. Many of the doctors still prefer this "store-and-forward" methods, possibly also due to lack of familiarity with the alternative real-time technologies.

With the emergence of internet-based communications in the late 1990's, telemedicine became more widely used in civilian practice. The internet provided a cost-efficient form of communication independent of the hardware. Initially used for teleconsultation between specialists, telemedicine started to be employed in emergency medical care to connect small and rural hospitals with specialty centers to address emergency situations. One of the first large centers that provided real-time consultation services was the University of California Davis Health System with its California Tele-health Network [8]. Today there are 14 Telehealth Resource Centers across the United States that focus on advancing effective use of telemedicine [9]. Telemedicine has also become more prevalent in emergency care to reduce overcrowding of emergency rooms and to provide support to rural areas. Recent meta-review of 38 reports on the emergency telemedicine in the US by Ward et al. [10] found overall positive results in terms of improving clinical processes, outcomes, and throughput.

With advances in mobile communications, the telemedicine technology can also be deployed in ambulances. Such systems can assist paramedics during triage and provide pre-hospital treatment under direct supervision of an expert physician by transmitting vital signs and video imaging to the care center [11]. In another example, Boniface et al. [12] performed a feasibility study of remotely guiding paramedics to obtain ultrasound imaging in the field for immediate diagnosis.

3   Current Limitations

Current real-time telemedicine technology, whether in military or civilian domain, faces several limitations. Upmost is the information overload as the data from various sources, such as video, vital signs, medical records, have to be interpreted concurrently by the expert/specialist for critical decision making. This often entails looking at several monitors or even using a camera to transmit vital signs information captured on the screen.

Next, instructions for the guided medical evaluation or procedure need to be conveyed to first responder, typically via audio communication. Although the modern telemedicine systems often include two-way video communication, the video is primarily used only to transmit the view of the patient. While some systems support pan-tilt-zoom cameras, if a different camera position is required, the expert has to instruct the responder to reposition the camera in order to obtain the desired view. When communicating with the responder, the expert cannot directly use gestures to provide instructions of the procedures since the video feedback is dislocated from patient's bedside and typically displayed on an external monitor.

Using only 2D video to display patient condition further limits the information available to the physician. By scanning and transmitting 3D surface information could provide additional cues to perceive the extent of the trauma as the expert may be able to detect bruising, swollen tissue, etc. In addition, combing the video feedback with other modalities could improve initial information needed to make informed decisions regarding emergency care and transportation.

4 Virtual and Augmented Reality

Use of virtual reality in telemedicine was first envisioned by Satava [13] who proposed using remote sensors, intelligent systems, telepresence surgery, and virtual reality surgical simulations, to improve combat casualty care in battlefield scenarios. In his view of the modern medical battlefield, he proposed using streaming video, vital signs information, and medical imaging transmitted to the telemedicine unit who would instruct the combat medic in the field. Before the evacuation, the critical care could be provided via remote surgery using an instrumented Trauma Pod, where the surgeon could combine live video data with VR models from a remote, safe location. Although significant advances have been made to date, the remote surgery using telepresence has only been accomplished on shorter distances in few cases due to network limitations in coverage and latency. The virtual reality has, on the other hand, been applied to considerable degree in training simulations to improve emergency care. In further review of VR technologies we limit ourselves only to those that can enhance real-time interaction and communication between geographically distributed individuals.

Recent advances in sensor technologies and miniaturization have made possible a robust and minimally intrusive digital acquisition of high quality video data (e.g., HD, 4K video), 360-degree video, real time 3D surface reconstruction (e.g., Microsoft Kinect, Intel RealSense), and acquisition of vital signs with various wearable sensors. Furthermore, modern smartphones and tablets, which are equipped with an array of sensors, high quality video camera, audio capabilities, and high bandwidth wireless network connectivity can be used in future telemedicine applications to provide better data acquisition. Visualization and interaction with collected data can be further enhanced by moving away from traditional computer displays to more immersive 3D stationary or wearable displays (i.e., head mounted displays). Another opportunity to reduce the information overload and provide the vital signs at the reach of the hand is to use augmented reality wearable displays which can show information overlain on the real world environment. The use of aforementioned technologies in remote collaboration for emergency telemedicine, however, requires a different paradigm of interaction.

Although the quality of experience with regard to visual and audio transmission has significantly improved over the years, the 2D video technology has several inherent drawbacks that cannot be mitigated easily. These include partial loss of non-verbal cues such as gestures and eye contact, which have been shown to increase trust, collaboration and productivity in video-enabled interactions [14]. In addition to the loss of non-verbal cues, there is a disconnect between the users and the content. In case of the telemedicine applications, the physician primarily conveys information back to the responder via verbal instructions. Video-based telepresence experience can be enhanced by 3D telepresence and 3D teleimmersion where remote interaction takes place in a virtual reality environment [15]. 3D teleimmersion technology for remote interaction has been explored by several researchers in the past decade (see the review in [16]), including our group at University of California, Berkeley. In our demonstration systems that we have developed over the years, we have investigated various aspects of interaction, networking, data compression, rendering, and others, while working with multi-disciplinary groups of users, including medical doctors. One of the lessons learned addressing the technological barriers includes the need to use low-complexity and off-the-shelf technologies that can be easily deployed and automatically calibrated in a real-world environment. In the proposed framework, we thus plan to facilitate real-time interaction between the physician and the emergency responder through the virtual and augmented reality technology that is already commercially available.

5   Augmented Telemedicine Platform

In this section we describe a novel telemedicine platform that addresses the existing technology gaps and breaks the information bottlenecks in current emergency telemedicine systems. The proposed platform shown in Fig. 1 consists of several compelling new features. First, a real-time patient data acquisition and visualization module captures patient's external trauma and vital signals in the field and precisely renders the signals for remote physicians via 3D teleimmersion. Second, an AR module allows physicians and first responders to examine patient data and collaborate in simple medical procedures via gestures and annotations. Finally, a telemedicine communication module enables secure and robust deployment of the above two modules over long distance through wireless network.

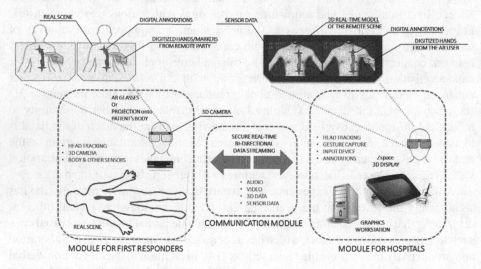

Fig. 1. Diagram of the augmented telemedicine system for remote interaction between a physician and an emergency responder.

In an example scenario, the augmented telemedicine platform can connect an ambulance with a local trauma center. A 3D image acquisition module is installed inside the ambulance. Once a patient is placed into the ambulance, the module scans the patient's body with millimeter accuracy. The acquired 3D representation of the patient accurately captures external trauma and the visual appearance of the injury. To examine for internal bleeding or hidden injuries, the first responder can use ultrasound to scan the patient's body and augment the patient's 3D avatar in real time. During the procedure, measured medical data of the patient are transmitted to the trauma center in real time. The attending physician at the trauma center can then review the patient's full-body medical condition through a virtual reality 3D display device and recommend treatments before and for the duration of the transportation until the patient arrives at the hospital. During this interaction, the physician is able to annotate the 3D avatar in the virtual environment to provide additional information. The annotations can be virtually attached to the patient's body by registering them to detected visual features on the skin or clothing. The first responder is subsequently able to view these annotations in real time via an augmented reality display device or a dynamic projection onto the body part of interest. The annotations can provide additional cues to guide the triage and can be retrieved when the patient arrives at the hospital. In this example, the augmented telemedicine platform is used to provide more seamless two-way interaction between the physician and first responder that cannot be easily replicated with traditional video communication.

In the reminder of this section we provide further details on each module of the proposed platform:

3D data acquisition and visualization. To improve the visual information that can be obtained by standard 2D cameras, we propose to use one or more RGB+D cameras that can generate the depth information of the captured scene in addition to high resolution texture. The depth information can be used to reconstruct a 3D model of the entire body or a body part. The principle of 3D acquisition can be based on multi-view stereo, stereo reconstruction with structured light or time-of-flight (ToF). Each of these technologies has certain advantages and disadvantages [17], which are beyond the scope of this paper. In our prototype implementation we use Microsoft Kinect sensor, which provides accurate (with errors between 2–4 mm [18]) real-time 3D reconstruction based on ToF with 30 Hz acquisition rate.

Figure 2 shows the output of the Kinect camera observing a mockup setup of an individual on a stretcher. The obtained depth and color data can be used to obtain the real-time 3D avatar representation of a patient's body and movement within the field of view of the acquisition system. The 3D acquisition from a stationary unit can be further combined with a handheld or adjustable scanner to provide a close-up and more detailed view of the injury. After the acquisition, the RGB+D video data are compressed and sent over the network. On the receiving end, the imagery data are converted into a 3D surface represented by a textured mesh (Fig. 3). This allows the viewer to select any viewpoint to examine the area of interest.

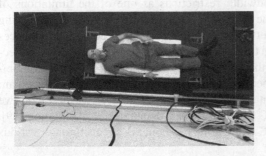 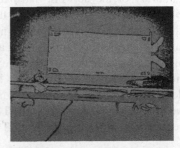

Fig. 2. RGB texture (left) and depth data output (right) generated by Kinect for Xbox One.

Fig. 3. Reconstructed 3D mesh with annotations rendered from an arbitrary point of view (left) and user interacting with the 3D data on zSpace system (right).

Immersive interaction. We will develop more intuitive virtual interaction methods that allow medical professionals to examine the patient remotely and also interact with the provider at the patient side. In particular, we are investigating remote collaboration with a stationary solution via zSpace virtual reality display technology[1] and a wearable solution via upcoming Microsoft HoloLens technology or other wearable AR glasses. The primary role of the display system is to receive the data from the 3D acquisition module and render them in real time as a 3D surface to be viewed by the medical professionals. The display system also provides tools to annotate the data virtually using a stylus. The advantage of using a stationary 3D display, such as zSpace, as opposed to more immersive wearable head mounted display, such as Oculus Rift, is in a more comfortable interaction that does not have adverse effects linked to head mounted displays (e.g., motion sickness, eye discomfort and other temporary visual changes). The zSpace display system also includes a stylus that can be used to directly interact with the 3D data, create annotations and gesture inputs. The annotations and gestures are then transmitted back to the responder in the field and displayed as augmented reality features that can be either projected onto the patient from a mounted projector or viewed via an AR display, such as the Microsoft HoloLens. The interaction module with the aforementioned features is aimed to guide the first responders during the initial triage and to provide critical care to the patient during transport.

Telemedicine communication. The robustness and reliability of the communication is critical during any remote interaction. As mentioned several studies have identified the availability of the network and bandwidth restrictions as one of the limitations of applying real-time telemedicine in the field. With the advances in mobile networking and increased coverage of 4G/LTE networks, it is now possible to connect ambulances in most urban and rural areas to a local trauma center without dedicated satellite connection. Our approach aims to leverage the open source real-time peer-to-peer communication standard WebRTC, which is becoming increasingly popular to securely stream video, audio and other multimedia data between different devices. In our past work we have investigated the use of WebRTC to stream Kinect data for telerehabilitation [19]. One of the main features of WebRTC is the ability to connect clients through various

---

[1] http://zspace.com.

firewalls while being able to dynamically adapt the multimedia transmission quality according to the available network bandwidth. We are currently investigating new compression methods for RGB+D video data that can be efficiently transmitted and adapted to the network while preserving important details in the captured data. Furthermore, the WebRTC connection will also be used to transmit vital signs data, medical imaging, and interaction data, such as gestures and annotation, in order to synchronize the two clients.

Medical imaging integration. For future work, we intend to further augment the visualization capabilities of the telemedicine platform with the integration of selected medical imaging modalities with the immersive telemedicine platform. In particular, we will integrate a portable ultrasound imaging module and overlay the ultrasound image on the patient's avatar that the physician will be able to review in real time. By having real time information available, the physician will be able to direct the first responder to perform the ultrasound examination with not just voice cues but also visual annotations. A key technology gap in this area is visual 3D localization (registration) with the patient body.

6 Discussion and Conclusion

The proposed platform combines off-the-shelf AR and VR technology to create a more interactive experience and improve the communication between first responders and emergency care physicians. As we develop this platform, we are interested in answering the following research questions:

- What is the required 3D resolution of the data acquisition to assess the extent of trauma remotely and add value to the current video technology? What is the minimal amount of information needed?
- Importance of certain features of the proposed platform to streamline the collaboration (e.g. real time 3D visualization, use of annotations, integration with vital signs data, etc.)
- How does network latency, jitter and overall connectivity affect the quality of experience (QoE)?
- How will communication with the VR/AR system change the interaction between the first responders and physician in time-critical scenarios?
- How to perform 3D reconstruction, automatic registration and data fusion of multiple depth-sensing cameras, each with different resolutions?
- How to track features of deformable objects to allow for real time registration of annotations to the human body?
- What methods are available to provide some form of effective haptic feedback to the remote user?

Some of the research questions will be examined during the development phase, where we will test the network connectivity and its effects on video resolution and interaction in terms of bandwidth and transmission delays/jitter. This information will be used to build in the mechanisms to adapt the 3D video transmission (e.g., reducing frame rate, increasing video compression ratio, etc.). We will work with our medical collaborators to understand the importance of various features for the specific emergency scenarios. Furthermore, we will collect user-feedback and collaboration performance metric [20] related to the interaction with the system (e.g., movement of the stylus, changes in viewpoint, user-interface interactions, etc.) and between users (e.g., use of annotations, references to visual markers, use of audio communication, etc.). This information will be used to further improve the system in future iterations.

We envision that the proposed augmented telemedicine system combining AR and VR can bring about disruptive new capabilities in telemedicine to achieve better patient triage and prehospital emergency care, combat casualty care in the battlefield, or during natural disasters. An important role of the augmented telemedicine platform will also be in the training of first responders and emergency care physicians. By taking advantage of AR technology, it will be possible to create various simulation scenarios with patient actors or mannequins to practice different situations. Using remote training capabilities of this platform, the first responders could be engaged in a training simulation scenario while waiting for a new on-site call.

Although the focus of this paper was on the emergency care, the proposed technology can be applied to other areas of telemedicine to facilitate more effective care by connecting patients with general and specialized providers. These include telerehabilitation services, occupational therapy, patient education, clinical trials, and others. Reducing the cost of transportation is an integral part of reducing the total cost of the current healthcare system.

Acknowledgements. This research was partially supported by Office of Naval Research (ONR) grant #N00014-09-1-0230.

References

1. Nesbitt, T.S., Marcin, J.P., Daschbach, M.M., Cole, S.L.: Perceptions of local health care quality in 7 rural communities with telemedicine. J. Rural Health **21**(1), 79–85 (2006)
2. Wilson, L.S., Maeder, A.J.: Recent directions in telemedicine: review of trends in research and practice. Health Inform. Res. **21**(4), 213–222 (2015)
3. Simpson, A.T.: A brief history of NASA's contributions to telemedicine. http://www.nasa.gov/content/a-brief-history-of-nasa-s-contributions-to-telemedicine. Accessed 10 Feb 2016
4. Freiburger, G., Holcomb, M., Piper, D.: The STARPAHC collection: part of an archive of the history of telemedicine. J. Telemed. Telecare. **13**(5), 221–223 (2007)
5. Garshnek, V., Burkle, F.M.: Applications of telemedicine and telecommunications to disaster medicine. J. Am. Med. Inform. Assoc. **6**(1), 26–37 (1999)
6. Nicogossian, A.E., Doarn, C.R.: Armenia 1988 earthquake and telemedicine: lessons learned and forgotten. Telemed. E-Health **17**(9), 741–745 (2011)
7. Ling, G.S., Rhee, P., Ecklund, J.M.: Surgical innovations arising from the Iraq and Afghanistan wars. Annu. Rev. Med. **61**, 457–468 (2010)
8. Nesbitt, T.S., Dharmar, M., Katz-Bell, J., Hartvigsen, G., Marcin, J.P.: Telehealth at UC Davis—a 20-year experience. Telemed. E-Health **19**(5), 357–362 (2013)
9. Telehealth Resource Center. http://www.telehealthresourcecenter.org. Accessed 10 Feb 2016

10. Ward, M.M., Jaana, M., Natafgi, N.: Systematic review of telemedicine applications in emergency rooms. Int. J. Med. Inform. **84**(9), 601–616 (2015)
11. Mandellos, G.J., Lymperopoulos, D.K., Koukias, M.N., Tzes, A., Lazarou, N., Vagianos, C.: A novel mobile telemedicine system for ambulance transport. Design and evaluation. In: Proceedings of the IEEE Engineering in Medicine and Biology Society (IEMBS), San Francisco, CA (2004)
12. Boniface, K.S., Shokoohi, H., Smith, E.R., Scantlebury, K.: Tele-ultrasound and paramedics: real-time remote physician guidance of the focused assessment with sonography for trauma examination. Am. J. Emerg. Med. **29**(5), 477–481 (2011)
13. Satava, R.M.: Virtual reality and telepresence for military medicine. Comput. Biol. Med. **25**(2), 229–236 (1995)
14. Doherty-Sneddon, G., Anderson, A., O'Malley, C., Langton, S., Garrod, S., Bruce, V.: Face-to-face and video-mediated communication: a comparison of dialogue structure and task performance. J. Exp. Psychol. Appl. **3**(2), 105–125 (1997)
15. DeFanti, T., Sandin, D., Brown, M., Pape, D., Anstey, J., Bogucki, M., Dawe, G., Johnson, A., Huang, T.S.: Technologies for virtual reality/tele-immersion applications: issues of research in image display and global networking. In: Earnshaw, R.A., Guedj, R.A., van Dam, A., Vince, J.A. (eds.) Frontiers of Human-Centered Computing, Online Communities and Virtual Environments, pp. 137–159. Springer, London (1999)
16. Kurillo, G., Bajcsy, R.: 3D teleimmersion for collaboration and interaction of geographically distributed users. Virtual Reality **17**(1), 29–43 (2013)
17. Sarbolandi, H., Lefloch, D., Kolb, A.: Kinect range sensing: structured-light versus time-of-flight Kinect. Comput. Vis. Image Underst. **139**, 1–20 (2015)
18. Yang, L., Zhang, L., Dong, H., Alelaiwi, A.El, Saddik, A.: Evaluating and improving the depth accuracy of Kinect for Windows v2. IEEE Sens. J. **15**(8), 4275–4285 (2015)
19. Anton-Saez, D., Kurillo, G., Goñi, A., Illarramendi, A., Bajcsy, R.: Real-time communication for Kinect-based tele-rehabilitation. Technical report (2014)
20. Damianos, L., Hirschman, L., Kozierok, R., Kurtz, J., Greenberg, A., Walls, K., Laskowski, S., Scholtz, J.: Evaluation for collaborative systems. ACM Comput. Surv. (CSUR) **31**(2), 15 (1999)

Advances and Tendencies: A Review of Recent Studies on Virtual Reality for Pain Management

Zhejun Liu[1], Sijia Wangluo[2], and Hua Dong[1(✉)]

[1] College of Arts and Media, Tongji University, Shanghai, China
{wingeddreamer,donghua}@tongji.edu.cn
[2] College of Design and Innovation, Tongji University, Shanghai, China
1539547470@qq.com

Abstract. In the progress of civilization, humans have developed various ways of pain management. Virtual reality (VR in short), a technology to create an illusion of presence in cyberspace is a new addition to this inventory. Because of its immersive and distractive nature, researchers believe that VR may be safer and more effective than traditional analgesic methods. There has been a number of studies in this field and the interest continues to grow. In order to summarize achievements obtained so far and figure out gaps for future research possibilities, by reviewing more than 100 articles, this article try to point out novel or unusual research perspectives so as to suggest future research possibilities.

Keywords: Virtual reality · VR · Pain management · Literature review

1 Introduction

1.1 Background

Pain, a feeling everyone tries to avoid, may come from disease, injury, retrogression, medical treatment and other sources. Despite our dislikes, pain serves as one of the bases for numerous lives on earth. It directs beings, not only humans but also other creatures, to notice danger, to avoid threat and to seek remedy so as to survive this competitive world. Therefore, human beings' strategy of coping with pain is not to eliminate it completely, which might be possible in the near future, but rather to relieve it and have it under control when necessary.

As history progresses, humans have developed various ways of pain relief, including chemical pharmacy, physical therapies as well as some mysterious yet effective treatments such as hypnosis and acupuncture. However, there has been no ultimate solution in this field till today, for these methods either have negative side effects or are not applicable or effective under some circumstances. In this situation, the explorations for new ways of pain relief have never stopped, among whose outcomes virtual reality is one of the latest inventions.

Virtual reality, usually abbreviated as VR, is a technology that exploits the latest advancements in computer science, in both hardware and software, to fabricate a virtual world for its users in order to create their illusion of presence in that cyberspace.

S. Lackey and R. Shumaker (Eds.): VAMR 2016, LNCS 9740, pp. 512–520, 2016.
DOI: 10.1007/978-3-319-39907-2_49

Furthermore, VR has the inherent potential of being interactive because its content is generated in real time, not ahead of time, which makes the experience even more immersive. Many scholars believe that VR has a promising value in pain relief mainly because of its capability, though not yet rigorously verified in a scientific manner, as a distractor. Despite the doubts whether VR actually helps to cure a disease or physical disorder, abundant evidences have been collected, showing its superiority in relieving pain and other kinds of discomfort caused by disease or the treatment procedures, and thus raising the acceptance of unpleasant therapies as well as patients' quality of lives.

There have been a number of studies concerning the application of VR technology in pain relief, and the interest in it continues to grow. A search for articles published between 1995 and 2015 (October) from the Web of Science databases with the keywords "virtual reality" and "pain" gave a report as shown in Fig. 1. A sharp increase in the number of articles published and cited in recent 20 years shows clearly that more and more attention has been drawn to this field.

Fig. 1. A search report from web of science

Also, there are quite a few review articles in this field, while this one aims to serve a different purpose from a different perspective. Besides giving a general overview of the existing research outcomes, this article also focuses on some special instruments, methods and results that are worthy of revisiting and further inspection. These articles, though small in ratio, may suggest future research directions and bear great potential value.

1.2   Procedures and Criteria

All the reviewed articles were collected from three important databases, which were Web of Science Core Collection, Medline database and EI Compendex database, via a search for articles published between 2006 and 2015 using key words "virtual reality" and "pain".

There were a total of 513 hits from 3 databases. The first pass filtering was conducted to remove apparently irrelevant articles by judging from their titles, and 245 remained (111 from Web of Science Core Collection, 99 from Medline Database and 35 from EI Compendex database). Then, a second pass filtering was conducted to remove duplicated ones found in multiple databases and 171 remained. These 171 articles were read carefully and filtered for a third time using the following inclusion criteria:

- VR technology was used to relieve pain (or other kinds of discomfort), not to evaluate symptoms, assist treatment planning or educate medical practitioners;
- The article must contain practical data from experiment, instead of merely presenting a protocol or a future research plan;
- VR technology must play an important role in the experiment, preferably as a subject for comparison, instead of being briefly mentioned or introduced;
- It should not be another review article. Review articles were used as references but not included in the final list;
- If more than one articles were written by the same author(s) and based on similar experiments, only the most cited one was kept. If the citation was unknown, the latest one was kept;
- The full text version must be available.

After filtering 43 articles remained in the final list. A spreadsheet was created to store extracted information in an organized way. In addition to general information such as the title, author, sponsors, source, time and etc., the other important labels of the classified information were as follows:

- Objective;
- Demographic information of the subjects;
- Sample size;
- Subject's health status;
- Kind or source of discomfort;
- Hardware and software used;
- Comparative targets;
- Research methods and procedures;
- Measures and instruments;
- Findings and conclusion.

Based on this organized information, we obtained the following review findings.

2 Common Research Patterns and General Conclusions

The application of VR technology in pain management has been investigated for many years. The research patterns used in most research projects are as follow:

2.1 Pattern A: To Evaluate the Efficacy of VR Therapies

The experiments done in this kind of researches were usually temporal. Researchers firstly inspected subjects' pain, anxiety and other relevant sensory and emotional levels. Then, after the subjects had receive VR therapies, they were evaluated again to check whether VR therapies contributed to the relief of pain and other discomfort. It was used to test the efficacy of VR therapy among patients suffering from complex regional injury [1], fibromyalgia [2], cancer [3] and motor dysfunction and associated neuropathic pain [4]. All these experiments shew positive result, which meant VR therapies helped the patients to improve their mental status.

Because only VR therapies were investigated, usually this pattern didn't require many experiment cycles and complex environments, making it simple and easy to implement. But the results might be questionable because it was difficult to tell whether VR treatment or self-recovery over time played the most important role. And it was also difficult to answer the question whether VR was a better choice since no other therapies were compared with it.

2.2 Pattern B: To Compare VR Therapies with Other Analgesic Methods

This was the commonest research pattern adopted by many researchers. In this pattern, VR therapies were usually compared with other kinds of chemical and/or physical analgesia to conclude whether (and/or how) VR therapies were superior in relieving pain and unpleasantness caused by a certain reason such as disease [5], burn [6–8], injury [9, 10], medical treatment [11, 12] and so forth. When healthy subjects participated in the experiment, pain was often inflicted artificially with heat stimulus [13], cold pressor [14, 15] or other equipment [16].

In these experiments, standard care without VR usually served as the baseline. In addition to it, the analgesic effect of VR was compared to a lot of other techniques, including TV programs, music, books or even lollipops [12, 17, 18].

As far as experiment design was concerned, there were two different kinds: the within-subject design and the between-subject design. In the former one, the same group of subjects received more than one treatment, randomized in order, and then underwent the same inquiry procedures to conclude which treatment worked better. In the latter one, subjects were randomly assigned to different groups to receive different treatments, and then similar procedures followed. In this research field, more studies used the within-subject design.

Finally, over 80 % of the reviewed articles drew positive conclusions. They supported the opinion that VR therapies might have great potential in pain management, not only because it was proven to be effective among sick and healthy subjects but also because it had very little side-effect and was much safer than other aggressive or offensive therapies.

2.3 Pattern C: To Explore the Factors Affecting the Effectiveness of VR Therapies

This pattern was used not so often, but the results were usually interesting and valuable. In addition to answering the questions whether VR therapies were useful and more effective than other traditional therapies, this research pattern tried to answer the question what might affect the usefulness of VR therapies.

This pattern was obviously valuable because the effectiveness of VR therapies could hardly get improved until the influential factors were clarified. However, this pattern was, from the reviewers' point of view, the most difficult one by far. Firstly, there might be a great number of influential factors, major or minor, superficial or profound, on users' side or VR's side. To figure out the most significant ones was not an easy job. Secondly, some variables on VR's side must be adjusted so as to assess their influence, which usually meant that those ready-made VR solutions from 3rd-party organizations could not be used. In this case, the researches would have to, if not by themselves, produce VR materials for intended experiments, which might be expensive and time-consuming. Thirdly, this pattern generally required stricter and more accurate variable control techniques to avoid unwanted overlapping and cross effects.

There were a few successful attempts. They will be introduced in Sect. 3.1.

3   Mentionable Research Projects

Among all the articles reviewed this far, some have uncommon features where future research opportunities possibly lie and are thus worth special attention.

3.1   In-Depth Analysis of Influential Factors

As mentioned in Sect. 2.3, pattern C, to explore the VR therapies' influential factors, was difficult but important. Many unique research projects and interesting findings were carried out and obtained with this pattern.

One of the article compared high tech VR, i.e. high quality VR content presented with more advanced hardware, with low tech VR, and concluded that the high quality one was more effective [19].

Another article used a series of experiments to verify the hypothesis that a cold VR environment might be more effective than a hot one when a subject was suffering from pain caused by heat and vice versa only to find that the difference between them was not significant [20].

There was another research trying to find out whether the same game played with a first-person view, which was believed to be more immersive, brought better analgesic effect than that played with a third-person view, and concluded that the they did not result in significantly different improvements in pain tolerance [21].

Similarly, one of the researches tried to test the hypothesis that increased body movement while steering a VR game led to the diminished experience of pain, but also failed to find significant relationship between body engagement and pain tolerance level [22].

There were also some experiments trying to measure the value of using HMDs (head mounted displays) in VR therapies, but they all concluded that the value of HMDs was questionable [16, 23, 24].

3.2 Unique Perspectives

In one study, 137 cancer patients receiving intravenous chemotherapy participated in 3 experiments to help to explore the influence of age, gender, state anxiety, fatigue and diagnosis on time perception with a VR distraction intervention [25]. PC games were used as the test material and were presented with HMDs. The author concluded that clinicians should not assume that all patients would become distracted and experience altered time perception while using VR and not all patients welcomed distraction during unpleasant medical treatments. Among all the reviewed articles, this was the only one trying to explore the influence of demographic properties.

Another article introduced an innovative pain management system, Epione, which formed a dynamic pain meter by using facial expression analysis, triggering biofeedback and augmented reality based destruction scenarios in an effort to maximize patient's pain relief [26]. Among all the reviewed articles, this was the only one that introduced the concept of intelligent self-adaptive VR system and community based mutual aid. The result was positive. According to the authors, the holistic approach and modular development of Epione allowed for flexible expansion to many user-scenarios, making it a supporting environment to the whole community, providing a better quality of life.

3.3 Unusual Results

Despite the fact that most research results were positive, there were still negative results denying the efficacy of VR therapies. Although they were small in number (only one found in our case) and might stem from imperfection in experiment design, these negative results might also suggest unnoticed or not yet understood defects in VR therapies. As a result, they well deserve revisiting and further verification.

This study used 86 adults suffering from burn pain to examine whether pre-procedural VR guided relaxation added to patient controlled analgesia with morphine reduced pain severity during awake dressing changes [27]. This study used cross-subject design and subjects were randomly assigned to 2 groups to receive either VR relaxation plus intravenous morphine PCA infusion or intravenous morphine PCA infusion alone. The result was that VR relaxation added to morphine PCA was associated with significantly greater pain intensity during and after awake dressing changes in the patients with burns.

4 Future Research Opportunities

Investigation of the application of VR technology in pain management started more than 10 years ago, and many valuable results have been already obtained. Researchers generally support its effectiveness, however, the underlying principles and mechanisms of VR therapies still remain in a black box. On the technology side, although VR is not a brand new concept, it is thriving and advancing rapidly these years thanks to the development of hardware and software industries. This tendency will also bring more research opportunities to this field.

In the authors' point of view, future research opportunities are very likely to be found in the following directions.

4.1 Better Understanding of VR Therapies

As introduced in Sect. 3.1, there are already researches trying to find out what are the influential factors of VR therapies. Only the experiment comparing high tech VR and low tech VR gave a conclusion that high quality ones are more effective. Other experiments all failed to establish a relationship between a potential influential factor and the effectiveness of VR therapies. But in common sense it is not reasonable to believe all VR therapies, no matter what their contents are and how their users are designed to experience them, will produce the same analgesic effect. This means more researches are needed to verify these results with larger sample sizes. Other potential influential factors are also to be discovered and estimated.

In addition, the underlying theories of VR therapies still remain a myth. Most researchers believe that its analgesic effects come from its power as a distractor. But what is actually happening on the psychological and neurological level remains to be unveiled. To make this kind of theoretical and profound discoveries is by no means easy, but it will bring about invaluable breakthroughs when successfully accomplished.

4.2 Better Segmented Subjects

Children, especially young kids are often dealt with as a specially group. The most likely reason is that they lack the ability to experience VR and express their feelings as well as adults. Expect for children, though, most research projects didn't differentiate subjects based on their demographic features and very few researches tried to how these features might affect experiment outcomes.

There ought to be differences between male and female users, well-educated and poorly-educated users, gamers and non-gamers. Adults shall also be divided into young, middle-aged and elderly people and they have different abilities of perception and comprehension. Moreover, Asian, American, European, African residents may also respond differently to the same VR therapy. There are even more criteria to be defined, and better segmented subjects will lead to more accurate and reliable results and conclusions.

4.3   Application of Latest Technologies

As mentioned above, VR technology is undergoing fast development lately. Many manufacturers are inventing new input and output devices to cater for the increasingly demanding requirements from VR users. Although most of the attention was paid to the entertainment field due to commercial motivations, new technologies may still well suit the need of the medical field. The reason is simple: the entertainment industries always try their best to make VR more immersive and attractive, and here lies the same power that distracts attention from pain, the essence of VR's analgesic effects.

So it's recommendable that researchers keep an eye on the latest technological advances, and when a new device or technology comes out, be the first to test it in pain management and other relevant fields.

Acknowledgements.   This article is a part of the results from the interdisciplinary research project "Arts and Wellbeing" supported by Tongji University.

References

1. Sato, K., et al.: Nonimmersive virtual reality mirror visual feedback therapy and its application for the treatment of complex regional pain syndrome: an open-label pilot study. Pain Med. 11(4), 622–629 (2010)
2. Botella, C., et al.: Virtual reality in the treatment of fibromyalgia: a pilot study. Cyberpsychology Behav. Soc. Netw. 16(3), 215–223 (2013)
3. Banos, R.M., et al.: A positive psychological intervention using virtual reality for patients with advanced cancer in a hospital setting: a pilot study to assess feasibility. Support. Care Cancer 21(1), 263–270 (2013)
4. Villiger, M., et al.: Virtual reality-augmented neurorehabilitation improves motor function and reduces neuropathic pain in patients with incomplete spinal cord injury. Neurorehabilitation Neural Repair 27(8), 675–683 (2013)
5. Schneider, S.M., Hood, L.E.: Virtual reality: a distraction intervention for chemotherapy. Oncol. Nurs. Forum 34(1), 39–46 (2007)
6. Hoffman, H.G., et al.: Virtual reality pain control during burn wound debridement in the hydrotank. Clin. J. Pain 24(4), 299–304 (2008)
7. Maani, C.V., et al.: Virtual reality pain control during burn wound debridement of combat-related burn injuries using robot-like arm mounted VR Goggles. J. Trauma-Injury Infect. Crit. Care 71, S125–S130 (2011)
8. Miller, K., et al.: A novel technology approach to pain management in children with burns: a prospective randomized controlled trial. Burns 37(3), 395–405 (2011)
9. Patterson, D.R., et al.: Virtual reality hypnosis for pain associated with recovery from physical trauma. Int. J. Clin. Exp. Hypn. 58(3), 288–300 (2010)
10. Hoffman, H.G., et al.: Virtual reality pain control during physical therapy range of motion exercises for a patient with multiple blunt force trauma injuries. Cyberpsychology Behav. 12(1), 47–49 (2009)
11. Gold, J.I., et al.: Effectiveness of virtual reality for pediatric pain distraction during IV placement. Cyberpsychology Behav. 9(2), 207–212 (2006)

12. Windich-Biermeier, A., et al.: Effects of distraction on pain, fear, and distress during venous port access and venipuncture in children and adolescents with cancer. J. Pediatr. Oncol. Nurs. **24**(1), 8–19 (2007)

13. Hoffman, H.G., et al.: The analgesic effects of oploids and immersive virtual reality distraction: evidence from subjective and functional brain imaging assessments. Anesth. Analg. **105**(6), 1776–1783 (2007)

14. Rutter, C.E., Dahlquist, L.M., Weiss, K.E.: Sustained efficacy of virtual reality distraction. J. Pain **10**(4), 391–397 (2009)

15. Loreto-Quijada, D., et al.: Differential effects of two virtual reality interventions: distraction versus pain control. Cyberpsychology Behav. Soc. Netw. **17**(6), 353–358 (2014)

16. Gordon, N.S., et al.: Interactive gaming reduces experimental pain with or without a head mounted display. Comput. Hum. Behav. **27**(6), 2123–2128 (2011)

17. Kipping, B., et al.: Virtual reality for acute pain reduction in adolescents undergoing burn wound care: a prospective randomized controlled trial. Burns **38**(5), 650–657 (2012)

18. Nilsson, S., et al.: Active and passive distraction in children undergoing wound dressings. J. Pediatr. Nurs.-Nurs. Care Child. Families **28**(2), 158–166 (2013)

19. Hoffman, H.G., et al.: Virtual reality helmet display quality influences the magnitude of virtual reality analgesia. J. Pain **7**(11), 843–850 (2006)

20. Muhlberger, A., et al.: Pain modulation during drives through cold and hot virtual environments. Cyberpsychology Behav. **10**(4), 516–522 (2007)

21. Dahlquist, L.M., et al.: Virtual-reality distraction and cold-pressor pain tolerance: does avatar point of view matter? Cyberpsychology Behav. Soc. Netw. **13**(5), 587–591 (2010)

22. Czub, M., Piskorz, J.: How body movement influences virtual reality analgesia? In: 7th International Conference on Interactive Technologies and Games, iTAG 2014, 16-17 October 2014. Institute of Electrical and Electronics Engineers Inc., Nottingham, Nottinghamshire, United Kingdom (2014)

23. Magora, F., Leibovici, V., Cohen, S.: Virtual reality methodology for pruritus and pain. In: 2009 Virtual Rehabilitation International Conference, VR 2009, June 29 2009 – July 2 2009. IEEE Computer Society, Haifa, Israel (2009)

24. Dahlquist, L.M., et al.: Effects of videogame distraction and a virtual reality type head-mounted display helmet on cold pressor pain in young elementary school-aged children. J. Pediatr. Psychol. **35**(6), 617–625 (2010)

25. Schneider, S.M., Kisby, C.K., Flint, E.P.: Effect of virtual reality on time perception in patients receiving chemotherapy. Support. Care Cancer **19**(4), 555–564 (2011)

26. Georgoulis, S., et al.: Epione: an innovative pain management system using facial expression analysis, biofeedback and augmented reality-based distraction. In: 2nd International Conference on Intelligent Networking and Collaborative Systems, INCOS 2010, 24-26 November 2010. IEEE Computer Society, Thessaloniki, Greece (2010)

27. Konstantatos, A.H., et al.: Predicting the effectiveness of virtual reality relaxation on pain and anxiety when added to PCA morphine in patients having burns dressings changes. Burns **35**(4), 491–499 (2009)

Hand Tracking and Haptic-Based Jugular Neonate Central Venous Access Procedure

Tatiana Ortegon-Sarmiento, Alvaro Uribe-Quevedo, Byron Perez-Gutierrez$^{(\boxtimes)}$, Lizeth Vega-Medina, and Gerardo Tibamoso

VR Center, Nueva Granada Military University, Bogota, D.C., Colombia
taxipiorsa@hotmail.com, {alvaro.j.uribe,byron.perez,lizvega}@ieee.org,
gtibap@gmail.com

Abstract. Medical simulators are important because they provide means to teach, learn, train, practice and develop skills necessary during medical practice. Simulation also allows exposing trainees to scenarios not possible during training, thus covering a wide range of life-like situations. Although widely used, simulation still faces challenges due to the high costs associated with the simulation equipment. Current advances in computer graphics and user interfaces provide affordable tools that allow exploring solutions in different medical fields. In this paper, we focus on the jugular central venous access performed on neonates, a procedure commonly practice to save lives through drug, nutrients and other medication administration. Simulation to practice this procedure is scarce and focused on adult simulation, yielding to transfer of knowledge to treat a neonate. Our approach focuses on developing a simulation prototype covering the preparation steps and execution of the procedure. To provide natural interactions, we integrated hand motion capture with haptics within a virtual environment representing the operation room. To study the prototype's user experience we asked 12 participants from last year of medical school to use the prototype.

Keywords: Simulator · Central venous access · Haptics · Neonate · Tracking · Virtual reality

1 Introduction

The central venous access (CVA) is an invasive medical procedure that demands great knowledge and skill during its execution. The skills are developed through training and refined during medical practice. The CVA is relevant for administering medication and nutrients directly into the circulatory system, in the case of neonatal patients; transfer of knowledge takes place as the training is performed on adult simulators or patients [27]. CVA is a feature available on some adult and pediatrics manikins, where trainees are able to measure vital signs, perform needle insertion and administration of medications, while the instructor controls and monitors the patient behavior to guarantee that the procedure is performed with proficiency [22]. Provided the scarce solution on neonatal CVA,

© Springer International Publishing Switzerland 2016
S. Lackey and R. Shumaker (Eds.): VAMR 2016, LNCS 9740, pp. 521–531, 2016.
DOI: 10.1007/978-3-319-39907-2_50

we focus our work on the jugular access because it allows better medication administration [4]. Transfer of knowledge presents challenges on its own as the anatomy of the neonate differs from the adult (e.g., skin is thinner and organs are closer) [28].

VR medical training research and development has resulted in solutions such as, surgeon virtual training systems [14, 34], navigation and 3D visualization of anatomic models [11], tools for image manipulation by hands tracking [29, 31], surgeries immersion systems [10, 20]. All of these provide alternative and complementary training tools that allow minimizing the probability of bad praxis or iatrogenesis. All these systems simulate the anatomic and physiologic characteristics of a patient with various levels of fidelity, determined by the quality, precision and realism.

Specifically, CVA adult simulation includes features that provide visual, physical and mechanical biological-like tissues. Many of surgical simulators [13, 25, 39], use different models including non linear elasticity, fluid simulation and finite elements analysis, allowing them to represent tissue displacements and deformations, making them more similar to real procedures. To provide interactions with touch feedback, some simulators include haptics devices to improve the user experience with the human anatomy [23, 24, 38]. Often, as an affordable approach, multimedia tools can be found focusing on learning the procedure in newborns [8], applications for the needle insertion in the virtual newborn jugular practice [37], systems that integrate physical models with virtual environments [17, 18], and ultrasound simulation [1].

Currently, virtual reality in medical simulation is still a demanding field due to its impacts in health professions education [3]. From the literature review, neonatal simulation is still on its infancy, providing grounds to research, and explore solutions to provide complementary training tools to address specific skills not relying on transfer of knowledge from current adult systems to the newborn. The goal of this work is develop a virtual simulator prototype to practice the jugular CVA using virtual reality as a mean to deliver an engaging realistic experience to the user. The paper is organized as follows, Sect. 1 describes previous and related Works, Sect. 2 presents proposed methodology and developed prototype, Sect. 3 described the user experience, the results are described in the Sect. 4, and Sect. 5 concludes the paper outlining future work.

2   CVA Simulator Development

From the characterization of real CVA procedure [15], three key elements were established to develop the simulator: interaction with a neonate patient including realism and suitable natural interactions using sight and touch senses, prior practicing with surgical tools and procedure steps.

In order to achieve these elements, we integrated virtual reality hardware (e.g., a Head Mounted Display, hand tracking, and a haptic device), to engage the user. In the application, we recreated an operation room using the Unity 3D 5.1.3

game engine [36] using 3D models for representing the required surgical tools [5,7,32,35] allowing the interaction between user with the patient and instruments. The virtual system is comprised of three modules including, a practice module, an evaluation module and an information module, as presented in Fig. 1. Our approach consisted of characterizing the CVA procedure to identify the systems input and outputs along with the required subsystems.

In the practice module, the user can manipulate all the tools with his/her own hands using a hand tracking system, increasing the dexterity and enhancing skills in instrument handling. In the evaluation module, the user performs the procedure as follows: (i) cleanliness of the hands (I know there is a medical name for this); (ii) wear the gloves; (iii) patient asepsis; (iv) needle insertion; (v) placing of the transparent bandage; and finally, a radiography analysis to ensure that the catheter was placed appropriately.

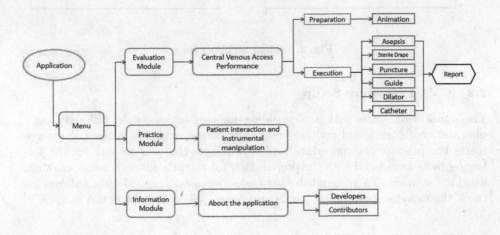

Fig. 1. System description

2.1 System Architecture

The system is composed by a haptic and visual system for a complete virtual reality experience. For the visual feedback, we decided to use a head mounted display to provide stereoscopic immersion. For this purpose we chose the Oculus Rift DK 2[21] that offers the user a wide vision field of 100 degrees diagonal FOV and 90 degrees horizontal FOV, characteristics sufficient for our scenario (neonates neck and surrounding regions). To provide natural user interactions, we decided to use the Leap Motion hand tracker [19], which allows the user to interact with the different objects of the scene, and also a Phantom Omni [12] haptic device that provides tactile feedback relevant to the CVA (Fig. 2).

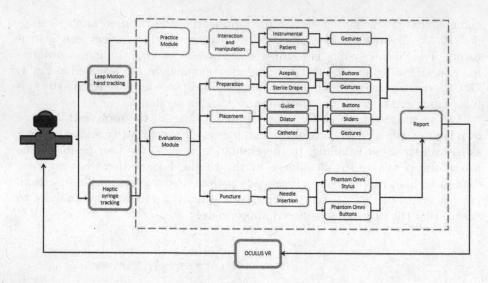

Fig. 2. System architecture

2.2   CVA Procedure Setup

The application starts with a menu allowing user to access the different modules and configure sound and language (english or spanish). When the trainee starts the practice the procedure begins requiring the user to perform the following tasks associated with the preparation for the procedure: i) hand washing; ii) glove wearing. To accomplish this tasks, we used Leap Motion features to track the movements of user's hands and wrists. Figure 3 depicts the tasks.

Fig. 3. Hand washing and gloves placement

The next step of the procedure is to prepare all equipment and instrumentation (shown in Fig. 8). To accomplish this task, our system uses hand tracking so the user can reach them in a natural manner (Fig. 4).

Then, the user performs the patient asepsis (Fig. 5a), for this task, we used the Leap Motion to take advantage of hand tracking to make interactions life-like.

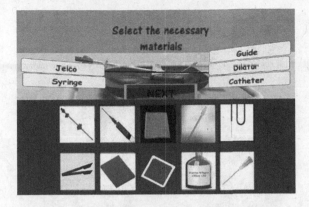

Fig. 4. Instrument selection [6,9,26,33]

When the user pinches the index and thumb, a gauze immediately appears so it can clean the patients areas of interest. As the user performs this action, a progress bar provides visual feedback on the task completion. Once finished, the user is required to place the sterile drapes as depicted on Fig. 5b.

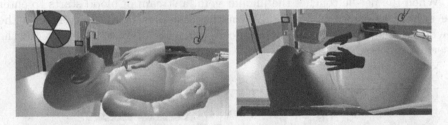

Fig. 5. (a) Patient asepsis and (b) sterile drapes placement

The next step is the catheter placement. This part is divided into four subsystems consisting on: (i) the needle insertion; (ii) the guide insertion; (iii) the use of the dilator; and finally, (iv) the catheter insertion. The needle insertion subsystem receives information from the Phantom Omni haptic device tracking yaw, pitch and roll and provides force feedback when the needle is inserted. Haptics interactions were implemented in Unity using Kirurobos C# wrapper for Phantom Omni [16]. To guarantee proper jugular vein puncture, the anatomical structures involved in the procedure were considered and so the organs, tissue and bone provide collision feedback. Even though the Digimation 3D models used (rib cage, heart, lungs, clavicle and blood vessels) [7] aren't anatomically correct, they provided all the information of its location and size. The perception of its physical properties are modeled by linear elasticity [38] (Fig. 6).

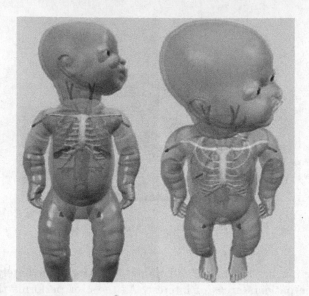

Fig. 6. 3D Models of the anatomical structures involved in the CVA procedure

When the needle touches the jugular vein, a stream of blood starts to enter the syringe as shown in Fig. 7a. When the user presses the button with the newborns image, the internal anatomical structures become visible to aid the insertion process.

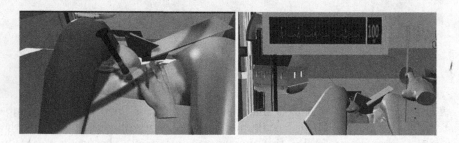

Fig. 7. (a) Needle insertion subsystem and (b) guide insertion subsystem

The guide insertion subsystem receives information from the Leap Motion device, the user must manipulate a slider to introduce the guide inside the jelco, as it is presented in Fig. 7b. The subsystem has an ECG, developed by Mike Austin, to control the patient cardiac frequency [2]. When the guide reaches the heart, an arrhythmia occurs, in this moment the user must back the guide until it stops. As soon as the guide is inserted, it is necessary to withdraw the jelco, for which, the user must to perform the swipe gesture with either hand.

Another subsystem that receives information from the Leap Motion, is the dilator (shown in Fig. 8a). The user manipulates the instrument through a circle gesture with the right hand, and with the left hand, by a swipe gesture, she or he removes the dilator.

To place the catheter, the user uses the same dynamics as with the guide, as it appears in Fig. 8b. Once properly positioned catheter, the guide is removed with the swipe gesture.

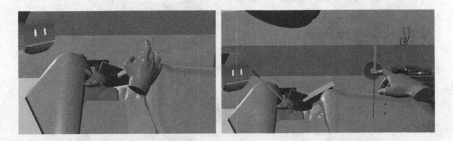

Fig. 8. (a) Dilator manipulation and (b) catheter insertion subsystem

Once completed the catheter placement, we proceed to place the transparent bandage to secure the catheter, as presented in Fig. 9a. Finally, the user takes a radiography to verify that the catheter placement as shown in Fig. 9b.

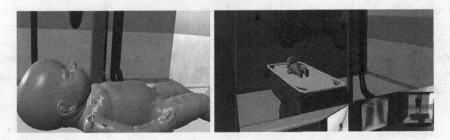

Fig. 9. (a) Final position of the catheter and fixation with transparent bandage and (b) radiography room (X-ray image [30])

3   User Experience

In order to analyze user perception with the developed tool, we carried out a series of test, which allowed us to verify if it contributes or not to learning the CVA procedure.

For the user experience evaluation, we use two computers with Windows 7 Enterprise 64-bit operating system, Intel Xeon processor, 8GB of RAM, NVidia

Quadro 4000 graphics card, IEEE-1394 and FireWire PCI Card. Also, we use two Oculus Rift, two Leap Motion, two Phantom Omni devices, and a pair of earphones, Fig. 10 shows one of the participants testing the system.

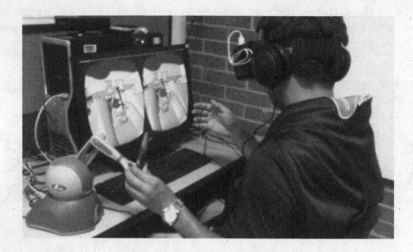

Fig. 10. User experience evaluation

At the time of evaluation, the first thing we did was to inform participants about the test, giving them a brief introduction to the game. Then, the experimenter indicated them to sit down, and put on the Oculus Rift and the headphones. At the puncture time, the experimenter gave participants the Phantom Omni stylus. Throughout the test, the application indicates the user the necessary instructions that this one has to perform. At the end of the test, we thanked the users for their participation, and asked them to answer an online survey in order to know their opinion about the application and their satisfaction.

4   Results

To analyze user experience using our solution, we gathered 12 participants from last year of medicine undergraduate program who did not have prior knowledge of the procedure. Once gathered the simulator was explained and participants were asked to used it navigating and exploring all features. The activity lasted 15 min per user and from the questionnaire and observation we highlight the following considerations:

– **Usability.** In this regard, we evaluated how easily turned out to be to the user to interact with the virtual patient (Fig. 11a). Most of the evaluated population agreed that it is normal, another part said that it was easy or that they needed practice, and a small minority answered that it was difficult.

- **User Experience.** In this part, we evaluate the degree of user satisfaction when our system was used, 100 % of the evaluated population enjoyed the application.
- **Immersion.** Regarding the immersion, most of the evaluated population experienced a presence sense in the implemented operations room, ensuring that the use of virtual reality devices contributed to this satisfactorily (Fig. 11b). Most of respondents rated as good the feedback force, and the other part rated this as regular.
- **Environment.** We ask the users to rate the implemented environment (Fig. 11c), most of them assigned a score of five (excellent), and the other part of them qualified it with four or three, none rated it with zero (deficient). Regarding the realism, many people considered it good.

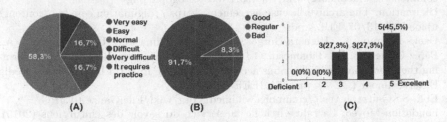

Fig. 11. Evaluation results: (a) Usability, (b) Immersion, (c) Environment

As to whether the application was useful in terms of learning, practice, and training in this area, big part of the study population (91.7 %) answered affirmatively. This is evident in that many of the users understood better the CVA procedure on having used our tool.

5 Conclusions and Future Work

According to user experience evaluation and analysis of results, we realized that the developed tool is helpful in the education and training of CVA, further by including various virtual reality devices, the user feels more immersed in the experience, which makes our application more appealing and entertaining, As future work, we will improve the force feedback including the modeling of vein rupture event, and we will implement a scoring system that will give to the user a qualification based on his/her performance.

Acknowledgments. This project was supported by the Research Division of Nueva Granada Mil. University through grant IMP ING 1776.

References

1. Amesur, N.B., Wang, D.C., Chang, W., Weiser, D., Klatzky, R., Shukla, G., Stetten, G.D.: Peripherally inserted central catheter placement using the sonic flashlight. J. Vasc. Interv. Radiol. **20**(10), 1380–1383 (2009)
2. Austin, M.: Ecg/ekg trace representation by creating a mesh (2014). http://ndunity3d.blogspot.com.co/2014/03/ecgekg-trace-representation-by-creating.html
3. Brydges, R., Hatala, R., Zendejas, B., Erwin, P.J., Cook, D.A.: Linking simulation-based educational assessments and patient-related outcomes: a systematic review and meta-analysis. Acad. Med. **90**(2), 246–256 (2015)
4. Cartwright, D.: Central venous lines in neonates: a study of 2186 catheters. Arch. Dis. Child. Fetal Neonatal Ed. **89**(6), F504–F508 (2004)
5. CGtrader: Free 3d models. https://www.cgtrader.com/free-3d-models
6. Wikimedia Commons: Database center for life science (dbcls) - needle. https://commons.wikimedia.org/wiki/File%3ANeedle_togopic.png
7. Digimation: The archive. license agreement. https://digimation.com/wp-content/uploads/2013/07/EULA.pdf
8. Dzeka-Lozano, N., Higuera-Burgos, N., Vega-Medina, L., Uribe-Quevedo, A., Perez-Gutierrez, B., Tibamoso, G.: Development of an application for performing the subclavian central venous access on neonates. In: 2014 IEEE Games Media Entertainment (GEM), pp. 1–4. IEEE (2014)
9. Ebli, S.: Gauze. https://commons.wikimedia.org/wiki/File:Gauze_01.JPG
10. Fondation-Moveo: La ralit virtuelle au service du savoir des chirurgiens (2015). http://www.fondation-moveo.fr/projets/realite-virtuelle/
11. Freire, F., Ramirez, W., Vallejo, H.: Sistema de entrenamiento virtual para medicina, June 2012. http://repositorio.cedia.org.ec/handle/123456789/289
12. Geomagic: Phantom   omni.   http://www.geomagic.com/en/products/phantom-omni/overview
13. Harders, M., Bachofen, D., Grassi, M., Bajka, M., Spaelter, U., Teschner, M., Heidelberger, B., Sierra, R., Steinemann, D., Tuchschmid, S., et al.: Virtual reality based simulation of hysteroscopic interventions. Presence Teleoperators Virtual Environ. **17**(5), 441–462 (2008)
14. Investigación: y desarrollo: Diseñan sistema de entrenamiento virtual para cirujanos, April 2015. http://www.invdes.com.mx/tecnologia-mobil/7111-disenan-sistema-de-entrenamiento-virtual-para-cirujanos
15. Jain, P., Pant, D., Sood, J.: Atlas of Practical Neonatal and Pediatric Procedures. JP Medical Ltd, London (2012)
16. Kirurobo: A c# (.net) wrapper for sensable phantom device. https://github.com/kirurobo/ManagedPhantom
17. Laerdal: Virtual   i.v.   simulator.   http://www.laerdal.com/us/doc/245/Virtual-I-V--Simulator
18. Larnpotang, S., Lizdas, D., Rajon, D., Luria, I., Gravenstein, N., Bisht, Y., Schwab, W., Friedman, W., Bova, F., Robinson, A.: Mixed simulators: augmented physical simulators with virtual underlays. In: 2013 IEEE Virtual Reality (VR), pp. 7–10. IEEE (2013)
19. Motion, L.: Motion controller for games, design, virtual reality and more. https://www.leapmotion.com/
20. Bizzotto, M.N., Costanzo, M.A., Bizzotto, M.L.: Leap motion gesture control with osirix in the operating room to control imaging: first experiences during live surgery. Surg. Innov. **21**(6), 655–656 (2014)

21. OculusRift: Developer center. https://developer.oculus.com/
22. Okuda, Y., Bryson, E.O., DeMaria, S., Jacobson, L., Quinones, J., Shen, B., Levine, A.I.: The utility of simulation in medical education: what is the evidence? Mt Sinai J. Med. J. Transl. Personalized Med. **76**(4), 330–343 (2009)
23. Pérez-Gutiérrez, B., Ariza-Zambrano, C., Hernández, J.C.: Mechatronic prototype for rigid endoscopy simulation. In: Shumaker, R. (ed.) Virtual and Mixed Reality, Part II, HCII 2011. LNCS, vol. 6774, pp. 30–36. Springer, Heidelberg (2011)
24. Perez-Gutierrez, B., Martinez, D.M., Rojas, O.E.: Endoscopic endonasal haptic surgery simulator prototype: a rigid endoscope model. In: 2010 IEEE Virtual Reality Conference (VR), pp. 297–298. IEEE (2010)
25. Picinbono, G., Delingette, H., Ayache, N.: Non-linear anisotropic elasticity for real-time surgery simulation. Graph. Models **65**(5), 305–321 (2003)
26. Pixabay: Antiseptic bottle. https://pixabay.com/es/botella-aceite-aceite-de-oliva-159249/
27. Rey, C., Álvarez, F., De La Rua, V., Medina, A., Concha, A., Díaz, J.J., Menéndez, S., Los Arcos, M., Mayordomo-Colunga, J.: Mechanical complications during central venous cannulations in pediatric patients. Intensive Care Med. **35**(8), 1438–1443 (2009)
28. Sanín, C.S., Sánchez, P., Darío, R., Rave, M.E.A., Varela, L.F.L.: Manejo y complicaciones de catéteres venosos centrales en niños: hospital universitario san vicente de paúl, medellín, colombia. Iatreia **21**, s8 (2008)
29. ScopisMedical: Touchless control of a surgical navigation system (2013). http://www.scopis.com/en/news/news/details/archive/2013/may/03/article/beruehrungslose-steuerung-eines-klinischen-navigationssystems/
30. Stillwaterising: Chest xray. https://commons.wikimedia.org/wiki/File%3AChest_Xray_PA_3-8-2010.png
31. TedCas: Natural user interfaces for healthcare, January 2016. http://www.tedcas.com/en/products
32. TF3DM: 3d models for free. http://tf3dm.com/
33. Torange.biz: Free phtobank - syringe. http://www.torange.us/Objects/medicine/syringe-19276.html
34. Tsagarakis, N.G., Caldwell, D.G.: A 5 dof haptic interface for pre-operative planning of surgical access in hip arthroplasty. In: Eurohaptics Conference, 2005 and Symposium on Haptic Interfaces for Virtual Environment and Teleoperator Systems, 2005, World Haptics 2005, First Joint, pp. 519–520. IEEE (2005)
35. Turbosquid: Royalty free license. all extended uses. https://support.turbosquid.com/entries/31030006-Royalty-Free-License
36. Unity: Game engine. http://unity3d.com/
37. Vega-Medina, L., Perez-Gutierrez, B., Tibamoso, G., Uribe-Quevedo, A., Jaimes, N.: Vr central venous access simulation system for newborns. In: 2014 IEEE Virtual Reality (VR), pp. 121–122. IEEE (2014)
38. Vega-Medina, L., Tibamoso, G., Perez-Gutierrez, B.: VR tool for interaction with the abdomen anatomy. In: Stephanidis, C. (ed.) HCI International 2013-Posters' Extended Abstracts. CCIS, vol. 374, pp. 235–239. Springer, Heidelberg (2013)
39. Wu, X., Downes, M.S., Goktekin, T., Tendick, F.: Adaptive nonlinear finite elements for deformable body simulation using dynamic progressive meshes. In: Computer Graphics Forum, vol. 20, pp. 349–358. Wiley Online Library (2001)

ANSIBLE: A Virtual World Ecosystem for Improving Psycho-Social Well-being

Tammy Ott[1], Peggy Wu[1(✉)], Jacki Morie[2], Peter Wall[1],
Jack Ladwig[1], Eric Chance[2], Kip Haynes[2], Bryan Bell[1],
Christopher Miller[1], and Kim Binsted[3]

[1] SIFT, LLC, Minneapolis, USA
{tott,pwu}@sift.net
[2] All These Worlds, LLC, Los Angeles, USA
jfmorie@gmail.com
[3] Univeristy of Hawaii, Honolulu, USA
binsted@hawaii.edu

Abstract. We describe preliminary results of ANSIBLE – A Network of Social Interactions for Bilateral Life Enhancement. ANSIBLE leverages virtual worlds to deliver evidence based wellness promoting strategies and virtual agents as tools to facilitate asynchronous human-human communication in order to counteract behavioral health challenges associated with prolonged isolation and deep space exploration. ANSIBLE was deployed in August 2015 in a 12 month study with six crew members in an isolation simulated Mars habitat facility. In this paper, we compare the data for the first five months of this mission to a previous control mission for which ANSIBLE was not used. We found initial support for ANSIBLE to increase perceptions of closeness and satisfaction with friend and family relationships (but not other crew members) during prolonged isolation as well as a trend in stress reduction and increased feelings of ANSIBLE usability over time.

Keywords: Virtual worlds · Virtual agents · Psychological support · Communications · Psychological health

1 Introduction

The social origin of humans is deeply integrated into our existence through millions of years of evolution, and is a major contributor to our survival as a species [1]. The unequivocal consequences of higher quality and quantity of social relationships on health outcomes have been demonstrated and widely accepted [2]. For future astronauts undertaking the envisioned 2.5 year Mars mission, sensory monotony and extreme work and living conditions serve as constant stressors to behavioral health. Astronauts will not only be physically separated from their social support for prolonged periods of time, but due to communication latencies, their timelines will also be detached. This will likely result in the magnification of the effects of social isolation seen with geographically distributed groups on earth, which permeate both the physiological and psychological systems [3]. In addition to the well-known effects on morbidity and

© Springer International Publishing Switzerland 2016
S. Lackey and R. Shumaker (Eds.): VAMR 2016, LNCS 9740, pp. 532–543, 2016.
DOI: 10.1007/978-3-319-39907-2_51

mortality [4], social isolation poses a significant threat to astronaut behavioral health and performance with research indicating loneliness is a risk factor for, and may contribute to, poorer overall cognitive performance, faster cognitive decline, poorer executive functioning, more negativity and depressive cognition, contagion that threatens social cohesion [5] and reduced physical activity [4].

Novel psychological support systems are crucial to help manage these stressors and help astronauts maintain their relationships with friends, family, and colleagues on Earth. Currently thousands of individuals all over the world are socializing, conducting commerce, collaborating, and essentially living their lives in a physically isolated environment, but are socially engaged through virtual environments. Digitally enabled connections are created independent of physical space and geography, forming genuine relationships at an unprecedented rate and scope. Research suggests that people derive the satisfaction they seek in the real world from their interactions in the virtual world [6]. Additionally, studies have shown that gameplay in virtual reality can influence prosocial behavior and traits [7] such as virtual "superpowers" leading to greater helping behavior in the real world, regardless of how participants used that power [8], as well as enhancing [9] and promoting empathy [10].

While the isolation experienced on a mission to Mars will likely surpass anything experienced on Earth, the positive effects of virtual environments for isolation on Earth provides hope that a similar approach will be effective to combat the expected negative effects of going to Mars. To meet this need we developed ANSIBLE - A Network of Social Interactions for Bilateral Life Enhancement. A virtual space where we are implementing evidence based strategies to promote social connectedness and psychological well-being while accommodating technical and environmental limitations of long duration space flight. Further details about ANSIBLE can be found in [11].

The purpose of the current paper is to determine ANSIBLE's effectiveness at maintaining the social connection between crew and family in an analog environment. To maximize the scientific value of the data collected during the long duration analog we have planned for various statistical comparisons between our experimental and control group, within our experimental group, and also with data collected from the crews friends and family. The current paper's focus is on comparisons between the first five months of our control group data and our experimental group data.

2 Materials and Methods

2.1 Participants

The current study is part of the overarching Hawaii Space Exploration Analog and Simulation (HI-SEAS, www.hi-seas.org), located on an isolated Mars-like site in the barren landscape of Mauna Loa, HI. Crews of six people (three female) live and work through long-duration exploration simulations with the aim of removing barriers to human exploration of Mars. Our research will span two missions. The first, HI-SEAS III, acted as our control group, was eight months long, and concluded on June 13, 2015. The second mission began on August 28, 2015 and will last 12 months. In addition to completing the same surveys as the control group, HI-SEAS IV will also utilize the

ANSIBLE virtual world ecosystem. In addition to our tasks, participants in both missions performed science research projects inside the habitat as well as Extra Vehicular Activities (EVAs) in the form of geological surveys or equipment maintenance tasks outdoors while donning prototype space suits.

2.2 Surveys

Social isolation refers to the lack of contact an individual has with others [12]. In the context of space flight, social isolation includes the lack of human contact outside the crew. Perceived social isolation (loneliness) is more closely related to the quality than quantity of social interactions [13, 14]. Therefore we measured perceived loneliness through a modified Circles of Closeness (COC) questionnaire. This is a four item questionnaire provided a pictorial measure of closeness and satisfaction, separately for mission control (MC) and friends and family (FF). Lower ratings indicated more closeness and satisfaction with the relationship. Previous implementations of COC found high alpha reliability, ranging from high .50 s to .92 depending on scale length [15].

In addition to a survey directly measuring perceived satisfaction/closeness with social support we included a survey on a consequence of lack of social support: stress [16]. For this we used the Perceived Stress Questionnaire (PSQ). This is a 30 item measure of subjectively experienced stress independent of a specific and objective occasion. It uses a 5 pt. Likert scale with higher scores indicating greater stress. The PSQ showed adequate reliability > 0.9 and was correlated with trait anxiety, Cohen's Perceived Stress Scale, depression, self-rated stress and stressful life events; with test-retest reliability varying by a factor of 1.9 over 6 months for past month ratings [17].

The ANSIBLE group completed additional surveys about their interactions with ANSIBLE. The first was the Short Feedback Questionnaire (SFQ) [18], a seven item measure of the sense of presence, perceived difficulty of the task and discomfort encountered during the experience. The first six questions are an abbreviated alternative to the Presence Questionnaire developed by Witmer and Singer [19]. This survey has been found to be suitable for various virtual environments and with different clinical populations [18] and has successfully tested other systems [20]. It uses a 5 pt. Likert scale with higher scores indicating higher levels of positive experience with the system. They also completed the System Usability Scale (SUS), a ten item measure providing a global view of subjective system usability [21]. It uses a 5 pt. Likert scale with higher scores indicating greater usability. Finally, we included seven 5 pt. Likert scale items tailored to specific ANSIBLE usability concerns: usefulness in social connection maintenance, well-being improvement, clearness of purpose, willingness to recommend to friend, working as wanted, wanting to use, and compatibility with schedule and workload.

2.3 Procedure

The subjects completed informed consent forms and explanations of the aims of our study prior to the commencement of the study. While in the Habitat all participants received self-paced training that described the procedures of completing the surveys. Those using ANSIBLE also received training on how to interact with the system.

The PI was available to answer questions or concerns of participants. Participants completed the COC at least once a week throughout the study, with the option to complete it up to three times a week. The PSQ was completed once a week during the duration of the study. Questionnaires were completed on the same schedule for both groups, with the exception that the ANSIBLE group completed the COC before and after ANSIBLE interactions, hence within this paper the after ANSIBLE COC measures were used for comparisons to the control group. Interactions within ANSIBLE lasted 20–30 min, where participants were given the ability to explore and interact as they pleased. For the control group we conducted an outgoing debrief after they exited the habitat, where we asked them about their experiences in the study as well as changes in social connections due to their participation. When the experimental group exits the habitat we will ask similar questions and additional questions about positive and negative experiences with the ANSIBLE system.

3   Results

Due to the nature of our data (multiple measurements per participant, missing data, and uneven spacing of repeated measurements; participants sometimes missed surveys or completed them off the given schedule), we used Mixed-Effect Model Repeated Measures (MMRM) to analyze results. In addition to overcoming the above limitations MMRM also allowed us to model time (i.e. each measurement occasion) as a Level 1 random effect and group (i.e. ANSIBLE or control) as a Level 2 fixed effect. We began with an initial unconditional model (i.e. no predictors) to determine if sufficient variability existed within our data set. We also modeled for random intercepts and slopes, with our repeated time measure using a first order autoregressive covariance structure, as well as including a squared time variable to determine if a quadratic relationship held more explanatory power for our data than a linear relationship. The assumptions of independent observations at the level above nesting, bivariate normality, and random residuals were checked and met. To control for initial differences in survey responses we used the difference between initial response and current response over time in our analyses, thus higher COC_{diff} scores indicate greater closeness and satisfaction and greater PSQ_{diff} scores indicate greater stress.

3.1   Circles of Closeness

COC Closeness. For the "how close do you feel to your family and friends" COC question, the unconditional repeated-measures model revealed significant variability in the COC_{diff} measure, suggesting it would be worthwhile to examine a conditional model to explain this variability. Time as a predictor of COC_{diff} approached significance, $F (1,126.72) = 3$, $p < .09$, with a slight increase over time ($\beta = .04$, $SE = .02$), the quadratic trend was n.s. There was significant with-in time variance (Var $= 9.9$, $SE = .38$, Wald $Z = 12.3$, $p < .001$), between subjects variance (Var $= .001$, $SE = .0004$, Wald $Z = 2.3$, $p < .05$) and covariance between different times once individual differences were accounted for, rho = .7, SE = .03, Wald Z = 26.8, p < .001, making the autoregressive structure appropriate for our data.

The model with group added as a predictor explained significantly more variance than the unconditional model, $-2LL\ \chi^2_{Change}(1) = 4.6$, p < .05. There was a significant effect of group, $F(1,109.7) = 5.5$, p < .05, with the ANSIBLE group reporting greater closeness to family and friends (M = 1.5) than Controls (M = −0.5). The linear [F (1,114) = 4.4, p < .05, β = .05, SE = .02] and quadratic [F(1,131.9) = 4.0, p < .05, β = −.0003, SE = .0001] trends both significantly describe the pattern of the data over time. There remains significant with-in time variance (Var = 9.4, SE = .78, Wald Z = 12.5, p < .001), between subjects variance (Var = .001, SE = .0006, Wald Z = 2.2, p < 05) and covariance between different times once individual differences were accounted for, rho = .7, SE = .03, Wald Z = 24.7, p < .001, see Fig. 1.

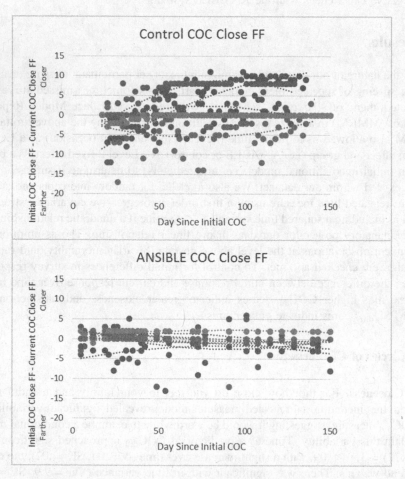

Fig. 1. Variability in "How close do you feel to your family and friends" COC question for each participant during the first five months within the HI-SEAS habitat. Top shows control data. Bottom shows ANSIBLE group data. Quadratic trend lines are shown (Color figure online).

For the "how close do you feel to other crew members" COC question, the unconditional repeated-measures model revealed significant variability in the COC_{diff} measure, suggesting it would be worthwhile to examine a conditional model to explain this variability. Time as a predictor of COC_{diff} was n.s., but the quadratic trend was significant, $F(1,104.6) = 6.2$, $p < .05$, $\beta = -.0002$, SE = .00008. There was significant with-in time variance (Var = 4.6, SE = .34, Wald Z = 12.2, $p < .001$), between subjects variance (Var = 5.16, SE = 1.8, Wald Z = 2.9, $p < .01$) and covariance between different times once individual differences were accounted for, rho = .59, SE = .05, Wald Z = 13.2, $p < .001$ making the autoregressive structure appropriate for our data. Adding group as a predictor did not explain significantly more variance than the unconditional model, $-2LL$ $\chi^2_{Change}(1) = .012$, $p > .05$, see Fig. 2.

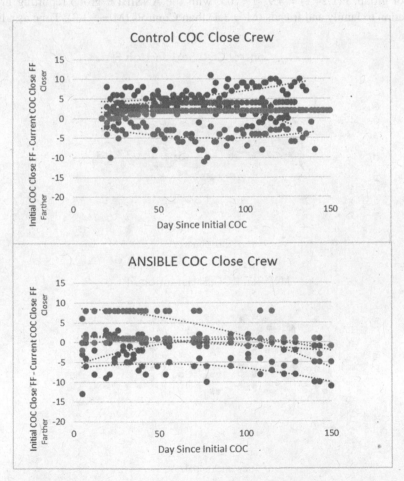

Fig. 2. Variability in "How close do you feel to fellow crew" COC question for each participant during the first five months within the HI-SEAS habitat. Top shows control data. Bottom shows ANSIBLE group data. Quadratic trend lines are shown (Color figure online).

COC Satisfaction. For the "how satisfied do you feel with your family and friends" COC question, the unconditional repeated-measures model revealed significant variability in the COC$_{diff}$ measure, suggesting it would be worthwhile to examine a conditional model to explain this variability. Time as a linear and quadratic trend were n.s. There was significant with-in time variance (Var = 4.8, SE = .43, Wald Z = 11.2, p < .001), between subjects variance (Var = 12.8, SE = 4.1, Wald Z = 3.2, p < .001) and covariance between different times once individual differences were accounted for, rho = .66, SE = .04, Wald Z = 16.5, p < .001 making the autoregressive structure appropriate for our data.

The model with group added as a predictor explained significantly more variance than the unconditional model, −2LL χ2Change(1) = 4.5, p < .05. There was a significant effect of group, F(1,24.1) = 4.9, p < .05, with the ANSIBLE group reporting greater satisfaction to family and friends (M = 3.1) than Controls (M = −1.3). Time as a linear

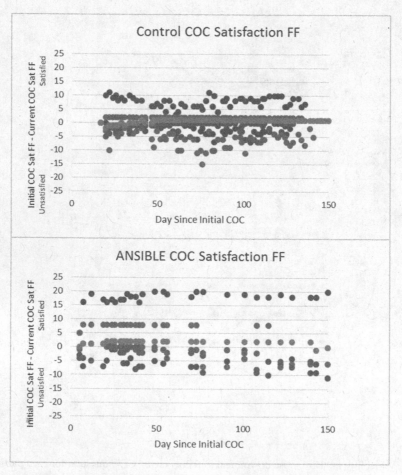

Fig. 3. Variability in "How satisfied do you feel with your family and friends" COC question for each participant during the first five months within the HI-SEAS habitat. Top shows control data. Bottom shows ANSIBLE group data (Color figure online).

and quadratic trend were n.s. There remains significant with-in time variance (Var = 4.8, SE = .43, Wald Z = 11.1, p < .001), between subjects variance (Var = 10.46, SE = 3.4, Wald Z = 3.1, p < 01) and covariance between different times once individual differences were accounted for, rho = .66, SE = .04, Wald Z = 16.5, p < .001, see Fig. 3.

For the "how satisfied do you feel with other crew members" COC question, the unconditional repeated-measures model did not reveal significant variability in the COC_{diff} measure, suggesting it is not worthwhile to examine a conditional model. Time as a linear and quadratic trend were n.s. There was significant with-in time variance (Var = 6.9, SE = .78, Wald Z = 8.8, p < .001) and covariance between different times once individual differences were accounted for, rho = .66, SE = .05, Wald Z = 13.4, p < .001 making the autoregressive structure appropriate for our data, but the between subjects variance was not significant (Var = 2.8, SE = 2.0, Wald Z = 1.4, p < .05). As

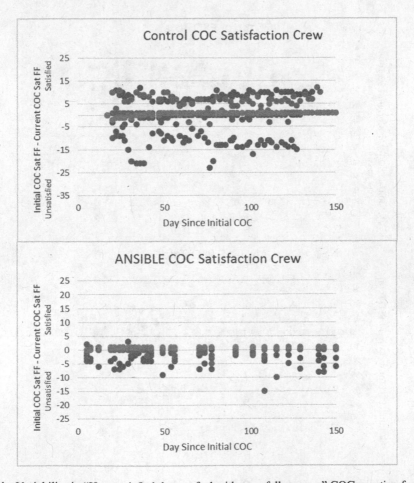

Fig. 4. Variability in "How satisfied do you feel with your fellow crew" COC question for each participant during the first five months within the HI-SEAS habitat. Top shows control data. Bottom shows ANSIBLE group data (Color figure online).

expected, adding group as a predictor did not explain significantly more variance than the unconditional model, $-2LL\ \chi^2_{Change}(1) = .043$, p > .05. See Fig. 4.

PSQ. The unconditional repeated-measures model revealed significant variability in the total PSQdiff measure, suggesting it would be worthwhile to examine a conditional model to explain this variability. Time as a linear and quadratic trend were n.s. There was significant with-in time variance (Var = 22.5, SE = 2.3, Wald Z = 9.8, p < .001), between subjects variance (Var = 39.6, SE = 12.7, Wald Z = 3.1, p < .01), but covariance between different times once individual differences were accounted for, rho = −.24, SE = .22, Wald Z = −1.1, p > .05 was not significant making the autoregressive structure unneeded for our data. However removing it did not significantly change model fit, $-2LL\ \chi^2 Change(1) = 0.57$, p > .05.

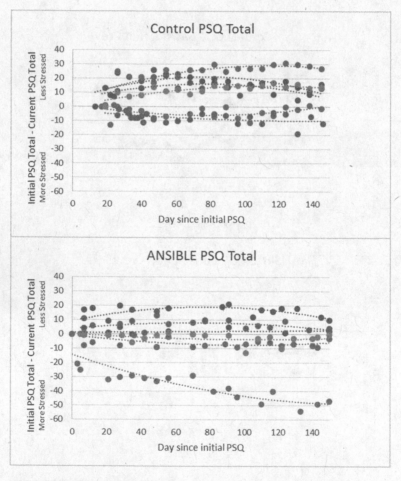

Fig. 5. Variability in Perceived Stress Questionnaire for each participant during the first five months within the HI-SEAS habitat. Top graph shows control data. Bottom graph shows ANSIBLE data. Quadratic trend lines are shown (Color figure online).

The model with group added as a predictor explained significantly more variance than the unconditional model, $-2LL$ $\chi^2_{Change}(1) = 3.85$, p < .05. The effect of group was marginally significant, $F(1, 24.9) = 3.16$, p < .09, with the ANSIBLE group reporting less stress (M = .1) than Controls (M = 6.7). Time as a linear trend was n.s and the quadratic trend approach significance, $F(1, 200) = 2.84$, p < .09, $\beta = -.0003$, SE = .0002. There remains significant with-in time variance (Var = 22.3, SE = 2.2, Wald Z = 10, p < .001) and between subjects variance (Var = 35.9, SE = 11.6, Wald Z = 3.1, p < 01), see Fig. 5.

ANSIBLE Usability. The ANSIBLE system is undergoing constant development and improvements as content is added. To determine the success of these improvements under continued system use we performed Pearson's Correlation analyses between questionnaires related to ANSIBLE use and time in the HI-SEAS habitat. We found a significant positive correlation between time and SUS total, r = .38, p < .01, and a sum of our ANSIBLE specific usability questions, r = .37, p < .01. We also found a negative correlation between SFQ total and time, r = −.42, p < .01, see Fig. 6.

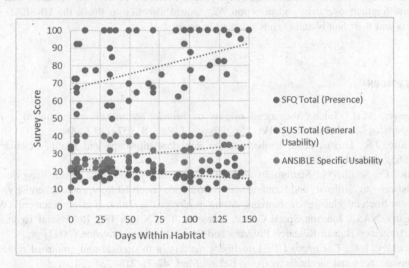

Fig. 6. Correlation between time in the HI-SEAS habitat and questionnaires related to ANSIBLE use. Linear trend lines are shown (Color figure online).

4   Summary and Conclusions

A main focus of the ANSIBLE ecosystem is to maintain the social connection between crew and family while crew members are participating in an isolated, long duration environments. Given this we expected ANSIBLE to impact the perception of friend and family relationships and not crew relationships. Accordingly we found ANSIBLE increased feelings of closeness and satisfaction with friends and family but not crew members, according to responses on the Circles of Closeness Questionnaire. Additionally we found ANSIBLE marginally decreased feelings of stress, a known consequence of social isolation. Given the significant trends of increased usability as ANSIBLE is used and improved upon, we expect the benefits of ANSIBLE to continue to grow.

This study is a first step in quantifying the considerable potential of communications through virtual environments in aiding isolated populations, particularly over prolonged durations such as future space exploration missions. However, the results are preliminary and data collection is ongoing. Future analyses will further examine the effects of ANSIBLE use on social connections compared to controls as well as deeper investigations into the within ANSIBLE group effects and ramifications of ANSIBLE use on friends and family. Further, additional analyses will examine the impact of the system to aid other expected consequences of the sensory monotony and extreme work and living conditions anticipated during long duration space missions are also planned, such as interventions to combat sensory and social monotony, social behavior modification, and social anxiety countermeasures.

Acknowledgments. The above work was sponsored by NASA's Human Research Program under contract #NNX14CJ06C. We would like to thank NASA personnel Lauren Leventon, Laura Bollweg, Jason Schneiderman, Diana Arias, Brandon Vessey, Al Holland, and Ron Moomaw for their oversight and direction. We would also like to thank the HI-SEAS crew members and their family and friends for their support.

References

1. Brewer, M.B.: Taking the social origins of human nature seriously: toward a more imperialist social psychology. Pers. Soc. Psychol. Rev. **8**, 107–113 (2004)
2. House, J.S., Landis, K.R., Umberson, D.: Social relationships and health. Science **241** (4865), 540–545 (2004)
3. Otto, C.: South Pole Station: an analogue for human performance during long-duration missions to isolated and confined environments: neurobiology, neurochemistry, and neurostructural changes in humans during prolonged isolation and confinement (White Paper). NASA Johnson Space Center, Houston, TX: NASA JSC Behavioral Health and Performance Human Research Program and Space Medicine Division (2007)
4. Hawkley, L.C., Cacioppo, J.T.: Loneliness matters: a theoretical and empirical review of consequences and mechanisms. Ann. Behav. Med. **40**(2), 218–227 (2010)
5. Cacioppo, J.T., Hawkley, L.C.: Perceived social isolation and cognition. Trends Cogn. Sci. **13**(10), 447–454 (2009)
6. Castronova, E., Wagner, G.G.: Virtual life satisfaction. Int. Rev. Soc. Sci. **64**(3), 313–328 (2011)
7. Gentile, D.A., Anderson, C.A., Yukawa, S., Ihori, N., Saleem, M., et al.: The effects of prosocial video games on prosocial behaviors: international evidence from correlational, longitudinal, and experimental studies. Pers. Soc. Psychol. Bull. **35**, 752–763 (2009)
8. Rosenberg, R., Baughman, S., Bailenson, J.N.: Virtual superheroes: using superpowers in virtual reality to encourage prosocial behavior. PLoS ONE **8**(1), e55003 (2013)
9. Greitemeyer, T., Osswald, S., Brauer, M.: Playing prosocial video games increases empathy and decreases schadenfreude. Emotion **10**, 796–802 (2010)

10. Gillath, O., McCall, C.A., Shaver, P., Blascovich, J.: Reactions to a needy virtual person: using an immersive virtual environment to measure prosocial tendencies. Media Psychol. **11**, 259–282 (2008)
11. Wu, P., Morie, J.F., Chance, E., Haynes, K., Hamell, J., Wall, P., Ladwig, J., Ott, T.: Maintaining psycho-social health on the way to mars and back. In: Virtual Reality International Conference (VRIC), 8–10 April, Laval, France (2015)
12. Cacioppo, J.T., Patrick, W.: Loneliness: Human Nature and the Need for Social Connection. WW Norton & Company, New York (2008)
13. Hawkley, L.C., Hughes, M.E., Waite, L.J., Masi, C.M., Thisted, R.A., Cacioppo, J.T.: From social structural factors to perceptions of relationship quality and loneliness: the Chicago health, aging, and social relations study. J. Gerontol. B Psychol. Sci. Soc. Sci. **63**(6), S375–S384 (2008)
14. Palinkas, L.A., Johnson, J.C., Boster, J.S.: Social support and depressed mood in isolated and confined environments. Acta Astronaut. **54**(9), 639–647 (2004)
15. Uleman, J.S., Rhee, E., Bardoliwalla, N., Semin, G., Toyama, M.: The relational self: closeness to ingroups depends on who they are, culture, and the type of closeness. Asian J. Soc. Psychol. **3**(1), 1–17 (2000)
16. Bachman, K.R.O.B., Otto, C., Leveton, L.: Countermeasures to Mitigate the Negative Impact of Sensory Deprivation and Social Isolation in Long-Duration Space Flight. NASA/TM-2012-217365 (2012)
17. Levenstein, S., Prantera, C., Varvo, V., Scribano, M.L., Berto, E., Luzi, C., Andreoli, A.: Development of the Perceived Stress Questionnaire: a new tool for psychosomatic research. J. Psychosom. Res. **37**(1), 19–32 (1993)
18. Kizony, R., Katz, N., Rand, D., Weiss, P.L.T.: Short Feedback Questionnaire (SFQ) to enhance client-centered participation in virtual environments. Cyberpsychology Behav. **9**(6), 687–688 (2006)
19. Witmer, B.G., Singer, M.J.: Measuring presence in virtual environments: a presence questionnaire. Presence Teleoperators Virtual Environ. **7**(3), 225–240 (1998)
20. Kizony, R., Raz, L., Katz, N., Weingarden, H., Weiss, P.L.T.: Video-capture virtual reality system for patients with paraplegic spinal cord injury. J. Rehabil. Res. Dev. **42**(5), 595–608 (2005)
21. Brooke, J.: SUS-a quick and dirty usability scale. Usability Eval. Ind. **189**(194), 4–7 (1996)

Immersive Gatekeeper Training System for Suicide Prevention in HMD Based Virtual Environments

Sinwoo Park and Changhoon Park[✉]

Department of Game Engineering, Hoseo University,
165 Sechul-ri, Baebang-myun, Asan, Chungnam 336-795, Korea
glsseact@imrlab.hoseo.edu, chpark@hoseo.edu

Abstract. This paper proposes an interactive role-playing simulation for gatekeeper training system designed for students. For the purpose of suicide prevention, this system provides an interactive and engaging virtual worlds using HMD (Head Mounted Display). To enhance the learning experience, immersive simulated conversation and realistic emotional communication are provided. In the immersive virtual environment, students can learn the common signs of psychological distress and how to refer troubled students to the counseling center. After completing the training, students will be better equipped to identify and correct common misconceptions about counseling.

Keywords: Suicide prevention · Gatekeeper · Immersive training system · Virtual reality · Head mounted display

1 Introduction

South Korea has the highest suicide rate among the OECD (Organization for Economic Cooperation and Development). An average of 29.1 people per 100,000 in Korea took their own lives in 2012, far surpassing the OECD average of 12, according to the OECD Health Data 2015. Hungary followed with 19.4 and Japan came next with 18.7 [1]. Furthermore, Suicide was also the No. 1 cause of death among teens and young people in Korea in 2011, with the suicide rate rising over the past decade, according to a report by Statistics Korea. The suicide rate per 100,000 for those aged 9–24 stood at 9.4, up from 5.3 in 2001. Between 2000 and 2010, the rate for youngsters aged 10 to 24 in OECD countries fell to 7.7 per 100,000 from 6.5, while that for South Koreans in the same age range soared 47 percent to 9.4 from 6.4, taking the fifth spot among the 34 member nations [2].

According to the result of sixth Korea Youth Risk Behavior Web-based Survey, 19.1 % of the total participants (72,623 of total adolescents aged 13 ~ 18years old) had experienced suicidal ideation and 4.9 % actually attempted suicide [1]. The suicide attempts in adolescence, in particular, have been suggested to be important indicators of suicide in adulthood. Therefore, the timely strategies of suicide prevention for adolescents is important to reduce the risk of suicide effectively.

© Springer International Publishing Switzerland 2016
S. Lackey and R. Shumaker (Eds.): VAMR 2016, LNCS 9740, pp. 544–551, 2016.
DOI: 10.1007/978-3-319-39907-2_52

There are several reasons that may lead to high youth suicide rate in Korea. First, adolescence itself can be a very turmoil period which causes the highest suicide attempt, compared to other developmental stages [3]. Second, lack of social service programs may lead to high suicide among adolescents. Korea Youth Counseling & Welfare Institute reported when Korean youth wanted to talk to someone about suicide, about 59 % of youth indicated that they could not find anyone to talk to. Third, it is well reported that adolescents have tendencies to confide in friends rather than helping professionals [4]. Therefore, approaching them with a traditional counseling method can be less effective (Fig. 1).

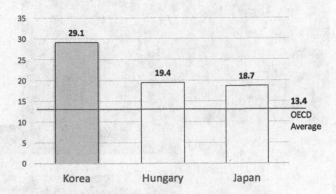

Fig. 1. Suicide rate in OECD

2 Related Works

2.1 Smart, Positive, Active, Realistic, X-Factor Thoughts (SPARX)

SPARX was developed by a team of University of Auckland adolescent depression specialists. And the software was designed by Auckland-based Media Interactive. This is a fantasy role-playing game designed to teach young people suffering from depression ways they can manage and overcome their condition. In the game, the player is the hero entrusted with the task of defeating the darkness and gloom that has engulfed the world. Players could learn ways of dealing with real-world problems by engaging with characters in the game. There is an in-game virtual guide who talks to the player and explains how they can apply the lessons learned in the game to real-life situations [7] (Fig. 2).

2.2 Beyond the Front (BTF)

Beyond the Front was developed by Lnincoln University and WILL Interactive. The BTF is a combination of interactive movie and computer game that will serve as a role-playing exercise for Army soldier. The game stars a fictional soldier, Specialist Kyle Norton who is suddenly experiencing a number of personal problems. During the video, questions appear on the screen at key moments, asking the player to decide whether to get help. Depending on the choices, Norton will feel better or sink deeper into suicidal thoughts. The goal is to immerse the viewer into Norton's life in a way that makes preventive lessons stick [5] (Fig. 3).

Fig. 2. Screenshots from SPARX

3   Immersive Gatekeeper Training System

In this paper, we proposed an innovate gatekeeper training system designed for students using HMD (Head Mounted Display) for the purpose of suicide prevention. This system provides an interactive and engaging virtual worlds to enhance the learning experience. In the immersive virtual environment, students can learn the common signs of psychological distress and how to refer troubled students to the counseling center (Fig. 4).

To enhance the learning experience, immersive simulated conversation and realistic emotional communication are provided like the below figure. Using virtual reality technology, we will provide a practice-based training simulation for students who can feel a sense of presence within a virtual world (Figs. 5 and 6).

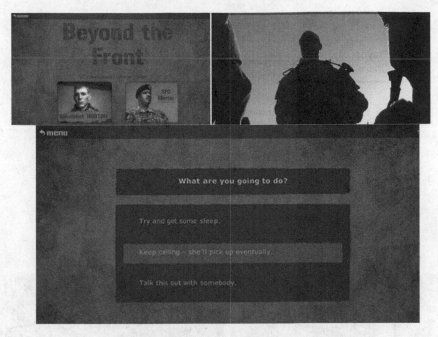

Fig. 3. Screenshots from BTF

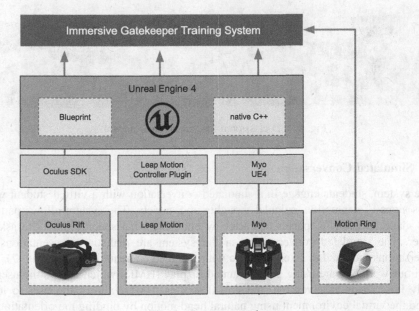

Fig. 4. System overview

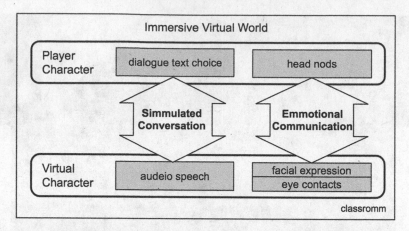

Fig. 5. Simulated conversation and emotional communication

Fig. 6. 3D classroom for virtual environment

3.1   Simulated Conversation

In the system, students engage in a simulated conversation with a virtual student who shows signs of depression, suicidal thoughts and anxiety. The system allows participants make decision for player character by choosing what specific things to ask or answer. The simulated conversations in the system are realistic representations of conversations they had or likely to have with troubled students in Korea (Fig. 7).

In our work, we are using head-mounted display (HMD) which allows the user to deeply immerse themselves into the virtual worlds. HMDs allows the user to look around the virtual environment using natural head motion by binding the orientation of the virtual camera to the orientation of the user's head. In this immersive virtual world, participants can practice having conversations with virtual character using open-ended

Fig. 7. Simulated conversation with text and audio speech

questions, reflective listening and other motivational interviewing techniques. During conversation, participants receive corrective feedback on their decisions with constructive criticism. By practicing speaking with virtual character, the training increases participants' confidence and ability to handle similar read-life situations.

Fig. 8. Making facial animation of virtual character

3.2 Emotional Communication

The proposed system aims to provide a fully animated and emotionally responsive virtual character that acts and responds like a real student exhibiting signs of psychological distress. Engaging in simulated conversations, the virtual character will present behaviors associated with depression, substance abuse, aggression and suicidal thoughts. For realistic virtual character, we implement 3D facial animation and naturalistic interaction. The movements of a real person's face and speech are captured at the same time. Then, these data are converted to build facial animations of 3D virtual character. For the naturalistic interaction, eye contacts and head nods are implemented by using head-tracking data from HMD. These forms of nonverbal interaction provide important social and emotional information during the simulated conversation (Figs. 8, 9 and 10).

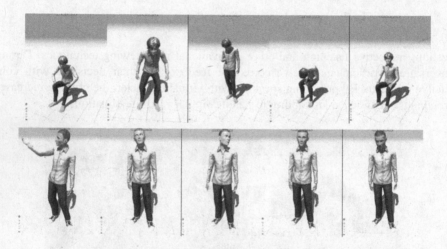

Fig. 9. Gesture animation of virtual character

Fig. 10. Title screenshot and example of study wearing HMD

4 Conclusion

This paper presented an interactive role-playing simulation for gatekeeper training. Students enter a virtual world and engage in a conversation with a virtual character who are fully animated and emotionally responsive. In the role-play scenarios, students practice and learn how to identify, approach, and refer troubled students by means of choosing dialogue options that appear on-screen. After completing the training, students will be better equipped to identify and correct common misconceptions about counseling.

Finding cost-effective solutions for suicide prevention and outreach program can be a challenge. We believe that the use of innovative and creative technology for suicide prevention programs can help to address these issues and promote widespread prevention and intervention. For example, there are effective programs, with cognitive behavioral therapy recommended as the preferred treatment for mild to moderate depressive disorder. However, fewer than a fifth of young people with depressive disorder receive treatment.

Acknowledgement. This work was supported by the National Research Foundation of Korea Grant funded by the Korean Government (NRF-2012S1A5A2A03034747).

References

1. OECD Health Data. Paris: OECD (2011)
2. Korean National Statistical Office 2013 Death and Cause of Death in Korea Korean National Statistical Of-fice, Daejeon (2013)
3. Kang, E., Hyun, M.K., Chio, S.M., Kim, J., Kim, G., Woo, J.: Twelve-month prevalence and predictors of self-reported suicidal ideation and suicide attempt among Korean adolescentsin a web-based nationwide survey. Aust. N. Z. J. Psychiatry **49**, 47–53 (2014)
4. Fremouw, W., Perczel, M., Ellis, T.: Suicide Risk: Assessment and Response Guidelines. Pergamon, Elmsford (1990)
5. Haines, C.V.: An evaluation of the proximal outcomes of a school based suicide awareness pro-gram: changes in knowledge, attitudes, and responses to analog scenarios (Unpublished doctoral dissertation). State University of New Jersey (2007)

Animation Validation of Obese Virtual Pediatric Patients Using a FLACC Pain Scale

Toni B. Pence[1]([⊠]), Lauren C. Dukes[2], and Larry F. Hodges[2]

[1] University of North Carolina at Wilmington, 601 S College Rd,
Wilmington, NC 28403, USA
pencet@uncw.edu
[2] Clemson University, 100 McAdams Hall, Clemson, SC 29634, USA
{lcairco,lfh}@clemson.edu

Abstract. We report on an experiment conducted to validate the non-verbal behaviors of our virtual patients as described by the standardized Face, Legs, Activity, Cry, Consolabiltiy scale [1] in relation to whether the virtual patient's gender or obesity has an affect on the participants' ability to correctly detect those animations. The results of this experiment provide insight into the feasibility of using a standardized pain scale as a method to validate virtual patients animations.

Keywords: Virtual characters · Virtual environment · Virtual patients · Simulation training · Virtual character animation

1 Introduction

Nursing students have limited opportunities for interaction with real patients, especially with pediatric patients, and often do not receive immediate and impartial feedback on their performance during their patient interaction. We created a virtual pediatric patient system for nursing students in order to provide an alternative educational method to practice their interviewing skills, with guidance, feedback and consistent experiences for all students.

During the development and previous usability evaluations of our system, we realized the importance of determining whether our virtual pediatric patients displayed nonverbal behaviors that were consistent with the behaviors nursing students would see in a real-word interaction with a pediatric patient. In order to investigate this we decided to validate our animations using a standard pediatric pain scale with four different virtual pediatric patients.

2 Related Work

2.1 Simulation Learning and Training

Simulation training is an effective strategy to help promote safe clinical practices [2] and impacts the development of self-efficacy and judgment skills for

© Springer International Publishing Switzerland 2016
S. Lackey and R. Shumaker (Eds.): VAMR 2016, LNCS 9740, pp. 552–564, 2016.
DOI: 10.1007/978-3-319-39907-2_53

nurses that are essential to provide the safest and most effective care possible [3]. Simulation learning that mimics real world scenarios is beneficial to nursing students and will provide standardized experiences in which students can practice problem solving techniques and clinical decision making abilities [3].

Researchers have used virtual patients to teach communications skills to medical students, and students have rated the virtual patient experience as being as effective as a standardized patient (actor) [3]. Medical students have also used virtual patients to help practice patient interviewing skills with a high level of immersion. Results indicate that using life-size virtual characters with speech recognition is useful in their education [4]. Adult virtual patients are fairly common, but virtual pediatric patients are rare.

Studies have shown that using virtual environments for simulation training can be effective [5] and that using life-like animated virtual characters can increase the level of realism of the training simulation [6]. The study done by Johnson et al. also showed that virtual patient systems with highly detailed human models create a more realistic experience [7]. Gulz et al. finds that the most established effect of animated agents in educational systems is the potential they provide to make the experience more engaging for the student [8].

2.2 Animation Validity

In an experiment conducted by Wu et al., they examined the impact of virtual human animations on the emotional responses of participants in a medical virtual reality simulation for education [9]. They conducted a between subjects experiment to study the difference between animated and non-animated characters by using an Electro Dermal Activity sensor. The results of their study suggests that participants' in the animated condition presented a higher sense of co-presence and a higher level of emotional response as the patient deteriorated in the simulation.

3 System Description

After a review of the literature and the results from our previous experiments, we became interested in exploring students' eye gaze patterns with different types of virtual pediatric patients, specifically obese virtual pediatric patients. Eye contact with patients is extremely important and is considered to be the most powerful form of nonverbal communication and that doctors' eye contact can deepen the bond with their patient, thereby affecting patient outcomes and safety [10]. There are differences in how much eye contact some medical professionals make with non-standard patients, including obese patients [11].

Our long term goal is to explore students' eye gaze patterns with different types of virtual pediatric patients, but before we can begin the eye tracking experiments, we need to validate the animations of our virtual patients. It is imperative that we are presenting the intended nonverbal behaviors to the students. We cannot expect to gain valuable insight from the eye tracking metrics if the nonverbal animations are incorrect or distracting. Also, we wanted to determine if there are other factors, like gender or obesity biases, that may affect how students look at the virtual patients.

For this experiment the virtual examination room for pediatrics from the original SIDNIE (Scaffolded Interviews Developed by Nurses in Education) [12] system that was used, as shown in Fig. 1a. The room consists of 3D objects created in Blender [13] and Unity [14]. The characters were created using Make-Human [15] and Blender. We created one parent to use in all conditions, since only the parents arm would be scene in the simulation, as shown in Fig. 1b.

(a) The room that the virtual characters were housed in.

(b) The mother used for all four virtual children.

Fig. 1. The virtual environment used in all experiment conditions.

4   Experiment Description

We conducted an animation validation experiment that compared the same animations between four different virtual characters that represented either an obese male, a non-obese male, an obese female or a non-obese female. We used the Face, Legs, Activity, Cry, Consolability (FLACC) pain scale [1], which is a common measurement tool used to assess pain for children between the ages of 2 months and 7 years, as our evaluation tool. There are many challenges in pediatrics with assessing pain in children, especially when they are nonverbal or too young to fully explain what they are feeling. Nurses are taught to use audio and visual cues to help figure out the pain level of a pediatric patient. The scale has five categories representing facial expressions, leg movement, activity level, crying and whether the child is consolable. Each category is assigned a score of 0, 1, or 2, and then each category is totaled for a score between 0 and 10, as shown in Table 1. To interpret the behavioral score, 0 = relaxed and comfortable, 1–3 = mild discomfort, 4–6 = moderate pain, and 7–10 = severe discomfort or pain or both. In this table, there are audio and visual descriptions to help guide the nurse determining the pain level of a pediatric patient. The descriptions provided by this pain scale provided the specific characteristics that were used to create a set of animations for our virtual pediatric patients.

Table 1. The FLACC pain scale. Each of the five categories are scored from 0–2, which results in a total score of zero to ten.

	Scoring		
Categories	0	1	2
Face	No particular expression or smile	Occasional grimace or frown, withdrawn, disinterested	Frequent to constant frown, quivering chin, clenched jaw
Legs	Normal position or relaxed	Uneasy, restless, tense	Kicking or legs drawn up
Activity	Lying quietly, normal position, moves easily	Squirming, shifting back and forth, tense	Arched, rigid or jerking
Cry	No cry	Moans or whimpers, occasional complaint	Crying steadily, screams or sobs, frequent complaints
Consolability	Content, relaxed	Reassured by occasional touching, hugging, or being talked to	Difficult to console or comfort

The goal of this experiment was to determine if our animations accurately represented the characteristics described in the FLACC pain scale. We also investigated whether there were differences in how the virtual patients animations were perceived between the male vs female virtual patient and the obese vs non-obese virtual patient. The virtual children were modeled to look similar, the only differences being gender and weight. We were not investigating any differences between ethnicity, so we made our virtual pediatric patients ethnically neutral to decrease any hidden biases the participants may have, as shown in Fig. 2.

4.1 Animation Set

We used the characteristics described in the FLACC pain scale to create the animations. As shown in Table 1, there are five categories (Face, Legs, Activity, Cry and Consolability) with three levels (0, 1 and 2) in each category. We decided to use Level 0 as the neutral level and we focused on Level 1 and Level 2,

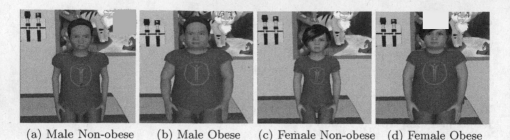

(a) Male Non-obese   (b) Male Obese   (c) Female Non-obese   (d) Female Obese

Fig. 2. The four different characters used in the animation validation experiment.

which gave us 10 specific characteristics to portray using animations. We had four different characters for a total of 40 animations, as shown in Table 2. To portray the characteristics of the FLACC category and level, Face 1, we created animations for our virtual character that contained an occasional frown or grimace and the characters head would look around the room as if he/she was disinterested in what was going on.

Since we were only interested in Face 1 for this test, we kept the FLACC categories of Legs, Activity, Cry and Consolability at Level 0 (neutral). The neutral position consisted of slight breathing motions and eye blinking with subtle movements to show that the virtual child was life-like. For the video labeled Face 1, we would expect the participant to score it as follows: Face = 1, Legs = 0, Activity = 0, Cry = 0 and Consolability = 0. For each of the tests, we were only interested in the visual cues being presented and did not provide any type of audio with any of the animations. For each of the 40 animation tests, we created a 30 second video where animations representing a single category and level from the FLACC pain scale were played on a loop.

Table 2. Videos coded by Category, Level, Gender and Obesity.

	Male obese	Male non-obese	Female obese	Female non-obese
Face 1	F1MO	F1MN	F1FO	F1FN
Face 2	F2MO	F2MN	F2FO	F2FN
Legs 1	L1MO	L1MN	L1FO	L1FN
Legs 2	L2MO	L2MN	L2FO	L2FN
Activity 1	A1MO	A1MN	A1FO	A1FN
Activity 2	A2MO	A2MN	A2FO	A2FN
Cry 1	Cy1MO	Cy1MN	Cy1FO	Cy1FN
Cry 2	Cy2MO	Cy2MN	Cy2FO	Cy2FN
Consolability 1	C1MO	C1MN	C1FO	C1FN
Consolability 2	C2MO	C2MN	C2FO	C2FN

Our *primary goal* of this research study was to determine if our virtual pediatric patients displayed the characteristics described in the FLACC pain scale through our virtual patients animations. We wanted to test if the characteristics of the animations we developed were interpreted in the way we expected by participants who graded our animations with the FLACC pain scale. We also wanted to test for any differences in the percent of correctly interpreted animations in relation to gender or obesity. We *hypothesized* that our animations would be correctly graded by the FLACC pain scale more than 50 percent of the time. We also *hypothesized* that we would see no significant difference in the amount of correctly graded animations in relation to gender. The literature mentioned previously suggests that there are issues with how medical professionals look at their obese patients, therefore we *expected* to see differences in the amount of correctly graded animations for the obese virtual pediatric patients.

4.2   Experiment Procedure

In all four conditions, participants were recruited through Amazon's Mechanical Turk system [16] and participated on-line using the Qualtrics Survey Software [17]. The entire experiment took around an hour and each participant was paid $4. Participants viewed a brief explanation on the FLACC pain scale and how to use it. Then each participant watched a 30 second video and scored the behavior shown in the video based on the FLACC pain scale. We gave the participants four practice questions to familiarize themselves with the format and the scoring. Next, participants watched 40 separate videos and used the FLACC scale to score each video. The ordering of these videos were randomized for each participant.

After the participants completed watching all of the videos, we then asked them to complete a survey containing questions about their demographics, computer use, weight characteristics, and exposure to virtual characters. Next, the participants completed the Attitudes Towards Obese Persons (ATOP) scale, which was designed to measure explicit attitudes and perceptions towards obese people [18]. Participants also completed the Beliefs About Obese Persons (BAOP) scale, which is an 8-item Likert-style scale that assesses a person's beliefs about the causes of obesity [19]. Finally, we asked participants to complete a Social Roles Questionnaire, which is comprised of a 24-item scale that measures attitudes toward gender roles [20].

4.3   Participants

There were 72 participants that started the experiment, but only 62 participants completed the experiment. There were 39 females and 23 males. Their ages ranged from 21 to 68 years old, with an average age of 39. The majority of participants classified themselves as white (46), while six were black or African-American, six were Asian, two were American Indian or Alaska Native, and two participants chose not to answer. Five participants classified themselves as under weight, 26 as healthy weight, 26 as over weight, four as obese and one participant chose not to classify their weight status. Participants reported a middling level of experience working with children (mean = 5.01, where 0 = no experience and 10 = a great deal, sd = 3.32), a low level of experience working in a health care setting (mean = 2.66, where 0 = no experience and 10 = a great deal, sd = 3.21), a high level of daily computer use (mean = 9.46, where 0 = no experience and 10 = a great deal), and a low level of exposure to virtual humans (mean = 3.66, where 0 = no exposure and 10 = a great deal).

5   Results and Discussion

Grading the Animations. Table 3 contains the grading results for the videos representing the Level 1 categories of the FLACC pain scale. For example, the Face 1 video contained the specific animations designed to represent the characteristics described in Level 1 of the categories in the FLACC pain scale. In the table, the values in bold and underlined in the column for Level 1 represent the videos where the category the participants selected matched the category we were portraying. 13 of the 20 videos for Level 1 were correctly categorized, but only 9 videos were correctly categorized at least 50 % of the time and 7 videos were correctly categorized at least 75 % of the time.

Table 4 contains the grading results for the videos representing the Level 2 categories of the FLACC pain scale. In the table, the values in bold and underlined in the column for Level 2 represent the videos where the category the participants selected matched the category we were portraying. 10 of the 20 videos for Level 2 were correctly categorized, but only 9 videos were correctly categorized at least 50 % of the time and 4 animations were correctly categorized at least 75 % of the time. From the table, we can see that for the videos representing the Legs 2 and Cry 2 categories of the FLACC pain scale were correctly categorized by the participants a majority of the time, regardless of condition. For Face 2, participants were able to correctly categorize the video for the non-obese condition (Pearson's = 0.0024*).

Overall, we are able to clearly identify which videos clearly portrayed the characteristics described in the FLACC pain scale and which videos did not represent the intended category. The results of this experiment give us insight on how to make our animations more realistic and representative. The FLACC pain scale has not been used in simulation training or in this manner before, but based on these results the FLACC pain scale provided a useful tool to use to test how we are portraying certain characteristics and expressions for our virtual patients.

5.1   Qualitative Feedback

In the post-questionnaire, we asked participants three five-scale Likert-style questions to gauge their beliefs on whether factors beyond the person's control could be the cause for obesity. The three questions we asked were (1) "How likely are genes to be a risk factor for obesity?", (2) "How likely are hormone problems to cause a person to be overweight or obese?", and (3) "How likely is medicine

Table 3. The average percent of participants that selected either Level 0, Level 1, or Level 2 for the videos that were intended represent Level 1 for each of the four conditions (male, female, obese, non-obese).

			Level		
			0	1	2
Face 1	Male	Obese	3	40	56
		Non-obese	11	**47**	42
	Female	Obese	5	**55**	40
		Non-obese	0	34	66
Legs 1	Male	Obese	18	35	47
		Non-obese	13	34	53
	Female	Obese	10	39	52
		Non-obese	15	42	44
Activity 1	Male	Obese	10	**84**	6
		Non-obese	8	**82**	10
	Female	Obese	8	**82**	10
		Non-obese	24	**68**	8
Cry 1	Male	Obese	40	**48**	11
		Non-obese	58	37	5
	Female	Obese	42	**56**	2
		Non-obese	44	**47**	10
Consolability 1	Male	Obese	24	**76**	0
		Non-obese	18	**79**	3
	Female	Obese	18	**82**	0
		Non-obese	13	**85**	2

to cause a person to gain weight?" In question (1) 72 % of the participants felt that genes were at least sometimes likely to be a risk factor for obesity (mean = 3.01). In question (2) 79 % of the participants felt that hormone problems could be the cause for a person to be overweight (mean = 3.22) and in question (3) 81 % of the participants thought medicine could be to blame for a person to gain weight (mean = 3.24). These three questions indicate that the majority of these participants do not blame the individual for their weight issues and that there may be other factors contributing to obesity. There was a correlation (p = 0.0006*) between the participants gender and how they answered the question "How likely is medicine to cause a person to gain weight?". Looking at the distribution of this question we can see that the female participants were more likely to believe that medicine could contribute to a person's weight gain.

Table 4. The average percent of participants that selected either Level 0, Level 1, or Level 2 for the videos that were intended represent Level 2 for each of the four conditions (male, female, obese, non-obese).

			Score (%)		
			0	1	2
Face 2	Male	Obese	13	56	31
		Non-obese	13	39	**48**
	Female	Obese	15	48	15
		Non-obese	8	29	**63**
Legs 2	Male	Obese	5	13	**82**
		Non-obese	5	10	**85**
	Female	Obese	5	6	**89**
		Non-obese	8	10	**82**
Activity 2	Male	Obese	8	63	29
		Non-obese	5	66	29
	Female	Obese	3	68	29
		Non-obese	3	68	29
Cry 2	Male	Obese	2	29	**69**
		Non-obese	3	39	**58**
	Female	Obese	0	31	**69**
		Non-obese	2	32	**66**
Consolability 2	Male	Obese	3	74	23
		Non-obese	3	73	24
	Female	Obese	6	69	24
		Non-obese	5	66	29

5.2   Beliefs About Obese People

Individual scores from the Beliefs About Obese People (BAOP) scale range from 0 to 48, with higher scores indicating the belief that obesity is not controllable. BAOP scores ranged from 2 (belief that obesity is controllable) to 35 (belief that obesity is not controllable) with an average BAOP score of 16.5. For the BAOP, an average score of 24 would indicate participants have a neutral belief that obesity is controllable, but for our experiment the average score of 16.5 means that participants lean towards the belief that obesity is controllable.

We conducted a one-way analysis of variance to compare the BAOP scores to the participants answers to the question "How likely are hormone problems to cause a person to be overweight or obese?" and we found a significant difference ($F = 0.0028^*$, $r^2 = 0.24$). We found that the average BAOP scores of those who also believe that hormones are very likely to cause obesity were much higher than the average BAOP scores of those who thought that hormones were somewhat likely (t = 0.0013*, n = 23), unlikely (t = 0.0281, n = 6), or very unlikely (t = 0.0295, n = 7).

Also, we were interested in how the BAOP scores would relate to how participants self-classified themselves as either underweight, healthy weight, overweight or obese. We conducted a one-way analysis of variance and we found a significant difference between these two questions (F = 0.0060*, r^2 = 0.22). We found that the average BAOP scores for the participants that classified themselves has having a healthy weight as being significantly lower than the participants that classified themselves as being underweight (t = 0.0094*, n = 5) or overweight (t = 0.0491*, n = 26). These results suggest that those who classify themselves as healthy weight are more likely to believe that obesity is controllable.

5.3   Attitudes Towards Obese People

Individual scores from the Attitudes Towards Obese People (ATOP) scale range from 0 to 120, with higher scores reflecting a more positive attitudes towards obese people. ATOP scores ranged from 17 (very negative view towards obese people) to 110 (very positive view towards obese people) with an average ATOP score of 65.66. The average ATOP score shows that a majority of participants had a neutral opinion towards obesity.

5.4   Social Roles Questionnaire

Gender Transcendent Attitudes. Each of the questions in the Gender Transcendent Attitudes (GTA) section are scored from 0 % to 100 % with higher scores indicating more traditional attitudes toward gender roles. The GTA scores ranged from 0 % (no difference in roles based on gender) to 60 % (higher belief that there are certain roles specific to gender) with an average GTA score of 11 %. These results suggest that our participants believe that any gender can do any task.

Gender Linked Attitudes. The Gender Linked Attitudes (GLA) questions are scored from 0 % to 100 % with higher scores indicating more traditional beliefs towards gender roles. Our scores ranged from 0 % (roles are not better performed by a specific gender) to 86 % (there are certain roles that specific genders are better performers) with an average GLA score of 33 % indicating that most participants do not believe that certain roles are performed better by a certain gender.

Gender Employed/Domestic Work Attitudes. The Gender Work Attitudes (GWA) scale goes from 0 % to 100 % with higher scores indicating more traditional beliefs when it comes to the divide between domestic work and employed work. Our GWA scores ranged from 14 % (jobs are not specific to gender) to 77 % (there are some jobs that certain genders should perform) with an average GWA score of 41 % indicating that almost half of the participants thought that there are distinct types of work that our better suited for specific genders.

5.5 Discussion

Our primary goal of this experiment was to see if we could create a set of animations that portrayed the characteristics described in the FLACC pain scale and then validate those animations (using videos) while also looking to see if the gender or obesity of the virtual patient had an effect on the outcome. In total 23 out of 40 videos were correctly categorized, regardless of condition. There were no significant differences in the animation identification pertaining to the characters gender which confirmed what we initially hypothesized.

The results of this experiment have provided us with insights on how to better develop our animations to represent the descriptions on the FLACC pain scale. Once the animations can be correctly identified using only visual representation, it would be interesting to see how the results would change when we add audio to the system.

Overall the Attitudes Towards Obese Persons (mean = 65.66 out of 120) and Beliefs About Obese Persons (mean = 16.5 out of 48) scores were neutral and had no significant effect on how participants scored the videos. Taking a look at the average scores of the Gender Transcendent Attitudes (11 %), the Gender Linked Attitudes (33 %) and the Gender Work Attitudes (41 %) we can come to the conclusion that for the majority of our participants they generally believe that roles should not be defined based on gender.

Using the descriptions from the FLACC scale to create a set of animations that can be validated proved to be successful. It provided us with a range of actions pertaining to the pediatric health domain. Once the animations have been fine tuned, it would be interesting to have pediatric health care professionals validate the videos using the FLACC pain scale and provide us with feedback on how it relates to the real world.

6 Future Work

The FLACC pain scale is a common measurement tool used to assess pain in children between the ages of 2 months and 7 years or individuals that are unable to communicate. Through a review of the literature we noticed that there were limited training opportunities for health care professionals to practice with the FLACC pain scale before using it in a real world situation. The validity of the FLACC pain scale as compared to the self-report pain measurement tools was proved in [21] but there is little documentation on how to train health care professionals to use it properly.

For future work, it would be possible to modify the SIDNIE system for use in training health care professionals on the proper use of the FLACC pain scale, while providing feedback, guidance, consistency and repetition. Additionally, it would be interesting to investigate the learning outcomes after FLACC pain scale training conducted with a modified SIDNIE in comparison with real world experience. Also, there is more to explore in determining if personal implicit or explicit biases affect how nursing professionals perceive pain in pediatric patients.

Acknowledgements. This research was supported, in part, by the NSF Graduate Research Fellowship Program (fellow numbers 2009080400 and 2011095211).

References

1. Merkel, S.I., Voepel-Lewis, T., Shayevitz, J.R., Malviya, S.: The FLACC: a behavioral scale for scoring postoperative pain in young children. Pediatr. Nurs. **23**(3), 293–297 (1997). LR: 20041117; JID: 7505804; ppublish
2. Hubal, R.C., Frank, G.A., Guinn, C.I.: Lessons learned in modeling schizophrenic and depressed responsive virtual humans for training. In: Proceedings of the 8th International Conference on Intelligent User Interfaces, pp. 85–92. ACM (2003)
3. Hockenberry, M.J., Wilson, D.: Wong's Nursing Care of Infants and Children. Mosby/Elsevier, St. Louis (2007)
4. Planas, L.G., Er, N.L.: A systems approach to scaffold communication skills development. Am. J. Pharm. Edu. **72**(2), 35 (2008)
5. Pruch, P., Vercher, J.L., Gauthier, G.M.: Acquisition of spatial knowledge through visual exploration of simulated environments. Ecol. Psychol. **7**(1), 1–20 (1995)
6. DeVault, D., Artstein, R., Benn, G., Dey, T., Fast, E., Gainer, A., Georgila, K., Gratch, J., Hartholt, A., Lhommet, M.: Simsensei kiosk: a virtual human interviewer for healthcare decision support. In: Proceedings of the 2014 International Conference on Autonomous agents and Multi-agent Systems, pp. 1061–1068. International Foundation for Autonomous Agents and Multiagent Systems (2014)
7. Johnsen, K., Dickerson, R., Raij, A., Lok, B., Jackson, J., Shin, M., Hernandez, J., Stevens, A., Lind, D.S.: Experiences in using immersive virtual characters to educate medical communication skills. In: Proceedings of Virtual Reality, pp. 179–186. IEEE (2005)
8. Gulz, A., Haake, M.: Design of animated pedagogical agents a look at their look. Int. J. Hum. Comput. Stud. **64**(4), 322–339 (2006)
9. Wu, Y., Babu, S.V., Armstrong, R., Bertrand, J.W., Luo, J., Roy, T., Daily, S.B., Dukes, L.C., Hodges, L.F., Fasolino, T.: Effects of virtual human animation on emotion contagion in simulated inter-personal experiences. IEEE Trans. Vis. Comput. Graph. **20**(4), 626–635 (2014)
10. Booth, T.L., McMullen-Fix, K.: Innovation center: collaborative interprofessional simulation in a baccalaureate nursing education program. Nurs. Educ. Perspect. **33**(2), 127–129 (2012)
11. Gudzune, K.A., Beach, M.C., Roter, D.L., Cooper, L.A.: Physicians build less rapport with obese patients. Obesity **21**(10), 2146–2152 (2013)
12. Pence, T.B., Dukes, L.C., Hodges, L.F., Meehan, N.K., Johnson, A.: The effects of interaction and visual fidelity on learning outcomes for a virtual pediatric patient system. In: IEEE International Conference on Healthcare Informatics (ICHI), pp. 209–218. IEEE (2013)
13. Blender. http://www.blender.org
14. UNITY: Game development tool. http://www.unity3d.com
15. MakeHuman. http://www.makehuman.org
16. Turk, A.M. http://www.mturk.com
17. Software, Q.S. http://www.qualtrics.com
18. Walter, M.E., Ragan, K., Sulak, T.N., Bagby, J.H.: Implicit and explicit biases toward obesity: Perspectives of school of education students. J. Community Med. Health Educ., vol. 3(212) (2013). doi:10.4172/2161-0711.1000212

19. Puhl, R., Masheb, R., White, M., Grilo, C.: Attitudes toward obesity in obese persons: a matched comparison of obese women with and without binge eating. Eat. Weight Disord. Stud. Anorexia, Bulimia Obes. **15**(3), 173–179 (2010)
20. Baber, K.M., Tucker, C.J.: The social roles questionnaire: a new approach to measuring attitudes toward gender. Sex Roles **54**(7–8), 459–467 (2006)
21. Willis, M.H., Merkel, S.I., Voepel-Lewis, T., Malviya, S.: Flacc behavioral pain assessment scale: a comparison with the child's self-report. Pediatr. Nurs. **29**(3), 195 (2003)

3DUI Electronic Syringe for Neonate Central Venous Access Procedure Simulation

Gerardo Tibamoso, Sergio Medina-Papagayo, Lizeth Vega-Medina,
Byron Perez-Gutierrez[✉], and Alvaro Uribe-Quevedo

VR Center, Nueva Granada Military University, Bogota, Colombia
gtibap@gmail.com, sergio.m.papagayo@gmail.com
{lizvega,byron.perez,alvaro.j.uribe}@ieee.org

Abstract. The central venous access is a highly complex medical procedure, which consists of accessing a central vein (e.g., femoral vein, jugular vein or the umbilicus) to deliver different drugs, anesthesia, fluids or treatments to the patient. This procedure requires a high degree of expertise and its malpractice can result in severe consequences for the patient leading to possible pneumothorax, hemothorax and even death, among many other health risks. In neonates, the procedure is even more challenging because of the anatomical features. The lack of training tools requires trainees to transfer knowledge from adult venous access to the neonate; therefore, it is highly necessary to create training tools for specialists. In this paper, the development of an interactive simulation system for practicing the needle insertion in the internal jugular vein in neonates is presented. A real model of a syringe coupled with inertial sensors was built to permit the interaction between the user and a neonate virtual model displayed on a touch screen. This system has been evaluated by users, who expressed great potential in this interactive simulation for training.

Keywords: Central venous access · Haptic · Syringe · Inertial measurement unit

1   Introduction

The central venous access (CVA) is an invasive medical procedure that allows accessing the big circulatory vessels (e.g., jugular, subclavian or femoral vein) to provide drugs, anesthesia, fluids or treatments to the patient in a critical condition [12]. It requires skilled specialists to successfully perform the technique and avoid any complications that may compromise the patients life [17,20]. In neonates, the procedure is even more challenging because of the size, gaps between organs, tissues and their mechanical properties. It has been shown that skills related to this procedure are improved with the use of training simulators [4,16,18,21], where virtual or real manikins are used to represent patient anatomy and vital functions in a controlled environment [8,15,27]. There are several CVA simulators for 5+ years old patients (CVC Insertion Simulator II

© Springer International Publishing Switzerland 2016
S. Lackey and R. Shumaker (Eds.): VAMR 2016, LNCS 9740, pp. 565–573, 2016.
DOI: 10.1007/978-3-319-39907-2_54

[1], Gen II Ultrasound Central Line Training Model [7], Internal Jugular Central Line Ultrasound Manikin [5], VascularAccessChild Training System [22]) designed for jugular, femoral and subclavian vein access, while CVA simulators for neonates are only focused on umbilicus, femoral and peripheral venous access and intraosseous access (Simbaby [13], SimNewB [14], BabySIM [6], Newborn PEDI Simulator [9]). However, neonatal CVA simulators for jugular and subclavian veins are scarce, lack to be remedied since the cannulation of these vessels is common in medical practice [25,26] and its realization requires greater skills obtained through practice [28].

An interactive simulation system for practicing the needle insertion in the access of the internal jugular vein in neonates is proposed. The system has a physical syringe coupled with inertial sensors and a virtual model of the neonatal patient displayed on a touch screen of a tablet device. During the simulation, the system generates a visual feedback for successful access to the internal jugular vein, or a failed attempt when the carotid artery is accessed. Both are closely spaced vessels. The response is based on a linear estimation of the intersection between the needle tip and the vessel, considering the insertion point on the patient skin, the angle chosen by the user and the position, orientation, and diameter of the target vessels. This paper is divided as follows: in Sect. 2 the medical procedure and the design of the proposed simulation system are described. In Sect. 3 the results of the user experience are presented. Finally, conclusions and future work are presented in Sect. 4.

2   3DUI Syringe Development

In real practice, an important and challenging step during CVA is the needle insertion using a syringe [17]. Anatomically, the access region for the internal jugular vein is bounded by the clavicle and the sternocleidomastoid muscle, as seen in the Fig. 1. A point within this region should be selected to insert the needle at an angle of 45 degrees relative to the coronal plane and in the direction of the ipsilateral nipple. Typically the vein is accessed less than 1.3 cm. A successful entry into the vessel is visually identified when venous blood returns into the syringe [11].

2.1   System Architecture

Using the needle insertion procedure in jugular CVA as a reference, we define the 3DUI inputs and outputs so our solution represents life-like interactions with a real syringe. For the proposed system a physical model of the syringe was built, coupled with inertial sensors to estimate its orientation, interacting with a virtual model of a neonate displayed on a touchscreen of a mobile device (tablet). During the procedure, the user can freely handle the syringe to select an access point on the touchscreen where the neonate is displayed. When the tip of the syringe touches the screen, the system estimates if the needle is accessing the internal jugular vein or the carotid artery, performing an extension of the

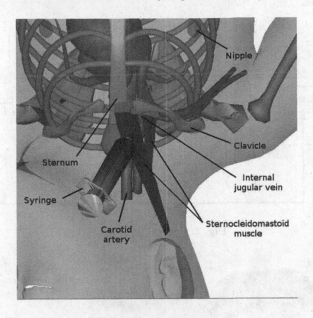

Fig. 1. Needle insertion

needle into the neonate, gradually, to a defined length, continuously evaluating the possible collision of the needle tip with the vessels represented by cylindrical geometric shapes. A description of the proposed system is presented in Fig. 2.

Over the skin of the neonate, a region access on the virtual model has been previously defined, as it is presented in Fig. 3. The spherical coordinates that compound this region are transformed into pixel coordinates to compare their position with the position chosen by the user with the syringe tip over the touch-screen. This transformation is done by using the visual model matrix, defined by the position and orientation of the camera, the features of the perspective projection and the display region on the screen [2]. When the system detects a collision between the tip of the syringe with any of the projected spheres, it can be determined the chosen position P_0 on the skin of the neonate doing an inverse transformation. If a collision with multiple spheres exists, the sphere closer to the camera is chosen.

With the information taken from the accelerometer (G) a magnetometer (B) coupled to the body of the syringe, an orthogonal basis estimation is stated $\langle i_s, j_s, k_s \rangle$, describing the orientation of the inertial sensors regarding to a general orthogonal reference system $\langle U, V, W \rangle$ defined by the magnetic and gravitational fields [19]. For this, taken as reference the normalized measure of the accelerometer $W = G/|G|$, without the effect of external accelerations besides gravity, we have

$$V = Wx\left(\frac{B}{|B|}\right) \tag{1}$$

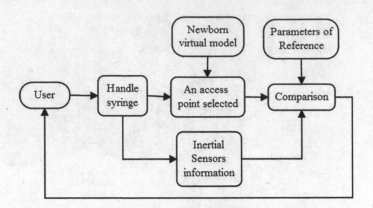

Fig. 2. System diagram

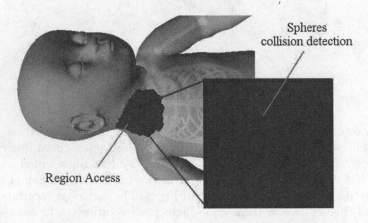

Fig. 3. Region access over the skin of neonate

and

$$U = V x W \qquad (2)$$

then, the orthogonal basis of the inertial sensors is defined by

$$i_s = (U_x, V_x, W_x) \qquad (3)$$
$$j_s = (U_y, V_y, W_y) \qquad (4)$$
$$k_s = (U_z, V_z, W_z) \qquad (5)$$

Therefore, the direction of the syringe is determined by the alignment of its central axis with i_s, j_s, k_s. With the position vectors P_0 and orientation vectors R of the tip of the syringe, the P vector representing the extension of the needle is defined, such as

$$P = P_0 + KR \qquad (6)$$

where the scalar $K > 0$ defines the magnitude of the vector. The value of K increases gradually in each iteration until a maximum value, a process where the collision between P and blood vessels is evaluated using the method described by Sunkel [24]. The method consists in projecting P to the reference vessel system, evaluating the resulting coordinates within the confines of the cylindrical body of the vessel. This projection is done by $P - P - C_0$, being C_0 the origin position of the vessel reference system and using the scalar product, such as

$$P' = (P \cdot i_v, P \cdot j_v, P \cdot k_v) \tag{7}$$

where i_v, j_v y k_v are the unit vectors that define the reference system of the vessel. If we assumed that central axis of the cylinder is i_v, the component x of $P'(P'_x)$ is evaluated between the length of the cylinder (L), while the components P'_y and P'_z are compared with the vessel radius ($radius$), as

$$\text{if} \left(min(L) \leq P'_x \leq max(L) \text{ and } \sqrt{P_y'^2 + P_z'^2} \leq radius \right) \text{ then collision} \tag{8}$$

If the collision exists, a graphical response is produced indicating the access to the jugular vein or the carotid artery. In Fig. 4 a graphical description of the actors in the collision detection is presented.

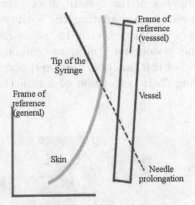

Fig. 4. Collision detection process between needle and jugular vein

The system requires an initial calibration of the measures taken by the magnetometer and also to align the framework of sensors with the reference frame of the virtual model. The calibration of the magnetometer consists in centering the data regarding the origin, finding maximum and minimum values of each component and normalize them, as proposed by [29]. On the other hand, to align the reference systems of the syringe and mobile device, they must be placed on a flat surface by making that the z-axis of the two coordinate systems points to the normal direction of the surface. Then, the central axis of the syringe is aligned with the x-axis of the virtual model that is parallel to one side of the mobile device.

3   Results

The virtual environment is composed by a 3D model considering the basic anatomical features described in anatomy books of a term neonate. This model is oriented in the Trendelenburg position with 15° of inclination which is the recommended for the jugular central venous access procedure. The software was built with Android Studio [10] using *libgdx* [30]. For the implementation of the syringe, it was used an Arduino Mini Pro [3], a 9-DOF inertial measurement unit MPU-9150 [23] which encapsulates an accelerometer, a gyroscope and a magnetometer, a Bluetooth interface for wireless transmission between sensors and the mobile device. This application was implemented on a Samsung Galaxy Note Tablet 8.0 as presented in Fig. 5.

The proposed system includes a user interface to manage different options in the virtual environment. The user has the possibility to adjust the camera in order to change the perspective view of the model with some hand gestures that enable to rotate the model, to approach or to take a distance from it. During the procedure, the user can freely manipulate the syringe to select an access point from the images of the neonate. There is a function that blocks the movement of the camera to help to find the point for performing the procedure.

To evaluate the usefulness of the system, user experience tests were performed. The test consisted of manipulating the syringe to access the internal jugular vein. The test was performed with 12 users. Each of the participants freely practiced with the system for 5 min, recognizing the components and method of use. At the end of this practice, users responded to a set of questions, with skill levels, regarding their perception of interaction and visual feedback during the procedure.

Fig. 5. Implemented prototype

3.1   User Experience

After the tests users stated:

- The visual representation of the neonate is realistic, however, it is important a further enhancement of anatomical landmarks such as the collarbone and nipple, which are key benchmarks for the procedure.
- The syringe allows adequate control of the position and orientation at the time of the puncture.
- Although the system allows the viewer to manipulate the virtual environment by changing the position of observation of the neonate, it is sufficient that the system allows a small lateral movements around it, as well as zoom in and out of the region of interest.

Within additional observations made by the users are: allowing a three-dimensional view of the virtual environment, for example by defining different views of the same scene on the screen to better identify the position of the observer with respect to the neonate; and to make known the bevel of the needle tip, since its orientation is important for access.

4   Conclusions and Discussion

An interactive simulation system for training puncture in the access of the internal jugular vein was developed. The system is an innovative tool that can complement traditional learning based on the information presented in books and videos, allowing the user to interact with the virtual anatomy and performing the puncture in different manners.

The system can be extended to simulate vital signs, breathing movements and sounds in the environment, under normal conditions and possible complications.

Force feedback is the next step. Using a vibrotactile actuator inside the syringe would be ideal for such applications to represent the rupture of the skin and vessels. This system can be complemented to perform the complete procedure step by step.

Acknowledgments. This project was supported by the Research Division of Nueva Granada Mil. University through grant IMP ING 1776.

References

1. 3-Dmed: CVC insertion simulator ii. https://www.3-dmed.com/product/cvc-insertion-simulator-ii
2. Angel, E.: Interactive Computer Graphics: A Top-Down Approach with OpenGL, 2nd edn. Addisson- Wesley, New York (2000)
3. Arduino: Pro mini microcontroller. https://www.arduino.cc/en/Main/Arduino BoardProMini

4. Barsuk, J.H., McGaghie, W.C., Cohen, E.R., Balachandran, J.S., Wayne, D.B.: Use of simulation-based mastery learning to improve the quality of central venous catheter placement in a medical intensive care unit. J. Hosp. Med. **4**(7), 397–403 (2009)

5. CAE: Internal jugular central line ultrasound manikin. https://www.bluephantom. com/product/Internal-Jugular-Central-Line-Ultrasound-Manikin_NEW!.aspx? cid=380

6. CAE-Healthcare: Babysim.   http://www.caehealthcare.com/eng/patient-simu lators/babysim

7. CAE-Healthcare: Gen ii ultrasound central line training model. https://www. bluephantom.com/product/Gen-II-Ultrasound-Central-Line-Training-Model_ Brand-NEW.aspx?cid=414

8. Engum, S., Jeffries, P., Fisher, L.: Intravenous catheter training system: computer-based education versus traditional learning methods. Am. J. Surg. **186**(1), 67–74 (2003)

9. Gaumard: Newborn pedi simulator. http://www.gaumard.com/s105

10. Google: Android studio. http://developer.android.com

11. Graham, A.S., Ozment, C., Tegtmeyer, K., Lai, S., Braner, D.A.: Central Venous Catheterization. New Engl. J. Med. **356**(21), e21 (2007)

12. Jain, P., Pant, D., Sood, J.: Atlas of Practical Neonatal and Pediatric Procedures. JP Medical Ltd, London (2012)

13. Laerdal: Simbaby. http://www.laerdal.com/us/SimBaby

14. Laerdal: Simnewb. http://www.laerdal.com/us/doc/88/SimNewB

15. Larnpotang, S., Lizdas, D., Rajon, D., Luria, I., Gravenstein, N., Bisht, Y., Schwab, W., Friedman, W., Bova, F., Robinson, A.: Mixed simulators: augmented physical simulators with virtual underlays. In: Virtual Reality (VR), IEEE 2013, pp. 7–10. IEEE (2013)

16. Ma, I.W., Brindle, M.E., Ronksley, P.E., Lorenzetti, D.L., Sauve, R.S., Ghali, W.A.: Use of simulation-based education to improve outcomes of central venous catheterization: a systematic review and meta-analysis. Acad. Med. **86**(9), 1137–1147 (2011)

17. McGee, D.C., Gould, M.K.: Preventing complications of central venous catheterization. New Engl. J. Med. **348**(12), 1123–1133 (2003)

18. Moureau, N., Lamperti, M., Kelly, L., Dawson, R., Elbarbary, M., Van Boxtel, A., Pittiruti, M.: Evidence-based consensus on the insertion of central venous access devices: definition of minimal requirements for training. Br. J. Anaesth. **110**(3), 347–356 (2013)

19. Pedley, M., Stanley, M.: Calculation of orientation matrices from sensor data.Technical report, Freescale, Inc. (2014)

20. Rey, C., Álvarez, F., Rua, V.D.L., Medina, A., Concha, A., Díaz, J.J., Menéndez, S., Los Arcos, M., Mayordomo-Colunga, J.: Mechanical complications during central venous cannulations in pediatric patients. Intensive Care Med. **35**(8), 1438–1443 (2009). http://icmjournal.esicm.org/Journals/abstract.html?=10.1007/ s00134-009-1534-0

21. Salazar Sanín, C., Sánchez, P., Darío, R., Arango Rave, M.E.,Lince Varela, L.F.: Manejo y complicaciones de catéteres venososcentrales en niños: Hospital universitario san vicente de paúl, medellín, colombia. Iatreia 21, p. s8 (2008)

22. Simulab: Vascularaccesschild training system. https://www.simulab.com/ products/vac-30

23. Sparkfun: Mpu-9150. http://www.sparkfun.com/products/11486

24. Sunkel, M.: Collision Detection for Cylinder-Shaped Rigid Bodies. Bachelor's thesis, Friedrich-Alexander-Universität Erlangen-Nürnberg (2010). https://www10. informatik.uni-erlangen.de/Publications/Theses/2010/Suenkel_BA_10.pdf
25. Trieschmann, U., ten Cate, F.U., Sreeram, N.: Central venous catheters in children and neonates? what is important? Images Paediatr. Cardiol. **9**(4), 1–8 (2007). http://www.ncbi.nlm.nih.gov/pmc/articles/PMC3232582/
26. Trieschmann, U., ten Cate, F.U., Sreeram, N.: Central venouscatheters in children and neonates (Part 2) ? Access via the internal jugular vein. Images Paediatr. Cardiol. **10**(1), 1–7 (2008). http://www.ncbi.nlm.nih.gov/pmc/articles/PMC3232585/
27. Ullrich, S., Kuhlen, T.: Haptic palpation for medical simulation in virtual environments. IEEE Trans. Vis. Comput. Graph. **18**(4), 617–625 (2012). http://dx.doi.org/10.1109/TVCG.2012.46
28. Verghese, S.T., McGill, W.A., Patel, R.I., Sell, J.E., Midgley, F.M., Ruttimann, U.E.: Ultrasound-guided internal jugular venous cannulation in infants: a prospective comparison with the traditional palpation method. J. Am. Soc. Anesthesiol. **91**(1), 71–77 (1999). http://anesthesiology.pubs.asahq.org/article.aspx?article id=1946253
29. Winer, K.: Simple and effective magnetometer calibration, August 2015. https://com/kriswiner/MPU-6050/wiki/Simple-and-Effective-Magnetometer-Calibration
30. Zechner, M.: libgdx. http://libgdx.badlogicgames.com/

Medutainment-Based AR Rally: Disaster Medical Learning Tool for Citizens

Ikushi Yoda[✉] and Momo Shiroyama

National Institute of Advanced Industrial Science and Technology (AIST),
Tsukuba, Japan
i-yoda@aist.go.jp, mm.shiroyama@google.com

Abstract. Various attempts have been made to teach first aid to the general public on how to deal with disaster medical situations, such as sending firemen to schools to give talks and hand out instructional pamphlets. But it is hard to determine whether the message is really getting through, or whether the students attend just because they have to. Now we have come up with a novel IT-based interactive educational tool based on a *medutainment* (medical edutainment) model for teaching basic first aid techniques to the public. Our initial assessment shows that this new medutainment-based approach is very effective for teaching first aid and disaster medicine to large numbers of people in situations where cost-effective experience-based training is impractical or not available.

Keywords: AR Rally · Disaster medicine · Medutainment · Edutainment · Education for first aid · Education for bystander

1 Introduction

Here we have developed an IT-based interactive educational tool tailored for young children and students based on *medutainment* (medical edutainment) [1] that entertains while teaching emergency medicine [2] (see Fig. 1). The application is called *AR Rally* and runs on a tablet computer or a smartphone. Players advance by solving quests (questions) presented on the tablet computer. Posters relating to the questions are put up the classroom or space where *AR Rally* is played. Key features of the prototype system include recognition of illustrations on the posters by the tablet's built-in camera, overlay representation using augmented reality (AR) functions, and game playing using touchscreen functions.

In the event of a mass casualty incident, the city or local community sets up special medical aid station and conducts triage, the process of determining priority of patients' treatments based on the severity of their wounds. Minor injuries may be treated onsite, while a hospital or other medical facility is designated as the destination to transport victims with moderate or more severe injuries. There may be a good number of locals or bystanders who can lend a hand if they have a basic understanding of first aid and disaster medical care, but unfortunately not many people have this basic knowledge. There is thus a critical need to improve people's knowledge of basic emergency medical care and first aid procedures. It was this insight that motivated the present

© Springer International Publishing Switzerland 2016
S. Lackey and R. Shumaker (Eds.): VAMR 2016, LNCS 9740, pp. 574–583, 2016.
DOI: 10.1007/978-3-319-39907-2_55

Fig. 1. AR Rally game

project to build a basic disaster medical education tool to help spread first aid knowledge and awareness among Japan's citizens.

The core content focuses on how to staunch bleeding (hemostasis), body position management, and other first aid procedures. It's hard to learn these techniques from a textbook, and the procedures themselves are not inherently interesting to most people. First aid is not the kind of thing that people flock to and are eager to learn. So one of our primary objectives in developing this tool was to provide people with basic disaster medical care knowledge in a light, digestible way that reduces any onerous sense of obligation.

As a model, we took the *edutainment* type handheld device used to guide people through museums [3, 4]. By interacting with the touchscreen display on these devices, people learn about the exhibits through content that is both educational and entertaining. This is very effective for two reasons. First, these devices effectively convert the passive learning process of simply viewing exhibits in a museum into a dynamic experience. Learning first aid is similarly a passive process. Lessons tend to be shrugged off by those who are really not that interested, so harnessing this edutainment approach could bring great benefits. Second, the handheld devices offer a way of building an interactive relationship between exhibits and viewers while moving through three-dimensional space. In emergency medical care, the procedures and the transport of injured cannot be separated from 3D motion and movement. This dimension is also critically important to enhance the edutainment value for younger elementary and middle school students. Real-time scoring and evaluation, and log functions are also important elements of medutainment applications.

The educational content of *AR Rally* primarily focuses on disaster medical care and medical aid stations in the form of a medutainment application tailored for the higher grades of elementary school and middle school. More specifically, *AR Rally* consists of a multiple-choice quiz (including use of an AR marker) regarding disaster medical care as well as a procedural game. The student's score and an explanation are provided immediately after the student gives her answers. Total results are tallied at the end to motivate the student to try harder. Note that while the story line is identical, two versions of *AR Rally* were developed—one for elementary students and the other for middle school students—with somewhat more advanced sentence structure and review quiz for the middle-school students.

We initially planned to implement *AR Rally* to run on iOS, but the programming was done in Unity [5] so it runs on both iOS and on Android. The application can thus be downloaded and run on tablet computers as well as on a variety of different smartphones, a capability that we think should help event organizers disseminate the software.

2 System Structure

Figure 2 shows an overview of all the chapters in *AR Rally*. Basic content is covered in Chapter 5. Note that two issues are addressed in each chapter. So, for example, Chapter 1 covers the game explaining the basics of disaster medical care and clothing-related considerations. Chapter 2 deals with hemostasis techniques (*i.e.*, ways to staunch bleeding). Chapter 3 is concerned with body position management. Chapter 4 deals with transport-related issues. And finally, Chapter 5 considers triage and includes a final review quiz. All of the content can be covered in about 20 min, and results are displayed for each question.

Let us next consider the features of *AR Rally* that make the content interesting even for students who have never shown much interest in disaster medicine. First, the students obtain information and explanations not by reading text, but by playing a game, so naturally this is much more interesting. Second, where teaching is involved, a quiz format is used which again engages and holds the attention of the students.

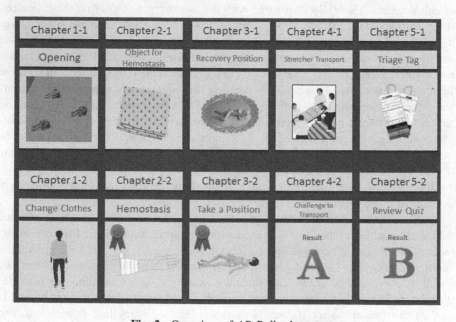

Fig. 2. Overview of *AR Rally* chapters

The quiz excites interest by putting up posters to represent question options, having the students choose a question as an AR marker, and by displaying results as interactive annotations in camera images. The hand skill games fully exploit the tablet computer's capabilities and help the student retain memory by manipulating and moving figures on the tablet using a finger tip for input. Finally, the review quiz at the end of the course helps students retain memory of the content.

Let us next take a closer look at three key features of AR Rally that help sustain interest in learning and remembering disaster medical care.

2.1 Opening: AR Triage Game

Writing a textbook about the procedures and significance of disaster medical care is easy, but presenting the content in a way that is retained in the mind of the reader is extremely difficult. First we applied gamification—game-design elements and game principles—to explain the concept of *triage*, which is at the very heart of emergency medical care. Triage involves the assignment of degrees of urgency to wounds or injuries to decide the order of treatment when there is a large number of casualties. At the site of an actual emergency, a paramedic or emergency medical technician writes triage information on a special tag called a *triage tag*, which is attached to the victims' arm. Victims are then sorted and moved to different areas as indicated by a color-coding scheme on the tags: green for minor injuries, yellow for moderate injuries, and red to severe injuries.

In the game version, first the floor plan of the medical aid station is captured by the tablet camera, AR is used to render the station in simple 3D which is overlaid with actual images, and then the game begins. As one can see from the screenshots in Fig. 3,

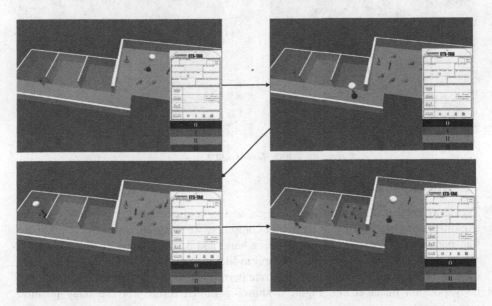

Fig. 3. Opening triage game (Color figure online)

the victims are brought into the medical aid station and color triaged by the system. Players merely select the victims one by one and transports them to the appropriate color-coded destination. Rather than launching into a detailed description of the procedure, a game is used to teach students the nature of triage through a game experience. A basic objective of the game is to teach children that in the event of a mass casualty incident when resources are stretched thin, even assistance from ordinary bystanders can make the difference between life and death.

2.2   AR Quiz

Here we will consider the AR-based interactive quiz scheme for teaching emergency medicine. The quiz is played on a tablet computer. First, several posters are put up on the wall at the event site highlighting the questions that will be asked (see Fig. 4). Or several questions could be combined on a single poster as illustrated in Fig. 5. A question is presented by the tablet, and the student has to choose the most appropriate poster image dealing with the question. The key here is that, if the student picks the wrong image, then augmented reality superimposes the question over the correct image. This sustains the student's interest while at the same time teaching the correct answer. If the student chooses the correct image, then the question returns to the tablet, and the rally continues. The opening game is similar, but the rally proceeds while going back and forth between real space and cyber space, and this too sustains the younger children's interest.

 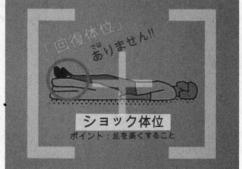

Fig. 4. AR Quiz

2.3   Hand Skill Games

Trying to teach first aid techniques using a textbook is exceedingly difficult. By fully exploiting the functionality of the tablet computer, we made this material much more transparent and easy to remember by using hand and finger gestures to manipulate 3D model figures on the screen. The 3D manikin-like models mimic the actual movements of people. We used the models to illustrate hemostasis (how to staunch bleeding) and body position management. Figure 6 shows gamified results for the body position management.

 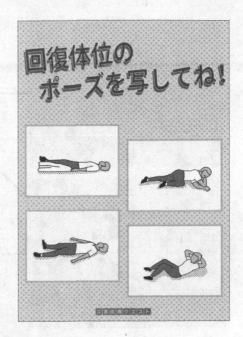

Fig. 5. AR Quiz posters

Figure 6 illustrates how to manipulate a figure lying on her back into the recovery position using finger gestures through a sequence of four steps. The actual maneuver is done by following the trajectories of the arrows shown in the figure with one's fingertip, and this causes the 3D model to actually change position and move in that direction. If at first the student does not succeed he can try again, and in the process learns how to put an injured person in the recovery position. Basically this is what we want the students to learn: the step-by-step procedure for putting someone into the correct position. While it's easy enough to glace skim over the procedure in a book, we think that our approach—exploiting the benefits of the touchscreen tablet and using one's finger to repeatedly perform the maneuver—is far better retained in the memory and also entertaining.

Emergency transport is covered in Chapter 4. In Chapter 4-2, we incorporated actual transport experience into the course by having the forth graders carry a 30-kg manikin on a stretcher. The idea was for the students to learn from experience what it is actually like to move a victim—a manikin that weighs about the same as a human child—without causing further injuries to the victim. For this exercise, a tablet computer is placed on the stretcher where its acceleration sensor measures up and down vibrations and jolts. This was used to simulate the shaking felt by the victim. High scores were given to students who could convey the stretcher with the least amount lateral shaking based on the assumption that this would result in less jostling and jolting of and injured victim. Obviously, this approach is not very accurate and does not guarantee no further injury to the victim. Rather than striving for accuracy, our primary goal was to promote learning

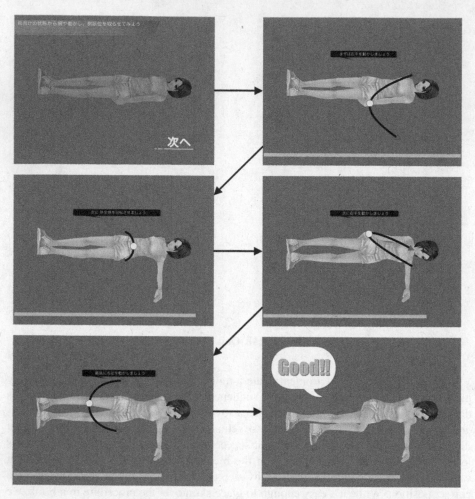

Fig. 6. Body position management game

while sustaining a feeling of tension and entertainment by incorporating real-life experience and a mechanical real-time scoring system (see figure on the right in Fig. 7).

3   Events and PDCA Cycle

3.1   Events

Up to now, about 780 students have participated in the stretcher-carrying exercise: roughly 600 students over four days at a shopping center, and 180 students during a one-day open house at AIST labs. Here's a brief overview of the event held at AIST labs.

Our assumption in developing this program is that it will be used as a training exercise at community medical aid stations—that is, to introduce people in the community to the local medical aid station. This prototype system is intended to simulate what one might experience in walking around a typical disaster site. One of the advantages of implementing the system on mobile devices is that the course can be tailored to a variety of different situations: people can learn disaster training procedures in their spare time, or the course can be used for training at actual medical aid stations, and so on. Figure 7 shows photos from one of the demonstration events. The participants at this event were about equally divided between children who came on their own and children who came with a parent.

Figure 8 shows the grade distribution of the student participants. A little more than half of the participants were third graders and older, so there were more younger children than we anticipated. The younger children worked through the questions with help from mom or dad.

Fig. 7. Event scenes

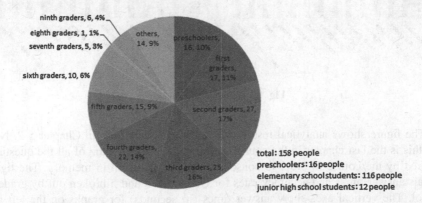

Fig. 8. Breakdown of participants

3.2 Evaluation and PDCA Cycle

Further refinement the course content of the prototype system will require qualitative assessment of the effectiveness of the hands-on experiential learning, comprehension and memory retention, and usability. Subjective surveys are normally used to gather this kind of information, but in our system the basic metrics are automatically compiled by the interaction of the subjects with their tablet computers. In other words, the tablets can be programmed to record correct/wrong answers on quizzes, time required to answer, the time it takes to read commentary, the time it takes to perform hand skill games, and so on. Moreover, by simply entering a student's grade in school, the program automatically determines the approximate difficulty of each question, the degree of interest the student will show in the commentary, and the ability of the child to understand and participate in the learning games. We are thus able to obtain useful feedback for all of the quiz questions based on quantitative data. Figure 9 illustrates the type of feedback that can be generated.

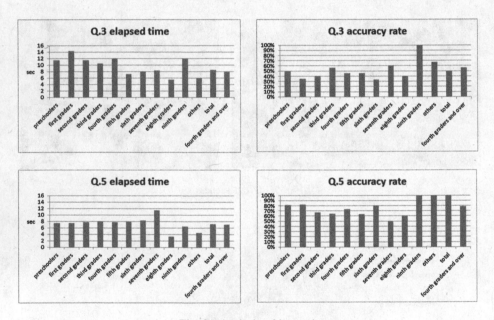

Fig. 9. Analysis of last quiz

The figure shows analytical results for the final review quiz in Chapter 5-2. Note that this is the last chapter in the course, and thus is a review quiz of all the questions covered by the course in order to consolidate the information in memory. The figure reveals answer times and accuracy rates for Questions 3 and 5 broken out by grade in school. The vertical axes show answer times (in seconds) for graphs on the left and accuracy rates (in percentages) for graphs on the right. The horizontal axes show grades in school of the subjects. One can see that there was considerable variation in the answer times and rather poor accuracy rates for Question 3 shown at the top. On the other hand, there was much less variation in the answer times and better accuracy for Question 5 shown at the bottom. We think that Question 5 was an appropriate review question, but since log functions were taken for all questions asked, we should be able to enhance the quality of the question over the course of repeated events.

4 Conclusions and Future Work

This work describes the development of *AR Rally*, a disaster medicine educational application tool that runs on tablet computers. Use of the tablet permits students to learn by doing as they move around, and also exploits a number of features that create interest in students and also helps them remember emergency medicine procedures. Some of these key features include explanation through games, quizzes based on augmented reality (AR) functions, and memory retention through repeated finger movements and gestures on the screen.

Up to now, the prototype system has been demonstrated at two public events—one event held over four days at a shopping center and the other event conducted during a one-day open house at AIST Labs—but more events are planned. The course content will be further enhanced and refined during three forthcoming events (a total of ten additional hands-on trial days) at science and technology museums and other venues.

It is not so much the end users as the sponsors and promoters of the demonstration events that will promote the widespread use of *AR Rally*. We will certainly do our part by making the software widely available for download so it can be used to disseminate disaster medical knowledge in science museums and in population centers from villages to major cities.

Acknowledgments. This study was partially carried out under the project, "Research and Development on Urban Disaster Reduction Communities based on Scientific analyses of Disaster Medicine and Rescue Training," under the R&D focus area, "Creation of Safe and Secure Cities and Regions Connected by Communities", of the JST Research Institute of Science and Technology for Society (RISTEX). The authors are grateful to the many supportive people and organizations for the cooperation.

References

1. Yoda, I., et al.: Critical review of Japanese disaster medical education for citizens: exploring the method of medutainment. J. Disaster Res. **10**, 919–928 (2015)
2. Ohta, S., et al.: Sustainable training-model development based on analysis of disaster medicine training. J. Disaster Res. **10**(5), 919–928 (2015)
3. Ohasi, Y., et al.: "Proposal of edutainment environment using a mobile phone in an aquarium," Information Processing Society of Japan Research Report, Entertainment Computing (EC), vol. 2008-EC-011, pp. 19–22, December 2008 (in Japanese)
4. Yatani, K., et al.: "Musex: a system for supporting children's collaborative learning in museum with PDAs," Information Processing Society of Japan Research Report, HI, Human Interface Study Group Report, no. 101, pp. 9–16, November 2002 (in Japanese)
5. Unity home page. http://unity3d.com/

VAMR in Industry, Design and Engineering

Interactive VR-based Visualization for Material Flow Simulations

Jan Berssenbrügge[1(✉)], Jörg Stöcklein[1], and Daniel Köchling[2]

[1] Fraunhofer Research Institution for Mechatronic Systems Design IEM, Paderborn, Germany
{jan.berssenbruegge,joerg.stoecklein}@iem.fraunhofer.de
[2] Heinz Nixdorf Institute, University of Paderborn, Paderborn, Germany
daniel.koechling@hni.upb.de

Abstract. The conventional way of visualizing the material flow in a production system is to use simulation tools and their integrated symbols and pictograms. By going this way, the reference to the real production system is very limited since conventional material flow models provide only an abstract view and are not very comprehensive for the user. This paper introduces a procedure which enables a Virtual Design Review of the planned process layout on a large-screen visualization facility. This enables production planners to conduct a virtual inspection of alternative concepts for a planned production system including the visualized material flow. As a result, planning certainty and system comprehension of all parties involved increase significantly, so that the presented procedure serves as a valuable decision support. This paper describes the steps to be taken from production data to an optimized material flow being verified by a Virtual Design Review.

Keywords: Virtual Design Review · Virtual Reality · Material flow optimization

1 Introduction

Future approaches for improving production systems have to consider a holistic view of production to avoid an isolated optimization of subsections at the expense of the overall system. To manage the resulting complexity in the analysis of all dependencies in manufacturing, computer-aided methods in simulation and visualization are suitable [1, 2]. These methods allow detecting weaknesses and bottlenecks without impairing the real production processes. Especially at the material flow simulation, a conflict arises inevitably between the need for models being as realistic as possible on the one hand, while not unnecessarily being too complex on the other hand, in order to keep the amount of required work for model preparation reasonable [3]. To resolve this conflict, useful assumptions have to be made, which simplify the models but do not weaken their significance [4]. The same applies to the visualization of procedures and facilities, which should be designed merely as realistically as necessary so that the user comprehension improvement is in adequate proportion to the modelling effort [5].

After developing a simulation-capable model, which is as close to reality as required, the simulation results must first be processed to allow an interpretation. Usually, this is

S. Lackey and R. Shumaker (Eds.): VAMR 2016, LNCS 9740, pp. 587–596, 2016.
DOI: 10.1007/978-3-319-39907-2_56

realized by selecting data, for example by analysing workload-diagrams and hence identifying possible bottlenecks. The data is normally aggregated to indexes and parameters using methods of statistics [6]. Furthermore, the processing of data includes a representation, which is suitable for interpretation, in order to provide a problem-specific and targeted decision support for the user. Here, one particular challenge is to provide simulation parameters and highly aggregated results for the user in a way that the user is not overburdened and the relevant results remain obvious. Thus, it is appropriate to merge the abstracted results from the material flow simulation by means of the established visualization methods based on the technology Virtual Reality (VR) with the aim to increase system comprehension of both, planners and decision makers.

Conventional simulation tools visualize the material flow simulation results based on 2D symbols, pictograms, and plausible 3D representations. This paper introduces a procedure, which enables users from the process layout planning to discuss questions concerning the planned layout (placement of machines, design of storage area, etc.) of a production system in the course of a Virtual Design Review of the layout on a large-screen visualization facility. For this purpose, an interactive visualization of the layout is provided for Virtual Design Review sessions. The interactive visualization of the layout illustrates the spatial localization of the flow of materials at a complex 3D model of a production system and facilitates the understanding of the complex dependencies. The procedure supports the assessment of different material flow concepts and consequently plays a part in contributing to increase planning certainty significantly.

In this paper, we focus on combining the material flow simulation with a 3D visualization in order to facilitate comprehension of the complex flow of materials. This requires building a 3D model of the production system and an interface for connecting the visualization system with the material flow simulation. In the following, we next describe the overall procedure for integrating VR-based visualizations into material flow simulations in Sect. 2, before we address specific aspects of the model acquisition in Sect. 3 and the design of the interface between the material flow simulation and the 3D visualization in Sect. 4, as well as, some implementation aspects in Sect. 5, respectively.

2   From Production Data to Virtual Design Review

To create an interactive visualization of the production layout, a lot of information is required. On the one hand, the dimensions of the production area, the machines and the material flow system are needed. On the other hand, data of the products, e.g. processing steps and time and required transport needs to be given. Figure 1 gives a rough overview of the processing of all this information and what basic elements are involved. The OMEGA model [7] serves as a detailed and transparent representation of the production processes. From there, the information is transferred to the material flow model in the tool *Plant Simulation* [8]. This material flow model maps the production processes in the form of executable code. The third element is the Virtual Design Review, which creates the three-dimensional illustration of the material flow model. This process comprises a few more sub steps, which are described in the following in some more detail.

Fig. 1. From production data to a Virtual Design Review

Data Collection of Existing Production: The reference system data is put together and analyzed. It is advisable to select representative product variants and map them in the form of OMEGA process models. These models have to include all information, which is required for the material flow model and the Virtual Design Review. Thus, they serve as an important basis for the interactive visualization. The OMEGA models are based on large amounts of production data, for example transaction data, stock quantities, product keys, etc. The data is transferred to the model in expert discussions and simultaneously translated to the material flow model. This process includes several cyclic repetitions so that the level of detail of the OMEGA model and the material flow model grows gradually. An advantage of this procedure is that changes and extensions can easily be added.

For the visualization of the material flow simulation, the production machines have to be modelled, but usually CAD data of the machines, a company applies, are not available. One solution for this problem is to use a 3D scanner to digitize all important parts and machinery of the production system. This method leads to a 3D model of the entire production system within a reasonable amount of time. The result of this phase is a database for the modeling and simulation of the material flow regarding the current situation.

Modeling and Simulation of an Existing Production System: By means of the coordinated database it is possible to build up a simulation model of the current production system, for example with the software tool *Plant Simulation*. First, this includes the modularization of the production resources and then, with the help of components from the Plant Simulation library, their creation and parameterization. Additionally, mobile objects like workers, forklifts, semi-finished and finished products are integrated. Finally, the production control is implemented and optimization potentials are identified.

Development of Alternative Concepts for the Production System: On the basis of the optimization potentials, different concepts of material flow optimization are developed. The concepts could for example be oriented towards principles like KANBAN or Just-in-Time. Based on the material flow model of the current situation they are created in the form of Plant Simulation models.

Evaluation of the Alternative Concepts: In accordance with the simulation results, the concept with the best outcome concerning economical and technical criteria is selected. This concept is the input data for the visualization in VR.

Virtual Design Review: Then, a VR model of the production system has to be built to illustrate the favored concept. While the material flow is implemented and simulated in Plant Simulation, the representation should happen in a visualization- or game-engine like *Unity3D* [9]. To achieve a collaboration between two different platforms, a synchronization of Plant Simulation and Unity3D is required. This synchronization is realized via a small interface, which transfers only a minimum of crucial high-level data from the material flow simulation to the interactive visualization. This is feasible by shifting parts of the application intelligence from the material flow simulation to the interactive visualization. That way, a lot of interface transfer traffic can be avoided. Thus, more complex simulation models can be connected and simulated in real time.

Virtual Inspection: Finally, the connection of the material flow simulation to the VR visualization can be presented in the course of a virtual inspection. Thereby, the advantages of the collaboration between material flow simulation and VR visualization become apparent. For example, the recognition value for the employees is higher and it is possible to identify problems which occur because of structural obstacles and which cannot be captured in Plant Simulation.

Figure 2 shows, which elements participate in the simulation environment and how the data is transferred between the different elements. While the data analysis and implementation in Plant Simulation has to be accomplished to a high extent manually, the synchronization needs to work automatically and fast to achieve a high-performance real time visualization. In respect to such a high-performance visualization, the

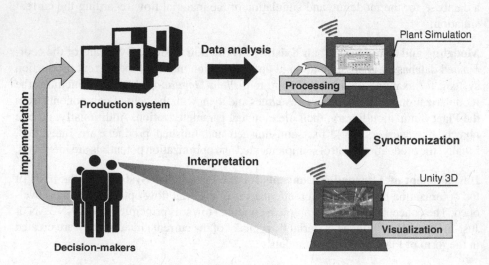

Fig. 2. Procedure of the simulation environment

subsequent sections describe in detail an easy and simple model acquisition, as well as, the communication interface between the material flow model and the Virtual Design Review.

3   Model Acquisition

A problem, that occurs when building up a complete factory floor, is to prepare a suitable 3D model of the production system and its components. Usually, CAD data of the production machines, a company applies, are not available. If CAD data exists, the CAD models are usually way too detailed to be used in an interactive virtual environment with an acceptable performance. In addition, optimizing high-polygon meshes is far too complex for achieving a reasonable result. But then, remodelling all machines as a low-polygon model suitable for interactive frame rates by hand is a time-consuming and cost-intensive task. One solution for this problem is to use a 3D scanner. In our case, a tablet-based 3D scanner was used to digitize all important machinery and components of the production system. Since the applied 3D scanner not only scans the 3D geometry but also generates a decent texturing of the model, the scanned production machines are suitable for an interactive visualization. With this method, we capture most of the machines of a specific production system within one day and place them inside a basic 3D model of the factory floor leading to a suitable 3D model of the entire production system (see Fig. 3).

Fig. 3. Scanned 3D model of a production machine (left) and scanned 3D models placed on a factory floor of a production system suitable for an interactive visualization.

Due to the nature of the scanning process, the scanned 3D-models of the production machines and facilities are geometrically not as exact as the corresponding CAD-models. But this was not crucial in our application context. The scanned 3D-models solely support the spatial orientation and localization of the material flow within the production facility and have no further function. In particular, the scanned 3D-models are not animated, in order to illustrate further details of the material flow. Since they merely make up the setting of the production facility their limited geometrical quality is sufficient in this application context.

4   Interfacing Material Flow Simulation and 3D Visualization

Material flow simulation is a typical example for a discrete event based simulation. That means, the simulation model is updated in discrete time steps. Typical data, which is updated in each time step is, e.g., actual position, attributes and states of production machines, material, devices, and workers, etc. If we want to visualize the simulation model in an external application outside of the material flow simulation system, we need to update our visualization with all the data from the material flow simulation model at every single time step. With complex simulation models and small time steps this leads to high data traffic on the network connection between the material flow simulation system and the visualization system. This is especially a problem when both systems run on different computers, which are connected via a network with limited bandwidth.

In general, material flow simulation, e.g. within the tool Plant Simulation, provides just an abstract model of the flow of materials, which is not illustrative and easy-to-understand by the user. The abstract model of the production system only provides a spatially idealized placement of the individual components of the production system. The pathways of the material between individual production components and machines are just modeled in an idealized way. Details within the material flow can only be modeled roughly, e.g. the time material needs to be transported along a path between production machines is specified by a single time value representing the necessary time for the material to be transported between two production machines.

Material flow simulation can simulate complex production processes over a long time period, in order to demonstrate a buffer workload over time. But this leads to large simulation time steps, which results in a material flow simulation being too fast to be illustrative and comprehensive for the user. Often, there is a need for parts of a material flow simulation to be visualized in real time, e.g. transportation processes along defined pathways, in order to be illustrative and comprehensive for the user.

In contrast to material flow models, a 3D model of the production system contains exact geometric properties of each component and its localization and thus provides spatially exact information about the pathways of the material flow within the production system. That way, it is more suitable to illustrate and visualize the material flow in a graphical and comprehensive way. The intrinsic geometric properties of a 3D model facilitate a more exact representation of the actual pathways of the material flow and thus a more exact simulation.

Furthermore, a 3D visualization system is also capable of simulating the real time aspects of a material flow simulation in more detail and thus more precise. E.g., in a 3D visualization system, a forklift transporting material between production machines on the before mentioned pathways, can be simulated with its real acceleration and speed profile instead of a single constant time value. This allows to model the real motion times of a forklift or human workers as part of a production system more precisely.

In the 3D visualization, the forklift motion can be modeled based on a physics model, which considers collisions between objects, such as a forklift and infrastructure or material. That way, we were able to model congestions due to geometric bottle necks, which occur e.g. when material is stored on an aisle or near doorways, due to storage space overflow at a production machine. By this, transport pathways can dynamically change or be closed over time, due to congestion etc., which facilitates a dynamic routing the material flow. All these aspects cannot be modeled in detail in a conventional material flow model.

5   Implementation of the Synchronization Interface

In order to utilizes the best of both worlds and to provide a graphical visualization, which is more intuitive and comprehensive, we connected the material flow simulation from Plant Simulation with a corresponding 3D visualization in Unity3D via an interface for data exchange. Both models run asynchronously and are synchronized only via a few synchronization points.

The material flow simulation provides simulation data over long time periods of production resulting into a rather abstracted or high-level overview of the whole process, while the 3D visualization simulates and illustrates single small time periods in real time, i.e. especially transportation processes, which are sparsely distributed over the complete simulation time period.

For these real time transportation processes, which are triggered by a synchronization event, the simulation is handed over from the material flow simulation to the 3D visualization. The 3D visualization enhances the material flow simulation by providing a more detailed simulation of the transportation action, based on a physics- and collision-based simulation and a geometric 3D-model covering the geometrical aspects of the actual routing of the transportation pathways. When the transportation simulation is finished, a synchronization event again triggers to hand back the results from the 3D visualization to the material flow simulation as feedback. That way, variable transportation times of forklifts due to changing pathways, which are based on a detailed motion simulation, are considered in the material flow simulation, instead of roughly estimated, constant time values.

For a better handling of the combined simulation, a fast-forward and a real-time mode were implemented. The material flow simulation basically covers long production time periods in fast forward mode, while the 3D visualization covers the actual transportation processes based on a physics simulation in real time mode, in order to enhance comprehension and a graphical illustration. The fast-forward mode demonstrated, how buffer workloads develop over longer production time periods, while the real-time mode illustrated real-time transportation processes, that are only fully comprehensible when shown in real-time. The switching between these two modes is done automatically via discrete synchronization events.

In a conventional material flow simulation a huge amount of data is generated while running. Sending all this information to the external visualization would cause flooding the interface, especially when running both programs on different computers. However, to be able to run both synchronously, we had to shift parts of the material flow simulation logic, such as routing via defined pathways, from the material flow simulation to the interactive visualization. Most of the data generated by the material flow simulation is updating the actual position of materials and workers. However, this information can be generated in the 3D visualization, since we know the start and destination and actual pathways of materials and workers due to the geometric 3D-model of the production system. Furthermore, we are also able to simulate collision avoidance for workers and a realistic walking speed within the 3D visualization, which is not considered by the material flow simulation at all.

Hence, the interface between the material flow simulation and the visualization only includes a few high-level commands, such as e.g. sending a signal from the material flow simulation to the visualization in order to trigger a motion and for sending a signal back from the 3D visualization back to the material flow when the destination is reached. That way, a lot of interface transfer traffic can be avoided and more complex simulation models can be connected and controlled in real time.

The technical implementation of the synchronization is as follows. For the communication with other programs, Plant Simulation provides a so-called socket module, which can operate as a host or a client. The communication interface consists of a subnetwork including 10 methods, the sockets 'receiver' and 'sender' and different tables. The elements are separated into four different application areas. The first area is the initialization and contains four methods to read information about the stationary and mobile entities and to initialize them. In the second area, named control, there are four methods, which direct the mobile entities and tell, if a part is ready for collection at a stationary entity. The third area is named communication and has two methods for receiving and sending messages. Furthermore, it contains the sockets receiver and sender and is responsible for the communication between Plant Simulation and Unity3D. The last area is called information and contains two tables, in which data about the entities is stored. The procedure of the synchronization using the described interface is as follows.

At the beginning, the initialization is executed. It sends the ID and x- and y-position of all existing stationary entities (e.g. machines) from Plant Simulation to the 3D visualization in Unity3D. In the 3D visualization the stationary entries are then instantiated and placed according to the submitted location. Additionally, the mobile entities (e.g. workers) with their ID and type are transferred. In the 3D visualization all mobile entries are placed inside their defined rest area waiting for incoming tasks. Beyond that, it is possible to add or remove both stationary and mobile entities to Plant Simulation during the simulation so that they can be sent to the 3D visualization, which then expands or reduces the already existing entities dynamically. During the simulation the 3D visualization is informed of what mobile entity should move from a starting entity to a destination entity. After the dispatch of this information, the mobile entity is unavailable for the simulation until the 3D visualization communicates, that the entity has reached its destination. When receiving such a motion command the 3D visualization sends a mobile entity from the actual position to the desired destination. The mobile entity then walks (if it is a worker) or drives (if it is a forklift) to that destination using a path finding algorithm, which takes the actual route situation into account. For example, if a path is dynamically blocked by some material, the mobile entity will take an alternative route to the destination. Also, if two mobile entities cross its paths, both try to avoid a collision, e.g. by an evasion maneuver or by waiting for the other to pass by. When reaching the destination, the 3D visualization informs Plant Simulation, which then unblocks the mobile entity in the material flow simulation.

Technically, the interface between Plant Simulation and Unity3D is realized using a UDP sender and receiver on both sides. Using the network device for communication allows the material flow simulation and the 3D visualization to run on different hardware. Based on the Open Sound Control (OSC) protocol [10], a set of communication commands was defined and implemented on both sides. The advantage of using OSC as protocol is that it is well defined, human readable and straightforward expandable, so that realizing new commands extending the protocol is very easy. Another advantage, especially while developing the communication protocol, is the use of already existing OSC tools (e.g. Line Lemur, Touch OSC, etc.), which enable the simulation of the communication counterpart.

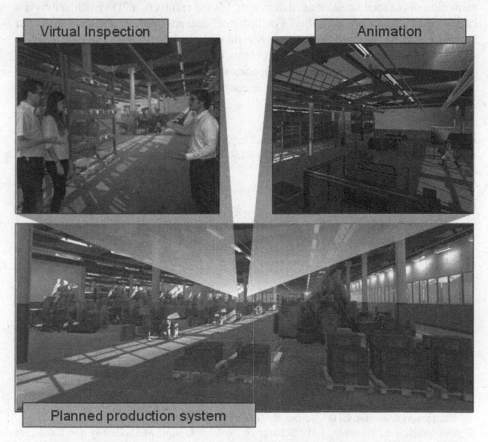

Fig. 4. Process planers utilizing an illustrative 3D visualization of the material flow within a planned production system during a virtual inspection at a large screen visualization facility.

6   Conclusion

The main goal of the proposed approach in this paper is to optimize the material flow of a production system. It extends the standard approach of material flow optimization with interactive, VR-based 3D visualizations of the optimized concepts. To realize this, a 6-stage approach was introduced. The new approach is based on applying a conventional material flow simulation system in combination with an VR-based 3D visualization, in order to facilitate system comprehension via an illustrative visualization of the material flow within the production system. For this, a synchronization interface between the material flow simulation and the 3D visualization was introduced.

The advantages of enhancing the simulation with visualization are obvious. Figure 4 shows an application scenario of a joint virtual inspection, where production system planers and decision makers inspect alternative material flow concepts for a production system based on an illustrative 3D visualization. The approach facilitates the animation of planned situations and demonstrates the results as a 3D visualization on a large screen visualization facility. For instance, the approach enables to obtain an impression of the planned production system without impairing the real production processes. Thus, it is easier to detect problems that may occur because of the planned changeover. The developed procedure supports the assessment of different material flow concepts and consequently plays a part in contributing to increase planning certainty significantly.

Acknowledgments. This work was supported in part by the Leading-Edge Cluster 'Intelligent Technical Systems OstWestfalenLippe (it's OWL)' and was funded by the Federal Ministry of Education and Research (BMBF).

References

1. Verein Deutscher Ingenieure (VDI): Digitale Fabrik – Grundlagen. VDI-Richtlinie 4499, Beuth-Verlag, Berlin (2006)
2. Bracht, U., Gecker, D., Wenzel, S.: Digitale Fabrik: Methoden und Praxisbeispiele. Springer, Heidelberg (2011)
3. Verein Deutscher Ingenieure (VDI): Simulation von Logistik-, Materialfluss- und Produktionssystemen – Grundlagen. VDI-Richtlinie 3633, Beuth-Verlag, Berlin (2010)
4. Bangasow, B.: Praxishandbuch Plant Simulation und SimTalk. Hanser-Verlag, München (2011)
5. Engelhardt-Nowitzki, C., Nowitzki, O., Krenn, B.: Praktische Anwendung der Simulation im Materialflussmanagement: Erfolgsfaktoren und Implementierungsszenarien. Gabler-Verlag, Wiesbaden (2008)
6. Schenk, M.: Digital Engineering – Herausforderungen für die Arbeits- und Betriebsorganisation. GITO-Verlag, Berlin (2009)
7. Gausemeier, J., Rammig, F.-J., Schäfer, W. (eds.): Design Methodology for Intelligent Technical Systems - Develop Intelligent Technical Systems of the Future. Springer, Heidelberg (2014)
8. Plant Simulation, Siemens PLM Software. http://www.plm.automation.siemens.com/en_us/products/tecnomatix/manufacturing-simulation/material-flow/plant-simulation.shtm
9. Unity3D Game Engine, Unity. http://unity3d.com
10. Open Sound Control. http://opensoundcontrol.org

Low-Cost Mixed Reality Simulator for Industrial Vehicle Environments

Daniel Kade[1][(✉)], Markus Wallmyr[1], Tobias Holstein[1,3], Rikard Lindell[1],
Hakan Ürey[2], and Oğuzhan Özcan[2]

[1] Mälardalen University, Västerås, Sweden
{daniel.kade,markus.wallmyr,tobias.holstein,rikard.lindell}@mdh.se
[2] Koç University, Istanbul, Turkey
{hurey,oozcan}@ku.edu.tr
[3] University of Applied Sciences, Darmstadt, Germany

Abstract. High-end industrial vehicle simulators are generally expensive and aim at providing a high level of realism. The access to such simulators is often a limited resource to researchers and developers who find themselves using a PC-based simulator instead. We challenge this approach by introducing a low-cost mixed reality simulator for industrial vehicles that allows to test new vehicle control concepts and design ideas in a rapid prototyping manner. Our simulator prototype consists of a head-mounted projection display, a CAVE-like room covered with a retro-reflective cloth and a rotatable chair with controls to steer an industrial vehicle. The created digital environment represents an obstacle course for an excavator and can be controlled by a joystick, a keyboard and can be explored by natural head movements.

Performed user tests with 21 participants showed that the mixed reality simulator is perceived as more realistic, natural to use and provides a more immersive experience than a PC-based simulator with the same environment and controls.

Keywords: Industrial vehicle simulator · Mixed reality · Head-mounted projection display

1 Introduction

Simulators, providing a virtual environment to users are nowadays available in different varieties and range from low-cost gaming simulators to highly realistic vehicle or industry simulators, such as professional car or flight simulators. Many development teams or researcher do not have access to high-end simulators. This might not be needed or cannot be afforded in many cases. Nonetheless, we argue that only using simple PC-based simulators might limit options for research, design and development teams when testing new concepts and ideas for industrial vehicles.

Generally, simulators provide advantages in terms of reproducibility, standardization and controllability of scenarios and tests. A simulator replicates

S. Lackey and R. Shumaker (Eds.): VAMR 2016, LNCS 9740, pp. 597–608, 2016.
DOI: 10.1007/978-3-319-39907-2_57

scenarios that might be difficult, expensive or even risky to reproduce in reality, such as a dangerous driving scenarios, where a driver would be physically at risk. Furthermore, it allows controlled simulation environments that are not affected by wind, weather and other external circumstances [7]. Additionally, the use of simulators and interactions with them can be evaluated without placing humans or physical objects in a real environment or before the real environment is ready, for example when evaluating improved operator environments.

These facts would argue for using a simulator in test and design scenarios. However, despite the progress in hardware and software used for simulators, there are still limitations. Industrial simulators are usually built with computer monitors or projection solutions that can be space consuming, require long setup times and pose high costs. Therefore, initial experiments, user evaluations or even trainings are often performed on simpler simulators. Fully featured simulation environments are used in later stages of a project, when previous stages indicated positive results. This limitation and way of working results in increased costs as well as it limits early evaluation of interaction with the technology or interface.

Another alternative when making the simulation is to use virtual reality (VR) glasses, which provide the ability to create an immersive virtual reality. Simulating a virtual environment in which the user can naturally look around by moving the head to interact with the virtual environment can be important in many scenarios, such as the simulation of complex industrial vehicles (cranes, excavators, fork lifts, etc.) or even normal driving scenarios (e.g. overtaking, parking, etc.) [13,16]. A mayor limitation with virtual reality is when physical artefacts like sliders, knobs and interior design of a real world prototype have to be used while performing in the virtual environment, e.g. mixed reality.

This paper introduces a low-cost mixed reality simulator that challenges many of the above-mentioned constraints. Our solution is easy to install, low-cost, consists of off-the-self hardware and a virtual environment that was created with the Unity game engine. In our prototype, we create a mixed reality environment while using physical controls and a projected virtual scenery. Our technology can be used in small setups where virtual windows or screens are in front of a user or to create larger CAVE-like simulations.

Furthermore, we evaluated if our mixed reality simulator provides the basic ability to be used in a scenario such as for industrial vehicles. Therefore, we created an industrial vehicle simulator resembling the physical controls and virtual representation of an excavator on a virtual obstacle course. In such environments it is of higher importance, compared to ordinary on-road cars, to be able to look up and down and to see the environment around the vehicle. In our simulator, users can explore the virtual environment freely by naturally moving their head in a CAVE-like setup.

The contribution of this paper is a low cost mixed reality simulator that can be used for testing and designing human machine interface (HMI) applications, such as evaluating new concepts to interact with vehicles, for education or for user training with industrial vehicles.

2   Related Work

Simulators have been used in many vehicle research areas to evaluate user behavior and HMIs as well as for education. These can range from specific replica simulators costing hundreds of thousands euros [24] to low cost simulators [3] and desk simulators [23]. The development of 3D engines with physics simulation and collision detection, as well as easy to use editors, also make it possible to build custom simulators [6]. For many purposes a more light weight simulator is sufficient, "as our ability to fill in the gaps to create strong cognitive representations has clear potential as an alternative to modeling every last detail of the space" [28]. In an on-road driving simulation, for example, it may be enough to look at a PC monitor to display the simulated environment in front of a car and to use a gaming steering wheel as input device. However this approach offers a very limited field-of-view (FOV), limiting simulations where operators need to move their head or body. This is especially a problem when interactions need to be tested that require to see the surrounding environment.

The interest to build virtual and mixed reality display systems [5, 25, 26] has increased, as new products are introduced to the market. Most of the see-through products offer a near-eye solution with a limited field of view, a constant focus, single eye usage (no stereoscopy), and limited depth of field. Many near-eye solutions come with a great deal of optical complexity in design, e.g., Google Glass [22], or Microsoft's HoloLens [19]. In [10] an additional specially made contact lens needs to be used to see the content. Thus, the users are having the challenge of interacting naturally with the physical world due to these optical limitations.

By disconnecting the user from the real world, the mentioned limitations are avoided. This is achieved via opaque wearable stereoscopic head-worn displays, e.g., Oculus Rift [8], also known as virtual reality glasses. Nonetheless, the challenge for real-life use cases remains the same or is even higher, as real world content now must be replicated into the virtual world [18].

While simulators are a great tool for assessing different scenarios and measuring driving performances, participants often face the problem of suffering from motion sickness [7]. This observation has been made in various research areas, including vehicle simulators [13] and flight simulators [17]. Motion sickness appears in mixed-reality and VR simulations respectively. Research showed, that the time spent in a simulator affects the likelihood of simulator sickness and that older participants have a greater likelihood of simulator sickness than younger participants [4]. However, participants react differently to simulation environments. Therefore, we found it important to get an indication on how our simulator behaves in this respect.

The use of laser scanning pico-projectors offers an interesting alternative, as these do not require any optical components to focus on the projection surface and the amount of pixels displayed stays constant with the increasing distance between the projector and the screen. Additionally, it comes with a coin size light engine [9] with further possibilities for miniaturization, thus making it even more wearable. The image qualities as well as the use of reflective material has been investigated before [2,12]. Image projections can also be made onto non-reflective surfaces [20,21]. However, in our setup we use a reflective material as this enables to mix physical controls with the virtual scenery without distortion and in different lighting conditions.

Wearable laser projectors, as we use it in our research, were used by Harrison et al. before [11]. They used a shoulder mounted projector combined with a depth camera to project images to non-reflective surfaces and to allow gestural interactions. In our approach we have further developed the idea of using a laser projector as a head-mounted mixed-reality device using a retro-reflective surface as screen. This technology was used before for motion capture acting support applications and for gaming tests [1,15]. Unlike other systems like e.g. from CastAR [14] or other research [27] this system does not require multiple projectors. Thus, problems originated from using multiple projectors such as the keystone or image registration effect are not an issue in our system.

3 Simulator Setup

The goal with our research was to build a low-cost simulator that allows to test new control concepts and design ideas in a fast and prototypical way. Therefore, it was of importance for us that the real and virtual world can be controlled and seen at the same time. We built a mixed reality simulator that allows to steer an excavator over an obstacle course by using a conventional joystick and wireless keyboard. Our mixed reality simulator setup consists of a head-mounted projection display, a room coated with a reflective cloth, input controllers mounted on a chair and software to drive and display the simulation.

3.1 Head-Worn Projection Display

Our head-worn projection display system, as shown in Fig. 1 consists of several off-the-shelf hardware: (1) a stripped-down laser pico projector, SHOWWX+ from Microvision, Inc., with external battery pack (2) a Samsung S4+ smartphone, (3) retro-reflective cloth covering the walls of our simulator room (can be seen Fig. 2), and (4) a headband with 3D printed housing holding the equipment.

A pico projector acts as a light engine in our head-mounted projection display. This has the ability that users who are wearing the prototype do not suffer from any key distortion effect, even when the reflective cloth used as a screen is distorted or not perfectly flat. This enables for a faster screen or CAVE-like setup by still allowing a clear and distortion free image. This lies in the optical abilities of the laser projector. The maximum native resolution of the projector is $848px \times 480px$ @60 Hz $vsync$ in size by a light emission of 15 lumen. To increase the image size, we attached a 180° fisheye lens which allows for a field of view of roughly 83.6° x 47.5°.

For our mixed reality application, we used the gyroscope sensor of the smartphone to look around in the digital environment and connected the pico projector through a MHL adapter to the smartphone. The overall system, has an expected uptime of 3 – 4 h.

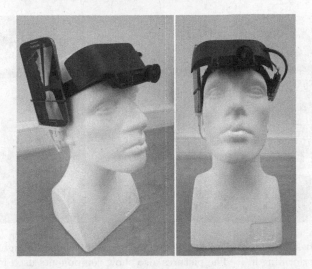

Fig. 1. Picture showing the head-mounted projection display including a smartphone, laser projector with battery pack and 3D printed housing

3.2 Projection Room

The simulator room was coated with a high-gain retro-reflective cloth no. 6101 from RB Reflektör. The cloth is used to reflect the projected light back to the source and has a high light gain. This effect allows users standing close to the projector to basically see a very bright image. We placed the reflective cloth in a 4×3 m room with a height of 3 m and also covered the floor in front and around the user. In this room we placed a rotatable chair and mounted a joystick and bluetooth keyboard on the chair. The setup of the room and the chair can be seen in Fig. 2.

3.3 Architecture and Software Description

Figure 3 provides a general overview of the technical components and the implemented architecture of our industrial simulator setup. The smartphone holds the digital simulator environment, developed in the Unity game engine version 5.2.3. The built-in gyroscope sensor of the smartphone is used to be able to look around in the digital environment with natural head movements. Moreover, we use the smartphone as a connection hub for the input devices and as a computation unit to show the digital environment through the connected projector. As joystick we used a Thrustmaster T.16000M which is connected to an Intel Compute Stick that runs a self-developed program converting joystick events into an XML format which is then sent via WIFI to the smartphone. Keyboard inputs were sent via Bluetooth to the smartphone. This data was thereafter used in the Unity engine to control the virtual environment.

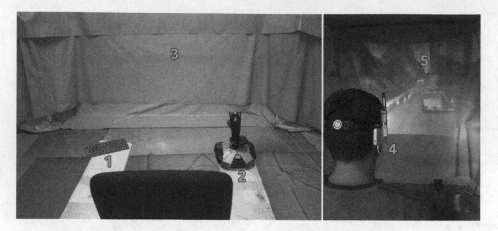

Fig. 2. The left-side picture depicts the simulator room while the right-side picture shows a user performing in it. The pictures also show components used for the simulator: 1. Bluetooth keyboard, 2. Joystick, 3. Reflective cloth, 4. Head-mounted projector, 5. Simulation projected to the screen

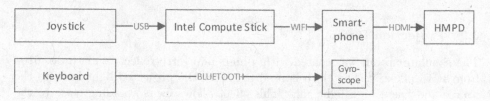

Fig. 3. Architecture overview of the mixed reality simulator

4   Functionality Test

For our informal functionality tests and to get a first impression from users about our industrial simulator, we conducted a test with 21 users (4 female and 17 male). Three testers were in the range of 20–25 years, 9 users were in the range of 26–35 and 9 were over 35 years old. Only one user had driven an excavator before; 8 testers have not experienced a wearable projector or display before and 13 tried it before. Moreover, 8 out of 21 users tried a vehicle or industrial simulator before.

To evaluate, if our mixed reality prototype could be useful as a simulator, we also built a PC-based simulator that held the same digital environment and controllers (joystick and keyboard). Figure 4 shows the PC-based test setup.

The user tests were conducted on one day and each user was given an introduction to both prototypes, its functionality and a minute of time to try out the controls. Users started with the PC-based simulator and performed an obstacle course where instructions were given during the test. Thereafter, the users performed the same tasks again in the mixed-reality simulator. We chose this order so that users were able to get familiar with the controls and the tasks

Fig. 4. PC-based simulator, with Bluetooth keyboard and directly connected joystick

at hand in a more familiar PC-based simulator environment. When testing the
mixed reality simulator, users already had an understanding on how to control
the excavator and what the tasks were.

Driving the excavator was set to the W, A, S, D keys of the keyboard and
steering the rest of the excavator was performed via the joysticks axes and buttons. Moving the lower excavator arm up and down was set to the vertical axis
of the joystick, moving the turret of the excavator to the horizontal axis, moving
the upper arm was controlled by twisting or turning the joystick around the
z axis and finally two buttons on the top of the joystick controlled the bucket
movement of the excavator. These controls do not fully resemble the controls of
a real excavator. This was intentionally chosen, as new control and design ideas
can be tested with our mixed reality prototype. The combination of choosing a
keyboard and a joystick might be rather unconventional in a real vehicle but fits
to our concept of exploring new control and design concepts for heavy machinery. This might especially be interesting as users and gamers are used to such
controls. Nonetheless, we did not focus on exploring this aspect in this research
further.

An overview of the obstacle course is given in Fig. 5. The general tasks were
to drive along the track, over and through different obstacles without hitting
objects or placed traffic cones. We placed 2 cube towers on the obstacle course
where users had to look up and use the excavator to push down the top 2 cubes
of each cube tower. This task was especially meant to test the controls of the
excavator and to evaluate the difference between the two simulators. Completing
one obstacle course in a simulator took about 5 min, the whole user test for one
user took 15 min to complete.

Fig. 5. Top-down view on the digital obstacle course with colored key elements

The user tests were also videotaped as reference material and as another source of data collection to evaluate the user reactions and comfort or discomfort while using the prototype. In addition, a questionnaire was filled out by the users to help evaluating their experiences with both prototypes.

In the questionnaire we asked the users three for us essential questions: "Which of the simulators felt more realistic?", "Which of the simulators felt more immersive?" and "Which of the simulators felt more natural to use and explore?".

Figure 6 shows the results of these three questions. From the answers, we can see that for all three questions, the users are indicating that the mixed reality simulator offers a more realistic feel.

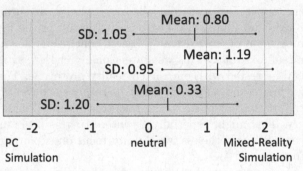

Which of the simulators ...

A) ... felt more realistic?

B) ... felt more immersive?

C) ... felt more natural to use and explore?

Fig. 6. Evaluation results for question based on immersion, realism and naturalness of use

Moreover, we asked the users if they experienced a feeling of nausea or discomfort while using the mixed reality simulator. The answers were fairly distributed and showed that 42.86 % of the users had no such feeling, 23.81 % felt a light feeling of discomfort, 4.76 % had a mild feeling of discomfort and 28.57 % perceived a clear feeling of discomfort. These results are depicted in Fig. 7. Previous research has performed user tests with a car simulator using Oculus Rift

DK2 VR glasses and tested 25 users [13]. They found that 84 % of their users felt motion sick in their tests. Our test results seem to show fewer issues with motion sickness. Nonetheless it needs to be tested with VR and even AR glasses in future research to solidify our findings.

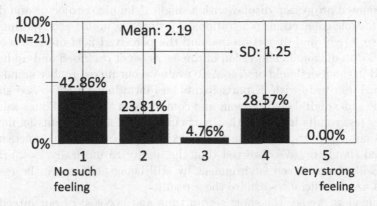

Fig. 7. Evaluation results for nausea and discomfort of the mixed reality simulator

Furthermore, we asked the user to rate their effort to complete the tasks in the two simulators. This indicated that it was slightly more difficult to complete the tasks in the mixed reality simulator, as can be seen in Fig. 8.

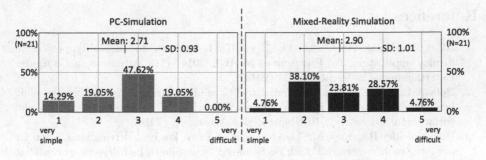

Fig. 8. Evaluation results for question based on the perceived efforts to complete the user tasks

Testing our mixed reality simulator has shown that the general perception was positive and that users showed an indication of preference towards the mixed reality simulator in comparison to a PC-based setup. During the user tests, we observed that the users were quite focused on the tasks at hand and the, for them, rather unknown way of controlling an excavator. Our mixed reality setup supported the users, as the real world controls were visible and could be touched and tested naturally.

5   Conclusion

In this paper, we have shown a low-cost mixed reality simulator for industrial vehicles. The simulator was built from off-the-self equipment and allows for flexible scenarios, e.g. CAVE-like or in-vehicle setups. Our simulator uses a head-mounted projection display with a single 15 lm pico projector and does not require a cable connection to a stationary processing unit. Perceived images are focus-free, bright and distortion-free and the perceived field-of-view is approximately 96° in diagonal. The vision of the users is not occluded and no hardware is placed in the users' field of vision. To evaluate our mixed reality simulator, we performed user tests with 21 participants and introduced a PC-based simulator using the same digital environment and controls as a baseline of our evaluations. The user test results indicated that participants had a more realistic, natural to use and immersive experience in the mixed reality simulator in contrast to the PC-based simulator. We observed that the ability to naturally look around in a CAVE-like large screen environment by still being able to see the real-world controls was beneficial to achieve these results.

In our view, we see the short set up time and low-cost of our mixed reality simulator prototype as a way to allow testing or developing prototypes and implementing design ideas for industrial vehicles or even other areas. Our tests were performed in a CAVE-like room but could even be installed inside a real vehicle cabin and combined with the controls of the vehicle. Therefore, we see our prototype as a basis for further research and a way to introduce simulators to different stages in designing and testing vehicular concepts.

References

1. Akşit, K., Kade, D., Özcan, O., Ürey, H.: Head-worn mixed reality projection display application. In: Proceedings of ACE 2014, 11th Advances in Computer Entertainment Conference. ACM (2014)
2. Bolas, M., Krum, D.M.: Augmented reality applications and user interfaces using head-coupled near-axis personal projectors with novel retroreflective props and surfaces. In: Pervasive 2010 Ubiprojection Workshop (2010)
3. Bretschneider-Hagemes, M.: Development of a new low cost driving simulation for assessing multidimensional task loads caused by mobile ICT at drivers' workplaces. – Objective-fidelity beats equipment-fidelity? In: Yamamoto, S. (ed.) Human Interface and the Management of Information. Information and Knowledge in Context. LNCS, vol. 9173, pp. 173–179. Springer, Heidelberg (2015)
4. Brooks, J.O., Goodenough, R.R., Crisler, M.C., Klein, N.D., Alley, R.L., Koon, B.L., Logan Jr., W.C., Ogle, J.H., Tyrrell, R.A., Wills, R.F.: Simulator sickness during driving simulation studies. Accid. Anal. Prev. **42**(3), 788–796 (2010). assessing Safety with Driving Simulators. http://www.sciencedirect.com/science/article/pii/S000145750900092X
5. Cakmakci, O., Rolland, J.: Head-worn displays: a review. J. Disp. Technol. **2**(3), 199–216 (2006)

6. Christodoulou, S., Michael, D., Gregoriades, A., Pampaka, M.: Design of a 3d interactive simulator for driver behavior analysis. In: Proceedings of the 2013 Summer Computer Simulation Conference, pp. 17:1–17:8, SCSC 2013, Society for Modeling & Simulation International, Vista, CA (2013). http://dl.acm.org/citation.cfm?id=2557696.2557716

7. De Winter, J., Van Leuween, P., Happee, P.: Advantages and disadvantages of driving simulators: a discussion. In: Proceedings of Measuring Behavior, pp. 47–50. Citeseer (2012)

8. Firth, N.: First wave of virtual reality games will let you live the dream. New Sci. **218**(2922), 19–20 (2013)

9. Freeman, M., Champion, M., Madhavan, S.: Scanned laser pico-projectors: seeing the big picture (with a small device). Opt. Photonics News **20**(5), 28–34 (2009)

10. Guillaumée, M., Vahdati, S.P., Tremblay, E., Mader, A., Bernasconi, G., Cadarso, V.J., Grossenbacher, J., Brugger, J., Sprague, R., Moser, C.: Curved holographic combiner for color head worn display. J. Disp. Technol. **10**(6), 444–449 (2014)

11. Harrison, C., Benko, H., Wilson, A.D.: Omnitouch: wearable multitouch interaction everywhere. In: Proceedings of the 24th Annual ACM Symposium on User Interface Software and Technology, pp. 441–450. ACM (2011)

12. Hua, H., Gao, C., Rolland, J.P.: Imaging properties of retro-reflective materials used in head-mounted projective displays (HMPDS). In: AeroSense 2002, pp. 194–201. International Society for Optics and Photonics (2002)

13. Ihemedu-Steinke, Q.C., Sirim, D., Erbach, R., Halady, P., Meixner, G.: Development and evaluation of a virtual reality driving simulator. In: Mensch und Computer 2015-Workshopband (2015)

14. Illusions, T.: Castar (2014). http://technicalillusions.com/castar/

15. Kade, D., Akşit, K., Ürey, H., Özcan, O.: Head-mounted mixed reality projection display for games production and entertainment. Pers. Ubiquitous Comput. **19**(3), 509–521 (2015)

16. Kemeny, A.: From driving simulation to virtual reality. In: Proceedings of the 2014 Virtual Reality International Conference, p. 32. ACM (2014)

17. Kolasinski, E.M.: Simulator sickness in virtual environments. Technical report, DTIC Document (1995)

18. McGill, M., Murray-Smith, R., Boland, D., Brewster, S.A.: A dose of reality: overcoming usability challenges in vr head-mounted displays. In: Proceedings of the 33rd Annual ACM Conference Extended Abstracts on Human Factors in Computing Systems, CHI EA 2015, p. 177, NY, USA (2015). http://doi.acm.org/10.1145/2702613.2732491

19. Microsoft: Hololens: a new way to see your world (2015). https://www.microsoft.com/microsoft-hololens/en-us/hardware

20. Mistry, P., Maes, P.: Sixthsense: a wearable gestural interface. In: ACM SIGGRAPH ASIA 2009 Sketches, p. 11. ACM (2009)

21. Mistry, P., Maes, P., Chang, L.: Wuw-wear ur world: a wearable gestural interface. In: Extended Abstracts on Human Factors in Computing Systems, CHI 2009, pp. 4111–4116. ACM (2009)

22. Olsson, M.I., Heinrich, M.J., Kelly, D., Lapetina, J.: Wearable device with input and output structures, 21 February 2013, US Patent 20,130,044,042

23. Politis, I., Brewster, S., Pollick, F.: Evaluating multimodal driver displays of varying urgency. In: Proceedings of the 5th International Conference on Automotive User Interfaces and Interactive Vehicular Applications, Automotive UI 2013, pp. 92–99, NY, USA (2013). http://doi.acm.org/10.1145/2516540.2516543

24. Ranta, P.: Added values of forestry machine simulator based training. In: International Conference on Multimedia and ICT Education, Linsbon, Portugal (2009)
25. Rolland, J., Thompson, K.: See-through head worn displays for mobile augmented reality. In: Proceedings of the China National Computer Conference (2011)
26. Rolland, J.P., Thompson, K.P., Urey, H., Thomas, M.: See-through head worn display (HWD) architectures. In: Chen, J., Cranton, W., Fihn, M. (eds.) Handbook of Visual Display Technology, pp. 2145–2170. Springer, Heidelberg (2012)
27. Sonoda, T., Endo, T., Kawakami, N., Tachi, S.: X'talvisor: full open type head-mounted projector. In: ACM SIGGRAPH 2005 Emerging Technologies, p. 32. ACM (2005)
28. Turner, P., Turner, S., Burrows, L.: Creating a sense of place with a deliberately constrained virtual environment, vol. 1, pp. 54–68. Inderscience Publishers, Geneva, Switzerland, May 2013. http://dx.doi.org/10.1504/IJCPS.2013.053554

Collaborative Design of Material Handling Systems Using Distributed Virtual Reality Environments

Orthodoxos Kipouridis[1]([✉]), Moritz Roidl[2], Marcus Röschinger[1], Michael ten Hompel[2], and Willibald A. Günthner[1]

[1] Institute for Materials Handling, Material Flow, Logistics, Technische Universität München, Munich, Germany
{kipouridis,roeschinger,kontakt}@fml.mw.tum.de

[2] Chair of Materials Handling and Warehousing, Technische Universität Dortmund, Dortmund, Germany
{moritz.roidl,michael.tenHompel}@tu-dortmund.de

Abstract. In order to integrate with an upcoming ecosystem of interconnected products and services, adaptive, intelligent and autonomous material handling systems (MHS) are being deployed in modern logistics facilities, enabling them to cope with requirements for high flexibility, configurability and reusability. Recent advances in virtual engineering and virtual reality (VR) technologies offer new possibilities for remote collaboration between companies regarding the design process of MHS, which involves several stakeholders. In this paper, we present a 3D collaborative virtual environment (3DCVE) as part of distributed multi-platform software for supporting MHS design tasks in logistics facilities. We describe how an in-memory data grid technology can be used for the distribution of data and the enabling of consistent user access to the virtual environment (VE). The main focus is put on the use-case of facility layout planning presenting the implementation of approaches regarding user interaction and collaboration.

Keywords: 3D collaborative virtual environments · Material handling systems design · Virtual reality

1 Introduction

Increasingly shorter product life cycles, growing product version ranges as well as more complex and global value chains pose new challenges to manufacturing and logistics. Against this background, industry and research have identified several courses of action which are often included in the frameworks of Industry 4.0 and the Industrial Internet. These aim for higher flexibility, changeability and efficiency within industrial processes. A promising approach is the introduction of intelligent, interconnected manufacturing and material handling systems (MHS) on the shop floor. Such systems -also called cyber physical systems (CPS), usually refer to embedded systems that can communicate with each other, targeting seamless integration towards an internet of things (IoT) and services. Because of their intelligent and decentralized control, CPS's are able to make

S. Lackey and R. Shumaker (Eds.): VAMR 2016, LNCS 9740, pp. 609–620, 2016.
DOI: 10.1007/978-3-319-39907-2_58

decisions autonomously and locally within a complex system and therefore increase flexibility and reactivity [1].

Enabled by advances in the fields of automation and communication, CPS's have also been introduced in materials handling. Initial industrial deployments have been brought to market as flexible conveyor belts, self-guided transport systems and autonomous, human-interacting robots [2]. Despite the advantages like high flexibility and reusability offered by these systems, their complexity, varied communication interfaces and lack of standardization have posed challenges to planning logistics facilities, particularly in the phases of system design and integration. Furthermore, the involvement of several stakeholders, such as facility and logistics planners, manufacturers of MHS's, system integrators and facility owners, complicates the planning and integration process.

We present a virtual engineering concept utilizing distributed 3DCVEs, which extends the work presented in [3] regarding a cloud-based software platform, with a view to support an integrated, effective and remote collaboration between the parties involved in the planning phase of heterogeneous MHS's. Furthermore, it is shown how planning activities, such as the plant layout design, visualization and testing of emulated and real MHS can be synchronized and collaboratively edited by different users.

This paper is structured as follows: it initially introduces virtual engineering and an overview of current approaches regarding collaborative planning of technical systems, investigating the potential of using VE's for collaboration in logistics facility planning. It then discusses the concept and its implementation details, demonstrating how an in-memory cloud-technology, primarily used for caching, can be used to enable distributed 3DCVEs. Following, we present our approach to topics like handling user interactions, transmission of data and virtual presence. Finally, it discusses the challenges and potential of the proposed concept, considering its generic aspects and portability with respect to other use cases outside the area of MHS.

2   Related Work

This chapter discusses the concepts of virtual engineering, its main methods and applications. In the second part, it provides an overview of the planning process for logistics facilities. Finally, current approaches regarding integration of virtual engineering in the planning process are presented.

2.1   Virtual and Collaborative Engineering

The term *virtual engineering* covers all information, communication, and visualization technologies that are used in a combined effort to optimize and accelerate the product development and production planning process [4, 5]. It covers three design elements, namely *concurrent*, *virtual* and *collaborative engineering*. Whereas concurrent engineering refers more to organizational aspects, enabling the parallel processing of traditionally successive design steps, in order to detect design or production problems earlier. Virtual and collaborative engineering focuses more technical concepts and are therefore subsequently described more in detail.

Virtual engineering applications incorporate computer graphics, sound, and networking to simulate the experience of real-time interaction in a shared, 3D virtual world. Virtual prototypes can be produced, reviewed and optimized in the early stages of the development process. In a multi-user environment, each user runs an interactive interface program on a client computer connected to a wide-area network (WAN). The interface program simulates the experience of immersion in a VE by rendering images and audio of the environment as perceived from the user's simulated viewpoint. Each user is represented in the shared VE by an entity rendered on every other user's computer, called an *avatar*. Multi-user interaction is supported by matching user actions to entity updates (e.g. motion and sound generation) in the shared VE.

Collaborative engineering denotes the cooperation of various actors, e.g. manufacturers, suppliers, customers and service providers in distributed networks with different IT infrastructures for development, planning and implementation projects. Most of the processes are supported by internet technologies and actors collectively work on tasks within a distributed environment. Collaborative engineering aims at the joint development of technological and competitive advantages which would not be achieved by single individuals. In order to achieve its goals, collaborative engineering requires intensive communication between partners and appropriate forms of organization to control inter-company workgroups. ICT products, and associated human resource activities, such as coaching, can be accommodated to increase the effectiveness of collaborative engineering process [6].

2.2 Collaborative Design of Material Handling Systems

There have been various methodologies proposed for planning warehouses and factories that include intelligent systems in the area of manufacturing and logistics [7, 8]. The following focuses on planning the deployment of MHS for logistics facilities.

In a typical logistics facility, a large number of software and hardware systems have to interoperate in order to accomplish tasks, such as storing, picking and transporting different goods. MHS, such as conveyors, picking systems, automated guided vehicles (AGV) and automated storage and retrieval system (AS/RS), include a large number of sensors, actuators and mechanical components as well as interfaces to software systems, like enterprise resource planning (ERP), and warehouse management systems (WMS) as shown in Fig. 1.

During the MHS design process various partners are required to work closely together in order to ensure the functionality and interoperability of the diverse system elements. In doing so, a large amount of data needs to be exchanged and reconciled, for which a variety of mediums and systems is used. Thus, the consistency and transparency of data, which are necessary for efficient and reliable decisions, can hardly be guaranteed. This inconsistency leads not only to further communication efforts, but also to additional time and monetary cost. Virtual engineering can address this need for collaboration by providing all stakeholders with suitable tools and techniques.

The design process of a heterogeneous MHS for a logistics facility is an iterative process, in which a simplified version of it is described in Fig. 2. In the preparation phase, the project stakeholders (e.g. systems manufacturers, clients and planners) are

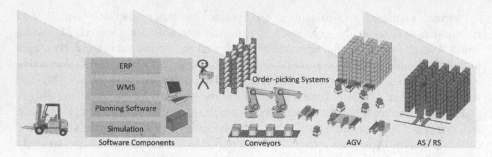

Fig. 1. Components of a modern logistics facility

responsible for generating the relevant project data, such as 3D models, interface specifications and building plans, for their respective systems, In the second step, the partners work together to create a rough general plan of the complete system under deployment. In the detailed planning phase, the communication interfaces between the systems have to be configured so that they can exchange information and interoperate. Finally, in the realization planning phase, the real systems have to be tested by executing test scenarios in order to prove their functionality, reliability and safety.

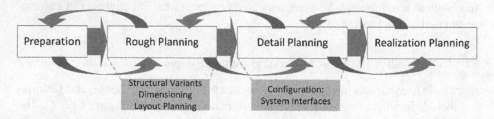

Fig. 2. Design Process of MHS (based on [9])

The concept proposed in this paper focuses on the rough planning phase, which also deals with the layout planning. With a view to create structural variants, the positions of systems are to be determined taking into consideration facility layout plans and previous installments. Current layout planning practices involve using a variety of CAD software as well as paper-printed layout plans. All these digital and non-digital plans are accessed and edited in a serial fashion by respective users, creating multiple versions of these plans. The documents are subsequently shared using conventional (e-mails) and modern methods (cloud shared folders).

2.3   Related Approaches for Collaborative Virtual Environments

In the past, various approaches and frameworks have been proposed to creating multiuser collaborative VE (such as those presented in [10, 11]), while recently, a number of single user software offerings, mostly involving CAD and product lifecycle management software (PLM), incorporate multi-user collaboration features. VR-Systems can in general be categorized as immersive (e.g. Cave Automatic Virtual Environment - CAVE), semi-immersive (Head Mounted Display - HMD) and non-immersive (displays). An extended review of the available desktop VR systems technologies is given in [12].

Following the advances in the VR, several tools have been proposed that target the integration of VR technology into the factory planning process. Examples of such efforts can be found in [13–15]. However, these approaches aim at factory planning processes, which, despite similarities with logistics facilities, do not specifically target heterogeneous MHS planning.

There is a number of challenges that are common to collaborative software engineering. Namely, following issues have been identified as most commonly occurring in collaborative software engineering tasks and should be avoided by newly developed engineering processes [16]:

• Storing information in different systems and at different locations
• Using different or incompatible formats of planning related files
• Lack of knowledge sharing mechanisms
• Parallel processing of different document versions.

With a view to address these challenges for the use case of supporting an enterprise-wide planning and realization of MHS, a multi-user distributed 3DCVE is presented in the following section.

3   Approach for a Multi-user, Distributed 3DCVE

As highlighted in the previous chapter, the design of modern MHS is a rather complex task that requires a high level of cooperation and awareness from every partner involved in the planning project.

With a goal to address the need for an effective, remote collaboration between stakeholders, a distributed software platform, named KoDeMat [17], has been developed. It supports designing and testing of decentralized controlled, heterogenous MHS in logistics facilities. The platform aims not only to support traditional planning processes, but also to enrich them with collaborative ones. It is based on a 3-tier, service-oriented architecture, as shown in Fig. 3, and is scalable to offer the provision of software-as-a-service according to project requirements.

In order to enable the collaboration between partners, a networking layer is required to distribute data between users. Based on the data distribution layer, the middle service-layer provides services that can support tasks in the MFS design process (e.g. interface definition, plant layout design and visualization of emulated and real systems). One of the main collaboration services of the platform is the 3DCVE. The services are made available to users through the presentation layer that includes topics such as interaction of users with other users as well as with the VE. The following paragraphs present the implementation, functionality and challenges of 3DCVE.

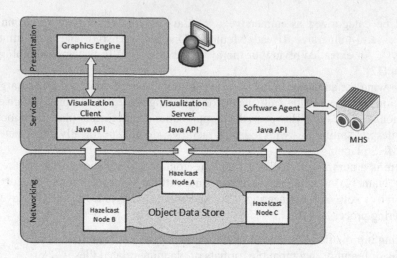

Fig. 3. Platform architecture for enabling distributed VE

3.1 Using an In-Memory Data Grid for Enabling Distributed VEs

A prerequisite to enable the synchronous collaboration of multiple remote users is the distribution of data. The proposed networking scheme is based on a concept of a data-centric, grid-based object distribution. The main idea of this concept is to deploy a NoSQL data store as a partitioned storage system that distributes data among nodes in a cluster. A similar approach of using a data-centric approach to coordinate distributed access to VE is presented in [18], though the networking layer differs from our concept as it uses a hierarchical peer-to-peer networking for the data store.

The KoDeMat platform introduces a networking scheme based on a tiered, object-sharing architecture that employs a framework for distributed computing, *Hazelcast*, which is primarily used in high-performance cloud computing. Hazelcast [19] addresses the transactional consistency as well as object serialization and duplication. Although in most cases transactional approaches are not favored for highly dynamic applications like visualization due to the increased message overhead that they introduce, this is not the case with the selected distribution technology, as it can support thousands of connected nodes with low latency. The drafted networking architecture is shown at the bottom layer of Fig. 3. A client plus member topology was selected as described in [20]. Every user in the network runs a node agent in a java virtual machine (JVM), which ensures the consistency and redundancy of the data.

In this design, users can join an ongoing session in the VE at any time. As soon as a new user joins, his client has access to the current state of objects that determine the state of the scene. The data distribution architecture ensures that all objects in the network have the same state. Similarly, if users disconnect (leave the session or crash), their data are not lost.

The process which communicates object changes to the graphics engine is executed in a separate thread (visualization server) that observes changes and updates the scene accordingly. Consequently, the proposed concept allows for cross-platform user interaction, independently of the graphics engine used. Figure 5 displays the test system, which was implemented using two different engines, an open-source java-based 3D engine named *javamonkey* (Fig. 5a) and a commercial Unity3D engine with the Oculus Rift HMD (Fig. 5b). Furthermore, using the distribution layer's java interface, technologies such as Web Graphics Library (WebGL) can be integrated in order to enable the deployment of the software to a thin client architecture via web browser.

In the following paragraphs we describe the VR-based tool focusing on implementation aspects for managing the concurrent user access, as well as user interaction such as steering, object selection and manipulation.

3.2   Event-Driven Architecture for Managing User Access in 3DCVE's

The networking architecture described in the previous paragraph offers robust, reliable and fast distribution of project-specific data amongst users participating in a joint planning project. Based on this architecture and using a data-centric model, visualization services were developed that enable the deployment of a multi-user VE via a client-server design. For this, the data-centric model describes the VE as collections of objects and their assigned attributes, such as translation, rotation etc. These collections are structured and synchronized among clients using the networking layer.

User actions are handled using an event-driven architecture, shown in Fig. 4. When a user evokes a change to an object in the scene using the UI (e.g. by rotating a 3D model), a change event is generated, encapsulated along with other changes on that object (e.g. pose) and sent to a command queue residing on a central server process. As described above, the server again resides on a separate JVM, which runs respectively on a Hazelcast node. The underlying distribution layer is also being used for the communication between clients and server through the change-command objects. The command

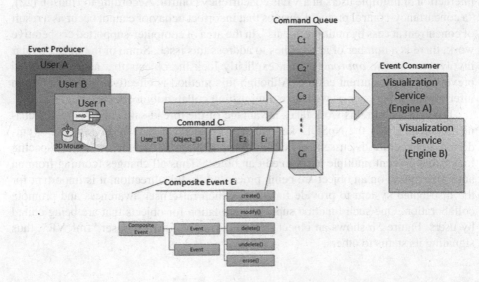

Fig. 4. Event-driven architecture for handling user actions (based on [17])

queue is executed serially processing every change, at which the server is authoritative over clients, being the only one that handles the requests that update the scene.

The above described architecture also sees for two important functions for a multiuser editor software, namely the creation of a full action history and the reversing of actions. Using the stored tagged events, a complete history of the actions of every user can be generated. This is particularly useful for documenting the design process and tracing back the users' decisions.

Another function, common to single-user software, is the undo/redo function, which offers the option to recover from errors and mishandlings. For a multiuser collaboration environment, the role of this function is even greater, since one user's errors can have a large impact on the actions of his collaborators. It is therefore important that errors can be quickly identified and reversed. The approach implemented in this work takes into account the model for a multiuser undo/redo function presented in [21], while modifying the concept to take advantage of the benefits that the data-centric distribution technology of KoDeMat platform offers. This was done using an additional, per-object buffer, which holds a history of changes performed on this object, as well as information about the user that performed the change. Applying a roles model that assigns rights to individual users or user groups, it is possible to manage the privileges of each user to "do" as well as to "undo" actions.

The concept also provides for the case of non-human triggered scene updates, namely for plain visualization of real and emulated MHS. In this case, there are highly volatile processes sending a large number of changes (e.g. position updates), a history of these changes in not desired and not meaningful. Each MHS needs only to provide status information about its own state into the VE and its agnostic of the changes that users perform. These machine clients communicate their data using the networking layer.

Managing Concurrent User Interaction. A challenge arising with simultaneous interaction of multiple users in a VE is concurrency control. According to Hudson [22], "a concurrency-control protocol ensures that incorrect behavior cannot occur as a result of concurrent access by multiple clients". In the area of computer-supported cooperative work, there is a number of approaches to address this issue. Some of the most popular involve *pessimistic approaches* that explicitly lock the objects that are being edited preventing its concurrent editing. Although this method is effective, it can lead to an inferior user experience as well as to diminishing collaboration effects.

The approach in this work takes advantage of the thread-safe concurrency mechanisms offered from the NoSQL, key-value store used for networking and the event-driven architecture discussed in the previous paragraph. There are no object-specific locks, that prevent multiple users to edit an object. Thus all changes (coming from an authorized user) on an object are being processed. In this direction, it is important for the distributed system to provide functions which raise user awareness and promote collaboration. One such function supports annotation for objects that are being edited by users. Figure 5b shows an object (robot) currently edited by user "fml_VR", thus signaling its status to others.

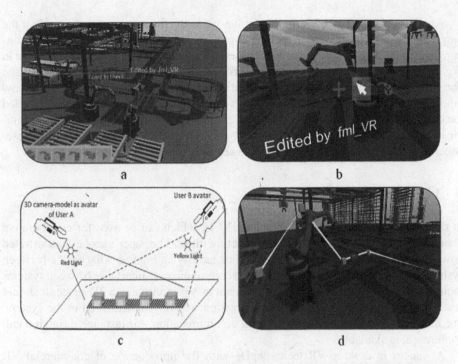

Fig. 5. Implemented 3D Collaborative Virtual Environment. (a): 3D Application with jmonkey 3D engine, (b) In-world menu for manipulating objects in Unity 3D, (c) camera models used as avatars, (d) definition of adjacencies between MHS in the VE

Orientation, Navigation and Object Manipulation in the 3D Space. As previously stated, this VR-enabled software uses the Unity 3D Engine and Oculus Rift HMD. In this VE, users can synchronously view and edit a 3D layout of the MHS as well as the surrounding facility infrastructure.

Egocentric orientation was used with a gaze-directed type of steering. Users can navigate in the 3D space, using a fly-through type of navigation. Through the integration of a 6 DOF controller in form of a 3D-mouse, and the head-tracking capabilities of the HMD, a 3D location-pointing concept was developed using a pointing arrow for the navigation in the 3D space to denote forward direction.

Various editing functions are implemented in order to enable the collaborative editing of a facility layout. Through an in-world 3D menu, users can perform actions such as moving, rotating and deleting of objects. The menu is context-based, displaying semi-transparent icons that depend on the selected object. Using a combination of raycasting and head-tracking techniques, users can select the desired function to execute, as shown in Fig. 5b. Further functions enable users to specify the adjacencies between MHS, by defining edges and vertexes of the material flow network (Fig. 5d). This way, alternative material flow matrices can be generated that can later be validated and used for the analysis of material flow.

Another important aspect in collaborative VE is the one of virtual presence. For the purposes of our facility planning tool, we chose to virtually represent users through non-human avatars. This approach represents users through a camera 3D model as shown in Fig. 5c. The benefits of such camera-avatars as collaboration tools are twofold. On the one hand, the avatar suggests the position of a user, on the other hand it is used to show other users in the collaborative VE a user's viewpoint. For this purpose, we extended the concept by using a type of telepointing approach. As a means to facilitate communication in the VE by attaching a light to the users' avatar, the viewing field of one user is being highlighted and so other users can see where someone is looking at.

4 Conclusion

In this work we presented a distributed 3DVCE, which can be used for collaborative planning of heterogeneous MHS's in logistics facilities. The paper's scope demonstrated how users can edit a 3D layout of a logistics facility and define adjacencies between systems. Further functions, such as specified communication interfaces between systems require editing digital documents, which is not as yet intuitive in a 3D space. It should also be noted that audio support communication was not implemented in the system. For this, it is assumed that a form of oral communication, for instance through a call conference, is available.

Advances in desktop-VR technologies with the introduction of commercial VR systems (the majority in the form of HMD) have made VR more accessible without requiring the large and expensive infrastructure of CAVE systems. This makes it possible to integrate VR technology in the planning processes of factories and logistics facilities. The introduction of 3DCVE's in planning processes can greatly assist in the early identification of misconceptions and uncover design-related production or implementation problems, while it contributes to more efficient and transparent processes and results in a significant reduction of costs and time (-to-market).

Nevertheless, a number of technical and non-technical challenges have been identified which need to be addressed in further research. The most important of the non-technical issues involves the integration of VR-technologies in existing planning workflows. The usability of 3DCVE should be extended by including more planning-specific tasks that should be identified based on concrete planning scenarios. Regarding technical challenges, immersive, VR-based tools and non-immersive (e.g. desktop-based) applications' interactions present still a major challenge. In order to achieve a truly cross-platform user planning interaction, the interplay between such systems should be enhanced to a degree where users can employ multiple platforms to achieve the same design tasks.

References

1. Kagermann, H., Wahlster, W., Helbig, J.: Recommendations for implementing the strategic initiative INDUSTRIE 4.0. Acatech, Frankfurt am Main (2013)
2. Mayer, S. H.: Development of a completely decentralized control system for modular continuous conveyor systems. Dissertation, University of Karlsruhe (TH) (2009)

3. Kipouridis, O., Roidl, M., Günthner, W.A., ten Hompel, M.: Cloud-based platform for collaborative design of decentralized controlled material flow systems in facility logistics. In: Kotzab, H., Pannek, J., Thoben, K.-L. (eds.) Dynamics in Logistics. Lecture Notes in Logistics, pp. 313–322. Springer, Heidelberg (2015)
4. Bullinger, H.-J., Potinecke, T., Tippmann, V., Rogowski, T.: Virtual engineering. Challenges and solutions. In: Proceedings of the 11th International HCI, vol. 5, p. 531 (2005)
5. Cecil, J., Kanchanapiboon, A.: Virtual engineering approaches in product and process design. Int. J. Adv. Manuf. Technol. **31**(9), 846–856 (2007). Springer
6. Siller, H.R., Vila, C., Estruch, A., Abellán, V., Romero, F.: Managing collaborative process planning activities through extended enterprise. In: Wang, L., Nee, L., Yeh Ching, A. (eds.) Collaborative Design and Planning for Digital Manufacturing, p. 153. Springer, Heidelberg (2009)
7. Bracht, U., Geckler, D., Wenzel, S.: Digitale Fabrik, Methoden und Praxisbeispiele, VDI. Springer, Heidelberg (2011)
8. Gausemeier, J., Rammig, F.J., Schäfer, W. (eds.): Design Methodology for Intelligent Technical Systems. Lecture Notes in Mechanical Engineering. pp. 12–19. Springer, Heidelberg (2014)
9. Grundig, C.: Fabrikplanung, Planungssystematik - Methoden - Anwendungen, pp. 37–40, Hanser, Munich (2014)
10. Frécon, E., Nöu, A.: Building distributed virtual environments to support collaborative work. In: Proceedings of the ACM Symposium on Virtual Reality Software and Technology, pp. 105–113 (1998)
11. Oliviera, J., Shen, X., Georganas, N.: Collaborative virtual environment for industrial training and e-commerce. IEEE VRTS (2000)
12. Wright, T., Madey, G.: Survey of Collaborative Virtual Environment Technologies. University of Notre Dame, USA (2008)
13. Pick, S., et al.: A 3D collaborative virtual environment to integrate immersive virtual reality into factory planning processes. In: 2014 International Workshop on Collaborative Virtual Environments (3DCVE) (2014)
14. Weidig, C., et al.: Future internet-based collaboration in factory planning. Acta Polytech. Hung. **11**(7), 157–177 (2014)
15. Menck, N., et al.: Collaborative factory planning in the virtual reality. In: 45th CIRP Conference on Manufacturing Systems (2012)
16. Mistrik, I., Grundy, J., van der Hoek, A., Whitehead, J.: Collaborative software engineering: challenges and prospects. In: Mistrik, I., Grundy, J., van der Hoek, A., Whitehead, J. (eds.) Collaborative Software Engineering, pp. 389–403. Springer, Heidelberg (2010)
17. ten Hompel, M., Günthner, W.A., Roidl, M., Kipouridis, O.: KoDeMat - Befähigung von KMU zur kollaborativen Planung und Entwicklung heterogener, dezentral gesteuerter Materialflusssysteme, Report, Lehrstuhl für Fördertechnik Materialfluß Logistik (fml) Technische Universität München - Lehrstuhl für Förder- und Lagerwesen (FLW) Technische Universität Dortmund, BVL (2014)
18. Sonnenfroh, M., et al.: Massively multiuser virtual environments using object based sharing. Electronic Communications of the EASST, vol. 17 (2009)
19. Veentjer, P.: Mastering Hazelcast, the Ultimate Hazelcast Book, Hazelcast Inc. (2015). http://www.hazelcast.com
20. Evans B.: An Architect's View of Hazelcast, White Paper, Hazelcast Inc. (2015). http://www.hazelcast.com

21. Choudhary, D.: A general multi-user undo/redo model. In: Proceedings of the Fourth European Conference on Computer-Supported Cooperative Work, ECSCW 1995 (1996)
22. Hudson, T.: Concurrency control for collaborative 3D graphics applications. Technical report, University of North Carolina at Chapel Hill, US (2000)

Investigating Low-Cost Virtual Reality Technologies in the Context of an Immersive Maintenance Training Application

Courtney McNamara(⊠), Matthew Proetsch, and Nelson Lerma

Naval Air Warfare Center Training Systems Division (NAWCTSD),
Orlando, FL, USA
{courtney.mcnamara,matthew.proetsch,
nelsom.lerma}@navy.mil

Abstract. This study evaluates the feasibility and limitations of integrating low cost commercial off the shelf (COTS) virtual reality (VR) technologies into immersive maintenance training applications. The Oculus Rift DK2, Microsoft Kinect V2, and Unity 3D Game Engine were evaluated for positional accuracy and signal chain latency in two distinct studies. Furthermore, the integration between hardware and software was also assessed to determine the limitations and challenges of developing a low cost immersive VR training system. The positional accuracy results showed that the Spine Mid, Spine Shoulder, and Neck joints had the lowest mean error and standard deviation when considering all joints tracked by the Kinect. The signal chain latency results showed 173–186 ms of delay from the time a user performed an action to the time the action was reflected in the virtual environment displayed to the headset. Overall, the integration of a low cost VR system including the Microsoft Kinect V2 and the Oculus Rift DK2 is feasible and could provide a realistic training environment that is deployable and reconfigurable.

Keywords: Virtual reality · Immersive environments · COTS · Maintenance training · Microsoft Kinect · Oculus rift

1 Introduction

The benefits of virtual reality (VR) immersive technologies have been demonstrated across numerous application domains, from behavior research and therapy to education and training [1]. Immersive VR brings a number of possible benefits for training applications [2, 3] that are of particular interest to the Navy Fleet which include spatial understanding, decreased information clutter, peripheral awareness, and increased information bandwidth. However, VR technology developers continue to address

---

Disclaimer: The views expressed herein are those of the authors, and do not necessarily reflect the official position of the Department of Defense or any of its components.

S. Lackey and R. Shumaker (Eds.): VAMR 2016, LNCS 9740, pp. 621–632, 2016.
DOI: 10.1007/978-3-319-39907-2_59

practical application and cost constraints pertaining to the utility, usability, and fidelity of VR systems. In many instances, these issues combine to override the otherwise beneficial elements that the immersive VR brings to the application.

Recently, significant advancements in the commercial entertainment industry and mobile computing market have led to the availability of improved low cost VR immersive technology components. Unlike previous generations of consumer-grade technologies, the newest wave of devices, including the Microsoft Kinect Version 2 (V2) and the Oculus Rift Development Kit 2 (DK2), provide promising alternatives to existing devices for creating VR-based training and performance support systems. These new and improved commercial off the shelf (COTS) solutions, when compared to existing Computer Assisted Virtual Environment (CAVE) systems, can provide significant savings for Department of Defense training systems. Furthermore, the rapid integration and wide compatibility support of multiple software platforms should further contribute to the final acceptance of VR technology for the purposes of training.

The progress in software and hardware has substantially increased the applicability of these technologies for the purposes of training. However, before these technologies are deployed two technical considerations must be addressed. These two considerations are real world positional accuracy and the overall system latency. Positional accuracy is an important quality of an immersive VR training environment because it contributes to the spatial awareness during training. Incorrect positional tracking in an immersive VR training environment can lead to incorrect spatial awareness and contribute to negative training. This study focuses on examining the positional accuracy of a tracked human body throughout the Microsoft Kinect field of view and examining whether its accuracy varies depending on the user's position relative to the sensor in two dimensions (near depth, mid-range, far depth; left, middle, and right) whereas previous studies have focused on accuracy only in the immediate vicinity of the user [4, 5]. System latency is also an important aspect in immersive VR training environments because it determines how fast information travels through the system to the end user's HMD. System latencies that that add significant delay can lead to motion sickness and cause training to be ineffective [9]. In this study system latency is defined as the amount of time between a user performing an action and the action being displayed on the HMD [8]. Therefore, understanding the system latency in low cost immersive VR environment can help adopters understand the limitations of applications.

The adoption of VR solutions for training systems is becoming widespread within the DoD; therefore, understanding the integration challenges of low cost VR systems is imperative to successfully implementing the technology in maintenance training systems. This study attempts to elucidate the capabilities and limitations of integrating low cost VR technologies by evaluating positional accuracy of tracked skeletons using the Microsoft Kinect V2, and by analyzing the latency of the signal chain between the user's motion and rendering changes on the Oculus Rift DK2. Understanding these two measures will allow developers to design scenarios for future applications based on the constraints imposed by the current low cost immersive VR technology.

2 Methodology

2.1 Equipment

This study utilized a desktop computer, Microsoft Kinect V2, Unity 3D game engine, and an Oculus Rift DK2 to create a low cost VR system. The specifications for the desktop computer used are listed in Table 1. The desktop computer integrated positional data from Microsoft Kinect using the Unity game engine to update the user's position in the virtual environment. The Oculus Rift DK2 was used to display stereoscopic 3D images of the virtual environment to the user. The maintenance training scenario used for this study featured a scaled model of the E-28 Arresting Gear engine, a large, land-based electromechanical system consisting of a gasoline engine, geared powertrain, and clutch assembly, and measuring approximately $8' \times 5' \times 5'$. The connection between the Kinect and the Unity game engine was established by using the Kinect Interface Application, a small lightweight application used to retrieve values from the sensor.

Table 1. Base station computer hardware specs

Processor	6-core Intel Xeon CPU X5660 @ 2.80 GHz with Hyper-Threading (12 logical cores)
Memory	4 GB DDR3 RAM @ 1333 MHz
GPU	NVIDIA GeForce GTX 580
HDD	WD 7200RPM 500 GB HDD
OS	Windows 8.1 operating system

2.2 Positional Accuracy Study

Setup. The positional accuracy study utilized a grid that was marked on the ground using tape which divided the extents of Kinect V2's operational range into 9 grid points. The grid point setup and the spacing between each of the 9 grid points can be seen in Fig. 1. The individual grid points and Microsoft Kinect were aligned such that they followed the manufacturer's provided specifications for optimal sensor performance, the so-called "sweet spot" [6].

Procedure. A total of ten participants were recruited for this study. Each participant was asked to stand on the middle of each of the 9 grid points in a consistent pose. Within each grid point each participant was instructed to rotate within their axis into each of four orientations: front, right, left, and back relative to the Kinect sensor. A snapshot of their 3D space position was recorded using the Kinect V2 in each orientation. The snapshot was repeated for each grid point. A total of 360 snapshots were taken for each of the 25 joints that Kinect V2 tracks. Each snapshot contained X, Y, and Z coordinates for each joint, in each of the four orientations at each grid point.

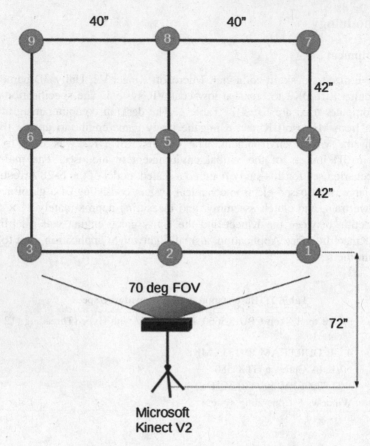

Fig. 1. Kinect positional accuracy setup with labeled grid point numbers

2.3 Signal Chain Study

Setup. The signal chain study measured the amount of latency in the system using 8 distinct stages. The sum of the delays between each stage captured the total latency between the real-world motion (such as a user waving a hand) and the time it was rendered on the HMD. Two conditions were used, local and remote, to assess the feasibility of different use cases. The local condition included the Kinect V2 sensor, Kinect Interface Application, Unity game engine, and Oculus Rift DK2 which were all connected and ran from the same base station. The remote condition had the same components as the local condition but included two separate base stations (computers). The first base station controlled the Kinect V2 sensor and the Kinect Interface Application which transmitted positional data over the network to a second base station which controlled the Unity game engine and the Oculus Rift DK2. The 8 stages used for to determine system latency for both local and remote conditions were defined as:

1. **Performed:** Motion data is performed in the real world when the user moves his or her body.
2. **Arrived:** Motion data enters the Arrived stage after the Kinect interface application acknowledges receipt of the data from the Kinect V2 sensor.
3. **Sent:** Motion data enters the Sent stage after the Kinect interface application sends the user motion data to the Unity game engine.
4. **Received:** Motion data enters the Received stage after the Unity game engine acknowledges receipt of the data.
5. **Integrated:** Motion data enters the Integrated stage after the game engine updates the state of smoothing filters. The smoothing filter used was a double exponential filter [10].
6. **Updated:** Motion data enters the Updated stage after the game engine calculates how the scene should respond to user movement.
7. **Prerender:** Motion data enters the Prerender stage immediately before the game engine begins issuing commands to the GPU for rendering.
8. **Postrender:** Motion data enters the Postrender stage after all GPU commands have completed. At this point, the user sees the results of his or her actions in the virtual environment.

Procedure. The delay between the Performed and Arrived stages was measured by using the experimental setup depicted in Fig. 2. The time elapsed between these two stages was measured using a 240 Hz high-speed camera. The framerate of the

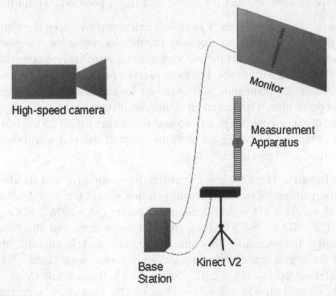

Fig. 2. Drop test setup for measuring the amount of latency between the Performed and Arrived stages

high-speed camera was used to determine time elapsed between the user event and its registration by the Kinect Client Application, which then reported the positional data on-screen. The elapsed time was calculated by correlating the real world action frames with the monitor displayed action frames (see Fig. 2).

The local condition latencies between stages 2–8 were measured by writing a time-stamped message to the system log that contained a unique identifier for position as it passed through each stage. This tracked a single snapshot of skeletal data from the Kinect as it moved through the VR system. This information was then analyzed to determine how much time was spent between each stage. The remote condition latency was measured by calculating the time between stages 2–8 similar to the local condition except in this scenario the two base stations clocks were synchronized using Network Time Protocol to sub-millisecond.

3   Results

3.1   Positional Accuracy Study Results

The results for the Kinect positional accuracy were divided into four sections. The first analysis computed the mean error and standard deviations for each of the 25 joints tracked by the Kinect regardless of the participant's orientation (front, back, left, and right) and position (forward, middle, back, left, center, and right) within the grid. The second analysis conducted was a one way ANOVA to ensure that the best tracking joints with the lowest mean error and standard deviation were significantly different from the joints that showed largest error means and standard deviations. The third and fourth analyses preformed were two 3×3 ANOVAs to verify if statistically significant differences were present between the lateral and depth positions within the grid.

Error Measure. The error for each joint was calculated by using the virtual distance provided by the Kinect's positional tracking capabilities minus the real world distance. All distances for both the real world and virtual environment were computed by using point two on the grid as a reference. For example, if a participant was on point nine, the real world distance for point nine was obtained by calculating the distance between point two and point nine. The virtual environment distance was similarly obtained by calculating the distance between point two and point nine for all 25 tracked joints. The error was then obtained by taking the absolute value of the real world distance minus each of the virtual joint distances.

Mean Error Results. The descriptive statistics for mean error and standard deviation for each joint regardless of orientation and position within the grid demonstrated that Spine Mid (M = .992", SD = .844"), Spine Shoulder (M = .936", SD = .797"), and Neck (M = .933", SD = .794") had the smallest mean error and standard deviations when compared to the remaining 22 joints, as seen in Fig. 3. In contrast, the joints that demonstrated the largest mean error and standard deviation were Hand left (M = 2.58", SD = .3.42"), Hand tip left (M = 2.61", SD = 3.42"), Thumb left (M = 2.91", SD = 3.34"), and Wrist Left (M = 2.52", SD = 3.31"). One way repeated measures ANOVA was conducted to verify if the differences between joints were statistically different. The results showed that Mauchly's sphericity assumptions had been violated, $\chi^2 = (299) = 11399$, $p < .001$, therefore Greenhouse-Geisser corrected tests were reported ($\varepsilon = .165$). The results indicated that there was a statistical significant difference between each of 25 joints mean error regardless of orientation or position on the grid, $F(3.95, 1261) = 26.683$, $p < .001$, $\omega^2 = .077$. A post hoc analysis using a Bonferroni correction was conducted to verify if the best tracking joints had significant mean differences from the other twenty two joints. The results revealed that Spine Mid, Spine Shoulder, and Neck joints regardless of orientation and position within the grid were statistical significant different from the remaining joints, $p < .05$, except when compared to ankle left which was not statistically significant, $p = 1.00$, from Spine Mid, Spine Shoulder, and Neck and ankle right which was not statistically significant, $p = .133$, from Spine Mid.

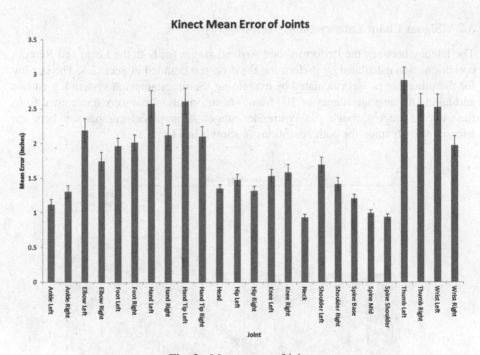

Fig. 3. Mean errors of joints

Grid Position Results. The grid position results were analyzed for differences in the lateral position and the depth positions with regards to the three best joints identified.

A 3 (Spine Mid, Spine Base, and Neck) X 3 (Left, Center, and Right) ANOVA was conducted to determine if differences existed within the best performing joints and three lateral positions regardless of orientation and depth position within the grid. For this analysis, the grid points for lateral were grouped by left (grid points 3, 6, and 9), center (grid points 2, 5, and 8), and right (grid points 1, 4, and 7). The results demonstrated that there were no statistically significant differences for Spine Mid,

F (2, 319) = 1.42, (p = .244), Spine Shoulder F (2, 319) = 2.142, (p = .119), and Neck F (2, 319) = 2.051, (p = .130), between left, center, and right lateral positions within the grid.

A 3 (Spine Mid, Spine Shoulder, and Neck) X 3 (front, middle, and rear) ANOVA was conducted to verify if significant differences existed between the best performing joints and the front, middle, and rear positions regardless of lateral positions within the grid. For this analysis, the grid points for depth were grouped by front (grid points 1, 2, and 3), middle (grid points 4, 5, and 6) and rear (grid points 7, 8, and 9). The results demonstrated that there were no statistically significant differences for Spine Mid, F (2, 319) = 2.120, (p = .122), Spine Shoulder F(2, 319) = 1.613, (p = .201), and Neck F(2, 319) = 1.447, (p = .237), between the front, middle, and rear lateral positions within the grid.

3.2   Signal Chain Latency Study Results

The latency between the Performed and Arrived stages for both the Local and Remote conditions was calculated by performing the drop test detailed in Sect. 2.3. The latency for the other stages was calculated by examining the timestamps on system log entries and taking the average latency of 300 frames of information that were transmitted from the Arrived stage through the Postrender stage. A graphical comparison between latency at each stage for both conditions is shown in Fig. 4.

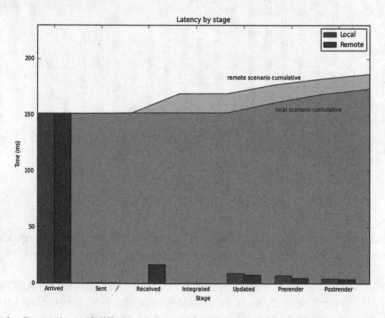

Fig. 4. Comparison of differing amounts of latency at each stage (Color figure online)

Local Condition. The latency between the Performed and Arrived stages was 151 ms. The remaining stages had a total combined latency 21.96 ms.

Remote Condition. The latency between the Performed and Arrived stages was 151 ms, similar to the local condition. The remaining stages had a total combined latency 35.10 ms.

4 Discussion

4.1 Positional Accuracy Study

The results of the positional accuracy experiment demonstrated that the Spine Mid, Spine Shoulder, and Neck joints had the lowest mean error and standard deviations when compared to the other 22 joints regardless of orientation and grid position. Identifying the joints that Kinect is capable of detecting and tracking accurately, regardless of user position and orientation, is of extreme importance to provide a realistic immersive VR experience. Based on the results obtained, Spine Mid, Spine Shoulder and Neck demonstrated a statistically significant difference when compared to the other twenty two tracked joints, except for Ankle Left and Ankle Right. This indicates that using these three joints could increase detection and tracking capabilities when operating within a free play environment. Furthermore, the results also confirmed that the differences between lateral and depth positions were not statistically significant for Spine Mid, Spine Shoulder, and Neck. This illustrates that the best three joints are unaffected by lateral or depth positions within the grid space. These results further supports the application of the Kinect as a low cost detection and tracking option for the purpose of tracking trainees in an immersive VR maintenance trainer.

4.2 Signal Chain Latency Study

The majority of latency incurred between an action happening in the real world and being rendered to the display of the Oculus DK2 device is due to the latency between the Performed and Arrived stages (151 ms) for both the local and remote conditions. The total latency after the system accepted positional information from Kinect was minimal when compared to the Performed and Arrived stages for both the local condition (21.96 ms, 12.7 %) and remote condition (35.10 ms, 18.8 %). These results were partly affected by CPU speed, memory, and GPU performance of the base stations used for this study. The latencies corresponding to each stage could be reduced by utilizing a more powerful computer which would reduce the time spent preparing the image for rendering by the HMD.

The most notable difference in latency between the Local and Remote conditions was incurred between the sent and received stages. The small inter-process communication latency of the Local condition was replaced in the Remote condition by a longer delay due to use of network communications. However, in the remote condition offloading the preprocessing of the Kinect data (Preformed, Arrived, and Sent stages) placed less of a load on the CPU allowing the dedicated machine running the Oculus

Rift DK2 to achieve better performance throughout the subsequent stages. Therefore care should be taken to select the appropriate system architecture when integrating these technologies on commodity hardware.

4.3   Integration Testing

During the process of integrating the targeted VR technologies for use in the experimental test bed, the researchers made several notable findings. The Oculus DK2 displayed multiple compatibility issues with several test computers. In particular, issues are prevalent with laptop computers which use hardware to switch between a dedicated, high performance GPU and a lower-power GPU, a feature commonly marketed as "NVIDIA Optimus" or "hybrid graphics". This was tested against multiple versions of the Oculus DK2 driver. Oculus DK2 also worked better with Windows 8 and Windows 8.1 than with Windows 7. Best results were obtained on a desktop computer with a dedicated graphics card and with Windows 8.1.

The Oculus DK2 uses stereoscopic rendering to create 3D viewing for the user. This stereoscopic rendering requires the computer to render the scene twice per frame, placing a significant demand on the CPU and GPU. While the test machine had no difficulties running the maintenance training application before the inclusion of VR, it struggled after adding support for the Oculus DK2 for this reason. When designing game scenes for use with VR, it may be necessary to optimize the 3D models, lighting, occlusion and other performance parameters to achieve the prescribed minimum of 60 fps.

Kinect V2 resolves joints most accurately when the user is standing and facing the sensor. Crouching, kneeling, bending at the waist, or turning away from the sensor causes Kinect V2 to "infer" the positions of joints which it cannot directly "see" with its line-of-sight depth and infrared sensors. This often results in an inaccurate estimation of their position.

Kinect V2 records and sends data at a rate of 30 Hz. Since the Oculus Rift DK2 HMD has a refresh rate of 75 Hz, there is a noticeable amount of stuttering when wearing the HMD. Specifically, if the user's position is updated only 30 times per second, while their view is updated 75 times per second, it can become disorienting. This update rate offset results in the user looking around with little to no noticeable lag but having their actions and viewpoint take longer to be updated.

5   Conclusion

This study indicates that Kinect V2 performs reasonably well on tasks of positional accuracy with a depth from 2m–4m, vertical 60 degree field of view, and horizontal 70 degree field of view. Within this 3D space, the Kinect V2 performs well at tracking a single user, as long as that user does not crouch, become partially obstructed, or turn away from the sensor. This makes it well-suited to utilize in tasks where a student needs to become familiar with a piece of equipment by walking around it in a virtual environment (with the assistance of the Oculus DK2 HMD), and making large, easily recognizable motions in order to interact with the virtual environment. Due to the limited precision of Kinect V2, it is not recommend for use in training tasks requiring recognition of small gestures. The Kinect V2 is also not recommended in cases where the user must kneel or twist their body. These behaviors cause the sensor to fail to accurately track a user.

The Oculus Rift DK2 HMD performed well in the study but had certain compatibility limitations. It is important to emphasize the necessity of supplying a machine compatible with the device (and its drivers). It is also important to note that the current version of this headset's display driver is not compatible with many gaming laptops. This restricts the user's ability to use the headset while untethered. Future display driver updates should be investigated to see if this problem is resolved. Other COTS virtual reality HMDs should also be investigated for this issue. Further research should be conducted as driver updates to existing technology becomes available and as new low cost virtual reality devices are released.

Acknowledgements. This work was funded by the Naval Air Systems Command (NAVAIR) Chief Technology Office (CTO) under the Section 219 Naval Innovative Science and Engineering (NISE) Program.

References

1. Ganier, F., Hoareau, C., Tisseau, J.: Evaluation of procedural learning transfer from a virtual environment to a real situation: a case study on tank maintenance training. Ergonomics **57**(6), 828–843 (2014). doi:10.1080/00140139.2014.89962
2. Bowman, D.A., McMahan, R.P.: Virtual reality: how much immersion is enough? Computer **40**(7), 36–43 (2007). doi:10.1109/MC.2007.257
3. Hirose, M., Schmalstieg, D., Wingrave, C.A., Nishimura, K.: Higher levels of immersion improve procedure memorization performance (2009)
4. Fürntratt, H., Neuschmied, H.: Evaluating pointing accuracy on Kinect V2 sensor. In: Proceedings of 2nd International Conference on Multimedia and Human-Computer Interaction (MHCI) (2014). http://avestia.com/MHCI2014_Proceedings/papers/124.pdf
5. Pino, A., Tzemis, E., Ioannou, N., Kouroupetroglou, G.: Using Kinect for 2D and 3D pointing tasks: performance evaluation. In: Kurosu, M. (ed.) HCII/HCI 2013, Part IV. LNCS, vol. 8007, pp. 358–367. Springer, Heidelberg (2013)
6. Kinect for Windows Human Interface Guidelines v2.0 [PDF]. Microsoft Corp, Redmond, WA (2014). https://go.microsoft.com/fwlink/p/?LinkID=403900
7. Wu, J.R., Ouhyoung, M.: On latency compensation and its effects on head-motion trajectories in virtual environments. Vis. Comput. **16**, 79–90 (2000)
8. Vincenzi, D.A., Deaton, J.E., Buker, T.J., Blickensderfer, E.L., Pray, R., Williams, B.: Mitigation of system latency in next generation helmet mounted display systems (NGHMDS). In: Proceedings of the Human Factors and Ergonomics Society Annual Meeting, vol. 55, No. 1, pp. 2163–2167, September 2011. Sage Publications

9. Kaber, D.B., Li, Y., Clamann, M., Lee, Y.S.: Investigating human performance in a virtual reality haptic simulator as influenced by fidelity and system latency. IEEE Trans. Syst. Man Cybern. Part A Syst. Hum. **42**(6), 1562–1566 (2012). doi:10.1109/TSMCA.2012.2201466. [6330028]

10. LaViola, J.J.: Double exponential smoothing: an alternative to Kalman filter-based predictive tracking. In: Proceedings of the Workshop on Virtual Environments 2003, pp. 199–206, May 2003. ACM

Tangible Augmented Reality and Engineering Product Dissection

Chloe McPherson[✉] and Rafael Radkowski

Virtual Reality Applications Center, Iowa State University, Ames, IA, USA
{cmcphe9,rafael}@iastate.edu

Abstract. Function-based design in engineering is an abstract approach to model the design space and to explore different design solutions. However, research results indicate that engineers and designers struggle to create function diagrams, especially when performing certain tasks such as product dissection. Augmented reality along with tangible objects can blend design aspect models such as the shape and topology in one AR presentation of the product and allow one to gain a better understanding of a product's functionality. We designed an AR application prototype that superimposes shape, functional groups, and component names onto a project of interest, which facilitates function diagram development and the understanding of the product's functionality.

Keywords: Tangible augmented reality · Product design · Engineering · Product dissection

1 Introduction

Function-based design is an engineering design method that utilizes the "function"-concept to structure and organize the components and activities of an engineering product. The term "function" combines and represents the intended inputs and outputs of a system and each of its subcomponents; a function is used to denote the transition from an input entity to an output entity. Functions are represented with different methods, for instance, a substantive and a verb [1], where the substantive describes the entity and the verb describes the activity that processes the entity. The entire functionality of the product is represented as a block diagram, connecting all functions. Knowledge of the product's functions helps engineers to determine and compare solutions based on meeting certain functional requirements, and is essential in a wide variety of design-related activities.

However, the function concept is a subject often difficult for novice designers to fully understand and apply successfully. Previous research has identified a deficiency in working knowledge [2, 3], especially when designers are asked to decompose a product into its sub-functions. An obstacle for them is the abstract nature of the entire function concept: functions are imaginary during product development, intangible, and quite often not visible. The designer must imagine the function, which has been identified as the source of many problems. Thus, instead of correctly dissecting the product, designers often default to selecting a functionality which appears to be correct based on their prior

© Springer International Publishing Switzerland 2016
S. Lackey and R. Shumaker (Eds.): VAMR 2016, LNCS 9740, pp. 633–642, 2016.
DOI: 10.1007/978-3-319-39907-2_60

knowledge and/or experience [2, 4]. Additionally, the components maintaining a function may also be hidden inside the main body or not ready for evaluation at a certain stage during product development. Product anticipation is required in this case. As a consequence, designers often do not share a common understanding, which is an obstacle when working on a team.

In our research we generally study the effect of augmented reality (AR), especially the connection of information, via visual cues, to the user's perception and understanding of his/her surrounding or particular objects. We focus on different domains and tasks. In this research, our efforts focus on AR-supported product dissection and its effectiveness in comparison to typical dissection approaches. In particular, we focus on tangible AR [5]. Tangible AR incorporates tangible objects, for example a printed prototype or a final product, and superimposes the prototype with virtual models. The physical device is used to interact with the AR application, whose main task is to change the user's perception of the object by showing additional information, blending layers, etc.

In conjunction with function models, we intend to reduce the abstract nature of the function concept and show additional information, such as hidden components and the links between components within the means of computer graphics. AR is used to superimpose a physical prototype with graphics to label the components of a product and to explain the interaction between different components. The goal is to improve the user's understanding of the product's functionality, thus, to allow him or her to generate better function models. Therefore, we study the effectiveness of AR-supported product dissection tasks.

This paper introduces theoretical aspects of this research and an application prototype, as well as discusses the first experience with AR-supported product dissection. The paper is structured as follows. The next section introduces the related work. We explain the research method in Sect. 3, followed by an introduction of the application prototype in Sect. 4. We close this paper with a summary and an outlook.

2   Tangible Augmented Reality and Product Dissection

Tangible AR describes the idea of using tangible objects to interact with AR content [5]. Tangible AR stems from the idea of tangible user interfaces. "Tangible user interfaces couple physical representations (e.g., spatially manipulable physical objects) with digital representations (e.g., graphics and audio) [6]." Tangible or graspable objects are easy to interact with. The user is able to move and rotate the objects. Physical objects allow for a detailed analysis of the shape of the object. However, they also hide information and do not allow one to abstract from the given shape and discover alternative solutions. Abstract models, such as functional models and computer-aided design (CAD) models, facilitate exploration of the design space. Concrete and abstract representations are important to the design of tangible interfaces [7]. On the opposite side, CAD models have a fundamental issue of intangibility. Viewing results on a computer monitor does not provide the same realistic and tactile feelings as mock-up models or other physical prototypes. There is a discrepancy between visual and tangible interfaces:

what we see is not what we touch [8]. AR allows one to blend physical and abstract models to mitigate this problem.

The following subsections explain the function concept and functional dissection, followed by the related work.

2.1 Functions and Product Dissection

Functions and function analysis are engineering approaches to structure a product under development. Different methods to describe functions have been introduced. But the most common method represents a function as a substantive and a verb [9], for instance, "*transform energy*." Common functions are classified into three groups related to the three major aspects for engineering: energy, material, and information [10].

Function models aggregate single functions yielding a representation of the functional relations of a product. Functional analysis methods can be of a hierarchical nature (top down or bottom up approaches), represented through a flow diagram (energy-flow approach), or captured in a list (enumeration approach). The top-down and energy-flow methods are the most common examples presented in design text books [9], and Eckert et al. found that professional designers using the top-down and energy-flow methods were able to find more functions than when using the enumeration approach. Figure 1 shows a typical energy flow function diagram. The rectangular blocks indicate the functions and the lines show the energy, material, or information connections between the functions. Each function block can have multiple connections, however, they must be compatible.

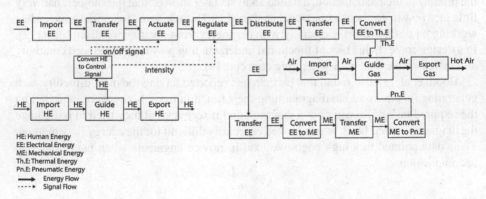

Fig. 1. Flow function diagram of a hair dryer according to [11]. It shows the functions as blocks and their connections via energy, material, and information flow.

Function diagrams help engineers explore solutions for a particular product. Functions and function models do not impose a particular solution. Typically, for each function more than one solution exists, thus, each solution can be considered as component neutral. This makes a function diagram an excellent measure for communicating ideas and determining a product solution in a team. This neutral description turns this model into an abstract model, which can also become a disadvantage: several users have different solutions in mind and communicate with a different notion in mind. This can cause confusion since people may believe that they are talking about the same item but do not notice that they found different alternatives. Consequently, this can end in different results when engineers perform certain design tasks.

Functional decomposition assists engineers with identifying essential functions while performing design tasks, including product dissection [9]. Simplified, an engineer analyzes a particular product and its functionality. Therefore, he or she takes it apart, physically or just in their imagination, and analyzes the components, functions, and how the components, in particular, the functions "interact." The abstract nature of the function model carries over to the dissection tasks: users have their own understanding of how a product is composed and which functionality is utilized for the product. This may explain why users' functional models result in mistakes. When users are asked to dissect a product and to develop a function diagram to show their knowledge of the product's function, they make mistakes [2, 9], and oftentimes each user generates a different diagram for the same product. Booth et al. [9] observed that there was a high rate of confusing functions with part names or design requirements, suggesting that students did not understand the distinction between a function and a design requirement.

Even engineers with the same background understand the notion of function and functional breakdown very differently. In one study, 20 designers with the same educational background in mechanical engineering were asked to analyze a given product in terms of the functions that occur in the product. They were asked to provide a summary in the form of a function tree in order to allow for comparison of their understanding. While each of the subjects left the experiment with the sense that they had understood the product to their satisfaction, detailed analysis later showed that the subjects had very little idea how to go about a functional analysis [2]. This phenomenon poses issues when working on design teams, especially with engineers from a variety of disciplines [12]. In a design context, this lack of functional understanding may lead to reduced creativity and increased fixation with generating concepts [9].

Booth et al. [9] also found that participants reported having the most difficulty with generating functions and in diagramming their function trees. Many were inhibited by the required task of drawing out a diagram, and it seemed that they tried to reorganize the diagrams in their head, which proved especially difficult for the energy flow method. Their data pointed to a high cognitive load in novice engineers when using function decomposition.

2.2 Tangible Augmented Reality in Product Development

Tangible AR blends multiple layers of information, and can improve user understanding of a physical part. Tangible AR has already been successfully applied to several physical prototypes, to enhance the user's perception of a product.

The Augmented Reality based Reconfigurable Mock-Up (ARMO), developed by Park et al. [13], enables interactive changes of shapes of products as well as colors, textures and user interfaces. Similarly, augmented foam (AF), another form of tangible AR was created to help designers make high-fidelity prototypes for design ideas very quickly [8]. The AF elevated the feeling of immersion for participants through multi-sense stimuli and spatial interaction between the designers and their results [8].

Gillet et al. [14] developed an AR system to allow virtual 3D representations of molecular properties to be overlaid only a tangible molecular model. "The physical model provide[d] a powerful, intuitive interface for manipulating the computer models, streamlining the interface between human intent, the physical model, and the computational activity [14]".

Balcisoy et al. [15] created an AR framework for testing product design, with the addition of virtual humans. In their proposed framework, a virtual human performed an evaluation test with an object composed of real and virtual components, increasing the realism of the interactive simulation.

The reported studies indicate the applicability of tangible AR to product development, and the developed prototypes clearly show that blending physical prototypes with AR has the potential to alter the users' understanding of a prototype for the better. However, tangible AR has been mostly utilized as a shape enhancer to improve the visible outcome with virtual finishing. We intend to enhance the understanding of the abstract level of functionality.

3   Method

Our approach to overcome the gap between concrete and abstract models is to blend the information that these models provide using augmented reality (AR). Figure 2 represents the basic idea. Engineering design typically addresses three aspects of a product: the shape, the structure/topology, and the functions/behavior of the product. These different aspects can be embodied by a set of models, for instance CAD models, part hierarchies, and functions diagrams, to mention three for instance. These models are created along the product development process, usually at different steps. In our research, we consider that the users already have a CAD model and a topology model of the product, at least, a first draft.

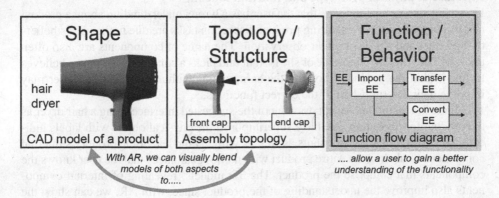

Fig. 2. Three aspects of engineering design, linked via tangible AR

Our goal is to improve the user's understanding of functionality through using representations of the two remaining aspects: shape and topology. A standard physical product dissection does not allow the user to know any information about either aspects of the product, though with the addition of AR we can also provide shape information, topology information, or both to the user. The information is visually linked to the associated physical components and functional groups. Using this additional information, our goal is to verify that this additional information provides the user with a better understanding of the product's underlying functions.

Following the obstacles found in the related work, we designed two interface concepts to present information about components and the relation between concepts (Fig. 3).

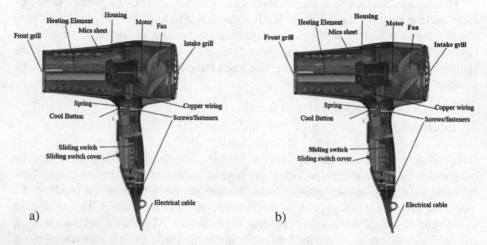

Fig. 3. Concept drawings: (a) Physical prototype superimposed with shape information, (b) Physical prototype superimposed with topology information

Interface 1: physical prototype and function labeling

Using function groups suggests that the user has a wrong understanding about a product and its composition. Errors during product dissection tasks are due to the user's beliefs of a product and not due to their observation. The name of components are also often unclear. Thus, the user thinks he or she is right and picks a component he or she believes to find within the product. Showing the components within a product to a user may improve their determination of the correct functions.

Figure 3(a) shows a concept drawing of the suggested interface using a hair dryer as the product for dissection. We have superimposed the physical object with labels indicating the names of all components as well as with 3D models of the product's internal components. Labeling the entire product with names guarantees that the user knows the components that comprise the product. The 3D models' revealing of internal components also improve the understanding of the product since, with AR, we can show the hidden components of the object.

Interface 2: physical prototype and topology information

Topology information allows a user to better understand which components interact with each other. Showing only the shape and the name of the components does not explain how the individual components interact with one another. The topology information explains which components are physically connected to each other to create an overall function, such as air flow.

Figure 3(b) presents a concept drawing that explains our solution. We intend to highlight groups of components that are physically connected to each other. In doing so, we reveal to users a function group, which is a group of components that fulfill a certain function.

Note, the topology information just shows which components interact together, they do not explain how the components interact together.

Relating this approach to a typical functional dissection task, the goal is that the user is able to generate a more accurate function diagram, or when comparing multiple users the variety of unique function diagram solutions decreases. This would imply that the user has a better understanding of the functionality of a product. A reduced variety would imply that a group of users share a more common understanding of the product.

Our challenge is to present users with the right amount of information to foster a better understanding without revealing the solution or creating a bias. In the worst case scenario, the additional information would govern the function diagram solutions that a group of users would create. Thus, instead of thinking, the users would literally model what they see. This might improve communication in a team setting but would also require that the shape and topology models always be exact. Conversely, too little information may not improve the capabilities of the user to work with functions.

To study this effect, we will conduct a user study to compare our AR application to a standard physical product dissection, through evaluating user's capability to generate accurate function diagrams. The user study follows a between-subject approach and compares a standard dissection task using pen & paper tools, with the two AR dissections. We work with two hypotheses that we intend to verify:

- Visual information, when combined with tactile information (AR-based dissection method), will contribute more to students' functional understanding than tactile information alone (physical product dissection)
- The more experienced users will perform better than the less experienced students

4   Application Prototype

We have developed a prototype of the AR application prototype for our study. Our hardware of choice is a tablet computer. Figure 4 shows the design concept of the main interface. The interface is designed so that the user can hold the tablet in landscape mode and easily access the buttons with little issue. We follow a typical border layout in horizontal orientation: the center of the main view is solely reserved for the AR view. Additional widget elements are placed along the right and left border of the application.

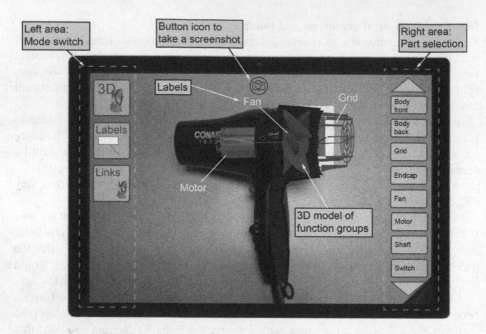

Fig. 4. Interface concept drawing

The main screen shows a video image of the physical world, superimposed with virtual objects of the product under investigation. The left border is reserved for button widgets that allow a user to switch between the three different visualizations according to the concepts in Sect. 3. The user can decide whether he or she would like to enable or disable the label view, model view, and function group view. For a study, some functions would be disabled depending on the mode under investigation. The right border presents button widgets that allow the user to switch between different components and functional group labels. Each button represents either a component of the product under investigation or a function group, depending on the mode that the user has selected. The components associated with the buttons are organized two-fold: first, all components and functions may be represented in alphabetical order. Second, components may be shown in a top-down organization, starting with all exterior components and ending with the internal components. The buttons are on/off-buttons, which allow a user to switch a model on or off.

The application also allows a user to take screenshots. Therefore, a screenshot button has been placed at the top of the application.

We use a marker-based AR application with template markers. The ARToolkit is used for tracking [16]. The ARToolkit uses template markers to track the marker with respect to a video camera. We attach a marker on the surface of each product under investigation in order to track its movements. The ARToolkit supports multiple markers so that we can associate each specific marker with a specific product. The widgets, in particular the labels on the buttons, change when the user analyzes a different product.

Right now, only one product can be used at a given time. The application would select the product associated with the marker with the lowest marker ID.

Figure 5 shows a user interacting with the AR application. The AR application has been implemented for a tablet computer, in this case, the Microsoft Surface Pro 4. It is our tablet of choice due to its large display and the camera's large field-of-view (FOV). The user may hold the tablet close to the product and still see the majority of the part. It is also possible for the user to hold an object in one hand and to use the tablet in the other.

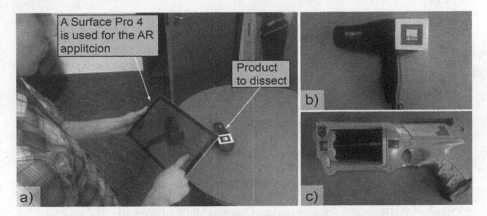

Fig. 5. (a) a user tests the application prototype. We use a (b) hair dryer and a (c) Nerf toy blaster as test objects in our study.

For our study, we work with two different products: a hair dryer and a toy Nerf dart blaster. Both products have been used for product dissection tasks in a several previous studies [3, 9], thus, using the same components facilitates comparison of the results.

The AR application is based on OpenSceneGraph and OpenCV. OpenSceneGraph is a scenegraph rendering API, which provides functions to model a 3D scene as a scene graph and to render an image. It also simplifies interaction handling. OpenCV is a computer vision library that is used mainly for video handling. In our case, we access the video camera, fetch images, and prepare them for rendering and for the ARToolkit. The entire application works in camera frame time.

5 Outlook

Currently, we work on a user study to evaluate the effectivity of AR. Users are asked to perform a product dissection task. We follow a between-subject design and compare the typical pen & paper approach along with a physical product dissection only to the AR-assisted dissection. Each participant in this study has to generate two function flow diagrams using a hair dryer and a Nerf toy blaster as shown in Fig. 5. The variance of different function flow diagrams and the deviation to a nominal diagram allow us to measure the outcome. We also ask the user in a pre-and post-questionnaire to identify a product from reading a function flow diagram. This question allows us to measure whether or not the user's understanding of those diagrams increases. Finally, the study results allow us to assess whether the AR-assisted dissection as support to the physical dissection improves understanding of the function-based design models.

References

1. Hirtz, J., Stone, R.B., McAdams, D.A., Szykman, S., Wood, K.L.: A functional basis for engineering design: reconciling and evolving previous efforts. Res. Eng. Des. **13**(2), 65–82 (2001)
2. Eckert, C., Ruckpaul, R., Alink, T., Albers, A.: Variations in functional decomposition for an existing product: experimental results. Artif. Intell. Eng. Des. Anal. Manuf. **26**(2), 107–128 (2012)
3. Booth, J.W., Bhasin, A.K., Reid, T., Ramani, K.: Evaluating the bottom up method for functional decomposition in product dissection tasks. In: ASME International Design Engineering Technical Conferences and Computers and Information in Engineering Conference, Buffalo, NY (2014)
4. Smith, E.E., Kosslyn, S.M.: Cognitive Psychology: Mind and Brain. Pearson/Prentice Hall, Englewood Cliffs (2007)
5. Billinghurst, M., Kato, H., Poupyrev, I.: Tangible augmented reality. In: 2008 Proceedings of the ACM SIGGRAPH Asia (2008)
6. Ullmer, B., Ishii, H.: Emerging frameworks for tangible user interfaces. IBM Syst. J. **39**(3/4), 915–931 (2000)
7. Marshall, P.: Do tangible interfaces enhance learning? In: Tangible and Embedded Interaction 2007, pp. 163–170 (2007)
8. Lee, W., Park, J.: Augmented foam: a tangible augmented reality for product design. In: IEEE and ACM International Symposium on Mixed and Augmented Reality, Vienna, Austria, pp. 106–109 (2005)
9. Booth, J.W., Reid, T., Eckert, C., Ramani, K.: Comparing functional analysis methods for product dissection tasks. J. Mech. Des. **137**(8), 1–10 (2015)
10. Hirtz, J., Stone, R., McAdams, D., Szykman, S., Wood, K.: A functional basis for engineering design: reconciling and evolving previous efforts. Res. Eng. Des. **13**(2), 65–82 (2002)
11. Otto, K., Wood, K.: Product Design: Techniques in Reverse Engineering and New Product Development. Prentice Hall, Upper Saddle River (2001)
12. Booth, J.W., Bhasin, A.K., Reid, T., Ramani, K.: Empirical studies of functional decomposition in early design. In: ASME International Design Engineering Technical Conferences and Computers and Information in Engineering Conference, Boston, MA (2015)
13. Jin, Y., Kim, Y., Park, J.: ARMO: augmented reality based reconfigurable mock-up. In: IEEE and ACM International Symposium on Mixed and Augmented Reality, Nara, Japan, pp. 273–274 (2007)
14. Gillet, A., Sanner, M., Stoffler, D., Olson, A.: Tangible interfaces for structural molecular biology. Structure **13**(3), 483–491 (2005)
15. Balcisoy, S., Kallmann, M., Fua, P., Thalmann, D.: A framework for rapid evaluation of prototypes with augmented reality. In: ACM Virtual Reality Software and Technology, Seoul, Korea, pp. 61–66 (2000)
16. Kato, H., Billinghurst, M.: Marker tracking and HMD calibration for a video-based augmented reality conferencing system. In: Proceedings of the 2nd International Workshop on Augmented Reality (IWAR 99), San Francisco, CA, pp. 85–94 (1999)

smARt.Assembly – Projection-Based Augmented Reality for Supporting Assembly Workers

Oliver Sand[1], Sebastian Büttner[2(✉)], Volker Paelke[3], and Carsten Röcker[1]

[1] Fraunhofer-Anwendungszentrum Industrial Automation, Lemgo, Germany
{Oliver.Sand,Carsten.Roecker}@iosb-ina.fraunhofer.de
[2] Ostwestfalen-Lippe University of Applied Sciences, Lemgo, Germany
Sebastian.Buettner@hs-owl.de
[3] Bremen University of Applied Sciences, Bremen, Germany
Volker.Paelke@hs-bremen.de

Abstract. In this paper we present *smARt.assembly* – a projection-based augmented reality (AR) assembly assistance system for industrial applications. Our system projects digital guidance information in terms of picking information and assembly data into the physical workspace of a user. By using projections, we eliminate the use of smart glasses that have drawbacks such as a limited field of view or low wearing comfort. With *smARt.assembly*, users are able to assemble products without previous knowledge and without any other assistance.

Keywords: Augmented reality · Projection · Assembly work · Manual assembly

1 Introduction

Current production systems are characterized by a very high degree of automation. However, a full automation of all production processes is not feasible. Changing markets cause product life cycles to become shorter and shorter. In addition, there is a shift from mass production to mass customization. Changing customer requirements result in mass customization where products have to be produced with a lot size of one [10]. These changes require a flexible production process where manual work will still be necessary. Workers at manual assembly stations (shown in Fig. 1) usually perform the manual tasks hand in hand with machines. Consequently, there will still be a place for humans during assembly in the production process of the future.

Embedding a manual assembly station into the production process results in high requirements for the worker. Due to mass customization, even two consecutive products can be completely different. This can result in highly demanding tasks for the worker, causing lower productivity and higher error rates. Due to a low availability of trained workers and concepts such as job rotation, training for the product assembly is required. However, training costs time and money,

© Springer International Publishing Switzerland 2016
S. Lackey and R. Shumaker (Eds.): VAMR 2016, LNCS 9740, pp. 643–652, 2016.
DOI: 10.1007/978-3-319-39907-2_61

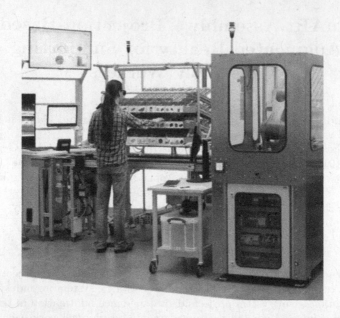

Fig. 1. Typical manual assembly station as part of a production line.

withdraws the worker from production, and is less applicable in case of ever changing products. An assistance system might also be used to support the worker at a manual assembly station, for example to train temporary workers in phases of high demand, in mass customization scenarios where exhaustive training of workers is difficult, for elderly people (whose quantity increases due to the demographic change [12]), or impaired workers that might need assistance during assembly due to various kinds of cognitive or motor skill impairments [13].

In previous research and industrial work, Augmented Reality (AR) assistance systems with smart glasses have been proposed as a way of training and assisting users, e.g. [5, 9, 17, 18, 20, 21]. However, systems with smart glasses often have drawbacks. First, the glasses currently available have limited wearing comfort due to the high weight of the electronic equipment, which makes them unsuitable for a workers' eight-hour shift. Second, people that require optical aids would either need a special version of the smart glasses (resulting in very high expenses) or need to rely on contact lenses. Wearing smart glasses in combination with prescription glasses is usually not an option. Third, the field of view is often reduced when wearing smart glasses, as described in [9]. To overcome these issues, we created *smARt.assembly* – an AR system that guides users through the steps of a manual assembly process by projecting digital artifacts into the physical space. This system has been developed as part of the SmartFactoryOWL – a factory for research purposes that aims on evaluating concepts and ideas for future manufacturing facilities [7]. Having presented first ideas in [4], we now show how *smARt.assembly* could support users with manual assembly tasks in future, without requiring smart glasses and with minimal installation effort on existing assembly stations.

2   Related Work

A large body of research has been done on the broad field of AR (e.g. [2,3,8, 17,20]). In this paper, we present the related work regarding two fields, which our work has been based on: projection-based (spatial) AR and AR assistance systems in industrial manufacturing.

2.1   Projection-Based Augmented Reality

Projection-based AR allows projecting digital artifacts on existing surfaces. The device itself can be much smaller than the area of the projection surface, which is an advantage in comparison with other approaches like normal displays – this even allows spanning whole rooms [11]. Today's broad availability and low costs make them an interesting choice for AR systems. Besides the early work of Cruz-Neira et al. on projections for virtual reality [6], one of the first uses of projection-based AR was the *Luminous Room* by Underkoffler et al. [22]. They built a room where both projection and image capturing was possible for all surfaces. Based on the room, they developed multiple use case examples for projection-based AR. The general issue with projection-based AR is the projection onto heterogenic surfaces. To cover this issue, cameras can be used in combination with the projector to implement a feedback loop, as demonstrated in the work of Jones et al. [11]. The information gathered by a depth-camera is used to prepare the image before projection in such a way, that it is correctly displayed after projection. An alternative solution is to use multiple projectors which all have different focus planes [14]. However, this approach is limited in case of complex geometry requiring many different focus planes. In industrial applications, Otto et al. [16] have used projections to augment floor surfaces to visualize layouts of assembly stations. While being inspired by the mentioned work, we focus on the case of giving assistance to untrained workers using projection-based AR.

2.2   Augmented Reality Assistance Systems

In current industrial practice, assembly instructions are often provided on paper or by a computer assisted instruction (CAI) system.

Assembly Support. Among others, Tang et al. [21] have shown that an AR manual on smart glasses is superior compared to paper manuals or CAI systems in terms of required mental effort as well as in the quality in terms of a reduced error rate. Billinghurst et al. [2] present a system for assembly with the help of AR presentations on mobile devices. Similarly, Gorecky et al. [8] developed an AR assembly assistance that uses tablets to show the instructions. While the mentioned works focus on the assembly, in industrial applications the picking of the relevant parts is also part of the manufacturing process. There are assistance systems for picking of parts that can be grouped into the following two concepts: Pick-by-Light and Pick-by-Vision systems.

For Pick-by-Light systems, a light is attached to every slot in a rack. The light indicates which part to pick next, in some systems combined with a number that displays the amount of parts to be picked. Proximity sensors attached to each slot can trigger the next light [9]. Pick-by-Light systems require a physical installation on the manual assembly station and therefore make the system inflexible and static. While these systems provide a good and spatial feedback to the user, they are expensive and are only economically in small installations with a high turnover [1].

Pick-by-Vision systems usually use smart glasses to display a picking highlight in the users' field of view. A build-in camera can be used for optical tracking to determine the users' point of view. One advantage is that no installation to the rack is required and a broader area can be used with one device [9]. From the domain of warehouse order picking there has been work on AR support for picking, e.g. Weaver et al. [23] showed that picking with smart glasses is much faster than picking based on paper instructions or audio signals.

Combined Picking and Assembly Support. While previous work on AR assembly usually omitted the picking, pick-by-vision systems with assembly support have been presented. For example, Paelke [17] presents an AR system that not only focuses on the assembly but also includes the picking step in the AR application based on smart glasses. The drawbacks of this specific smart glasses approach are described in [18].

While all of the listed assistance systems use smart glasses, we focus on the use of projection-based AR for combined picking and assembly assistance. While previous work has shown that AR applications with smart glasses are very useful in the industrial context of manual assembly, we believe that presenting the same information as a projection is superior to smart glasses, since projection-based AR eliminates some of the drawbacks, such as a lack of comfort and limited field of view.

3   smARt.assembly

With *smARt.assembly* we show an AR-supported manual assembly station that uses projection-based AR to project virtual artifacts into the physical space. Two types of information are projected into the users' workspace: picking information in terms of highlighting the box, where the next part is located and assembly information for each of the assembly steps.

The highlighting on the box is realized by multiple nested white rectangles that are animated and move towards the center of the related label of the boxes. The presentation was created in multiple prototype iterations and was chosen for two reasons: First, it was the most visible presentation on the multicolored box labels; second, the evaluation of earlier prototypes showed that the animations successfully catches the users' attention, even if the box is not in their focus. The highlighting can be seen in Fig. 2(a).

The assembly steps are shown on a white panel on the right side of the assembly stations. With this projection surface of a size of 30 cm × 20 cm, each assembly step is shown individually. The presentation for one assembly step itself is a 2D image taken from a digital 3D model. The presentation shows the current work piece including the next part to mount, where the next part to mount is highlighted. Each of the 2D images is turned in a way that the new part to mount is clearly visible. The way of presenting the information was also developed over multiple iterations. Our evaluations of the first iterations indicated that the projection onto a surface located at the side of the station is superior to a presentation in the center, since assembly instructions do not overlap with the actual working space. The presentation can be seen in Fig. 2(b).

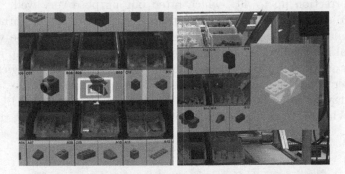

Fig. 2. Presentation of (a) picking information and (b) assembly instruction.

The projector for the installation is mounted above the head of the user (Fig. 3) and very close to the assembly station, so that information can be projected right onto the workstations without disturbing the user and without casting shadows from the user on the work area.

When using our current prototype, users have to indicate the next step manually to the system. For this purpose, we use foot pedals with two buttons: one for the next step and one for the previous step. With this approach we enable users to switch forward and backward, without having to move their hands away from the current work piece. We are currently investigating other input methods like gesture control or computer vision to improve the interaction with the system from an ergonomic perspective by eliminating the foot pedals.

To cope with changing products or changing production environments the system has to be flexible. A configuration mode allows to change the spatial location of the assembly instructions and to adapt the system to different box layouts. Therefore the system can easily be attached to existing racks or be adapted to changes in the setup.

4   Implementation

For the manual assembly station that is presented here we had to cover a projection area of approximately 100 cm × 60 cm, where the boxes are arranged in three rows, with either a size of 12 cm × 18 cm or 6 cm × 18 cm. It comes with a flat projection surface (see Fig. 3). However, a real world assembly station comes with a more complex arrangement to fit the users ergonomic needs, in the future we also want to support such configurations. Since the projector must not obstruct the users' view on the assembly station, nor should the user cast shadows from the projector onto the assembly station, the projector had to be mounted very close to the rack. We used the Optoma GT670 projector that has a very small throw ratio of 0.52, a resolution of 1280 × 800 (WXGA) and has keystone correction up to 40°, which fitted our purpose very well. The main issues of projectors in an assembly assistance scenario are the brightness of the projected image and the lifetime of the devices. For our prototype we choose a traditional lamp based projector, however the lifetime of the lamp is limited, resulting in additional maintenance time and costs. Other technologies, such as LED or laser projectors, are better suited for long running scenarios and come with warranty for 24/7 operation. The projector is attached to a PC running Microsoft Windows 7 and the software was developed in C++ using the Metaio SDK [15].

Fig. 3. Prototype of projection-based AR assembly station, with the projector attached above the users' head.

5   Evaluation

In our ongoing study we focus on the usability of our presented assistance system for manual assembly and compare it with a previous prototype of an AR-based assistance system with smart glasses. The previous system has been presented in [19]. Within our study, participants are asked to assemble two out of three LEGO sets, which each consists of 18–19 bricks. The participants have to build each of the sets without prior knowledge and training. Each participant has to build one set with *smARt.assembly* and one set with smart glasses (within-subject-design). The build order is randomly selected as well as the LEGO set to be build is assigned randomly, always by making sure that no participant builds two identical sets. The time for the build process is monitored and errors in picking and in the build process are observed and logged. After the assembly of the two sets the participants fill out a survey asking the participants to classify statements about usefulness and joyfulness of the two approaches on a Likert-Scale. The participants were recruited at our university, resulting in eight male participants, aged 21–30 yr. (average 24.25 yr.), who all are students.

While the study is still ongoing, the results of the first eight participants are promising. The study clearly shows that the assembly time per step are lower for *smARt.assembly* compared with the previous system based on smart glasses. Participants in the study took between 5.4 s and 14.4 s (average: 9.3 s) with *smARt.assembly*, which is half the time compared with the previous prototype that resulted in a range between 13.9 s and 32.9 s (average: 24.4 s).

In the same way the results for the error rate was influenced by the technology used: while users had an average picking error rate of 10.1 % with smart glasses, with *smARt.assembly* not a single participants made a picking error. When it comes to the assembly process, the results were all free of errors when using *smARt.assembly*, while we observed one participant with a build error when using the smart glasses in the study. The study is ongoing and we will evaluate more participants to be able to prove that the results are significant. Futhermore, we will also present the results of the survey at a later point. For now, we can state that most of the participants showed excitement about this presentation of assembly instructions and expressed this exitement in the survey as well.

6   Conclusion

With *smARt.assembly* we presented a projection-based AR system that helps untrained workers to assemble products without any previous knowledge or trainings. The system shows both picking information for the next part to assemble as well as assembly instructions in the physical workspace of the user.

Even though a formal evaluation of the system is not part of this paper, we presented some first insights into our ongoing evaluation. We are currently continuing our user study that compares various presentation techniques, such as smart glasses, projection-based AR, and paper manuals in the context of industrial manufacturing. While doing this study, many people did already work with the *smARt.assembly* system presented in this paper and showed already promising results: Compared to our previous prototype with smart glasses [19], the projection-based system seem to be much more robust with respect to changing light conditions. The ongoing evaluation indicates that users working with the projection-based instructions are able to assemble products faster and with a lower error rate, compared to the system based on smart glasses. Furthermore, users working with *smARt.assembly* showed excitement about this presentation of assembly instructions. All users have been able to assemble the products without any previous knowledge about the assembly steps, just by following the guidance given by our system. We will continue our study to get more and significant results about the impact of different presentation techniques.

In addition to the ongoing evaluation, future work could contain an integration of other input modalities into the assembly station, such as gesture control or computer vision technologies for the detection of the obtained step as well as a mean for quality control.

References

1. Baumann, H.: Order picking supported by mobile computing. Ph.D. thesis, University of Bremen, January 2013. http://elib.suub.uni-bremen.de/edocs/00102979-1.pdf
2. Billinghurst, M., Hakkarainen, M., Woodward, C.: Augmented assembly using a mobile phone. In: Proceedings of the 7th International Conference on Mobile and Ubiquitous Multimedia MUM 2008, NY, USA, pp. 84–87 (2008). http://doi.acm.org/10.1145/1543137.1543153
3. Büttner, S., Cai, T., Cramer, H., Rost, M., Holmquist, L.E.: Using computer vision technologies to make the virtual visible. In: Mobile AR: Design Issues & Opportunities Workshop at MobileHCI 2011. ACM (2011)
4. Büttner, S., Sand, O., Röcker, C.: Extending the design space in industrial manufacturing through mobile projection. In: Proceedings of the 17th International Conference on Human-Computer Interaction with Mobile Devices and Services Adjunct MobileHCI 2015, NY, USA, pp. 1130–1133 (2015). http://doi.acm.org/10.1145/2786567.2794342
5. Caudell, T., Mizell, D.: Augmented reality: An application of heads-up display technology to manual manufacturing processes. In: Proceedings of the Twenty-Fifth Hawaii International Conference on System Sciences, vol. 2, pp. 659–669, January 1992
6. Cruz-Neira, C., Sandin, D.J., DeFanti, T.A.: Surround-screen projection-based virtual reality: the design and implementation of the cave. In: Proceedings of the 20th Annual Conference on Computer Graphics and Interactive Techniques, SIGGRAPH 1993, pp. 135–142 (1993)
7. Fraunhofer, I.-I.: SmartFactoryOWL - Home. http://www.smartfactory-owl.de/index.php/en/. Accessed 2 June 2015
8. Gorecky, D., Campos, R., Chakravarthy, H., Dabelow, R., Schlick, J., Zühlke, D.: Mastering mass customization - a concept for advanced, human-centered assembly. Assembly Manufact. Eng. 11, 62 (2013)

9. Günthner, W.A., Blomeyer, N., Reif, R., Schedlbauer, M.: Pick-by-Vision: Augmented Reality unterstützte Kommissionierung. Lehrstuhl für Fördertechnik Materialfluss Logistik - Technische Universität München, Garching (2009). http://www.fml.mw.tum.de/fml/images/Publikationen/Abschlussbericht%20Pick-by-Vision.pdf

10. Hinrichsen, S., Jasperneite, J., Schrader, F., Lücke, B.: Versatile assembly systems - requirements, design principles and examples. In: Villmer, F.J., Padoano, E. (eds.) 4th International Conference on Production Engineering and Management PEM 2014, Lemgo, September 2014

11. Jones, B.R., Benko, H., Ofek, E., Wilson, A.D.: Illumiroom: Peripheral projected illusions for interactive experiences. In: ACM SIGGRAPH 2013 Emerging Technologies SIGGRAPH 2013, no. 7 (2013)

12. Korn, O., Funk, M., Schmidt, A.: Towards a gamification of industrial production: A comparative study in sheltered work environments. In: Proceedings of the 7th ACM SIGCHI Symposium on Engineering Interactive Computing Systems EICS 2015, NY, USA, pp. 84–93 (2015). http://doi.acm.org/10.1145/2774225.2774834

13. Korn, O., Schmidt, A., Hörz, T.: Augmented manufacturing: A study with impaired persons on assistive systems using in-situ projection. In: Proceedings of the 6th International Conference on PErvasive Technologies Related to Assistive Environments PETRA 2013, NY, USA, pp. 21:1–21:8 (2013). http://doi.acm.org/10.1145/2504335.2504356

14. Low, K., Welch, G., Lastra, A., Fuchs, H.: Life-sized projector-based dioramas. In: Proceedings of the ACM Symposium on Virtual Reality Software and Technology VRST 2001, NY, USA, pp. 93–101 (2001). http://doi.acm.org/10.1145/505008.505026

15. Metaio GmbH: meatio — SDK Overview. http://www.metaio.com/products/sdk/. Accessed 19 Mar 2015

16. Otto, M., Prieur, M., Rukzio, E.: Using scalable, interactive floor projection for production planning scenario. In: Proceedings of the Ninth ACM International Conference on Interactive Tabletops and Surfaces ITS 2014, NY, USA, pp. 363–368 (2014). http://doi.acm.org/10.1145/2669485.2669547

17. Paelke, V.: Augmented reality in the smart factory: Supporting workers in an industry 4.0. environment. In: Emerging Technology and Factory Automation (ETFA), pp. 1–4. IEEE, September 2014

18. Paelke, V., Röcker, C.: User interfaces for cyber-physical systems: Challenges and possible approaches. In: Proceedings of the International Conference on Human-Computer Interaction HCII 2015 (2015)

19. Paelke, V., Röcker, C., Koch, N., Flatt, H., Büttner, S.: User interfaces for cyber-physical systems: expanding the designer's toolbox. at-Automatisierungstechnik 63(10), 833–843 (2015). Walter de Gruyter GmbH

20. Schreiber, W., Alt, T., Edelmann, M., Malzkorn-Edling, S.: Augmented reality for industrial applications - a new approach to increase productivity? In: Proceedings of the 6th International Scientific Conference on Work With Display Units WWDU 2002. pp. 380–381 (2002)

21. Tang, A., Owen, C., Biocca, F., Mou, W.: Comparative effectiveness of augmented reality in object assembly. In: Proceedings of the SIGCHI Conference on Human Factors in Computing Systems CHI 2003, pp. 73–80 (2003)

22. Underkoffler, J., Ullmer, B., Ishii, H.: Emancipated pixels: Real-world graphics in the luminous room. In: Proceedings of the 26th Annual Conference on Computer Graphics and Interactive Techniques SIGGRAPH 1999, pp. 385–392. ACM Press/Addison-Wesley Publishing Co., New York (1999). http://dx.doi.org/10.1145/311535.311593

23. Weaver, K.A., Baumann, H., Starner, T., Iben, H., Lawo, M.: An empirical task analysis of warehouse order picking using head-mounted displays. In: Proceedings of the SIGCHI Conference on Human Factors in Computing Systems CHI 2010, pp. 1695–1704 (2010)

All links were last followed on December 18, 2015.

Virtual Tailor for Garment Design

Andrea Vitali[✉], Lorenzo D'Amico, and Caterina Rizzi

Department of Management, Information and Production Engineering,
University of Bergamo (BG), Dalmine, Italy
{andrea.vitali1,caterina.rizzi}@unibg.it

Abstract. This paper presents an application, named TLAB (i.e., Tailor's LABoratory) to support virtual clothing design. In particular, it focuses the attention to the first step of garment design process, i.e., customers' measure acquisition. TLAB is based on low-cost innovative technology (e.g., Oculus Rift SDK 2, Leap Motion device and Microsoft Kinect v2) to permit the interaction by hand and emulate the work traditionally done by tailors to manufacture a garment. In this paper, firstly we present the technology used for creating TLAB by describing hardware and software solutions adopted. Then, the design of a Natural User Interface (NUI) is depicted. The NUI design allows simplifying the interaction with hands through the use of the Leap Motion device as hand-tracking device. Finally, preliminary tests are discussed and conclusion presented.

Keywords: Mixed reality · Garment design · Augmented interaction

1 Introduction

Virtual clothing environments have been made available by exploiting 3D technology enhancements. In particular, three-dimensional scanners and three-dimensional virtual clothing simulation applications have been developed, and thus, incorporated into solutions for the fashion industry. Furthermore, many companies are using automated systems to improve working efficiency and reduce costs in technical areas through the use of digital data, which come from the optimization of virtual clothing design [1–3]. Both 2D and 3D CAD/CAM systems are available to design virtual garments and textiles. 2D CAD systems permit to design the 2D patterns composing the garment and used to manufacture it. The 3D systems can be used to re-create and simulate the garment behavior assembling the 2D patterns on a 3D digital mannequin [4]. In a fully virtual approach, the tailor designs the garment around the customer's avatar acquired by using body-scanner.

However, these systems do not take into account a previous phase, which is usually executed by the tailor on a mannequin in order to derive the standard measures and size of the final user. In this phase, the tailor gets the necessary measurements by using a flexible tape measure around the mannequin or the final customer in different postures. This paper introduces the Taylor's LABoratory (TLAB), a low-cost mixed reality application that permits to emulate this phase as traditionally done by the tailor. First, we introduce the low cost technology available to develop mixed reality applications. Then,

© Springer International Publishing Switzerland 2016
S. Lackey and R. Shumaker (Eds.): VAMR 2016, LNCS 9740, pp. 653–661, 2016.
DOI: 10.1007/978-3-319-39907-2_62

the TLAB is described as well as the developed Natural User Interface (NUI). Finally, preliminary tests and results are presented and discussed.

2   Low Cost Devices for Mixed Reality

In the last years, many devices have been designed to make possible the interaction with a virtual environment in a natural way where the user can interact with the application, as he/she should do in a real situation [5–7]. Many of them come from entertainment sector, are low cost and make available Software Development Kits (SDKs) for application development.

Among the several IT devices for mixed reality, there are two important categories: devices for 3D visualization and those for hand-tracking to interact with 3D environment in a natural way. The first category is represented by the last generation of head mounted displays, which permits to visualize a 3D virtual environment in the same way we can see the real world [8, 9]. In the last two years, the most important low-cost HMDs have been Oculus Rift (Fig. 1a.), HTC Vive (Fig. 1b.) and Google CardBoard (Fig. 1c.). The cost is reasonably low and, therefore, easily affordable for both users and developers.

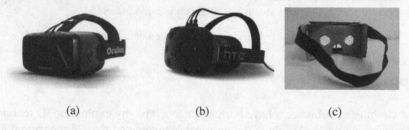

(a)   (b)   (c)

Fig. 1. Head mounted displays: (a) Oculus Rift SDK 2, (b) HTC Vive and (c) Google CardBoard.

The second type of devices concerns the augmented interaction with 3D objects and worlds by using hands. Hand-tracking devices allow detecting hands with high precision with have the ability to track each single finger and thin objects held in hand. Among them, the most important and cheapest devices are the Leap Motion (Fig. 2a.) [10] and the Duo3D (Fig. 2b.) [11].

(a)   (b)

Fig. 2. Low-cost hand-tracking devices: (a) Leap Motion device and (b) Duo3D

In our research context, a third type of devices has to be taken into account, i.e. the 3D laser scanners to acquire 3D models of human body. Also in this case, low cost solutions, such as Microsoft Kinect v2 [12], are available. There are other low cost 3D scanners, which have been exploited for taking measures along human body, such as Apple PrimeSense Carmine (Fig. 3b.) and Occipital Structure Sensor (Fig. 3a.). Apple PrimeSense Carmine acquires 3D human model as a Microsoft Kinect, but it can be only used on IOs platform. For example, Apple PrimeSense Carmine has been used in an innovative solution where the sensors were positioned inside a cabin in order to acquire all measures of human body for custom made garments. Occipital Structure Sensors permits 3D scanning by using Apple mobile devices. Occipital Structure Sensor device makes 3D scanning technology portable and suitable for mobile applications.

(a)   (b)

Fig. 3. Occipital Structure Sensor (a) and Apple PrimeSense Carmine (b)

3 Tailor's Laboratory

Our main goal has been to develop a virtual environment where the tailor can interact with the virtual customer as s/he traditionally performs. The Oculus Rift as head mounted display and the Leap Motion device as hand-tracking device have been selected since we have already positively experienced for other design applications. A body

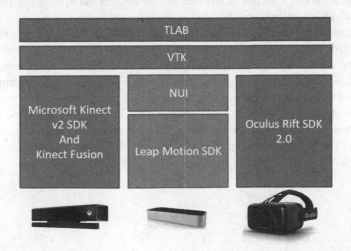

Fig. 4. Software architecture of TLAB

scanner solution based on four Microsoft Kinect v2 has been considered to acquire the customer's body.

Figure 4 shows the TLAB software architecture where:

- The Visualization ToolKit (VTK) [13] is used to manage the 3D rendering of the virtual environment. TLAB is composed by a set of widgets, such as sliders, buttons and the virtual tape measurement. Each operation inside TLAB is possible through the use of VTK.
- Microsoft Kinect Fusion for Microsoft Kinect v2 is used for the 3D acquisition of human avatar.
- The Leap Motion SDK for hand tracking permits to get data about hands/fingers position and orientation, which are detected by Leap Motion device in, real-time. The interaction with the 3D environment has been studied to provide the user with a long lasting interaction and reducing fatigue for arms and shoulders.
- The Oculus Rift SDK 2.0 to track the head position and orientation permits the visualization of the 3D virtual environment with depth perception. Also in this case, Oculus Rift SDK is strictly linked with the 3D rendering of the scene.

Virtual widgets are automatically visualized in the user's field of view of the Oculus Rift when 3D body shape is detected and thus, the user can start to take the standard measures using hands/fingers detected by the Leap Motion device. Each virtual object is rendered through the use of Oculus Rift SDK.

3.1 Framework for Synchronization

The synchronization among mentioned SDKs is possible thanks to a software framework developed in house, which contains a set of basic class able to simplify the use of the whole system. The framework is general purpose and fully independent of the application the developer wants to implement. In fact, it has been also used in other mixed reality applications that permit to emulate the traditional manufacturing process of a product, such as lower limb prosthesis.

This framework permits to exploit Oculus Rift SDK with VTK and Leap Motion SDK with no direct access to their basic SDKs. Furthermore, a set of methods are available to create a Natural User Interface [14] with the developed VTK widgets for mixed reality. In this way, each existent application can be re-designed in very simple way in order be used with a mixed reality environment.

As showed in Fig. 5, a simple application can be developed in few rows of code. A 3D model has been added inside the basic 3D environment that is rendered through Oculus Rift. The presented source code executes the following actions:

```
 1  ⊟#include "stdafxMR.h"
 2   #include "FrameworkMR.h"
 3
 4  ⊟int main(int argc, char* argv[])
 5   {
 6      vtkSmartPointer<FrameworkMR> frameworkMR = vtkSmartPointer<FrameworkMR>::New();
 7      frameworkMR->Init();
 8
 9      vtkSmartPointer<vtkSTLReader> reader = vtkSmartPointer<vtkSTLReader>::New();
10      reader->SetFileName("3D_s_body.stl");
11      reader->Update();
12      vtkSmartPointer<vtkPolyDataMapper> mapper = vtkSmartPointer<vtkPolyDataMapper>::New();
13      mapper->SetInputConnection(reader->GetOutputPort());;;
14      vtkSmartPointer<vtkActor> actor = vtkSmartPointer<vtkActor>::New();
15      actor->SetMapper(mapper);
16
17      frameworkMR->GetUserSceneManager()->AddActor("3D_s_body", actor);
18      frameworkMR->ResetCamera(actor->GetBounds());
19
20      frameworkMR->Start();
21
22      return EXIT_SUCCESS;
23  }
```

Fig. 5. The framework source code.

- Framework initialization.
- Load the model in STL file format.
- Add the loaded 3D model inside 3D environment.
- Set the of field of view according to the position of 3D model.
- Start the rendering into Oculus Rift.

3.2   Development of the Virtual Tape Measure

By starting from the VTK widget named contour widget, a virtual tape measure has been implemented. It is a 3D line that can be modified using its control points. The customized version of the contour widget can be applied on a surface and each modification follows the surface of the 3D mesh on which it lies. The TLAB graphically and numerically visualizes on the avatar all the taken measures, so that the tailor can easily compares and evaluates their correctness. Figure 6 shows some examples.

The interaction with the virtual tape is done through Leap Motion device, which tracks the gestures to use the virtual tape measure.

The virtual tape can be selected and modified adding/removing/moving its control points using the index finger. To modify the path/length of the tape measure, the user has to touch the contour for 10 s, a new point is added and the length recalculated; if an existent control point is selected for more than 5 s, it becomes green and the user can move it along the customer digital body until he reaches the right position to get the measure. The measure is visualized in the field of view of Oculus Rift and changes each time the tape measure is modified.

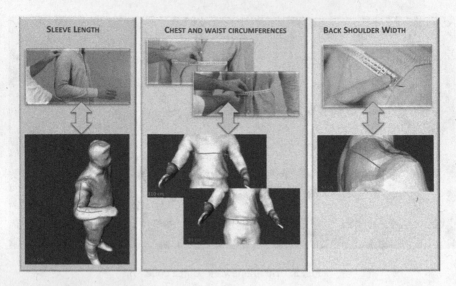

Fig. 6. Basic measurements usually acquired by the tailor for a shirt.

4   Natural User Interface for TLAB

The NUI (Natural User Interface) can be defined as the set of gestures and actions made by the user during the interaction with the virtual environment. In our case, the traditional operations performed by the tailor have been analyzed when s/he manufactures a garment, such as a shirt or a jacket.

S/he uses continually the hands to take measurements around the human body as well as moving legs or arms of the customer to define the best posture to get correct measurements. Figure 6 shows some examples of measures taken by the tailor to design a man shirt and related postures. A limited set of gestures have been defined as follows:

- Movements of index finger. If the virtual tape measure state has been activated, the user can interact with the tape measure as previously described.
- Palm rotation. The palm rotation permits the rotation of the human avatar.
- Horizontal movement of both palms. Leap Motion detects the distance between palms. Then, the increasing and the decreasing permit to zoom–in and out of 3D models.

The NUI has been implemented using the basic framework previously mentioned to synchronize Oculus Rift and Leap Motion device with the 3D environment. To manage the various interaction modes and the defined gestures, the NUI is constituted by a limited number of states, represented by a finite state machine (FSM) shown in Fig. 7. The legend explains how TLAB changes interaction mode according to the selected gesture.

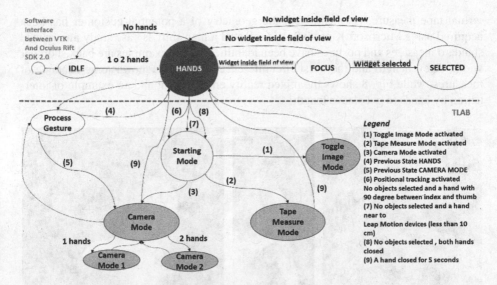

Fig. 7. Finite State Machine developed for TLAB.

The upper part is the software interfaces to interact with Leap Motion device and Oculus Rift, the lower part describes the several modes developed to use TLAB.

Hands state permits the link between the basic software interface of Leap Motion device and TLAB. It controls the following events if there are no selected virtual widgets (e.g., virtual sliders and 3D buttons):

1. Hand with 90 degree between index and thumb and positional tracker of Oculus Rift deactivated. This event activates the Camera Mode.
2. Hand with 90 degree between index and thumb and positional tracker of Oculus Rift activated. This event activates the Object Mode.
3. Hand near to Leap motion (less than 10 cm). This event activates the Toggle Image Mode.
4. Both hands closed. This event activates the Rule Mode.

The *Starting Mode* state permits to monitor activation gestures, and update the indicators of the actual interaction mode (i.e., icons and images).

The *Tape Measure* state allows interacting with the virtual tape measure through a set of gestures that permits to define the path of the tape along the human body and thus, take the measurement for garment design (Fig. 7).

The *Process Gesture* state monitors the execution of basic gestures (e.g., circle, swipe and pinch) and permits to execute the actions associated to a particular gesture in the activated mode.

5   Tests and Preliminary Results

Preliminary tests have been carried out to verify the potential of the implemented solution especially with regard to the interaction with Leap Motion device and the use of the virtual tape measure. As mentioned, the geometry of a potential customer has been acquired using Microsoft Kinect v2. We selected a man shirt as case study and related standard measures and postures have been identified. Some examples are back shoulder width, sleeve length and the waist circumference. The Fig. 6 shows some example of measures, while Fig. 8 shows the mixed reality environment and an example of interaction by hands to get sleeve length.

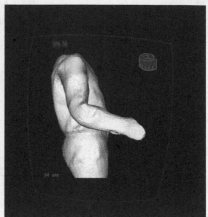

Fig. 8. Initial interaction for taking sleeve measure and TLAB visualized inside Oculus Rift.

The application permitted to define necessary postures and acquire all customer's measurements that have been also compared with the real ones. In general they are comparable and the differences were no more than ±5 mm. The most critical measures were the waist and chest circumferences that require a tailor's expertise. However, further tests have been planned. First, we will consider different types of garments, such as pant, skirt, and dress, since different avatar postures could be necessary. Secondly, a significant numbers of testers, including tailors, with different levels of skills about IT tools will be involved. This will permit to perform a more detailed analysis of measures acquisition in a virtual environment and their reliability. Furthermore, a comparison between real and virtual tasks will be carried out.

6   Conclusions

This paper presents an application that permits to emulate the first phase of garment design process, i.e. customer's measurements, allowing the tailor to interact with customer's avatar as s/he traditionally does. Acquired measures can be later used to define the 2D patterns of the garment and, using a 3D CAD system, numerically simulate its behavior on the avatar. Therefore, integrated with a body scanner and a 3D clothing system, it will permit to fully virtualize the garment development process.

Even if first trials were successfully, further tests are necessary considering the variety of garments and users with different skills and expertise. This will not only allow us to validate the applications but also to acquire the tailor's knowledge that could be embedded within the system.

Future developments have been planned to include a first automatic generation of the 2D garment patterns starting from taken measurements and integrate TLAB with 2D and 3D systems. New modules will be added to manage a database of postures and movements to be automatically applied to the customer's avatar and guide the users during measures detection. Finally, this research work has been developed within the framework of a national industrial project, named BODY-SCAN and we have planned to test the developed application with the textile-clothing companies involved in the project.

Acknowledgments. The authors would like to thank MISE (Ministry of Economic Development), Italy for co-funding the Industria 2015 – BODY-SCAN project.

References

1. Fontana, M., Rizzi, C., Cugini, U.: A CAD-oriented cloth simulation system with stable and efficient ODE solution. Comput. Graph. (Pergamon) **30**(3), 391–407 (2006)
2. Fontana, M., Carubelli, M., Rizzi, C., Cugini, U.: ClothAssembler: a CAD module for feature-based garment pattern assembly. Comput.-Aided Des. Appl. **2**(8), 795–804 (2005)
3. Zhang, D., Wang, J., Yang, Y.: Design 3D garments for scanned human bodies. J. Mech. Sci. Technol. **28**(7), 2479–2487 (2014)
4. Porterfield, J.A.: Exploring 3D Garment Simulation as a Prototype Validation Tool for Costume Design, North Carolina State University, 122p. (2015). http://gradworks.umi.com/36/90/3690349.html
5. Kim, M., Cheeyong, K.: Augmented reality fashion apparel simulation using a magic mirror. Int. J. Smart Home **9**(2), 169–178 (2015)
6. Bordegoni, M., Ferrise, F.: Designing interaction with consumer products in a multisensory VR environment. Virtual Phys. Prototyping **8**, 1–21 (2013)
7. Colombo, G., Facoetti, G., Rizzi, C., Vitali, A.: Socket virtual design based on low cost hand tracking and haptic devices. In: Proceedings of the 12th ACM SIGGRAPH International Conference on Virtual-Reality Continuum and its Applications in Industry, pp. 63–70 (2013)
8. Hoffman, H.G., Meyer, W.J., Ramirez, M., Roberts, L., Seibel, E.J., Atzori, B., Sharar, S.R., Patterson, D.R.: Feasibility of articulated arm mounted oculus rift virtual reality goggles for adjunctive pain control during occupational therapy in pediatric burn patients. Cyberpsychology Behav. Soc. Netw. **17**(6), 397–401 (2014)
9. Ohta, Y., Tamura, H.: Mixed Reality: Merging Real and Virtual Worlds. Springer Publishing Company Incorporated, Heidelberg (2014)
10. Leap Motion. https://www.leapmotion.com/
11. Duo3D. https://duo3d.com/
12. Vitali, A., Comotti, C., Colombo, G., Regazzoni, D., Rizzi, C.: Low cost 3D scanners along the design of lower limb prosthesis. In: Proceedings of the 6th International Conference on 3D Body Scanning Technologies, pp. 147–154 (2015)
13. VTK-Visualization ToolKit. http://www.vtk.org/
14. Kaushik, D., Jain R.: Natural user interfaces: trend in virtual interaction (2014). arXiv Prepr. arXiv:1405.0101

An Interactive Augmented Reality Furniture Customization System

Tzu-Chien Young and Shana Smith[(⊠)]

Department of Mechanical Engineering,
National Taiwan University, Taipei, Taiwan
ssmith@ntu.edu.tw

Abstract. Shopping on the Internet has many advantages, compared to shopping on-site. However, shopping on the Internet has limited user experiences, especially for large and heavy furniture products. In addition, users cannot change the materials and dimensions of the online furniture products. As a result, online shoppers often cannot make right purchasing decisions. This paper presents an augmented reality furniture customization system, which provides users the abilities to view and change the materials and dimensions of three-dimensional virtual furniture, within the contexts of real environments. A Kinect is used to track the human body motions. Occlusions for real and virtual objects in different depths are considered to increase the realism of the system. A calibration algorithm is developed to find the depth, IR image, and RGB image information of the Kinect, to improve the image quality in the augmented reality environment. Furniture customization functions are provided to improve user experiences. User test results show that users consider the augmented reality-based furniture customization system realistic and natural to use.

Keywords: Augmented reality · Occlusion · Furniture display

1 Introdcution

Augmented Reality (AR) is a technology which combines virtual objects with real scene captured from cameras. Applications of AR are various. For example, Ling and Shuyu used AR technology in textbook design to improve students' learning [1]. Carozza et al. used AR technology in city design [2]. In order to improve the realism of AR scenes, virtual objects and real objects must have correct spatial relationships. However, traditional AR always places virtual objects in front of the real objects. It may confuse users and cause decision failure. Therefore, solving occlusion problems becomes an important issue in AR. Hayashi et al. solved the occlusion problems by combining stereo information to find the depth of a moving object [3]. Fortin and Hebert fixed the locations of cameras and physical scenes to find depth information of real objects to solve the occlusion problems [4].

Interaction between users and virtual objects is another important issue in AR. Seo and Lee tracked the positions and motions of hands [5]. When users clicked an image on a plane board, they could interact with the virtual objects. Radkowski and Stritzke

© Springer International Publishing Switzerland 2016
S. Lackey and R. Shumaker (Eds.): VAMR 2016, LNCS 9740, pp. 662–668, 2016.
DOI: 10.1007/978-3-319-39907-2_63

used a Kinect to track human bodies to control a virtual cursor for assembly and disassembly training [6].

Correct occlusion and smooth interaction can improve the realism of an AR application. Most previous AR furniture display systems do not allow users to view virtual furniture with accurate relative positions, orientations, and sizes, in the context of the physical environment. In addition, they do not allow users to change the dimensions and materials of virtual furniture in the AR environment.

In order to allow users to directly, intuitively, and naturally interact with virtual objects, in this study, a Kinect was used to obtain the depth information of the real world. A two-step method was developed to align the depth images and RGB images. Z-buffer was overlapped with the calibrated depth image to solve the occlusion problem. This study built a furniture display system to verify the developed method. A user test was conducted to evaluate the effectiveness of the system.

2 Method

2.1 Calibration of Kinect

Although the Kinect is capable of providing depth information, the depth images and RGB images are mismatched, as shown in Fig. 1. Because of different angles and positions of the infrared camera and color camera, the Kinect needs to be calibrated to align the depth images and RGB color images. An object in the world coordinate first needs to be projected to the camera coordinate by the external parameters of the camera, and then projected to the image coordinate by the internal parameters of the camera.

Fig. 1. Mismatch between the depth image and RGB image

Stereo Calibration. Kinect camera calibration (stereo calibration) needs to find the external parameters between the color camera and infrared camera to obtain the correct relative rotation, translation, and scaling relationships between the two cameras.

This study used the internal parameters of the color camera and infrared camera and the image pairs, which were taken simultaneously by the two cameras, to perform stereo calibration. The calculation method was carried out using the Matlab Camera Calibration Toolbox.

Translation Correction Between Depth Image and Infrared Image. The translation correction was performed with a star-shaped calibration board and an ellipse fitting method. The depth image and infrared image were taken simultaneously. The system detects ellipse edges in the depth image and find the corresponding edges in the infrared image to calculate the least square deviation for translation, as shown in Fig. 2. Figure 3 shows the images before and after translation. The result shows that the depth images and infrared image can fit together.

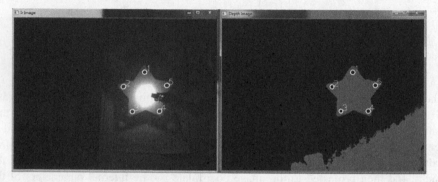

Fig. 2. Corresponding points between the depth image (left) and the infrared image (right)

Fig. 3. Before (left) and after (right) translation

2.2 Occlusions in AR

AR is a computer-generated environment combined with real scene and virtual objects. The key to construct a realistic AR environment is to have a correct transformation relationship between the camera coordinate system and the world coordinate system.

This study uses NyARtoolkit (http://nyatla.jp/nyartoolkit/wp/) as the development toolkit. NyARtoolkit is an open source, based on marker tracking. This study verifies the correctness of the AR coordinate system by placing a virtual block of 160 mm (width) × 80 mm (height) on a marker of 160 mm (width) × 160 mm (height), as shown in Fig. 4. The result shows that the dimension of the virtual object can correctly fit with the real object in the AR environment.

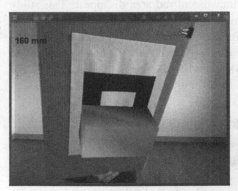

Fig. 4. Verify the size of the virtual object

Occlusions. The occlusion problem was solved by overlapping the calibrated depth image with the Z-buffer of the DirectX. Thus, the Z-buffer represents the real depth of the physical world. Before rendering the virtual objects, the z coordinates of the virtual objects are compared with the depth information in the Z-buffer. If the virtual objects are nearer to the observers, they are rendered. Otherwise, the virtual objects are occluded. In this study, a 32bit Z-buffer and DirectX 9.0c were used. Figure 5 shows an example of the occlusion results.

Fig. 5. An example of the occlusion

2.3 Interaction in AR

This study creates a cubic event trigger which is used to fire the interaction event. To improve the stability in controlling virtual objects, a bigger cube which is apart from the event trigger 200 mm was created as a separation detector. When users' hands touch or enter into the event trigger, an interaction event happens and the event trigger will show up as a transparent red area. When users' hands move out the separation detector, the interaction event ends and the transparent red area disappear. This study created four kinds of basic interactions, which were resize, translation, rotation and animation. The four interactions should be triggered by both hands. With Kinect's body tracking capability, the positions and parameters of both hands can be obtained to manipulate the virtual objects. Figure 6 shows that when the user's hands enter into the event trigger, a transparent red area appears to show the interaction mode.

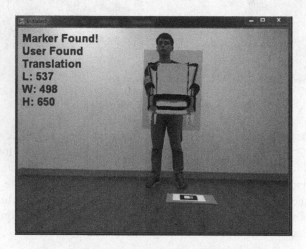

Fig. 6. Interact with virtual objects

3 Experiment

Two experiments were carried out to test the developed AR furniture display system. Furniture models were taken from the TF3DM open source (http://tf3dm.com/3d-models/furniture). There were 12 men and 11 women in the test. In the first experiment, subjects needed to interact with the virtual furniture and place the virtual furniture at the correct locations, Fig. 7 shows an example. A questionnaire with a Likert scale of 1 (extremely disagree) to 7 (extremely agree) was used to evaluate the AR system, after the subjects finished the task. Table 1 shows the questionnaire results. Most subjects considered the AR system helpful, interesting, and smooth to use. Most subjects also would like to use this system when purchasing furniture online.

The second experiment tested the effects of occlusion. Subjects first arranged the furniture as the first experiment. Then, subjects followed the instruction to go to certain

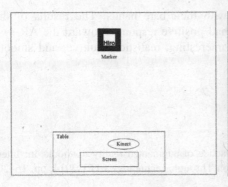 

Fig. 7. User experimental environment

Table 1. User experience in AR

	AR	
	Mean	Std. deviation
The system can help me to estimate the size of the furniture	5.870	0.7571
I like to interact with virtual furniture using the AR system	6.304	0.8221
The interaction with furniture is intuitive	5.957	0.9283
The operation of the system is smooth	5.478	0.790
The AR system is interesting	6.585	0.590
The system can help me to purchase the right furniture	6.044	0.878
I would like to use this system when purchasing furniture online	6.130	0.757

locations, with and without occlusions. Another questionnaire was used to evaluate the occlusion effects. Table 2 shows that the AR system with occlusion is significantly more realistic and intuitive than that without occlusion.

Table 2. With and without occlusion in AR

	No occlusion		Occlusion	
	Mean	Std. deviation	Mean	Std. deviation
The system is realistic	1.826	0.887	6.652	0.573
The system is intuitive	2.000	1.087	6.609	0.583

4   Conclusions

With the advance of computer hardware and software, AR applications are becoming more popular. Correct occlusion and direct interaction can improve the realism of an AR environment and help users be immersed in the AR environment. This study developed an interactive AR system using natural user interface with occlusion. The discrepancy between the depth image and infrared image was resolved. Users can directly interact with the virtual objects with their bare hands. The results of the experiments also show that most subjects had positive responses toward the AR system. They considered the system helpful, interesting, realistic, intuitive, and smooth to use.

References

1. Ling, Z., Shuyu, Z.: Design research and practice of augmented reality textbook. In: International Conference of Educational Innovation Through Technology EITT 2014, pp. 16–20, Brisbane (2014)
2. Carozza, L., Tingdahl, D., Bosché, F., Gool, L.: Markerless vision-based augmented reality for urban planning. Comput.-Aid. Civil Infrastruct. Eng. **29**(1), 2–17 (2014)
3. Hayashi, K., Kato, H., Nishida, S.: Occlusion detection of real objects using contour based stereo matching. In: Proceedings of the 2005 International Conference on Augmented Tele-Existence, New York, USA, pp. 180–186 (2005)
4. Fortin, P.A., Hebert, P.: Handling occlusions in real-time augmented reality: dealing with movable real and virtual objects. In: The 3rd Canadian Conference on Computer and Robot Vision, pp. 54–54 (2006)
5. Seo, D.W., Lee, J.Y.: Direct hand touchable interactions in augmented reality environments for natural and intuitive user experiences. Expert Syst. Appl. **40**(9), 3784–3793 (2013)
6. Radkowski, R., Stritzke, C.: Interactive hand gesture-based assembly for augmented reality applications. In: The 5th International Conference on Advances in Computer-Human Interactions, Valencia, Spain, pp. 303–308 (2012)

Novel Virtual Environments

Ghost Hunter – An Augmented Reality Ghost Busting Game

Stuart Armstrong[1](✉) and Kyle Morrand[2]

[1] QinetiQ, Orlando, FL, USA
Stuart.armstrong@qinetiq.com
[2] 302 LLC, Orlando, FL, USA
kmorrand@302llc.com

Abstract. In Ghost Hunter the player can walk into any environment and hunt for ghosts. The game automatically generates a real time physical representation of the room using a combination of motion tracking, area learning and depth perception technologies. Looking through a mobile sight attached to a mock up ghost gun the player is able to spot and destroy ghosts that can emerge from any surface in the room.

This paper covers the design and technology of developing a mobile, augmented reality, game aimed at exploiting current advances in mobile AR. We aim to cover tracking challenges of an untethered device that does not rely on physical markers, design challenges of integrating tablet based technology with a portable mock weapon system, and game design principles that cover the integration.

Keywords: Augmented reality · Mobile · Game · AR · Ghost · Tango

1 Introduction

1.1 Augmented Reality

Augmented Reality (AR) is the name given to the process of overlaying virtual and synthetic information on to the live world. Application areas include navigation, advertising, entertainment and education. With the convergence of technologies in modern mobile phones, accessibility to hardware that can support augmented reality has never been easier.

An example of AR applications includes Golfscape GPS Rangefinder by Shotzoom Software that uses the Global Positioning System (GPS) and compass within your mobile phone to provide golf course summary and information. This information is displayed when you look at the course through the inbuilt camera on the phone (Fig. 1).

S. Lackey and R. Shumaker (Eds.): VAMR 2016, LNCS 9740, pp. 671–678, 2016.
DOI: 10.1007/978-3-319-39907-2_64

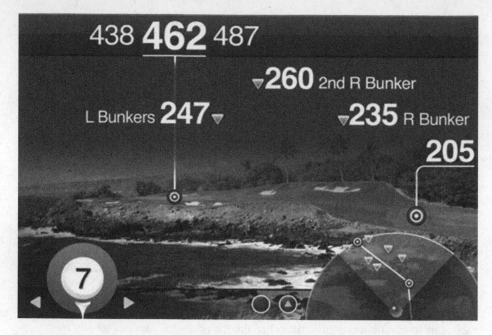

Fig. 1. Example of AR application – Golfscape rangefinder by Shotzoom software

1.2 AR Games

Being able to mix real world and virtual environments can introduce interesting game play elements into the real world. Up until recently, the technology required to

Fig. 2. Drakerz-confrontation by Drakerz

implement AR in a mobile gaming environment hasn't been accessible to the general consumer. However, with the rapid advancements in mobile technologies, in particular high quality camera's, accurate geo-location and increased processing capabilities on the mobile device, games that mix real world locations with innovative game play are beginning to emerge. Some examples include:

- Google's Ingress (iOS), a game that involves 'hacking' real world locations to gain control of portals for your faction. This game uses the players position, orientation and camera to overlay game play information onto the mobile device screen.
- Drakerz-Confrontation, a Pokémon style game where the creatures 'pop off' the cards. This game uses the phone camera to capture and correlate the location of the card and place a 3D character model of creature on top of the card as soon through the phone (Fig. 2).

Current generation AR based games either use broad location settings, which are accurate to within a few meters, or fiducial markers, high contrast, distinct patterns that computer vision algorithms can accurately determine orientation and position to correlate between the real world and game worlds.

2 Ghost Hunter

Ghost Hunter is a short, augmented reality, game in which the player's objective is to search around their real-world environment looking for ghosts. The game was designed to be fully mobile but retain some gameplay physical characteristics of a first person shooter as the focus is on a complete game that you can use in any real world indoor location and interact with the environment around you.

2.1 Design Challenges

As briefly discussed earlier, most AR games on the market rely on one of two technologies to track user movements and align the game world with the real world.

The first set of technologies rely on using the inbuilt location tracking of the phone or mobile device. Although accuracy does vary with each device, a position accuracy of less than a couple of meters is about average. Combined with the inbuilt compass (and potentially inertial sensors), the device is able to understand its position and orientation. This approach works very well outdoors, and has been used as the basis of navigation for the last ten years, however it doesn't enable real time, accurate position tracking required for real time gaming. In addition, the system itself is not able to generate information about its environment so is entirely reliant on pre-built information.

The second set of technologies relies on a computer vision technique (often referred to as Fiducial markers). A fiducial marker is an object or image placed within the scene which the image system can use as a point of reference or measure. For instance, within the Drakerz-Confrontation game detailed above, the playing cards are used as the reference marker. The system knows the exact dimensions of the card and from the pattern is able to determine the orientation and position of the card within the image and from that extrapolate the position of the device in relation to the card. This allows the system to accurately overlay game world features over their real world counterparts. The system often has to recalculate and redraw the scene many times per second in order to maintain a stable image.

For Ghost Hunter we required the ability to not only know the accurate location of the device but also for the game environment to be able to interpret the real world around it. The preferred method for being able to generate this understanding of the real world location is to use 3D depth sensor. A number of depth sensors are available:

- Structured Light sensor – Illuminates the real world with a structured IR light pattern. From the size of the dots and the pattern the system can determine 3D geometry.
- Time of Flight Camera – Depth is measured based on the time it takes for an IR beam to transmit, reflect and return to the sensor. A scene can be built by building up this depth information over time.
- Stereo – An image is captured from two cameras a small distanced apart and by comparing the two images depth and 3D geometry can be determined.

Combining these methods can enable for very accurate real time capture of the real world environment in a number of different lighting conditions (Fig. 3).

2.2 Google's Project Tango Yellowstone Tablet

Google released its Project Tango "Yellowstone" tablet in June 2014 marking one of the first consumer devices to combine both depth sensing and color camera within a single mobile device.

Fig. 3. Google's project Tango Yellowstone tablet

The Yellowstone is a 7-inch tablet that features a 2.3 GHz quad-core Nvidia Tegra K1 processor, 128 GB flash memory, 1920 × 1200-pixel touchscreen, 4MP color camera, fisheye-lens (motion-tracking) camera, integrated depth sensing, and 4G LTE connectivity.

Tango uses a combination of motion tracking, depth perception and area learning to accurately map the physical location around the player and position the tablet exactly within the real world space. With this information we have the potential to accurately generate and incorporate, in real time, physical spaces into the game environment without having to spend significant time and money (Fig. 4).

Fig. 4. Point cloud image captured by Project Tango

Ghost Hunter was a short game designed to explore using real time real world map generation as a game play mechanic.

2.3   Top Shot Firearm Controller

For the game controller, the Top Shot Elite Firearm Controller from Activision was selected. This controller includes built in wireless technology, twin analogue sticks, D-Pad, action buttons as well as a pump action feature (Fig. 5).

Fig. 5.   Top shot elite firearm controller, modified to hold tablet

The Top Shot was modified to accommodate the Yellowstone tablet as a 'ghost sight', and a wireless interface was created to pick communicate between the gun and the tablet.

2.4 Gameplay

The player uses the Yellowstone's Depth Perception camera to ping a surface in front of them, such as a table, floor, wall, etc. and check if there's a ghost inside. If the ping sensor is red, a ghost will appear and the ghost(s) will be forced out of the surface. The ghost(s) will then approach the player, and can be avoided by moving around in the environment, as well as use the gun to shoot them down.

The player scores points by successfully shooting the ghost and loses points if the ghost manages to reach the player. The player is also able to move within the physical space to avoid the ghost creating a dynamic environment where the player has to be conscious of not only the game space but also their physical surroundings. Each round is timed and the speed, number and health of ghosts can be increased with difficulty (Fig. 6).

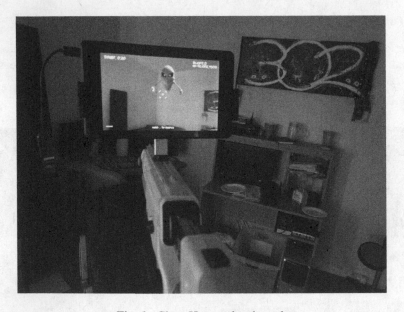

Fig. 6. Ghost Hunter play through

2.5 User Interface

The player is presented with a simple screen that details the time left in the current round, current score and players all time hi-score. In the middle of the screen is a red reticle which displays the current aim point of the player (Fig. 7).

Fig. 7. Early user interface for Ghost Hunter

If the player moves the gun around the environment and presses the ping button (x on the controller) a small circle is drawn on the real world surface. This circle represents a search area and will remain gray if no ghost is present, but turn red if a ghost has been detected. After a small amount of time, a ghost will spawn out of any red circle areas and turn and advance towards the player. The player has to shoot the ghosts before they reach their location and each ghost takes a number of hits depending on the difficulty. The player is able to 'super charge' their weapon by using the pump action and is physically able to move around the room and dodge the ghosts in order to avoid being hit.

2.6   Challenges

During game development a number of challenges were encountered that highlighted some potential issues with our approach:

- Accurately determining the direction of physical surface in relation to the camera so that the ghost perpendicularly floats out of the surface proved to be a demanding task. The Tango builds up a complex model of the room over time and often starts with incomplete information, so occasionally our system would either not locate a surface or misinterpret a surface so the ghost would come out at a strange angle. The longer the Tango was able to build the depth image then the less likely there was of errant ghosts.
- Changes in lighting within the environment conflicts with the depth sensors. IR doesn't work as well outdoors, in sunlight or in a very bright room and depth information can be degraded in these conditions. In addition, dark surfaces also will reduce the quality of the depth information again leading to strange ghost behavior.
- In order to reduce processing requirements, the game would only interrogate the 3D model of the environment when a pulse was fired from the gun. However, this meant that if you moved around the room physical objects wouldn't obscure the ghost as it advances towards you leading to a break in immersion. Moving to a design where the environment is interrogated each frame would allow real world objects to obscure

the ghosts, even when in flight allowing players to truly interact with their environment (such as hiding behind the table). However, this significantly increases processing requirements and can reduce frame rate.

3   Conclusion

Although very simple, Ghost Hunter shows a good example of being able to mix virtual and game play elements with the real world. By exploiting the feature rich functionality of the Tango tablet and integrating with a commercially available gun controller we were able to rapidly produce a short game that enables you to hunt ghosts anywhere.

This short project has demonstrated that AR games can now be developed on today's mobile platform and with the continued advancement in mobile technologies and computer vision techniques we will see a proliferation in AR based game play and games.

Immersive Journalism in VR: Four Theoretical Domains for Researching a Narrative Design Framework

Gary M. Hardee(✉)

University of Texas at Dallas, Richardson, USA
ghardee@utdallas.edu

Abstract. A major focus of research in Virtual Reality (VR) media examines the technological affordances for creating immersion, which in turn can generate presence – the feeling of being there – in a virtual environment. This research has given rise to an emerging form of fact-based storytelling called immersive journalism, a term used to describe digitally produced stories designed to provide a first-person, interactive experience with news events. This paper examines the concept of immersive journalism and discusses both its potential and its limitations as a narrative and journalistic genre. Immersive journalism will require a new narrative design framework, and four theoretical domains are discussed as underscoring this framework. The four are VR presence, narrative, cognition and journalistic ethics.

Keywords: Journalism · Virtual reality · Embodiment · Interactive narrative · Situated cognition · Ethics

1 Introduction to Immersive Journalism

Immersive journalism is a term used to describe an emerging form of news reporting that seeks to capitalize on the technological enhancements of virtual environments and Virtual Reality (VR) displays. Immersive journalism is described as an evolution of long-held, ongoing news reporting practices that attempt to elicit "a connection between the audience and the news story" [1]. In the 1950s, journalists Edward R. Murrow and Fred Friendly worked to create stronger audience connection in their broadcast series See It Now [2]; later, this form of journalistic reporting was presented in the You Are There radio and television series, re-created moments in history produced by former CBS news anchor Walter Cronkite [3]. Today, some journalists are beginning to use VR technology, and specifically Head Mounted Display (HMD) devices, to explore the narrative and technological possibilities and limitations for creating enhanced connection. The goal is to generate a greater sense of presence in a virtual representation of a news event. This paper analyzes the primary objective of immersive journalism – to create presence – and examines four interdisciplinary theoretical domains that underscore a design framework that can optimize communications potential of VR as a channel for journalism. Those four theoretical domains include VR, narrative, cognition and journalistic ethics.

© Springer International Publishing Switzerland 2016
S. Lackey and R. Shumaker (Eds.): VAMR 2016, LNCS 9740, pp. 679–690, 2016.
DOI: 10.1007/978-3-319-39907-2_65

Before examining each of these, however, it is important to note how immersive journalism has arisen from decades of research into VR theory and HMD technologies. Renowned VR researcher Morton Heilig filed a patent for his first HMD in 1957 [4]. In the 1990s, Biocca and Levy specifically analyzed VR as a potential journalism channel. They noted that the history of communications media is "a history of interfaces that deliver information to more sensorimotor channels with increased sensory realism in each channel" [5]. The authors foresaw the need for interdisciplinary research into VR, one that combined cognitive psychology, haptic studies, multimedia design, communication theory and socio-cultural studies. They surmised that the ultimate communications interface "will never arrive" but is instead an always-moving target [6]. Still, such a Holy Grail caution has not abated the allure of using multisensory computer interfaces to give an audience a greater sense of presence in the virtual experience, and immersive journalism is yet another demonstration of the ongoing attraction to travel this fossilized path.

Advances in VE technology – 3D computer-generated graphics software, web-based videogame engines, 360-degree video technology, and HMD devices – are making VR in general, and immersive journalism as well, a less expensive, more commercially viable proposition. Biocca and Levy viewed VR as moving steadily closer to fulfilling "the oldest dream of the journalist, to conquer time and space. … the ability to create a sense on the part of audiences of being present at distant, newsworthy locations and events" [5, p. 137]. Creating a sense of presence in distant events – in terms of both time and space – is the chief motivation underscoring immersive journalism research. The objective is to create connections that can elicit a first-person, perhaps even emotional, reaction. Further, greater connection to the story could potentially address a concern about "compassion fatigue" in audiences, the "desensitization and emotional burnout, as a phenomenon associated with pervasive communication about social problems" [7, p. 687].

2   Four Research Domains for Immersive Journalism

The first theoretical domain to consider in researching a design framework for immersive journalism is an overview of the theory and research on presence, which is most commonly defined as the feeling of being in the virtual environment (VE). This definition is examined further in the next section. For the purposes of this paper, presence is viewed not as an absolute but as a continuum. At its optimal communicative state, presence is a product of what Mel Slater defines as both Place Illusion (PI) and Plausibility Illusion (Psi) [8]. PI is the feeling of a virtual embodied transformation into the VR experience, and Psi is the belief that events are really happening even though the audience knows they are not real. These two illusions can contribute to response-as-if-real actions (RAIR) by the user, which in turn enhances the expressive power of the story and contributes to the audience's willingness to suspend disbelief – a critical factor in any successful narrative [8].

The second theoretical domain is what one early VR engineer, William Bricken, proclaimed as the physics of VR – cognitive psychology [9]. Marshal McLuhan wrote that all media "are extensions of some faculty, psychic or physical" [10]. In this paper, two lines of cognitive theory are discussed as the foundation that supports presence and VR's potential as a communications channel – be it for journalism or other uses. One is embodied cognition, which holds that the bodily activity shapes the world of human experience and presupposes higher forms of decision-making. The second is situated cognition theory, which contends that learning emerges through actions in specific, cultural, contextual arenas. More than other communications media, VR holds promise as a channel for embodied activity, multisensory information within the virtual representation of a contextual, lived experience.

A third perspective that will be examined briefly is narrative theory. At its core, journalism is about telling stories, and narrative theory supports storytelling as a time-tested, psychological organizing mechanism for understanding time, space and causality – for making sense of the world. Philosopher Paul Ricoeur identifies narrative as the way in which humans understand time and flat out declares that narrative is the "guardian" of time [11]. Psychologist Jerome Bruner contends that narrative "gives shape to things in the real world and often bestows on them a title to reality" [12, p. 8]. The challenge in immersive journalism is to design a framework that makes the handling of time, space and causality credible in an interactive medium – credibility that Slater contends can be difficult to maintain and easily lost [8]. Well-designed, interactive narrative, however, can support the goal of presence.

Finally, the principles, standards and ethics of professional journalism will be discussed. For a fact-based storytelling genre in a new medium to be embraced as journalism, these standards and codes of ethics stand at the gate as the guardian of professionalism and credibility. Immersive journalism is and will be held accountable to the current and historical ethics of the profession, standards such as accuracy, fairness, thoroughness, context, transparency, accountability and awareness of bias. Journalistic codes of ethics [13, 14], common to many news organizations, are critical to maintaining journalism's credibility with an audience but could potentially conflict with immersion techniques used to create the illusion of presence. Each of the next sections discusses these four domains in greater detail.

3   VR and the Pursuit of Presence

As stated above, the chief motivation for creating immersive journalism is to create a stronger connection to a news story by enhancing the audience's presence in the virtual representation of the real-world event. Presence is a term VR researchers use, often quite liberally, to define a phenomenological "feeling of being there" in the virtual environment (VE). Immersion is commonly reserved as the term used to define the level of fidelity – visual, auditory, haptic – afforded by the technology [8, 15, 16].

Some journalists and news organizations use the term presence to describe their 360-degree videos that cover a wide range of news topics, such as the demographic and economic changes impacting Iowa farmers [17] and the flight of immigrants from war in Syria [18]. In introducing its first 360 video series, The New York Times described them as a new form of storytelling that "enables an uncanny feeling of connection with people whose lives are far from our own. By creating a 360-degree environment that encircles the viewer, virtual reality creates the experience of being present within distant worlds ..." [18]. ABC states on its website the VR opens the door to "boundless possibilities, allowing viewers to be anywhere we are at any time" [19]. De la Peña develops immersive journalism using a videogame engine, 3D computer graphics, animation software, motion-tracking technology and HMDs to report on a wide range of topics, from hunger in Los Angeles and domestic violence to the war in Syria [20].

The concept of presence in VR applications typically includes the ability of the audience to take actions within the VE model, which in turn responds to the interactivity with perceptual and sometimes physiological feedback. The Handbook of Virtual Environments states that virtual environments and virtual reality provide a "model of reality with which a human can interact, getting information from the model by ordinary human senses such as sight, sound, and touch and/or controlling the model using ordinary human actions such as position and/or motion of body parts and voice" [21, p. 33]. Further, based on a body of research, Slater contends that the qualia of presence, meaning the internal and subjective component of sense perceptions, arises from the affordances of virtual reality media in which "people respond with their whole bodies, treating what they perceive as real" [8, p. 3549].

Using these definitions as criteria to define presence in VR, there is little surprise that one founder of a VR startup company criticizes the most common form of immersive journalism – 360-degree video – that is presented by numerous news organizations. Writing about The New York Times' 360 videos and its initiative to distribute 1 million Google Cardboard display devices, Smith states that this should not be called VR [22]. Smith writes, "Never, ever take control of the camera away from the viewer. .... The bad news for applications like the NYT VR application and 360 video as a whole is that it's impossible to avoid breaking this rule with 360 video. 360 video is inherently limited ..." [22].

Smith's criticism highlights the problem of, as he says, "shoehorning old formats into new technologies." This is a particular challenge for immersive journalism and points to the need for new content design practices that can transition passive journalistic storytelling into practices that create higher levels of presence in VR media. Still, the critique that 360 video does not qualify as VR seems too strident. Instead, immersive journalism should be viewed as a continuum from low to high based on how well the narrative creates presence and handles narrative time, space and causality.

The history of storytelling is replete with experimentation in ways to transport an audience to a specific time and place and help them understand the causality of events through the organizing mechanisms of narrative. From cave paintings and ancient oral storytellers to paintings, photographs, newspapers, television and now VR narratives, storytelling represents time, space and offers some level of causality, either through the communication of a sequence of events or through information that the audience itself organizes. These core aspects of narrative are discussed further below. Arguably, 360 video enhances temporal and spatial presence not provided in 2D and allows modest enhancements to embodied presence by allowing the audience to turn their heads and bodies to see a broader contextual landscape of the story. Thinking of VR as a continuum, 360 video should be placed at the low end.

Slater's research provides both a language and framework for examining what immersive journalism should accomplish to move to the upper end of a presence continuum. As mentioned above, presence is shaped by both Place Illusion (PI) and Plausibility Illusion (Psi). Slater contends that PI is a factor of the level "sensorimotor contingencies" (SC) that are afforded by the VR system. "SCs refer to the actions that we know to carry out in order to perceive. … The SCs supported by a system define a set of valid actions that are meaningful in terms of perception within the virtual environment depicted. For example, turn your head or bend forward and the rendered visual images ideally change the same as they would if you were in an equivalent physical environment" [8, p. 3550]. The closer that SCs align to those used in physical reality, Slater states, the greater the sense of "placeness" or PI.

As an example, Slater collaborated with Maria Sanchez-Vives and De la Peña in the development of an immersive journalism story about detainees in the United States federal prison at Guantanamo, Cuba. De la Peña, a former Newsweek magazine reporter and documentary filmmaker, states that her research lab strives to create stories that elicit visceral reactions [18]. She calls immersive journalism an "empathy machine" [23]. The motion-tracking technology that De la Peña uses affords enhanced kinesthetics, allowing the virtual environment to respond to movement of the viewer. The Guantanamo Bay journalism experiment [24] allows viewers to undergo an illusionary transformation of their physical body and to enter perceptually the body of a detainee. To enhance physical presence, viewers are asked to sit in a chair with their hands behind the back. The virtual image presented is of a detainee with his hands behind his and squatting on a wooden box in a cell.

For immersive journalism to move higher on a presence continuum and optimize VR as a journalistic communications channel, then enhancing embodied engagement with the VE and the narrative is key. As Biocca and Levy note, "If the mass audience must be forced to view passively, then this experience fails to deliver the full promise of virtual reality. It becomes just another form of passive television, even if it is stereoscopic" [5, p. 139]. Eastgate et al. write that "it is reasonable to suppose that VE technology can offer more representations of the types of interactivity commonly encountered in real life" [25, p. 372]. The authors note that interactivity can mean both affording the user to take action to change a virtual object or virtual scene as well as updating the VE in response to the user's movement and position. As well, the authors consider a theory of presence a complex, multidimensional perception formed by multisensory data and cognitive processes [25]. The next section discusses two cognitive theory domains that are notably applicable to presence and immersive journalism.

4   Cognitive Theory, Presence and Immersive Journalism

The value of creating enhanced presence in a news story to create better understanding is supported by literature on cognitive theory. Two theoretical domains that are notably applicable to VR media share the concept of human activity as a central theme. These two are embodied and situated cognition.

Biocca notes that VR technology promises the potential for the artist – or in this case the journalist – to make "the creations of the imagination more literal" by engaging the user in an embodied experience. Biocca contended that a theory of presence rests on discovering what is going on when people use their senses to understand and interpret their surrounding environment and when they interact with objects in that environment [26]. He contended that the mind is at the heart of presence, and the mind is anchored by the body.

This contention aligns with the literature on embodied cognition. Maurice Merleau-Ponty argued that the body structures human understanding and experience in the real world [27]. He viewed physiology and psychology not as "parallel sciences, but rather two characterizations of behavior, the first concrete and the second abstract" [27, p. 33]. Hubert Dreyfuss and Samuel Todes amplified this philosophical perspective in their research. Dreyfus wrote that humans make themselves at home in the world "by moving so as to organize a stable spatiotemporal field in which we use our skills to make determinate the determinable objects that appear in that field. The skills we acquire then feed back into the perceptual world, which becomes more and more determinate as we learn to make more refined discriminations and have more reliable anticipations. Merleau-Ponty calls this feedback phenomenon the intentional arc" [28, pp. xvi-xvii].

Narrative in general, and journalism specifically, is about representing the world of human experiences. Bodily activity within a virtual mediation of real-world experiences can enhance understanding of the narrative. Todes contended that the "existence of the human body as capable of activity is necessary for" understanding the world of human experience. The primary form of directed action is an intention of the body, a body-directedness, which first gives us the global sense of space and time presupposed by all our higher personal forms of directed activity, principally those of will and judgment" [28, p. 65]. Or as cognitive theorist Andy Clark states: "… to be conscious is to be a subject of experience – to feel the toothache, to taste the bananas, to smell the croissant, and so on" [29, p. 37] Clark cites Dreyfus, who wrote about the "thickness of understanding" that comes from extensive bodily and real-world experience [29, p. 37]. Intelligent behavior, Clark wrote, stems from "the complex interplay of neural operations, bodily actions, and the use of multiple aids, props, and artifacts" [29, p. 161].

The potential of immersive journalism rests in the technological affordance of bodily actions and the amplification of multisensory feedback, adding kinesthetic, haptic and olfactory information to the visual and auditory. Biocca and Levy wrote that "virtual reality facilitates the imagination not by depressing the senses but by immersing the senses in information from the illusory space" [5, p. 136].

In addition to embodiment, the illusory space in VR affords contextual, situated activity. Situated cognition theory holds that cognition is a complex social phenomenon that involves persons solving problems in a specific arena – a culturally contextual time and space. Situated cognition theory holds that cognition "observed in everyday practice is distributed – stretched over, not divided among – mind, body, activity and culturally organized settings" [30, p. 1]. Lave researched the use of math in real-world settings – such as a grocery store– as a means of analyzing cognitive psychology's accounts for "stability and continuity of cognitive activity across settings through the psychological mechanism of learning transfer. That is, knowledge acquired in 'context free'

circumstances is supposed to be available for general applications in all contexts. ..."
[30, p. 8]. The conclusion that arose from her studies was that the more appropriate unit
of analysis of cognition "is the whole person in action, acting with the settings of that
activity" [30, p. 17].

VEs and VR can serve as a stage for representing culturally contextual, lived experiences. When VR and VEs afford psychological and embodied actions – allowing users
to problem solve – they become arenas for practicing and experimenting situated cognition. Immersive journalism, as both a VR stage and a narrative, can afford audiences the
opportunities to explore time, space and causality based on a fact-based reporting. Both
embodied activity and problem solving in specific contextual arenas can be exercised,
contributing to a better understanding of news events represented, to the audience's
sense of presence and a connection to the story. Riva et al. wrote that "characteristics
of the 'story' created when a subject is exploring a VE plays a key role in enhancing the
sense of presence: to be a part of a narration, to play a more or less defined role in the
story could influence the sense of identification ... and the state of presence during a
virtual experience" [9, p. 654]. Mantovani and Catelnuovo reference the relationship of
situated activity to Csikszentmihalyi's theory of flow, which "refers to a merging of
action and awareness, during which a person loses self-consciousness and a sense of
time, focusing on the present, and blocking out the past and the future" [31,
Sect. 11.3.2.4].

5   Narrative and Presence

Psychologist Jerome Bruner wrote that stories are not innocent; they always have a
message [12, p. 15]. Kovach and Rosensteil wrote that journalism is "storytelling with
a purpose. That purpose is to provide people with information they need to understand
the world" [32, p. 214]. What both perspectives express is the critical role of narrative
as means of guiding the audience to understanding information. It is in such perspectives
that immersive journalism practitioners see such great potential in VR as a new emerging
canvas for storytelling.

Just as storytellers have reconfigured narrative frameworks from medium to medium –
from oral storytelling, to novels, to film, to videogames – designing stories for VR will
require new practices. As Biocca and Levy point out, "Conceptually, VR journalism may
be no different than present-day journalism. Certainly, the tools will change. But
constructing a news space will increase the level of complexity of the news tasks by a
power of 10.... Undoubtedly, the art and science of journalism will change" [5, p. 146].

A key research question for narrative in any medium, and certainly for immersive
journalism, is what characteristics of storytelling are medium-free, or transmedial, and
which are medium-specific to VR. As a starting point, Marie-Laure Ryan proposes that
certain core characteristics of storytelling are medium-free: character, events, setting,
time, space, and causality [33]. Two other concepts – immersion and presence – should
be added as transmedial. The chapter structure of a printed novel can create page-turning
immersion in the linear progression of the plot; film techniques and camera angles can
be used to create a sense of presence. Both readers and audience can be technologically

induced to feel a strong connection to and presence in a story. In VEs and VR, however, immersion and presence hold particular significance. Presence is arguably the VR's core aesthetic. As multiple speakers at the first Vision Summit 2016, a conference on VR and Augmented Reality, emphasized, presence supplies VR media a special communications power, the "magic of being transported to another place" [34].

Technological possibilities and limitations for immersion can shape the level of presence in VR and will dictate what types of immersive journalism stories work best and how they should be designed and reported. Oral storytellers understand that the "live performance of face-to-face interaction makes a difference as to what kind of stories are told, how they are told, and why they are told" [33, p. 28]. The same holds for VEs and VR.

Practitioners of immersive journalism will have to consider how to move beyond thinking of VEs and VR as virtual containers for information and begin thinking of how to build fact-bound storyworlds that are channels for embodied activity and imaginative exploration. Alex McDowell, film producer and narrative scholar at the University of Southern California, contends that designing storyworlds is the must-have framework for VR that will disrupt the linear storytelling of other media [35]. In Storyworlds across Media, Ryan writes: "Storyworlds hold a greater fascination for the imagination than the plots that take place in them, because plots are self-enclosed, linear arrangements of events that come to an end while storyworlds can always sprout branches to their core plots that further immerse people, thereby providing new pleasures" [33, p. 19]. Designing storyworlds, and presence within them, will complicate the journalistic processes of story design and reporting, placing greater emphasis on recording specific timelines and spatial characteristics.

Techniques from other media, such as the fade-ins and fade-outs to communicate the passage of time in film, could break presence, necessitating the consideration of new methods for handling time. Storytellers will need to understand and design VR, medium-specific narrative clues that will help audiences transition from passive media that are largely based on literary frameworks and into interactive, embodied spaces – in other narrative spaces more like lived experiences in the real word.

The critical starting point for research into new narrative design methods is from the perspective of presence. The design of storytelling will have to grow from solely repre-sentations of "what is" and expand to explorations of "what if," to think of VR as space to engage in "acts of imagination" [33] that a feeling of presence allows. Immersive journalism stories will need to afford levels of reactivity in the VE and interactivity by the user in order to support both place illusion and plausibility illusion. To optimize the medium, immersive journalism will need to enhance the responses-as-if-real by the user. This aligns with what Rosensteil contends is the current evolution of journalism, which has moved from an ethic of "trust me" to an ethic of "show me" [36]. Immersive jour-nalism practitioners will have to move away from passive authorship that speaks at the audience and towards narrative that immerses and guides the audience along potentially multiple narrative paths that provide varying changing perspectives and responsive environments.

6   Journalism Ethics in a New Medium

A fourth consideration for designing immersive journalism will undoubtedly be the current journalism practices and codes of ethics that professional journalism associations and news organizations typically embrace. Two representative examples are The American Press Institute's elements of journalism [13] and the Society of Professional Journalists' Code of Ethics [14]. Commonly these ethics define what journalists and news organizations should do and how they view their role in society – as informer, interpreter or sometimes advocate [37]. Values that are typically codified are the zeal for accuracy and context through thorough, fair and transparent reporting. Kovach and Rosenstiel contend that, although every generation creates its own journalism largely in reaction to technological advances, the purpose, underlying elements and essential values remain "remarkably constant" across countries, cultures and political systems [32, pp. 19–20].

Journalists have long viewed their profession – the Fourth Estate – as a virtuous guardianship of the public interest, and there is reason to expect this ethic to bridge new communications channels. Still, the language and mediation mechanics of VR appear inconsistent with journalism's objectives of realism and transparency. The art of creating presence in VR is described as the "illusion" of place and plausibility. VR developers speak of technological methods for tricking the brain or fooling the senses to create what some call consensual hallucination [5].

Biocca and Levy note that all news reporting is some kind of simulation: the print journalist re-creates an event with colorful language; the television news crew controls and edits what the viewer sees. An ever-present ethical question for journalism in many media is one of balancing engagement and reality. In television, CBS producer Don Hewitt called the balancing act a fine line between show business and news business, in which "some people stay so far away from the line that nobody wants to watch" and others keep crossing the line. Hewitt said the trick "is to walk up to that line and touch it with your toe but don't cross it" [38, p. 254]. Kovach and Rosenstiel contend engagement should be journalism's ethical commitment to the citizenry. They state that engaging storytelling and information are not in conflict, but instead are points on a continuum. Good storytelling pushes the two points together. [32, p. 214].

As practitioners of immersive journalism develop new frameworks for storytelling in VR, new journalism practices, standards and ethics will likely evolve to address the unique technological capabilities of VR. De la Peña, a leading developer of immersive journalism, acknowledges that VR media, given the possibilities for creating a robust illusion of presence, could easily allow for propaganda and mistruth as much, if not more, than other media. In an interview with The New York Times, she said, "What does transparency look like when you have goggles on? I don't know the answer, but it is something I think about a lot" [23]. Kovach and Rosenstiel state that whatever form journalism takes, its main purpose is distillation, storytelling that extracts the essential meaning, engages the public and provide "critical analytical thinking that illuminates the matter under consideration" [32, p. 215]. The engaging potential of presence in a fact-based narrative will need to be balanced with new methods for communicating the accuracy of the facts, the fairness of multiple perspectives and the thoroughness of reporting that are used to support the simulation.

7 Summary

As in many fields of research into VR, immersive journalism seeks to take advantage of ongoing enhancements to the technology in an effort to provide an audience a greater sense of presence in virtual stories about news vents, and perhaps creating a stronger connection to the events portrayed. This goal requires new design considerations for storytelling in a nascent medium. To optimize the communicative potential of VR, this paper has proposed that ongoing development of immersive journalism should be an interdisciplinary effort that crosses four domains. Those four are theories on VR presence, narrative, cognition and journalistic ethics. VR presence is a core aesthetic of the technology and a primary motivator for storytelling in the medium. Narrative theory provides a starting point for determining what core characteristics of storytelling transcend all media and which are unique to VR. Cognition theory, specifically focusing on embodied and situated cognition, underscores the possibilities and limitations of VR as a communications channel that is potentially more powerful than other media. Finally, professional journalistic standards and ethics should be examined given the theories of presence that emphasize illusion. Accuracy, fairness, thoroughness and transparency will likely have to be redefined for immersive journalism applications.

References

1. de la Peña, N., Weil, P., Llobera, J., Giannopoulos, E., Pomes, A., Spanlang, B., Slater, M.: Immersive journalism: immersive virtual reality for the first-person experience of news. Presence **19**, 291–301 (2010)
2. Simon, R.: Museum TV. See it Now: U.S. Documentary Series (n.d): http://www.museum.tv/eotv/seeitnow.htm
3. Siegel, R., Norris, M. NPR, 23 October 2003. Walter Cronkite: history's lessons: http://www.npr.org/templates/story/story.php?storyId=1480691. Accessed 23 Oct 2003
4. mortonheilig.com (n.d): http://www.mortonheilig.com/TelesphereMask.pdf
5. Biocca, F., Levy, M.R.: Communication applications of virtual reality. In: Biocca, F., Levy, M.R. (eds.) Communication in the Age of Virtual Reality, p. 128. Lawrence Erlbaum Associates, Publishers, Hillsdale (1995)
6. Biocca, F., Levy, M.R.: The vision of virtual reality. In: Biocca, F., Levy, M.R. (eds.) Communication in the Age of Virtual Reality. Lawrence Erlbaum Associates, Publishers, Hillsdale (1995)
7. Kinnick, K.N., Krugman, D.M., Cameron, G.T.: Compassion fatigue: communication and burnout toward social problems. Journal. Mass Commun. Q. **73**(3), 687–707 (1996)
8. Slater, M.: Place illusion and plausibility can lead to realistic behaviour in immersive virtual environments. Philos. Trans. Roy. Soc. B **364**, 3549–3557 (2009)
9. Riva, G., Davide, F., IJsselsteijn, W. (eds.): Being There: Concepts, Effects and Measurements of User Presence in Synthetic Environments (vol. 5 of Emerging Communication: Studies on New Technologies and Practices in Communication). Ios Press, Amsteradam (2003)

10. McLuhan, M., Fiore, Q., Agel, J.: The Medium is the Massage. Ginko Press, Corte Madera (1967)
11. Ricoeur, P.: Time and Narrative, vol. 1. The University of Chicago Press, Chicago (1984)
12. Bruner, J.: Making Stories: Law, Literature, Life, Paperback edn. Harvard University Press, Cambridge (2005)
13. American Press Institute: The elements of Journalism (n.d). http://www.americanpressinstitute.org/journalism-essentials/what-is-journalism/elements-journalism/. Accessed 19 July 2015
14. SPJ Code of Ethics, 6 September 2014. Society of Professional Journalists: http://www.spj.org/ethicscode.asp. Accessed June 2015
15. Slater, M.: Measuring presence: a response to the Witmer and Singer presence questionnaire. Presence: Teleoper. Virtual Environ. **8**(5), 560–565 (1999)
16. Slater, M., Steed, A., Usoh, M.: Being There Together: Experiments on Presence in Virtual Environments. Collection of Papers for Lecture Series, University College London, Department of Computer Science (2013). http://publicationslist.org/melslater. Accessed 19 July 2015
17. Jackson, S., Gannon, C.: Harvest of Change (2015). The Des Moines Register: http://www.desmoinesregister.com/pages/interactives/harvest-of-change/
18. Silverstein, J.: The New York Times Magazine. The New York Times: http://www.nytimes.com/2015/11/08/magazine/the-displaced-introduction.html?_r=0. Accessed 5 Nov 2015
19. ABC News VR See The Whole Picture. ABC News (n.d): http://abcnews.go.com/US/fullpage?id=33768357
20. Emblematic Group (n.d): http://www.emblematicgroup.com/#/content/
21. Hale, K.S., Stanney, K.M. (eds.): Handbook of Virtual Environments: Design, Implementation, and Applications, 2nd edn. CRC Press Taylor & Francis Group, Boca Raton (2016)
22. Smith, W.: Wired. Wired Culture: http://www.wired.com/2015/11/360-video-isnt-virtual-reality/. Accessed 16 Nov 2015
23. Manly, L.: Arts, 19 November 2015. The New York Times: http://www.nytimes.com/2015/11/22/arts/a-virtual-reality-revolution-coming-to-a-headset-near-you.html?_r=1. Accessed Feb 2016
24. de la Peña, N.: Towards Immersive Journalism: The IPSRESS Experience, 15 July 2009. YouTube: https://www.youtube.com/watch?v=_z8pSTMfGSo. Accessed Feb 2016
25. Eastgate, R.M., Wilson, J.R., D'Cruz, M.: Structured development of virtual environments. In: Hale, K.S., Stanney, K.M. (eds.) Handbook of Virtual Environments: Design, Implemntation, and Applications, 2nd edn. CRC Press Taylor & Francis Group, Boca Raton (2015)
26. Biocca, F.: Preface. In: Riva, G., David, F., IJsselsteijn, W. (eds.) Being There: Concepts, Effects and Measurements of User Presence in Synthetic Environments, p. 344. IOS Press, Amsterdam (2003). http://www.neurovr.org/emerging/volume5.html. Accessed Feb 2016
27. Merleau-Ponty, M.: Phenomenology of Perception. Taylor and Francis e-Library ed., Routledge, New York (2015). Accessed 26 July 2015
28. Todes, S.: Body and World. The MIT Press, Cambridge (2001)
29. Clark, A.: Mindware: An Introduction to the Philosophy of Cognitive Science. Oxford University Press, Oxford (2001)
30. Lave, J.: Cognition in Practice: Mind, Mathematics and Culture in Everyday Life. Cambridge University Press, Cambridge (1988)

31. Mantovani, F., Catelnuovo, G.: Sense of presence in virtual training: enhancing skill acquisition and transfer of knowledge through learning experience in virtual environments. In: Riva, G., David, F., IJsselsteijn, W. (eds.) Being There: Concepts, Effects and Measurements of User Presence in Synthetic Environments. IOS Press, Amsterdam (2003)

32. Kovach, B., Rosenstiel, T.: The Elements of Journalism. Three Rivers Press, New York (2014)

33. Ryan, M.-L., Thon, J.-N. (eds.): Storyworlds Across Media: Toward a Media-Conscious Narratology. University of Nebraska Press, Lincoln (2014)

34. Riccitiello, J.: Vision Summit 2016 Keynote. Los Angeles, California, USA, 10 Feb 2016. https://www.youtube.com/watch?v=2hYDtxCtzdA. Accessed 11 Feb 2016

35. McDowell, A.: Vision Summit 2016 Keynote. Los Angeles, California, USA, 10 Feb 2016. https://www.youtube.com/watch?v=2hYDtxCtzdA. Accessed 11 Feb 2016

36. Rosensteil, T.: The Future of Journalism: Tom Rosensteil at TEDxAtlanta. Atlanta, GA, USA: TEDx Talks (2013). https://www.youtube.com/watch?v=RuBE_dP900Y. Accessed 28 May 2013

37. Ward, S.J.: Journalism Ethics. In: Wahl-Jorgensen, K., Hanitzsch, T. (eds.) The handbook of Journalism Studies, pp. 295–307. Routledge Taylor & Francis, New York (2009)

38. Newton, E. (ed.): Crusaders, Scoundrels, Journalists: The Newseum's Most Intriguing Newspeople. Times Books a division of Random House Inc., New York (1999)

Virtual Environments as Communication Technologies of Faith

John F. Kay$^{(\boxtimes)}$

University of Texas at Dallas, Richardson, TX, USA
John.kay@utdallas.edu

Abstract. His paper analyzes virtual environments (V.E.'s) as possible technologies for the communication of the belief system known as the Christian faith. V.E. technologies are computer-generated, 3D-appearing, multi-sensorial, interactive, graphical simulations. Some V.E.'s, such as virtual reality (V.R.), some augmented reality (A.R.), and desktop digital games *with* head-mounted displays (H.M.D.'s), are immersive technologies, while other V.E.'s, such as desktop digital games *without* H.M.D.'s and some A.R., are not immersive technologies. These technologies may be considered communication technologies because they communicate or represent reality. The faith that has been, and can be, communicated is multi-dimensional and consists of sensory information, thoughts, and a variety of emotions. The first-hand study of immersive V.E.'s, although not the "dominant means of communication" as the bound book has been for Christianity (Lundby 2013), might be able to reveal that V.E.'s can communicate dimensions of the faith that earlier technologies have been unable to do.

Keywords: Virtual environments · Christianity · Faith · Communication · Communication technologies

1 Introduction

Although virtual environments (V.E.'s) could simulate many different faiths, i.e., systems of religious beliefs, the focus here is on Christianity. The Christian faith has been communicated along the historical path leading from New Testament times to the Church of today. That faith needed communication to survive. The Apostle Paul asked the Roman Christians, "And how are they to believe in one of whom they have never heard? And how are they to hear without someone to proclaim him?" (Romans 10:14, [New Revised Standard Version]). Paul sent people to preach. Others since him have used communication technologies to communicate the faith.

While earlier scholars (Mazuryk and Gervautz 1996) equate V.E. with virtual reality (V.R.), V.E. is the broader term. V.E. technologies are computer-generated, three-dimensional-appearing, multi-sensorial, interactive, graphical simulations. Figure 1 shows that some V.E.'s, such as virtual reality, some augmented reality, and desktop digital games with head-mounted displays (H.M.D.'s), are immersive technologies, while other V.E.'s, such as desktop digital games without H.M.D.'s and some augmented reality, are not immersive technologies. As this paper will show, immersive

© Springer International Publishing Switzerland 2016
S. Lackey and R. Shumaker (Eds.): VAMR 2016, LNCS 9740, pp. 691–701, 2016.
DOI: 10.1007/978-3-319-39907-2_66

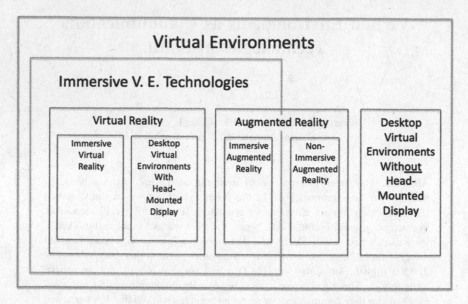

Fig. 1. Immersive and Non-immersive virtual environment technologies.

refers to the technologies rather than the experiences of the users. These technologies may be considered communication technologies because they communicate or represent reality. This paper analyzes V.E.'s as possible communication technologies of Christian faith.

2   Dimensions of Faith

What are the dimensions of faith that Christians have communicated? The dimensions are the component aspects of the belief system and the many actions Christians have taken to proclaim that faith. Christians have spoken, written, read, and heard proclaimed texts about Bible stories and verses, moral teachings, theological teachings, Christian-living examples, and inspiring stories of Christians throughout the millennia. They have read and said the liturgy. They have read and sung words to the hymns and songs. They have heard music of instruments and the voices of worship leaders and fellow parishioners. They have felt the waters of baptism, the wood of the communion railing, and the cups of communion. For holy communion/the Eucharist, they have tasted the bread and the grape juice, which Welch originally developed as a substitute for communion wine. They have tasted their own tears in response to an affective sermon or after learning the news of the death of a fellow church member. They have smelled the scent of the flowers on the altar or the overpowering perfume or cologne on the person sitting in front of them. If a virtual environment could be used to communicate the faith, then the V.E. could draw upon many of these dimensions.

3   Virtual Environments

3.1   Inherent Qualities of V.E. Technologies

For McLuhan (1994, p. 34), all media are extensions of people's senses. Most media extend what we see and hear, but some extend other senses as well. Virtual reality and augmented reality extend the human mind and body into the world. Both of these V.E. technologies immerse human users, not their avatars.

1. Of Virtual Reality

Virtual reality (V.R.) or immersive V.R. is one of three virtual environments (V.E.) on which this research is focusing. The other two V.E.'s of concern are augmented reality and desktop V.E., such as serious games and simulations. Ivan Sutherland developed the idea of the first V.R. system in 1968 (Mazuryk and Gervautz 1996, p. 2).

Writing a decade before the introduction of the Oculus Rift and other reasonably-priced head mounted displays (H.M.D.'s), Burdea and Coiffet provide the following definition:

> Virtual reality is a high-end user-computer interface that involves real-time simulation and interactions through multiple sensorial channels. These sensorial modalities are visual, auditory, tactile, smell, and taste (Burdea and Coiffet 2003, p. 3).

V.R. has many beneficial inherent qualities. Immersive V.R. allows users to interact with a virtual environment. Users can transverse the V.E. by moving their feet, their hands, the rest of their bodies, and their heads in physical space by donning H.M.D.'s and wearing haptic sleeves and gloves. The adjective haptic refers to the quality of touch.

Virtual reality technology, especially desktop V.E., affords the creation of virtual environments and virtual worlds, which are a type of V.E. Schroeder (2008, p. 2) sees virtual worlds as "virtual environments that people experience as ongoing over time and that have large populations which they experience together with others as a world for social interaction." The development of reasonably-priced, commercially-manufactured V.R. head-mounted displays (H.M.D.'s) such as the Oculus Rift, which probably will cost approximately $300 instead of $10,000 for earlier H.M.D.'s, should lead to an explosion of V.R. applications. V.R. H.M.D.'s and headphones allow people to step into V.E.'s and see and hear 3D worlds. The addition of haptic technologies will afford the ability to touch and feel the contents of the V.E. If a worship service were simulated in V.R. with haptic capabilities, for example, the user could touch and feel a virtual holy-communion cup.

2. Of Augmented Reality

This research is focusing also on augmented reality (A.R.). Like those of V.R., the technologies of A.R. can be immersive. Broll et al. (2008), for example, presents A.R. games on mobile phones, but these technologies are not immersive. Milgram et al. (1995, p. 283) define A.R. broadly as "augmenting natural feedback to the operator with simulated cues" and more narrowly as "a form of virtual reality where the participant's head-mounted display is transparent, allowing a clear view of the real world."

Klopfer and Squire (2008, p. 205) "define 'augmented reality' broadly as a situation in which a real world context is dynamically overlaid with coherent location or context sensitive virtual information". Milgram's stricter definition focuses on the technology, while the definition of Klopfer and Squire lifts the experience. However, Klopfer and Sheldon (2010, p. 86) refer to A.R. as a "technology that blends real-and virtual-world experiences". As with the recommendations for V.R., the understanding of A.R. should start with technological definitions before advancing to the affordances; otherwise, the result is a comparison of incompatibles.

Augmented reality has beneficial qualities that can lead to many interesting applications of the technology. Studying the educational uses of A.R., Wu et al. (2013) states that A.R. "enables students to use 3D synthetic objects to augment the visual perception of the target system or environment." Wu describes A.R.'s benefits:

> With mobile devices, wireless connection, and location-registered technology, the pervasive or mobile-A.R. system could enable ubiquitous, collaborative and situated learning enhanced by computer simulations, games, models, and virtual objects in real environments.... The affordances of such a system could include portability, social interactivity, context sensitivity, connectivity, and individuality. (Wu et al. 2013, pp. 43–44).

The benefits found by Arvanitis et al. (2009) particularly interest this research. They found that A.R. helps students to visualize complex and invisible concepts. In an example of non-immersive A.R., Wagner (2012, pp. 89–91) declares that a digital screen at the Abbey at Cluny, France, allows visitors to peer through it and see not war-ravaged ruins but an overlay of how the Abbey looked hundreds of years ago when it was in good repair. She proposes that a temple created in Second Life could be located in the physical world. Only people wearing A.R. H.M.D.'s could see the temple. In an example of immersive A.R., a hologram of Christ or biblical characters could be projected into a room. Visitors could see the projected hologram from multiple points of view, or visitors with A.R. H.M.D.'s could see the image, with which they interact via artificial intelligence programs. Such uses of the technologies could help people to learn more about the faith and possibly provide spiritual insights unavailable through other means.

3.2 Theology of Virtual Environments

The study of virtual environments raises fascinating theological issues and questions. What is virtual, and what is real? What is the locus of the virtual? Blascovich and Bailenson (2011, p. 22) state, "Historically, virtual reality is perhaps most commonly found in religion." French social scientist Durkheim (2012, p. 381) declares, "But religion exists; it is a system of given facts; in a word, it is a reality." Christianity and other religions believe in the existence of the unseen spiritual realm. Lewis (1952) wrote, "If we find ourselves with a desire that nothing in this world can satisfy, the most probable explanation is that we were made for another world."

The writer of the Gospel of John contends that Jesus Christ came from God and that after His death, burial, resurrection, and ascension returned to God. Since our earthly lifespan measures only a blip compared with the rest of eternity, Blascovich and Bailenson (2011, p. 23) ask if this corporeal life really is the virtual. Bryson (1996) reminds the reader that "virtual reality is an effect, not an illusion." Wagner (2012, p. 4) states, "Both religion and virtual reality can be viewed as manifestations of the desire for transcendence". Many Christians recite the Nicene Creed, which at the end speaks of the hope for this transcendence, "We look for the resurrection of the dead, and the life of the world to come. Amen" (*United Methodist Hymnal* 1989, p. 880).

3.3   Non-immersive Virtual Environment Technologies

N.I.V.E. technologies include desktop virtual environments without H.M.D.'s and non-immersive A.R. Although not immersive these technologies have communicated and may communicate the Christian faith or at least dimensions of it.

4   Desktop Virtual Environments Without Head-Mounted Displays

While the Internet helps congregations to communicate their message and make connections within and without the church, the key communication technology event of the creation and use of non-immersive virtual environments (N.I.V.E.'s) has and will afford the user opportunities for more-involved interaction. Linden Lab moved N.I.V.E.'s online with Second Life, but few churches have taken advantage of offering worship there. Even though Second Life (Linden Lab 2014) considers itself "The largest-ever 3D virtual world created entirely by its users" and even though The United Methodist Church (U.M.C.), for example, has eleven-million members worldwide, only ninety-one people belonged to the U.M.C. group in Second Life in 2014. The largest Christian church on Second Life was LifeChurch.tv. Avatars visited that church, which posted their times of worship. During worship services the avatars sat, stood, walked around, or flew around the worship space as a video showed a live-action sermon. People used their church-going experience on Second Life as a supplement to the physical church where they belong, whether that church is one of the twenty LifeChurch.tv locations in the United States or other churches, as their primary church, or in other ways.

A socio-cultural analysis of Second Life churches reveals some foundational changes in what "going to church" means. LifeChurch.tv and other churches have online churches as well. People can "go to church" by attending a church only online. They can watch a video of a worship service, submit prayer requests, and give their offerings online, but they probably use their real name. "Going to church" on Second Life takes the online worship experience to a more-involved level. People's avatars can enter the three-dimensional virtual environment, turn around, see and hear all around them, and interact with other avatars and virtual agents. But having the ability to create their avatars as people or even things dissimilar to them provides them with different identities with which to interact in a virtual worship space. LiveChurch.tv has discontinued their Second Life ministry, but a few dozen other churches still worship in that online V.E.

5   Non-immersive Augmented Reality

While non-immersive V.R. and non-immersive V.E. show people other worlds, non-immersive augmented reality (N.I.A.R.) technologies provide more information about this world. N.I.A.R. technologies can or could allow people to recognize more dimensions of reality than they can humanly sense. Such capabilities complement the Christian understanding that two realms coexist: the spiritual realm lies over the physical realm. As described earlier in this review, Christians believe that they are not of this world because their Founder was not from this world. In John 17:14–15, the author of the Fourth Gospel writes a prayer that Jesus prayed for his disciples on the original Maundy Thursday: "I have given them your word, and the world has hated them because they do not belong to the world, just as I do not belong to the world. I am not asking you to take them out of the world, but I ask you to protect them from the evil one." Even though the disciples "do not belong to the world," Jesus did not want them to leave the world; rather, Jesus wanted to send them into it and thus continue his ministry after his death. A.R. gives its users located in this world the ability to see and/or hear information that humans cannot naturally sense.

People have responded to N.I.A.R. mobile applications by their expecting more from a photograph on a mobile device than only a picture. Currently, N.I.A.R. mobile applications allow people to take a photograph with the camera on their smartphone, tablet, or other mobile device and superimpose on the photograph information about the photo's subject. Bolter and Grusin (2000) would label such use as "hypermediation," in which the medium of the screen calls attention to itself. The mobile device knows its location from triangulation among cell towers and/or from a global positioning system (G.P.S.). The A.R. app identifies the subject in the photograph by knowing the geotag of the camera's subject. This identification coupled with connectivity to the Internet give the A.R. app the online information related to that geotag. As a result people with A.R.-equipped mobile devices might have less social interaction with local people because they can read their "hypermediated" smartphones rather than ask people for information.

The information provided by A.R. includes audio as well as video. In fact, Sony introduced the Walkman portable cassette audio-player in July, 1979 (Verma n.d.). Museums began loaning them to their patrons so that the guests could take guided tours and stop at paintings and listen to descriptions of what they were seeing. That technological system worked well as long as the patrons traveled through the museum along the proscribed path because the Walkman did not know its location. Auditory A.R. on a digital mobile device, on the other hand, knows its location. Applications can say more information about museum items in any order of presentation, direct the blind where to walk, alert drivers, and speak in the dark.

The ubiquity of mobile digital devices and the reasonable cost and multiple affordances of N.I.A.R. technology proffer the church many possible uses of N.I.A.R. People could take self-guided tours of church buildings. They could aim the phone's camera at the ruins of a cathedral in Europe and see on their screen a representation of how the building looked and how worshipers used it during the Middle Ages. They could aim at an empty piece of land today and see on their screens the architect's vision of a proposed church building. They could take it to the Holy Land and see and hear not only buildings as they appeared during the first century, but also, virtual reenactments of the Bible stories that occurred in the places. United Methodists could take A. R.-equipped devices to Epworth, England, and point them at the parsonage of Reverend Samuel and Susanna Wesley and see on their tablet a virtual reenactment of six-year-old John Wesley's being rescued from the second-story window as the house burned. These uses of N.I.A.R. technology could assist people, especially those who prefer visual and auditory styles of teaching, in their learning about the faith. Also, they could repeat the experiences in order to help them better remember and understand.

Critics could argue that N.I.A.R. technologies promote private engagements with places and things. If they were alive, Plato (1892) and Ong and Hartley (2012) could levy the same complaint against written materials. N.I.A.R. technologies make possible self-guided tours and solitary learning. Their users turn to the printed characters on the screen or the simulated voice coming from the speakers rather than ask the docent in the museum, the fellow traveler on the sidewalk, or the religious leader in the church. However, they could look at the process in the reverse: the users of N.I.A.R. could become the ones who tell others what they have learned, what their human senses could not impart to them.

5.1 Immersive Virtual Environment Technologies

I.V.E. technologies add the benefit of immersion. Churches have participated in the event of the creation and use of immersive virtual environment technologies (I.V.E. T.'s) less than they have in all of the other key communication technology events. The high cost of earlier H.M.D.'s, the related-scarcity of immersive virtual reality (I.V.R.) equipment, and the public's unfamiliarity with the application of the technologies have precluded churches and individual Christians from developing and using I.V.E.T.'s. However, the upcoming advent of reasonably-priced and widely-available consumer H. M.D.'s such as the Oculus Rift should open the market for I.V.R. applications.

1. Immersive Virtual Reality

Widespread use of I.V.R. has yet to happen, but Western culture might be ripe for the church to utilize I.V.R. when the technology is broadly available. Ryan (2001, 1) observes, "the idea of V.R. is very much a part of our cultural landscape," such as witnessed in science fiction books and films and, as this research contends, in the church. Christians and even non-Christians, especially during times of crisis or turbulence, have sought solace, the sacred, and occasionally political asylum by entering a sanctuary. The worship services, prayer services, and even the room itself have provided spiritual meaning in an environment set apart for worship. Via a "cultural sociological approach". Lynch (2012, p. 87) argues, "Sacred meanings are not, therefore, free-floating signifiers but materially mediated".

While the physical sanctuary can serve as a material medium, I.V.R. can present a digital version of sanctuary because I.V.R. can be defined as "an immersive digital environment that is isolated from the real world" (Rhodes and Allen 2014). I.V.R. made for churches could serve as sanctuary by helping people, especially spiritual seekers, to temporarily escape from worrying about the problems of this world and to explore another world, such as a possible three-dimensional depiction of heaven. Although the possibility exists that users might exchange a hunger for the future heaven for a desire for the immediate simulacrum (Baudrillard 1981), an I.V.E.T. representing a New Testament view of heaven could pique people's interest in the spiritual, provide a respite, and encourage people to learn more about the faith.

Churches could use I.V.R. developed for them so that people could "act within a world and experience it from the inside" (Ryan 2001, p. 20). Ryan's observation about activity within the virtual world is instructive for the church because her contention prepares a seedbed for ideas for possible future development. She (Ryan 2001, p. 20) writes, "In V.R. we act within a world and experience it from the inside". Animations on television and film show the viewer scenes, but I.V.R. allows the viewer to enter the inside of a digital scene and interact with that environment from a first-person perspective or as a third-person avatar in what Second Life (Johnson 2014) calls "the third-person object view". Users of the V.F.E. could "experience [the learning and cultic worship of various faiths] from the inside" (Ryan 2001, p. 20).

A possible additional feature of I.V.R. technologies, haptic ability could uniquely communicate dimensions of the faith. The "laying on of hands" appears throughout the New Testament, especially in the Book of Acts. In the history of the church, this impartation has signified important events, such as at baptisms, confirmations, ordinations, weddings, and healing services. For those receiving the touch, the "laying on of hands" indicates the congregation's affirmation and the Holy Spirit's activity. A user of I.V.R. could don not only a H.M.D. and headphones, but also, haptic sleeves and gloves, which would afford the sensations of touch. Kinesthetic learners especially might appreciate and/or benefit from using haptic technologies because touching helps facilitate their learning.

If a Christian worship service were simulated in V.R. with haptic capabilities, the user could touch and feel a virtual holy-communion cup, a bound Bible, and the water of a baptismal fount. Haptic clothing, such as vests, shirts, pants, boots, and hats could proffer the wearer the abilities to feel a pat on the back, the hardness of a bare wooden pew, the softness of a pew or chair cushion, the water and towel of a foot-washing, and the imposition of ashes on the forehead. Christians believe that God entrusts humans to care for the divinely-created earth and that the Second Person of the Trinity put on flesh and bones in the person of Jesus of Nazareth. Such theologies of stewardship and incarnation respectively encourage Christians to appreciate the physical realm, which we humans can lovingly touch. The use of I.V.R.'s haptic features thus could foster an appreciation for creation and the incarnation in ways that other key communication technology events cannot.

2. Immersive Augmented Reality

As with the relationship between non-immersive V.R. and I.V.R., immersive qualities can greatly enhance A.R. While the graphics of N.I.A.R. appear from only one point of view, graphics surround the user(s) in immersive A.R. (I.A.R.). Google Glass and other see-through H.M.D.'s are examples of I.A.R. Google Glass wearers can walk, drive, and operate in the world while seeing both the physical world and the virtual overlay of information. They can turn their heads, move their bodies, and see from different points of view.

Religious uses of I.A.R. might act as hierophanies within the culture. History of Religions Professor Eliade (1987, p. 7) identifies a hierophany as happening when "something sacred shows itself to us". In other words, a hierophany is a "manifestation of sacred realities" (Eliade 1987, p. 11). Lynch (2012) disagrees with the sacrality's being an ontological reality. For him a group in the culture, rather that the thing itself, determines sacredness; however, that collective could identify a religious use of I.A.R. as a hierophany. Wagner (2012) asks if an I.A.R. projection of Christ into a room coupled with an A.I. interface could be labeled as a hierophany. She (Wagner 2012, 91) contends, "With augmented reality, the virtual world steps out of the computer 'box' and into our lives with incredibly powerful implications for religious experience".

I.A.R. serves well as a metaphor for a Christian understanding of reality. The Apostle Paul wrote to the church at Corinth, Greece, "...we look not at what can be seen but at what cannot be seen; for what can be seen is temporary, but what cannot be seen is eternal" (II Corinthians 4:18). In other words, the seen physical world is temporary in comparison to the unseen eternal realm of God. As the H.M.D.'s of I.A.R. allow the wearers to look through the lens into the physical world while reading the writing on the lens, a person of faith can look at the physical realm but know that the unseen spiritual realm overlaps what he or she naturally sees. Faith as trust is required to see what cannot be seen.

6   Conclusion

While reviewing interdisciplinary literature, this research has shown the importance of technologies for the communication of Christian faith. Marshall McLuhan's (1962) insistence that new communication technologies do not replace old ones; rather, new ones add to the repertoire of possible technologies that people, in this case Christians, may use to communicate the faith.

The use of the newest communication technologies, virtual environments, affords communication of dimensions of the faith not possible with earlier technologies. N.I.V. E.T.'s such as N.I.V.R., N.I.A.R., and desktop digital games offer high amounts of interactivity for users, such as students in Sunday School. Since the 3D-graphical representation of Bible accounts, historical events, worship services, and possibly abstract theological concepts in V.E.'s allows them to be experienced "from the inside" (Ryan 2001, p. 20), students can glean a first-person perspective of the faith. A.R., especially I.A.R., can uniquely represent the Christian understanding that people of faith simultaneously reside in the physical and spiritual realms. As "an immersive digital environment that is isolated from the real world" (Rhodes et al. 2014), I.V.R. uniquely makes possible the creation of virtual sanctuary and the representation of the otherworldliness of heaven.

Knut Lundby (2013, p. 226) realizes, "Religions are to a large extent shaped by their dominant means of communication". For most of church history, that medium has been the book. Will the faith of the future pin such high importance on the bound book? The first-hand study of I.V.R., I.A.R., and desktop V.E.'s with H.M.D.'s, although not the "dominant means of communication", might be able to reveal that V. E.'s can communicate dimensions of the faith that other, earlier technologies have been unable to do or do as well.

References

Arvanitis, T.N., Petrou, A., Knight, J.F., Savas, S., Sotiriou, S., Gargalakos, M., Gialouri, E.: Human factors and qualitative pedagogical evaluation of a mobile augmented reality system for science education used by learners with physical disabilities. Pers. Ubiquitous Comput. **13** (3), 243–250 (2009)

Atwood, C.D.: Handbook of Denominations in the United States, 13th edn. Abingdon Press, Nashville (2010)

Barrick, A.: Most Americans still believe in god. The Christian Post (2011). http://www. christianpost.com/news/most-americans-still-believe-in-god-nonbelief-rises-50791/

Baudrillard, J.: Simulacra and Simulation. University of Michigan Press, Ann Arbor (1981)

Bible: New Revised Standard Version. Division of Christian Education of the National Council of the Churches of Christ in the United States of America, The Holy Bible, New Revised Standard Version (1989)

Blascovich, J., Bailenson, J.: Infinite Reality: The Hidden Blueprint of our Virtual Lives. William Morrow & Co, New York (2011)

Bolter, J.D., Grusin, R.: Remediation: Understanding New Media. MIT Press, Cambridge (2000)

Broll, W., Lindt, I., Herbst, I., Ohlenburg, J., Braun, A.-K., Wetzel, R.: Toward next-gen mobile AR games. IEEE Comput. Graph. Appl. **28**(4), 40–48 (2008)

Burdea, G., Coiffet, P.: Virtual Reality Technology, 2nd edn. Wiley, Hoboken (2003)

Davie, G.: Resacralization. In: Turner, B.S. (ed.) The New Blackwell Companion to the Sociology of Religion, pp. 160–180. Wiley, Chichester (2010)

Duke, J.: History of Christianity II. Brite Divinity School, Texas Christian University, Fort Worth (1992)

Durkheim, E.: The Elementary Forms of the Religious Life. Courier Dover Publications, Mineola (2012). http://ambounds.org/Class/ReligionReading1.pdf

Eliade, M.: The Sacred and the Profane: The Nature of Religion. Harcourt Brace Jovanovich Publishers, San Diego (1987). Translated by Trask, W.R.

Garner, R.L.: Humor in pedagogy: how ha-ha can lead to aha! Coll. Teach. **54**(1), 177–180 (2006)

Hinrichs, R., Wankel, C. (eds.): Transforming Virtual World Learning, vol. 4. Emerald Group Publishing, Bradford (2011)

Johnson, E.: Second Life Creator Linden Lab Says Virtual Worlds and Virtual Reality Belong Together, 27 June 2014. http://recode.net/2014/06/27/second-life-creator-linden-lab-says-virtual-worlds-and-virtual-reality-belong-together/

Kinnaman, D.: You Lost Me: Why Young Christians Are Leaving Church… and Rethinking Faith. Baker Books, Grand Rapids (2011)

Klopfer, E., Sheldon, J.: Augmenting your own reality: student authoring of science-based augmented reality games. New Dir. Youth Dev. **2010**(128), 85–94 (2010)

Klopfer, E., Squire, K.: Environmental detectives—the development of an augmented reality platform for environmental simulations. Educ. Tech. Res. Dev. **56**(2), 203–228 (2008)

Lewis, C.S.: Mere Christianity. Scribner/Simon & Schuster Inc., New York (1952)

Linden Lab (2014). www.LindenLab.com

Lundby, K.: Theoretical frameworks for approaching religion and new media. In: Campbell, H. A. (ed.) Digital Religion: Understanding Religious Practice in New Media Worlds, pp. 225–237. Routledge, Abingdon (2013)

Lynch, G.: The Sacred in the Modern World: A Cultural Sociological Approach. Oxford University Press, Oxford (2012)

Mazuryk, T., Gervautz, M.: Virtual Reality-History, Applications, Technology and Future. Vienna Institute of Technology, Vienna (1996)

McKim, D.K.: Westminster Dictionary of Theological Terms. Westminster/John Know Press, Louisville (1996)

McLuhan, M.: The Gutenberg Galaxy: The Making of Typographic Man. University of Toronto Press, Toronto (1962)

McLuhan, M.: Understanding Media: The Extensions of Man. MIT Press, Cambridge (1994)

Milgram, P., Takemura, H., Utsumi, A., Kishino, F.: Augmented reality: a class of displays on the reality-virtuality continuum. In: Photonics for Industrial Applications, pp. 282–292. International Society for Optics and Photonics (1995)

MW2014: Museums and the Web, #Taull1123 Immersive Experience in a World Heritage Site (or Augmented Reality Without Devices) (2014). http://mw2014.museumsandtheweb.com/bow/taull1123-immersive-experience-in-a-world-heritage-site-or-augmented-reality-without-devices/. Accessed 24 Oct 2014

Ong, W.J., Hartley, J.: Orality and Literacy: The Technologizing of the Word, 30th Anniversary edn. Routledge, Abingdon (2012)

Plato: Phaedrus. In: The Dialogues of Plato, 3rd edn. revised and corrected, vol. 1. Oxford University Press, Oxford (1892). http://oll.libertyfund.org/title/111. Accessed 28 Oct 2013, translated into English with Analyses and Introductions by Jowett, B., in Five Volumes

Prensky, M.: Digital natives, digital immigrants, Part 1. On Hori. **9**(5), 1–6 (2001)

Rhodes, T., Allen, S.: Performing Arts in the Wearable Age. Carnegie Mellon University, Pittsburgh (2014). http://static.squarespace.com/static/51d98be2e4b05a25fc200cbc/t/5392084de4b0037d4d325314/1402079309465/ThomasRhodesSamuelAllen_PerformingArtsInTheWearableAge_6.6.2014.pdf

Ryan, M.-L.: Narrative as Virtual Reality. Johns Hopkins University Press, Baltimore (2001)

Schroeder, R.: Defining virtual worlds and virtual environments. J. Virtual Worlds Res. **1**(1), 1–3 (2008)

United Methodist Hymnal, The Book of United Methodist Worship. The United Methodist Publishing House, Nashville (1989)

Wagner, R.: Godwired: Religion, Ritual, and Virtual Reality. Routledge, Abingdon (2012)

Wu, H.-K., Lee, S.W.-Y., Chang, H.-Y., Liang, J.-C.: Current status, opportunities and challenges of augmented reality in education. Comput. Educ. **62**, 41–49 (2013)

Geometry Explorer: Facilitating Geometry Education with Virtual Reality

Chengyuan Lai[(✉)], Ryan P. McMahan, Midori Kitagawa, and Iolani Connolly

University of Texas at Dallas, Richardson, TX, USA
{Chengyuan.Lai,rymcmaha,midori,lani.connolly}@utdallas.edu

Abstract. A key to learning high-level geometry concepts is an individual's ability to understand spatial dimensions and to mentally transform 3D shapes. However, prior research indicates that many students do not have adequate spatial understanding skills. On the other hand, immersive virtual reality (VR) has been shown to afford greater spatial understanding. In this paper, we present the Geometry Explorer, a VR system designed to facilitate geometry education by leveraging increased spatial understanding. The system uses a Samsung Gear VR to allow users to view and manipulate the dimensions of 3D shapes. We have created a game based on the goal of manipulating shapes to reach target volumes. We informally evaluated our initial prototype using the Rapid Iterative Testing and Evaluation (RITE) approach. In this paper, we present our modifications based on the usability issues discovered during RITE testing. We conclude by discussing the future of the Geometry Explorer.

Keywords: Virtual reality · Geometry education · Head-mounted display

1 Introduction

Geometry is important and exists in every aspect of people's daily lives. Analysis of two-dimensional (2D) and three-dimensional (3D) shapes and the study of geometric relationships are used in fields ranging from architecture to manufacturing. As a fundamental component of mathematics [1], geometry provides a means of applying mathematical ideas to the concrete things that we can see in the real world. According to a study on high school students [2], a good knowledge of geometry plays a critical role in developing expertise in STEM[1] domains. Being knowledgeable of geometry helps people to understand the world better and to think in different ways.

Although geometry is so important in everyday life, many people are not equipped with essential geometry knowledge and ability. This is due to the fact that geometry is difficult to learn and to teach [3]. One critical aspect to geometry education is the ability to understand and convey spatial relationships. Spatial understanding is not an ability that people are born with. Like many other skills, it requires practice to develop [4]. Formative experiences constructing and actively manipulating shapes and models play an important role in the development of spatial understanding and geometric knowledge [3].

---

[1] STEM is the acronym of Science, Technology, Engineering and Math.

© Springer International Publishing Switzerland 2016
S. Lackey and R. Shumaker (Eds.): VAMR 2016, LNCS 9740, pp. 702–713, 2016.
DOI: 10.1007/978-3-319-39907-2_67

However, traditional methods of teaching geometry do not support these types of activities. Instead, texts and 2D figures are used as attempts to illustrate 3D shapes and convey 3D concepts. Considering these issues, new technologies provide opportunities to improve geometry education.

One technology that has potential to drastically improve geometry education is immersive virtual reality (VR). Immersive VR provides computer graphics that appear to surround the user, in turn allowing the user to naturally look around a virtual environment [5]. This capability, combined with stereoscopic graphics, allows immersive VR to greatly facilitate spatial understanding [6]. Additionally, VR can allow the user to interact with and manipulate 3D shapes. These advantages make VR an ideal technology for improving geometry education.

By taking advantage of modern immersive VR technologies, we have built a VR system for facilitating geometry education that we call the *Geometry Explorer*. Currently, the system focuses on teaching the user how to calculate the volume of different 3D shapes by directly manipulating the dimensions of the shapes to achieve desired volumes. Prior to creating the Geometry Explorer, we identified several system requirements in order for it to be a usable and feasible solution to geometry education problems. With these requirements in mind, we used the Samsung Gear VR head-mounted display (HMD) to implement the system and a game based on the objective of manipulating 3D shapes to achieve target volumes. We used the Rapid Iterative Testing and Evaluation (RITE) approach [7] to informally assess the efficacy of the system and to identify problems with the preliminary prototype. After several improvements, we are now ready to conduct a summative evaluation to compare the effectiveness of the Geometry Explorer to traditional geometry education methods.

2 Related Work

Several technologies have been proposed to aid in teaching and learning geometry. Most of these are either desktop-based applications or immersive systems.

2.1 Desktop-Based Geometry Applications

Numerous desktop-based applications have been created for teaching geometry. Dynamic geometry systems (DGS) are the most common type among these and include applications such as *Cabri*, *Cinderella*, and *GeoGebra* [8]. These DGS applications allow users to carry out a set of operations on different geometry shapes in order to create and manipulate geometric constructions. According to prior research studies [9, 10], such applications work effectively in improving students' understanding of planar geometry and 2D geometric concepts. But they have not been demonstrated to significantly improve students' understanding of 3D geometry and concepts [10].

While the above-mentioned systems are helpful for improving some aspects of geometry education, particularly for 2D shapes, they are less effective for conveying 3D geometry concepts. There are several potential reasons why. First, these desktop-based systems do not usually support stereoscopic viewing, which deprives the user of an important depth cue. Second, motion parallax cues are only supported through virtual camera movements controlled with the mouse and keyboard. Finally, due to limitations of the mouse and keyboard, 3D manipulations are only supported through complex modal interactions, like those found in 3D modeling applications [5].

2.2 Immersive Geometry Systems

As mentioned before, immersive systems provide several advantages that desktop-based interfaces do not. These advantages include large fields of regard (FOR; i.e., the total size of the visual field surrounding the user [6]), stereoscopy, and head tracking for natural viewing. Furthermore, these advantages yield additional benefits, such as improved spatial understanding [6] and a greater sense of presence (i.e., the sense of "being there" in a virtual environment [11]).

Realizing the potential benefits of using VR to promote geometry education, Kaufmann and his colleagues have developed an immersive augmented reality system called Construct3D [12]. The Construct3D system uses an optical see-through HMD to provide stereoscopic views of virtual objects within the real-world space. The system uses a two-handed 3D interaction tool called the Personal Interaction Panel (PIP), which acts as a handheld tablet. Using the PIP, users can place predefined solids, planes, lines, and points within the virtual environment. These open-ended construction features make Construct3D similar to a 3D modeling application.

In a series of usability evaluations conducted with teachers, Kaufmann identified three key strengths of the Construct3D system [13]. First, the construction of 3D dynamic geometry is a major educational asset for explorative learning. Second, the ability to dynamically place and modify shapes allows users to visual objects that are composites of traditional shapes. Third, users can actively walk around objects, which supports better spatial understanding. However, Kaufmann acknowledged that Construct3D was not a feasible classroom solution due to the expensive cost of the Construct3D hardware, the technical complexity required to set up the system, and its inability to support more than a few students [13].

With these limitations in mind, we set out to develop an immersive VR system that would provide benefits similar to Kaufmann's Construct3D, but in a form that was both usable and feasible for classroom instruction. Additionally, we chose to focus on a specific learning objective for geometry education, in the form of calculating the volume of various 3D shapes.

3   System Requirements

The primary purpose of our research was to develop a VR system that would facilitate learning how to calculate the volumes of various 3D shapes and how manipulating a 3D shape would affect its volume. Prior research has indicated that students frequently encounter difficulties in understanding volume formulas and measurements [14]. One noted issue is that students tend to memorize volume formulas without understanding their meaning [3]. This is likely due to a lack of spatial understanding skills [4]. Hence, one system requirement was that it could facilitate spatial understanding and support the development of such skills. An additional learning requirement was that the system should be interesting to use, as research has shown that students are intrinsically motivated to learn when they find the process interesting [15].

With regard to helping students learn how to calculate volumes, we had to decide on which 3D shapes, and their corresponding volume formulas, to focus. We consulted the Common Core State Standards (CCSS), an educational initiative in the United States that details what students should know about English and mathematics at the end of each grade, kindergarten through high school [16]. According to the CCSS for math, the first shape that students should learn how to calculate its volume is the right rectangular prism (5.MD.C.5.A), in 5th grade. Later on, during high school geometry, students should learn how to use the volume formulas for cylinders, pyramids, cones, and spheres (HSG.GMD.A.3). Hence, the system needed to support learning of all five shapes.

Outside of learning requirements, we identified several requirements in order for the system to be feasible for use in an educational environment. The first of these was universal usability (i.e., the system must be usable for every user) [17]. A particular concern related to universal usability was accommodating users with visual impairments, as many VR systems are not usable with glasses [5]. Ergonomics was another concern, as some VR systems cause fatigue when the user must sustain uncomfortable positions or weights [18]. One feasibility concern was whether schools could afford the system hardware. Some schools struggle to maintain in-class computers, especially those in poorer socioeconomic districts. Hence, the solution needed to be inexpensive. Finally, the system had to be easy to use, as any good interface should be [17].

4 System Design

To address our system requirements, we designed a game for the Samsung Gear VR HMD that involves manipulating 3D shapes to achieve target volumes.

4.1 Hardware: Samsung Gear VR

Immersive VR has been shown to facilitate greater spatial understanding by providing more depth cues, such as stereopsis, motion parallax, perspective, and occlusion [6]. Hence, we decided to utilize immersive VR to address our requirement of facilitating spatial understanding. In turn, we expected VR to better support understanding volume formulas, as opposed to just memorizing them.

Considering all of our requirements, we decided to use the Samsung Gear VR for our system hardware (see Fig. 1). With a 96° field of view (FOV), 360° field of regard (FOR [6]), a resolution of 1280 × 1440 per eye, and an internal tracker for rotational head tracking, the Gear VR provides an immersive user experience. Unlike most other HMDs, the Gear VR provides a focal adjustment that accommodates nearsightedness and farsightedness. The device also only weighs 318 g and provides adjustable head straps for an ergonomic form factor. These two features make the Gear VR more universally usable than other VR hardware options. The Gear's integrated touchpad and back button afford easy-to-use interactions without the need for additional devices, such as a game controller. Finally, the Gear VR is inexpensive and costs less than most classroom desktop computers.

Fig. 1. High school students using the Gear VR to interact with the Geometry Explorer

4.2   Interactions: 3D Volume Manipulations

To facilitate learning how manipulating a shape affects its volume, we designed the Geometry Explorer to directly provide the ability to manipulate a shape's dimensions and, in turn, its volume. As seen in Fig. 2, context-sensitive widgets afford scaling along each of the three individual axes of a shape. Using head orientation to control a cursor, the user first selects one of the context-sensitive widgets with a tap of the touchpad. Once selected, the widget moves along its indicated axis to remain centered in the user's view as the user rotates his or her head. As the widget moves, the scale of the corresponding dimension changes accordingly. At any point, the user can tap the touchpad again to release the widget and stop manipulation of the dimension.

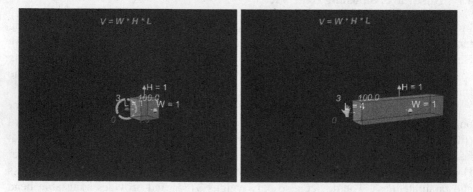

Fig. 2. The Geometry Explorer uses context-sensitive widgets for 3D volume manipulations.

While every shape has three dimensions, we developed the Geometry Explorer in a manner to provide manipulations that correspond to the shape's volume calculation. For both the right rectangular prism and pyramid, all three dimensions (XYZ) could be independently manipulated. However, for the cylinder and cone, the widgets for the horizontal axes (XZ) were linked. Hence, manipulating the X-axis widget would result in the Z-axis widget being manipulated in the same manner. Finally, all three widgets were linked for the sphere, as dragging one would manipulate all three.

4.3 Motivation: Manipulation Game

In order to make the Geometry Explorer interesting to use, we decided to create a game around the concept of manipulating the volumes of the shapes. Other researchers have had success with making mathematics interesting by developing intrinsically motivating games [15], so we took a similar approach. Our game's objective was to manipulate a unit-sized shape to a randomly generated target volume as quickly as possible. Users would receive higher scores for achieving the target volume faster and lower scores for solving the volume problem slower. To further motivate the importance of scoring high (i.e., efficiently solving the volume problem), we retain a leaderboard of the ten highest scores and indicate if the user's score is among them.

5   RITE-Based Modifications

After developing a preliminary prototype of the Geometry Explorer, we used the RITE approach [7] to determine the potential efficacy of our system and to quickly improve its overall design. We conducted a series of RITE sessions with high school students, high school teachers, college students, and college educators over the course of three months. We identified and fixed several issues with our original prototype through these sessions. The following subsections are a summary of our major RITE-based modifications.

5.1   Multiplication Look-up Matrix

The most important issue that we identified during our RITE sessions is that mentally calculating the volume of a 3D shape is extremely challenging. The high school and college students were not able to successfully calculate target volumes while immersed, due to the inability to write down interim calculations. Instead, they resorted to manipulating the shapes in an ad hoc fashion, comparing the current volume to the target volume. Even the high school and college educators struggled with the mental calculations, likely due to the relatively small capacity of working memory [19].

Because we were interested in helping students learn what the volume formulas represented and not how to multiple numbers, we have added a multiplication look-up matrix. The concept of the matrix is similar to a two-factor multiplication look-up table, in which the user can find a target result and determine the two numbers that yield it when multiplied. However, because volume calculations require at least three factors, we had to create a three-factor look-up matrix.

Seen in Fig. 3, the matrix consists of a single plane of cubes with 12 columns and 12 rows, representing the X and Y-axis values, respectively. At the top of the matrix, the current Z value is also provided, which is initially set to 1. Each cube contains the numerical result of multiplying its row number, column number, and the Z value. In order to find results in which Z is greater than 1, the user can swipe forward on the Gear VR touchpad to increase the value of Z. Similarly a backward swipe decreases Z. This matrix now allows users to quickly determine three factors that can be multiplied to find a target volume and to focus on learning what the formulas represent, as opposed to using cognitive resources to mentally make the calculations.

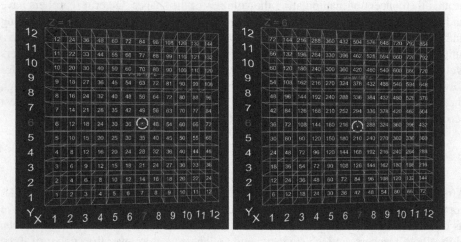

Fig. 3. The new multiplication look-up matrix allows students to focus on learning the volume formulas, as opposed to mentally multiplying numbers.

5.2 Head-Referenced Formula

In our original prototype, we positioned the shape's volume formula within the world to initially appear in the center of the user's FOV. If the user looked left or right, the formula would no longer be visible. We initially chose this world-referenced positioning to avoid the occlusion issues that accompany head-referenced objects [5]. Additionally, we thought it would force users to memorize the formula. However, during the RITE evaluations, we discovered that users struggled and became frustrated with not being able to see the formula and manipulate the shape at the same time. This was particularly the case for users not familiar with the formulas.

To remedy this issue, we modified the formula to be head-referenced instead of world-referenced. Now, the formula is always visible just above the center of the user's FOV, as seen in Fig. 2. Though we originally avoided making the formula head-referenced to adhere to view-occlusion guidelines [5], our modification now adheres to Shneiderman's guideline on minimizing short-term memory loads [17].

5.3 Target Number of Manipulations

As described in Sect. 4.3, our game was originally focused on only how quickly the user could achieve the target volume. However, during RITE sessions, we found that many users would only solve for the easiest calculation. For example, if the target volume for a rectangular prism was 12, many users would only scale one dimension to a length of 12, leaving the other two dimensions at their initial value of 1 unit. Few users would manipulate all three dimensions, such as $X = 2$, $Y = 2$, and $Z = 3$.

We have since included a target number of manipulations for each shape to address this issue. To randomly generate target volumes, we were already randomly selecting an integer value between 1 and 12 for each dimension. We used this information to set a target number of manipulations based on the number of dimensions that were not randomly set to 1. For example, if X and Y were randomly set to numbers greatly than 1, but Z was set to 1, the target number of manipulations would be two.

We also devised a new scoring mechanism to reinforce the importance of performing the exact number of target manipulations. In addition to decreasing with every second used to achieve the target volume, the user's score is also now based on the ratio of performed manipulations to target manipulations. Hence, performing too few or too many manipulations will decrease the overall score. This rewards those users that manipulate all three dimensions in a pre-calculated manner.

5.4 Informative Cursor

In our original implementation, the cursor was simply a crosshair, as seen in Fig. 4 on the left. We provided the target and current volume information as head-referenced objects in the lower periphery of the user's FOV to avoid occlusions. However, during the RITE sessions, we found that many users struggled to read the peripheral text.

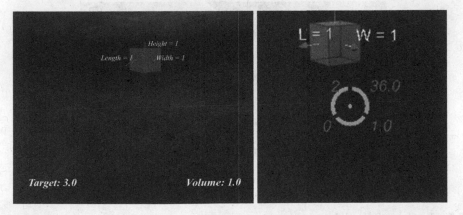

Fig. 4. Comparison of the original information layout (left) and the new cursor (right)

To solve this readability issue and to support the inclusion of the new information regarding the target and current number of manipulations, we designed an informative cursor, as seen in Fig. 4 on the right. We placed the volume information in the right corners of the cursor, with the target volume above the shape's current volume. We placed the manipulation information in the left corners of the cursor, again with the target number being above the current number of manipulations. To further visually separate the numbers and avoid confusion, we colored the target information values red and the current information values green. Altogether, this new cursor ensures that the information needed for the game is readily available in the user's fovea.

5.5 Shape Rendering

In our initial prototype, we used the standard shader and directional lighting provided by Unity 5, our software development platform, for rendering the 3D shapes. This can be seen in Fig. 4 on the left. However, during the evaluations, some users reported difficulties the dimensions of the shapes at certain dimensions. To fix this issue, we have switched to using a wireframe shader to highlight the dimensions of each shape, as seen in Fig. 4 on the right.

5.6 Environment Change

Another seemingly minor aspect to the Geometry Explorer game that became evidently important was the surrounding environment. Originally, we chose to a vibrant space-related scene with an asteroid belt as the environment for our shape manipulations (see Fig. 5). However, during RITE testing, most of the high school students were more interested in looking around the environment instead of focusing on the shape-manipulation task. To remedy this issue, we switched to another space-related scene, but without distracting asteroids or vibrant colors.

Fig. 5. This environment was deemed too distracting during our RITE sessions.

5.7 In-Game Tutorial

A major issue that we encountered during RITE testing was the inability to see what the user was viewing on the Samsung Gear VR. With computer-based HMDs, such as the Oculus Rift, the user's point of view (POV) can be duplicated on another screen.

However, due to the Gear VR's graphics running on a mobile phone screen, we were unable to view the user's POV on another display.

This issue was most problematic for explaining how to use the interface to play the game. Firstly, while immersed, the users could not see the touchpad or back button, and had to rely on tactile sensations to distinguish the two. Often, we had to physically place the user's hand over these inputs. Secondly, we found it difficult to effectively describe how to interact with the widgets, as we did not know where the user was looking. While most users would eventually figure it out, a few users became frustrated with the disconnection in communication and quit.

To alleviate the above issues, we have created an in-game tutorial. The tutorial first covers the inputs on the Samsung Gear VR and has the user practice using them, similar to the setup tutorial that accompanies the Gear VR. Next, the tutorial explains the assets seen within the environment, starting with the informative cursor, what each number represents, the formula displayed above, and finally the context-sensitive widgets. The tutorial then explains to the user how to solve a rectangular prism volume calculation by manipulating all three widgets to specified dimensions. We have found the system much easier to introduce to new users with this in-game tutorial (Fig. 6).

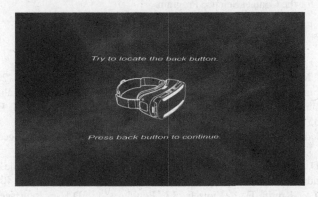

Fig. 6. Our new in-game tutorial covers both the hardware features of the Gear VR and the mechanics of the volume-manipulation game.

6   Conclusions and Future Work

Understanding geometry is an important skill, especially for STEM fields. However, many students struggle to learn geometry due to a lack of spatial understanding. VR offers the potential to drastically improve geometry education by enhancing spatial understanding and allowing students to interact with and manipulate 3D shapes. As such, we have developed a VR system for facilitating geometry education that we call the Geometry Explorer. The system uses a Samsung Gear VR HMD to view and manipulate the dimensions of 3D shapes in order to learn how such manipulations affect the volumes of the shapes. To make learning volume formulas interesting, we created a game that assesses how quickly a user can manipulate a shape to correctly obtain a target volume. Using the RITE approach with students and educators, we identified several issues with our initial Geometry Explorer prototype and made modifications to address them. In this paper, we have shared those insights and modifications, in hopes to inform future research on using VR for educational purposes.

Currently, the Science and Engineering Education Center (SEEC) at the University of Texas at Dallas is using the Geometry Explorer as an exhibit in its Contact Science Program. As part of the program, the Geometry Explorer is taken to public libraries on a regular basis for youth from the general population to interact with the system. We are also working with local school districts to integrate the system into their geometry curriculum.

Furthermore, we are currently in the process of conducting a summative evaluation to compare the efficacy of the Geometry Explorer to traditional classroom materials and to online materials, such as Khan Academy. We are using a between-subjects design to compare the efficacies of the three conditions. We hypothesize that the Geometry Explorer will yield greater increases in accurately remembering the volume formulas and applying them to given problems.

Acknowledgements. This research has been partially supported by an award from Texas Instruments Inc. for the Contact Science Program.

References

1. Boyer, C.B., Merzbach, U.C.: A History of Mathematics. Wiley, Hoboken (2011)
2. Wai, J., Lubinski, D., Benbow, C.P.: Spatial ability for STEM domains: aligning over 50 years of cumulative psychological knowledge solidifies its importance. J. Educ. Psychol. **101**, 817–835 (2009)
3. Fuys, D., Geddes, D., Tischler, R.: The van Hiele model of thinking in geometry among adolescents. J. Res. Math. Educ. Monogr. **3**, 1–196 (1988)
4. Ben-Haim, D., Lappan, G., Houang, R.T.: Visualizing rectangular solids made of small cubes: analyzing and effecting students' performance. Educ. Stud. Math. **16**, 389–409 (1985)
5. Bowman, D.A., Kruijff, E., LaViola Jr., J.J., Poupyrev, I.: 3D User Interfaces: Theory and Practice. Addison-Wesley, Boston (2005)
6. Bowman, D.A., McMahan, R.P.: Virtual reality: how much immersion is enough? IEEE Comput. **40**, 36–43 (2007)
7. Medlock, M.C., Wixon, D., Terrano, M., Romero, R., Fulton, B.: Using the RITE method to improve products: a definition and a case study. In: Usability Professionals Association, Orlando, FL (2002)
8. Hohenwarter, M., Fuchs, K.: Combination of dynamic geometry, algebra and calculus in the software system GeoGebra. In: Computer Algebra Systems and Dynamic Geometry Systems in Mathematics Teaching Conference, Pecs, Hungary (2004)
9. Lima, C., Alves, G., Soares, A.: Geometric visualization: how to acquire it using dynamic geometry systems? In: IEEE International Conference on Systems (ICONS), pp. 306–311 (2008)
10. Baki, A., Kosa, T., Guven, B.: A comparative study of the effects of using dynamic geometry software and physical manipulatives on the spatial visualisation skills of pre-service mathematics teachers. Br. J. Educ. Technol. **42**, 291–310 (2011)
11. Slater, M., Usoh, M., Steed, A.: Taking steps: the influence of a walking technique on presence in virtual reality. ACM Trans. Comput. Hum. Interact. (TOCHI). **2**, 201–219 (1995)

12. Kaufmann, H., Schmalstieg, D.: Mathematics and geometry education with collaborative augmented reality. Comput. Graph. **27**, 339–345 (2003)
13. Kaufmann, H.: Virtual environments for mathematics and geometry education. Themes Sci. Technol. Educ. **2**, 131–152 (2009)
14. Huang, H.-M.E.: An exploration of computer-based curricula for teaching children volume measurement concepts. In: 36th Conference of the International Group for the Psychology of Mathematics Education, pp. 315–322, Taipei, Taiwan (2012)
15. Habgood, M.P.J., Ainsworth, S.E.: Motivating children to learn effectively: exploring the value of intrinsic integration in educational games. J. Learn. Sci. **20**, 169–206 (2011)
16. Porter, A., McMaken, J., Hwang, J., Yang, R.: Common core standards the new US intended curriculum. Educ. Researcher **40**, 103–116 (2011)
17. Shneiderman, B.: Designing the User Interface: Strategies for Effective Human-Computer Interaction. Addison Wesley, Boston (1998)
18. Nichols, S.: Physical ergonomics of virtual environment use. Appl. Ergon. **30**, 79–90 (1999)
19. Johnson, J.: Designing with the Mind in Mind: Simple Guide to Understanding User Interface Design Guidelines. Morgan Kaufmann, Burlington (2010)

Intelligent Virtual Environment Using a Methodology Oriented to Agents

Sandra Mateus[1](✉) and John Branch[2]

[1] Politécnico Colombiano Jaime Isaza Cadavid, Medellín, Colombia
spmateus@elpoli.edu.co
[2] Universidad Nacional de Colombia, Medellín, Colombia
jwbranch@unal.edu.co

Abstract. This paper describes a Virtual Environment with Intelligent Agents, using an agent-oriented methodology called Prometheus. This technique was incorporated in the perception and reasoning of a character in the Intelligent Virtual Environment (IVE), in order to react intelligently to given warning signs. The main objective of the character in the developed IVE is finding the optimum path without having to do extra shifts. The used technique achieves an optimal solution using only probability calculations, without requiring additional data to be supplied. This solution is obtained given the repetitions and the number of ants in the character agent. The virtual environment was created with the UDK tool to identify warning signs in a work environment. UDK is used because of its importance in the development of world-renowned games.

Keywords: Intelligent virtual environment · Intelligent agents · Ant colony algorithm

1 Introduction

Intelligent Virtual Environments (IVE) are a hybrid between Virtual Reality (VR) and Artificial Intelligence (AI). They can achieve great capabilities of complex and interactive behaviors to reach a high level of realism [1]. This realism is based on the elements allowing smart performance such as perception, reasoning, learning and communication using natural language.

One of the techniques in artificial intelligence is the so called technique of Intelligent Agents. An agent can be a reactive or deliberative system which has a degree of autonomy. This means that a task can be delegated to it the system itself determines the best way to perform this task. These systems are called agents, because they are active beings, useful producers of actions: they are sent to a given environment to achieve goals and actively pursue these goals, finding out by themselves the best way to achieve these objectives [2].

In the literature, there are intelligent tutoring systems oriented to virtual environments. For instance, Buche and Querrec [3] developed an intelligent tutoring system with some 3D virtual environments. They integrated a tutorial system adaptable with multi-agent systems for pedagogical decisions. Clement et al. [4] presented an intelligent

© Springer International Publishing Switzerland 2016
S. Lackey and R. Shumaker (Eds.): VAMR 2016, LNCS 9740, pp. 714–723, 2016.
DOI: 10.1007/978-3-319-39907-2_68

tutoring system as part of an IVE for training. In this system, the proposed student model uses an ontology as a pedagogical and diagnostic approach for conflict resolution, in order to infer learning goals that the student has acquired eventually testing it in a 3D virtual biotechnology laboratory. Moreover, the use of agents has also been applied to intelligent vehicles. They have been used for different applications ranging from the physical simulation to full scale tests, using different virtualization levels for sensors, actors, scenarios and environments [5]. Simulations of evacuation are widely used to represent human emergencies. As an example, Xi and Smith [6] address this topic using a virtual environment with gaming technology and intelligent agents.

In IVEs centered on a character, Liu et al. [7] developed a framework for modeling virtual humans with a high level of autonomy at the behavioral and movement levels in a virtual environment. Their framework included a perception module, a decision module and control module of autonomous movement. Gilbert and Forney [8] developed a tour guided by an avatar in a virtual clothes store in a 3D world of Second Life Game using virtual agents and a robust variant of Artificial Intelligence Markup Language (AIML) having as challenge the Turing Test.

In this paper, we used an agent-oriented methodology called Prometheus, which consists of three phases to follow [9]: system specification, architecture design and detailed design. In the system specification, general objectives, functionalities and scenarios applied to the detection of risks in a work environment were defined. In the architecture design, agents (character agent and virtual environment agent), perceptions, actions, protocol and coupling data are defined. In the detailed design, the agents and their reasoning are described.

This paper is organized as follows: in Sect. 2, the concepts of perception and reasoning are discussed, and the 3D virtual environment created is displayed; in Sect. 3, the Intelligent Agents implemented in the virtual environment is explained; in Sect. 4, the experiments and results are presented; and Finally, the conclusions.

2   Perception and Reasoning

The Intelligent Virtual Environments must reach large capacities of complex and interactive behaviors to achieve a high level of realism [1]. This realism is based on elements enabling intelligent performance such as perception, learning, and communication through natural language and reasoning. According to the above, this paper focuses only on the perception and reasoning, cognitive and behavioral levels of a Virtual Environment.

According to Marthino et al. [10], perception is considered as all events of the virtual environment that are filtered according to the interests and location of the character and is based on two principles: (1) A limited perception, in which a character perceives all events, but only perceives its associated area; and (2) An inaccurate perception, in which the character perceives the virtual environment as it is, but only receives relevant events associated with it. They also describe the reasoning as a process performed by a set of production rules which are conditions. These conditions are based on the model of the world, in the state of the target, the characteristic behavior and the internal state information.

Given the above concepts, the reasoning of the character implemented in the IVE is based on the impact of its internal target and priority of the action to perform on the cognitive and behavioral levels.

Based on aforementioned, a model of IVE is proposed using a game engine. This model incorporates AI techniques such as agents. The goal is to produce, from a given perception of a character, a reasoning respect to the Virtual Environment.

In this model, this can be seen as a set classifier S, which takes a set of perceptions P1…Pn and combines them to make adequate reasoning R1…Rn. This reasoning to perform a certain action is supported on one of the techniques of Artificial Intelligence named in the model. Thus the system decides and selects an action A, according to the reasoning made (Eq. 1).

$$S(\{P_1, R_1\}, \{P_2, R_2\}, \ldots \{P_n, R_n\}) \to A \qquad (1)$$

With this model, the following characteristics of an Intelligent Virtual Environment described by [1] want to be achieved: Decisive: any action taken by the character will be reflected in an effective plan; Real Time: The character should respond in real time to the perceptions of the environment and in the same way, adequate reason to perception form received; Ordered: That is, the agent follows the proper sequence in their behavior.

Perceptions were simulated in this virtual environment and their respective actions to perform through reasoning with the AI technique are shown in Table 1.

Table 1. Perceptions and actions that the character executes in the virtual environment

Perception	Action run
Detects fire	Activate the fire alarm
Detects electrical risk	Turn off light switches
Detects wet floor	Call the cleaning staff
Workplace - do not know what to do	Use the intercom for help

Fig. 1. Virtual environment developed with UDK

In Fig. 1 it is shown a rendering of the Virtual Environment. This environment is the one that the character will interact with as disclosed in Table 1 and to which AI techniques are applied as explained in the following sections.

3   Intelligent Virtual Environment with Intelligent Agents

In this work is used the agent-oriented methodology called Prometheus. This methodology consists of three stages [9]: System specification, architectural design and detailed design (Fig. 2).

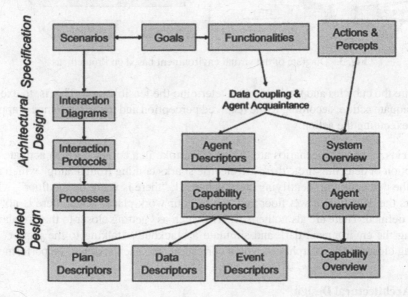

Fig. 2. Stages of prometheus methodology [9]

3.1   System Specification

Based on the proposed and developed virtual environment, Fig. 3 shows a general vision of the system specifications of the IVE developed on this work.

General Objectives. For the study case of providing warning signals on a work environment, the objectives are four: (Objective #1) Providing to people graphical information regarding what should be done upon perceiving a signal that might represent any kind of danger; (Objective #2) based on (Objective #1), maximizing the security on the work environment; (Objective #3) Surpass some kind of obstacle and (Objective #4) avoiding a possible accident.

Functionalities. Two functionalities have been defined in order to manage and operate the interaction during the execution of the virtual environment. They are focused on achieving the proposed objectives: (1) Identify possible obstacles which, for the study

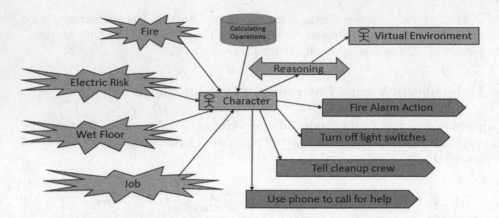

Fig. 3. Diagram of the virtual environment based on Prometheus

case, are the cubicles and walls and (2) Determine the feasible path. This is, to execute the adequate action, according to the received perception and to the randomness applied when executing the action.

Scenarios. The used scenarios are: "There is smoke in a corner", which activates the perception of detecting fire; "there are electric sparks coming from a lamp" which activates the perception of identifying electric hazard; "there is water on the floor", which triggers the detection of wet floor and "go to your work place" when there is not any action defined. There are also other scenarios such as "getting closer to the fire alarm", "getting the environment dark and simulate a blackout", "talking to the janitor" and "getting closer to the interphone" which corresponds to each action to be performed.

3.2 Architectural Design

Agents. There are two kinds of agents involved in the architectural design: Character agent and virtual environment agent. The character is the main actor, capable to respond, react and interact with the environment by using the ant colony algorithm. This algorithm is used to calculate the adequate path for the action to be performed in real time. On the other hand, the virtual environment agent is the agent which the character agent interacts with.

Perceptions. The perceptions of the character are the same ones described on Fig. 3: detect fire (P#1), detect electrical hazard (P#2), detect wet floor (P#3) and the work place (P#4).

Actions. The actions to perform are defined according to the perception: Start the fire alarm (A#1), turn off the light switches (A#2), call cleaning staff (A#3) and use the interphone to ask for help (A#4).

Protocol. It defines the interaction between character agent and virtual environment agent. Also, it defines the action to be performed or feasible path. It is compsed by the following messages:

- Location update: This is an informational message. It is sent from the character agent to the environment agent. Whenever the character agent changes its location, it must inform it to the environment. ·
- Environment change: This is a request-response message. Whenever the character agent performs a change on the environment (such as to activate an alarm), it informs to the environment agent which must respond whether this change is allowed or not. Also, it must update the environment information.

Data Coupling. It shows the process of data transfer in the system, in the environment agent as well as to transfer as to receive from the character agent.

Data is stored in a database management system which may be accessed by the two agents. The shared data are: character agent location and actions to be performed in the environment.

3.3 Detailed Design

Character Agent. This is a deliberative agent. It determines the action to be performed given the reasoning that it does from the received perception. The diagram of this agent can be observed in Fig. 4.

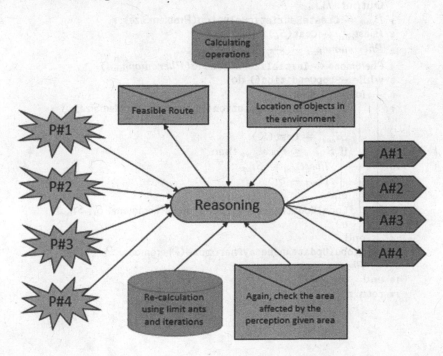

Fig. 4. Character agent

When the agent begins to interact with the environment, it receives information about the location of objects in this environment. The calculation of operations and the re-calculation of the algorithm have the information of the managed data. The action to be performed is calculated by the ant colony algorithm.

The ant colony system has as principle to use the techniques of swarm and pheromone generation as the communication mechanism to create paths with destinations as the same swarm and places with food.

As metaphor, when the creation of a swarm begins, the ants go around in a random way in order to create paths spreading their pheromones. Thus, multiple travels are performed to shape an organized pattern. For this purpose the algorithm proposed by Brownlee [11] was used.

Virtual Environment Agent. This agent provides to the character agent the location of objects in the environment. Also, it is on charge to graphically show the actions performed by the character.

4   Experiments and Results

As explained in the previous section, the ant colony algorithm was implemented in the character agent. This algorithm is shown on Fig. 5.

Input: ProblemSize, $Population_{size}$, m, ρ, β, σ, $q0$
Output: P_{best}

1 $P_{best} \leftarrow$ CreateHeuristicSolution(ProblemSize);
2 $Pbest_{cost} \leftarrow$ Cost(S_h);
3 $Pheromone_{init} \leftarrow \frac{1.0}{ProblemSize \times Pbest_{cost}}$;
4 Pheromone $\leftarrow$ InitializePheromone($Pheromone_{init}$);
5 **while** $\neg$StopCondition() **do**
6   **for** $i = 1$ **to** m **do**
7        $S_i \leftarrow$ ConstructSolution(Pheromone, ProblemSize, β, $q0$);
8        $Si_{cost} \leftarrow$ Cost(S_i);
9   **if** $Si_{cost} \leq Pbest_{cost}$ **then**
10          $Pbest_{cost} \leftarrow Si_{cost}$;
11          $P_{best} \leftarrow S_i$;
12   **end**
13   LocalUpdateAndDecayPheromone(Pheromone, S_i, Si_{cost}, σ);
14   **end**
15   GlobalUpdateAndDecayPheromone(Pheromone, P_{best}, $Pbest_{cost}$, ρ);
16 **end**
17 **return** P_{best};

Fig. 5.   The ant colony algotihm [11]

This algorithm is known by performing a large amount of recursive cycles to achieving an optimal solution. Because of this, it requires some limits in order to achieve that result. These limits are determined by the amount of ants and a given amount of cycles and repetitions to achieve the optimal calculation. What is desired is that the agent calculation be higher than the randomness in the least possible number of repetitions.

In this algorithm, two structures are used to store data. One structure stores the places that are going to be visited by the ants and the other one stores temporarily the data of the most adequate place, which are the actions to be performed. The maximum number of iterations and the maximum number of ants are considered.

The main function of this algorithm calls the search function (Fig. 6) whose goal is identifying which is the optimal path. That is to say, in each state of the character, the whole algorithm must be solved, and the character agent may only go onto the next state if it fulfills the condition of having an optimal value lower than the proposed one.

The search function has the objective of finding using probabilistic calculations from other functions the best path given some distances. To calculate those distances, the traveler salesman problem algorithm is used.

In the algorithm described in Fig. 6 the random permutation will make a shift of the places. Thus, it will always have a different objective and the calculations will always be different although the goal will be the same. The cost function delivers the calculation of the distance between the places. The pheromone matrix helps in the calculation of the path followed by the character.

Later, calculations are performed according to a random result indicating whether going through a greedy path or a probabilistic path. The differences is that the greedy

```
AgentsSearch ()
      best.vec = permutation_random (places)
      best.cost = cost (best.vec, places)
      init_pheromone = 1.0 / (places.size * best.cost)
      pheromone = init_pheromone_mat ( places.size , init_pheromone )
      For (s_i=0, s_i < max_it, 1) do
            For (s_j=0, s_j < num_ants, 1) do
                  candidate.vec = stepbystep (places, pheromone, heuristic,greed)
                  candidate.cost = cost (candidate.vec,places)
                  If (candidate.cost < best.cost) then
                        best= candidate
                  EndIf
            EndFor
      EndFor
      Return best
EndAgentsSearch
```

Fig. 6. Search function in the ant colony algorithm

path uses a calculation previously given whereas the probabilistic path recalculates the given probability trying to obtain a more adequate result.

There is also a greedy function which compares some values previously generated to identify which one is the highest within a list and then delivering the next place to go to. The probabilistic selection recalculates, using the previous probability values, the next best place to visit.

Finally, in Fig. 7 the IVE can be seen, when it is executed with the smart agents. In this case, it is executing the reasoning upon detecting electric hazard due to a blackout in the environment.

Fig. 7. IVE with agents

5 Conclusions

The objective of the main character in the Virtual Environment is to find the optimal path without requiring extra movements. The technique used in this paper solves this using only probabilistic calculations without requiring that real data be provided. This approach can achieve different optimal solutions, given the repetitions and the number of ants in the character agent. As much time this technique has to solve the problem, it will provide a more adequate result.

The technique has a system of calculations which, in spite of being simple, becomes complex when performing operations with a tool such as the videogame engines. By requiring so many interactions, giving the parameters of maximum number of ants and interactions, the established limits for each tool might be saturated.

In this case, UDK has a limit of iterations for each frame per second. Once it is surpassed, the tool just stops working. This makes that the implementation and potential of this technique becomes reduced by the limitations of the used software. It is proposed as future to evaluate the implementation of this IVE using a different algorithm in the agents.

References

1. Cavazza, M., Lugrin, J.-L., Hartley, S., Renard, M., Nandi, A., Jacobson, J., Crooks, S.: Intelligent virtual environments for virtual reality art. Comput. Graph. 29(6), 852–861 (2005). Elsevier
2. Bordini, R., Hübner, J., Wooldridge, M.: Programming Mulit-agent Systems in AgentSpeak Using Jason. Wiley, London (2007)
3. Buche, C., Querrec, R.: An expert system manipulating knowledge to help human learners into virtual environment. Expert Syst. Appl. 38(7), 8 (2011)
4. Clemente, J., Ramirez, J., De Antonio, A.: Applying a student modeling with non monotonic diagnosis to intelligent virtual environment for training/instruction. Expert Syst. Appl. 41(2), 508–520 (2014). Elsevier
5. Kurt, A., Vernier, M., Biddlestone, S., Redmill, K., Özgüner, Ü.: Chapter 2 – testing of intelligent vehicles using virtual environments and staged scenarios. In: Advances in Intelligent Vehicles, pp. 45–64. Academic Press (2014)
6. Xi, M., Smith, S.: Simulating cooperative fire evacuation training in a virtual environment Using Gaming Technology. In: IEEE Virtual Reality 2014, pp. 139–140. IEEE, Minneapolis, Minnesota, USA: ©2014
7. Liu, W., Zhou, L., Xing, W., Liu, X., Yuan, B.: Creating autonomous, perceptive and intelligent virtual humans in a real-time virtual environment. Tsinghua Sci. Technol. 16(3), 233–240 (2011)
8. Gilbert, R., Forney, A.: Can avatars pass the turing test? Intelligent agent perception in a 3D virtual environment. Int. J. Hum. Comput. Stud. 73, 30–36 (2015)
9. Padgham, L., Winikoff, M.: Prometheus: A Practical Agent-Oriented Methodology. Ed. TermLing (2005)
10. Martinho, C., Paiva, A., Gomes, M.: Emotions for a motion: rapid development of believable panthematic agents in intelligent virtual environments. Appl. Artif. Intell. 14, 14–33 (2000)
11. Brownlee, J.: Clever Algorithms - Nature Inspired Programming Recipes. Creative Commons, Australia (2012). ISBN 978-1-4467-8506-5

Applying Virtual Reality in City Planning

Minh-Tu Nguyen[1]([✉]), Hai-Khanh Nguyen[1], Khanh-Duy Vo-Lam[2],
Xuan-Gieng Nguyen[2], and Minh-Triet Tran[1]

[1] Faculty of Information Technology, University of Science, VNU-HCM,
Ho Chi Minh City, Vietnam
{nmtu,nhkhanh}@apcs.vn, tmtriet@fit.hcmus.edu.vn
[2] Artificial Intelligence Laboratory, University of Science, VNU-HCM,
Ho Chi Minh City, Vietnam
{vlkduy,nxgieng}@mmhci.org

Abstract. The rapid growth of virtual reality in recent years has brought this technology to a wide variety of common users. Realizing the potential of this technology in building and planning cities; the authors introduce a system in which architectures are brought together into a 3-dimensional virtual environment in order to collaborate in building cities. This system uses the Oculus Rift as the VR device, combining with Leap Motion to detect user's hand-gestures. The authors walkthrough all the details in building such systems including object modeling, communication protocols and gesture recognition technique.

Keywords: Urban planning · City planning · Virtual reality · Collaborative environment · Human computer interaction

1 Introduction

Urban planning, building prototype designing or interior design are now becoming more common in fast growing industry. This inspires the authors to build a system that help the prototype designing feature more effective and intuitive by using Virtual Reality technology and Leap Motion. The system also provides interactive analysis communication between investors and the architectures. Since the customers are usually not sure about what they really want from the architectures; it is the architectures job to design and propose the idea to the customers via meetings and presentations; this process usually takes up from weeks to months. The authors propose a system that allow architectures to be able to present the prototype to the investors, receive their feedbacks and adjust the prototype instantly at real time without having to leave their offices. This helps save a lot of time during the customers (usually investors) analysis procedure to come up with an approval between investors and architectures.

Furthermore, the system also allows collaborating between architectures; each architecture or team will contribute to separate areas to avoid conflicts between members and can commit their work easily in real time; they should see the whole virtual environment gets updated as they commit their work. This feature is innovative since it provides intuitive perspective in designing construction prototypes. Hence, the team can easily

© Springer International Publishing Switzerland 2016
S. Lackey and R. Shumaker (Eds.): VAMR 2016, LNCS 9740, pp. 724–735, 2016.
DOI: 10.1007/978-3-319-39907-2_69

compromise in designing and come up with an agreement of the construction prototype in real time.

There are many visual and computational tools and applications for city planning (or a general system); there are even tools for collaborating, team-working between multiple computers. However, despite all the visual technology they can display on a computer, it would be more productive and innovative if architectures can see the whole project in a real 3-dimensional environment and modify or make adjustments using hand gesture instead of mouse manipulation. By using gesture, the system provides users an interactive experience with the model; especially, manipulating with gesture is easier in the virtual world. In this article, we propose a system called City Planning for architectures in which they can visualize the whole city planning project in a virtual 3-D world by applying virtual reality technology and interact with them via gestures. The authors decide to use Oculus Rift as the virtual reality device and Leap Motion for gesture recognition. The contributions are as follow:

- Architects can collaborate, discuss and design city together in real-time without having to leave their offices. All of the actions are synchronized between all users. Each member or team will contribute to an area or part of the project; they can commit their work separately to avoid conflicts. The environment will get updated once they have committed the changes.
- The system can also be used to present the project to the clients. The system simulates a virtual environment of the city project in front of users. Users can communicate with each other by voice-call application such as Skype, Hangout… For architecture users, they can modify, insert, delete objects… i.e. they have complete control over the system. On the other hand, client users such as investors, contractor or venture capitalists…are given a limited amount of task such as rotating, zooming and pointing at object. Therefore, client users can give their feedbacks on the project that is being presented and architectures or designing team can adjust the prototype instantly until both sides agree on the design.

In this article, the authors walkthrough step-by-step technique in building such system. Section 2 introduces the background concept and related works. Section 3 introduces the proposed system in general. Section 4 describes the architectures that are used to develop the application. Section 5 presents techniques to recognize user's hand-gestures. Section 6 gives an insightful view of the applications and scenarios of usage of the system. Conclusion and future work are discussed in Sect. 7.

2   Background & Related Works

2.1   Virtual Reality Technology

Virtual reality (VR) is described as a 3-dimensional, computer generated environment which can be explored and interacted with by a person [12]. The technology has been around since the 90 s but is not well-known by the community. Since 2010, with the vast technology outburst of the 21th century, large tech corporations such as Google, Facebook, Sony, Samsung, etc. started to invest in this technology and make it available worldwide to basic users. In 2014, Facebook bought Oculus VR for $2 billion, Google introduced Cardboard and Sony announced its Project Morpheus (code name for Play Station VR). In 2015, Samsung released Gear VR [8]: its first portable VR device that comes with Samsung smartphones. Realizing the future of VR technology in the next few years, the authors decide to integrate this beautiful technology in this project in order to bring an immersive graphics and intuitive experience to users. Furthermore, VR has been applied in many other fields such as education and healthcare [11].

2.2 City Planning

City planning, urban zoning, designing buildings, structures, etc. have always been a time-consuming task. There are many phases and procedures one has to go through from proposing ideas, seeking for investment, presenting, adjusting the designs, etc. before their ideas got approved and they can launch the construction. These procedures usually take up to months or even years. And many projects got rejected from funding because the investors could not realize the potential of these projects; many of which are due to lack of visualization and intuitive observation of how the projects look like in reality.

There are also many aspects to consider in planning constructions, such as the physical environment (location, climate, resources, etc.), the social environment (ordering the city to proper area to satisfy the social needs) and the economic environment (supporting to businesses) [1]. It is necessary to inspect these variables by a 3D rendering application. VR is also researched to be applied in urban or city planning many times before as in [12–14].

There has been many software systems that support city planning. Esri City Engine [5] appears to be one of the most popular and powerful. It is an advanced city planning software, which has many essential and useful features. We can get the overview of the city from any angle, many options included such as lighting, shadowing, skybox. The content of the city can get to the tiny detail, we can have flyovers, bridges, parking lots, harbors, etc. The details are also really close to realistic. Figure 1 shows the main UI of Esri City Engine.

Fig. 1. Esri city engine overview

Cybercity3D [6] is also a very popular software that support city planning. This software focuses on creating realistic 3D models from real world. These models can be imported in different 3D rendering engines including Esri City Engine, Unity Engine.

In this paper, we focus only on how we create a simple prototype of a city or urban area, which is a full representation of a city. However, by integrating VR in this project, we want to put city planning to a new level; that is, to give users immersive experience by letting them interact with the model in a 360-degree visualization. Or further more, help users inspect their project as a first person perspective, i.e. let them walk around streets and buildings with real physics. A real city would have a lot of details, from the basic ones such as roads, buildings, trees to more complex ones like road intersection, roundabout, flyovers, signs, traffic lights, etc. To keep it simple, we only put into the application the most basic components: Roads, Buildings and Trees.

2.3 Collaboration in Human Computer Interaction

While VR has been widely used, even to support robotic system for the disabled [11], there will be even more applications if people in a VR system can collaborate. Collaboration in Human Computer Interaction can be applied in many fields: learning, designing, simulating, presentation, etc. Huang et al. [2] attempted to build a collaborative virtual reality learning system for medical education. Dos Santos et al. [3] proposed a multi-user interacted simulation of the oil and gas workflow to predict the outcome of an experiment before it goes to the real life. Another interesting application is the collaborative big data visualization and exploration system in virtual reality from Donalek et al. [4]. It helps the data mining process becomes easier and more natural (Fig. 2).

Fig. 2. From left to right: The collaborative virtual environment in medical learning, in oil and gas workflow simulation and the big data visualization and exploration.

Inspired from the idea of collaborative virtual environment, we wish to help architectures and designers to innovate their ideas together in VR. Plus, by integrating collaborative contributing feature, we make the communication between architectures and clients become easier. We give clients and investors the ability to experience the city prototype, give their ideas, feedbacks and watch the architectures adjust the prototype instantly. Hence, shorten the time of project analysis between architectures and investors. There will be less presentation slides and pictures in those fund raising meetings; but instead an intuitive way to experience the project with VR.

3 Proposed System

Our idea is to established a 3-dimensional environment in which users are connected together via internetworking protocols. Users are categorized into different classes; each class is provided with different permissions and controls over the model. In this paper, we introduce two primary user classes: Architecture and client. Architecture users are able to inspect (rotating, zooming), modify, insert, remove objects; client users are more limited since they are only allowed to inspect the model. We use Unity 3D Game Engine as our 3D renderer; Oculus Rift and Leap Motion technology are the visualization and gesture recognition protocols respectively.

3.1 Unity 3D Engine

We use Unity as our 3D renderer engine since it provides a flexible powerful development platform for creating 3D environment. We can easily define building models or import models from other 3D platform. Unity also support us with physics and visual effects so we can integrate and inspect in our environment. In addition to its powerful 3D support, Unity also allows multiplatform development which give us the ability to export our work on multiple operating systems, especially mobile platforms.

3.2 Oculus Rift with Leap Motion Technology

The combination of VR and gestures recognition in our project brought user experience to a whole new level. We decide to use Oculus Rift as our VR device since it is well integrated with Unity and its handful SDK support for multiple platforms from Windows, Mac OS to mobile. We use Leap Motion technology as our primary gestures recognition device as Leap Motion supports detail detection of the arm and hand structures like fingers and joints. Leap Motion also provides recognitions of simple hand gestures such as swipe, screen tap, key tap, circle; these gestures are then translated into control commands like mouse click, mouse drag, or screen zoom.

3.3 Application Overview

Figure 3 shows the UI overview of the application we built. There are 4 main components:

- Item box: appears in Item mode, shows list of the available items (buildings, trees, roads, etc.). When we click on an item, they will be active (to be drawn). We can choose many items to mix them together when drawing down onto the map.
- Properties box: appears when we select an item, showing their properties.
- Manipulation box: appears when we change to Manipulation mode, shows the list of controls you have, including selecting, transforming, scaling, etc.
- Users list: list of connected users. When we click on someone, we can see their perspective.

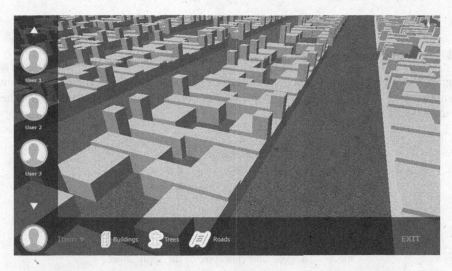

Fig. 3. The UI overview of the application. Click item to reveal other modes like selection, manipulation, etc.

3.4 Usage Workflow

Our target is to provide a fast way to create a city planning prototype. To do this, we focus on dividing the city in multiple areas. Each area can be auto generated, instead of putting items one by one, with custom properties like list of models to be generated, probability of occurrence, etc.

Figure 4 illustrates the normal usage workflow of the application. The main 4 steps are: design the roads system, generate city areas, then modify the details (change, add, delete items) and merge areas together. In that way, multiple users can control different areas independently, then connect their work afterward.

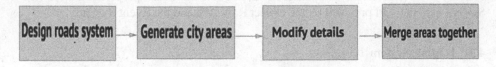

Fig. 4. Normal usage workflow

Designing Roads System. Designing realistic roads system is a very difficult problem. In this application, we only consider a simple kind of road, with fixed width and straight direction. Intersections are automatically generated if two roads cross each other.

Generate City Area. This is the most important part of the usage of the application. You can auto-fill an area of the city, with custom-define sized, either big like the whole city or small like a tree zone. The generated items are automatically stepped out from the roads.

4   System Architecture

4.1   Architecture Overview

Figure 5 demonstrates the general architecture of the application. There are 4 main components: The Object Raw API, the Raw Network API, the Event System and the Items System.

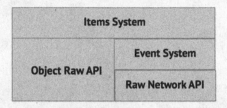

Fig. 5. The general architecture of the application

Object Raw API. This is the abstraction of the item manipulation on the map. It provides the raw item control, such as put item on a specific position, with a specific transform, scale; check for object position violation, etc.

Raw Network API. This is the abstraction of networking events, responsible for sending and receiving messages from the server or other clients.

Event System. The higher abstraction of networking. It provides methods of event manipulation, event that can be delivered to the other clients. It uses the Raw Network API inside.

Items System. The abstraction of all items in the city (buildings, trees, roads, area, map, etc.). The Items System defines the base and the specific methods and properties of every items (e.g. trees and buildings has different methods and properties). The Items System uses the API provided by the Object Raw API and the Event System.

4.2   Editing System

The Editing System here refers to the system of editing, manipulating the city plan, including the item sets can be drawn on the map, the selection tool and the manipulation tool.

Figure 6 shows the hierarchy of items. Each kind of item has distinct methods and properties. Map is the overall map (or world), it is also an item which we can change the perspective, lighting, etc. Area is the one we can define after creating map, each area has the method of auto-fill with custom Shapes. Shape is the abstraction of buildings and miscellaneous things like trees, signs, etc.

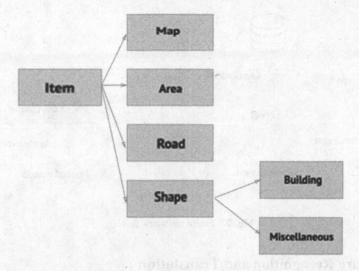

Fig. 6. The hierarchy of items

The selection and manipulation tool is also categorized to each kind of item. We have distinction between Map selection, Area selection, Road selection and Shape selection. This helps us increase the accuracy of picking what we want (e.g., selection between area and shape can be messed up).

4.3 Networking System

There are 2 kinds of event: DataEvent and ViewingEvent. DataEvent is the kind of event that affect the City data, such as moving a position of an item, rotating, changing specific properties. ViewingEvent is the special event for the purpose of presentation, sharing your perspective to others. We use TCP/IP to transfer DataEvent messages, to ensure data commitment. UDP is used in transferring ViewingEvent messages, as it need speed but not necessary integrity of data.

Figure 7 describes the basic event network flow. DataEvent will be sent to the Server, which will then be checked for conflict and stored in the database. Meanwhile, the ViewingEvent will be send peer to peer, directly to other clients, as it not necessary to store that information. Both kind of events when received will be pushed into something called Pool of events that each client has. Those events will sequentially be applied to change the offline city data in each client. To check the network status, every second a client will send an acknowledgement message to the server or the other client and reverse. If there is no acknowledgement after 4 s, each side will decide the other side is out of connection.

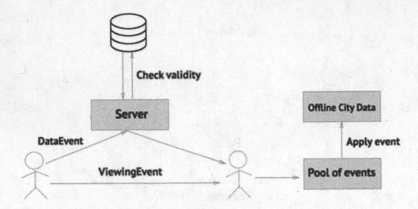

Fig. 7. Event network flow

5 Gesture Recognition and Translation

5.1 Navigating and Controlling Mode

In this section, we also introduce two primary navigating and controlling modes of the system, the view mode and the locating mode. In view mode, user can rotate the system by 360 degrees in space and zoom in/out the system. In this mode, user is provided the ability to view every aspect of details in the system from any angle.

The second mode is locating mode. In this mode, user is given the ability to locate objects onto the city such as buildings, trees, etc. as well as adjusting their rotations.

5.2 Gesture Recognition and Translation

Gestures Recognition. The authors define 3 primary gestures in order to control and navigate the system: grab gesture, circle gesture, screen-tab gesture. Circle gesture and screen-tab gesture are recognized using built-in Leap motion API while grab gesture is recognized by calculating the distance between finger joints as discussed below.

Grab Gesture. Grab gesture is recognized when the user hand is holding as a fist. Leap Motion technology provides us with strong recognition of the hand and arm structure including positions of joints and fingertips. As the hand is holding, the thumb fingertip will be close to the joints of other fingers. Therefore, by traversing and calculating the distance between the thumb fingertip and other fingers' joints, we can check weather the user is holding his hand to grab the object.

Grab gesture is translated as the action of pressing and holding the left mouse button (mouse dragging). User uses this gesture to rotate the city model or dragging objects.

Circle Gesture. Circle gesture is recognized by using Leap Motion built-in gesture API [10]. User triggers this gesture by rotating their hand in a circle shape at a fast enough speed.

As in view mode, user can use this gesture to zoom in or out the city model by circling clockwise or counterclockwise respectively. In locating mode, user users this gesture in order to adjust the rotation of the objects. Each clockwise circle will rotate the object by 90 degrees clockwise and each counterclockwise circle will rotate the object by 90 degrees counterclockwise.

Screen-Tap Gesture. Screen-tap gesture is also provided by Leap Motion built-in gesture API [10]. Screen-tab gesture is identified when the tip of a finger pokes forward and then springs back to approximately the original position. Screen-tap gesture is translated as a mouse click. User users this gesture in order to select any object in locating mode or interact with the application GUI interface.

6 Scenario of Usage

6.1 Improve Client-Architecture Design Development

Figure 8 demonstrates the design development procedure of an architecture. Usually this process takes up from weeks to months since most clients are not sure what they really want from their ideas. Furthermore, in the professional industry, this procedure has to go through many layers between the architectures and the client.

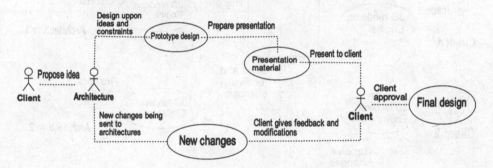

Fig. 8. Design development procedure

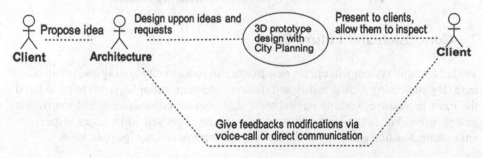

Fig. 9. Design development directly in real time with city planning

With City Planning, we can shorten the time for design development by allow direct communication, instant modifications between architectures and clients; furthermore, we bring immersive user experience to both client and architecture. This way, the client can have an intuitive view of the project instead of viewing it over presentation slides and images. This scenario is illustrated in Fig. 9.

6.2   Productive Collaborating Between Architectures

Another scenario of usage is collaboration architecting as discussed above. We are inspired by the idea of multiple software engineer working on the same project. Each member or team will work on different area of the city and commit their work separately. The server will check for conflicts, update the changes and notify all of its clients about the new changes; this will update environment of all users as well. With the integration of VR and gestures controlling, we hope to build a new frontier of working environment that inspires collaboration and innovation between users. Figure 10 illustrates the system as well as the permissions given to each class of user.

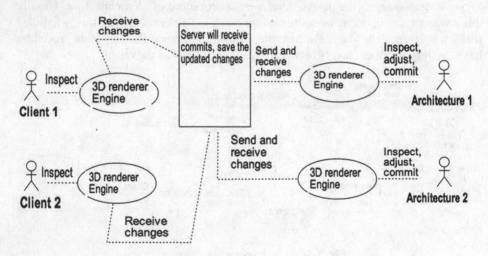

Fig. 10.   Collaborating between architectures and clients

7   Conclusion and Future Work

We believe this system will open a new frontier in modern city zoning and urban planning. By combining virtual reality and motion detection technology, we hope to build the most productive working environment that inspires collaboration and innovation among users. For future works, this system can be improved to let users inspect the environment as first person or to expand into an interior designing application.

References

1. Urban Planning Basic. http://science.howstuffworks.com/environmental/green-science/urban-planning2.htm
2. Huang, H.M., Liaw, S.S., Teng, Y.C.: Developing a collaborative virtual reality learning system. J. Inf. Technol. Appl. Edu. (JITAE) **1**(2), 74–79 (2012)
3. Dos Stantos, I.H.F., Soares, L.P., Carvalho, F., Raposo, A.: A collaborative virtual reality oil & gas workflow. Int. J. Virtual Reality **11**(1), 1–13 (2012)
4. Donalek, C., Djorgovski, S.G., Davidoff, S., Cioc, A., Wang, A., Longo, G., Norris, J.S., Zhang, J., Lawler, E., Yeh, S., Mahabal, A., Graham, M., Drake, A.: Immersive and collaborative data visualization using virtual reality platforms. In: IEEE International Conference on Big Data, p. 609 (2014). ISBN: 978-1-4799-5665-4
5. Esri CityEngine. http://www.esri.com
6. CyberCity3D. http://www.cybercity3d.com
7. Virtual Reality Basic. http://www.vrs.org.uk/virtual-reality/what-is-virtual-reality.html
8. Samsung Gear VR. https://www.oculus.com/en-us/gear-vr/
9. Stanislav, R.: Virtual environments as situated techno-social performances. In: CAADRIA2010: New Frontiers, The 15th International Conference on Computer Aided Architectural Design Research in Asia (2010)
10. Leap Motion Gestures. https://developer.leapmotion.com/documentation/csharp/api/Leap.Gesture.html
11. Hu, F., Lu, J., Zhang, T.: Virtual Reality Enhanced Robotic Systems for Disability Rehabilitation. In: Gallery, p. 49 (2016). ISBN: 978-1466697409
12. Bourdakis, V.: Virtual Reality: A Communication Tool for Urban Planning. http://fos.prd.uth.gr/vas/papers/CAAD-TNDC/
13. Sunesson, K., Allwood, C.M., Paulin, D., Heldal, I., Roupé, M., Johansson, M., Westerdahl, B.: Virtual reality as a new tool in the city planning process. Tsinghua Sci. Technol. **13**(1), 255–260 (2008). ISSN: 1007-0214 41/67
14. Roupé, M.: Development and Implementations of Virtual Reality for Decision-making in Urban Planning and Building Design. Chalmers University of Technology, Göteborg (2013). ISBN: 978-91-7385-799-4.- 170 s

A Role of Augmented Reality in Educational Contents: Intermediating Between Reality and Virtual Reality

Shohei Tsuchida and Shu Matsuura[✉]

Faculty of Education, Tokyo Gakugei University,
4-1-1 Nukuikita, Koganei, Tokyo 184-8501, Japan
shumats0@gmail.com

Abstract. Many science education materials exhibit simplified models of nature. This simplification is beneficial to represent the essential characteristics of nature, but it forces the learners to cognitively assign the model to reality. This paper describes a traditional content exhibiting the lunar phase, which is taught in the elementary school. The use of multiple frames of observation and the necessity of dual concept required for perceiving the lunar orbital motion and Earth's rotational motion around its axis creates an extraneous cognitive load. This study introduces a simple desktop model of the planets and a multi-view display of the model planets using augmented reality (AR) and virtual reality (VR). Eye-tracking experiments are performed to examine the role of AR to intermediate between the spatial arrangement of real objects and the VR display observed from a fixed position on an object that represents the Earth. The results indicate that participants who experimented with the desktop model took more time to check and move their eye gaze between AR, VR, and the real model, in the beginning phase of the trials. Therefore, it is suggested that AR intermediates cognition of a view outside of the orbit and a surface of the Earth.

Keywords: Cognitive load · Learning · Desktop model

1 Introduction

Traditional learning materials of science education are usually based on simplified models that illustrate the essential character of nature or the essence of theories. Although this simplification or idealization enables clear scientific understanding of the complex natural phenomena, 2D illustrations on paper sometimes generate a high cognitive load for less-experienced learners.

In this study, the description of the lunar phases is used as an example to investigate the effect of augmented reality (AR) on learners' cognition load. Elementary school students learn the basic principles of planetary movements theoretically and through observations, which are often conducted at home. Although students are capable of changing their understanding of the lunar phases in a scientifically accurate way, they might continue to hold views inconsistent with the scientific perspective [1, 2]. Learners have to relate the lunar phases to the orbital motion of the moon. Here, multi-frame of observation brings about extraneous cognitive loads for the learners [3].

© Springer International Publishing Switzerland 2016
S. Lackey and R. Shumaker (Eds.): VAMR 2016, LNCS 9740, pp. 736–745, 2016.
DOI: 10.1007/978-3-319-39907-2_70

One frame of observation is the view from outside the Earth's orbit, where the sun looks still (universe view). The other frame of observation is the view from a fixed position (usually the location of the learner's country) on the surface of the Earth (earth view). The Shape of the moon that is observed from the earth view is determined by the relative positions of the sun, the Earth, and the moon. Although this is not taught at elementary schools, the angle between the Earth's axis and the orbital plane also has to be considered.

To tackle the cognitive load produced by using multiple frames, constructivistic activities using balls and a light are often conducted in classrooms [4–7]. In addition, digital learning materials provide a synchronized animation of the planet motions on the display, and the multi-view display enables learners to observe from both the universe and earth views. A virtual observation using AR proves effective for junior high school students [8].

In this study, an AR system is used, which includes a tabletop model that represents the sun, the Earth, and the moon displayed in both the universe view (AR) and the earth view (virtual reality, VR). It is hypothesized that the AR display plays a role in supporting the learner to relate the arrangement of the real tabletop blocks with the moon phases exhibited in the VR display. We discuss the gaze time on AR display, VR display, and real objects in a simple problem-solving process using eye-tracking equipment.

2   Method

2.1   Tabletop Toy-Model of the Sun, the Earth, and the Moon

Two of 50 mm × 50 mm square blocks with a thickness of 10 mm representing the Earth and the moon, on a worksheet with a sun marker, were used to show the eight location of the moon around the Earth, which result in the different phases of the moon (Fig. 1). The AR application was created using Vuforia (Qualcomm) AR package on the development environment Unity v.5.3.2.f1 (Unity Cooperation). The Vuforia

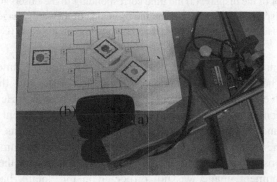

Fig. 1. The worksheet and blocks with the planet markers. (a) the blocks with the earth and the moon markers; (b) the worksheet with a sun marker; (c) the web camera to capture the scene on the worksheet. The view is of the participant.

"frame markers" (35 mm × 35 mm) for AR detection were pasted on the block surface. The size of the markers was set to be smaller than the block size to avoid occlusion by the participants' fingers. The worksheet where the blocks were placed, was the size A4. A web camera (Logicool C920R) captured the images of the markers. The participants watched the AR and VR view displayed on a 27' monitor (Apple Thunderbolt Display) set at around 70–100 cm from the face of the participant.

2.2   The Moon Phase Question

The participants of the experiments were students at a teacher's training university aged from 20 to 22. Nine students participated in the sessions. They were majoring in science education for elementary school. Thus, they have experience in establishing understanding of the moon phases.

The participants were asked to arrange the blocks in order to reproduce an indicated moon phase. The moon phases requested were the waxing crescent moon in the east, the waning crescent moon in the west, or the waxing gibbous moon in the west.

Fig. 2. A screen shot of the display. (a) the time corresponding to the observations in (b) and (c). (b) AR (RB mode) display. A gray blue zone in the right side of the earth image shows the visible area from the view position. VR display from the view position on the earth (Color figure online).

The display consists of three windows, i.e., AR, VR, and the time presentation as shown in Fig. 2. The AR window displays the graphics of the sun, the Earth, and the moon from the universe view superimposed on the block markers. Here, we examined two types of representations. First, the video image of the environment was exhibited in the "real background video (RB)" mode. The AR display consists of two types of images, namely, the image of a real scene captured by the web camera, and the AR graphics superimposed on the real scene. The RB consists of these components. Second, the environment image was not projected in the "blank background (BB)" mode, because the BB mode lacks a visual cue for three-dimensional cognition. The RB mode provides three-dimensional perspective in the real scene, together with the planet configurations in the universe view. This mode augments the real model, and it is expected to stimulate a three-dimensional sensation.

The VR window shows the moon lit by the sun from the earth view. The corresponding viewing position was predetermined on the marker of the earth block. The right side of the window corresponds to the east, and the left side indicates the west. The shape of the moon and its position correspond to the arranged planet model. Finally, the time presentation shows a clock to indicate the time corresponding to the arrangement of the model blocks.

The participants were asked to sit in front of the display to solve the problem by manipulating the blocks. The eye-tracking measurement was performed using "ViewTracker" (DITECT Corporation), a head-mounted-type eye tracker. Eye tracking continued for fewer than 100 s, and the participants solved the problems within this period.

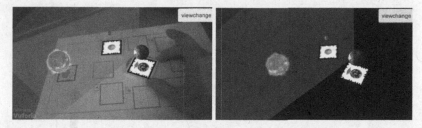

Fig. 3. Comparison of the RB (left) and BB (right) modes of the equivalent scene.

Each participant engaged in two successive sessions with different problems. In these sessions, the types of AR windows, RB, and BB, were changed. Participants had another set of successive sessions, with the order of RB-BB converted, on another day. This conversion was done to avoid a memory effect, which would result in the participants' solving the new problem too fast. After each session, the participants were interviewed on how they solved the problem.

3 Results and Discussion

3.1 Types of Problem Solving

Approach Types. The solution to the questions involves two phenomena, namely the lunar orbital motion (LOM) and the Earth's rotational motion around its axis (ERM). Based on the interview, the participants' approaches to this problem are grouped into three types. In the first type, the participant tries to solve the lunar orbital motion (LOM), namely the phase of the moon. In the second approach, the participant attempts to solve the Earth's rotational motion (ERM), namely the direction of the moon seen from the Earth. The explanations of the third type were vague in solving ERM and LOM separately.

Behavior Types. In addition, there are two types of behaviors. Students of the first type immediately manipulate the model, experimenting until he/she finds the solution (experiment-oriented type). Another type of student tries to solve the problem conceptually, reaches a satisfactory answer, which he/she tests by manipulating the model (think-first type).

Table 1. Number of cases for three approach and two behavior types. Each cell is divided into two orders of real background (RB) and blank background (BB) conditions.

	ERM			Vague			LOM		
Experiment oriented	8	RB → BB	4	0	RB → BB	0	9	RB → BB	4
		BB → RB	4		BB → RB	0		BB → RB	5
Think first	7	RB → BB	4	3	RB → BB	2	3	RB → BB	2
		BB → RB	3		BB → RB	1		BB → RB	1

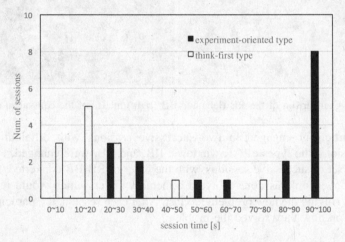

Fig. 4. Histogram of session times for experiment-oriented and think-first type participants

The students' sessions are grouped according to the types described above. Table 1 shows the number of sessions of these six groups, and further, the table shows the number of sessions under two types of AR viewing. Accordingly, the ERM and LOM numbers are almost equivalent for experiment-oriented students. However, ERM is more frequent than LOM in think-first type students. Since ERM has only two possible choices of east or west, the think-first type participants might feel ERM consideration is an easier task to begin with and therefore chose to perform this one first.

Figure 4 shows a comparison of the session times for experiment-oriented and think-first type participants. The figure shows that think-first type participants finish earlier, while many experiment-oriented participants require a longer session time. This result suggests that experiment-oriented participants make full use of the visualization to solve the problem.

3.2   Gaze Time on the Visual Components

The times of the participants' sessions were divided into dwell time on the AR display component (AR-dwell), the VR component (DR-dwell), and the real model blocks (real-dwell), and motion time gazing point from one component to the other (motion).

Comparison Between the Real Background (RB) and the Blank Background (BB). As seen in Fig. 3, the background scene display seems effective for the spatial cognition of planet CG. Here, we compare the total dwell times on the AR display with and without the environment image in Fig. 5. The figure includes the sessions of both experiment-oriented and think-first types. The dwell time on AR with RB exhibits a peek within a small time-range of 10–20 s. On the other hand, the dwell time on BB exhibits a high peak at a long time-range of 90–100 s. This result implies that the AR display without a background video requires a larger load for spatial cognition as compared with AR with the real scene.

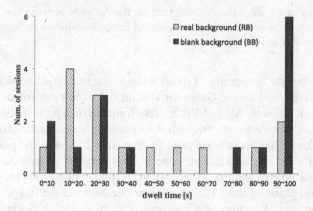

Fig. 5. Histogram of total dwell time of each session on AR display with the real and the blank background (RB and BB, respectively).

We now discuss the effect of the change of RB and BB in the successive two sessions, i.e., we compare the change from RB to BB, and the change from BB to RB. Let us denote the total dwell time on the AR display in the first session as T_{AR1}, and the time in the second session as T_{AR2}. Then, the difference in dwell time between the two sessions is $\Delta T = T_{AR1} - T_{AR2}$.

Figure 6 shows the comparison of the time difference ΔT for successive RB-to-BB and BB-to-RB sessions. The BB-to-RB sessions show a positive ΔT, decreasing AR viewing. This implies that less time is required for cognition using the RB type AR, as compared with the BB type, in addition to an effect of practice. On the other hand, the RB-to-BB sessions show positive and negative ΔT. Negative or small ΔT implies that the cognition of BB requires more gaze, regardless of the effect of practice.

Comparison of Dwell Times in Three Time Zones. To characterize the time change in the display and object model, each session is divided into three time zones. The first one-third of a session is called "time zone 1," the middle one-third is "time zone 2," and the final period is referred to as "time zone 3."

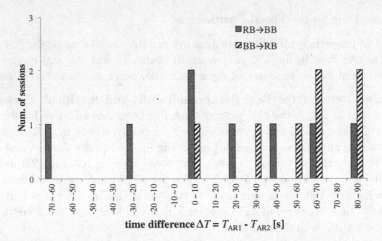

Fig. 6. Histogram of the difference of dwell time on the AR view between two successive two sessions. In successive sessions, the real background image is switched on from BB to RB, or switched off, from RB to BB.

Figure 7 shows the histograms of dwell times in the real object model, AR and VR display in the three time zones. Gazes for around 0.2 s are most frequent on the real objects. Although gazes on AR and VR are less frequent than on real objects in a small time-range, $\sim$2-s gazes are more frequent than gazes on real objects. Gazes on the AR for more than 2 s are particularly frequent in time zone 2. Moreover, gazes on the VR for more than 1 s are observed in time zone 3. This suggests an intermediating role of AR between real objects and the VR image from a view of the object.

Furthermore, gazes on the AR area often concentrate on the image of the participant's finger image taken from the camera, as seen in Fig. 8. Seeing their fingers implies that they try to collect visual feedback that will supplement muscular sensory feedback. The participants rotate the block, watching the AR display, and getting a visual feedback from the image of their hands. Then, from time to time, they confirm the resultant moon phase from the earth view represented in the VR display. In this way, the AR display intermediates between the universe view and earth views through the visual feedback of their manipulation.

The aim of the original question is to get a correct VR image by arranging the blocks. Thus, it is natural to begin with seeing and manipulating the blocks and to certify the result in the VR window at the end. AR in this study provides pictorial cues to help understand both the moon phase lit by the sun and the earth view at short notice.

The percentages of dwell time in the cells were shown in the top middle of the cells. Participant's fingers are inside the center and center bottom cells, which show high percentages.

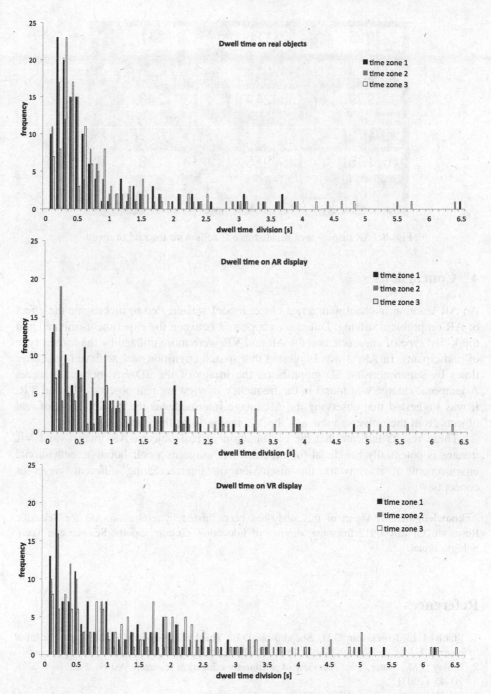

Fig. 7. Histogram of the dwell time on real objects (top), and AR (middle) and VR (bottom) displays for three successive time zones of the sessions.

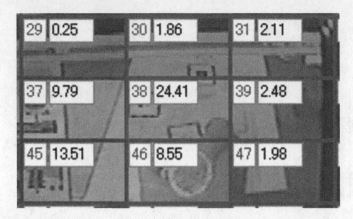

Fig. 8. AR display area divided into 9 cells with the rate of dwell.

4 Conclusions

An AR learning material with a real object model was created to investigate the effect of AR on problem solving. Differences appeared between the experiment-oriented and think-first type of approach, and the AR and VR were more utilized by the former type of participants. In AR, it was suggested that spatial cognition was achieved in shorter times by superimposing 3D graphics on the image of the 3D environmental scene. A temporal change was found in the frequency of viewing real objects, AR, and VR. It was suggested that observing the AR image intermediates the manipulation of real objects from the universe view and the VR image from the earth view.

These results indicate that the combination of real objects, AR images, and VR images is potentially beneficial for experimental usage in a collaborative, educational environment, if it activates the discussion on intermediating different views or concepts.

Acknowledgments. A part of this study has been funded by a Grant-in-Aid for Scientific Research (C) 15K00912 from the Ministry of Education, Culture, Sports, Science and Technology, Japan.

References

1. Stahly, L.L., Krockover, G.H., Shepardson, D.P.: Third grade students' ideas about the lunar phases. J. Res. Sci. Teach. **36**(2), 159–177 (1999)
2. Bailey, J.M., Slater, T.F.: A review of astronomy education research. Astron. Edu. Rev. **2**(2), 20–45 (2003)
3. Sweller, J.: Cognitive Science **12**(2), 257–288 (1988)
4. Suzuki, M.: Conversations about the moon with prospective teachers in Japan. Sci. Educ. **87**(6), 892–910 (2003)

5. Foster, G.W.: Look to the moon, students learn about the phases of the moon from an "Earth-centered" viewpoint. Sci. Child. **34**(3), 30–33 (1996)
6. Abell, S., George, M., Martini, M.: The moon investigation: instructional strategies for elementary science methods. J. Sci. Teach. Educ. **13**(2), 85–100 (2002)
7. Kavanagh, C., Agan, L., Sneider, C.: Learning about phases of the moon and eclipses: a guide for teachers and curriculum developers. Astron. Educ. Rev. **4**(1), 19–52 (2005)
8. Tian, K., Endo, M., Urata, M., Mouri, K., Yasuda, T.: M-VSARL system in secondary school science education: lunar phase class case study. In: IEEE 3rd Global Conference on Consumer Electronics, pp. 321–322 (2014)

Author Index

Printed in the United States
By Bookmasters